COOK, WELTON & GEMMELL

SHIPBUILDERS OF HULL AND BEVERLEY

1883 – 1963

BY

MICHAEL THOMPSON

WITH

DAVE NEWTON, RICHARD ROBINSON

AND TONY LOFTHOUSE

HUTTON PRESS

1999

Published by
The Hutton Press Ltd.,
130 Canada Drive, Cherry Burton,
Beverley, East Yorkshire HU17 7SB

ISBN 1 902709 02 0

Printed and bound by
Fretwells Limited, Hull

CONTENTS

Front cover (top): A View of the Grovehill Shipyard facing west during 1952 at a time when the yard was working at full capacity with all seven berths in use. The trawler in the foreground is the ELLA HEWETT (Yard No.871). At the fitting out jetty is one of the oil barges BLAKEDALE.H (Yard No.872) and the trawler BOSTON JAVELIN (Yard No.863). Photo by courtesy of Stan Thompson.

Front cover (bottom): On 9 March 1950 the tug ACETUT guides the newly completed trawler KINGSTON ZIRCON (Yard No.817) out of Humber Dock, Hull to run her trials on the River Humber. Photo:- Beverley Shipyard Collection.

Back cover: The sideways launching of vessels into the River Hull was quite spectacular. Crowds of local people would gather on the bankside to watch the proceedings taking care to keep clear of the resulting waves which swept across the river. Being launched on 21 November 1956 is the trawler SWANELLA (Yard No.919). Photo by courtesy of Andrew Marr.

ACKNOWLEDGEMENTS

The compilation of this book represents almost five years of painstaking research carried out by a group of four shipping enthusiasts. They would like to express their most grateful thanks to a number of people who have assisted in the project.

Arthur G. Credland, Keeper of Maritime History, Hull Maritime Museum.

Anne Cowne, Information Administrator, Lloyds Register of Shipping, London.

Jack Daussy, French Trawler Historian, Fecamp, France.

G.W. Oxley, City Archivist, Hull City Archives.

John Wilson, Archivist and Carol Moss, Assistant, North East Lincolnshire Archives, Grimsby.

The Staff of the Local Studies, Technical and Reference Libraries, Hull Central Library.

Library Staff of the National Fishing Museum, Grimsby.

John Cooper, Shipyard Archive Material, Beverley.

Paul Bryan, Fishery Officer, Grimsby for Archive Material.

Sigtryggur Eythorsson and Edward M. Swan for Icelandic Information and Translation.

Phil Thomas, World Ship Society Tug Specialist.

Asa Magnusson, Magnus Andersson, Leif and Gunilla Fjellstedt, Swedish Tug Information.

David Slinger, Paul Whiting, Dave Buckley, Malcolm Stockdale, George Scales. Steve Pulfrey, Jonathan Grobler, Ron Pett.

David Tyler of "Railtourer" Travel Hull. For providing complimentary rail travel to London for research.

Unless otherwise stated the photographs and plans have been supplied by the Hull Maritime Museum:- Barnard & Straker Collection, The Harry Cartlidge Collection and the Beverley Shipyard Collection.

INTRODUCTION

The iron and steel shipbuilding firm of Cook, Welton & Gemmell was established at Hull in 1883 by three partners who had formerly been colleagues in Earle's Shipbuilding & Engineering Co Ltd. the city's largest shipbuilding enterprise[1].

All three men were incomers; William James Cook[2] was born in Deptford, London in 1883, Charles Keen Welton[3] was born in Deptford, London in 1848, the former having served his apprenticeship as a boilermaker and the latter as plater in their home town. Both worked as platers for Earle's, Cook then served as a boilermaker. William M Gemmell, was born in Port Glasgow, Scotland in 1847, was apprenticed as a shipwright to C & W Earle and later worked as a draughtsman and naval architect[4]. He left Earle's and was then yard manager of David Parkinson Garbutt's shipyard until it went into liquidation in November 1883[5].

William M. Gemmell. Photo: courtesy of Dr. I. M. M. Gemmell

Cook, Welton & Gemmell's office was located in South Bridge Road near to the Humber Iron Works Shipbuilding and Engineering Yard[6], where the partners leased premises and shared the patent slip from which vessels could be launched into the River Humber, close to Sammy's Point[7] at the entrance to the River Hull.

On Wednesday 21 January 1885 the company celebrated the launch of their first vessel the PRECURSOR, an iron hulled sailing smack built for Robert Hellyer, a member of the great pioneering family of fishing vessel owners who had come to Hull from Devon in the middle of the century. Fitted with a steam winch and all modern improvements she was the largest fishing smack built in Hull up to this time. The naming ceremony was performed by Miss Maggie Gemmell[8].

During 1885 a total of eight sailing smacks were built but with the advent of steam powered trawlers (Earle's had launched the steam trawler ZODIAC in 1882[9]) more and more owners were turning to the 'new technology'. By the end of that year the yard's first steam trawler, the IRRAWADDY had been completed for George Beeching and Thomas Kelsall[10] to the order of Messrs Charles D Holmes & Co, who supplied the engines, boiler and trawling machinery (winches etc). The trawler ran her trials on Monday 28 December 1885 in squally weather off Withernsea where she achieved an average speed of 11 knots over the measured mile.

From the outset the company built the hull and superstructure and contracted out all the engineering work. Two local marine engineering companies, Charles D Holmes and Amos & Smith[11], were to form long-lasting relationships with Cook, Welton & Gemmell and the successor companies.

The phenomenal development of the Hull and Grimsby fishing industries encouraged the expansion of shipbuilding in the area. Both Cook, Welton & Gemmell in Hull and Cochranes[12] of Beverley, were to specialise in trawler building throughout their existence, and their development was a direct result of the demand for ever larger and more efficient trawlers. Although the Hull yard built a small number of tugs and other vessels, it was for their trawlers that the company became renowned. During the 1890's Britain's trawlers began to fish further afield and started to exploit the rich Icelandic grounds during the summer months. This development led in turn to the construction of yet bigger and more powerful vessels with increased capacity for fish storage and fuel bunkers. Even so part of the fish room was filled with coal for the outward journey and it was so calculated that as the fishing grounds were reached the coal would have been used up enabling the space to be scrubbed clean ready to receive the catch.

By the early 1900's Hull fishermen took advantage of these larger vessels to explore the distant Arctic grounds off Norway and in the Barents Sea. The success of these trips led to the formation of a distant water fleet and the need to fish all the year round, so the naval architects were called upon to design vessels with good sea-keeping qualities to withstand the severe weather conditions encountered in the winter months. For many years, however, the North Sea remained the most important source of fish caught by the Hull and Grimsby fleets. The North Sea grounds were largely fished by the box fleets comprising small steam trawlers which stayed fishing five or six weeks at a stretch. Each morning the fish would be transferred in boxes (hence the term box fleet) to a fast cutter which would rush the fish to market in Hull or London's Billingsgate whilst the catch was still fresh[13].

In 1901 Cook, Welton & Gemmell acquired the Grovehill shipyard (on the River Hull) at Beverley, previously occupied since 1884 by Cochrane, Hamilton and Cooper. After going into liquidation in 1901 the latter were reformed as Cochrane and Sons at the Ouse Shipyard, Selby.

The first vessel launched by Cook, Welton & Gemmell at Beverley was the steam tug HUNTSMAN, built for Thomas Gray & Co Hull[14]. During 1902, twenty vessels were launched in Hull and the same number at the new yard. At first the yard numbers allocated to the two yards were mingled but from 1903 Beverley was allocated its own numbers, starting at twenty-one. Throughout the history of the yard, vessels after launch, were towed as empty shells down the river for fitting out in Hull.

In 1904 having failed to renegotiate any secure tenure of the Hull premises all the shipbuilding was concentrated in Beverley[15]. Launched on the 2 February, the trawler THOMAS HAMLING[16] was the last vessel built at the Hull yard and the following month the plant was auctioned off. During twenty-two years since the foundation some 336 vessels had been built, comprising 8 sailing smacks, 300 trawlers (222 for Hull, 62 for Grimsby and 16 for other fleets), 16 tugs, 6 War Department vessels, 2 drifters, 2 yachts, I steam lighter and 1 lightship.

As the twentieth century progressed, Grimsby trawler owners embarked upon a considerable expansion program and eventually the port would have the largest fishing fleet in the world. The intense rivalry between Hull and Grimsby led to claim and counterclaim and for most of the twentieth century Hull could claim the largest total catch (in weight) and Grimsby the highest value as a result of premium fish caught by mid-water vessels. Hull concentrated on distant-water grounds and bulk fish.

Between 1902 and 1917, Cook, Welton & Gemmell obtained orders for 370 trawlers to be built at the Beverley yard - 232 for Grimsby. The most prominent of the Grimsby owners was Alec Black for whom 71 vessels were launched (for his own and various subsidiary companies) and George F Sleights who ordered 50 trawlers. The majority of the Grimsby vessels were for the North Sea fishery, and were of the well proven design with bridge aft of the funnel.

For the Hull fleet 125 trawlers were built, predominantly for Hellyer's Steam Fishing Co Ltd, and their subsidiary Imperial Steam Fishing Co Ltd for which a total of 52 vessels were constructed. Twenty-nine vessels were built for the Hull Steam Fishing and Ice Co (The Red Cross Fleet)[17].

1907 saw Cook, Welton & Gemmell registered as a limited company and very much in the van of trawler design and development. During that year a length of 140 ft and gross tonnage of 300 was exceeded for the first time with the of ROMAN *(Yard No. 141)*, VERA *(Yard No. 150)* and SAXON *(Yard No. 154)*. Built in 1910 The Hull Steam Fishing & Ice Co's North Sea box fleet trawlers ST. JOHNS *(Yard No. 198)* and STORNOWAY *(Yard No. 199)* were the first trawlers fitted with electric lighting.

In 1913 more 'box men' this time for Hellyer's BARDOLPH *(Yard No.217)*, and CALIBAN[18] *(Yard No. 218)*, were among the first to be fitted with Marconi Marine radio sets. The same year saw the completion of the world's largest distant water trawler to date the PASSING *(Yard No. 261)*, 160ft long and 459 tons (gross) built for the Alec Black subsidiary, the South Western Steam Fishing Co Ltd. of Grimsby.

From September 1914, following the outbreak of the Great War, the Admiralty began to requisition large numbers of trawlers for auxiliary patrol and minesweeping duties with the Royal Navy. Newly completed trawlers were amongst those requisitioned and it was expected that orders placed by mercantile owners would diminish but surprisingly in 1915 - 1916, forty-five new trawlers were built.

By 1916 war losses and increased naval requisition, some 1400 of the 1900 British registered trawlers, had hugely depleted the fishing fleet, so the Admiralty bought 14 trawlers off the stocks from the Beverley yard; 2 were completed as Non-Standard Mersey Class and the remaining 12 as Non-Standard Castle Class. This was followed by orders for 51 Castle Class trawlers, and 14 Kil Class patrol gunboats from the Cook, Welton, & Gemmell yard.

Because of the severe reduction of fishing opportunities caused by enemy action (including extensive minefields) it was decided on 29 May 1917 that all remaining trawlers would be requisitioned and placed under the white ensign in a special ' fishery reserve'. These vessels continued to fish, but in small fleets, some of the number being given guns for self-protection.

Following the end of hostilities on 11 November 1918, 7 Castle Class trawlers and 10 Kil Class patrol gunboats orders were cancelled. Of the 44 Castle class built for the Admiralty, 25 were completed as warships, 19 as fishing trawlers arid the 7 cancelled vessels were completed and sold to mercantile owners. Only 4 of the 14 Kil Class patrol gunboats ordered, were completed.

The company was now able to complete Yard Numbers 365-371 which had been delayed by the war and in 1920 the Beverley yard was kept busy completing the Admiralty contracts and a number of mercantile contracts. Between 1920 and 1922 the Admiralty sold off large numbers of its surplus trawlers many of which had been built with the purpose of re-building the British fishing fleet to compensate for the war losses. This sudden influx of vessels, however, had an adverse effect on trawler builders as the market became overcrowded with ready made vessels.

Cook, Welton & Gemmell suffered a severe slump and from 1921 until the middle of 1924 no trawler orders were received. In 1921 only four coasters and two lighters were built and to make matters worse, when the original purchaser of the coaster FARFIELD *(Yard No. 439)* built at a cost £38,000, failed to take up the vessel on completion, the builders had reluctantly to accept Thomas Coppack's offer of £12,000. The situation remained grim when in 1922 with only one light float and two tugs on the books the company decided to build three small trawlers on 'spec' to provide some employment for the work force. These were eventually sold in 1923, during which year not a single vessel was launched.

The fishing industry enjoying a spell of post-war prosperity and the Hull owners began an expansion programme which included orders for seven large distant water trawlers placed with Cook, Welton & Gemmell in 1924. The company was to play a major roll in the 1924-1937 expansion of the Hull fishing fleet, which led to Hull becoming the premier distant water fishing port in the world.

1924 also saw the beginnings of a major financial fiasco when the company tendered for the building of an oceanographic research vessel required by the Crown Agents for the Colonies. Intended for oceanographic research in the South Atlantic and combining the characteristics of a whaler and trawler Cook, Welton & Gemmell's bid of £29,375 was accepted and work began on Yard No.477, a vessel to be named WILLIAM SCORESBY(19). Amos & Smith supplied the machinery with a boiler which could be fired using either coal or oil and indeed this was the first oil-burning vessel built by Cook, Welton & Gemmell.

A Crown Agents surveyor supervised the building at Beverley and there were continual disputes with the shipyard management over the specification and constructional details. Much of the blame should probably be placed on the Crown Agents who were not only lacking in experience of ship design but were totally out of their depth when it came to the construction of a research vessel. Most of their clients in the colonies were interested in acquiring river and lake steamers and these were readily obtainable from companies (e.g. Yarrows) with a long tradition of building these types of vessels. Much of the time the Crown Agents seem to have regarded the WILLIAM SCORESBY as a glorified gentleman's yacht rather than a working vessel for use in the South Atlantic, some of the fiercest waters in the world.

Progress on the vessel was slow and there were claims that priority was being given to various trawlers under construction at the time but in fact the work force had been greatly reduced by the lack of orders between 1921-1923. Eventually the WILLIAM SCORESBY was launched on 31 December 1925 and accepted on 14 June 1926. When the contract was completed Cook, Welton & Gemmell Ltd were unable to pay their creditors and faced bankruptcy. They had no option but to go into voluntary liquidation, but managed to continue trading in the hands of the Receiver.

The knock-on effect to local engineering firms was serious and C D Holmes & Co Ltd were very concerned at the potential loss of business if the Beverley yard was to close down. This led to a complete restructuring of the business with Holmes taking the largest holding of £l shares.

Charles D Holmes & Co Ltd	3,998 shares	Francis G B Gemmell	1,500 shares
Herbert H Butterfield	1,500 shares	Alfred S Twidle	1,000 shares
Charles D Holmes	I share	Harold E Sheardown	1 share

A total of 8000 shares were taken up and H. E. Sheardown nephew of Charles Denton Holmes(20) was appointed chairman of the new company. A. S. Twidle was a director and secretary and the other shareholders were directors and under this new management the yard began to flourish.

By the 1930's the quantity and quality of trawlers resulted in a fleet that was all too efficient and the result was large landings of fish and depressed prices. This became just another component of a severe commercial and industrial depression world-wide, and large amounts of good quality fish left unsold were turned into fish meal. Trawlers were laid up or traded at a loss and 1931 was a particularly bad year for the British fishing industry. In the following year only four trawlers were built at the Beverley yard.

In 1933 Hellyer Bros. Ltd ordered five trawlers *(Yard No's 578, 579, 580, 581 and 587)*. which were to be the last of the company's trawlers to be built at Beverley. Future orders were placed with Smiths Dock Co Ltd Middlesbrough, a move which ended nearly fifty years association with Cook, Welton & Gemmell. 1933 saw the introduction of the cruiser stern which improved speed and efficiency; the first vessel to incorporate the feature was the LADY LILIAN *(Yard No. 575)* and thereafter it became the norm.

Two of the main customers of the shipyard, Kingston Steam Trawling Co Ltd[21], and Thomas Hamling & Co Ltd both of Hull, continually pushed the company's designers and engineers to produce bigger and faster trawlers. In 1934 Thomas Hamling's ordered the impressive PENTLAND FIRTH *(Yard No. 577)* length 164 ft 6 in, 456 tons (gross); this and her sister ship ST. ACHILLEUS *(Yard No. 595)* were the first Beverley built trawlers which achieved service speed of 12 knots.

Also in 1934 Kingston Steam Trawling Co ordered eight trawlers to be furnished with a compound engine fitted with an exhaust steam turbine. This engine could achieve 20% more power if required or could save 20% of the coal fuel bill at normal speed. The KINGSTON CORNELIAN *(Yard No. 593)*, length 160 ft 6 in, 449 tons (gross) was the first British trawler fitted with this type of engine.

The Hull North Sea box fleet ceased operations in March 1936 and Kelsall Bros. & Beeching went into liquidation. The catching power of the distant-water fleet had outstripped them and these small inefficient vessels, many rather old, were now no longer viable, killed off by the relatively high cost of crews and fuel. Indeed the irrelevance of the 'box fleet' to the market is emphasised the next year by a record total catch for the Hull fleet of no less than 328,447 tons of fish. This oversupply caused a collapse in prices and in recognition of these large fluctuations in the fortunes of the fishing fleet an 'economic investigation' research unit was established. Uneconomic trawlers were laid up, sold or scrapped, and no orders were placed for new trawlers in 1938. The shipyard was kept going with orders for four tugs, two pleasure boats, one water boat and a pontoon! Towards the end of 1938, the worst effects of the overall economic depression were ameliorating and once again orders for trawlers resumed.

As the political situation in Europe deteriorated, the Admiralty began to order warships for the Royal Navy including two corvettes and two minesweepers from the Beverley yard. Also in 1939 during the month of August the Admiralty purchased several large trawlers for conversion to anti-submarine vessels. War was declared in September and once again the majority of the British fishing fleet was requisitioned to serve as minesweepers and anti-submarine vessels and in a variety of auxiliary roles. This included five trawlers *(Yard No's 650,651,654,655 and 656)* ordered in 1939. While six trawlers *(Yard No's 657-652)* which had been planned for civilian owners were cancelled because of the war situation. Grovehill was completely turned over to production for the Admiralty and between 1939 and 1945 Cook, Welton & Gemmell Ltd built 88 vessels for the Royal Navy, and 5 for the Ministry of War Transport.

Towards the end of 1944 when the invasion of Europe was well under way the Admiralty began to return requisitioned vessels to their owners for conversion and re-equipping as fishing vessels. At the same time the Government allowed shipbuilders to allocate turns (Yard No's) to prospective ship-owners for when peace-time ship building operations resumed. In 1945 projected costs for building new distant water trawlers had escalated to £60,000, double the £30,000 figure in 1939. Many trawler owners were unhappy with the situation and adopted a 'wait and see' approach. A few owners, however, ordered as many 'turns' as possible. Basil Parkes[22] (Boston Deep Sea Fishing Co Ltd) and J Marr & Son Ltd[23] were the first to place orders closely followed by Thomas Hamling & Co, Kingston Steam Trawling Co and the Grimsby firm of A.W. Butt. Those who moved to complete orders immediately after the war were proven to have taken the right decision since by 1948 the cost of building a distant water trawler had risen to over £100,000.

Following the launching of the last of the Admiralty and Ministry of War Transport orders the Grovehill yard was able to return to building civilian vessels, commencing with five home water trawlers. The first of these the ABY *(Yard No. 755)* was laid down at berth No. 1 on 18 May 1945, ten days after the VE-day celebrations.

In 1945, Edward Sheardown brought Ambrose Hunter to Beverley as managing director, an appointment which proved a great success as the yard diversified into the production of a wider variety of vessels. As opposed to the shipbuilding slump after the Great War the peace of 1945 brought a big demand for new ships. The Grovehill yard was soon working to capacity with a work force of about 700 including office staff, riveters, drillers, platers, caulkers, blacksmiths, burners, welders, shipwrights, joiners, painters and a French polisher. Arthur Bell was yard manager, Eric Hunter, chief draughtsman and Derek Massey, naval architect, and in this new era the design team working in conjunction with the Parkes and Marr families were credited with most of the technological advances within the British trawler fleet.

During the war, oil-fired steam vessels had proved highly successful in generating more steam power than the equivalent coal burners. This led to the yard receiving an order for five oil-fired distant water vessels for completion in 1946, the ST. JOHN *(Yard No. 763)*; ST. MATTHEW *(Yard No. 764)*; BREUGHEL *(Yard No. 765)*; REUBENS *(Yard No. 767)* and SOUTHELLA *(Yard No. 768)*. The ST. JOHN had the distinction of being the first oil-fired distant water trawler built for a British owner. The two Belgian trawlers were built for Motorvisserij of Ostend who had close links with Basil Parkes through his North Cape Fishing Company.

In 1946 and 1947 Cook, Welton & Gemmell built six trawlers for the French government and ten for the Icelandic government, the designs reflecting the particular fishing traditions and methods of these two nations and they are an interesting contrast to their British counterparts.

Completed in 1948 the ST. CHAD *(Yard No. 794)* was to herald a new design feature. Unlike their coal-burning predecessors, the oil-fired vessels did not require a tall funnel to keep smoke clear of the bridge. The funnel was reduced in size and incorporated into the bridge structure allowing a more streamlined design.

In 1949 Lesley Marr who was a skilled pilot purchased an aircraft, flew to South Africa and was able to sell a number of J Marr & Son Ltd surplus vessels. This venture resulted in a number of Beverley built trawlers being purchased by the National Trawling & Fishing Co, Cape Town an associate company of Irvin & Johnson also of Cape Town. The success of these vessels fishing in southern waters lead to a number of orders being placed with Cook Welton & Gemmell in 1953 for coal fired steam trawlers.

1949 also saw the appearance of the first of the big 'triple deck' bridge trawlers to be ordered, this was the KINGSTON GARNET *(Yard No. 816)*. She was laid down on 14 July that year, framed 30 August, plated 12 October and launched on 8 November. Towed from Grovehill on the evening tide of 5 January 1950 she arrived at the Albert Dock three days later, needing seven high tides to complete her journey! The completed trawler ran her trials on 7 February 1950.

In 1953, Coronation year, Edward Sheardown was appointed C.B.E. for his contribution to British industry after nearly thirty years as chairman and he died on 22 July the following year to be succeeded by John Wood.

J Marr & Son Ltd and Boston Deep-Sea Fisheries were instrumental in the construction of the yard's first motor trawlers. Beginning in 1946 the two companies had co-operated in the building of the two experimental motor trawlers the THORINA *(Yard No. 766)* and ALAN WATER *(Yard No. 777)*. In 1949 orders were placed for four home water trawlers, VELIA *(Yard No. 839)*, HILDINA *(Yard No. 852)*, IRVANA *(Yard No. 855)* and IDENA *(Yard No. 856)* but there was long delays in receiving the engines from Mirrlees. The manufacturers were experiencing production problems with these marine diesel engines the first such built by the company. Jimmy Mewse the superintendent engineer of J Marr must take much credit for their successful development for use in the trawler fleet and he spent a considerable amount of time developing lubricants and bearings which would allow the required torque and power to be generated. Delivered in 1953 the PRINCESS ANNE *(Yard No. 830)* and the BRUCELLA *(Yard No. 867)* were considered to be the first successful distant water motor trawlers.

Most owners, however, remained faithful to steam until the new motors had undergone several years of development and proved their worth at sea.

1958 saw the last steam trawler to be built at Beverley for British owners. This was the ARSENAL *(Yard No. 928)* which was also the only trawler built by Cook, Welton & Gemmell for Consolidated Fisheries Ltd of Grimsby.

Finally in 1959 the South African trawler DISA *(Yard No. 941)* built for Irvin & Johnson (Cape Town) had the distinction of being the last steam-powered vessel to be built at Beverley.

From the mid 1950's experiments were carried out to establish a practical system for freezing fish at sea. The traditional method of storing fish in crushed ice imposed a severe limitation on the time the vessel could spend at sea. After fifteen days fish preserved in this way declines rapidly in quality. This often meant a vessel returning home only partly filled in order to land any fish still in a saleable condition for eating, otherwise it would end up as fish meal. As it turned out the first vessel in the Hull fleet with freezing capability was the stern trawler LORD NELSON (H330) built by, Rickmers Werft of Bremerhaven in Germany for Associated Fisheries Ltd Hull. She arrived in the port on the 30 June 1961, which was to herald a new era in fishing. The net towed directly behind, not from the side, was brought up a ramp at the stern, an idea borrowed from the whale factory ships.

Managing director Ambrose Hunter left Beverley in 1960 to return to Scotland and R.J. Jackson was appointed. In recognition of their service to the company Eric Hunter and Derrick Massey were both made directors and served along with H. Brockman and H.C. Sargent.

In 1961 four distant-water trawlers were ordered LORD JELLICOE *(Yard No. 979)*, NORTHERN REWARD *(Yard No. 980)*, LORD ST VINCENT *(Yard No. 981)* and NORTHERN GIFT *(Yard No. 982)*. These were the last traditional side-fishing trawlers to be built for Associated Fisheries.

After the annual shareholders meeting in October 1962, the chairman of Cook, Welton & Gemmell, John Wood announced that the company was to cease trading once the contracts in hand had been completed. The 240 employees were each handed a notice to this effect and three main reasons were given why the closure was inevitable.

The Government deciding to subsidise, through the White Fish Authority, the building of trawlers for British owners in foreign yards was one major factor. In addition, following the amalgamation of so many of the trawler owning firms the number of potential customers had been greatly reduced and also the location of the yard presented a serious practical problem. The new trawlers in demand were getting bigger and bigger and could not be readily accommodated in the confined waters of the River Hull and its sinuous course between Beverley and Hull[24].

On 31 March 1963, eighty years of shipbuilding by Cook, Welton & Gemmell came to an end. By the time of its demise the company had earned a reputation for designing some of the finest trawlers ever built. A glance at the record books of all the major fishing ports show Beverley - built vessels to be amongst the most successful.

The yard produced several of the prestigious Silver cod winners, a trophy awarded for the highest total catch of the year, including the SOMERSET MAUGHAM *(Yard No.965)* which won the trophy no less than four times in 1962, 1965, 1966 and 1967.

The tug LADY ELSIE launched on 31 October 1962 had the sad distinction of being the last vessel built by Cook Welton & Gemmell and in February 1963 the company went into voluntary liquidation.

In total the company built 1317 vessels, 336 at Hull and 981 at Beverley. These consisted of :- Sailing Smacks 8, Steam Drifters 5, Coal Fired Steam Trawlers 883, Oil Fired Steam Trawlers 86, Motor Trawlers 60, Diesel Electric Trawlers 3, Admiralty vessels 160, HM War Office Vessels 15, Coasters 17, Steam Tugs 26, Motor Tugs 7, Light Floats 9, Boat Beacons 7, Estuarial Spirit Lighters 6, Passenger Pleasure Ships 4 and Mixed Others 21.

At the present time twenty-nine vessels are still in service (excluding light-vessels). The oldest of these is the IMDAT ex DUCHESS OF YORK (Yard No. 106) built at Hull in 1893.

The closure of Cook, Welton & Gemmell was the end of a chapter but the yard was re-opened under the ownership of C.D. Holmes a firm which had since the beginning supplied many of the engines, winches and other fittings(25). After a decade of production, the yard became part of the Drypool Shipbuilding and Engineering Co, which also included Cochrane of Selby(26). This firm went into liquidation in 1976 and the yard was then acquired by Whitby Shipbuilders Ltd subsequently, renamed Phoenix Shipbuilders Ltd. The next year, 21 May, a Receiver was called in by the Yorkshire Bank and this proved to be the end of the Grovehill site for shipbuilding.

An unnamed ramped transport ferry left unfinished was launched by the Yorkshire Dry Dock Co on 2 March 1979, the last vessel to leave the yard. It was moved to William Wright dock after the sale of the machinery and fittings at Beverley. At the end of 1981 the craft was taken to the Central Dry Dock (Hull) for conversion into a seismic survey vessel by Messrs. Ruscador(27).

NOTES

1. Joyce M Bellamy' The history of C. and W. Earle and Earles Shipbuilding and Engineering Co Ltd' **Business History** vol 6, no. 1, December 1963.

2. Died in Cottingham, near Hull, 20 February 1917.

3. Died in London, 29 August 192 1.

4. Died in Hull, 2 May 1926.

5. David Garbutt, shipbuilder, appears in the Hull trade directory for 1882 at a Spyvee Street address and in 1885 David Parkinson Garbutt is located on Garrison Side. Born 1845 his lasting achievement is as a developer of the Avenues estate which made him very rich but the shipbuilding venture lost him his fortune. Garbutt recovered his finances by further speculation this time in East Hull and in 1903 helped found the Hull City Mission. He died 15 November 1915 at Wyton Lodge. See Hull Times 14 July 1934, p6 and K Elson **Hull Personalities - Pearson Park and The Avenues**, Hull, 1990, pp7-8.

6. The Humber Iron Works were acquired in 1882 by Bailey and Leetham, steamship owners for fitting and repairing vessels of their fleet. The company was bought by Thomas Wilson and sons in 1903.

7. So called after Martin Samuelson who ran the shipyard on this site 1857-1864; succeeded by Humber Iron Works 1864 etc.

8. Presumably the daughter of William Gemmell.

9. A detailed description of the ZODIAC appears in the **Bulletin of the United States Fish Commission**, vol 8, 1888 (1890)

Washington, pp 183-6.

10. Kelsall and Beeching established a fleet of trawlers which operated the 'box system' in the North Sea. Because of the distinctive cockerel emblem on the funnel their vessels were known as the Gamecock fleet.

11. Founded in 1874 by Charles Frederick Amos and Henry Wilson Ringrose Smith in partnership with Arthur Wilson of the Wilson Line; the latter was Smiths brother-in-law. The three men purchased the former Albert Dock (Neptune Street) works of Martin Samuelson and set up business as marine and general engineers, boilermakers and iron and bronze founders. Amos's father had been a partner in an engineering firm in Essex and had sent his son to serve an apprenticeship at Earles yard where Smith was doing the same. After the 1939-1945 war the company merged with Brigham and Cowan, Engineers and Ship repairers and the name of Amos and Smith was discarded.

12. Transferred their business to Selby making way for Cook, Welton & Gemmell's transfer from Hull to Beverley in 1901.

13. For a description of the box fleet see; Malet Lambert Local History Originals vol. 27 **The Boxing Fleet - Fishing Log Book, 1929-1923 of Skipper John Glanville**; edited by A.G. Credland, 1985.

14. Then Hull's largest towing company; led the way to an amalgamation with a number of rival firms to form the United Towing Co in 1920; the naming system of vessels ending in -man was retained by the new firm; see Alan Ford **United Towing 1920-1990 - a history**, Hull 1990 and second revised edition 1997.

15. Though Bailey and Leethams fleet had been purchased by the Wilson Line in 1903 there were several years of wrangling by the former directors over the liquidation of the remaining assets. Presumably this prevented any long term lease being signed with Cook, Welton & Gemmell for use of this site (see note 6).

16. Thomas Hamling founded the company in 1893 which pioneered fishing at Bear Island. Ceased trading in 1983; see M Thompson **Hull's Side Fishing Trawling Fleet**, Hull, 1987.

17. A box fleet which rivalled that of Kelsall and Beeching who eventually took it under control; the Gamecock and Red Cross fleets remained in service until 1936 when they were forced into liquidation.

18. Hellyer trawlers were frequently named after Shakespearian characters.

19. The research ship **WILLIAM SCORESBY** used for whale-marking during the **DISCOVERY** expeditions (1925-1939) to the Antarctic Ocean. She was named after William Scoresby, (1789-1957) of Whitby, whaler and Arctic scientist.

20. Like Gemmell, as well as Charles Amos and Henry Smith, Charles Denton Holmes was apprenticed at Earles Shipyard. In 1869 Holmes (1848-1938) was taken into partnership with Messrs Brownlow Lumsden after being assistant manager at their Junction Foundry, Alfred Street. This had originally been the works of T and W Pim who in 1840 had fitted new boilers in the **SIRIUS**, the first vessel to cross the Atlantic east to west entirely under steam. In 1843 they launched Hull's first screw-driven steamer the ss **ARCHIMEDES**.
The firm of Brownlow Lumsden were the direct descendants of Brownlow and Pearson managers of the city's first steamship company the Hull Steam Packet Co. Richard Pearson of Thome in 1821 constructed the paddle-steamer **KINGSTON**; wooden-hulled it was the first sea-going steamer to be built in the region and was fitted with engines by Overton of Hull.
Holmes became the full owner of the firm in 1893 and it became known as C.D. Holmes and Co, registered in 1908 as a private limited company. See F.H. Pearson **The Early History of Hull Steam Shipping**, Hull, 1890 (Howden 1984) and A.G. Credland **Iron and Steel Shipbuilding on the Humber**: Earles of Hull, Hull, 1982.

21. The Kingston Steam Trawling Co was formed in 1897; in 1960 control of the company passed to Hellyers.

22. See memoir by his son Sir Basil Parkes O.B.E, **Trawlings of a Lifetime**, Isle of Man, 1991.

23. J. Marr and Son Ltd operated out of Hull and Fleetwood and their yellow hulled vessels are still a familiar sight in the Hull fish dock - see Michael Thompson **The Marr Story - the history of a fishing family**, Hull, 1995.

24. See **Trawling Times**, October 1962.

25. After the crash of the Hull fishing industry, as a result of the imposition of the 200 mile limit around Iceland, C.D. Holmes went into terminal decline and closed in 1979.

26. The Drypool Group (founded as Drypool Engineering in 1916) by 1966 owned five dry-docks including Union Dry-Dock and Central Dry-Dock, acquired Selby Shipyard in 1961 and Beverley in 1973, but overreached themselves and went into liquidation in 1976, badly hit by the collapse of orders for new distant water trawlers and over- capacity in the shipbuilding industry generally.

27. See A. G. Credland **Iron and Steam Ship-building**, p.37 (see note 20).

THE SHIPYARD

This view of the shipyard facing east is dated 15 September 1950 (Taken just prior to the shed being built for the construction of the Admiralty mine-sweepers). The framework alongside the vessels on to which wooden walkways were fitted were known as 'spalls'. To the right of the picture is one of the fixed crane and two crawler cranes used to lift heavy pieces of the ship into position.
Photo:- Beverley Shipyard Collection.

Bow shot of the trawler ELLA HEWETT (Yard No.871) showing the close framework which gave the added strength required by trawlers. The plating on the ship's side is known as the template straker (with the ribbon above), this plate acts as a guide to the positioning of the other plates.
Photo by courtesy of Stan Thompson.

At berth No.4, on 6 September 1948, shipyard workers are preparing the ST. APOLLO (Yard No.798) for launching. The launch ways were greased with soft-soap and tallow. The ropes placed over the ships side were stapled to the timber which formed 'the cradle' to stop them floating away, so they could be re-used. After the launch a boat collected any flotsam to keep the river clean. For the launch, the water level had to be just right about two inches below the jetty edge.
Photo:- Beverley Shipyard Collection.

One of the great shipbuilding traditions was the launching ceremony. Mrs Harold Davidson the wife of the secretary of J Marr & Son Ltd christens one of the company's vessels with a bottle of champagne smashed against the ship's bow. Also present on the platform are left Harold Edward Sheardown, chairman of Cook Welton & Gemmell and centre Don Campey a director.
Photo by courtesy of Andrew Marr.

On 26 September 1949 shipyard workers and their families watch the launch of the trawler NORTHERN PRINCE (Yard No.814). For the men who had worked on the ship the event brought a tremendous feeling of pride and achievement.
Photo:- Beverley Shipyard Collection.

This picture taken from Weel Bridge in 1957 shows the extent of the Grovehill Shipyard. Fitting out are the trawlers JOSEPH CONRAD (Yard No.924) and ARSENAL (Yard No.928). These vessels were the last oil fired steam trawlers to be built for British owners at Beverley.
Photo:- Beverley Shipyard Collection.

Moored in the River Hull awaiting the next high tide on passage from Beverley to Railway Dock, Hull is the trawler KIRKELLA (Yard No.861) assisted by the Peter Foster tugs LANCELOT and ACETUT. The trawler left Grovehill under tow on 12 February 1952 and arrived in Hull on 15 February the trip having taken seven high tides. The photograph highlights the confines of the river, and explains why all vessels were built with their bows pointing towards Hull.
Photo:- by courtesy of J Marr & Son Ltd.

Boilermakers at work tubing boiler No.1841 which was for the trawler ELLA HEWETT (Yard No.871).
Photo by courtesy of Hull Maritime Museum.

The tractor and trailer of Charles D Holmes & Co Ltd, transporting a triple expansion steam engine to the Albert Dock for installing aboard a trawler.
Photo by courtesy of Hull Maritime Museum.

With the trawler moored alongside the sheer-legs at Albert Dock, the engine is lowered into the engineroom.
Once the engine, boiler and winches had been installed the vessel was towed to C D Holmes fitting out berth in Princes Dock.
Photo by courtesy of Hull Maritime Museum.

On a visit to Hull in 1948 H.R.H. Prince Philip inspected the newly completed Grimsby trawler PRINCESS ELIZABETH (Yard No.800). To the right of Prince Philip is Harold Edward Sheardown chairman of Cook Welton & Gemmell and to the Prince's left is Ambrose Hunter the managing director.
Photo by courtesy of Hull Maritime Museum.

THE WORK FORCE

In the plating shed, the plater and plater's helpers are pulling a frame from the furnace. This operation needed a line of at least four men who linked hands to move the heavy frame from the furnace. On the floor to the right is the template to which the frame had to be bent to shape. Because of the heat and exhaustive work they were issued with Barley Water to replace body fluid.
Photo:- Beverley Shipyard Collection.

Two riveters at work on the stem of the KINGSTON JACINTH (Yard No.836) in 1951. The plates were first bolted into place prior to being riveted. One man holds the rivet in place whilst the other man hammers it into shape, the third man catches the hot rivets for the riveters. The chalk marks on rivets are made by the tallyman to work out the piece work pay rate.
Photo:- Beverley Shipyard Collection.

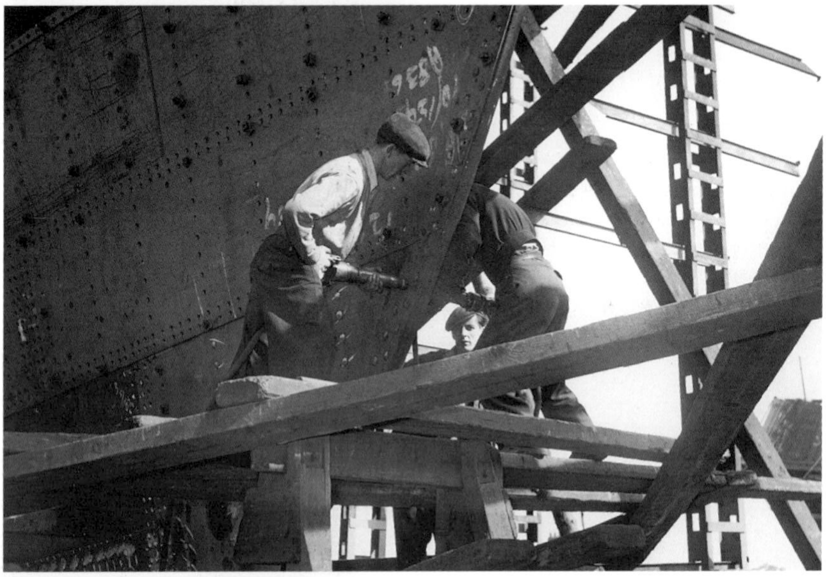

The burner is cutting a plate to shape, every single piece of plate was made to a template. The templates were made in the mould loft from plans which were drawn up in the shipyard's drawing office.
Photo:- Beverley Shipyard Collection.

A Welder at work on the deck plates of a vessel. As time progressed increasing use was made of welding until eventually riveted ships disappeared from the scene.
Photo:- Beverley Shipyard Collection.

Joiners fitting a cabin door frame. Interiors were completed to a very high standard with top quality wood and brass fittings used. The shipyard employed a French Polisher to complete the interior work.
Photo:- Beverley Shipyard Collection.

Shipwrights at work measuring up the interior of a trawler's bridge, for the positioning of the various equipment. The coils of wire cable were awaiting installation by electricians. The electrical work was contracted out to Broady's.
Photo:- Beverley Shipyard Collection.

CASUALTIES

The ATHELSTAN (Yard No.222/1911) was one of the many trawlers lost in Wartime. Presumed to have been mined, she was last seen on 27 April 1940. The trawler was Posted Missing :- Lost with all hands.
Photo by courtesy of Henry Hartley

The CUCKOO (Yard No.154/1896) has managed to return safely to St. Andrew's Dock, having sustained severe collision damage. Collisions were one of the main causes of North Sea trawler losses.
Photo by courtesy of Jonathan Grobler

On 13 February 1933, the ST. DELPHINE (Yard No.491/1928) lies stranded in the mud on the bank of the River Humber, having run aground in thick fog. Because of her strong construction the trawler was not in danger and was floated off on the next high tide.
Photo Author's Collection

May 1924, the HESSONITE (Yard No.398/1918) lies wrecked under high cliffs, two miles from Birsay, Orkney Isles. Despite the high seas, the Stromness lifeboat managed to rescue all twelve crew off the stricken trawler.
Photo Author's Collection

March 1939, the LADY JEANETTE (Yard No.616/1937) lies capsized off Hessle foreshore, in the River Humber. Nine crew were lost in the tragedy. Salvage attempts failed and the wreck was dispersed with explosives.
Photo Author's Collection

April 1947, the SHERATON (Yard No.115/1906) lies wrecked near Hunstanton Lighthouse. The trawler was on charter to the R.A.F. for use as a Target Towing Vessel at the time of her loss.
Photo Author's Collection

September 1953, the HASSETT (Yard No.521/1929) lies wrecked at Aukeingill, 10 miles north of Wick. Fifteen of the trawler's crew were rescued by the Coastguard using breeches buoy equipment, five crew were lost in the tragedy.
Photo Author's Collection

March 1968, the ROSS TARIFA (Yard No.795/1948) sinks into the Goodwin sands, where she came to rest after breaking free of the tug MOORCOCK in bad weather, whilst on tow from Hull to a shipbreakers yard in Belgium.
Photo Author's Collection

Yard No.1 1885 PRECURSOR *Photo by courtesy of David Taylor*

Yard No.9 1885 IRRAWADDY *Photo by courtesy of Lynne Petersen*

Vessels built at Hull 1885 to 1904.

NAME Official No. Port Letters Numbers	Yard No. Launched Registered	Registered G Ton N Ton	 L Ft B Ft	Engine Builder Horse Power Reg'd Speed	OWNER (Built for)
PRECURSOR 91399 H1426 Sailing Smack	1 21.01.1885 27.03.1885	92 92	81.4 20.3	N/A	Robert Hellyer Hull
27.04.1898 Sold to William D Crooks, Plymouth. 1909 to John H Tope, Plymouth for use as cargo vessel. 11.07.1914 Vessel sank following a collision with the s.s WILLIAM BALLS (2483 gt/ b 1894) of North Shields 5 miles north of Shipwash Light-vessel in approx Position 52°04.3'N 001°38'E on passage from Plymouth towards Hull with a cargo of china clay.					
BASSANIO 91404 H1432 Sailing Smack	2 04.03.1885 18.04.1885	92 92	81.4 20.3	C.D.Holmes 40 NHP 9.5 knots	Robert Hellyer Hull
Aug 1888 Converted to a steam trawler and *(Lengthened to 96.7 ft 119.6 Gross tons 54.6 Net tons).* 16.08.1888 Re-registered as a steam trawler and renamed HERMIONE. 10.09.1900 Sold to Soc des Pecheries du Gulfe de Gascogne, Bordeaux, France. renamed PHOQUE II (ARC8524). 1929 to G F Castaing, La Rochelle. 1923 Vessel sold to shipbreakers and broken up.					
MAGNETA 91421 H1447 Sailing Smack	3 00.05.1885 18.06.1885	89 89	81.2 20.2	C.D.Holmes 40 NHP 9.5 knots	Francis & Thomas Ross Ltd Hull
Oct 1888 Converted to a steam trawler *(Lengthened to 95.7 ft 116 Gross tons 56 Net tons).* 15.10.1888 Re-registered as a steam trawler. 24.01.1908 Vessel wrecked at Creek Point near Hayburn Wyke, Yorkshire.					
PLOVER 91437 H1466 Sailing Smack	4 00.09.1885 26.10.1885	89 89	81.0 20.2	N/A	John William Hellyer Hull
23.11.1895 Vessel sank following a collision with the ss WHARFE (914 gt/ b 1890) at the entrance to the River Humber.					
UNITY 91429 H1455 Sailing Smack	5 00.06.1885 01.08.1885	89 89	81.0 20.3	N/A	Francis & Thomas Ross Ltd Hull
18.11.1890 Sold to Hull Steam Fishing & Ice Co Ltd, Hull. 05.03.1896 Sold to Norwegian owners. 1908 Vessel deleted from Lloyds Register of Shipping.					
ARIEL 91446 H1473 Sailing Smack	6 00.09.1885 11.11.1885	89 89	81.0 20.5	C.D.Holmes 43 NHP 9.5 knots	Charles Hellyer Hull
July 1888 Converted to a steam trawler *(Lengthened to 95.5 ft 117.4 Gross tons 61 Net tons).* 30.07.1888 Re-registered as a steam trawler and renamed OBERON.25.02.1901 Sold to E Soloman & Co, L'Orient, France. 17.02.1913 Vessel sank off Cape Castellas on passage Port de Boue towards Valencia with a cargo of fish.					
ELEANOR MARIA M 91542 GY1036 Sailing Smack	7 00.06.1885 13.08.1885	89 89	81.4 20.3	N/A	Henry Morris Grimsby
27.08.1886 Sold to James Revler, Grimsby. 26.02.1887 Sold to Robert Hellyer, Hull renamed NARCISSUS (H12). 28.01.1898 to John Flett, Kirkwall, Orkney. 1900 Vessel deleted from Lloyds Register of Shipping.					
GOOD & BLANCHARD 91545 GY1040 Sailing Smack	8 00.09.1885 03.10.1885	89 89	81.4 20.3	N/A	Jesse Good & Henry Blanchard Grimsby
17.09.1887 Sold to Robert Hellyer, Hull renamed INVICTA (H26). 31.08.1900 to Joseph Jewell, Bideford, Devon. 1913 to A C S Store, Bideford, Devon. 1914 to Portuguese owners. 1914 Vessel deleted from Lloyds Register of Shipping.					
IRRAWADDY 93063 H1479 Steam Trawler	9 00.12.1885 30.12.1885	126 66	100.0 20.0	C.D.Holmes 45 NHP 10 knots	George Beeching & Thomas Kelsall Hull
05.11.1889*(Tonnage adjusted 133.1 Gross Tons 84.9 Net Tons).* 06.12.1889 Sold to The British Steam Fishing Co Ltd, Hull. 13.04.1910 to Thomas Stephen, Aberdeen (A313). 1914 to J N Sanne, Uddevalla, Sweden renamed ALBATROSS. 1923 Vessel sold to shipbreakers and broken up.					
HOPE Sailing Smack	10 1886	Order cancelled vessel not built			
HERON 93073 H1489 Steam Trawler	11 22.03.1886 08.05.1886	106 46	90.0 20.4	Muir & Houston 37 NHP 9.5 knots	William Henry Putt Hull
14.08.1889 Sold to Liverpool Steam Fishing Co Ltd, Liverpool (LL99). 1902 to Soc. des Pecheries de Gulfe de Gascogne, Bordeaux, France renamed LAMANTIN (ARC8474). 1914 to J F Caistaing, La Rochelle, France. Feb 1916 Vessel posted missing:- Lost with all hands.					

NAME Official No. Port Letters Numbers	Yard No. Launched Registered	Registered G Ton N Ton	 L Ft B Ft	Engine Builder Horse Power Reg'd Speed	OWNER (Built for)
LARK 93077 H1493 Steam Trawler	12 00.05.1886 15.05.1886	102 52	90.0 20.4	C.D.Holmes 30 NHP 9.2 knots	Christopher Pickering & Samuel L Haldane Hull
24.10.1888 *(Tonnage adjusted 105.6 Gross Tons & 68.4 Net Tons).* 15.11.1904 Sold to Joshua J Neale & Henry West Ltd, Cardiff (CF12). 1909 to Societa Ilva, Naples, Italy renamed AQUILA. Jul 1912 Vessel sold to shipbreakers and broken up.					
LINNET 93079 H1495 Steam Trawler	13 04.06.1886 03.07.1886	102 52	90.0 20.4	C.D.Holmes 30 NHP 9.2 knots	Christopher Pickering & Samuel L Haldane Hull
09.11.1886 Sold to H J Julius, Geestemunde, Germany renamed AMALIE (PG7). Feb 1900 Vessel posted missing:- Lost with all hands.					
ELECTRA 93080 H1498 Steam Trawler	14 00.05.1886 19.06.1886	102 54	90.0 20.4	C.D.Holmes 30 NHP 9 knots	Francis & Thomas Ross Ltd Hull
01.06.1900 Sold to E Douville, Dieppe, France renamed PIERRE FRANÇOIS (DI365). 1916 to Mme Vve A Lecat, Dieppe. 1930 to Soc. Anon des Chalutiers du Littoral, Arcachon. 1935 to Gaston Le Corrone, L'Orient. 1937 Vessel sold to shipbreakers and broken up.					
ADVENTURE 93083 H1500 Steam Trawler	15 00.06.1886 28.07.1886	122 50	89.8 20.7	Bailey & Leetham 35 NHP 9.5 knots	Richard Simpson Hull
08.02.1889 Vessel sank during a storm in the North Sea.					
BRITANNIA 93088 H1506 Steam Trawler	16 21.07.1886 13.08.1886	122 51	89.8 20.7	C.D.Holmes 35 NHP 9.5 knots	Richard Simpson Hull
27.08.1894 Sold to Edward P Maxstead & Walter S Bailey, Hull. 05.07.1902 to Vivda de J B Otermin, San Sebastian, Spain renamed ELCANO. 1920 to Ana Huarle, San Sebastian. 1922 to S A & F Gorgonio, Valencia. 08.02.1930 Vessel foundered off Valencia.					
ROSE 93097 Steam Lighter	17 00.01.1887 28.02.1887	67.5 49	81.4 15.2	E. Wales 20 NHP 6 knots	J Hobson York
18.04.1901 Sold to Henry Leetham, York. 23.11.1901 *(Converted to a Dumb barge).*					
INDUSTRIA 93104 H14 Steam Trawler	18 00.02.1887 10.03.1887	133 62	95.0 20.7	C.D.Holmes 35 NHP 9.5 knots	Francis & Thomas Ross Ltd Hull
30.04.1917 Vessel captured by U-boat and sunk by time bombs in the North Sea.					
BOURNEMOUTH 93107 H17 Steam Trawler	19 00.03.1887 19.04.1887	135 62	97.0 20.6	C.D.Holmes 40 NHP 10 knots	Charles Hellyer Hull
13.12.1889 Sold to Western Steam Trawling Co Ltd, Bristol (BL2). 1912 to Fiskeriaktieb, Gothenburg, Sweden renamed TARNAN. 1917 to Italian owners. 1919 Vessel sold to Italian shipbreakers and broken up.					
FRANCES 93135 Steam Yacht	20 00.04.1888 15.05.1888	20 7	56.0 11.0	Robey & Co 9 NHP 8 knots	George W Long Hull
20.09.1913 Sold to Walter Crampin, Grimsby.09.11.1915 to A Bannister and registered as a fishing vessel (GY903). 28.06.1917 Vessel captured by U Boat and sunk by time bombs 10 miles north-east of Spurn Point Yorkshire.					
CHINDWIN 92123 H34 Steam Trawler	21 03.12.1887 31.12.1887	127 59	100.0 20.1	C.D.Holmes 45 NHP 10 knots	George Beeching & Thomas Kelsall Hull
06.02.1895 Vessel wrecked Port Patrick West Scotland.					
VANGUARD 93128 H36 Steam Trawler	22 01.03.1888 30.03.1888	134 59	98.6 20.3	C.D.Holmes 45 NHP 10 knots	Charles Hellyer Hull
19.07.1889 Sold to Cia Portuguezade Pescarias, Lisbon, Portugal renamed FERNANDO. 09.06.1890 Vessel wrecked near Cape Roca. All crew rescued.					

NAME Official No. Port Letters Numbers	Yard No. Launched Registered	Registered G Ton N Ton	 L Ft B Ft	Engine Builder Horse Power Reg'd Speed	OWNER (Built for)
GENERAL ROBERTS 93132 H38 Steam Trawler	23 01.03.1888 28.03.1888	142 62	100.0 20.3	C.D.Holmes 45 NHP 10 knots	Christopher Pickering Samuel L Haldane Henry A L Russell Hull
22.01.1891 Sold to W Wolfe, Milford Haven. 1903 G Pettit, Milford Haven. 05.06.1906 Vessel foundered 12 miles north-east of Round Island Isles of Scilly.					
HEREWOOD 93138 Steam Tug	24 23.04.1888 25.05.1888	108 20	98.2 20.8	C.D.Holmes 60 NHP 11 knots	Thomas Gray & Co Ltd Hull
04.0.91888 Sold to The Peninsular & Oriental Steam Navigation Co Ltd, London for use at Bombay, India. 1915 to Mazagon Dock Co, Bombay, India. 28.11.1918 Vessel sold to shipbreakers and broken up.					
RANGOON 93140 H45 Steam Trawler	25 00.05.1888 15.06.1888	129 54	100.4 20.1	C.D.Holmes 45 NHP 10 knots	George Beeching & Thomas Kelsall Hull
08.01.1897 Vessel transferred to Fleetwood (FD149).07.04.1899 Returned to Hull (H87) by Kelsall Bros. & Beeching. 23.05.1912 Sold to Gjerdajö & Balkkevig, Haugesund, Norway renamed ATLE . 1934 to Steffen Staalesen, Haugesund, Norway renamed MIMIR. 1948 renamed ATLE *(diesel engine fitted by Nils Finnöy Motorfbk).* 09.09.1955 Vessel sank following a collision east of Langanes.					
DOGGER BANK 93143 H47 Steam Trawler	26 00.06.1888 21.07.1888	135 55	95.3 20.9	C.D.Holmes 45 NHP 10 knots	George Bowman Hull
24.12.1890 Sold to Edward Cargill, Hull. 18.04.1893 Vessel sank following a collision with the German barque THEKLA in the North Sea.					
PRIME MINISTER 93145 H48 Steam Trawler	27 28.07.1888 28.08.1888	135 57	95.3 20.8	C.D.Holmes 45 NHP 10 knots	Richard Simpson Hull
09.11.1889 Sold to The Humber Steam Trawling Co Ltd, Hull. 27.08.1894 to Edward P Maxstead & Walter S Bailey, Hull. 19.09.1903 Vessel wrecked south of Hayburn Wyke near Whitby, Yorkshire.					
LORD CHANCELLOR 93149 H50 Steam Trawler	28 00.09.1888 06.10.1888	135 57	95.3 20.8	C.D.Holmes 45 NHP 10 knots	Humber Steam Trawling Co Ltd Hull
05.07.1906 Sold to James Hall Sunderland (SD86) 1915 to W Grant Grimsby (GY711) 16.04.1917 Vessel captured by U-boat and sunk 50 miles north-east of Longstone (Holy Island).					
RESOLUTE 95772 H52 Steam Trawler	29 00.10.1888 12.11.1888	131 57	98.8 20.3	C.D.Holmes 45 NHP 10 knots	Robert Hellyer Hull
03.04.1890 Sold to Cia Portugueza de Pascaria, Lisbon, Portugal renamed NISARD. 1895 to Cia Colonial de Buzi, Beira, Mozambique renamed AÇOR. 1906 *(Converted to a storage hulk).*					
MIZPAH 95776 H56 Steam Trawler	30 00.11.1888 14.12.1888	131 57	98.8 20.3	C.D.Holmes 45 NHP 10 knots	Robert Hellyer Hull
06.02.1890 Sold to Fischdampfer Rhederie Nordsee, Altona, Germany renamed NORDSEE. Dec 1894 Vessel posted missing:- Lost with all hands.					
ZEBEDEE 95778 H62 Steam Trawler	31 00.12.1888 17.01.1889	131 57	98.8 20.3	C.D.Holmes 45 NHP 10 knots	Robert Hellyer Hull
21.12.1889 Sold to Ei Sine a Resuluen F do Asqueta, San Sabastian, Spain renamed ALFREDO. 1889 to Mercader & Hije, San Sebastian, Spain renamed BASCONIA renamed (1899) MAMELENA No.4. 15.11.1901 Vessel wrecked after stranding on the coast of Mimezan Landes.					
SIR ALBERT ROLLIT 95775 H55 Steam Trawler	32 30.11.1888 14.12.1888	135 57	95.3 20.8	Bailey & Leetham 45 NHP 10 knots	Humber Steam Trawling Co Ltd Hull
27.05.1894 Sold to Edward P Maxtead & Walter S Bailey, Hull. 14.07.1906 to James Hall, Sunderland (SD88). 1913 to G M Suinhofvud, Gothenburg, Sweden renamed NANNA. 1919 Vessel deleted from Lloyds Register of Shipping.					

Yard No.35
1889 EDWARD ROBSON
Photo:- Barnard and Straker Collection

Yard No.49
1890 LYCURGUS
Photo:- Barnard and Straker Collection

Yard No.53
1890 MANDALAY
Photo:- Barnard and Straker Collection

<table>
<tr><th rowspan="2">NAME
Official No.
Port Letters Numbers</th><th rowspan="2">Yard No.
Launched
Registered</th><th colspan="2">Registered</th><th rowspan="2">Engine Builder
Horse Power
Reg'd Speed</th><th rowspan="2">OWNER
(Built for)</th></tr>
<tr><th>G Ton
N Ton</th><th>L Ft
B Ft</th></tr>
<tr><td>NIL DESPERANDUM
95785
H66 Steam Trawler</td><td>33
16.03.1889
28.03.1889</td><td>140
50</td><td>100.5
20.9</td><td>Bailey & Leetham
45 NHP
10 knots</td><td>Humber Steam
Trawling Co Ltd
Hull</td></tr>
<tr><td colspan="6">22.11.1894 (Tonnage adjusted 148.0 gt 57.7 nt).
15.04.1913 Sold to Progress Steam Trawling Co Ltd, Scarborough (SH186).
25.09.1916 Vessel sunk by U-boat 20 miles north-east of Scarborough. One of 13 trawlers captured and sunk by a U-boat during the hours of darkness 24/25.09.1916. on Whitby Fine Ground. The German commander stopped a Norwegian cargo ship and arranged for the 126 captured fishermen to be landed at a British port (South Shields).</td></tr>
<tr><td>EXCELSIOR
95795
H70 Steam Trawler</td><td>34
01.06.1889
18.06.1889</td><td>140
50</td><td>100.6
20.9</td><td>Bailey & Leetham
45 NHP
10 knots</td><td>Humber Steam
Trawling Co Ltd
Hull</td></tr>
<tr><td colspan="6">09.10.1894 (Tonnage adjusted 148.0 gt 57.7 nt).
09.01.1905 Vessel wrecked in severe weather on rocks at the "Grand" Egilsay Island, Orkney. Sister trawler EDWARD ROBSON tried to tow the EXCELSIOR free but failed. She took off all nine crew and landed them at Kirkwall.</td></tr>
<tr><td>EDWARD ROBSON
95798
H73 Steam Trawler</td><td>35
1889
15.07.1889</td><td>140
50</td><td>100.6
20.9</td><td>Bailey & Leetham
45 NHP
10 knots</td><td>Humber Steam
Trawling Co Ltd
Hull</td></tr>
<tr><td colspan="6">09.10.1894 (Tonnage adjusted 148.0 gt 57.7 nt).12.01.1914 Sold to Fiskaktie "Mars", Gothenburg, Sweden renamed MARS.
01.01.1923 Vessel sank after a collision 10 miles off Vinga.</td></tr>
<tr><td>TORFRIDA
95783
Steam Tug</td><td>36
1889
28.02.1889</td><td>126
14</td><td>106.0
19.5</td><td>C.D.Holmes
75 NHP
11.5 knots</td><td>Thomas Gray & Co Ltd
Hull</td></tr>
<tr><td colspan="6">23.12.1893 Sold to J C Egea, Almera, Spain renamed SAN JACINTO.
1898 to J Davis Towage & Salvage Ltd, Liverpool renamed TORFRIDA.
01.03.1950 Vessel sold for scrap to John Ford & Sons Ltd, and broken up at Cardiff.</td></tr>
<tr><td>UNDINE
96195
GY204 Steam Trawler</td><td>37
1889
11.05.1889</td><td>163
69</td><td>106.3
20.5</td><td>C.D.Holmes
50 NHP
10 knots</td><td>Grimsby Union Steam
Fishing Co Ltd
Grimsby</td></tr>
<tr><td colspan="6">31.10.1910 Sold to N V Zeeviss Maats de ver Wachting , Ijmuiden, Holland renamed NEELTJE CATHARINA (IJM160).
Jan 1916 Vessel posted missing in the North Sea (possibly mined):- Lost with all hands.</td></tr>
<tr><td>PHILIP MAXTED
95793
H69 Steam Trawler</td><td>38
13.05.1889
27.05.1889</td><td>140
50</td><td>100.6
20.9</td><td>Bailey & Leetham
45 NHP
10 knots</td><td>Humber Steam
Trawling Co Ltd
Hull</td></tr>
<tr><td colspan="6">16.11.1894 (Tonnage adjusted 148 gt 57 nt). 19.12.1912 Sold to Thomas Lauder, Aberdeen (A537).
1920 to C Larsson, Gothenburg, Sweden renamed GREYHOUND. 1923 to Rederiet Ester, Gothenburg renamed ESTER.
1925 Vessel reported to have been wrecked.</td></tr>
<tr><td>FOXHOUND
95803
H75 Steam Trawler</td><td>39
26.08.1889
10.09.1889</td><td>140
50</td><td>100.7
20.9</td><td>Bailey & Leetham
45 NHP
10 knots</td><td>Humber Steam
Trawling Co Ltd
Hull</td></tr>
<tr><td colspan="6">27.01.1909 Vessel sank following a collision with the Grimsby trawler OLYMPIA GY62 (see Bev Yard No. 71) off Spurn Head. The OLYMPIA sustained considerable damage in the collision but was able to reach Grimsby.</td></tr>
<tr><td>DEERHOUND
95815
H81 Steam Trawler</td><td>40
1889
26.11.1889</td><td>140
60</td><td>100.7
20.9</td><td>Bailey & Leetham
45 NHP
10 knots</td><td>Humber Steam
Trawling Co Ltd
Hull</td></tr>
<tr><td colspan="6">15.02.1900 Vessel sank in the North Sea with the loss of all nine crew. One of five Hull trawlers which disappeared in the "great gale and blizzard" which caused considerable damage to shipping and to coastal towns.</td></tr>
<tr><td>OSTRICH
95801
H74 Steam Trawler</td><td>41
1889
13.08.1889</td><td>140
49</td><td>100.7
20.9</td><td>C.D.Holmes
45 NHP
10 knots</td><td>William Henry Putt
Hull</td></tr>
<tr><td colspan="6">08.01.1895 Sold to St Andrews Steam Fishing Co Ltd, Hull. 09.11.1900 to T H Peverall, Hartlepool (HL61).
1914 to F W Mason, Hartlepool. 10.02.1917 Vessel captured by U-boat and sunk 135 miles off Longstone.</td></tr>
<tr><td>GRAPHIC
95807
H78 Steam Trawler</td><td>42
1889
10.10.1889</td><td>141
68</td><td>103.7
20.3</td><td>C.D.Holmes
45 NHP
10 knots</td><td>Charles Hellyer &
James Chant
Hull</td></tr>
<tr><td colspan="6">19.03.1890 Sold to Parceria de Pescarais Norte, Oporto, Portugal renamed CHIRE.
21.05.1917 to George F Sleight, Grimsby renamed VIOLET CAIE (GY1051).
1917 Rqd by the Royal Navy as a fishing trawler (Fishery Reserve). 1919 returned.
04.12.1925 to Moreau & Cayrouse, Dieppe, France renamed JACQUELINE-LOUISE.
1937 Vessel sold to shipbreakers and broken up.</td></tr>
</table>

NAME Official No. Port Letters Numbers	Yard No. Launched Registered	Registered G Ton N Ton	 L Ft B Ft	Engine Builder Horse Power Reg'd Speed	OWNER (Built for)
GREYHOUND 95817 H84 Steam Trawler	43 27.11.1889 16.12.1889	140 60	100.6 20.9	Bailey & Leetham 45 NHP 10 knots	Humber Steam Trawling Co Ltd Hull
20.01.1914 Sold to Swedish owners. 1919 Vessel deleted from Lloyds register of shipping.					
ENGLISHMAN 95814 Steam Tug	44 1889 15.11.1889	169 32	116.0 22.0	C.D.Holmes 96 NHP 12 knots	Thomas Gray & Co Ltd Hull
14.01.1898 Sold to A Bazile fils ainé & Co, Rouen, France renamed INDUSTRIE. 1900 to Öhrvikens Aktieb, Skellefteå. 1904 to J Block, Cheefoo, China. 1906 to Japanese Government (Navy Dept). 1909 Vessel deleted from Lloyds Register of Shipping.					
STAGHOUND 95818 H85 Steam Trawler	45 1889 23.01.1890	152 53	101.1 20.9	Bailey & Leetham 45 NHP 10 knots	Humber Steam Trawling Co Ltd Hull
21.12.1894 Vessel sank in the North Sea with the loss of all nine crew. One of six Hull trawlers and nine smacks which were lost in the severe storms which raged through the North Sea during December 1894.					
BLOODHOUND 95821 H89 Steam Trawler	46 08.02.1890 05.03.1890	150 52	100.4 20.9	Bailey & Leetham 45 NHP 10 knots	Humber Steam Trawling Co Ltd Hull
16.12.1912 Sold to Thomas Lauder, Aberdeen (A533). 1920 to Oberon Shipping Co Ltd, Hull (H57). 1922 Sessions & Sons Ltd, Cardiff. 1937 Vessel sold to shipbreakers and broken up.					
RICHARD SIMPSON 95823 H91 Steam Trawler	47 22.02.1890 28.03.1890	185 65	110.6 20.5	C.D.Holmes 60 NHP 10.5 knots	Humber Steam Trawling Co Ltd Hull
11.05.1899 Vessel wrecked after stranding on the south coast of Iceland.					
OTTERHOUND 95824 H92 Steam Trawler	48 1890 21.04.1890	150 52	100.5 20.9	Bailey & Leetham 45 NHP 10 knots	Humber Steam Trawling Co Ltd Hull
06.04.1914 Sold to Nigel S Clarke, Scarborough . 25.9.1916 Vessel captured by U-boat and sunk 20 miles north-east of Scarborough *(see Yard No. 33)*.					
LYCURGUS 95828 H93 Steam Trawler	49 1890 12.05.1890	146 49	102.6 20.3	C.D.Holmes 50 NHP 10 knots	Charles Hellyer Hull
11.06.1897 Hellyer Steam Fishing Co Ltd, Hull. 22.12.1908 Vessel sank following a collision with the Hellyer Trawler EUDOCIA H130 *(see Yard No. 61)* in the North Sea.					
VICTORIA 95831 H96 Steam Trawler	50 1890 28.05.1890	155 55	104.5 20.3	C.D.Holmes 50 NHP 10 knots	Pickering & Haldane's Steam Trawling Co Ltd Hull
02.12.1910 Sold to Thomas Hudson, Hull. 20.12.1912 to Hudson Fishing Co Ltd, Fleetwood. 01.06.1915 Vessel captured by U-103 (Claus Rucker) and sunk by time bombs 145 miles from St Ann's Head Nr Milford Haven. Whilst trying to escape the trawler was shelled and the skipper and five crew were killed.					
ANGLIA 96223 GY254 Steam Trawler	51 1890 02.07.1890	147 50	102.0 20.4	C.D.Holmes 50 NHP 10 knots	Henry Bennett Grimsby
05.01.1895 Sold to Anchor Steam Fishing Co Ltd, Grimsby. 25.05.1901 to George R Nicholson, Liverpool (LL127). 1903 to James Hall, Sunderland (SD80). 1913 to J N Sanne, Uddevalla, Sweden renamed FISKMÅSON. 1927 to Fiskeri A/B Neptun, Gothenburg renamed NEPTUN. 1940 Vessel sold to shipbreakers and broken up.					
CEYLON 95842 H103 Steam Trawler	52 1890 02.08.1890	169 65	106.0 21.0	C.D.Holmes 50 NHP 10 knots	Hull Steam Fishing & Ice Co Ltd Hull
03.12.1904 Vessel sank after a collision with the Hull trawler VANCOUVER H299 (139 gt/ b 1895) in the North Sea. After affecting temporary repairs an attempt was made to sail the CEYLON home escorted by the trawler HOBART H555 *(see Yard No. 7)* but by the following day she settled by the stern and sank. All nine crew were taken aboard the HOBART.					
MANDALAY 95845 H105 Steam Trawler	53 1890 27.08.1890	148 48	103.2 20.0	C.D.Holmes 50 NHP 10 knots	George Beeching & Thomas Kelsall Hull
08.01.1897 Vessel transferred to Fleetwood (FD146). 01.01.1899 Returned to Hull (H77) by Kelsall Bros & Beeching. 22.10.1904 Damaged on the Dogger Bank North Sea by the Russian Navy Baltic Fleet which was en route to the Pacific and mistook the Hull trawler fleet for Japanese torpedo boats and opened fire on them. *(The Dogger Bank Incident)*. 14.02.1908 Vessel wrecked after stranding at Ravenscar in thick fog. All crew rescued.					

NAME	Yard No.	Registered		Engine Builder	OWNER
Official No.	Launched	G Ton	L Ft	Horse Power	(Built for)
Port Letters Numbers	Registered	N Ton	B Ft	Reg'd Speed	
PRINCE CONSORT	54	154	104.0	C.D.Holmes	Pickering & Haldane's Steam
98702	1890	55	20.3	50 NHP	Trawling Co Ltd
H106 Steam Trawler	11.09.1890			10 knots	Hull
03.02.1911 Sold to Thos Davidson, Aberdeen (A358). 18.04.1917 to Joseph R Mordant Grimsby (GY1036). 1917 Rqd by the Royal Navy as a fishing trawler (Fishery Reserve). 1919 returned. 23.10.1917 to Record Steam fishing Co Ltd, Grimsby. 22.03.1918 to Brent Steam Fishing Co Ltd, Grimsby . 26.02.1919 to James Mathorn, London. 22.10.1920 to Bank Steam Fishing Co Ltd, Grimsby. 28.11.1924 Registration closed on advice that the vessel was broken up.					
ZENOBIA	55	145	100.3	C.D.Holmes	Charles Hellyer &
98705	1890	48	20.2	45 NHP	James Chant
H110 Steam Trawler	17.10.1890			10 knots	Hull
30.10.1891 Sold to Charles Hellyer, Hull. 05.08.1897 to Hellyer Steam Fishing Co Ltd, Hull. 26.11.1905 to R R Pastor, Corunna, Spain renamed HISTORIA renamed (1906) ZENOBIA. 1915 to L Lamigueiru, Corunna, Spain. 1919 to Soc Française des Pecheries du Calvados, Caen, France renamed BARBUE. 1924 to E Leveau, Dieppe, France.1940 Requisitioned by the French Navy.24.07.1943 Vessel sunk by mine near to Ile de Rè					
SAN PEDRO	56	130	93.0	C.D.Holmes	Richard L Coller
98703	1890	45	20.7	45 NHP	Birkenhead
Steam Trawler	03.10.1890			10 knots	
04.10.1890 Sold to F L Roxas Manilla, Philippines. 1895 to Atlantic & Gulf & Pacific Improvement Co Ltd, Manilla. 1909 Deleted from Lloyds register of shipping.					
MARTABAN	57	148	103.6	C.D.Holmes	George Beeching & Thomas
98710	1890	49	20.0	50 NHP	Kelsall & Co
H115 Steam Trawler	20.11.1890			10 knots	Hull
08.01.1897 Vessel transferred to Fleetwood (FD147). 04.04.1899 Returned to Hull (H82) by Kelsall Bros & Beeching. 05.12.1912 Robert Moon, Aberdeen (A527). 20.05.1915 Vessel captured by U-boat and sunk by gunfire 22 miles east by north of Aberdeen.					
GIBRALTAR	58	146	100.4	C.D.Holmes	Hull Steam Fishing
98713	1890	51	20.5	45 NHP	& Ice Co Ltd
H119 Steam Trawler	29.12.1890			10 knots	Hull
24.07.1907 Sold to A Agafleff Archangel, Russia renamed OPYT. 1911 *(Rebuilt as a cargo vessel tonnage adjusted 170 Gross Tons).* 1915 to Russian Navy as a mine-sweeper No. T10. 14.10.1916 Vessel wrecked at Observatornia Bay, Sviatoinos Gulf. All crew rescued.					
TASMANIA	59	146	100.5	C.D.Holmes	Hull Steam Fishing
98716	1891	50	20.5	45 NHP	& Ice Co Ltd
H122 Steam Trawler	17.01.1891			10 knots	Hull
18.01.1912 Sold to Active Fishing Co Ltd, Fleetwood. (FD171). 1917 Rqd by the Royal Navy as a fishing trawler (Fishery Reserve). 1919 returned. 1918 H E Stroud, Aberdeen (A737). 1920 C W Robinson , Aberdeen. 1924 Vessel sold to shipbreakers and broken up.					
EGYPT	60	145	100.5	C.D.Holmes	Hull Steam Fishing
98721	1891	53	20.5	45 NHP	& Ice Co Ltd
H126 Steam Trawler	18.02.1891			knots	Hull
03.05.1907 Sold to Haller & Odenburg, Smögen, Sweden. 1928 Vessel sold to shipbreakers and broken up.					
EUDOCIA	61	147	101.3	C.D.Holmes	Charles Hellyer
98727	10.02.1891	56	20.3	45 NHP	Hull
H130 Steam Trawler	06.03.1891			10 knots	
24.08.1897 Sold to Hellyer Steam Fishing Co Ltd, Hull. 26.11.1914 to Thomas Lauder, Aberdeen (A205). 1917 Rqd by the Royal Navy as a fishing trawler (Fishery Reserve). 1919 returned. 10.05.1917 to Henry Smethhurst, Grimsby (GY1049). 22.02.1924 to James H Mein, Grimsby. 28.11.1924 to Consolidated Steam Fishing Co Ltd, Lowestoft (LT113). 1941 to Dinas Steam Trawling Co Ltd, Fleetwood . 1945 to Odafoam Ltd, Liverpool. Oct 1950 Vessel sold for scrap to Thos W Ward Ltd and broken up at Preston.					
PRINCE OF WALES	62	158	106.0	C.D.Holmes	Pickering & Haldane's Steam
98733	1891	59	20.5	50 NHP	Trawling Co Ltd
H136 Steam Trawler	13.04.1891			10 knots	Hull
01.07.1891 Sold to Pickering & Haldane's Steam Trawling Co Ltd, Hull. 03.04.1912 Sold to Port of Blyth Steam Fishing & Ice Co Ltd, Blyth (BH80). 1915 to James Pattison, Hartlepool (HL8). 25.03.1917 Vessel captured by U-boat and sunk 17 miles off Girdleness.					

Yard No.59
1891 TASMANIA
Photo:- Barnard and Straker Collection

Yard No.63
1891 SPARTA
Photo:- Barnard and Straker Collection

Yard No.79
1891 FIDELIA
Photo:- Barnard and Straker Collection

NAME Official No. Port Letters Numbers	Yard No. Launched Registered	Registered G Ton N Ton	 L Ft B Ft	Engine Builder Horse Power Reg'd Speed	OWNER (Built for)
SPARTA 98737 H140 Steam Trawler	63 07.04.1891 11.05.1891	146 56	101.3 20.3	C.D.Holmes 45 NHP 10 knots	Charles Hellyer Hull
11.06.1897 Sold to Pickering & Haldane's Steam Trawling Co Ltd, Hull. 25.11.1905 Sold to R R Pastor, Corunna, Spain renamed ESPARERTO . 1908 to L Lamigueiro, Corunna. 1917 to Marine Nationale Francaise (French Navy) renamed CAPELAN. 1919 to Numa Lurie, d'Arcachon (ARC1726). 1920 Vessel sold for scrap to shipbreakers.					
CITY OF WAKEFIELD 98729 H132 Steam Trawler	64 1891 24.03.1891	143 44	99.0 20.9	Tindall & Co 48 NHP 10 knots	George Bowman Hull
19.12.1892 Sold to Pickering & Haldane's Steam Trawling Co Ltd, Hull. 30.12.1898 to Pebferay Peberay, Boulogne, France renamed PADOUE (B2582). 1916 to Soc Salazar Y Marqueze, San Sabastian, Spain. 1931 Vessel sold to shipbreakers and broken up.					
SLEUTH HOUND 98709 H114 Steam Trawler	65 1890 13.11.1890	153 49	101.0 20.8	Bailey & Leetham 45 NHP 10 knots	Humber Steam Trawling Co Ltd Hull
27.10.1897 Vessel wrecked at Filey Brigg, Yorkshire whilst homeward bound to Hull. All nine crew rescued.					
BOAR HOUND 98722 H125 Steam Trawler	66 05.01.1891 12.02.1891	153 57	101.0 20.8	Bailey & Leetham 45 NHP 10 knots	Humber Steam Trawling Co Ltd Hull
28.09.1911 Sold to Fiskiaktieb Avane, Gothenburg, Sweden renamed ARNE. 1927 Vessel sold to shipbreakers and broken up.					
WOLF HOUND 98738 H141 Steam Trawler	67 25.04.1891 14.05.1891	151 58	100.9 20.9	Bailey & Leetham 45 NHP 10 knots	Humber Steam Trawling Co Ltd Hull
04.12.1896 Vessel wrecked at Kettleness, near Whitby, Yorkshire.					
BUCK HOUND 98741 H143 Steam Trawler	68 08.05.1891 04.06.1891	151 58	100.9 20.9	Bailey & Leetham 45 NHP 10 knots	Humber Steam Trawling Co Ltd Hull
27.07.1902 Vessel stranded at Torsminde on the Danish Coast and subsequently re-floated. 12.01.1914 Sold to Fiskeriaktieb Mars, Gothenburg, Sweden and renamed VENUS. 1919 Vessel deleted from Lloyds Register of Shipping.					
BASSET HOUND 98749 H151 Steam Trawler	69 09.06.1891 06.07.1891	150 57	100.2 20.9	Bailey & Leetham 45 NHP 10 knots	Humber Steam Trawling Co Ltd Hull
12.01.1914 Sold to Fiskeriaktieb Merkur, Gothenburg, Sweden and renamed MERKUR. 1927 Vessel sold to shipbreakers and broken up.					
NORTH SEA 98745 H147 Steam Trawler	70 22.05.1891 12.06.1891	145 55	100.9 20.9	C.D.Holmes 45 NHP 10 knots	Edward Buckton Cargill Hull
26.05.1897 Sold to Cargill Steam Trawling Co Ltd, Hull . 25.09.1899 *(Lengthened to 110.5 ft 155 Gross Ton & 63 Net Tons)* and renamed OTTOMAN EMPIRE . 03.05.1913 to Clevedon Steam Trawling Co Ltd, Fleetwood (FD180). 23.08.1917 to William Grant, Grimsby renamed NAVENBY (GY1094). 1917 Rqd by the Royal Navy as a fishing trawler (Fishery Reserve). 1919 returned. 19.08.1924 Registration closed on advice that the vessel was broken up.					
CAMBRIA 99178 GY371 Steam Trawler	71 27.06.1891 20.08.1891	147 59	102.1 20.4	C.D.Holmes 50 NHP 10 knots	Sir Henry Bennett Grimsby
17.11.1893 Vessel left Grimsby for the fishing grounds not heard of again. Posted missing:- Lost with all hands.					
GAZE HOUND 98759 H161 Steam Trawler	72 1891 25.08.1891	138 49	95.5 20.8	Bailey & Leetham 45 NHP 10 knots	Humber Steam Trawling Co Ltd Hull
05.07.1906 Sold to James Hall Sunderland (SD87). 05.06.1915 Vessel captured by U-boat and sunk by gunfire 50 miles off Aberdeen.					

NAME Official No. Port Letters Numbers	Yard No. Launched Registered	Registered G Ton N Ton	 L Ft B Ft	Engine Builder Horse Power Reg'd Speed	OWNER (Built for)
DESIDERATUM 98752 H154 Steam Trawler	73 08.07.1891 01.08.1891	150 59	100.5 20.8	Bailey & Leetham 45 NHP 10 knots	Richard Simpson Hull
23.01.1899 Sold to London & Yorkshire Steam Trawling & Fish Carrying Co Ltd, Hull. 1904 to Lancashire Steam Fishing Co Ltd, Fleetwood (FD45). 1914 to Westerburg & Berglund, Gothenburg, Sweden renamed PYSEN (GG481).1926 to M A Fridberg, Lindköping. 07.03.1928 Vessel wrecked at Espevser, Norway.					
SETTER 98761 H163 Steam Trawler	74 22.08.1891 09.09.1891	150 58	100.6 20.9	Bailey & Leetham 45 NHP 10 knots	Humber Steam Trawling Co Ltd Hull
13.02.1907 Vessel sank in the North Sea.					
MASTIFF 98762 H164 Steam Trawler	75 05.09.1891 28.09.1891	150 58	100.6 20.9	Bailey & Leetham 45 NHP 10 knots	Humber Steam Trawling Co Ltd Hull
01.01.1914 *(Tonnage adjusted 62.5 Net Tons).* 29.05.1914 Sold to Fiskeriaktieb Svea, Gothenburg, Sweden. 1923 Vessel deleted from Lloyds Register of Shipping.					
TERRIER 98768 H171 Steam Trawler	76 17.09.1891 16.10.1891	149 57	100.5 20.7	Bailey & Leetham 45 NHP 10 knots	Humber Steam Trawling Co Ltd Hull
01.01.1914 (*Tonnage adjusted 62.5 Net Tons).* 29.09.1916 Vessel wrecked on Wrecher Head, Scotland whilst homeward bound to Hull.					
HERON 98732 H135 Steam Trawler	77 14.03.1891 16.04.1891	145 53	100.9 20.9	Bailey & Leetham 45 NHP 10 knots	William J Cook Charles K Welton William M Gemmell Hull
Vessel built for the owners of the shipyard. William M Gemmell appointed as manager. 08.01.1895 Sold to St Andrews Steam Fishing Co Ltd, Hull. 04.05.1898 The HERON sank the Grimsby lugger WILLIAM in collision near Middle Bank Buoy, River Humber. 10.12.1898 to F W Jacobs, Geestemunde, Germany renamed ANNA (PG76). 1909 to Kolenberg & Putz, Geestemunde, renamed LOKI. 1910 to Actieselskabet Loki, Haugesund, Norway. 1913 to T Bakkevig & Sön, Haugesund, renamed MAGNE. 07.06.1923 to H Hendriksen, Siggufjord, Iceland renamed RIFSNES (SI16). 26.06.1926 to Sigurdi Jonssyni Gordunum & Simoni Sveinbjararsyni, Reykjavik (RE272). 20.05.1937 to Hafsteini Bergthorssyni, Reykjavik. 1942 *(8 cyl R A Lister diesel engine fitted).* 12.09.1965 Vessel capsized and sank at Bjarnarey, Iceland.					
CITY OF BIRMINGHAM 98760 H162 Steam Trawler	78 1891 31.08.1891	143 50	99.0 20.9	C.D.Holmes 45 NHP 10 knots	George Walter Bowman Hull
21.12.1894 Vessel sank in the North Sea with the loss of all nine crew. One of six Hull trawlers and nine smacks which were lost in the severe storms which raged through the North Sea during December 1894.					
FIDELIA 99544 H177 Steam Trawler	79 06.10.1891 09.11.1891	147 56	100.0 20.5	C.D.Holmes 50 NHP 10 knots	Francis & Thomas Ross Ltd Hull
1918 Rqd by the Royal Navy as a boom defence vessel. 1919 returned. 13.01.1925 Sold to Consolidated Steam Fishing & Ice Co Ltd, Lowestoft (LT187). 1940 Rqd by the Royal Navy as a boom defence vessel. 05.05.1941 Vessel sunk by German aircraft in Lowestoft Harbour.					
RETRIEVER 99547 H180 Steam Trawler	80 21.10.1891 21.11.1891	147 56	100.5 20.7	Bailey & Leetham 45 NHP 10 knots	Humber Steam Trawling Co Ltd Hull
17.09.1900 Vessel sank following a collision with the Hull Trawler DANUBE H240 (149 gt/ b 1894) in the River Humber.					
MERRIE ISLINGTON 99551 H183 Steam Trawler	81 19.11.1891 17.12.1891	147 56	100.4 20.7	Bailey & Leetham 45 NHP 10 knots	Humber Steam Trawling Co Ltd Hull
06.05.1915 Vessel captured by U-boat and sunk 6 miles off Whitby Yorkshire.					
BULLDOG 99562 H192 Steam Trawler	82 03.03.1892 26.03.1892	148 57	100.4 20.7	Bailey & Leetham 45 NHP 10 knots	Humber Steam Trawling Co Ltd Hull
30.07.1915 Sold to Walter H Beeley, Grimsby (GY576). 1917 Rqd by the Royal Navy as a fishing trawler (Fishery Reserve). 1919 returned. 18.07.1919 to N Ashworth, Fleetwood (FD328). 1924 Vessel sold to shipbreakers and broken up.					

<table>
<tr><th rowspan="2">NAME
Official No.
Port Letters Numbers</th><th rowspan="2">Yard No.
Launched
Registered</th><th colspan="2">Registered</th><th rowspan="2">Engine Builder
Horse Power
Reg'd Speed</th><th rowspan="2">OWNER
(Built for)</th></tr>
<tr><th>G Ton
N Ton</th><th>L Ft
B Ft</th></tr>
<tr><td>ACTIVE
99561
H191 Steam Trawler</td><td>83
16.02.1892
08.03.1892</td><td>149
62</td><td>102.4
20.6</td><td>C.D.Holmes
45 NHP
10 knots</td><td>Pickering & Haldane's Steam Trawling Co Ltd
Hull</td></tr>
<tr><td colspan="6">18.01.1909 Sold to Benjamin J Ridge, Newlyn, Cornwall.
10.05.1912 to Active Fishing Co Ltd, Fleetwood (FD157). 1916 to J W Smethurst, Aberdeen (A776).
26.4.1917 Vessel captured by U-boat and sunk by time-bombs 80 miles off St Abb's Head.</td></tr>
<tr><td>SWIFT
99556
H186 Steam Trawler</td><td>84
02.01.1892
26.01.1892</td><td>149
62</td><td>103.4
20.6</td><td>C.D.Holmes
45 NHP
10 knots</td><td>Pickering & Haldane's Steam Trawling Co Ltd
Hull</td></tr>
<tr><td colspan="6">28.6.1911 Sold to NV Maats Swift, Ijmuiden, Holland (IJM1). 1920 to L M & N Parlevliet, Ijmuiden.
1922 to P J Schipper, Ijmuiden. 1924 to NV Stoomv Maats Luctor, Ijmuiden.
1930 to W Kramer & G P Booij, Ijmuiden renamed VIOS III. 1936 Vessel sold to shipbreakers and broken up.</td></tr>
<tr><td>PRESIDENT LUDWIG

Steam Tug</td><td>85
1892
1892</td><td>174
27</td><td>116.0
22.0</td><td>C.D.Holmes
80 NHP
12 knots</td><td>Soc. Anonyme de Remorquage a' Helice
Antwerp</td></tr>
<tr><td colspan="6">02.09.1917 Chartered by the Royal Navy renamed LUDGATE. 15.02.1918 Vessel wrecked in Wigtown Bay.</td></tr>
<tr><td>DIRECTOR GERLING

Steam Tug</td><td>86
1892
1892</td><td>174
27</td><td>116.0
22.0</td><td>C.D.Holmes
80 NHP
12 knots</td><td>Soc. Anonyme de Remorquage a' Helice
Antwerp</td></tr>
<tr><td colspan="6">1927 Vessel sold to shipbreakers and broken up.</td></tr>
<tr><td>SLEDMERE
99570
H196 Steam Trawler</td><td>87
28.03.1892
18.05.1892</td><td>148
57</td><td>102.5
20.5</td><td>C.D.Holmes
45 NHP
10 knots</td><td>Charles Hellyer
Hull</td></tr>
<tr><td colspan="6">05.08.1897 Sold to Hellyer Steam Fishing Co Ltd, Hull.. 10.10.1898 to M. Noé, Nante, France renamed CORMORAN.
1906 to Pecheries Franc d Arachon Soc. Anon, Arcachon renamed INTREPIDE .
05.07.1907 Vessel wrecked at Chaucre Ile d' Oléon.</td></tr>
<tr><td>CYPRUS
99572
H198 Steam Trawler</td><td>88
1892
03.06.1892</td><td>132
57</td><td>95.6
20.5</td><td>C.D.Holmes
35 NHP
9.5 knots</td><td>Hull Steam Fishing & Ice Co Ltd
Hull</td></tr>
<tr><td colspan="6">15.02.1900 Vessel sank in the North Sea with the loss of all nine crew. One of five Hull trawlers which disappeared in the "great gale and blizzard" which caused considerable damage to shipping and to coastal towns.</td></tr>
<tr><td>QUEBEC
99573
H199 Steam Trawler</td><td>89
1892
10.06.1892</td><td>132
57</td><td>95.6
20.5</td><td>Amos & Smith
35 NHP
9.5 knots</td><td>Hull Steam Fishing & Ice Co Ltd
Hull</td></tr>
<tr><td colspan="6">20.01.1916 Sold to Neville S Clarke, Scarborough (SH208).
25.09.1916 Vessel captured by U-boat and sunk by gunfire 20 miles north-east of Scarborough (see Yard No. 33).</td></tr>
<tr><td>MELBOURNE
99578
H200 Steam Trawler</td><td>90
1892
23.06.1892</td><td>132
57</td><td>95.6
20.5</td><td>C.D.Holmes
35 NHP
9.5 knots</td><td>Hull Steam Fishing & Ice Co Ltd
Hull</td></tr>
<tr><td colspan="6">31.03.1912 Sold to W A Massey & Son Ltd, Hull.
02.05.1913 to Bloomfields Ltd, Great Yarmouth renamed OCEAN COMRADE (YH405).
1914 Rqd by the Royal Navy as a minesweeper No. FY 160. 1918 returned.
1918 Rqd by the Royal Navy as a fishing trawler (Fishery Reserve). 1919 returned.
1923 to A Lewis, Aberdeen. 1929 to NV Viss Maats Beka, Ijmuiden, Holland renamed BEKA.
31.01.1931 to W Barnard, Lowestoft renamed OCEAN COMRADE (LT244).
26.04.1937 Vessel sold to German shipbreakers and broken up.</td></tr>
<tr><td>SYDNEY
99576
H202 Steam Trawler</td><td>91
1892
11.07.1892</td><td>132
57</td><td>95.6
20.5</td><td>Amos & Smith
35 NHP
9.5 knots</td><td>Hull Steam Fishing & Ice Co Ltd
Hull</td></tr>
<tr><td colspan="6">20.09.1905 Vessel sank following a collision in the North Sea.</td></tr>
<tr><td>PICTON CASTLE
99566
H194 Steam Trawler</td><td>92
1892
26.04.1892</td><td>148
57</td><td>100.5
20.8</td><td>C.D.Holmes
50 NHP
10 knots</td><td>George H D Birt
Hull</td></tr>
<tr><td colspan="6">28.04.1897 Sold to Castle Steam Fishing Co Ltd, London (LO148) vessel transferred to Milford Haven.
02.02.1903 to Silhouette Freres, Bayone, France renamed ST. JOSEPH (BA478).
21.11.1904 to SA Des Pecheries de Biarritz.
1908 to Soc Anon Mamelina, San Sabastian, Spain renamed MAMELINA No.8.
1917 to Marine Nationale Francaise (French Navy) renamed ETOURNEAU I.
1918 to C M Lemos, Piræus, Greece renamed ETOURNEGU. 1923 Vessel deleted from Lloyds Register of Shipping.</td></tr>
</table>

Yard No.89
1892 QUEBEC
Photo:- Barnard and Straker Collection

Yard No.100
1893 QUEENSLAND
Photo:- Barnard and Straker Collection

Yard No.119
1894 CONDOR
Photo:- Barnard and Straker Collection

<table>
<tr><th rowspan="2">NAME
Official No.
Port Letters Numbers</th><th rowspan="2">Yard No.
Launched
Registered</th><th colspan="2">Registered</th><th rowspan="2">Engine Builder
Horse Power
Reg'd Speed</th><th rowspan="2">OWNER
(Built for)</th></tr>
<tr><th>G Ton
N Ton</th><th>L Ft
B Ft</th></tr>
<tr><td>DALE CASTLE
99566
H195 Steam Trawler</td><td>93
14.04.1892
13.05.1892</td><td>148
57</td><td>100.5
20.8</td><td>C.D.Holmes
50 NHP
10 knots</td><td>George H D Birt
Hull</td></tr>
<tr><td colspan="6">28.04.1897 Sold to Castle Steam Fishing Co Ltd, London (LO149) vessel transferred to Milford Haven.
05.07.1904 to Silhouette Freres, Bayone, France renamed ST. PIERRE (BA883).21.09.1904 to SA Des Pecheries de Biarritz.
1908 to Soc Anon Mamelina, San Sabastian, Spain renamed MAMELINA No. 10 .
1917 to Marine Nationale Francaise (French Navy) renamed PASSEREAU.
1919 to Henri Lerenard, Cherbourg (CH2478). 28.08.1928 to Joseph Hamel, Cherbourg.
17.02.1931 to Les Chalutiers Cherbourgeois, Cherbourg.
1940 Rqd by the French Navy as a mine-sweeper escaped to Southampton and used by the Royal Navy.
1945 Vessel deleted from Lloyds Register of Shipping (War loss).</td></tr>
<tr><td>GAME COCK
99583
H205 Steam Trawler</td><td>94
22.09.1892
13.10.1892</td><td>151
63</td><td>103.9
20.6</td><td>C.D.Holmes
50 NHP
10 knots</td><td>Pickering & Haldane's Steam
Trawling Co Ltd
Hull</td></tr>
<tr><td colspan="6">13.06.1902 Sank the Grimsby trawler CANADIAN GY392 (134 gt/ b 1891) in collision 80 miles east of Spurn Point.
03.04.1912 Sold to Blyth Steam Fishing & Ice Co Ltd, Blyth. 1913 to Jack S Ellis, Scarborough (SH191).
25.09.1916 Vessel captured by U-boat and sunk by gunfire 20 miles north-east of Scarborough (see Yard No. 33).</td></tr>
<tr><td>STORM COCK
99586
H207 Steam Trawler</td><td>95
22.10.1892
14.11.1892</td><td>151
63</td><td>104.0
20.6</td><td>C.D.Holmes
50 NHP
10 knots</td><td>Pickering & Haldane's Steam
Trawling Co Ltd
Hull</td></tr>
<tr><td colspan="6">06.02.1902 Sold to G R Nicholson, Liverpool (LL303). 1913 to The Sunrise Fishing Co Ltd, Fleetwood (FD148).
1917 Rqd by the Royal Navy as a fishing trawler (Fishery Reserve). 1919 returned.
1918 to Armitage's Steam Trawling Co Ltd, Hull (H405). 1919 to E W Hall, Lowestoft (LT393).
1924 to C Huish, Plymouth. 1934 to Mrs J Huish, Plymouth. 1935 to R Hancock & Sons, Plymouth.
1937 Vessel sold to shipbreakers and broken up.</td></tr>
<tr><td>BROXHOLME
99587
H208 Steam Trawler</td><td>96
08.11.1892
09.12.1892</td><td>154
61</td><td>105.2
20.5</td><td>C.D.Holmes
55 NHP
10 knots</td><td>Hellyer Steam
Fishing Co Ltd
Hull</td></tr>
<tr><td colspan="6">21.03.1906 Sold to Spanish owners renamed BOHEMIO.
1916 to the Italian Navy as a mine-sweeper renamed STROMBOLI.
1919 to Maltese Fishing Co Ltd, Malta renamed NAUTILUS.
1922 to F S Mizzi, renamed SIR FILIPPO SCEBERRAS. 1924 to Malta Steam Shipping Co Ltd, renamed WEMBLE.
1935 to Giuseppe Pappa, Syracuse, Italy renamed CARMELO PAPPA.
1937 to Fratelli Savaco, Palermo renamed FORTUNATO . 1938 Vessel sold to Italian shipbreakers and broken up.</td></tr>
<tr><td>CHIEFTAIN
99685
GY476 Steam Trawler</td><td>97
04.02.1893
21.02.1893</td><td>120
39</td><td>88.5
20.1</td><td>C.D.Holmes
44 NHP
10 knots</td><td>Thomas Robinson
Grimsby</td></tr>
<tr><td colspan="6">22.01.1901 Sold to Onward Steam Fishing Co Ltd, Grimsby.
17.03.1906 to Joseph Malandain Et Ses Gendres, Fecamp, France renamed JEAN EDMÉE (F1930).
1913 to Veuve Joseph Malandain Et Ses Gendres, Fecamp.
29.07.1915 Rqd by the Marine Nationale for war service. 08.01.1919 returned.
1917 to Charles Prentout, Fecamp. 1921 to C Carrasset A Pochez et J De Vibraye, Fecamp.
1923 Jacques De Vibraye, Fecamp.
14.05.1935 Vessel sprang a leak and foundered 62 miles south-east of de Groix. All eleven crew rescued.</td></tr>
<tr><td>MONTREAL
99595
H211 Steam Trawler</td><td>98
30.03.1893
19.05.1893</td><td>139
63</td><td>99.0
20.5</td><td>C.D.Holmes
33 NHP
9.5 knots</td><td>Hull Steam Fishing
& Ice Co Ltd
Hull</td></tr>
<tr><td colspan="6">31.03.1913 Sold to George J Wheeler, Hull. 18.03.1914 to J White Hull (diesel engine fitted Torbinia Eng Co 23 NHP).
1920 to D Petrie Hull renamed LADYLOAN. 1929 to R A Gray, Hull renamed EDMEE.
1930 to J Weser, Groningen, Holland renamed LAUWERS (converted to a cargo vessel tonnage unchanged).
08.01.1931 Vessel sank in heavy weather off Vegiland.</td></tr>
<tr><td>HERCULES
99594
Steam Tug</td><td>99
1893
04.05.1893</td><td>82
19</td><td>80.6
18.1</td><td>Earle's
45 NHP
10 knots</td><td>Hull Dock Co
Hull</td></tr>
<tr><td colspan="6">1893 to North Eastern Railway Co Ltd, Hull. 1924 to London & North Eastern Railway Co, Hull.
24.06.1936 Vessel sold to South Stockton Shipbreaking Co Middlesbrough and broken up.</td></tr>
</table>

NAME Official No. Port Letters Numbers	Yard No. Launched Registered	Registered G Ton N Ton	 L Ft B Ft	Engine Builder Horse Power Reg'd Speed	OWNER (Built for)
QUEENSLAND 99596 H212 Steam Trawler	100 01.05.1893 31.05.1893	139 63	99.0 20.5	Earle's 35 NHP 9.5 knots	Hull Steam Fishing & Ice Co Ltd Hull
06.02.1913 Vessel sank after collision with the Hull trawler KLONDYKE H420 *(see Yard No. 216)* in the North Sea.					
STORK 99598 H214 Steam Trawler	101 1893 09.06.1893	151 60	102.6 20.8	Bailey & Leetham 45 NHP 10 knots	William H Putt & Co Ltd Hull
17.02.1896 Sold to St Andrews Steam Fishing Co Ltd, Hull. 08.01.1899 to The Dundee Fishing Co Ltd, Dundee (DE115). 13.04.1917 Vessel captured by U-boat and sunk by time bombs 20 miles east of St Abbs head.					
EDITH 99591 Steam Tug	102 1893 10.08.1893	33	60.1 14.0	C.D.Holmes 20 NHP 9 knots	John Scott Hull
29.06.1964 Vessel sold to shipbreakers and broken up.					
GEORGE 99600 H216 Steam Trawler	103 12.06.1893 03.07.1893	150 58	100.8 20.8	Bailey & Leetham 45 NHP 10 knots	Richard Simpson & John Brocklesby Hull
01.12.1902 Sold to London & Yorkshire Steam Trawling & Fish Carrying Co Ltd, Hull. 27.10.1904 to Neale & West Ltd, Cardiff (CF7). 1911 to W Lewis, Aberdeen. 03.01.1911 Vessel wrecked on Hammonds Knoll off Yarmouth on delivery passage from Cardiff towards Aberdeen.					
LABORE ET HONORE 102914 H217 Steam Trawler	104 03.07.1893 27.07.1893	150 58	100.8 20.7	Bailey & Leetham 45 NHP 10 knots	Richard Simpson Hull
01.12.1902 Sold to London & Yorkshire Steam Trawling & Fish Carrying Co Ltd, Hull. 27.10.1904 to Neale & West Ltd, Cardiff (CF5). 1911 to G Shoulder, Swansea (SA110). 1913 Mrs M E Newman, Swansea. 1919 to G Shoulder, Swansea. 1917 Rqd by the Royal Navy as a fishing trawler (Fishery Reserve). 1919 returned. 1926 Vessel sold to shipbreakers and broken up.					
DUKE OF YORK 102922 H224 Steam Trawler	105 1893 12.09.1893	150 58	100.8 20.7	Bailey & Leetham 45 NHP 10 knots	Richard Simpson Hull
01.12.1902 Sold to London & Yorkshire Steam Trawling & Fishing Carrying Co Ltd, Hull. 27.10.1904 to Neale & West Ltd, Cardiff (CF4). 1911 to R W Lewis, Aberdeen (A422). 09.02.1917 Vessel captured by U-boat and sunk by time bombs 34 miles from Girdleness.					
DUCHESS OF YORK 102926 H227 Steam Trawler	106 1893 20.11.1893	150 58	101.1 20.8	Bailey & Leetham 45 NHP 10 knots	Richard Simpson & Edward Brown Hull
22.02.1899 Sold to London & Yorkshire Steam Trawling & Fish Carrying Co Ltd, Hull. 17.09.1902 to Soc. Anon. de Pesca Algecirreña, Algecira, Spain renamed CARMEN . 1916 to Marine Nationale Francaise (French Navy) renamed ŒILLET later renamed GINETTE. 1919 to Ramon Carranzer Huelva Spain. 1920 to D Demetriades & Co, Piræus, Greece renamed ALEXANDRA D *(converted to a cargo vessel tonnage unchanged).* 1923 to C Viahus, Piræus. 1927 to Mrs Anna Sachtouris, Piræus renamed THEMISTOCLES. 1929 to Soc.Anon Turque Les Houilleres Turques, Constantinople, Turkey renamed IMDAT. 1935 to Haci Arifzade Temel Effendi, Istanbul. 1936 *(3 cyl 50 NHP Widdop & Co Ltd diesel engine fitted).* 1939 to Temel Sunar, Istanbul.1947 to Sevki Hantal, Istanbul. 1993 to Imdat Gemicilik Sanay Ltd, Sirketi, Istanbul. 1999 Vessel still in service.					
PRIDE OF THE HUMBER 102930 H231 Steam Trawler	107 11.12.1893 10.01.1894	150 58	101.1 20.8	Bailey & Leetham 45 NHP 10 knots	Richard Simpson Hull
23.02.1899 Sold to London & Yorkshire Steam Trawling & Fish Carrying Co Ltd, Hull. 27.10.1904 to Neale & West Ltd, Cardiff (CF10). 02.01.1910 Vessel sank after stranding at Flat Holm.					
CHAMPION 102933 H233 Steam Trawler	108 11.01.1894 03.02.1894	150 58	101.1 20.8	Bailey & Leetham 45 NHP 10 knots	Richard Simpson Hull
23.02.1899 Sold to London & Yorkshire Steam Trawling & Fish Carrying Co Ltd, Hull. 27.10.1904 to Neale & West Ltd, Cardiff (CF6). 1913 to R W Lewis, Aberdeen (A637). 1920 to R W Crawford, Scarborough (SH350). 1922 to James Pattison, Hartlepool (HL37). 1929 to J D Irvin Jnr, Hartlepool. 1931 Vessel sold to shipbreakers and broken up.					

NAME Official No. Port Letters Numbers	Yard No. Launched Registered	Registered G Ton N Ton	 L Ft B Ft	Engine Builder Horse Power Reg'd Speed	OWNER (Built for)
HUMBER	109 1893 1893		70.0 15.6		HM War Office Whitehall London
Government Boat. No details of type or service record.					
SPARTAN 99703 GY520 Steam Trawler	110 12.07.1893 29.07.1893	120 40	88.5 20.1	C.D.Holmes 45 NHP 10 knots	Thomas Robinson Grimsby
22.01.1901 Sold to Onward Steam Fishing Co Ltd, Grimsby. 20.03.1907 to Colin R Seller Peterhead (PD206) *(converted to a drifter).* 1912 to Lighthouse Fishing Co Ltd, Yarmouth (YH20). 1915 to T L Devlin, Granton (GN63) . 1917 Rqd by the Royal Navy as a fishing trawler (Fishery Reserve). 1919 returned.1920 to J Inglis, Granton. 1921 to A Thomson, Leith . 1926 to D Allen, Granton. 1926 Vessel sold to shipbreakers and broken up.					
PETREL 102920 H222 Steam Trawler	111 10.08.1893 29.08.1893	151 64	101.5 20.6	C.D.Holmes 45 NHP 10 knots	Pickering & Haldane's Steam Trawling Co Ltd Hull
30.01.1912 Sold to James Hall, Sunderland (SD5). 1915 to H Wood, Grimsby (GY609). 30.03.1917 Vessel captured by U-boat and sunk 120 miles east of Aberdeen.					
OSPREY 102924 H225 Steam Trawler	112 14.09.1893 05.10.1893	151 64	101.5 20.6	C.D.Holmes 45 NHP 10 knots	Pickering & Haldane's Steam Trawling Co Ltd Hull
23.10.1908 Sold to Elias Stefansson, Reykjavik, Iceland renamed ISLENDINGUR (RE120). 1915 to Actieselsk Fram Reykjavik. 09.12.1926 Vessel sank at Eidisuik Reykjavik. 1942 Salvaged and re-registered (RE73). 02.02.1961 Icelandic Fishing Registration closed on advice that the vessel was broken up.					
VALKYRIE 102925 H226 Steam Trawler	113 07.10.1893 22.11.1893	150 48	103.0 20.5	C.D.Holmes 45 NHP 10 knots	Charles Hellyer Hull
11.06.1897 Sold to Hellyer Steam Fishing Co Ltd, Hull. 22.12.1910 to L Calamel, Le Treport, France renamed WALKERIE (DI617). 1942 Rqd by the German Navy as a mine-sweeper No. M4612. 13.08.1944 Scuttled to block the port of St Malo.					
SPRINGFIELD 102928 H228 Steam Trawler	114 11.10.1893 06.12.1893	150 48	103.0 20.5	C.D.Holmes 45 NHP 10 knots	Charles Hellyer Hull
24.08.1897 Sold to Hellyer Steam Fishing Co Ltd, Hull. 22.05.1905 to Soc Anon des Pecheries de Biarritz, Bayonne, France renamed SOKORRI. 1910 to Soc Anon Mamelina, San Sabastian, Spain renamed MAMELINA NO.4. 1927 to Pesquera Malagueña, Malaga renamed PUNTA BELLILLA. 1932 Vessel reported wrecked.					
NORMAN 104162 GY579 Steam Trawler	115 08.02.1894 22.02.1894	119 38	90.1 20.1	C.D.Holmes 45 NHP 10 knots	Thomas Robinson Grimsby
22.01.1901 Sold to Onward Steam Fishing Co Ltd, Grimsby. 25.06.1907 to John Mitchell & Sons Peterhead (PD502). Jun 1915 Rqd by the Royal Navy as a net layer. 1919 returned. 1927 to J Alexander Glasgow (GW20). 1940 to J A Kyles Glasgow. 1948 to Clyde Herring Carriers Ltd, Glasgow. 16.10.1950 Vessel sold for scrap to A McNeill and broken up at Greenock.					
SATELLITE	116 1894 1894		65.0 14.6		HM War Office Whitehall London
Government Boat. No details of type or service record.					
ADELAIDE 102938 H239 Steam Trawler	117 10.03.1894 10.04.1894	139 57	99.0 20.5	Amos & Smith 34 NHP 9.5 knots	Hull Steam Fishing & Ice Co Ltd Hull
10.01.1912 Sold to William Robbens & Sons, Lowestoft (LT1164). 1915 to H Smethurst, Grimsby (GY604). 06.02.1917 Vessel captured by U-boat and sunk 30 miles east north-east of the Tyne.					
LABRADOR 102946 H246 Steam Trawler	118 05.04.1894 25.04.1894	139 57	99.0 20.5	Amos & Smith 35 NHP 9.5 knots	Hull Steam Fishing & Ice Co Ltd Hull
27.02.1912 Sold to William Robbens & Sons Lowestoft (LT1165). 23.01.1915 Vessel left Lowestoft for the fishing grounds not heard of again. Posted missing:- Lost with all hands.					

Yard No.123
1894 CITY OF EXETER
Photo:- Barnard and Straker Collection

Yard No.128
1894 FLORENCE
Photo:- Barnard and Straker Collection

Yard No.138
1895 PORTIA
Photo:- Barnard and Straker Collection

NAME Official No. Port Letters Numbers	Yard No. Launched Registered	Registered G Ton N Ton	 L Ft B Ft	Engine Builder Horse Power Reg'd Speed	OWNER (Built for)
CONDOR 102947 H247 Steam Trawler	119 1894 09.05.1894	151 64	101.5 20.6	C.D.Holmes 45 NHP 10 knots	Pickering & Haldane's Steam Trawling Co Ltd Hull
10.02.1912 Sold to Port of Blyth Steam Fishing & Ice Co Ltd, Blyth (BH84). 1915 to Dick Crawford, Scarborough (SH12). 29.05.1915 Vessel sunk by mine 30 miles north-east of Scarborough. All nine crew lost.					
UGANDA 104167 GY601 Steam Trawler	120 04.05.1894 28.05.1894	131 46	93.5 20.3	Earle's 44 NHP 10 knots	Grimsby Union Steam Fishing Co Ltd Grimsby
16.02.1899 Sold to Dundee Steam Trawling Co Ltd, Dundee (DE108). 1902 to A H Peigné, Nantes, France renamed ALCYON (N627). 28.03.1907 Vessel foundered in the Bay of Biscay.					
ULUNDI 104167 GY606 Steam Trawler	121 04.05.1894 09.06.1894	131 46	93.5 20.3	Earle's 44 NHP 10 knots	Grimsby Union Steam Fishing Co Ltd Grimsby
10.02.1899 Sold to Dundee Steam Trawling Co Ltd, Dundee (DE107). 02.10.1911 Vessel sunk following a collision off Bell Rock.					
CHANTICLEER 102955 H254 Steam Trawler	122 05.06.1894 22.06.1894	150 62	103.3 20.8	C.D.Holmes 45 NHP 10 knots	Samuel T White George T Armitage James Chant Hull
12.08.1898 Sold to Mr J Chant & Mrs M J Paddon, Plymouth (PH402). Nov 1914 Rqd by the Royal Navy as a minesweeper No. FY 921. 1918 returned. 1919 to Wharncliffe Steam Fishing Co Ltd, Grimsby (GY124). 1919 to N Sinderson Grimsby. 1925 to Boston Deep Sea Fishing Co Ltd, Grimsby. 1926 to G Honoré, Boulogne, France renamed HENRIVILLE. 1938 Vessel sold to shipbreakers and broken up.					
CITY OF EXETER 102961 H256 Steam Trawler	123 03.07.1894 19.07.1894	148 60	100.4 20.8	C.D.Holmes 45 NHP 10 knots	George W Bowman Hull
09.04.1912 Sold to Port of Blyth Steam Fishing Co Ltd, Blyth renamed LORD COLLINGWOOD (BH96). 10.12.1914 to The Beacon Steam Fishing Co Ltd, Grimsby (GY405). 23.10.1915 to Aldersyde Steam Fishing Co Ltd, Grimsby. 08.11.1916 to Richard W Crawford, Scarborough. 22.02.1917 Vessel captured by U-boat and sunk 129 miles from Longstone.					
CORNELIA 102963 H257 Steam Trawler	124 21.07.1894 09.08.1894	149 60	102.5 20.5	C.D.Holmes 45 NHP 10 knots	Charles Hellyer Hull
05.08.1897 Sold to Hellyer Steam Fishing Co Ltd, Hull. 26.10.1906 to T Luenge, Corunna, Spain renamed COLON. 06.09.1916 Vessel wrecked at Cadiz, Spain.					
WELSHMAN 102957 Steam Tug	125 1894 05.07.1894	72 1	76.5 17.0	Tindall & Co 39 NHP 9 knots	Thomas Gray & Co Ltd Hull
15.10.1895 Sold to Societe L' Economique, Bordeaux, France renamed LE CHARLES DESPEAUX . 1938 Vessel sold to Jos de Smedt (Shipbreakers), Belgium and broken up.					
FRANCONIA 104180 GY630 Steam Trawler	126 01.08.1894 22.08.1894	154 65	102.2 20.7	C.D.Holmes 50 NHP 10 knots	Great Grimsby & East Coast Steam Fishing Co Ltd Grimsby
01.03.1912 Sold to Blyth Steam Fishing Co Ltd, Blyth. 1914 to Soc Anon Pesquera Malagueña, Malaga, Spain. 1916 to Marine Nationale Francaise (French Navy) renamed EPERVIAR. 1919 to Soc Provencale D'Aff & D'Armenent, Marseilles, France renamed CELTIQUE. 1925 to N Melchiorrti, Rome, Italy renamed CLARETTA. 1946 *(6 cyl Ansaldo diesel engine fitted).* 1948 to Florio Tonnare Di Favignana E Formica, Trapani1. 1959 Vessel sold to shipbreakers and broken up.					
CLAUDIA 102967 H263 Steam Trawler	127 1894 18.09.1894	149 60	102.5 20.5	C.D.Holmes 45 NHP 10 knots	Charles Hellyer Hull
05.08.1897 Sold to Hellyer Steam Fishing Co Ltd, Hull. 29.12.1895 Stranded on rocks near Buckton Hall, Filey Yorkshire. 03.01.1896 Towed off but foundered in deep water nearby.					
FLORENCE 102969 H265 Steam Trawler	128 1894 29.09.1894	149 60	102.6 20.5	C.D.Holmes 45 NHP 10 knots	Samuel T White & Co Hull
23.11.1896 Sold to Armitage's Steam Trawling Co Ltd, Hull. 11.07.1912 to Reliable Steam Fishing Co Ltd, Scarborough (SH144). 13.07.1916 Vessel captured by U-boat and sunk 10 miles north-east of Scarborough.					

NAME Official No. Port Letters Numbers	Yard No. Launched Registered	Registered G Ton N Ton	 L Ft B Ft	Engine Builder Horse Power Reg'd Speed	OWNER (Built for)
RAMESES 104189 GY715 Steam Trawler	129 16.10.1894 30.10.1894	155 65	102.2 20.7	C.D.Holmes 45 NHP 10 knots	Robert W Roberts & James Ruthven Ltd Grimsby
18 04.1917 Vessel captured by U-boat and sunk 60 miles off Blyth.					
CLYDE	130 1894 1894		70.0 15.6	Amos & Smith NHP knots	HM War Office Whitehall London
Government Boat. No details of type or service record.					
SAXON 104190 GY722 Steam Trawler	131 20.10.1894 10.11.1894	119 37	88.5 20.1	C.D.Holmes 43 NHP 10 knots	Alfred Bannister Grimsby
22.01.1901 Sold to Onward Steam Fishing Co Ltd, Grimsby. 1915 Rqd by the Royal Navy as a mine-sweeper renamed SAXON II. 1918 reverted on return. 08.03.1920 to W Lilburn, North Shields (SN22). 1926 to J D Irvin, North Shields. 22.04.1931 Vessel foundered 15 miles off the Tyne.					
Unnamed Lightship	132 1894		40.0 15.5	N/A	Trinity House Hull
For use in marking part of the navigable deep water channel of the River Humber.					
GUERNSEY 105023 H271 Steam Trawler	133 12.02.1895 04.03.1895	138 57	98.7 20.5	Amos & Smith 35 NHP 9.5 knots	Hull Steam Fishing & Ice Co Ltd Hull
28.11.1913 Sold to Sven Olsson, Gullholmn, Sweden renamed SONJA. 1927 Vessel deleted from Lloyds Register of Shipping reported lost.					
ALDERNEY 105029 H273 Steam Trawler	134 27.02.1895 15.03.1895	138 57	98.7 20.5	Amos & Smith 35 NHP 9.5 knots	Hull Steam Fishing & Ice Co Ltd Hull
23.06.1914 Sold to V Putz & Co, Geestamunde, Germany renamed OST. 24.06.1915 Vessel captured by Royal Navy submarine No. S1 in the North Sea and requisitioned by the Royal Navy as a minesweeper No. FY 1881 renamed CROMSIT renamed (08.11.1915) CROMSIN. 18.05.1920 Sold to A Robertson, Aberdeen Official No 144795 (A333). 1924 to A Bruce, Aberdeen. 1929 to T T Irvin, Aberdeen renamed ARO. 1930 to Crater Steam Fishing Co Ltd, North Shields. 1936 Vessel sold to shipbreakers and broken up.					
ALBATROSS 105037 H277 Steam Trawler	135 11.03.1895 27.04.1895	151 65	101.7 20.7	C.D.Holmes 45 NHP 10 knots	Pickering & Haldane's Steam Trawling Co Ltd Hull
1914 Rqd by the Royal Navy as a minesweeper No. FY 772 renamed ALBATROSS II. 1918 reverted on return. 04.12.1917 Sold to J S Ellis, Scarborough. 1926 to R de Carranza, Malaga, Spain renamed PUNTA PALOMA. 1948 to Navegacion y Pesca, Aviles renamed CASTIFUYADO. 1958 to Iriberri SA, Aviles renamed PUNTA ASTONDO. Aug 1969 Vessel sold to Garcia y Cia (shipbreakers) Spain and broken up at Pasajes.					
PENGUIN 105042 H284 Steam Trawler	136 11.05.1895 12.06.1895	151 65	101.7 20.7	C.D.Holmes 45 NHP 10 knots	Pickering & Haldane's Steam Trawling Co Ltd Hull
22.12.1914 Sold to Reginald White, Grimsby (GY420). 1915 Rqd by the Royal Navy for harbour services. 1918 returned. 25.03.1916 James Johnson, Scarborough. 1919 to H W Barker Scarborough (SH223). 1926 to R de Carranza, Malaga, Spain renamed PUNTA ALCAZAR. Sep 1969 Vessel sold to Garcia y Cia (shipbreakers) Spain and broken up at Pasajes.					
OSPREY Steam Tug	137 1895 1895	153 22	110.0 20.0	Amos & Smith 51 NHP 9 knots	HM War Office Whitehall London
Government Boat. No details of type or service record. 1923 Sold to Cox & Danks Ltd, Portsmouth renamed FERRODANKS Official No. 147985. 1933 Vessel sold for scrap to Metal Industries, Charlestown. 18.04.1934 Breaking up completed.					
PORTIA 105038 H280 Steam Trawler	138 1895 09.05.1895	178 76	108.8 20.6	C.D.Holmes 55 NHP 10 knots	Charles Hellyer & Co Ltd Hull
07.05.1897 Sold to Hellyer Steam Fishing Co Ltd, Hull. 29.12.1915 Sold to South Western Fishing Co Ltd, Grimsby (GY828). 30.08.1917 to Alec Black Grimsby. 1917 Rqd by the Royal Navy as a fishing trawler (Fishery Reserve) renamed PORTA III. 1919 returned and reverted. 1931 Vessel sold for scrap to Thos W Ward Ltd Preston. 26.01.1932 Registration closed on advice the vessel was broken up .					

NAME Official No. Port Letters Numbers	Yard No. Launched Registered	Registered G Ton N Ton	 L Ft B Ft	Engine Builder Horse Power Reg'd Speed	OWNER (Built for)
CURLEW 105031 H274 Steam Trawler	139 16.03.1895 05.04.1895	134 56	95.2 20.3	C.D.Holmes 55 NHP 10 knots	Pickering & Haldane's Steam Trawling Co Ltd Hull
27.09.1898 Sold to T Hanlow, Dublin. 03.01.1900 to Dublin Steam Trawling Co Ltd, Dublin. 1906 to James Hall, Sunderland (SD78). 05.06.1915 Vessel captured by U-boat and sunk by gunfire north-east of Aberdeen.					
VALERIA 105057 H305 Steam Trawler	140 10.07.1895 02.08.1895	149 59	102.5 20.5	C.D.Holmes 45 NHP 10 knots	Charles Hellyer & Co Ltd Hull
24.08.1897 Sold to Hellyer Steam Fishing Co Ltd, Hull. 11.04.1910 to Naam Venn Stoomv " Nil Desperandum",Ijmuiden, Holland renamed MARTHA (IJM165).*(Herring Lugger).* 1918 to Scheepsexplottatie Maats, Ijmuiden. 1920 to N V Zee Visscherij Maats "Shamrock 1" , Ijmuiden. 1939 to J V Pronk Ijmuiden. 1942 Vessel reported missing in the North Sea presumed mined:- Lost with all hands.					
ARGONAUT 105058 H291 Steam Trawler	141 27.07.1895 26.08.1895	149 59	102.5 20.5	C.D.Holmes 45 NHP 10 knots	Charles Hellyer & Co Ltd Hull
24.08.1897 Sold to Hellyer Steam Fishing Co Ltd, Hull. 18.01.1913 to Leon Feron, Boulogne, France renamed FRANCETTE (B284). 1914 Rqd by Marine Nationale Francaise (French Navy) . 1919 returned. 30.04.1920 to Alexandre et Andre Merrienne Freres, Fecamp (F441). 28.06.1937 Vessel sold for scrap to Arie Rijsdijk, Holland and broken up at Hendrik-Ido-Ambracht .					
PENELOPE 105065 H295 Steam Trawler	142 07.09.1895 30.09.1895	149 59	102.5 20.5	C.D.Holmes 45 NHP 10 knots	Charles Hellyer & Co Ltd Hull
11.06.1897 Sold to Hellyer Steam Fishing Co Ltd, Hull.12.05.1911 to NV Stoomvissch Maats Praxis, Ijmuiden (IJM64). 31.12.1942 Vessel reported missing in the North Sea presumed mined:- Lost with all hands.					
ARIADNE 105061 H293 Steam Trawler	143 19.08.1895 11.09.1895	149 59	102.5 20.5	C.D.Holmes 45 NHP 10 knots	Charles Hellyer & Co Ltd Hull
11.06.1897 Sold to Hellyer Steam Fishing Co Ltd, Hull. 05.07.1911 to NV Stoomvissch Maats "de Een" ,Ijmuiden, Holland renamed De EEN (IJM7). 31.07.1917 Vessel reported missing in the North Sea presumed mined:- Lost with all hands.					
SIR REDVERS BULLER	144 1895 1895	370 143	130.0 23.0	Amos & Smith NHP knots	HM War Office Whitehall London
Government Boat. No details of type or service record.					
PELICAN 105046 H285 Steam Trawler	145 05.05.1895 25.06.1895	156 63	104.3 20.8	C.D.Holmes 50 NHP 10 knots	St Andrews Steam Fishing Co Ltd Hull
30.12.1909 Vessel wrecked off Bempton Cliffs, East Yorkshire on passage from Farne Islands towards Hull. All nine crew rescued from the rigging in darkness by the Flamborough lifeboat FORESTER .					
MARGUERITE 105051 H288 Steam Trawler	146 24.06.1895 11.07.1895	151 62	103.4 20.8	C.D.Holmes 45 NHP 10 knots	Armitage's Steam Trawling Co Ltd Hull
15.10.1913 Sold to W A Leith, Aberdeen (A594). 1915 to R W Crawford, Scarborough (SH214). 24.09.1916 Vessel captured by U-boat and sunk by gunfire 20 miles off Scarborough.					
CITY OF GLOUCESTER 105069 H298 Steam Trawler	147 18.09.1895 14.10.1895	152 59	101.5 20.8	C.D.Holmes 45 NHP 10 knots	George W Bowman Hull
01.09.1911 Sold to NV Stoomvissch Maats Praxis, Ijmuiden, Holland renamed PLEJADEN (IJM44). 21.01.1916 Vessel left Ijmuiden for the fishing grounds not heard of again. Posted missing:- Lost with all hands.					
JACKDAW 105072 H300 Steam Trawler	148 16.10.1895 09.11.1895	150 64	101.5 20.8	C.D.Holmes 45 NHP 10 knots	Pickering & Haldane's Steam Trawling Co Ltd Hull
09.11.1895 Sold to J Duncan & Sons Ltd, Liverpool. 22.12.1897 Vessel sank in the River Mersey later salved and returned to service 01.04.1898 Registration re-opened. 22.11.1915 to Andrew Lewis, Aberdeen. 02.12.1915 Vessel wrecked at Barra Ness, Yell Island, Shetland.					

Yard No.145
1895 PELICAN
Photo:- Barnard and Straker Collection

Yard No.151
1895 CRYSTAL (At Scarborough)
Photo by courtesy of George Scales

Yard No.160
1896 HONORIA
Photo:- Barnard and Straker Collection

NAME **Official No.** **Port Letters Numbers**	**Yard No.** **Launched** **Registered**	**Registered** **G Ton** **N Ton**	 **L Ft** **B Ft**	**Engine Builder** **Horse Power** **Reg'd Speed**	**OWNER** **(Built for)**
ARCADIA 105766 Steam Tug	149 1895 1895	180 63	109.1 21.5	Earle's 71 NHP 12 knots	W Watkins London
04.08.1914 Rqd by the Royal Navy No. N66 / (1918) N24 renamed CHICHESTER. 29.05.1919 returned. 1952 renamed BADIA. 1955 Sold to Shiptowage Ltd, London. 1957 Vessel sold to shipbreakers and broken up.					
MANILA 105775 Steam Tug	150 1895 1895	180 63	109.1 21.5	Earle's 71 NHP 12 knots	W Watkins London
1902 Sold to Table Bay Harbour Board, Cape Town, South Africa. 1916 to British Africa Shipping & Coaling Co Ltd, Cape Town. 1920 to C E Zalocastas, Piræus, Greece renamed ELSI Z. 1926 to Loucas Matsos & Sons, Piræus renamed AGHIOS NICOLAUS. 1957 Vessel sold to shipbreakers and broken up.					
CRYSTAL 105079 H303 Steam Trawler	151 20.11.1895 16.12.1895	149 57	100.0 20.8	C.D.Holmes 45 NHP 10 knots	Kingston Steam Trawling Co Ltd Hull
1917 Rqd by the Royal Navy as a fishing trawler (Fishery Reserve) . 1919 returned. 21.03.1919 Sold to Trident Steam Fishing Co Ltd, Hull. 16.11.1929 to Gibson & Mumby, Hull. 13.02.1934 to Filey United Steam Trawling Co Ltd, Scarborough (SH58). 1943 to Boston Deep Sea Fishing Co Ltd, Scarborough. 26.06.1943 Vessel sunk by mine 12 miles off Scarborough.					
TOPAZ 105081 H307 Steam Trawler	152 18.12.1895 09.01.1896	149 57	100.0 20.8	C.D.Holmes 45 NHP 10 knots	Kingston Steam Trawling Co Ltd Hull
23.01.1908 Vessel sunk following a collision with the Hull trawler JESSICA H870 *(see Yard No. 97)* in the River Humber later salved. 10.07.1908 Sold to Hull Steam Trawling Mutual Insurance & Provident Co Ltd, Hull. 17.08.1908 to William Nettleton, Hull. 13.12.1910 to Fiskeriaktieb Hvalen, Gothenburg, Sweden. 1931 to E Waxen, Oslo, Norway. 15.12.1941 Vessel sunk off the west coast of Norway by aircraft bombs All crew lost.					
GRECIAN 105540 GY15 Steam Trawler	153 18.01.1896 13.02.1896	119 38	88.5 20.1	Earle's 45 NHP 10 knots	Thomas Robinson Grimsby
07.12.1915 Sold to Charles Dobson, Grimsby. 11.10.1916 to Thomas Whitehead, Scarborough. 20.04.1917 Vessel captured by U-boat and sunk by time bombs north-east of Longstone Light-vessel.					
CUCKOO 105083 H309 Steam Trawler	154 30.01.1896 19.02.1896	156 55	103.5 20.9	C.D.Holmes 50 NHP 10 knots	John McCann Hull
03.12.1897 Sold to Yorkshire Steam Fishing Co, Hull. 1914 Rqd by the Royal Navy as a minesweeper No. FY 388 (1918) renamed NIGHTJAR . 1919 returned and reverted. 04.12.1917 to Ellis Steam Trawling Co Ltd, Scarborough. 1923 to R de Carraza, Malaga, Spain renamed PUNTA AZAMOR. 03.07.1946 Vessel wrecked off San Esteban Pravia in dense fog on passage from Aviles towards Grande Sole.					
MAGPIE 105084 H311 Steam Trawler	155 04.02.1896 05.03.1896	156 55	103.5 20.9	C.D.Holmes 50 NHP 10 knots	Pickering & Haldane's Steam Trawling Co Ltd Hull
1904 Damaged by Russian Warships in the "Dogger Bank incident". 05.12.1916 Sold to George F Sleight, Grimsby (GY1010). 1918 Rqd by the Royal Navy as a fishing trawler (Fishery Reserve) renamed MAGPIE III. 1919 returned and reverted. 29.10.1920 to A Walker, Aberdeen (A495). 1928 to P Valkaniar & Yak, Ijmuiden, Holland. 1936 Vessel sold to shipbreakers and broken up.					
BRITSH EMPIRE 105085 H313 Steam Trawler	156 27.02.1896 23.03.1896	159 63	104.6 20.8	C.D.Holmes 50 NHP 10 knots	Edward B Cargill & Co Hull
27.02.1900 Vessel wrecked off White Cliffs Speeton 5 miles south of Filey Yorkshire. All nine crew rescued by rocket apparatus (Breaches Buoy).					
KESTREL 105099 H318 Steam Trawler	157 02.04.1896 23.04.1896	160 64	105.0 20.8	C.D.Holmes 50 NHP 10 knots	Pickering & Haldane's Steam Trawling Co Ltd Hull
21.02.1915 Vessel sank following a collision with the ss HYDRA in the North Sea.					

<table>
<tr><th rowspan="2">NAME
Official No.
Port Letters Numbers</th><th rowspan="2">Yard No.
Launched
Registered</th><th colspan="2">Registered</th><th rowspan="2">Engine Builder
Horse Power
Reg'd Speed</th><th rowspan="2">OWNER
(Built for)</th></tr>
<tr><th>G Ton
N Ton</th><th>L Ft
B Ft</th></tr>
<tr><td>FALCON
106701
H321 Steam Trawler</td><td>158
16.04.1896
08.05.1896</td><td>160
64</td><td>105.0
20.8</td><td>C.D.Holmes
50 NHP
10 knots</td><td>Pickering & Haldane's Steam Trawling Co Ltd
Hull</td></tr>
<tr><td colspan="6">15.02.1900 Vessel sank in the North Sea with the loss of all nine crew. One of five Hull trawlers which disappeared in the "great gale and blizzard" which caused considerable damage to shipping and to coastal towns.</td></tr>
<tr><td>IRISHMAN
105093
Steam Tug</td><td>159
1896
13.04.1896</td><td>99
--</td><td>85.9
17.1</td><td>Tindall & Co
70 RHP
10.5 knots</td><td>Thomas Gray & Co Ltd
Hull</td></tr>
<tr><td colspan="6">09.05.1898 Sold to Medina Steam Tug & Water Co Ltd, Cowes Isle of Wight. 30.07.1914 Rqd by the Royal Navy.
1919 returned. 1920 to Cowes Steam Tug Co Ltd, Cowes. 25.02.1926 Vessel offered for sale but withdrawn.
1940 to Vectis Transport Co Ltd Cowes. 08.05.1941 Vessel sunk by mine off Portsmouth.</td></tr>
<tr><td>HONORIA
106704
H325 Steam Trawler</td><td>160
11.05.1896
23.06.1896</td><td>159
62</td><td>105.0
20.5</td><td>Earle's
55 NHP
10.5 knots</td><td>Charles Hellyer & Co Ltd
Hull</td></tr>
<tr><td colspan="6">11.06.1897 Sold to Hellyer Steam Fishing Co Ltd, Hull.
09.01.1906 Stranded at Redcar Cleveland subsequently re-floated and rebuilt (178 Gross Tons Length 118 ft 9in).
23.07.1915 Vessel captured by U-boat and sunk by gunfire 35 miles north north-west of Cape Wrath.</td></tr>
<tr><td>IOLANTHE
106709
H328 Steam Trawler</td><td>161
30.05.1896
14.07.1896</td><td>159
62</td><td>105.0
20.5</td><td>Earle's
55 NHP
10.5 knots</td><td>Charles Hellyer & Co Ltd
Hull</td></tr>
<tr><td colspan="6">11.06.1897 Sold to Hellyer Steam Fishing Co Ltd, Hull.
03.05.1915 Vessel captured by U-boat and sunk by time bombs 140 miles east north-east of Hornsea, East Yorkshire.</td></tr>
<tr><td>TORONTO
105091
H316 Steam Trawler</td><td>162
04.03.1896
08.04.1896</td><td>147
61</td><td>98.4
20.5</td><td>Amos & Smith
35 NHP
9.5 knots</td><td>Hull Steam Fishing Co Ltd
Hull</td></tr>
<tr><td colspan="6">15.03.1912 Sold to Akties Sildfangst , Trondheim, Norway renamed (1916) BORGAROY.
1919 to Akties Sortland Fiskeriselskop, Sortland renamed GAVLFJORD.
1932 to Akties Stortind, Sigerfjord renamed STORTIND.
Nov 1944 Vessel badly damaged by an explosion whilst lying at Hillefjord. Sold for breaking up.</td></tr>
<tr><td>JAMAICA
105098
H317 Steam Trawler</td><td>163
26.03.1896
22.04.1896</td><td>146
60</td><td>98.4
20.5</td><td>Amos & Smith
35 NHP
9.5 knots</td><td>Hull Steam Fishing Co Ltd
Hull</td></tr>
<tr><td colspan="6">02.02.1912 Sold to Duder & Brother, Bahia, Brazil.
1920 to Aymar Johnson, New York, USA renamed BELLA, (converted to a Tug).
1922 to St Lawrence Transportation Ltd, Montreal, Canada renamed JAMAICA.
1932 to A Janin, Montreal renamed CLAIRE JANIN. 1951 Vessel sold to shipbreakers and broken up.</td></tr>
<tr><td>TRINIDAD
106720
H366 Steam Trawler</td><td>164
12.09.1896
12.10.1896</td><td>147
61</td><td>98.4
20.5</td><td>Amos & Smith
35 NHP
9.5 knots</td><td>Hull Steam Fishing Co Ltd
Hull</td></tr>
<tr><td colspan="6">25.09.1916 Vessel captured by U-boat and sunk by gunfire 23 miles north-east of Whitby (see Yard No. 33).</td></tr>
<tr><td>ALERT
106703
H324 Steam Trawler</td><td>165
16.05.1896
23.06.1896</td><td>150
57</td><td>101.5
20.8</td><td>C.D.Holmes
45 NHP
10 knots</td><td>John Wilkins &
Alfred Barrett
Milford Haven</td></tr>
<tr><td colspan="6">18.03.1899 Sold to Neale & West Ltd, Cardiff (CF22). 1914 to D G Jones, Milford Haven (M3).
1917 Rqd by the Royal Navy as a fishing trawler (Fishery Reserve) renamed ALERT IV. 1919 returned & reverted.
1919 to J R McKnight, Milford Haven. 1926 to Ramon de Carranza, Malaga, Spain renamed PUNTA SABINAL.
Nov 1969 Vessel sold for scrap to Garcia y Cia. Pasajes and broken up.</td></tr>
<tr><td>SETI
106659
GY72 Steam Trawler</td><td>166
15.06.1896
21.07.1896</td><td>160
60</td><td>101.8
20.8</td><td>C.D.Holmes
45 NHP
10 knots</td><td>Robert W Roberts &
James Ruthven Ltd
Grimsby</td></tr>
<tr><td colspan="6">26.08.1914 Vessel sunk by the German cruiser ALBATROSS (B 1907) in the North Sea 80 miles SW of the Spurn Point.</td></tr>
<tr><td>MONARCH
106712
H331 Steam Trawler</td><td>167
1896
05.08.1896</td><td>163
65</td><td>105.0
20.6</td><td>Bailey & Leetham
45 NHP
10 knots</td><td>Richard Simpson & Co Ltd
Hull</td></tr>
<tr><td colspan="6">23.02.1899 Sold to London & Yorkshire Steam Trawling & Fish Carrying Co Ltd, Hull.
01.12.1902 to Neale & West Ltd, Cardiff (CF9). 1913 to R W Lewis, Aberdeen.
26.11.1915 to Harry Robinson & William Grant, Grimsby renamed MONS (GY806).
1917 Rqd by the Royal Navy as a fishing trawler (Fishery Reserve). 1919 returned.
19.08.1924 Registration closed on advice that the vessel was broken up.</td></tr>
</table>

NAME Official No. Port Letters Numbers	Yard No. Launched Registered	Registered G Ton N Ton	 L Ft B Ft	Engine Builder Horse Power Reg'd Speed	OWNER (Built for)
PREMIER 106715 H344 Steam Trawler	168 28.07.1896 20.08.1896	163 65	105.0 20.6 -	Bailey & Leetham 45 NHP 10 knots	Richard Simpson & Co Ltd Hull
23.02.1899 Sold to London & Yorkshire Steam Trawling & Fish Carrying Co Ltd, Hull. 17.09.1902 to Soc Anon de Pesca Algecireña, Algeciras, Spain renamed ALGECIRAS. 1905 to P Gutierrez Feu, Algeciras. 1919 Vessel deleted from Lloyds Register of Shipping (War loss).					
COUNCILLOR 106721 H337 Steam Trawler	169 26.08.1896 28.10.1896	162 63	105.0 20.5	Bailey & Leetham 45 NHP 10 knots	Richard Simpson & Co Ltd Hull
23.02.1899 Sold to London & Yorkshire Steam Trawling & Fish Carrying Co Ltd, Hull. 17.09.1902 to Soc Anon de Pesca Algecireña, Algeciras, Spain renamed PALMA. Jan 1913 Vessel wrecked at Cape Malabat.					
TURQUOISE 106718 H335 Steam Trawler	170 12.08.1896 15.09.1896	164 67	105.4 20.7	Earle's 50 NHP 10.5 knots	Kingston Steam Trawling Co Ltd Hull
1918 Rqd by the Royal Navy as a fishing trawler (Fishery Reserve). 1919 returned. 25.10.1923 Sold to William Mitchell, Aberdeen (A951). 1926 to Andrew M Watson, Aberdeen. 1927 to N V Stoom Viss Maats de Drie, Ijmuiden, Holland renamed DE DREE (IJM311). 1935 Vessel sold to shipbreakers and broken up.					
JACINTH 106725 H340 Steam Trawler	171 24.08.1896 24.12.1896	164 67	105.4 20.7	Earle's 50 NHP 10.5 knots	Kingston Steam Trawling Co Ltd Hull
14.05.1912 Sold to NV Maats Erin Ijmuiden, Holland renamed ERIN (IJM88). 27.12.1915 Vessel sunk by mine in the North Sea.					
BENGAL 106719 H287 Steam Trawler	172 07.09.1896 02.10.1896	149 64	100.6 21.0	Amos & Smith 35 NHP 9.5 knots	Hull Steam Fishing & Ice Co Ltd Hull
1914 Rqd by the Royal Navy as a minesweeper No. FY 1203. 1918 returned. 09.06.1919 Sold to Arthur Gouldby, Lowestoft (LT575). 1923 to NV Stoomv Maats de Onderneming, Ijmuiden, Holland renamed COBI (IJM41). 1927 to NV Visscherij Maats Roode Zee, Ijmuiden renamed ROODE ZEE.1937 Vessel sold to shipbreakers and broken up.					
COMRADE 106723 H338 Steam Trawler	173 10.10.1896 14.11.1896	162 63	105.5 20.7	C.D.Holmes 50 NHP 10 knots	J Duncan Sons & Co Liverpool
14.08.1909 Sold to NV Stoomv Maats Pesca, Ijmuiden renamed INVIERNO(IJM158). 1937 Vessel sold to shipbreakers and broken up..					
LORD C. BERESFORD 106726 H341 Steam Trawler	174 1896 22.12.1896	162 63	105.5 20.7	C.D.Holmes 50 NHP 10 knots	Pickering & Haldane's Steam Trawling Co Ltd Hull
25.10.1897 Sold to Yorkshire Steam Trawling Co Ltd, Hull. 29.11.1899 to Dublin Trawling Ice & Cold Storage Co Ltd, Dublin (D199). 1926 to Lincolnia Steam Fishing Co Ltd, Fleetwood. 1926 Vessel sold for scrap to J Hornsby & Son and broken up.					
SABRINA 106734 H346 Steam Trawler	175 04.01.1897 24.02.1897	158 61	105.5 20.5	Earle's 55 NHP 10.5 knots	Charles Hellyer & Co Ltd Hull
02.08.1897 Sold to Hellyer Steam Fishing Co Ltd, Hull. 21.05.1915 Vessel sunk by mine 160 miles east north-east off Spurn Light- vessel.					
HARRIER 106728 H342 Steam Trawler	176 21.12.1896 21.01.1897	162 64	105.5 20.7	C.D.Holmes 50 NHP 10 knots	Pickering & Haldane's Steam Trawling Co Ltd Hull
16.07.1914 Sold to The Alliance Steam Trawling Co Ltd, Scarborough (SH36). 25.09.1916 Vessel captured by U-boat and sunk 20 miles north-east of Scarborough .					
WILBERFORCE 106731 H344 Steam Trawler	177 24.12.1896 01.02.1897	162 64	105.5 20.7	C.D.Holmes 50 NHP 10 knots	National Steam Trawling Co Ltd Hull
18.11.1906 Sold to R de Carranza, San Sebastian, Spain renamed ALFONSO XIII. 1926 to Painset & La Font, Boulogne, France renamed CHEVETTE. 1937 Vessel sold to shipbreakers and broken up.					

Yard No.171
1896 JACINTH
Photo:- Barnard and Straker Collection

Yard No.190
1897 FARADAY
Photo:- Barnard and Straker Collection

Yard No.199
1898 SARPEDON as
LORD SHREWSBURY
Photo by courtesy of George Scales

NAME Official No. Port Letters Numbers	Yard No. Launched Registered	Registered G Ton N Ton	 L Ft B Ft	Engine Builder Horse Power Reg'd Speed	OWNER (Built for)
LANSDOWNE	178 1897 1897	170 97	120.0 20.0	Amos & Smith 35 NHP 9.5 knots	HM War Office Whitehall London
Government Boat. No details of type or service record.					
LORD NELSON 106733 H345 Steam Trawler	179 21.01.1897 15.02.1897	162 63	105.5 20.7	C.D.Holmes 50 NHP 10 knots	National Steam Trawling Co Ltd Hull
18.11.1906 Sold to R de Carranza, San Sebastian, Spain renamed REINA VICTORIA. 1946 to Isaac Lloret Rojo, San Sabastian. 1965 Vessel sold for scrap to shipbreakers and broken up in Spain.					
DOURO 108465 GY310 Steam Trawler	180 08.03.1897 05.04.1897	150 63	96.0 20.5	Earle's 45 NHP 10 knots	Ocean Steam Trawling Co Ltd Grimsby
1917 Rqd by the Royal Navy as a fishing trawler (Fishery Reserve). 1919 returned. 09.04.1919 Sold to Fred Bacon, Grimsby. 06.06.1919 to Economy Steam Fishing Co, Grimsby. 05.03.1920 to Harold Bacon, Grimsby . 26.03.1920 Sold to Trawlers White Sea & Grimsby Ltd, Grimsby. 04.06.1937 Registration closed on advice that the vessel was broken up at Bo'ness Scotland.					
CONGO 108458 GY274 Steam Trawler	181 16.02.1897 17.03.1897	152 58	96.0 20.5	Earle's 45 NHP 10 knots	Ocean Steam Trawling Co Ltd Grimsby
1917 Rqd by the Royal Navy as a fishing trawler (Fishery Reserve). 1919 returned. 09.04.1919 Sold to Fred Bacon, Grimsby. 06.06.1919 to Economy Steam Fishing Co, Grimsby. 05.03. 1920 to Harold Bacon, Grimsby . 27.03.1920 Sold to Trawlers White Sea & Grimsby Ltd, Grimsby. 04.06.1937 Registration closed on advice that the vessel was broken up at Bo'ness Scotland.					
SCOTLAND 106739 H348 Steam Trawler	182 17.03.1897 14.04.1897	152 63	101.8 20.6	Amos & Smith 35 NHP 10 knots	Hull Steam Fishing & Ice Co Ltd Hull
01.01.1914 *(Tonnage adjusted 63.2 net tons).* 31.01.1919 Sold to Benjamin Knowles, Hull. 07.03.1919 Vessel sunk off Flamborough Head, East Yorkshire (possibly mined).					
IRELAND 106741 H351 Steam Trawler	183 15.04.1897 07.05.1897	152 63	101.8 20.6	Amos & Smith 35 NHP 9.5 knots	Hull Steam Fishing & Ice Co Ltd Hull
01.01.1914 *(Tonnage adjusted 63.2 net tons).* 10.02.1917 Vessel captured by U-boat and sunk by gunfire105 miles from Girdleness in approx position 57° 01'N 001°10'E					
SARGON 108464 GY305 Steam Trawler	184 02.03.1897 06.04.1897	167 68	108.7 20.7	C.D.Holmes 50 NHP 9.5 knots	Standard Steam Fishing Co Ltd Grimsby
01.03.1912 Sold to Port of Blyth Steam Fishing Co Ltd, Blyth renamed LORD SELBORNE (BH91). 10.12.1914 to Beacon Steam Fishing Co Ltd, Grimsby (GY392). 14.09.1916 to The Allen Steam Fishing Co Ltd, Grimsby renamed (12.12.1916) CYNTHIA. 1917 Rqd by the Royal Navy as a fishing trawler (Fishery Reserve). 1919 returned. 09.04.1919 to Fred Bacon, Grimsby. 04.06.1919 to Economy Steam Fishing Co Ltd, Grimsby. 26.03.1920 to Trawlers White Sea & Grimsby Ltd, Grimsby. 05.11.1945 to London (Grimsby) Ltd, Grimsby. 08.04.1948 to Ravendale Trawlers Ltd, Grimsby. 22.12.1951 to James Mowatt, Aberdeen (A697). 1953 Vessel sold to BISCO and allocated to Malcolm Brechin, Granton. 18.03.1953 Registration closed on advice that the vessel was broken up.					
SOLON 108469 GY326 Steam Trawler	185 23.03.1897 07.05.1897	160 55	101.8 20.6	C.D.Holmes 50 NHP 9.5 knots	Standard Steam Fishing Co Ltd Grimsby
01.03.1912 Sold to Port of Blyth Steam Fishing & Ice Co Ltd, Blyth renamed LORD SCARBOROUGH (BH92). 10.12.1914 to The Beacon Steam Fishing Co Ltd, Grimsby. (GY393). 02.04.1917 Vessel captured and sunk by U-boat in the North Sea 100 miles east of May Island.					
IMPERIAL QUEEN 106752 H357 Steam Trawler	186 19.05.1897 18.06.1897	173 68	108.5 20.6	C.D.Holmes 58 NHP 10 knots	Hellyer Steam Fishing Co Ltd Hull
1906 Sold to Soc Anon Pesqueria Gallega, Corunna, Spain renamed DRAGON. 1915 to Marine Nationale Francaise (French Navy) renamed RUSE. 1919 to Soc Les Affreteurs Reunis, L'Orient. renamed PAN (L1939). 17.06.1926 to M' Emile Avry, L'Orient. renamed JULIENNE 1938 Vessel sold for scrap to Belgium shipbreakers. Jul 1938 breaking up commenced.					

NAME Official No. Port Letters Numbers	Yard No. Launched Registered	Registered G Ton N Ton	 L Ft B Ft	Engine Builder Horse Power Reg'd Speed	OWNER (Built for)
RECORDIA 106744 H352 Steam Trawler	187 1897 31.05.1897	167 68	108.5 20.6	C.D.Holmes 58 NHP 11 knots	Hellyer Steam Fishing Co Ltd Hull
17.09.1906 Sold to Soc des Pêcheries, Français d'Arcachon, France renamed AUDACIEUX. 1910 Vessel reported to have been lost.					
LARK 106754 H359 Steam Trawler	188 31.05.1897 03.07.1897	182 65	110.0 21.0	C.D.Holmes 58 NHP 10 knots	Pickering & Haldane's Steam Trawling Co Ltd Hull
13.12.1911 Vessel wrecked at Bempton Cliffs 5 miles north of Flamborough Head, Yorkshire on passage to Hull in a gale. All nine crew rescued by the Flamborough lifeboat.					
LINNET 106757 H363 Steam Trawler	189 03.06.1897 13.07.1897	182 65	110.0 21.0	C.D.Holmes 58 NHP 10 knots	Pickering & Haldane's Steam Trawling Co Ltd Hull
25.01.1902 Vessel sank off the north coast of Scotland.					
FARADAY 106761 H366 Steam Trawler	190 19.06.1897 23.07.1897	177 60	108.0 21.0	C.D.Holmes 50 NHP 10 knots	Francis & Thomas Ross Ltd Hull
13.10.1907 Vessel wrecked off Croseipoll Bay, Isle of Coll, Outer Hebrides.					
INDIAN EMPIRE 106765 H 369 Steam Trawler	191 1897 13.08.1897	193 65	110.0 21.0	C.D.Holmes 60 NHP 10.5 knots	Cargill Steam Trawling Co Ltd Hull
15.02.1900 Vessel foundered in the North Sea.					
CELESTIAL EMPIRE 106769 H371 Steam Trawler	192 05.09.1897 17.09.1897	182 65	110.0 21.0	C.D.Holmes 60 NHP 10.5 knots	Cargill Steam Trawling Co Ltd Hull
24.02.1901 Stranded at Hilston near Withernsea, East Yorkshire subsequently re-floated and rebuilt. 31.10.1901 Sold to W Cooper, Hull. 1908 to W Johnson Liverpool renamed CELESTIAL. 1908 to E Salmon, L'Orient, France renamed JUPITER (L236). 1908 to Canadian Fishing Co Ltd, Vancouver renamed CELESTIAL EMPIRE. 1920 to Pacific Coyle Navigation Co Ltd, Vancouver, renamed CAPE SCOTT *(converted to a tug)*. 1947 Vessel stripped for spares and hull sunk in Puget Sound as a breakwater. 1956 Raised for scrap and broken up.					
DANE 108480 GY403 Steam Trawler	193 1897 18.09.1897	160 61	100.2 21.0	Earle's 45 NHP 10 knots	"D" Line Steam Fishing Co Ltd Grimsby
03.06.1912 Sold to NV Stoomv Maats Praxis V, Ijmuiden, Holland renamed PERSEUS (IJM45). 1940 Escaped to England and fished from Fleetwood. 1945 returned to Ijmuiden. Jan 1951 Vessel sold to shipbreakers and broken up at Ijmuiden.					
DOVEY 108481 GY425 Steam Trawler	194 1897 01.10.1897	160 61	100.2 21.0	Earle's 45 NHP 10 knots	"D" Line Steam Fishing Co Ltd Grimsby
25.04. 1913 Sold to Alfred Bannister, Grimsby. 21.05.1913 to East Anglia Steam Fishing Co Ltd, Grimsby. 11.06.1915 Vessel sunk by mine in the North Sea 50 miles east by south of Spurn Point.					
DURBAN 106778 H378 Steam Trawler	195 09.09.1897 06.11.1897	152 57	101.8 20.6	Amos & Smith 35 NHP 9.5 knots	Hull Steam Fishing & Ice Co Ltd Hull
01.01.1914 *(Tonnage adjusted 60.3 net tons)*. Dec 1914 Rqd by the Royal Navy as an auxiliary patrol vessel No. FY 1209. Oct 1915 returned. 1917 Rqd by the Royal Navy as a fishing trawler (Fishery Reserve). 1919 returned. 15.03.1919 Vessel posted missing:- Lost with all hands (possibly mined) in the North Sea.					
DOUGLAS 106773 H375 Steam Trawler	196 15.09.1897 08.10.1897	152 57	101.8 20.6	Amos & Smith 35 NHP 9.5 knots	Hull Steam Fishing & Ice Co Ltd Hull
03.12.1901 Vessel sunk following a collision with the fish carrier AUSTRALIA H1328 (238 gt/ b 1882) in the North Sea. The AUSTRALIA was disabled and was unable to come to the aid of the DOUGLAS. Eight crew lost and one rescued.					
DUKE OF WELLINGTON 109015 H388 Steam Trawler	197 1898 18.03.1898	182 65	110.0 21.0	C.D.Holmes 58 NHP 10 knots	National Steam Trawling Co Ltd Hull
18.05.1915 Vessel captured by German Torpedo boat and sunk on the Dogger Bank. All crew taken prisoner.					

NAME Official No. Port Letters Numbers		Yard No. Launched Registered	Registered G Ton N Ton	 L Ft B Ft	Engine Builder Horse Power Reg'd Speed	OWNER (Built for)
SIHON 109520 GY581	 Steam Trawler	198 24.02.1898 07.04.1898	172 62	108.7 20.7	C.D.Holmes 50 NHP 10 knots	Standard Steam Fishing Co Ltd Grimsby
01.03.912 Sold to Port of Blyth Steam Fishing & Ice Co Ltd, Blyth renamed LORD STRATHMORE (BH93). 10.12.1914 to The Beacon Steam Fishing Co Ltd, Grimsby (GY394). 20.01.1917 Vessel wrecked off Bamburgh Castle, Northumberland.						
SARPEDON 109534 GY686	 Steam Trawler	199 1898 25.05.1898	167 53	101.8 20.8	C.D.Holmes 45 NHP 9.5 knots	Standard Steam Fishing Co Ltd Grimsby
01.03.1912 Sold to Port of Blyth Steam Fishing & Ice Co Ltd, Blyth renamed LORD SHREWSBURY (BH94). 10.12.1914 to The Beacon Steam Fishing Co Ltd, Grimsby (GY395). 1918 Rqd by the Royal Navy as a fishing trawler (Fishery Reserve). 1919 returned. 29.12.1918 to Stringer's Steam Fishing Co Ltd, Grimsby. 03.12.1919 to The Brent Steam Fishing Co Ltd, Grimsby. 03.05.1920 to Banks Fishing Co Ltd, Grimsby. 25.03.1924 to Great Central Co-op Eng & Ship Repair Co Ltd, Grimsby. 19.06.1928 to Trawlers White Sea & Grimsby Ltd, Grimsby. 08.12.1941 Vessel posted missing:-Lost with all hands presumed mined near the Humber Estuary.						
HAWK 109016 H389	 Steam Trawler	200 27.01.1898 25.03.1898	181 65	110.0 21.0	C.D.Holmes 58 NHP 10 knots	St Andrews Steam Fishing Co Ltd Hull
19.04.1916 Vessel sunk following a collision with the Brazilian ss CORCOVADO (3046 gt/ b 1890) in the North Sea 5 miles north-east of Spurn Light-vessel whilst outward bound from Hull towards Iceland.						
BUTTERFLY 109026 H393	 Steam Trawler	201 10.02.1898 16.05.1898	182 68	110.0 21.0	C.D.Holmes 58 NHP 10 knots	British Steam Fishing Co Ltd Hull
29.02.1912 Sold to Naam Venn Stoomv Praxis IV, Ijmuiden, Holland renamed POSEIDON (IJM74). 1936 Vessel sold to shipbreakers and broken up.						
RAMBLER 109034 LL10	 Steam Trawler	202 12.03.1898 06.06.1898	162 55	105.4 20.7	C.D.Holmes 50 NHP 10 knots	John Duncan & Sons Co Ltd Liverpool
1915 Rqd by the Royal Navy as a boom defence vessel. 1920 returned. 25.03.1919 Sold to Andrew Walker, Aberdeen (A150). 1929 to Walker Steam Trawling & Fishing Co Ltd, Aberdeen. 1936/37 Vessel sold to shipbreakers and broken up.						
HELVETIA 109803 GY767	 Steam Trawler	203 09.05.1898 01.07.1898	167 53	101.8 20.8	C.D.Holmes 50 NHP 10 knots	Great Grimsby & East Coast Steam Fishing Co Ltd Grimsby
01.08.1916 Vessel captured and sunk in the North Sea by U-boat 5 miles east of Seaham.						
CITY OF HULL 109030 H396	 Steam Trawler	204 26.02.1898 26.05.1898	181 65	110.0 21.0	C.D.Holmes 58 NHP 10 knots	City Steam Fishing Co Ltd Hull
27.05.1907 Sold to Dublin Steam Trawling Co Ltd, Dublin renamed DEAN SWIFT (D335). 1917 Rqd by the Royal Navy as a fishing trawler (Fishery Reserve). 1919 returned. 1925 to Mrs J M F A Nierinck, Dublin. 1928 to Thorneley & Co, Fleetwood (FD29) . 1929 to Dalby Steam Fishing Co Ltd, Fleetwood. 1959 Sold for scrap to Hammond Lane Foundry, Dublin. 27.01.1959 Arrived Dublin for breaking up.						
FORWARD 109042 H407	 Steam Trawler	205 06.06.1898 23.07.1898	182 62	110.0 21.0	C.D.Holmes 60 NHP 10.5 knots	John Hollingsworth & Charles H Double Hull
04.03.1901 Sold to Pickering & Haldane's Steam Trawling Co Ltd, Hull renamed SEA LARK. 1915 Rqd by the Royal Navy as a auxiliary patrol vessel No. FY 1213 renamed SEA LARK II . 30.09.1918 Vessel sunk in collision off John's Point, County Down.						
EDWARD B. CARGILL 109051 H412	 Steam Trawler	206 1898 23.08.1898	182 65	110.0 21.0	C.D.Holmes 60 NHP 10 knots	Cargill Steam Trawling Co Ltd Hull
01.01.1914 *(Tonnage adjusted 73.7 net tons)*. 15.11.1915 Vessel sunk by mine in the North Sea off Spurn Point .						
SHAKESPEARE 109041 H406	 Steam Trawler	207 1898 21.07.1898	182 60	110.0 21.0	C.D.Holmes 55 NHP 10 knots	National Steam Trawling Co Ltd Hull
11.12.1907 Vessel wrecked near Spoil Point Stromness, Brakness, Orkney Island. Four crew lost.						

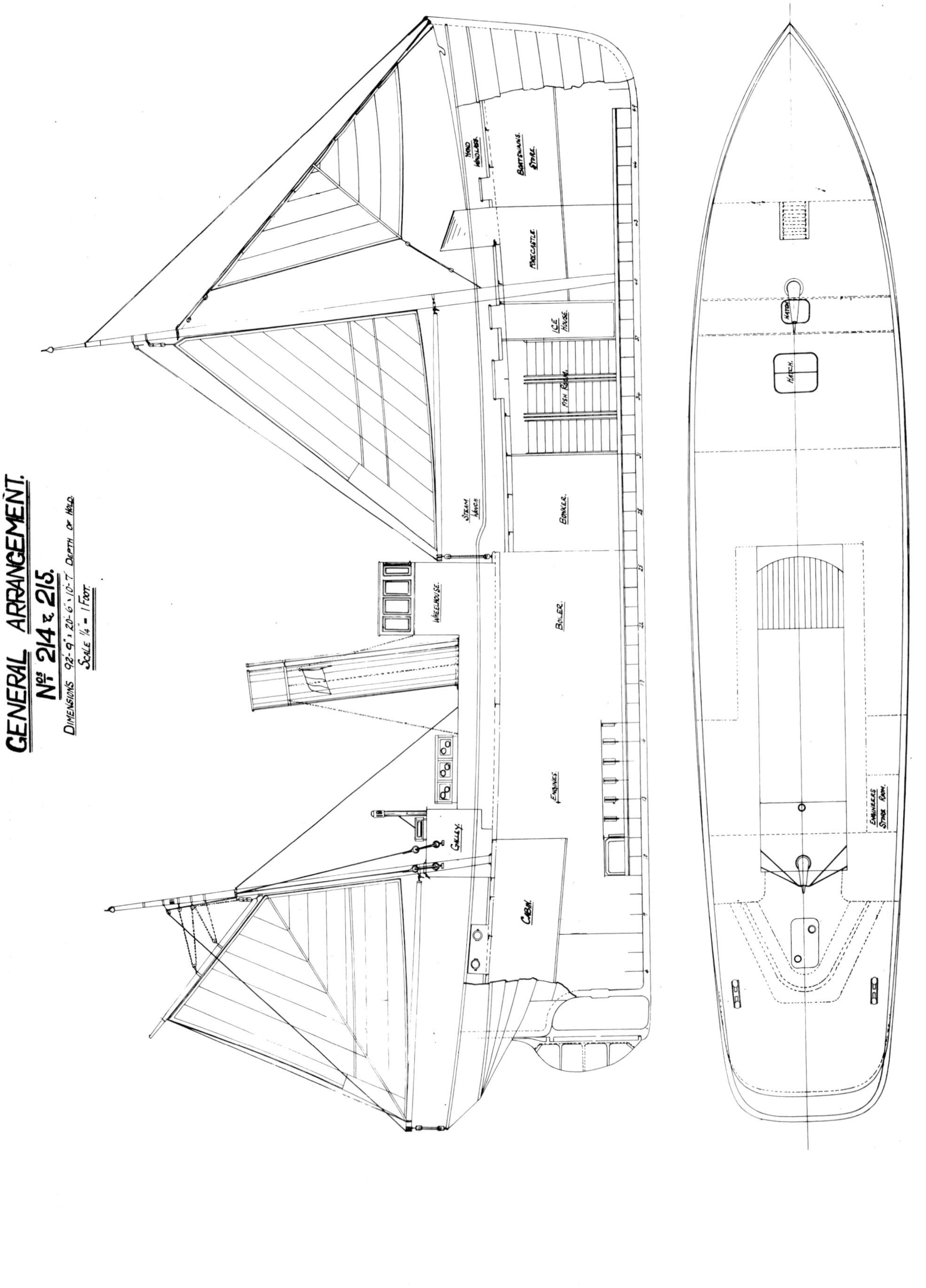
GENERAL ARRANGEMENT.
Nos 214 & 215.
DIMENSIONS 92'-9" x 20'-6" x 10'-7" DEPTH OF HOLD.
SCALE 1/4" = 1 FOOT.
WHEELHOUSE.
GALLEY.
CABIN.
ENGINES.
BOILER.
BUNKER.
STEAM WINCH
FISH ROOM.
ICE HOUSE.
FORECASTLE.
BOATSWAINS STORE.
HAND WINDLASS.
HATCH.
HATCH.
ENGINEERS STORE ROOM.

<table>
<tr><th rowspan="2">NAME
Official No.
Port Letters Numbers</th><th rowspan="2">Yard No.
Launched
Registered</th><th colspan="2">Registered</th><th rowspan="2">Engine Builder
Horse Power
Reg'd Speed</th><th rowspan="2">OWNER
(Built for)</th></tr>
<tr><th>G Ton
N Ton</th><th>L Ft
B Ft</th></tr>
<tr><td>ROYALIST
109078
H428 Steam Trawler</td><td>207A
01.09.1898
31.10.1898</td><td>183
66</td><td>111.7
21.0</td><td>C.D.Holmes
58 NHP
10 knots</td><td>George Walton
Hull</td></tr>
<tr><td colspan="6">05.09.1901 Sold to Dublin Steam Trawling Co Ltd, Dublin (D206).
31.07.1917 to George Frederick Sleight, Grimsby (GY1090).
1917 Rqd by the Royal Navy as a fishing trawler (Fishery Reserve). 1919 returned.
30.11.1920 to A Walker, Aberdeen (A498). 1929 to Hewell Fishing Co Ltd, London (LO17).
1935 Vessel sold to shipbreakers and broken up.</td></tr>
<tr><td>POINTZ CASTLE

LO167 Steam Trawler</td><td>208
26.08.1898
00.10.1898</td><td>162
52</td><td>105.2
20.7</td><td>C.D.Holmes
50 NHP
10 knots</td><td>Castle Steam Trawling Ltd
London</td></tr>
<tr><td colspan="6">1906 Vessel transferred to Milford Haven. 1907 Sold to J Wurthmann, Bremerhaven, Germany renamed OSKAR (BX 70).
1908 to J A Steenken, Bremerhaven. 30.01.1910 Vessel wrecked near Tor.</td></tr>
<tr><td>COLONIAL EMPIRE
109038
H404 Steam Trawler</td><td>209
07.04.1898
17.06.1898</td><td>162
53</td><td>105.4
20.7</td><td>Tindall & Co
55 NHP
10 knots</td><td>Cargill Steam
Trawling Co Ltd
Hull</td></tr>
<tr><td colspan="6">12.12.1911 Sold to NV F Maats Praxis III, Ijmuiden, Holland renamed PALLAS (IJM84).
1936 Vessel sold to shipbreakers and broken up.</td></tr>
<tr><td>WALWYNS CASTLE
109049
H411 Steam Trawler</td><td>209A
23.06.1898
13.08.1898</td><td>162
52</td><td>105.2
20.7</td><td>C.D.Holmes
50 NHP
9.5 knots</td><td>Castle Steam Trawling Ltd
London</td></tr>
<tr><td colspan="6">19.09.1906 Vessel transferred to Swansea (SA9). 1907 to J N Sonne, Uddevalla, Sweden renamed HAFSÖRNEN.
1920 to A/B Fiskmasen, Uddevalla .1938 to Fiskeri A/B Greta, Gothenburg. 1952 Vessel sold to shipbreakers and broken up.</td></tr>
<tr><td>EASTWARD HO
109058
H415 Steam Trawler</td><td>210
1898
13.09.1898</td><td>162
53</td><td>105.2
20.7</td><td>Tindall & Co
55 NHP
10 knots</td><td>Samuel T White & Co Ltd
Hull</td></tr>
<tr><td colspan="6">1915 Rqd by the Royal Navy as a mine-sweeper. 1919 returned.
12.02.1920 Sold to Monkshaven Fishing Co Ltd, Whitby (WY106). 1924 to W Barton, Whitby.
20.12.1924 to Consolidated Fisheries, Lowestoft (LT95). 1936 Vessel sold to shipbreakers and broken up.</td></tr>
<tr><td>HENE CASTLE
109056
H414 Steam Trawler</td><td>210A
08.08.1898
10.09.1898</td><td>162
53</td><td>105.5
20.7</td><td>C.D.Holmes
50 NHP
9.5 knots</td><td>Castle Steam Trawlers Ltd
London</td></tr>
<tr><td colspan="6">23.10.1906 Transferred to Swansea.1908 to Kisen Giogye Kabushiki Kaisha, Nagasaki, Japan renamed FUKAYE MARU.
1938 to Mitsubishi Kogyo KK, Wakamatsu. Dec 1941 Vessel deleted from the fishing register:- (War Loss).</td></tr>
<tr><td>ROCHE CASTLE
109064
H419 Steam Trawler</td><td>211
05.09.1898
01.10.1898</td><td>168
60</td><td>110.0
20.7</td><td>C.D.Holmes
50 NHP
9.5 knots</td><td>Castle Steam Trawlers Ltd
London</td></tr>
<tr><td colspan="6">15.09.1906 Vessel transferred to Swansea. 1907 to Captain Kopitoff, Archangel, Russia renamed NIKALOI.
1911 to Gebr. P & C Malachoff, Archangel renamed NICOLAI. 1919 to an Estonian owner renamed SAAREMAA.
Jun 1921 Vessel deleted from Lloyds Register of Shipping (Reported sunk in the Baltic).</td></tr>
<tr><td>NARBERTH CASTLE
109077
H427 Steam Trawler</td><td>212
06.10.1898
24.10.1898</td><td>168
60</td><td>110.0
20.7</td><td>C.D.Holmes
50 NHP
10 knots</td><td>Castle Steam Trawlers Ltd
London</td></tr>
<tr><td colspan="6">06.07.1906 Vessel transferred to Swansea. Nov 1906 Sold to W Richmond, Grimsby (GY203).
06.04.1917 Vessel captured and sunk by U-boat 30 miles north north-west off Dennis Head.</td></tr>
<tr><td>NEW ZEALAND
109056
H413 Steam Trawler</td><td>213
1898
29.08.1898</td><td>290
111</td><td>146.78
22.6</td><td>Amos & Smith
65 NHP
11 knots</td><td>Hull Steam Fishing
& Ice Co Ltd
Hull</td></tr>
<tr><td colspan="6">Used as a company carrier transporting "boxing fleet" catches of fish to London's Billingsgate Fish Market.
1916 Rqd by the Royal Navy as a Boom defence vessel renamed HOKIANGA. 1920 returned and reverted.
11.02.1937 Vessel sold to Dutch shipbreakers and broken up.</td></tr>
<tr><td>TEUTON
109809
GY795 Steam Trawler</td><td>214
1898
08.08.1898</td><td>141
34</td><td>93.2
20.6</td><td>Crabtree & Co
45 NHP
10 knots</td><td>Alfred Bannister
Grimsby</td></tr>
<tr><td colspan="6">22.01.1901 Sold to Onward Steam Fishing Co Ltd, Grimsby.1915 Rqd by the Royal Navy as a minesweeper No. FY 780
(1918) as a fishing trawler (Fishery Reserve) renamed (18.03.1918) ANGOLIAN. 1920 returned.
18.03.1934 to Andrew Wilson, Buckie renamed HAZELDENE (BCK47).
1953 Vessel sold for scrap to Thos W Ward Ltd. 30.04.1953 Arrived Barrow for breaking up.</td></tr>
</table>

NAME Official No. Port Letters Numbers	Yard No. Launched Registered	Registered G Ton N Ton	 L Ft B Ft	Engine Builder Horse Power Reg'd Speed	OWNER (Built for)
TROJAN 109819 GY848 Steam Trawler	215 06.08.1898 08.09.1898	140 33	93.2 20.6	Crabtree & Co 45 NHP 10 knots	Thomas Robinson Grimsby
1914 Rqd by the Royal Navy as a minesweeper No. FY 782 renamed TROJAN II . 1919 returned and reverted. 01.03.1920 Sold to Eddystone Steam Fishing Co Ltd, Grimsby. 23.08.1922 to Herbert W Chant, Grimsby. 01.06.1932 to James Chant, Plymouth. 29.06.1932 to Alfred H C Wilson, Plymouth. 1940 Rqd by the Royal Navy as a boom defence vessel No. Z.218. 1945 returned. 31.07.1950 to Percy V Semour, Plymouth. 17.05.1952 Vessel sunk in collision with the Liberian tanker KIKI NAESS (4519 gt/ b 1928) off the Eddystone Lighthouse. All ten crew rescued.					
KLONDYKE 109066 H420 Steam Trawler	216 20.08.1898 06.10.1898	155 55	105.0 20.6	Amos & Smith 50 NHP 9 knots	Hull Steam Fishing & Ice Co Ltd Hull
01.01.1914 *(Tonnage adjusted 61.7 net tons).* 1914 Rqd by the Royal Navy as a minesweeper No. FY 647. 04.06.1916 Vessel sunk following a collision near Owers Light-vessel.					
ROMAN EMPIRE 109082 H431 Steam Trawler	217 26.10.1898 18.11.1898	182 63	110.0 21.0	C.D.Holmes 60 NHP 10.5 knots	Cargill Steam Trawling Co Ltd Hull.
01.01.1914 *(Tonnage adjusted 72.7 net tons).* 25.05.1920 Sold to Jutland Amalgamated Trawlers Ltd, Hull . 27.12.1923 Vessel sprang a leak and sank 40 miles east north-east of Flamborough.					
STREPHON 109820 GY852 Steam Trawler	218 24.08.1898 04.10.1898	162 52	101.8 20.8	C.D.Holmes 45 NHP 9.5 knots	Standard Steam Fishing Co Ltd Grimsby
01.03.1912 Sold to Port of Blyth Steam Fishing Co Ltd, Blyth renamed LORD STANHOPE (BH95) . 10.12.1914 to The Beacon Steam Fishing Co Ltd, Grimsby (GY401). 14.11.1914 Vessel lost in collision with Inner Dowsing Light-vessel.					
FAWN 109842 GY1008 Steam Trawler	219 26.11.1898 22.12.1898	191 64	107.5 21	Amos & Smith 50 NHP 10 knots	Thomas E Fisher & Henry Morris Co Ltd Grimsby
11.09.1916 Sold to Henry Croft Baker, Grimsby. 26.04.1917 to John Green, Grimsby. 1918 Rqd by the Royal Navy as a fishing trawler (Fishery Reserve). 1919 returned. 24.08.1919 Vessel posted missing Lost with all hands presumed mined off Hartlepool.					
OSIRIS 109838 GY986 Steam Trawler	220 16.11.1898 08.12.1898	173 62	108.8 21.0	C.D.Holmes 50 NHP 10 knots	Roberts & Ruthven Ltd Grimsby
23.09.1919 Sold to Brent Steam Fishing Co Ltd, Grimsby. 09.11.1923 to Richard W Lewis, Aberdeen. 1932/33 Vessel sold to shipbreakers and broken up.					
GENERAL GORDON 110686 H3 Steam Trawler	221 17.01.1899 17.02.1899	211 72	116.8 21.2	C.D.Holmes 58 NHP 10.5 knots	Yorkshire Steam Fishing Co Ltd Hull
28.07.1900 Sold to L Bouclet , Boulogne, France renamed DORADE (B2690). Feb 1911 Vessel posted missing :- Lost with all hands.					
BOADICEA 110689 H17 Steam Trawler	222 09.02.1899 16.03.1899	193 61	113.6 21.0	Amos & Smith 53 NHP 10 knots	Hellyer Steam Fishing Co Ltd Hull
07.02.1905 Sold to Nicto y Pérez, Corunna, Spain renamed ONCE AMIGOS. 1906 to V Nicto, Corunna renamed BOADICEA. 1914 to Ramon Carranza, Corunna. 1919 Vessel deleted from Lloyd Register of Shipping:- (War loss).					
FULMAR 110694 H25 Steam Trawler	223 23.02.1899 30.03.1899	205 68	116.9 21.2	C.D.Holmes 58 NHP 10.5 knots	Pickering & Haldane's Steam Trawling Co Ltd Hull
10.09.1912 Sold to William J Barrett (GY769). 14.03.1913 to G E Forum, Denmark *(Nominal owner to allow vessel to fish in Moray Firth, as all British trawlers were banned from the area).* 31.03.1915 to William J Barrett, Grimsby (GY470). 1915 Rqd by the Royal Navy as a minesweeper No. FY 1756. 17.01.1916 Vessel sunk by mine in the Gulf of Sollum.					
BELOVAR 109847 GY1036 Steam Trawler	224 17.12.1898 18.01.1899	178 62	108.7 21.0	C.D.Holmes 50 NHP 10 knots	Alec L Black Grimsby
18.04.1905 Sold to Soc de Pesca Y Salvamenta "Neptune" , Vigo, Spain. 1924 to Drouilet, Arcachon, France renamed ECUREUIL. 1929 to J Tissot, Arcachon, France. 28.12.1930 Vessel wrecked after stranding near Rourtin.					

Yard No.213
1898 NEW ZEALAND
Photo:- Barnard and Straker Collection

Yard No.217
1898 ROMAN EMPIRE
Photo:- Barnard and Straker Collection

Yard No.225
1898 NEWLAND
Photo:- Barnard and Straker Collection

NAME Official No. Port Letters Numbers	Yard No. Launched Registered	Registered G Ton N Ton	 L Ft B Ft	Engine Builder Horse Power Reg'd Speed	OWNER (Built for)
NEWINGTON 110697 H33 Steam Trawler	225 02.03.1899 01.04.1899	193 61	115.3 21.0	C.D.Holmes 58 NHP 10.5 knots	City Steam Fishing Co Ltd Hull
31.05.1907 Sold to the Government of Canada, Vancouver. 1915 Rqd by the Royal Navy as an auxiliary patrol vessel served in Canadian waters. 1919 returned. 1920 to Pacific Coyle Navigation Co Ltd, Vancouver, *(converted to a tug).* 1956 to Straits Towing Ltd, Vancouver . 22-24.08.1959 Vessel foundered whilst laid up in Vancouver harbour. May 1961 declared a constructive total loss.					
PERTH 109070 H421 Steam Trawler	226 21.09.1898 19.10.1898	155 55	105.0 20.6	Amos & Smith 35 NHP 9 knots	Hull Steam Fishing & Ice Co Ltd Hull
10.11.1912 Vessel sunk following a collision with the Hull trawler MAURITIUS H547*(see Yard No. 310)* in the North Sea.					
AUCKLAND 109097 H441 Steam Trawler	227 15.12.1898 11.01.1899	155 55	105.0 20.6	Amos & Smith 35 NHP 9 knots	Hull Steam Fishing & Ice Co Ltd Hull
01.01.1914 *Tonnage adjusted 61.0 net tons).* 1914 Rqd by the Royal Navy as a minesweeper No. FY 648. 1919 returned. 28.03.1919 Sold to Arthur Gouldby, Lowestoft (LT445). 1936 to H B Garrood, Lowestoft. 1936 Vessel sold to shipbreakers and broken up.					
CLEOPATRA 110701 H46 Steam Trawler	228 13.03.1899 12.04.1899	193 61	113.6 21.0	Amos & Smith 53 NHP 10 knots	Hellyer Steam Fishing Co Ltd Hull
13.02.1901 Vessel wrecked whilst steaming between the Westmost Islands and Thorlvik Roads, Iceland. On passage towards Hull. Ten crew lost and one man was rescued off the beach by local farmers.					
RHODESIA 110681 H443 Steam Trawler	229 31.12.1898 25.01.1899	155 55	105.0 20.6	Amos & Smith 40 NHP 9 knots	Hull Steam Fishing & Ice Co Ltd Hull
01.01.1914 *(Tonnage adjusted 61.0 net tons).* 1915 Rqd by the Royal Navy as an auxiliary patrol vessel No. FY 1215. 19.04.1915 Vessel wrecked near Stornoway.					
VIKING 110709 H451 Steam Trawler	230 29.03.1899 01.05.1899	180 65	110.2 21.0	C.D.Holmes 58 NHP 10.5 knots	John Henry Robins & Co Ltd Hull
29.10.1906 Sold to T Luengo, Corunna, Spain. 1918 to L Lamigueiro, San Sebastian. 19.09.1926 Vessel wrecked after stranding 30 miles South of Casablanca, Moroccan coast.					
NORTHWARD HO 110713 H455 Steam Trawler	231 08.04.1899 05.05.1899	180 67	110.2 21.0	Tindall & Co 55 NHP 10.25 knots	S T White & Co Ltd Hull
03.05.1915 Vessel captured by U-boat and sunk by time bombs 145 miles east north-east of Hornsea, East Yorkshire.					
ISIS 110883 GY75 Steam Trawler	232 29.04.1899 29.05.1899	175 65	108.1 21.0	C.D.Holmes 50 NHP 9.5 knots	Roberts & Ruthven Ltd Grimsby
1917 Rqd by the Royal Navy as a fishing trawler (Fishery Reserve). 1919 returned. 28.05.1920 Sold to George Pearce, Grimsby. 28.05.1925 Registration closed on advice that the vessel was broken up.					
SOPHRON 110882 GY58 Steam Trawler	233 26.04.1899 19.05.1899	198 61	140.0 21.0	Amos & Smith 50 NHP 10 knots	Standard Steam Fishing Co Ltd Grimsby
29.09.1902 Vessel foundered off Sule Skerry, Orkney.					
ISERNIA 110887 GY164 Steam Trawler	234 10.05.1899 10.06.1899	198 60	114.0 21.0	Amos & Smith 50 NHP 10 knots	Great Grimsby & East Coast Steam Fishing Co Ltd Grimsby
03.04.1914 Sold to Strand Steam Fishing Co Ltd, Grimsby. 1915 Rqd by the Royal Navy as a minesweeper No. FY 1746. 1920 returned. 16.03.1928 to Gibson & Mumby, Hull (H443). 23.02.1934 to J S Ellis, Scarborough. 1938 to A A Davidson, Aberdeen. 1938 Vessel sold to shipbreakers and broken up.					
SATYRION 110890 GY197 Steam Trawler	235 24.05.1899 21.06.1899	198 62	114.0 21.0	Amos & Smith 50 NHP 10 knots	Standard Steam Fishing Co Ltd Grimsby
07.01.1905 Vessel posted missing:- Lost with all hands whilst fishing at Iceland.					

NAME Official No. Port Letters Numbers	Yard No. Launched Registered	Registered G Ton N Ton	 L Ft B Ft	Engine Builder Horse Power Reg'd Speed	OWNER (Built for)
STRATON 110891 GY208 Steam Trawler	236 12.06.1899 07.07.1899	198 67	114.0 21.0	Amos & Smith 50 NHP 10 knots	Standard Steam Fishing Co Ltd Grimsby
04.02.1911 Sank the Grimsby trawler SILVERDALE GY999 (169 gt/ b 1898) in a collision near Spurn lightship. 26.01.1914 Sold to John L Green & Henry Croft Baker, Grimsby.02.04.1914 Sold to Strand Steam Fishing Co Ltd, Grimsby. 05.05.1915 Vessel captured by U-boat and sunk by gunfire 40 miles off Hartlepool.					
HORUS 110909 GY691 Steam Trawler	237 08.08.1899 15.09.1899	173 61	108.8 21.0	C.D.Holmes 50 NHP 9.5 knots	Roberts & Ruthven Ltd Grimsby
27.04.1916 Vessel captured by German Navy surface vessels in the North Sea taken to Willhelmshavn renamed KRIEGSHILFE. 1919 returned. 1925 to Dalby Pogson & Symonds, Grimsby renamed DALBY (GY154). 1930 to Dalby Steam Fishing Co Ltd, Fleetwood. 1939 Sold to for scrap to Thos W Ward Ltd, Preston and broken up.					
JERIA 110903 GY496 Steam Trawler	238 26.07.1899 25.08.1899	197 61	114.0 21.0	Amos & Smith 50 NHP 10 knots	Great Grimsby & East Coast Steam Fishing Co Ltd Grimsby
21.11.1913 Sold to Edward Bacon, Grimsby. 15.12.1913 to Spartan Steam Fishing Co Ltd, Grimsby renamed STALKER. 06.09.1915 to Lindsey Steam Fishing Co Ltd, Grimsby. 1915 Rqd by the Royal Navy as a minesweeper No. FY 1838. 1919 returned. 15.01.1941 Damaged by enemy aircraft bombs Hawke Road, River Humber. 01.04.1944 by the Royal Navy as a fuel trawler renamed CHOICE. 25.08.1944 Vessel foundered off Normandy following a collision with the tug EMPIRE SAMSON (261 gt/ b 1943).					
VULTURE 110731 H470 Steam Trawler	239 28.06.1899 31.07.1899	190 57	115.5 21.0	C.D.Holmes 58 NHP 10 knots	St Andrews Steam Fishing Co Ltd Hull
Aug 1914 Rqd by the Royal Navy as a minesweeper No. FY 310 renamed VULTURE II. 16.03.1918 Vessel sunk following a collision with a wreck in Loch Eriboll.					
STRYMON 110915 GY912 Steam Trawler	240 09.09.1899 02.10.1899	198 62	114.0 21.0	Amos & Smith 55 NHP 10 knots	Standard Steam Fishing Co Ltd Grimsby
26.01.1914 Sold to John L Green & Henry Croft Baker, Grimsby. 02.04. 1914 to Strand Fishing Co Ltd, Grimsby. 1918 Rqd by the Royal Navy as a minesweeper No. FY 1842. 27.10.1917 Vessel sunk by mine off Shipwash Light-vessel mine laid by UC 11 on 26.10.1947.					
KHARTOUM 110734 H472 Steam Trawler	241 11.07.1899 17.08.1899	303 119	148.6 22.5	Amos & Smith 85 NHP 11 knots	Hull Steam Fishing & Ice Co Ltd Hull
Used as a company carrier transporting "boxing fleet" catches of fish to London's Billingsgate Fish Market. 26.03.1916 Vessel sunk by mine 6 miles north-east of Longships Light-vessel.					
Not Built	242				
PERSIAN EMPIRE 110743 H476 Steam Trawler	243 21.08.1899 27.10.1899	195 49	115.5 21.0	C.D.Holmes 63 NHP 10.5 knots	Cargill Steam Trawling Co Ltd Hull
01.01.1914 *(Tonnage adjusted 75.0 net tons).* Dec 1914 Rqd by the Royal Navy as a minesweeper No. FY 799. 1919 returned. 03.06.1921 Sold to Jutland Amalgamated Trawlers Ltd, Hull. 01.01.1926 to Cook & Ireland, Fleetwood (FD83). 1930 to J S Ellis & Co Ltd, Fleetwood. 1938 to R F Cammish, Fleetwood. 1943 to Don Fishing Co Ltd, Fleetwood. 1948 to Standard Steam Fishing Co Ltd, Grimsby (GY49). 26.01.1953 Vessel sold for scrap to J W Draper, (Shipbreakers) and broken up at Grimsby.					
GRECIAN EMPIRE 110750 H479 Steam Trawler	244 09.10.1899 29.11.1899	195 49	115.5 21.0	C.D.Holmes 63 NHP 11 knots	Cargill Steam Trawling Co Ltd Hull
01.01.1914 *(Tonnage adjusted 75.0 net tons).* Jan 1915 Rqd by the Royal Navy as a minesweeper No. FY 792. 1919 returned. 03.06.1921 Sold to Jutland Amalgamated Trawlers Ltd, Hull. 06.04.1925 Camloun Fishing Co Ltd, Aberdeen (A115) renamed (1934) GOLDEN SCEPTRE. 19.01.1937 Sailed from Aberdeen towards Shetland fishing grounds. Jan 1937 Vessel posted missing:- Lost with all nine crew.					

<table>
<tr><th rowspan="2">NAME
Official No.
Port Letters Numbers</th><th rowspan="2">Yard No.
Launched
Registered</th><th colspan="2">Registered</th><th rowspan="2">Engine Builder
Horse Power
Reg'd Speed</th><th rowspan="2">OWNER
(Built for)</th></tr>
<tr><th>G Ton
N Ton</th><th>L Ft
B Ft</th></tr>
<tr><td>HORNSEA
110761
H485 Steam Trawler</td><td>245
08.11.1899
26.01.1900</td><td>305
126</td><td>148.7
22.8</td><td>Amos & Smith
85 NHP
10 knots</td><td>Hull Steam Fishing
& Ice Co Ltd
Hull</td></tr>
<tr><td colspan="6">Used as a company carrier transporting “boxing fleet” catches of fish to London’s Billingsgate Fish Market.
1916 Rqd by the Royal Navy as an auxiliary patrol vessel.1920 returned.
10.02.1937 Sold for scrap to Dutch shipbreakers and broken up.</td></tr>
<tr><td>MAYFLY
110745
H477 Steam Trawler</td><td>246
07.10.1899
11.11.1899</td><td>191
64</td><td>113.8
21.0</td><td>C.D.Holmes
48 NHP
10 knots</td><td>British Coast Steam
Fishing Co Ltd
Hull</td></tr>
<tr><td colspan="6">22.11.1912 Sold to James Bruce Graham, Hartlepool (HL72). 31.07.1916 to J W & H Smethurst, Grimsby (GY899).
24.04.1917 Vessel captured by U-boat in the North Sea and sunk 70 miles north-east by north of Spurn Light-vessel.</td></tr>
<tr><td>TOBAGO
110756
H482 Steam Trawler</td><td>247
15.11.1899
16.12.1899</td><td>159
56</td><td>106.8
21.0</td><td>Amos & Smith
45 NHP
10 knots</td><td>Hull Steam Fishing
& Ice Co Ltd
Hull</td></tr>
<tr><td colspan="6">1917 Rqd by the Royal Navy as a fishing trawler (Fishery Reserve). 1919 returned.
22.12.1923 Sold to George D Utting, Lowestoft (LT1293) renamed (1930) TRESCO.
1945 to Respondo Trawlers Ltd, Lowestoft. 1947 to F Uglow & Son, Lowestoft.
Oct 1951 Vessel sold to shipbreakers and broken up at Milford Haven.</td></tr>
<tr><td>SINGAPORE
113559
H505 Steam Trawler</td><td>248
03.05.1900
29.05.1900</td><td>159
58</td><td>106.8
21.0</td><td>Amos & Smith
45 NHP
10 knots</td><td>Hull Steam Fishing
& Ice Co Ltd
Hull</td></tr>
<tr><td colspan="6">1917 Rqd by the Royal Navy as a fishing trawler (Fishery Reserve). 1919 returned.
12.01.1920 Vessel sank following a collision with the cruiser H M S ADVENTURE (b 1904) which was anchored off Immingham River Humber. Six crew lost, three rescued.</td></tr>
<tr><td>SHAMROCK
110788
H483 Steam Trawler</td><td>249
23.10.1899
30.12.1899</td><td>184
65</td><td>110.2
21.1</td><td>C.D.Holmes
50 NHP
10 knots</td><td>John Duncan & Sons Co Ltd
Liverpool</td></tr>
<tr><td colspan="6">01.01.1914 (Tonnage adjusted 73.0 net tons). 1918 Rqd by the Royal Navy as a fishing trawler (Fishery Reserve).
1920 returned. 13.10.1928 Sold to Consolidated Fisheries, Lowestoft (LT406).
1939 Rqd by the Royal Navy as a mine-sweeper (1940) boom defence vessel No. FY 768. 1944 returned.
1945 Deleted from the fishing register probably used as a target vessel.</td></tr>
<tr><td>OLIVER CROMWELL
110767
H490 Steam Trawler</td><td>250
20.11.1899
05.02.1900</td><td>222
74</td><td>125.1
21.5</td><td>C.D.Holmes
60 NHP
10.5 knots</td><td>Yorkshire Steam
Fishing Co Ltd
Hull</td></tr>
<tr><td colspan="6">07.08.1905 Vessel wrecked off Akranes, Faxe Bay, Iceland .</td></tr>
<tr><td>ROSALIND
110764
H487 Steam Trawler</td><td>251
08.12.1899
20.01.1900</td><td>198
59</td><td>117.0
21.0</td><td>Amos & Smith
55 NHP
10 knots</td><td>Hellyer Steam
Fishing Co Ltd
Hull</td></tr>
<tr><td colspan="6">10.08.1905 Sold to E Somoza y Cia, Corunna, Spain. 1912 to S A Pesquera Malagueña, Malaga .
1919 Vessel deleted from Lloyds Register of shipping (reported lost).</td></tr>
<tr><td>SEAGULL
110775
H494 Steam Trawler</td><td>252
14.12.1899
02.03.1900</td><td>225
77</td><td>125.1
25.5</td><td>C.D.Holmes
60 NHP
10 knots</td><td>Pickering & Haldane’s Steam
Trawling Co Ltd
Hull</td></tr>
<tr><td colspan="6">12.02.1907 Sold to Fiskveidihlllutafelgie, Reykjavik, Iceland renamed MARZ (RE114).
26.10.1916 Vessel wrecked at Gerdaholmi near, Gardour, Iceland.</td></tr>
<tr><td>LIVINGSTONE
110784
H496 Steam Trawler</td><td>253
19.01.1900
28.03.1900</td><td>213
71</td><td>120.0
21.5</td><td>C.D.Holmes
60 NHP
10 knots</td><td>National Steam
Trawling Co Ltd
Hull</td></tr>
<tr><td colspan="6">01.01.1914 (Tonnage adjusted 83.0 net tons). 02.11.1917 Sold to East Riding Steam Fishing Co Ltd, Hull.
1914 Rqd by the Royal Navy as a minesweeper No. FY 256.
12.12.1917 Vessel sunk in the North Sea by the German Cruiser EMDEN (B 1909) and three escort destroyers.</td></tr>
<tr><td>PURITAN
110786
H497 Steam Trawler</td><td>254
03.02.1900
02.04.1900</td><td>219
66</td><td>120.0
21.5</td><td>C.D.Holmes
60 NHP
10 knots</td><td>George Walton
Hull</td></tr>
<tr><td colspan="6">04.05.1903 Vessel wrecked after stranded in thick fog near the Ravenscar Hotel off Peak Point, Blea Wyke, Ravenscar. After six hours in the ship’s boat the crew were picked up by the Hull trawler HERO H886 (see Yard No.105) and landed at Scarborough.</td></tr>
</table>

Yard No.245
1900 HORNSEA
Photo:- Barnard and Straker Collection

Yard No.253
1900 LIVINGSTONE
Photo:- Barnard and Straker Collection

Yard No.257
1900 KASTORIA as SCOOPER
Photo by courtesy of George Scales

NAME Official No. Port Letters Numbers	Yard No. Launched Registered	Registered G Ton N Ton	 L Ft B Ft	Engine Builder Horse Power Reg'd Speed	OWNER (Built for)
STORK 110788 H498 Steam Trawler	255 17.02.1900 18.04.1900	219 69	120.0 21.5	C.D.Holmes 60 NHP 10 knots	St Andrews Steam Fishing Co Ltd Hull
28.11.1912 Vessel wrecked on a reef off the west coast of Iceland.					
SERAPION 113161 GY1154 Steam Trawler	256 20.02.1900 26.04.1900	195 64	120.0 21.5	Amos & Smith 55 NHP 10 knots	Standard Steam Fishing Co Ltd Grimsby
28.10.1913 Sold to John E Rushworth, Grimsby. 05.08.1915 Sold to Henry G Hopwood & Henry L Taylor, Grimsby. 1917 Rqd by the Royal Navy as a fishing trawler (Fishery Reserve). 1919 returned. 16.10.1922 to Diamonds Steam Fishing Co Ltd, Grimsby. 26.11.1939 Rqd by the Royal Navy as a mine-sweeper. 27.01.1940 returned. 05.11.1946 Vessel sunk in the North Sea following a collision with the trawler ATHENIAN GY357 *(see Yard No. 365)* 4 miles off the Humber Light-Vessel in thick fog. All the crew were taken aboard the ATHENIAN.					
KASTORIA 113162 GY1155 Steam Trawler	257 06.03.1900 11.04.1900	195 64	113.6 21.5	Amos & Smith 55 NHP 10 knots	Great Grimsby & East Coast Steam Fishing Co Ltd Grimsby
21.11.1913 Sold to Edwin Bacon, Grimsby. 15.12.1913 to Spartan Steam Fishing Co Ltd, Grimsby renamed SCOOPER. 1915 Rqd by the Royal Navy as a boom defence vessel No. FY 1745. 1919 returned. 24.10.1918 to E Bacon, Grimsby. 06.09.1915 to Lindsey Steam Fishing Co Ltd, Grimsby. 1961 Sold for scrap to AC Slooten Wormer, Holland. 11.05.1961 Arrived Den Helder for breaking up.					
LACONIA 113179 GY1173 Steam Trawler	258 30.04.1900 02.06.1900	195 64	113.6 21.5	Amos & Smith 55 NHP 10 knots	Great Grimsby & East Coast Steam Fishing Co Ltd Grimsby
17.05.1911 Vessel lost following a collision in the North Sea with ss LOCH LOMOND (2619 gt/ b 1888) approx 3 miles east north-east of Flamborough Head Yorkshire.					
CHRYSOLITE 110791 H499 Steam Trawler	259 20.03.1900 07.05.1900	222 72	121.8 21.5	C.D.Holmes 63 NHP 10.5 knots	Kingston Steam Trawling Co Ltd Hull
19.05.1915 Vessel captured by U-boat and sunk by time bombs 25 miles off Lerwick.					
SETHON 113174 GY1167 Steam Trawler	260 29.03.1900 10.05.1900	195 64	113.6 21.0	Amos & Smith 55 NHP 10 knots	Standard Steam Fishing Co Ltd Grimsby
23.11.1913 Sold to Edwin Bacon, Grimsby. 15.12.1913 to Spartan Steam Trawling Co Ltd, Grimsby renamed (1914) SLASHER. 06.09.1915 to Lindsey Steam Fishing Co Ltd, Grimsby. 1915 Rqd by the Royal Navy as a minesweeper No. FY 1744. 1919 returned. 01.06.1940 Vessel sunk in the North Sea by German aircraft off the River Humber.					
CORNELIAN 113558 H506 Steam Trawler	261 15.04.1900 09.06.1900	222 76	121.8 21.5	C.D.Holmes 60 NHP 11 knots	Kingston Steam Trawling Co Ltd Hull
14.01.1916 Vessel posted missing :- Lost with all hands.					
SILANION 113184 GY1179 Steam Trawler	262 16.05.1900 02.07.1900	195 63	113.6 21.0	Amos & Smith 55 NHP 10 knots	Standard Steam Fishing Co Ltd Grimsby
05.12.1902 Vessel stranded at Duncansby Head but later salved. 01.03.1904 Registry re-opened. 01.03.1904 Sold to Grimsby Victor Steam Fishing Co Ltd, Grimsby renamed ST. BERNARD (GY1280). 04.11.1916 to H Croft Baker, Grimsby. 01.05.1917 to J L Green, Grimsby. 02.06.1917 Vessel captured by U-boat and sunk 65 miles north by west of Noup Head, Orkney Island.					
MORAVIA 113185 GY1180 Steam Trawler	263 24.05.1900 17.07.1900	195 63	113.6 21.0	Amos & Smith 55 NHP 10 knots	Great Grimsby & East Coast Steam Fishing Co Ltd Grimsby
15.12.1913 Sold to Spartan Steam Fishing Co Ltd, Grimsby renamed SCOUTER (GY1180). 06.09.1915 to Lindsey Steam Fishing Co Ltd, Grimsby. Jul 1915 Rqd by the Royal Navy as a minesweeper No. FY 1600. 1919 returned. 1956 Vessel sold for scrap to B J Nijkerk SA, Antwerp. 04.03.1956 Registration closed on advice that the vessel was broken up.					

NAME Official No. Port Letters Numbers	Yard No. Launched Registered	Registered G Ton N Ton	 L Ft B Ft	Engine Builder Horse Power Reg'd Speed	OWNER (Built for)
ST. BERNARD 110794 H501 Steam Trawler	264 19.04.1900 19.05.1900	186 78	113.6 21.0	Bailey & Leetham 60 NHP 10.5 knots	Humber Steam Trawling Co Ltd Hull
11.10.1901 Vessel sank off the Færoe Islands. A shore party from the British fishery protection cruiser BELLORAN found wreckage from the ST. BERNARD but no survivors from the crew of nine.					
VICTORIAN 113194 GY1189 Steam Trawler	265 25.06.1900 24.08.1900	195 62	113.6 21.0	Amos & Smith 55 NHP 10 knots	William Butt & Willie Hill Grimsby
10.07.1912 Sold to Loyal Steam Fishing Co Ltd, Grimsby. 3.10.1913 to William Ellis, Grimsby. 1915 Rqd by the Royal Navy as a minesweeper No. FY 1841 renamed VICTORIAN II . 1920 returned and reverted. 03.09.1918 to James Coombes, Grimsby. 04.06.1925 to South Western Steam Fishing Co Ltd, Grimsby. 02.11.1925 to Earl Steam Fishing Co Ltd, Grimsby. 29.03.1928 to T C & F Moss Ltd, Grimsby renamed CROXTON. 11.01.1940 Vessel sunk in the North Sea by German aircraft.					
GENERAL GORDON 113575 H515 Steam Trawler	266 31.07.1900 29.09.1900	201 71	113.4 21.0	C.D.Holmes 60 NHP 10.5 knots	Pickering & Haldane's Steam Trawling Co Ltd Hull
02.08.1905 Sold to Del Rio e Cia, Ferrol, Spain. 1921 to Lamigueiro y Jove, San Sabastian. Apr 1922 Vessel wrecked on the Basque coast:- Lost with all hands.					
RUGBY 113193 GY1188 Steam Trawler	267 14.06.1900 18.07.1900	205 67	113.8 21.5	C.D.Holmes 60 NHP 10.5 knots	William Grant Grimsby
04.05.1915 Vessel captured by U-boat in the North Sea and sunk by time bombs 100 miles north-east of Spurn Point.					
TOR BAY 113568 H511 Steam Trawler	268 18.06.1900 25.07.1900	198 60	117.0 21.0	C.D.Holmes 60 NHP 10.5 knots	Hellyer Steam Fishing Co Ltd Hull
02.03.1905 Sold to Valle & Co, Corunna, Spain renamed GLADIATOR. 10.09.1907 Vessel wrecked after stranding at Corme.					
ROYALLIEU 113197 GY1191 Steam Trawler	269 11.07.1900 15.08.1900	203 67	113.8 21.5	C.D.Holmes 60 NHP 10.5 knots	William Grant Grimsby
16.05.1905 Sold to Pelham Steam Fishing Co Ltd, Grimsby. 06.05.1906 Vessel wrecked after stranding on Bempton Cliffs, Yorkshire.					
TUGELA 113591 H521 Steam Trawler	270 05.11.1900 17.12.1900	233 85	125.0 21.5	C.D.Holmes 70 NHP 11 knots	Neptune Steam Fishing Co Ltd Hull
10.09.1912 Sold to Thomas Hudson, Hull. 14.03.1913 to East Riding Steam Fishing Co Ltd, Hull. 1915 Rqd by the Royal Navy as a mine-sweeper / auxiliary patrol vessel No. FY 1817. 26.06.1916 Vessel sunk by mine in the North Sea off Lowestoft.					
Not Built	271				
QUEEN 113203 GY1197 Steam Trawler	272 01.08.1900 14.09.1900	161 46	100.0 21.0	C.D.Holmes 50 NHP 9.5 knots	Queen Steam Fishing Co Ltd Grimsby
1914 Rqd by the Royal Navy as a minesweeper No. FY 691 renamed (1915) QUEEN II renamed (1917) QUEST. 1919 returned and reverted. 1951 Vessel sold to BISCO and allocated to J J King & Co Ltd, Gateshead 23.11.1951 Registration closed on advice that the vessel was and broken up.					
POINTER 113571 H513 Steam Trawler	273 02.07.1900 21.08.1900	228 83	125.0 21.5	Bailey & Leetham 60 NHP 11 knots	Humber Steam Trawling Co Ltd Hull
11.06.1907 Sold to Akties P.J Thorsteinsson & Co, Copenhagen, Denmark renamed SNORRI STURLUSON (RE134). 09.10.1910 Registration transferred to Reykavik, Iceland. 09.03.1914 Registration transferred to Copenhagen, Denmark. 20.04.1915 to Thor Jensen, Reykavik, Iceland. 08.12.1919 to T H Plater, Grimsby renamed BRIGAND (GY787). Jan 1924 to J Potts, Grimsby. Oct 1924 Vessel sold to shipbreakers and broken up.					
CYRANO 113209 GY1203 Steam Trawler	274 27.08.1900 20.10.1900	179 62	108.7 21.0	C.D.Holmes 55 NHP 10 knots	Alec Black & Walter Olney Grimsby
04.03.1905 Vessel lost following a collision in the North Sea with the Grimsby trawler DEVONSHIRE GY766 (148 gt/ b 1898) 130 miles north-east by north of Spurn Point.					

Yard No.261
1900 CORNELIAN
Photo:- Barnard and Straker Collection

Yard No.270
1900 TUGELA
Photo:- Barnard and Straker Collection

Yard No.282
1900 ENCORE
Photo:- Barnard and Straker Collection

NAME Official No. Port Letters Numbers	Yard No. Launched Registered	Registered G Ton N Ton	 L Ft B Ft	Engine Builder Horse Power Reg'd Speed	OWNER (Built for)
PHAROS 113217 GY1211 Steam Trawler	275 10.12.1900 18.01.1901	197 62	113.7 21.0	C.D.Holmes 50 NHP 10 knots	Roberts & Ruthven Ltd Grimsby
25.09.1906 Vessel posted missing:- Lost with all hands. Left Grimsby on 23.09.1906 bound for the Færoe Islands fishing grounds and was not heard of again.					
ROMANOFF 113210 GY1204 Steam Trawler	276 10.09.1900 09.11.1900	178 63	108.7 21.0	C.D.Holmes 55 NHP 10 knots	Alec Black Grimsby
20.05.1905 Sold to Pelham Steam Fishing Co Ltd, Grimsby. 29.01.1909 to Christian M Evensen, Thorshaven, Færoe Islands renamed CECELIE. 21.06.1911 to Earl Steam Fishing Co Ltd, Grimsby renamed ROMANOFF (GY639). 28.05.1914 to Savoy Steam Fishing Co Ltd, Grimsby. 02.08.1917 to William Baynton & Walter Jagger, Grimsby. 1917 Rqd by the Royal Navy as a fishing trawler (Fishery Reserve). 1919 returned. 23.03.1920 to Headway Steam Fishing Co Ltd, Grimsby. 06.06.1922 to F Whitehead, Scarborough (SH373). 1930 to J Pattison & Others, Hartlepool. 1934 to Wiggleswork & Good, Aberdeen (A275). 1937 Vessel sold to shipbreakers and broken up.					
LADYBIRD 113595 H524 Steam Trawler	277 27.11.1900 07.01.1901	219 73	120.0 21.5	C.D.Holmes 63 NHP 10.5 knots	British Steam Trawling Co Ltd Hull
30.09.1906 Vessel wrecked off Colliston near Aberdeen.					
MERCURY 113584 H518 Steam Trawler	278 13.09.1900 29.11.1900	222 74	121.8 21.5	C.D.Holmes 60 NHP 10.5 knots	William Widdowson William H Welstead G H Clark J S Smithers Hull
15.07.1909 Sold to Kingston Steam Trawlers Ltd, Hull. 02.05.1915 Vessel captured by U-boat in the North Sea and sunk by gunfire 14 miles from Aberdeen.					
MINERVA 113590 H520 Steam Trawler	279 27.09.1900 10.12.1900	222 74	121.8 21.5	C.D.Holmes 60 NHP 10.5 knots	William Widdowson Hull
21.07.1909 Sold to Kingston Steam Trawlers Ltd, Hull. 10.05.1914 Vessel sank following a collision in the North Sea 160 miles east north-east of May Island.					
EMU 113579 H516 Steam Trawler	280 08.10.1900 31.10.1900	164 57	105.0 21.0	Amos & Smith 40 NHP 10 knots	Great Northern Steam Ship Fishing Co Ltd Hull
1915 Rqd by the Royal Navy as a auxiliary patrol vessel / boom defence vessel. 1919 returned. 24.06.1918 Sold to H Croft Baker, Grimsby (GY1227). Feb 1919 to Tena Blau & H Wood, Grimsby renamed OUR TENA. May 1919 to Henry Wood, Grimsby. 1924 to Charles Dobson, Grimsby. 1935 to A Summers, Peterhead. 1937 Vessel sold to shipbreakers and broken up.					
ENDYMION 113588 H519 Steam Trawler	281 10.11.1900 30.11.1900	164 57	105.0 21.0	Amos & Smith 40 NHP 10 knots	Great Northern Steam Ship Fishing Co Ltd Hull
1917 Rqd by the Royal Navy as a fishing trawler (Fishery Reserve). 1919 returned. 24.08.1918 Sold to Alliance Steam Fishing Co Ltd, Hull. 24.10.1918 to Richard Scotter & Richard Cammish, Hull. 07.07.1920 to Endymion Steam Trawling Co Ltd, Scarborough. 28.02.1925 to Bay Steam Trawlers Ltd, Fleetwood (FD62). 1929 to A M Goldsmith, Fleetwood. 1934 Vessel sold to shipbreakers and broken up.					
ENCORE 113594 H523 Steam Trawler	282 03.12.1900 22.12.1900	164 59	105.0 21.0	Amos & Smith 40 NHP 10 knots	Great Northern Steam Ship Fishing Co Hull
1918 Rqd by the Royal Navy as a fishing trawler (Fishery Reserve). 1919 returned. 17.05.1919 Sold to Stanley Bell, Lowestoft (LT929). 1926 to G D Utting, Lowestoft. 1929 to Utting & Gamble, Lowestoft.1932 to J H Gamble, Lowestoft. 1936 Vessel sold to shipbreakers and broken up.					
MERCIA 113218 GY1212 Steam Trawler	283 24.12.1900 28.01.1901	175 51	105.0 21.0	C.D.Holmes 55 NHP 9.5 knots	East Anglian Steam Fishing Co Ltd Grimsby
20.03.1915 Vessel posted missing:- Lost with all hands. Left Grimsby for the North Sea Fishing Grounds and was not heard of again.					
BERNICIA 113220 GY1215 Steam Trawler	284 24.01.1901 11.02.1901	175 51	105.0 21.0	C.D.Holmes 55 NHP 9.5 knots	East Anglian Steam Fishing Co Ltd Grimsby
01.02.1915 Vessel posted missing:-Lost with all hands. Left Grimsby for the North Sea Fishing Grounds not heard of again.					

NAME Official No. Port Letters Numbers	Yard No. Launched Registered	Registered G Ton N Ton	 L Ft B Ft	Engine Builder Horse Power Reg'd Speed	OWNER (Built for)
SCOTSMAN 113605 Steam Tug	285 09.03.1901 18.05.1901	172 8	110.0 20.0	Crabtree & Co 75 NHP 12 knots	Thomas Gray & Co Ltd Hull
31.12.1901 Sold to H M Government and served with the Royal Navy (No. C3781). 19.04.1921 Vessel placed on disposal list and sold at Simonstown, South Africa.					
DAUNTLESS 113607 Steam Tug	286 03.04.1901 22.05.1901	132 9	90.0 18.1	Bailey & Leetham 55 NHP 10 knots	North Eastern Railway Co Hull
Ordered by Mrs F M Singer USA as a schooner but completed as a tug for North Eastern Railway Company, Hull. 30.12.1922 Under the Railway Act of 1921 the ownership passed to the London and North Eastern Railway Company. 1932 to James Dredging Towage & Transport Ltd, Hull. 23.04.1937 Sold to Dutch shipbreakers and broken up.					
SHIELDS 113612 H528 Steam Drifter	287 06.05.1901 15.06.1901	72 34	76.0 18.1	Crabtree & Co 20 NHP 9.5 knots	British Coast Steam Fishing Co Ltd Hull
From new vessel based at Great Yarmouth. 1915 Rqd by the Royal Navy as a netlayer No. FY 1880, based at Great Yarmouth. 1919 returned. 15.08.1919 Sold to Jesse Spring, Hull 23.03.1923 to William Massey & Sons Ltd, Hull. 22.04.1924 Vessel sold to shipbreakers and broken up.					
GRIMSBY 113613 H529 Steam Drifter	288 06.05.1901 23.07.1901	72 34	76.0 18.1	Crabtree & Co 20 NHP 9.5 knots	British Coast Steam Fishing Co Ltd Hull
From new vessel based at Great Yarmouth. 16.12.1916 Sold to John Halifax, Yarmouth (YH444). 1917 to C Durrant, Lowestoft (LT913). 1920 to G W Keable, Lowestoft. 1924 Vessel sold to shipbreakers and broken up.					
CITY OF LONDON 114294 FD201 Steam Trawler	289 17.06.1901 1901	195 76	115.0 21.0	C.D.Holmes 55 NHP 10 knots	T F Kelsall Fleetwood
1915 Rqd by the Royal Navy as a boom defence vessel. 1919 returned. 1920 Sold to J Robson, Stranraer (SR1). 1923 to A Lewis, Aberdeen (A113). 1926 to Regent Fishing Co Ltd, Aberdeen renamed DANURIE. 1937 Vessel sold to shipbreakers and broken up.					
NEPTUNE O126 Steam Trawler	290 06.07.1901 03.08.1901	199 72	112.0 21.5	C.D.Holmes 66 NHP 10.5 knots	H Aspeslagh & C F Zonnekeijn Ostend
26.12.1916 Vessel captured and sunk by U-boat in the Irish Sea near the Smalls.					
CONQUEROR 113225 Steam Tug	291 31.07.1901 31.08.1901	41 7	60.0 14.1	Tindall Earle & Hutchinson 28 NHP 9 knots	George P Letten Grimsby
11.05.1905 Sold to Great Central Railway Shipping Company, London renamed No. 3. 12.05.1923 Under the Railway Act of 1921 the ownership passed to the London and North Eastern Railway Company. 21.06.1932 Registration closed on advice that the vessel was broken up.					
QUEEN ALEXANDRA 113614 H530 Steam Trawler	292 20.07.1901 24.08.1901	231 93	121.7 21.5	C.D.Holmes 63 NHP 10.5 knots	Armitage's Steam Trawling Co Hull
07.01.1920 Sold to Thomas H Smith, Fleetwood (FD364). 1923 to Sun Steam Trawling Co Ltd, Fleetwood. 1927 to Mason Trawlers Ltd, Fleetwood. 1952 Vessel sold for scrap to Thos W Ward Ltd. 11.09.1952 Arrived Barrow for breaking up.					
KING EDWARD VII 113618 H531 Steam Trawler	293 15.08.1901 06.09.1901	204 59.6	116.66 21.0	C.D.Holmes 63 NHP 10.5 knots	Cargill Steam Trawling Co Ltd Hull
12.01.1907 Vessel wrecked on Cape Utskalar west coast of Iceland.					
OTHELLO 113619 H532 Steam Trawler	294 29.10.1901 03.10.1901	240 88	125.0 21.5	Amos & Smith 74 NHP 10.5 knots	Hellyer Steam Fishing Co Ltd Hull
23.10.1906 Sold to Canasa Trillo & Cia, Spain renamed AVISPA. 1916 Sold to the Russian Navy No. T28. 1920 passed to USSR Archangel fleet renamed (1923) KAMBALA No. 2. 1941 Vessel sunk by German aircraft bombs off Olenii Island Murmansk coast.					
SOUTH COATES 113626 H536 Steam Trawler	295 20.10.1901 29.11.1901	232 92	125.0 21.5	C.D.Holmes 63 NHP 10.5 knots	City Steam Fishing Co Ltd Hull
14.02.1906 Vessel wrecked on Ingollshöfdi south coast of Iceland.					

Yard No.301
1901 LORD ROSEBERY
Photo:- Barnard and Straker Collection

Yard No.316
1902 WALTER S. BAILEY
Photo:- Barnard and Straker Collection

Yard No.325
1902 MACKENZIE
Photo:- Barnard and Straker Collection

<table>
<tr><th rowspan="2">NAME
Official No.
Port Letters Numbers</th><th rowspan="2">Yard No.
Launched
Registered</th><th colspan="2">Registered</th><th rowspan="2">Engine Builder
Horse Power
Reg'd Speed</th><th rowspan="2">OWNER
(Built for)</th></tr>
<tr><th>G Ton
N Ton</th><th>L Ft
B Ft</th></tr>
<tr><td>DESDEMONA
113624
H535 Steam Trawler</td><td>296
03.10.1901
08.11.1901</td><td>242
88</td><td>125.0
21.5</td><td>Amos & Smith
74 NHP
10.5 knots</td><td>Hellyer Steam
Fishing Co Ltd
Hull</td></tr>
<tr><td colspan="6">14.03.1906 Vessel wrecked near Stokkseyri south-west coast of Iceland.</td></tr>
<tr><td>PLATO
113625
Steam Tug</td><td>297
24.10.1901
26.11.1901</td><td>135
49</td><td>90.0
22.1</td><td>Amos & Smith
65 NHP
10.5 knots</td><td>Thomas Wilson & Co
Hull</td></tr>
<tr><td colspan="6">01.02.1917 Sold to Ellerman's Wilson Line, Hull. 10.03.1939 to James A White, Leith renamed PLETO.
28.12.1939 Rqd by the Royal Navy as a harbour tug. 27.07.1946 returned.
1962 Vessel broken up by James A White at Inverkeithing.</td></tr>
<tr><td>BRITON
113628
H538 Steam Trawler</td><td>298
30.11.1901
06.01.1902</td><td>242
88</td><td>125.0
21.5</td><td>Amos & Smith
74 NHP
10.5 knots</td><td>Imperial Steam Fishing Co
Hull</td></tr>
<tr><td colspan="6">04.03.1902 Vessel wrecked at Stapi south-east coast of Iceland.</td></tr>
<tr><td>SEA HORSE
113621
H533 Steam Trawler</td><td>299
17.09.1901
19.10.1901</td><td>229
91</td><td>120.0
21.75</td><td>Amos & Smith
70 NHP
10 knots</td><td>Pickering & Haldane's Steam
Trawling Co Ltd
Hull</td></tr>
<tr><td colspan="6">30.11.1916 Sold to George F Sleight, Grimsby (GY1011).
06.10.1925 to Enrique Gonzalez Rodrigues, Malaga, Spain renamed SANTA TEOLINDA.
29.06.1933 Vessel sank following a collision with the Spanish cargo vessel RITA SISTER (2845 gt/ b 1900).
All crew rescued.</td></tr>
<tr><td>SAXON
113634
H541 Steam Trawler</td><td>300
14.01.1902
18.02.1902</td><td>242
88</td><td>125.0
21.5</td><td>Amos & Smith
74 NHP
10.5 knots</td><td>Imperial Steam
Fishing Co Ltd
Hull</td></tr>
<tr><td colspan="6">14.08.1906 Sold to D Tejero, Perez, Corunna, Spain renamed MARY.
1919 Vessel deleted from Lloyds Register of Shipping.</td></tr>
<tr><td>LORD ROSEBERY
113627
H537 Steam Trawler</td><td>301
22.11.1901
11.12.1901</td><td>229
91</td><td>120.0
21.75</td><td>Amos & Smith
70 NHP
10 knots</td><td>Yorkshire Steam
Fishing Co Ltd
Hull</td></tr>
<tr><td colspan="6">15.02.1908 Vessel lost following a collision with the Hull trawler GAUL H761 (see Yard No. 64) off Cape Utskalar, Iceland. All crew picked up by the GAUL.</td></tr>
<tr><td>LA CHAMPAGNE

B2758 Steam Trawler</td><td>302
16.12.1901
1902</td><td>231
83</td><td>125.0
22.0</td><td>Tindall Earle &
Hutchinson
70 NHP10 knots</td><td>Altazin-Fourny et Cie
Boulogne
France</td></tr>
<tr><td colspan="6">1917 Rqd by Marine Nationale Francaise (French Navy) . 1919 returned.
1926 Sold to Gournay - Delpierre & Co, Boulogne renamed NOTRE DAME DES MIRACLES.
1936 Vessel sold to shipbreakers and broken up.</td></tr>
<tr><td>SEA KING
113630
H540 Steam Trawler</td><td>303
23.12.1901
24.01.1902</td><td>228
91</td><td>120.0
21.5</td><td>C.D.Holmes
63 NHP
10 knots</td><td>John Henry Robins & Co Ltd
Hull</td></tr>
<tr><td colspan="6">02.04.1914 Sold to J V Barraquer, Barcelona, Spain renamed MISERICORDIA.
1917 to Marine Nationale Francaise (French Navy) renamed SÈVERÉ.
1919 to Deschaud & Co, Marseilles, France (converted to a cargo vessel).
1922 to Seb Malandrino, Syracuse, Italy renamed OLIVERI SEBASTIANO.
05.05.1925 Vessel wrecked 20 miles from Benghazi whilst on passage to Derna with a cargo of wood and benzene</td></tr>
<tr><td>SEA LION
113635
H542 Steam Trawler</td><td>305
10.02.1902
03.03.1902</td><td>231
93</td><td>121.0
21.75</td><td>Amos & Smith
70 NHP
10 knots</td><td>Pickering & Haldane's Steam
Trawling Co Ltd
Hull</td></tr>
<tr><td colspan="6">1914 Rqd by the Royal Navy as a minesweeper No. FY 259. 1919 returned.
04.11.1918 Sold to Walter W Crampin Steam Fishing Co Ltd, Grimsby (GY1221).
1927 to Trawlers White Sea & Grimsby Ltd, Grimsby. 1934 Vessel sold to shipbreakers and broken up.</td></tr>
<tr><td>MARIE

B2763 Steam Trawler</td><td>306
11.02.1902
1902</td><td>231
83</td><td>125.0
22.0</td><td>C.D.Holmes
70 NHP
10.5 knots</td><td>Francois Fourny et Cie
Boulogne
France</td></tr>
<tr><td colspan="6">1914 Rqd by Marine Nationale Francaise (French Navy) 20.02.1915 Vessel sunk by mine off Dunkirk.</td></tr>
<tr><td>CANDACE
116133
Steam Yacht</td><td>313
19.11.1902
13.03.1903</td><td>432
90</td><td>175.0
23.0</td><td>Bailey & Leetham
99 NHP
13 knots</td><td>Walter S Bailey
Hull</td></tr>
<tr><td colspan="6">27.04.1907 Vessel sold to USA owners.</td></tr>
</table>

NAME Official No. Port Letters Numbers	Yard No. Launched Registered	Registered G Ton N Ton	 L Ft B Ft	Engine Builder Horse Power Reg'd Speed	OWNER (Built for)
CAVALIER 113638 H544 Steam Trawler	314 13.02.1902 16.04.1902	244 98	125.0 22.0	C.D.Holmes 63 NHP 10 knots	George Walton Hull
13.11.1906 Sold to Marine Steam Fishing Co Ltd, Hull. 1911 to R De Carranza, Cadiz, Spain renamed SAN RAFAEL. 1916 to Marine Nationale Francaise (French Navy) renamed FIER. 1920 Vessel deleted from Lloyds register.					
LA FLANDRE B2777 Steam Trawler	315 09.04.1902 1902	231 81	125.0 22.0	Tindall Earle & Hutchinson 65 NHP 10 knots	Altazin-Fourny et Cie Boulogne France
1913 Sold to A Coppin, Boulogne, France. 1915 Rqd by Marine Nationale Francaise (French Navy) . 01.02.1919 returned. 1926 to Huret-Delforge, Boulogne. 1955 Vessel sold for scrap to Van Heyghen Freres, Belgium. 23.01.1956 Breaking up commenced at Ghent.					
WALTER S BAILEY 113643 H546 Steam Trawler	316 12.04.1902 23.05.1902	244 98	125.0 22.0	C.D.Holmes 63 NHP 10.5 knots	Humber Steam Trawling Co Ltd Hull
1914 Rqd by the Royal Navy as a Q (decoy ship) No. FY 265. 1919 returned. 11.12.1919 Sold to Fresh Fish Supplies Ltd, Hull. 16.07.1924 to Dinas Steam Trawling Co Ltd, Fleetwood (FD19). 1932 to Viking Steam Trawling Co Ltd, Hull (H335).1935 Line Fishing Co Ltd, Grimsby renamed TROCADERO (GY129). 06.09.1936 Vessel wrecked after stranding on the south coast of Iceland.					
JOHN SHERBURN 116086 H644 Steam Trawler	317 21.07.1902 19.09.1902	244 97	125.0 22.0	C.D.Holmes 63 NHP 10 knots	Humber Steam Trawling Co Ltd Hull
1914 Rqd by the Royal Navy as an auxiliary patrol vessel No. FY 815. 06.03.1915 Vessel wrecked near Dover.					
CECIL RHODES 116075 H554 Steam Trawler	318 04.02.1902 10.07.1902	244 94	125.0 21.5	C.D.Holmes 63 NHP 10 knots	John Hollingsworth Hull
02.04.1905 Vessel wrecked near Önundarfjordr north-west coast of Iceland.					
PERSIAN 113226 GY1226 Steam Trawler	319 24.06.1902 30.07.1902	171 41	101.0 21.16	C.D.Holmes 55 NHP 9.5 knots	Thomas Robinson Grimsby
14.12.1911 Vessel posted missing:- Lost with all hands left Grimsby for North Sea fishing grounds and not heard of again.					
WESSEX 113231 GY1231 Steam Trawler	320 23.07.1902 22.09.1902	171 41	101.0 21.16	C.D.Holmes 55 NHP 9.5 knots	East Anglian Steam Fishing Co Ltd Grimsby
05.11.1914 Vessel posted missing:- Lost with all hands left Grimsby for North Sea fishing grounds and not heard of again.					
MACKENZIE 116093 H691 Steam Trawler	325 16.09.1902 16.10.1902	256 93	128.3 22.0	C.D.Holmes 75 NHP 11 knots	Neptune Steam Fishing Co Ltd Hull
12.12.1910 Vessel wrecked near Portland south coast of Iceland.					
WINDWARD HO 116097 H692 Steam Trawler	326 18.08.1902 23.10.1902	226 78	121.8 21.5	C.D.Holmes 63 NHP 10 knots	S T White & Co Ltd Hull
09.05.1917 Vessel sunk by mine 3 miles south of Peterhead.					
SCOTSMAN 116114 Steam Tug	327 13.11.1902 02.01.1903	141 11.5	98.0 19.0	Amos & Smith 60 NHP 9.5 knots	Thomas Gray & Co Ltd Hull
18.08.1908 Sold to Scotsman Co Ltd, Halifax, Nova Scotia, Canada. 1921 to The All Seas Marine Salvage Co Halifax Nova Scotia. 1923 to Thompson Towage Ltd, Hull. 23.10.1926 to United Towing Co Ltd, Hull. 11.02.1927 Vessel sold for scrap to Henry Scarr Hessle and broken up.					
SWAN 116103 H700 Steam Trawler	335 20.09.1902 15.11.1902	239 84	125.0 21.75	Amos & Smith 70 NHP 10.5 knots	Pickering & Haldane's Steam Trawling Co Ltd Hull
1915 Rqd by the Royal Navy as a minesweeper No. FY 811 renamed SWAN II. 1919 returned. 04.10.1918 Sold to W Crampin, Grimsby (GY1223). 1919 to W Crampin Steam Fishing Co Ltd, Grimsby. 1920 to Bunch Steam Fishing Co Ltd, Grimsby. 1930 to The Hewett Fishing Co Ltd, London (LO47). 1940 Rqd by the Royal Navy as a minesweeper No. FY 1880 (1941) boiler cleaning vessel. 1945 returned. 1949 Vessel sold to shipbreakers and broken up.					

NAME Official No. Port Letters Numbers	Yard No. Launched Registered	Registered G Ton N Ton	 L Ft B Ft	Engine Builder Horse Power Reg'd Speed	OWNER (Built for)
LORD SALISBURY 116105 H702 Steam Trawler	336 15.10.1902 28.11.1902	239 84	125.0 21.75	Amos & Smith 70 NHP 10.5 knots	Yorkshire Steam Fishing Co Ltd Hull
04.05.1911 Sold to Machado & Cie, Lisbon, Portugal renamed MACHADO IX. 1912 to F M Quadros, Rio de Janerio, Brazil renamed QUADROS then renamed GARIBALDI. 18.09.1917 to Chem de Fer de L'Etat Francais, Havre (H1614). 16.02.1924 to Alexandre et André Merrienne, Fecamp, renamed FORTIS (F564). 1927 to Merrienne Freres, Fecamp. 19.12.1937 Vessel made final landing. 1940 Stripped down to a hulk. 1942 Rebuilt by German forces as an armed trawler (FH41). 1943 (FC43). 1944 Transferred to Havre. 11.09.1944 Vessel sunk during an air raid by allied forces.					
TYNDRUM 115339 LL375 Steam Trawler	337 21.10.1902 27.11.1902	191 64	110.0 21.0	C.D.Holmes 55 NHP 9.5 knots	John Duncan & Sons Co Ltd Liverpool
1919 Sold to Stepney Steam Fishing Co Ltd, Scarborough (SH35). 1923 to Co-operative Fishing Society Ltd , Scarborough. 1936 Vessel sold to shipbreakers and broken up.					
HELIOS 113238 GY784 Steam Trawler	338 03.12.1902 21.01.1903	201 62	115.0 21.5	C.D.Holmes 55 NHP 9.5 knots	Roberts & Ruthven Ltd Grimsby
1915 Rqd by the Royal Navy as an auxiliary patrol vessel / 1917 fishing trawler (Fishery Reserve). 1919 returned. 13.11.1925 Sold to Sir T Robinson, Grimsby. 29.11.1941 to J Bennett, Grimsby. 14.06.1945 to Thornton Trawlers, Fleetwood. 17.10.1946 to Lewis Isaacs, Grimsby. 01.11.1946 to Producers Steam Fishing Co Ltd, Grimsby. 1951 Vessel sold to BISCO and allocated to C W Dorkin & Co Ltd Gateshead. 17.07.1951 Breaking up completed.					
OPHIR 116137 H725 Steam Trawler	341 14.02.1902 06.04.1903	230 84	125.0 21.75	Amos & Smith 70 NHP 10.5 knots	Pickering & Haldane's Steam Trawling Co Ltd Hull
1915 Rqd by the Royal Navy as a minesweeper No. FY 1204 renamed OPHIR III. 1919 returned. 04.10.1918 Sold to Crampin Steam Fishing Co Ltd, Grimsby (GY1220). 1933 to Walker Steam Trawling Co Ltd, Aberdeen renamed STAR OF MORAY (A232). 1934 to Hewett Fishing Co Ltd, London renamed LADYLOVE (LO167). 30.08.1941 Vessel posted missing - Lost with all fourteen crew off Iceland (possibly torpedoed by U202 on 27.08.1941).					
SIR FRANCIS DRAKE 116126 H720 Steam Trawler	345 20.12.1902 13.02.1903	256 93	128.4 22.0	C.D.Holmes 75 NHP 11 knots	National Steam Trawling Co Ltd Hull
18.03.1910 Vessel wrecked in Medalland Bay south coast of Iceland.					
GOOD HOPE 116128 H722 Steam Trawler	346 17.01.1903 23.02.1903	256 93	128.4 22.0	C.D.Holmes 75 NHP 11 knots	Cargill Steam Trawling Co Ltd Hull
1914 Rqd by the Royal Navy as a minesweeper No. FY 355. 1919 returned. 12.08.1918 Sold to Joseph R E Mardaunt , Grimsby (GY1187). 27.01.1919 to William H Rachkind, Grimsby. 02.11.1920 to William Power, Grimsby. 30.04.1923 to Ernest J Baskcomb, Grimsby. 04.05.1923 to Great Central Co-op Engineering & Ship Repair Co Ltd, Grimsby. 28.08.1923 to Good Hope Ltd, Grimsby. 08.11.1927 to Good Hope Ltd, Halifax, Nova Scotia, Canada. 16.03.1929 Vessel sank following a collision at the entrance of Halifax harbour.					
OSTRICH 116141 H729 Steam Trawler	347 12.03.1903 09.04.1903	244 89	125.0 22.0	C.D.Holmes 63 NHP 10.25 knots	St Andrews Steam Fishing Co Ltd Hull
1915 Rqd by the Royal Navy as a mine-layer (1916) renamed OSTRICH II. 1920 returned and reverted. 11.06.1926 Sold to Rederi A/B Titania, Gothenburg, Sweden renamed TITANIA . 1959 Vessel sold to shipbreakers and broken up.					
SOPHRON 113244 GY1270 Steam Trawler	348 25.05.1903 17.06.1903	195 62	113.7 21.0	Amos & Smith 59 NHP 10 knots	Standard Steam Fishing Co Ltd Grimsby
1914 Rqd by the Royal Navy as a minesweeper No. FY 725. 22.08.1917 Vessel sunk by mine in the Firth of Tay mine laid by UC41.					
ATHENIAN 113247 GY1273 Steam Trawler	349 14.07.1903 08.08.1903	171 41	101.0 21.0	C.D.Holmes 55 NHP 10 knots	Onward Steam Fishing Co Ltd Grimsby
10.02.1917 Vessel captured by U-boat in the North Sea and sunk 105 miles east by south of Aberdeen.					

Yard No.347
1903 OSTRICH
Photo:- Barnard and Straker Collection

Yard No.350
1903 PRINCESS VICTORIA
Photo:- Barnard and Straker Collection

Yard No.357
1903 ST. CLAIR
Photo:- Barnard and Straker Collection

NAME Official No. Port Letters Numbers	Yard No. Launched Registered	Registered G Ton N Ton	 L Ft B Ft	Engine Builder Horse Power Reg'd Speed	OWNER (Built for)
PRINCESS VICTORIA 118769 H766 Steam Trawler	350 27.08.1903 23.09.1903	272 84	128.4 22.5	C.D.Holmes 75 NHP 10.5 knots	Armitage's Steam Trawling Co Ltd Hull
1915 Rqd by the Royal Navy as a minesweeper No. FY 1971. 07.11.1915 Vessel sunk following a collision off Ushant.					
REFINO 113245 GY1271 Steam Trawler	351 08.06.1903 14.07.1903	181 54	105.0 21.0	C.D.Holmes 55 NHP 9.5 knots	George Frederick Sleight Grimsby
23.09.1916 Vessel captured by U-boat in the North Sea and sunk by gunfire south-east by south of Spurn Light-Vessel.					
RADO 113246 GY1272 Steam Trawler	352 29.06.1903 24.07.1903	182 54	105.0 21.0	C.D.Holmes 55 NHP 9.5 knots	George Frederick Sleight Grimsby
04.10.1916 Vessel captured by U-boat in the North Sea and sunk by time bombs 15 miles NE by E of Spurn Light-Vessel.					
NUBIA 113250 GY1275 Steam Trawler	353 27.08.1903 28.08.1903	196 62	113.5 20.8	Amos & Smith 59 NHP 10 knots	Great Grimsby & East Coast Steam Fishing Co Ltd Grimsby
15.02.1937 Sold to Henry G Hopwood & Charles Taylor, Grimsby. 20.05.1937 Sold to Japan Fishing Co Ltd, Grimsby. Nov 1939 Rqd by the Royal Navy as an auxiliary patrol vessel. 17.10.1941 Vessel sank in the North Sea following a collision 6 miles off the River Tyne. Six crew lost.					
DEFENDER 118914 GY1279 Steam Trawler	354 10.10.1903 20.10.1903	206 67	113.8 21.5	C.D.Holmes 60 NHP 10.5 knots	Alec Black Grimsby
14.11.1909 Vessel wrecked on Mackenzie Rock south-west of Skerryvore Lighthouse.					
BRISBANE 118915 GY1281 Steam Trawler	355 10.10.1903 09.11.1903	207 66	113.8 21.5	C.D.Holmes 60 NHP 10.5 knots	William Grant & Henry Croft Baker Grimsby
1918 Rqd by the Royal Navy as a fishing trawler (Fishery Reserve). 1919 returned. 22.06.1918 Sold to A Grant, Grimsby. 15.01.1920 to Sylvia Steam Fishing Co Ltd, Grimsby. 13.03.1922 to Dobson Steam Fishing Co Ltd, Grimsby. 25.02.1931 to C Dobson, Grimsby. 29.12.1941 to Dinas Steam Trawling Co Ltd, Fleetwood. 01.03.1945 to Great Grimsby & East Coast Steam Fishing Co Ltd, Grimsby. 22.05.1954 Vessel sold for scrap to J W Draper & Sons Ltd, Grimsby and broken up.					
SILANION 118918 GY1284 Steam Trawler	356 24.10.1903 23.11.1903	199 62	115.0 21.5	Amos & Smith 59 NHP 10 knots	Standard Steam Fishing Co Ltd Grimsby
25.02.1928 Whilst outward bound from Grimsby towards the Færoe fishing grounds the SILANION ran ashore in dense fog onto rocks near Cruden Bay, Aberdeenshire. She managed to pull clear but started taking on water forward. The skipper managed to beach the stricken vessel in Cruden Bay. All ten crew were rescued and tended by local Whinnyfold fishermen .					
ST. CLAIR 118797 H803 Steam Trawler	357 23.11.1903 01.01.1904	255 94	128.33 22.25	C.D.Holmes 70 NHP 10.5 knots	Thomas Hamling & Co Ltd Hull
1915 Rqd by the Royal Navy as a minesweeper No. FY 1844 renamed SUNSPOT. 1919 returned and reverted. 02.10.1924 Sold to Dinas Steam Trawling Co Ltd, Fleetwood (FD15). 1946 to Northern Trawlers Ltd, Grimsby (GY387). 1948 to Associated Trawlers Ltd, Great Yarmouth. 23.08.1949 Vessel stranded on the Isle of Stroma, Pentland Firth in thick fog whilst homeward bound to Yarmouth. The ST. CLAIR was re-floated and the tide carried her across the Firth were she ran aground again on rocks off Swona. The local lifeboat came alongside and took off all the crew. The vessel was sold to shipbreakers and broken up in situ.					
CRUSADER 118800 H5 Steam Trawler	358 22.12.1903 21.01.1904	259 92	130.0 22.25	C.D.Holmes 70 NHP 10.5 knots	Marine Steam Fishing Co Ltd Hull
23.03.1914 Sold to Canosa y Reboredo, Barcelona, Spain renamed HABANA. 1916 Sold to the Russian Navy No. T.29. 1920 Passed to the USSR Fleet renamed NAVAGA. 1928 Vessel deleted from Lloyds Register of Shipping.					
THOMAS HAMLING 118801 H6 Steam Trawler	359 02.01.1904 08.02.1904	256 95	128.33 22.25	C.D.Holmes 70 NHP 10.5 knots	Neptune Steam Fishing Co Ltd Hull
13.01.1910 Vessel wrecked near Portland on the south coast of Iceland. Eight of the crew survived an arduous overland trek to safety but three men perished.					

Vessels built at Beverley 1902 to 1919.

<table>
<tr><th rowspan="2">NAME
Official No.
Port Letters Numbers</th><th rowspan="2">Yard No.
Launched
Registered</th><th colspan="2">Registered</th><th rowspan="2">Engine Builder
Horse Power
Reg'd Speed</th><th rowspan="2">OWNER
(Built for)</th></tr>
<tr><th>G Ton
N Ton</th><th>L Ft
B Ft</th></tr>
<tr><td>HUNTSMAN
113637
Steam Tug</td><td>304 Bev 1
13.02.1902
29.04.1902</td><td>126
12.5</td><td>95.0
18.0</td><td>Crabtree & Co
50 NHP
10 knots</td><td>Thomas Gray & Co Ltd
Hull</td></tr>
<tr><td colspan="6">02.11.1904 Sold to Impresa Adriatica di Lavori Potruali, Trieste, Italy renamed AQUILEIA A.
1923 Vessel deleted from Lloyds Register of Shipping.</td></tr>
<tr><td>KING EDWARD
113641
Schooner</td><td>307 Bev 2
15.03.1902
13.05.1902</td><td>355
155</td><td>149.0
24.0</td><td>Amos & Smith
84 NHP
11 knots</td><td>James Halliday
Quebec
Canada</td></tr>
<tr><td colspan="6">27.06.1910 Sold to Dept of Naval Service of Canada renamed LAURENTIAN.
1917 Royal Canadian Navy auxiliary patrol vessel. 1919 to Canadian Steamship Lines, Quebec (Passenger Vessel).
1947 Vessel sold to shipbreakers and broken up.</td></tr>
<tr><td>GOZO
113639
H545 Steam Trawler</td><td>308 Bev 3
27.02.1902
19.04.1902</td><td>172
64</td><td>108.3
21.3</td><td>Amos & Smith
45 NHP
10 knots</td><td>Hull Steam Fishing
& Ice Co Ltd
Hull</td></tr>
<tr><td colspan="6">Oct 1914 Rqd by the Royal Navy as a minesweeper No. FY 644. 1919 returned.
19.11.1930 Sold to C H Brand, Hull. 12.10.1939 to Boston Deep Sea Fishing Co Ltd, Hull.
12.03.1941 to Yolland Trawling Co Ltd, Milford Haven. 17.02.1945 to Milford Fisheries Ltd, Milford Haven.
24.07.1945 Vessel sunk by mine 25 miles south south-west off The Old Head of Kinsale . All crew rescued.</td></tr>
<tr><td>THANET
113649
H549 Steam Trawler</td><td>309 Bev 4
10.05.1902
13.06.1902</td><td>172
64</td><td>108.3
21.3</td><td>Amos & Smith
45 NHP
10 knots</td><td>Hull Steam Fishing
& Ice Co Ltd
Hull</td></tr>
<tr><td colspan="6">Sep 1915 Rqd by the Royal Navy as a boom defence vessel . 1919 returned.
May 1936 Vessel sold (£340) for scrap to Metal Industries, Fife. 25.11.1936 Breaking up commenced at Charlestown.</td></tr>
<tr><td>MAURITIUS
113646
H547 Steam Trawler</td><td>310 Bev 5
10.04.1902
03.06.1902</td><td>172
64</td><td>108.3
21.3</td><td>Amos & Smith
45 NHP
10 knots</td><td>Hull Steam Fishing
& Ice Co Ltd
Hull</td></tr>
<tr><td colspan="6">17.5.1915 Vessel posted missing:- lost with all hands whilst fishing in the North Sea.</td></tr>
<tr><td>CAIRO
116071
H550 Steam Trawler</td><td>311 Bev 6
10.05.1902
23.06.1902</td><td>172
64</td><td>108.3
21.3</td><td>Amos & Smith
45 NHP
10 knots</td><td>Hull Steam Fishing & Ice
Co Ltd
Hull</td></tr>
<tr><td colspan="6">Oct 1914 Rqd by the Royal Navy as a base ship for minesweepers.1916 minesweeper No. FY 635. 1919 returned.
19.11.1930 Sold to C H Brand, Hull. 30.11.1939 to Boston Deep Sea Fishing Co Ltd, Hull.
22.05.1941 to Cairo Fishing Co Ltd, Hull. 12.03.1945 to Milford Fishing Ltd, Milford Haven.
1945 to G Mitchell, Lowestoft (LT154).
1959 Vessel sold for scrap to Thos W Ward Ltd, Preston. 18.11.1959 Arrived Grays River Thames for breaking up.</td></tr>
<tr><td>HOBART
116076
H555 Steam Trawler</td><td>312 Bev 7
24.05.1902
11.07.1902</td><td>172
64</td><td>108.4
21.3</td><td>Amos & Smith
45 NHP
10 knots</td><td>Hull Steam Fishing
& Ice Co Ltd
Hull</td></tr>
<tr><td colspan="6">Sep 1915 Rqd by the Royal Navy as a boom defence vessel. 1919 returned.
May 1936 Vessel sold (£340) for scrap to Metal Industries, Fife. 10.06.1936 Breaking up commenced at Charlestown.</td></tr>
<tr><td>HAWTHORN
113228
GY1228 Steam Trawler</td><td>321 Bev 8
07.07.1902
05.08.1902</td><td>179
55</td><td>108.3
21.0</td><td>C.D. Holmes
55 NHP
9.5 knots</td><td>William Grant &
Dawson Robinson
Grimsby</td></tr>
<tr><td colspan="6">1917 Rqd by the Royal Navy as a fishing trawler (Fishery Reserve) renamed HAWTHORN II. 1919 returned and reverted.
28.05.1927 to A Grant, Grimsby. 07.03.1929 to F Robinson, Grimsby. 01.11.1929 to A J Mumby, Milford Haven (M68).
1932 Hawthorn Fishing Co Ltd, Milford Haven. 1937 Vessel sold to shipbreakers and broken up.</td></tr>
<tr><td>ROSCO
113232
GY1232 Steam Trawler</td><td>322 Bev 9
24.07.1902
10.09.1902</td><td>166
50</td><td>101.0
21.0</td><td>C.D. Holmes
55 NHP
9.5 knots</td><td>George F Sleight
Grimsby</td></tr>
<tr><td colspan="6">1917 Rqd by the Royal Navy as a fishing trawler (Fishery Reserve). 1919 returned.
29.11.1938 Sold to Consolidated Fisheries, Lowestoft renamed LAVENHAM (LT274).
08.10.1939 Transferred to Grimsby (Consolidated Fisheries).1944 to Elkington Estates Ltd, / C Dobson, Grimsby (GY3).
1947 to Yolland Bros Ltd, Milford Haven. 1951 Vessel sold to shipbreakers. Nov 1951 Broken up at Milford Haven.</td></tr>
</table>

<table>
<tr><th>NAME
Official No.
Port Letters Numbers</th><th>Yard No.
Launched
Registered</th><th colspan="2">Registered</th><th>Engine Builder
Horse Power
Reg'd Speed</th><th>OWNER
(Built for)</th></tr>
<tr><th></th><th></th><th>G Ton
N Ton</th><th>L Ft
B Ft</th><th></th><th></th></tr>
<tr><td>ROSARENO
113233
GY1233 Steam Trawler</td><td>323 Bev 10
24.07.1902
06.10.1902</td><td>166
49</td><td>101.0
21.0</td><td>C.D. Holmes
55 NHP
9.5 knots</td><td>George F Sleight
Grimsby</td></tr>
<tr><td colspan="6">1917 Rqd by the Royal Navy as a fishing trawler (Fishery Reserve). 1919 returned.
01.10.1933 Sold to George F Sleight & Ramond L Humphery, Grimsby.
05.12.1938 to Consolidated Fisheries, Lowestoft renamed RENDLESHAM (LT265).
05.11.1940 Vessel wrecked after striking a submerged rock on the north west point of Cape Clear.</td></tr>
<tr><td>COLLINGWOOD
113229
GY1229 Steam Trawler</td><td>324 Bev 11
11.07.1902
23.08.1902</td><td>179
55</td><td>108.7
21.0</td><td>C.D. Holmes
55 NHP
9.5 knots</td><td>William Grant &
Harold C Baker
Grimsby</td></tr>
<tr><td colspan="6">1917 Rqd by the Royal Navy as a fishing trawler (Fishery Reserve). 1919 returned.
01.1920 Sold to Sylvia Steam Fishing Co Ltd, Grimsby. 30.08.1922 to Dobson Steam Fishing Co Ltd, Grimsby.
01. 02.1931 to C Dobson, Grimsby.
1940 Rqd by the Royal Navy as a boom gate vessel renamed FIELDGATE. 1945 returned and reverted.
26.03.1945 to Wembley Steam Fishing Co Ltd, Grimsby. 1949 Vessel sold for scrap to Pounds, Portsmouth.
11.06.1949 Registration closed on advice that the vessel was broken up.</td></tr>
<tr><td>REINDEER
113236
GY1236 Steam Trawler</td><td>328 Bev 12
18.09.1902
17.11.1902</td><td>192
52</td><td>112.7
21.5</td><td>Amos & Smith
62 NHP
10 knots</td><td>Morris & Fisher Ltd
Grimsby</td></tr>
<tr><td colspan="6">Nov 1914 Rqd by the Royal Navy as a minesweeper No. FY 816 renamed (1915) REINDEER II.1920 returned and reverted.
10.11.1926 Sold to Walter Garratt, Grimsby. 26.11.1931 to Thomas Fisher, Grimsby.
1937 Vessel sold for scrap to South Stockton Shipbreaking Co Ltd . 30.04.1937 Arrived Thornaby for breaking up.</td></tr>
<tr><td>ELK
113235
GY1235 Steam Trawler</td><td>329 Bev 13
21.08.1902
31.10.1902</td><td>181
46</td><td>108.7
21.0</td><td>Amos & Smith
62 NHP
10 knots</td><td>Morris & Fisher Ltd
Grimsby</td></tr>
<tr><td colspan="6">Dec 1914 Rqd by the Royal Navy as a minesweeper No. FY 706 renamed (1918) ELK II. 1919 returned.
02.09.1918 Sold to Victoria Steam Fishing Co Ltd, Grimsby. 27.09.1929 to Oliver Curphey, Milford Haven (M36).
1938 to W.H.E. Nichols, Milford Haven. 1939 Rqd by the Royal Navy as a danlayer. No. FY 4.24
27.11.1940 Vessel sunk by mine off Ile Point, Cornwall. All crew rescued.</td></tr>
<tr><td>PRETORIA
116104
H701 Steam Trawler</td><td>330 Bev 14
22.09.1902
24.11.1902</td><td>180
64</td><td>109.0
21.5</td><td>Amos & Smith
45 NHP
10 knots</td><td>Hull Steam Fishing
& Ice Co Ltd
Hull</td></tr>
<tr><td colspan="6">Oct 1914 Rqd by the Royal Navy as a minesweeper No. FY 368. 1920 returned.
18.01.1924 Vessel sank following a collision in the North Sea with the trawler ELLESMERE H767 (183 gt/ b 1903).
All Nine crew were taken aboard the ELLESMERE and then transferred to the JULIET GY660 which was returning to port.</td></tr>
<tr><td>KIMBERLEY
116111
H707 Steam Trawler</td><td>331 Bev 15
04.10.1902
16.12.1902</td><td>181
65</td><td>109.0
21.5</td><td>Amos & Smith
45 NHP
10 knots</td><td>Hull Steam Fishing
& Ice Co Ltd
Hull</td></tr>
<tr><td colspan="6">Oct 1915 Rqd by the Royal Navy as a minesweeper renamed KIMBERLEY II . 1919 returned and reverted.
1936 Vessel sold (£340) for scrap to Metal Industries Charlestown, Fife, Scotland. 16.12.36 Breaking up commenced.</td></tr>
<tr><td>NORMAN
116123
H717 Steam Trawler</td><td>339 Bev 16
15.11.1902
23.02.1903</td><td>270
104</td><td>130.0
22.0</td><td>Amos & Smith
78 NHP
10.5 knots</td><td>Imperial Steam
Fishing Co Ltd
Hull</td></tr>
<tr><td colspan="6">25.05.1910 Sold to P Feixas, Barcelona, Spain renamed PEDRO.
1919 Vessel deleted from Lloyds Register of Shipping (1914 - 1918 War Loss)</td></tr>
<tr><td>JOHANNESBURG
116117
H711 Steam Trawler</td><td>333 Bev 17
19.11.1902
06.01.1903</td><td>181
65</td><td>109.0
21.5</td><td>Amos & Smith
45 NHP
10 knots</td><td>Hull Steam Fishing
& Ice Co Ltd
Hull</td></tr>
<tr><td colspan="6">Oct 1915 Rqd by the Royal Navy as a minesweeper No. FY 1796. 1919 returned.
02.10.1931 Sold to W Normandale Scarborough renamed NORDALE (SH89). 1938 to Torbay Trawlers Ltd, Scarborough.
15.1.1942 Vessel wrecked on the Mull of Kintyre, Scotland.</td></tr>
<tr><td>MAFEKING
116123
H716 Steam Trawler</td><td>332 Bev 18
19.11.1902
30.01.1903</td><td>181
65</td><td>109.0
21.5</td><td>Amos & Smith
45 NHP
10 knots</td><td>Hull Steam Fishing
& Ice Co Ltd
Hull</td></tr>
<tr><td colspan="6">Oct 1914 Rqd by the Royal Navy as a minesweeper No. FY 637. 1919 returned.
18.10.1922 Vessel wrecked on The Binks off Spurn Point in an easterly gale whilst outward bound for the fishing grounds. The nine crew took to the ship's boat and safely landed at Immingham. Spurn lifeboat came to investigate the wreck but found it abandoned.</td></tr>
</table>

Yard No.3
1902 GOZO
Photo:- Barnard and Straker Collection

Yard No.20
1902 ROMEO
Photo:- Barnard and Straker Collection

Yard No.28
1903 MALABAR
Photo:- Barnard and Straker Collection

NAME Official No. Port Letters Numbers	Yard No. Launched Registered	Registered G Ton N Ton	 L Ft B Ft	Engine Builder Horse Power Reg'd Speed	OWNER (Built for)
LADYSMITH 116138 H726 Steam Trawler	334 Bev 19 02.02.1903 24.03.1903	181 65	109.0 21.5	Amos & Smith 45 NHP 10 knots	Hull Steam Fishing & Ice Co Ltd Hull
25.12.1911 Vessel sank in the North Sea following a collision with the fish carrier AUSTRALIA H1328 (238 gt/ b 1882). Badly holed the LADYSMITH sank rapidly. All nine crew took to the ship's boat and were picked up by the AUSTRALIA.					
ROMEO 116127 H721 Steam Trawler	340 Bev 20 17.12.1902 21.02.1903	270 104	130.0 22.0	Amos & Smith 78 NHP 10.5 knots	Hellyer Steam Fishing Co Ltd Hull
02.08.1912 Sold to Walter Crampin, Grimsby (GY735). 06.11.1912 Left Grimsby for the Icelandic fishing grounds and disappeared during a spell of very bad weather off Iceland. Nov 1912 Vessel posted missing:- Lost with all hands.					
PLUTARCH 116134 H724 Steam Trawler	21 15.01.1903 16.03.1903	270 105	130.0 22.0	Amos & Smith 78 NHP 10.5 knots	Hellyer Steam Fishing Co Ltd Hull
30.04.1912 Sold to Bakker and Dijksen, Ijmuiden, Holland renamed ERNESTINE PAULINE (IJM95). 1915 to Maats Ernestine Pauline, Ijmuiden . 27.07.1917 Vessel posted missing:- sunk by mine in the North Sea.					
DANE 116144 H730 Steam Trawler	22 03.03.1903 18.04.1903	267 100	130.0 22.0	Amos & Smith 78 NHP 10.5 knots	Imperial Steam Fishing Co Ltd Hull
03.04.1908 Sold to Canosa Trillo y Cia, Barcelona, Spain renamed ARAÑA. 1917 to Marine Nationale Francaise (French Navy) renamed ANNIBAL based at La Rochelle. 1919 to Oscar Dahl, La Rochelle renamed HEROS 1920 to The French Government. 1922 Vessel deleted from Lloyds Register of Shipping.					
PERICLES 116147 H735 Steam Trawler	23 13.03.1903 02.05.1903	267 103	130.0 22.0	Amos & Smith 78 NHP 10.5 knots	Hellyer Steam Fishing Co Ltd Hull
02.04.1908 Sold to Akties Trawling Kompagniet, Christiania, Norway renamed FLYING FISH. 1910 to Akties Bas, Sandefjord renamed BAS. 1916 to Laegter Akties Christiania renamed VESLEFJELL renamed (1918) SCOUT. 1919 Converted to a Tug for A/S Laegter Trafik, Porsgrund renamed STOREGUT. 1928 to Empresa Brazileiro de Nav, Rio de Janeiro, Brazil renamed SANTA CRUZ. 1933 Vessel deleted from Lloyds Register of Shipping.					
TITAN 113241 GY1259 Steam Trawler	24 31.01.1903 13.03.1903	171 41	101.0 21.16	Amos & Smith 55 NHP 9.5 knots	Thomas Robinson Grimsby
26.10.1916 Vessel captured by U-boat and sunk by gunfire 56 miles south east of Girdle Ness.					
POONAH 116151 H737 Steam Trawler	25 31.03.1903 20.05.1903	171 57	105.0 21.25	Amos & Smith 45 NHP 10 knots	Hull Steam Fishing & Ice Co Ltd Hull
Nov 1914 Rqd by the Royal Navy as a minesweeper No. FY 530. 18.08.1915 Vessel sank following a collision in Sulva Bay Turkey during the Dardanelles Campaign.					
LUCKNOW 116152 H739 Steam Trawler	26 14.04.1903 25.05.1903	171 57	105.0 21.25	Amos & Smith 45 NHP 10 knots	Hull Steam Fishing & Ice Co Ltd Hull
Oct 1914 Rqd by the Royal Navy as a minesweeper No. FY 649. 18.05.1917 Vessel sunk by mine off Portsmouth. Mines laid by UC 36 on the same day.					
MALABAR 118761 H754 Steam Trawler	27 27.01.1903 19.08.1903	171 57	105.0 21.25	Amos & Smith 45 NHP 10 knots	Hull Steam Fishing & Ice Co Ltd Hull
20.12.1915 Vessel left Hull for a fishing trip in the North Sea. 27.12.1915 Vessel posted missing :-lost with all nine crew during severe weather.					
DELHI 118751 H742 Steam Trawler	28 14.04.1903 30.06.1903	171 57	105.0 21.25	Amos & Smith 45 NHP 10 knots	Hull Steam Fishing & Ice Co Ltd Hull
1917 Rqd by the Royal Navy as a fishing trawler (Fishery Reserve). 1919 returned. 10.11.1930 Sold to N J Chamberlain, Hull. 05.07.1937 to W James, Hull. 10.05.1940 to Pair Fishing Co Ltd, Hull. 15.03.1945 to W H Kerr Lowestoft (LT111). 1947 to A C Mitchell & Others, Milford Haven 1949 to W H Kerr, (Ship-chandler), Milford Haven. 1957 Vessel sold for scrap to Thos W Ward Ltd, Preston. 16.05.1957 Arrived Milford Haven for breaking up.					

<table>
<tr><th rowspan="2">NAME
Official No.
Port Letters Numbers</th><th rowspan="2">Yard No.
Launched
Registered</th><th colspan="2">Registered</th><th rowspan="2">Engine Builder
Horse Power
Reg'd Speed</th><th rowspan="2">OWNER
(Built for)</th></tr>
<tr><th>G Ton
N Ton</th><th>L Ft
B Ft</th></tr>
<tr><td>TANJORE
118766
H759 Steam Trawler</td><td>29
27.01.1903
12.09.1903</td><td>168
55</td><td>105.0
21.25</td><td>Amos & Smith
45 NHP
10 knots</td><td>Hull Steam Fishing
& Ice Co Ltd
Hull</td></tr>
<tr><td colspan="6">Oct 1914 Rqd by the Royal Navy as a minesweeper No. FY 634. 1919 returned.
18.02.1924 Vessel sank following an explosion caused by a freak accident during fishing operations in the North Sea. Thick fog came down when the TANJORE was due to send her boats to a fish carrier. To alert other vessels of her position the skipper fired a signal rocket. As the missile rose the stick broke and it fell and exploded close to the ship's side. This caused a split in the ship's plates and she began to sink. All nine crew took to the ship's boat and were picked up by another trawler.</td></tr>
<tr><td>EMPEROR
116170
H741 Steam Trawler</td><td>30
14.05.1903
23.06.1903</td><td>181
62</td><td>109.0
21.5</td><td>Amos & Smith
46 NHP
10 knots</td><td>Great Northern Steam Ship
Fishing Co Ltd
Hull</td></tr>
<tr><td colspan="6">Sep 1914 Rqd by the Royal Navy as a minesweeper No. FY 552. 1915 as a fishing trawler. 1919 returned.
14.12.1918 Sold to Richard F Scotter & Richard Cammish, Scarborough.
23.06.1920 to Emperor Steam Trawling Co Ltd, Scarborough. 11.09.1925 to F Thornley, Bolton.
29.10.1928 to Thomas T Brown, Leith. 16.11.1929 to Mark M Robson, Milford Haven.
30.03.1937 Registration closed on advice that the vessel was broken up.</td></tr>
<tr><td>ESMERALDA
118753
H747 Steam Trawler</td><td>31
13.06.1903
18.07.1903</td><td>181
62</td><td>109.0
21.5</td><td>Amos & Smith
46 NHP
10 knots</td><td>Great Northern Steam Ship
Fishing Co Ltd
Hull</td></tr>
<tr><td colspan="6">1917 Rqd by the Royal Navy as a fishing trawler (Fishery Reserve). 1919 returned.
30.11.1918 Sold to Richard F Scotter & Richard Cammish, Scarborough.
14.07.1920 to Esmeralda Steam Trawling Co Ltd, Scarborough. 26.01.1925 Richard W Lewis, Aberdeen (A80).
30.03.1937 Vessel sold to shipbreakers and broken up.</td></tr>
<tr><td>ERMINE
118760
H753 Steam Trawler</td><td>32
11.07.1903
14.09.1903</td><td>181
62</td><td>109.0
21.5</td><td>Amos & Smith
46 NHP
10 knots</td><td>Great Northern Steam Ship
Fishing Co Ltd
Hull</td></tr>
<tr><td colspan="6">May 1915 Rqd by the Royal Navy as a minesweeper No. FY 1776. 1919 returned.
24.04.1918 Sold to Hull Steam Fishing & Ice Co Ltd, Hull. 26.03.1930 H E Rees, Milford Haven (M90).
1943 J F Gwyther, Milford Haven. 1948 Mrs M Gwyther, Milford Haven.
1952 Vessel sold for scrap to K E Rees & Co Ltd. 26.08.1952. Arrived Grays, River Thames for breaking up.</td></tr>
<tr><td>ERIN
118764
H757 Steam Trawler</td><td>33
11.07.1903
02.09.1903</td><td>181
62</td><td>109.0
21.5</td><td>Amos & Smith
46 NHP
10 knots</td><td>Great Northern Steam Ship
Fishing Co Ltd
Hull</td></tr>
<tr><td colspan="6">Sep 1914 Rqd by the Royal Navy as a minesweeper No. FY 381 renamed (1915) ERIN II.
19.10.1915 Vessel sunk by mine in the English Channel laid by UC5 on the same day off South Foreland Kent.
Seven crew lost.</td></tr>
<tr><td>EROS
118775
H768 Steam Trawler</td><td>34
28.07.1903
29.09.1903</td><td>181
62</td><td>109.0
21.5</td><td>Amos & Smith
46 NHP
10 knots</td><td>Great Northern Steam Ship
Fishing Co Ltd
Hull</td></tr>
<tr><td colspan="6">1917 Rqd by the Royal Navy as a fishing trawler (Fishery Reserve).
08.06.1918 Vessel sunk by mine in the North Sea. Six crew lost including the skipper.</td></tr>
<tr><td>HERCULES
118780
H771 Steam Trawler</td><td>35
26.08.1903
09.10.1903</td><td>261
95</td><td>128.33
22.0</td><td>C.D. Holmes
70 NHP
10.5 knots</td><td>Anglo - Norwegian Steam
Fishing Co Ltd
Hull</td></tr>
<tr><td colspan="6">15.11.1912 Sold to Lancashire Steam Fishing Co Ltd, Fleetwood (FD172).
Mar 1915 Rqd by the Royal Navy as a minesweeper No. FY 1361 renamed HERCULES IV. 1919 returned.
1932 J Marr & Son Ltd, Fleetwood. 1937 Vessel sold for scrap to Thos W Ward Ltd, Preston and broken up.</td></tr>
<tr><td>MARCONI
118784
H777 Steam Trawler</td><td>36
02.10.1903
30.10.1903</td><td>261
98</td><td>130.0
22.0</td><td>C.D. Holmes
70 NHP
11 knots</td><td>Francis & Thomas Ross Ltd
Hull</td></tr>
<tr><td colspan="6">06.03.1909 Vessel wrecked off Ingolfshofde, south coast Iceland.</td></tr>
<tr><td>GOLDEN ERA
118792
H798 Steam Trawler</td><td>37
08.10.1903
01.12.1903</td><td>261
95</td><td>128.33
22.0</td><td>C.D. Holmes
70 NHP
10.5 knots</td><td>Hall Leyman & Co
Hull</td></tr>
<tr><td colspan="6">17.12.1905 Vessel sank off the coast of Iceland.</td></tr>
</table>

Yard No.31
1903 ESMERALDA
Photo:- Barnard and Straker Collection

Yard No.35
1903 HERCULES
Photo:- Barnard and Straker Collection

Yard No.53
1904 ROTO
Photo:- Barnard and Straker Collection

NAME Official No. Port Letters Numbers	Yard No. Launched Registered	Registered G Ton N Ton	 L Ft B Ft	Engine Builder Horse Power Reg'd Speed	OWNER (Built for)
LYSANDER 118794 H800 Steam Trawler	38 10.10.1903 21.12.1903	264 96	130.0 22.0	Amos & Smith 78 NHP 10.5 knots	Hellyer Steam Fishing Co Ltd Hull
Aug 1914 Rqd by the Royal Navy as a minesweeper No. FY 255 renamed (1915) LYSANDER II. 1919 returned. 07.11.1917 Sold to Mersey Steam Trawling Ltd, Fleetwood (FD352). 1926 to Magnolia Steam Fishing Co Ltd, Fleetwood renamed SYDNELSIE. 1928 to R L Hancock, Milford Haven. 28.06.1935 Vessel sank after striking rocks near Blasketts Islands, off the west coast of Ireland. The crew abandoned the stricken vessel in the lifeboat and were picked up by another trawler.					
IMPERIALIST 118798 H2 Steam Trawler	39 07.11.1903 11.01.1904	264 96	130.0 22.0	Amos & Smith 78 NHP 10.5 knots	Imperial Steam Fishing Co Ltd Hull
19.01.1907 Vessel driven ashore in severe weather on to the 'Blinders' a row of jagged rocks near Bredde Bright, Gruden Fjord west coast of Iceland. A boat was launched and after ten hours the crew managed to reach the uninhabited island of Knifsey. With the aid of an Icelandic rescue party all the crew landed safely in Stichohalme.					
WATCHFUL 114900 PD498 Drifter - Liner	40 02.12.1903 1903	88 32	86.0 18.0	Crabtree & Co 35 NHP 9.5 knots	W H Leask Peterhead
1912 Sold to A & B Buchan & W H Leask, Peterhead (a friend of W M Gemmell). Sep 1915 Rqd by the Royal Navy as a Boom defence vessel. 1919 returned. 1919 to J Alexander & J Kyles, Glasgow (GW19) *(Herring Carrier).* 1938 Vessel sold to shipbreakers and broken up at Troon.					
VALKYRIE 119654 BF1436 Steam Trawler	41 23.12.1903 1904	88 32	86.0 18.0	Crabtree & Co 33 NHP 9.5 knots	J M Slater Banff
1907 Sold to J Muir, Portknockie (WK116). Mar 1915 Rqd by the Royal Navy harbour service renamed VALKYRIE II No. FY 3010. 1919 returned and reverted. 1935 Vessel sold to shipbreakers and broken up.					
CARIAMA 118920 GY4 Steam Trawler	42 04.02.1904 15.03.1904	216 93	119.75 21.5	C.D. Holmes 60 NHP 10.5 knots	Thomas Bascomb Grimsby
15.01.1907 Sold to Reading & Dickinson Swansea (SA41). 1908 to Hector Steam Trawling Co Ltd, Swansea. 1915 to Mersey Steam Trawling Co Ltd, Fleetwood renamed MEUSE (FD107). 1917 Rqd by the Royal Navy as a fishing trawler (Fishery Reserve). 1919 returned. 1926 to W Morley & Co, Fleetwood. 1932 to Oceanic Trading Corp, Fleetwood. 1933 to Hewett Fishing Co, Fleetwood. 1935 Vessel sold to shipbreakers and broken up.					
COURSER 118921 GY1287 Steam Trawler	43 08.02.1904 25.03.1904	216 93	119.75 21.5	C.D. Holmes 60 NHP 10.5 knots	Thomas Bascomb Grimsby
10.04.1905 Vessel wrecked near The Sow west coast of Hoy.					
ALFREDA	44 31.03.1904 00.00.1904	111 1	93.5 18.75	Amos & Smith NHP knots	HM War Office Whitehall London
No details of type of vessel, or service record has been found. 1947 Sold to Quebec River Transport Canada renamed RINA B Official No. 190963, *(converted to a coastal tanker).* 04.08.1965 Vessel sank off St Augustion, Quebec.					
MOONSTONE	45 19.05.1904 04.08.1904	74 3	87.0 17.5	Amos & Smith NHP knots	HM War Office Whitehall London
No details of type of vessel, or service record has been found.					
LOUISE	46 19.05.1904 04.08.1904	74 3	87.0 17.5	Amos & Smith NHP knots	HM War Office Whitehall London
No details of type of vessel, or service record has been found.					
PRINCE CHARLES O26 Steam Trawler	47 17.02.1904 28.03.1904	245 120	120.0 21.87	C.D. Holmes 63 NHP 10.5 knots	A T Goulder & Co Ostend Belgium
1933 Sold to Dobson Ship repair Co Ltd, Grimsby renamed LANGWITH (GY517). 1937 Vessel sold to shipbreakers and broken up.					

NAME Official No. Port Letters Numbers	Yard No. Launched Registered	Registered G Ton N Ton	 L Ft B Ft	Engine Builder Horse Power Reg'd Speed	OWNER (Built for)
THE PRINCE 117564 YH878 Steam Drifter	48 20.04.1904 31.05.1904	77 22	78.0 18.0	Crabtree & Co 28 NHP 9 knots	Crown Steam Drifters Ltd Lowestoft
Apr 1915 Rqd by the Royal Navy as a netlayer No. FY 1432. 1920 returned. 1924 Sold to J Copeland , Tynemouth. 1927 to J Cormack, Banff renamed MAGNELPHYL (BF294). 1933 Vessel sold to shipbreakers and broken up.					
THE PRINCESS 117566 YH879 Steam Drifter	49 20.04.1904 13.06.1904	77 22	78.0 18.0	Crabtree & Co 28 NHP 9 knots	Crown Steam Drifters Ltd Lowestoft
Feb 1915 Rqd by the Royal Navy boom defence vessel No. FY 1091. 1919 returned. 1924 Sold to J Wood & A Donaldson, Portknockie, Banffshire (BF40). 1927 to L Smith & John Mair, Portknockie. 1937 Vessel sold (£215) for scrap to Metal Industries, Fife, Scotland. 12.06.1937 Arrived Charlestown, for breaking up.					
REVERTO 118927 GY13 Steam Trawler	50 18.05.1904 07.07.1904	177 54	105.0 21.0	C.D. Holmes 55 NHP 9.5 knots	George F Sleight Grimsby
1906 The was changed to GY104 because 13 was considered unlucky. 18.09.1916 Vessel posted missing:- lost with all hands whilst fishing in the North Sea.					
RECTO 118928 GY16 Steam Trawler	51 18.05.1904 20.07.1904	177 54	105.0 21.0	C.D. Holmes 55 NHP 9.5 knots	George F Sleight Grimsby
06.04.1917 Vessel captured by U-boat and sunk by time bombs 45 miles north east of Kinnaird Head.					
SYRIAN 118930 GY25 Steam Trawler	52 29.06.1904 03.08.1904	175 45	101.0 21.0	C.D. Holmes 55 NHP 9.5 knots	Frank & Thomas Robinson Grimsby
11.07.1915 Vessel captured by U-boat in the North Sea and sunk by gunfire 45 miles east north-east of Hornsea.					
ROTO 118931 GY22 Steam Trawler	53 29.06.1904 16.08.1904	170 59	105.0 21.0	C.D. Holmes 55 NHP 9.5 knots	George F Sleight Grimsby
Jan 1915 Rqd by the Royal Navy as a minesweeper / bomb thrower No. FY 947. 1920 returned. 17.11.1933 Sold to George F Sleight & Ramond L Humphery, Grimsby. 21.11.1938 Sold to Consolidated Fisheries, Lowestoft renamed SAXMUNDHAM (LT286). 1945 Cranbrook Shipping Co Ltd, London. 1952 Vessel sold to BISCO and allocated to Clayton & Davie Ltd. Jul 1952 Arrived Dunston on Tyne for breaking up.					
RENOVO 118933 GY23 Steam Trawler	54 16.07.1904 09.09.1904	170 59	105.0 21.0	C.D. Holmes 55 NHP 9.5 knots	George F Sleight Grimsby
1917 Rqd by the Royal Navy as a fishing trawler (Fishery Reserve). 1919 returned. 17.11.1933 Sold to George F Sleight & Ramond L Humphery, Grimsby. 21.11.1938 Sold to Consolidated Fisheries, Lowestoft renamed WALSINGHAM (LT279). 08.10.1939 transferred back to Grimsby. 30.03.1940 Vessel sank following a collision in the North Sea 25 miles south-east of Harwich.					
ADMIRAL TOGO 118832 H259 Steam Trawler	55 13.08.1904 01.10.1904	249 88	126.66 22.0	Amos & Smith 76 NHP 10.5 knots	Pickering & Haldane's Steam Trawling Co Ltd Hull
07.03.1913 Vessel wrecked off Stafsnes, Iceland. All twelve crew lost.					
LORD WOLSELEY 118836 H263 Steam Trawler	56 27.08.1904 14.10.1904	249 88	126.66 22.0	Amos & Smith 76 NHP 10.5 knots	Yorkshire Steam Fishing Co Ltd Hull
22.03.1907 The skipper and crew of the LORD WOLSELEY rescued all eighteen crew from the schooner PROMISE OF DUNKERQUE, which was in distress in the North Atlantic in severe weather. 1913 Sold to Duchene & Legrand Freres, Boulogne, France renamed ELISABETH. 20.09.1915 Rqd by the French Navy. 13.03.1917 Vessel sank off Flandres.					
JAPAN 118839 H580 Steam Trawler	57 14.08.1904 02.11.1904	248 88	126.66 22.0	Amos & Smith 76 NHP 10.5 knots	Pickering & Haldane's Steam Trawling Co Ltd Hull
05.11.1908 Vessel wrecked at Medalland Bay, Iceland. Two crew lost ten rescued .					

Yard No.57
1904 JAPAN
Photo:- Barnard and Straker Collection

Yard No.64
1905 GAUL
Photo:- Barnard and Straker Collection

Yard No.81
1905 MIKADO
Photo:- Barnard and Straker Collection

<table>
<tr><th rowspan="2">NAME
Official No.
Port Letters Numbers</th><th rowspan="2">Yard No.
Launched
Registered</th><th colspan="2">Registered</th><th rowspan="2">Engine Builder
Horse Power
Reg'd Speed</th><th rowspan="2">OWNER
(Built for)</th></tr>
<tr><th>G Ton
N Ton</th><th>L Ft
B Ft</th></tr>
<tr><td>ELECTRA
118840
H661 Steam Trawler</td><td>58
14.09.1904
14.11.1904</td><td>269
102</td><td>130.0
22.25</td><td>C.D. Holmes
70 NHP
10.5 knots</td><td>Francis & Thomas Ross Ltd
Hull</td></tr>
<tr><td colspan="6">Jul 1915 Rqd by the Royal Navy as a minesweeper No. FY 1743 renamed ELECTRA II. 1919 returned.
12.12.1934 Sold to Henry Elliot & Sons Ltd, Fleetwood.
1940 Rqd by the Royal Navy as auxiliary patrol vessel No. FY 4.159 later as a boom defence vessel. 1946 returned.
21.12.1942 to Alfred Fishing Co Ltd, Fleetwood. 18.02.1946 Laid up at Alexandra Dock Grimsby.
1946 Vessel sold for scrap to John R Hepworth, Hull. 06.11.1946 Left Grimsby to be broken up at Paull.</td></tr>
<tr><td>ST. KILDA
118838
H355 Steam Trawler</td><td>59
30.08.1904
20.10.1904</td><td>187
68</td><td>108.33
21.5</td><td>Amos & Smith
45 NHP
10 knots</td><td>Hull Steam Fishing
& Ice Co Ltd
Hull</td></tr>
<tr><td colspan="6">1917 Rqd by the Royal Navy as a fishing trawler (Fishery Reserve). 1919 returned.
May 1936 Vessel sold (£340) for scrap to Metal Industries Charlestown Fife. 16.09.1936 Breaking up commenced.</td></tr>
<tr><td>IONA
118843
H709 Steam Trawler</td><td>60
24.09.1904
16.11.1904</td><td>187
68</td><td>108.33
21.5</td><td>Amos & Smith
45 NHP
10 knots</td><td>Hull Steam Fishing
& Ice Co Ltd
Hull</td></tr>
<tr><td colspan="6">1917 Rqd by the Royal Navy as a fishing trawler (Fishery Reserve). 1919 returned.
May 1936 Vessel sold (£340) for scrap to Metal Industries Charlestown Fife. 09.12.1936 Breaking up commenced.</td></tr>
<tr><td>COURTLAND
118938
GY35 Steam Trawler</td><td>61
13.10.1904
02.12.1904</td><td>211
76</td><td>115.33
21.5</td><td>Amos & Smith
65 NHP
10 knots</td><td>Alec L Black
Grimsby</td></tr>
<tr><td colspan="6">29.06.1908 Sold to Naam Ven Stoomv Grotius, Ijmuiden, Holland renamed GROTIUS.
1910 to Sold to Christian M Evensen, Thorshaven, Færoe Islands renamed PAULINE.
12.03.1915 to Earl Steam Fishing Co Ltd, Grimsby renamed EARL GRANARD (GY449).
Apr 1915 Rqd by the Royal Navy as a minesweeper No. FY 2653. 1919 returned.
24.09.1915 to Rushworth Steam Fishing Co Ltd, Grimsby. 16.03.1918 to Isaac Bunch, Grimsby.
22.12.1923 to Great Central Co-op Eng & Rep Co Ltd, Grimsby. 15.06.1928 to Harold Bacon, Grimsby.
26.09.1930 to T C & F Moss Ltd, Grimsby renamed (01.04.1931) CASTLETON.
Nov 1939 Rqd by the Royal Navy as an auxiliary patrol vessel. Jan 1940 returned.
26.06.1940 Vessel sunk by torpedo in the North Sea by U62 (Kapitan Michalowski) off Orkney Islands. All ten crew lost.</td></tr>
<tr><td>KINGSWAY
118940
GY37 Steam Trawler</td><td>62
09.11.1904
13.01.1905</td><td>211
76</td><td>115.33
21.5</td><td>Amos & Smith
65 NHP
10 knots</td><td>Alec L Black
Grimsby</td></tr>
<tr><td colspan="6">08.04.1914 Sold to Strand Steam Fishing Co Ltd, Grimsby.
Dec 1914 Rqd by the Royal Navy as a boom defence vessel . 1919 returned.
28.10.1929 to Samuel Chapman & Sons, Grimsby. 20.04.1931 to Charles Dobson, Grimsby.
Nov 1939 Rqd by the Royal Navy as an auxiliary patrol vessel . Jan 1940 returned.
26.03.1941 Bombed and damaged by German aircraft 10 miles east of Bell Rock.
24.12.1941 to The City Steam Fishing Co Ltd, Hull. 01.10.1943 to R Cammish , Scarborough.
May 1954 Vessel sold to BISCO and allocated to J J King & Co Ltd. Gateshead and broken up.</td></tr>
<tr><td>BASSANIO
118850
H732 Steam Trawler</td><td>63
27.10.1904
02.01.1905</td><td>270
94</td><td>130.0
22.0</td><td>Amos & Smith
80 NHP
10.5 knots</td><td>Hellyer Steam Fishing Co Ltd
Hull</td></tr>
<tr><td colspan="6">15.04.1913 Sold to Imperial Steam Fishing Co Ltd, Hull.
Aug 1914 Rqd by the Royal Navy as a minesweeper No. FY 309. 1919 returned.
07.11.1917 to Talbot Steam Trawling Co Ltd, Fleetwood (FD207). 1927 to Neptune Steam Trawling Co Ltd, Hull (H318).
12.03.1928 C Duggleby, Hull. 22.12.1931 to Viking Steam Trawling Co Ltd, Hull.
1935 Vessel sold to shipbreakers and broken up.</td></tr>
<tr><td>GAUL
121030
H761 Steam Trawler</td><td>64
24.11.1905
30.01.1905</td><td>270
94</td><td>130.0
22.0</td><td>Amos & Smith
65 NHP
10.5 knots</td><td>Imperial Steam
Fishing Co Ltd
Hull</td></tr>
<tr><td colspan="6">Feb 1915 Rqd by the Royal Navy as a minesweeper / bomb thrower No. FY 733. 1920 returned.
02.11.1917 Sold to New Docks Steam Trawling Co Ltd, Fleetwood (FD143).
30.03.1926 During a gale the GAUL was driven into Ballerullen Bay, Tiree, North Hebrides and wrecked. The crew of nine took to the lifeboat but this overturned and seven men were lost, two succeeded in reaching the shore. The GAUL had been on charter carrying fish from Iceland to Grimsby and was being returned to Fleetwood when she was lost.</td></tr>
</table>

<table>
<tr><th rowspan="2">NAME
Official No.
Port Letters Numbers</th><th rowspan="2">Yard No.
Launched
Registered</th><th colspan="2">Registered</th><th rowspan="2">Engine Builder
Horse Power
Reg'd Speed</th><th rowspan="2">OWNER
(Built for)</th></tr>
<tr><th>G Ton
N Ton</th><th>L Ft
B Ft</th></tr>
<tr><td>BUFFALO
118946
GY52 Steam Trawler</td><td>65
10.01.1905
17.03.1905</td><td>230
92</td><td>122.0
21.5</td><td>Amos & Smith
65 NHP
10 knots</td><td>Henry Morris &
Thomas E Fisher
Grimsby</td></tr>
<tr><td colspan="6">Jul 1915 Rqd by the Royal Navy as a minesweeper No. FY 1597 renamed BUFFALO IV. 1919 returned and reverted.
11.11.1926 Sold to Walter Garrett, Grimsby. 26.11.1931 to Thomas Fisher, Grimsby.
1937 Vessel sold for scrap to South Stockton Shipbreaking Co Ltd . 27.04.1937 Arrived Thornaby for breaking up.</td></tr>
<tr><td>ANSON
118943
GY47 Steam Trawler</td><td>66
08.12.1904
21.02.1905</td><td>211
76</td><td>115.33
21.5</td><td>Amos & Smith
65 NHP
10 knots</td><td>William Grant
Grimsby</td></tr>
<tr><td colspan="6">Feb 1915 Rqd by the Royal Navy as a minesweeper No. FY 1090 renamed (1917) ANSON II. 1920 returned and reverted.
16.01.1920 Sold to Sylvia Steam Fishing Co Ltd, Grimsby. 30.08.1922 to Dobson Steam Fishing Co Ltd, Grimsby.
27.02.1931 to Charles Dobson, Grimsby.
1939 Rqd by the Royal Navy as an auxiliary patrol vessel (1940) water tender (1941) renamed COCKADE (1944) renamed STOCKADE. 1946 returned and reverted. 26.03.1945 to Wembley Steam Fishing Co Ltd, Grimsby.
03.07.1945 Vessel laid up at Grimsby.1949 Vessel sold to BISCO and allocated to J J King & Co Ltd, Gateshead.
26.08.1949 Left Grimsby for breaking up on the Tyne.</td></tr>
<tr><td>SISAPON
118942
GY42 Steam Trawler</td><td>67
26.11.1904
11.02.1905</td><td>211
76</td><td>115.33
21.5</td><td>Amos & Smith
65 NHP
10.5 knots</td><td>Standard Steam
Fishing Co Ltd
Grimsby</td></tr>
<tr><td colspan="6">23.05.1917 Vessel captured by U-boat and sunk by gunfire on the Færoe Bank.</td></tr>
<tr><td>SALACON
118948
GY55 Steam Trawler</td><td>68
10.01.1905
25.03.1905</td><td>211
76</td><td>115.33
21.5</td><td>Amos & Smith
65 NHP
10.5 knots</td><td>Standard Steam
Fishing Co Ltd
Grimsby</td></tr>
<tr><td colspan="6">1917 Rqd by the Royal Navy as a fishing trawler (Fishery Reserve). 1919 returned.
15.02.1937 Sold to Henry G Hopwood & Charles Taylor, Grimsby. 24.05.1937 to Japan Fishing Co Ltd, Grimsby.
07.09.1940 Vessel sunk by mine in the North Sea 5.3 miles from Spurn Lighthouse. Eight crew lost four rescued.</td></tr>
<tr><td>MOORE</td><td>69
24.12.1904
09.03.1905</td><td>115
3</td><td>97.0
18.75</td><td>Amos & Smith
65 NHP
10.6 knots</td><td>HM War Office
Whitehall
London</td></tr>
<tr><td colspan="6">No details of type of vessel, or service record has been found. Based at Portsmouth</td></tr>
<tr><td>ABYDOS
118949
GY73 Steam Trawler</td><td>70
08.02.1905
01.04.1905</td><td>230
92</td><td>122.0
21.5</td><td>C.D. Holmes
60 NHP
10 knots</td><td>Roberts & Ruthven Ltd
Grimsby</td></tr>
<tr><td colspan="6">20.03.1907 Vessel stranded near Reyjkanes Lighthouse, Iceland.</td></tr>
<tr><td>OLYMPIA
122687
GY62 Steam Trawler</td><td>71
23.01.1905
26.05.1905</td><td>221
91</td><td>120.0
21.5</td><td>Amos & Smith
66 NHP
10.5 knots</td><td>Great Grimsby & East Coast
Steam Fishing Co Ltd
Grimsby</td></tr>
<tr><td colspan="6">03.08.1916 Vessel captured by U-boat and sunk by gunfire 3 miles off Coquet Island.</td></tr>
<tr><td>BERMUDA
122681
GY56 Steam Trawler</td><td>72
08.02.1905
07.04.1905</td><td>211
76</td><td>115.33
21.5</td><td>C.D. Holmes
60 NHP
10 knots</td><td>Grant & Baker Steam
Fishing Co Ltd
Grimsby</td></tr>
<tr><td colspan="6">Dec 1914 Rqd by the Royal Navy as a minesweeper No. FY 712. 1920 returned. 17.07.1926 Renamed BARBUDA.
11.12.1928 Sold to Sir Thomas Robinson & Son Ltd, Grimsby renamed (22.01.1934) THRACIAN.
1955 Vessel sold for scrap to Van Heyghen Freres, Belgium. 17.12.1955 Arrived Ghent for breaking up.</td></tr>
<tr><td>SENATOR
122685
GY61 Steam Trawler</td><td>73
08.03.1905
15.05.1905</td><td>211
76</td><td>115.33
21.5</td><td>C.D. Holmes
60 NHP
10 knots</td><td>Pelham Steam Fishing Co Ltd
Grimsby</td></tr>
<tr><td colspan="6">02.07.1910 Sold to Earl Steam Fishing Co Ltd, Grimsby. 13.12.1912 to Marshall Line Steam Fishing, Grimsby.
09.05.1913 to John L Green, Grimsby. 20.12.1914 to Reunion Steam Fishing Co Ltd, Grimsby.
14.12.1915 to Walter Crampin, Grimsby. Aug 1915 Rqd by the Royal Navy as a minesweeper No. FY 295.
08.05.1917 Vessel sunk by mine off Tory Island. Mine laid by U80.</td></tr>
</table>

<table>
<tr><th rowspan="2">NAME
Official No.
Port Letters Numbers</th><th rowspan="2">Yard No.
Launched
Registered</th><th colspan="2">Registered</th><th rowspan="2">Engine Builder
Horse Power
Reg'd Speed</th><th rowspan="2">OWNER
(Built for)</th></tr>
<tr><th>G Ton
N Ton</th><th>L Ft
B Ft</th></tr>
<tr><td>EARL WARWICK
122694
GY77 Steam Trawler</td><td>74
18.05.1905
12.07.1905</td><td>208
77</td><td>117.0
21.5</td><td>C.D. Holmes
60 NHP
10 knots</td><td>Earl Steam Fishing Co Ltd
Grimsby</td></tr>
<tr><td colspan="6">19.01.1909 Sold to Christian M Evensen Færoe Island renamed THORA.
10.03.1915 Earl Steam Fishing, Grimsby renamed EARL WARWICK (GY446).
Mar 1915 Rqd by the Royal Navy as a minesweeper No. FY 2652. 1919 returned.
24.09.1915 to Rushworth Steam Fishing Co, Grimsby. 22.03.1918 to Yarborough Steam Fishing Co, Grimsby.
28.05.1919 to United Steam Fishing Co, Grimsby. 21.11.1919 to Vincent Steam Fishing Co, Grimsby.
24.08.1923 to Great Central Co-op Eng & S Rep Co Ltd, Grimsby. 15.06.1928 to Harold Bacon, Grimsby.
26.09.1930 to T C & F Moss Ltd, Grimsby renamed (11.04.1931) CLACTON.
1954 Vessel sold for scrap (for £1924) to Jacques Bakker en Zonen, Belgium. 02.10.1954 Arrived Bruges for breaking up.</td></tr>
<tr><td>EARL OF SHAFTESBURY
121055
H815 Steam Trawler</td><td>75
11.03.1905
25.05.1905</td><td>262
93</td><td>130.0
22.25</td><td>C.D. Holmes
70 NHP
10.5 knots</td><td>National Steam
Trawling Co Ltd
Hull</td></tr>
<tr><td colspan="6">10.08.1908 Vessel reported wrecked off Cape Kanin, north coast of Russia.</td></tr>
<tr><td>ALEXANDRA
122689
GY60 Steam Trawler</td><td>76
22.04.1905
20.06.1905</td><td>179
61</td><td>108.33
21.0</td><td>C.D. Holmes
55 NHP
9.5 knots</td><td>Queen Steam Fishing Co Ltd
Grimsby</td></tr>
<tr><td colspan="6">28.01.1917 Vessel captured by U-boat and sunk by time bombs 60 miles from Longstone Lighthouse (Holy Island).
The skipper was taken prisoner.</td></tr>
<tr><td>SANDRINGHAM
122688
GY59 Steam Trawler</td><td>77
23.03.1905
20.06.1905</td><td>179
61</td><td>108.33
21.0</td><td>C.D. Holmes
55 NHP
9.5 knots</td><td>Queen Steam Fishing Co Ltd
Grimsby</td></tr>
<tr><td colspan="6">Dec 1914 Rqd by the Royal Navy as a boom defence vessel. 1919 returned.
03.03.1930 Sold to Arthur Grant & Sons Ltd, Grimsby renamed PENN.
07.04. 1940 Left Grimsby for a fishing trip in the North Sea. Her empty lifeboat was recovered at Cley Norfolk and wreckage was sighted in approx position 53° 22' N 000° 40' E. 17.04.1940 Vessel posted missing:- lost with all nine crew.</td></tr>
<tr><td>COURSER
122698
GY79 Steam Trawler</td><td>78
18.05.1905
01.08.1905</td><td>227
95</td><td>124.75
22.0</td><td>C.D. Holmes
63 NHP
10.5 knots</td><td>Thomas Baskcomb
Grimsby</td></tr>
<tr><td colspan="6">Oct 1916 Rqd by the Royal Navy as a boom gate vessel. 1920 returned.
02.02.1916 Sold to H Croft Baker & John L Green, Grimsby.
28.02.1916 to S & T Wood, Grimsby. 17.09.1924 to Charles Dobson, Grimsby.
1940 Rqd by the Royal Navy as a minesweeper No. FY 1823 renamed CAVALCADE . Dec 1946 returned and reverted.
08.07.1940 to Consolidated Fisheries Ltd, Grimsby. 09.03.1942 to J Bennett, Grimsby.
30.01.1947 to Planet Fishing Co Ltd, Granton (GN33).
21.04.1952 Vessel sold to BISCO and allocated to Malcolm Brechin Granton and broken up.</td></tr>
<tr><td>CONDOR
122703
GY85 Steam Trawler</td><td>79
04.07.1905
13.08.1905</td><td>227
95</td><td>124.75
22.0</td><td>C.D. Holmes
63 NHP
10.5 knots</td><td>Thomas Baskcomb
Grimsby</td></tr>
<tr><td colspan="6">22.11.1914 Vessel sunk by mine in the North Sea on Newcomb Sand, off Lowestoft.</td></tr>
<tr><td>BARBADOS
122693 / 166635
GY71 Steam Trawler</td><td>80
22.04.1905
05.07.1905</td><td>211
76</td><td>115.33
21.5</td><td>C.D. Holmes
60 NHP
10 knots</td><td>Grant & Baker Steam
Fishing Co Ltd
Grimsby</td></tr>
<tr><td colspan="6">Dec 1914 Rqd by the Royal Navy as a boom defence vessel.1919 returned.
14.12.1928 Sold to Sir Thomas Robinson & Sons Ltd, Grimsby.
1939 Rqd by the Royal Navy as an auxiliary patrol vessel (1940) Royal Navy miscellaneous uses. 1945 returned.
30.05.1940 Registration closed. 30.05.1940 New registration opened No. 166635 renamed ALSATION (GY323).
1944 to Dominion Steam Fishing Co, Grimsby.
1955 Vessel sold to BISCO and allocated to Metal Industries Ltd, Fife. 20.05.1955 Arrived Charlestown for breaking up.</td></tr>
<tr><td>MIKADO
121063
H823 Steam Trawler</td><td>81
05.06.1905
04.08.1905</td><td>265
102</td><td>130.0
22.25</td><td>Amos & Smith
79 NHP
10.5 knots</td><td>Pickering & Haldane's Steam
Trawling Co Ltd
Hull</td></tr>
<tr><td colspan="6">Feb 1915 Rqd by the Royal Navy as a minesweeper No. FY 1222. 1919 returned.
01.11.1918 Sold to W Baker & W Jagger, Grimsby (GY1238). 1920 to Headway Steam Fishing Co Ltd, Grimsby.
1922 to W Goodwin, Halifax, Nova Scotia, Canada. 25.05.1924 Vessel wrecked 15 miles west of Louisbourg, Nova Scotia.</td></tr>
</table>

Yard No.83
1905 PRINCESS LOUISE
Photo:- Barnard and Straker Collection

Yard No.86
1905 CHIEFTAIN
Photo:- Barnard and Straker Collection

Yard No.101
1906 AUCUBA (At Scarborough)
Photo by courtesy of George Scales

<table>
<tr><th rowspan="2">NAME
Official No.
Port Letters Numbers</th><th rowspan="2">Yard No.
Launched
Registered</th><th colspan="2">Registered</th><th rowspan="2">Engine Builder
Horse Power
Reg'd Speed</th><th rowspan="2">OWNER
(Built for)</th></tr>
<tr><th>G Ton
N Ton</th><th>L Ft
B Ft</th></tr>
<tr><td>DYNAMO
121066
H825 Steam Trawler</td><td>82
20.06.1905
24.08.1905</td><td>275
105</td><td>131.66
22.25</td><td>Amos & Smith
79 NHP
10.5 knots</td><td>Francis & Thomas Ross Ltd
Hull</td></tr>
<tr><td colspan="6">28.04.1914 Sold to Canosayy Rebor, Spain renamed VILL de CEE.
1916 to the Russian Navy renamed T25. 1920 to the USSR Navy (1923) renamed SALOA.
1940 Vessel deleted from Lloyds Register of Shipping (War Loss).</td></tr>
<tr><td>PRINCESS LOUISE
121084
H837 Steam Trawler</td><td>83
31.08.1905
10.10.1905</td><td>289
113</td><td>133.33
22.5</td><td>C.D. Holmes
70 NHP
10.5 knots</td><td>Armitage's Steam
Trawling Co Ltd
Hull</td></tr>
<tr><td colspan="6">24.12.1913 Vessel stranded. 03.11.1914 returned to service (H140). Feb 1915 Rqd by the Royal Navy as a minesweeper No. FY 1176 renamed PRINCESS LOUISE II . 1919 returned and reverted.
10.11.1916 to Armitage's Steam Trawling Co Ltd, Fleetwood. 1920 Sun Steam Trawling Co Ltd, Fleetwood (FD365).
1927 to Cie Belge de Pécheries Maritimes, Ostend, Belgium renamed PASTOOR PYPE. (O.176).
1930 to Dewsland Trawlers Ltd, Fleetwood renamed DANELAND (FD58).
1938 to Dinas Steam Trawling Co Ltd, Fleetwood.
06.04.1941 Vessel sunk by German aircraft 30 miles north ½ west of Rathin O'Birne Island. All twelve crew rescued.</td></tr>
<tr><td>KINGFISHER
121072
H830 Steam Trawler</td><td>84
03.08.1905
27.09.1905</td><td>261
93</td><td>130.0
22.25</td><td>C.D. Holmes
70 NHP
10.5 knots</td><td>St Andrews Steam
Fishing Co Ltd
Hull</td></tr>
<tr><td colspan="6">22.04.1912 Vessel wrecked off Portland the south point of Iceland.
When an Icelandic search party reached the wreck it was being swept by heavy seas and there was no sign of the crew. Later the ship's lifeboat was found in a wrecked condition. All twelve crew lost.</td></tr>
<tr><td>FRANKLIN
121088
H841 Steam Trawler</td><td>85
05.08.1905
01.09.1905</td><td>275
103</td><td>131.66
22.25</td><td>C.D. Holmes
70 NHP
10.5 knots</td><td>Francis & Thomas Ross Ltd
Hull</td></tr>
<tr><td colspan="6">1914 Sold to Ramon Canosa, Barcelona, Spain renamed SANTIAGO.
1916 to Russian Navy No. T26. 1920 to the USSR Navy (1923) renamed TRESKA RT26.
1940 Served with the Baltic fleet during World War II . 1949 to USSR fleet based at Murmansk .
1960 Vessel deleted from Lloyds Register of Shipping.</td></tr>
<tr><td>CHIEFTAIN
121095
H847 Steam Trawler</td><td>86
28.09.1905
02.12.1905</td><td>278
105</td><td>133.44
22.25</td><td>C.D. Holmes
70 NHP
10.5 knots</td><td>Marine Steam Fishing Co Ltd
Hull</td></tr>
<tr><td colspan="6">Jan 1915 Rqd by the Royal Navy as a minesweeper / bomb thrower No. FY 945. 1919 returned.
30.10.1918 Sold to East Riding Steam Fishing Co Ltd, Hull. 1926 to Robson Trawlers Ltd, Fleetwood (FD30).
1933 to Transvaal Steam Trawling Co Ltd, Fleetwood. 1936 Vessel sold to shipbreakers and broken up.</td></tr>
<tr><td>TUSCAN
122700
GY82 Steam Trawler</td><td>87
06.07.1905
18.08.1905</td><td>178
58</td><td>105.0
21.25</td><td>C.D. Holmes
55 NHP
9.5 knots</td><td>Onward Steam
Fishing Co Ltd
Grimsby</td></tr>
<tr><td colspan="6">1917 Rqd by the Royal Navy as a fishing trawler (Fishery Reserve). 1919 returned.
09.01.1925 Sold to Olasaboa Soc Ltd, a, San Sabastian, Spain renamed GURE AMETZA.
Nov1968 Vessel sold for scrap to Albizu Y Cia (Iron), Spain and broken up.</td></tr>
<tr><td>BENGAL
122712
GY108 Steam Trawler</td><td>88
30.10.1905
01.01.1906</td><td>211
76</td><td>115.33
21.5</td><td>C.D. Holmes
60 NHP
10.5 knots</td><td>Grant & Baker Steam
Fishing Co Ltd
Grimsby</td></tr>
<tr><td colspan="6">Feb 1915 Rqd by the Royal Navy as a minesweeper No. FY 1150 renamed BENGAL II. 1919 returned and reverted.
14.12.1928 Sold to Sir Thomas Robinson & Sons Ltd, Grimsby.
1939 Rqd by the Royal Navy as a minesweeper No. FY 1591 renamed STAUNCH. 1945 returned and reverted.
1955 Vessel sold to BISCO and allocated to Metal Industries, Fife. 20.05.1955 Arrived Charlestown for breaking up.</td></tr>
<tr><td>ROSALIND
121085
H839 Steam Trawler</td><td>89
02.09.1905
26.10.1905</td><td>174
55</td><td>108.5
21.5</td><td>Amos & Smith
45 NHP
9.5 knots</td><td>Hellyer Steam
Fishing Co Ltd
Hull</td></tr>
<tr><td colspan="6">Oct 1915 Rqd by the Royal Navy as a minesweeper No. FY 1780 renamed ROSALIND II.
1919 returned and reverted. 13.04.1918 Sold to A Gouldby, Hull. 1920 to A E Stock, Lowestoft (LT977).
1926 to Baxter & Catchpole, Lowestoft. 1943 to Rosalind Fishing Co Ltd, Lowestoft. 1954 to Jackson Mills, Fleetwood.
1955 Vessel sold for scrap to West of Scotland Shipbreaking Co Ltd. 13.09.1955 Arrived at Troon for breaking up.</td></tr>
</table>

NAME Official No. Port Letters Numbers	Yard No. Launched Registered	Registered G Ton N Ton	 L Ft B Ft	Engine Builder Horse Power Reg'd Speed	OWNER (Built for)
ARIEL 121091 H843 Steam Trawler	90 30.09.1905 14.11.1905	174 55	108.5 21.5	Amos & Smith 45 NHP 9.5 knots	Hellyer Steam Fishing Co Ltd Hull
Sep 1914 Rqd by the Royal Navy as a minesweeper No. FY 616 renamed (1915) ARIEL II . 1919 returned and reverted. 04.09.1917 Sold to Iago Steam Trawling Co Ltd, Milford Haven. 14.12.1927 to Ocean Steam Fishing Co Ltd, Hull. 25.10.1935 to R Walkington, Fleetwood. 02.08.1945 Vessel sank following a collision with the cargo ship BENLEDI (5943 gt/ b 1930) in thick fog south-west of the Chickens Rock, Irish Sea. The ten crew abandoned the stricken trawler into a lifeboat lowered by the BENLEDI. After being rescued they were landed at Liverpool. The ARIEL had just resumed fishing after delivering a live mine (which she had trawled up) to Douglas I.O.M. were it had been disposed of by Naval authorities.					
BIANCA 121093 H845 Steam Trawler	91 16.10.1905 21.11.1905	174 55	108.5 21.5	Amos & Smith 45 NHP 9.5 knots	Hellyer Steam Fishing Co Ltd Hull
Sep 1914 Rqd by the Royal Navy as a minesweeper No. 600. 1919 returned. 04.07.1917 Sold to C Dobson, Grimsby (GY686). 1920 to Dobson Steam Fishing Co, Grimsby. 14.12.1923 to Kelsall Bros & Beeching Ltd, Hull (H907). 06.03.1936 to Crescent Trawler Co Ltd, Milford Haven. 20.03.1941 Vessel sank in the Irish Sea following an explosion after trawling up a mine or bomb whilst fishing approx 14 miles off Holyhead. Five crew lost four rescued.					
CASSANDRA 121096 H848 Steam Trawler	92 16.10.1905 02.12.1905	174 55	108.5 21.5	Amos & Smith 45 NHP 9.5 knots	Hellyer Steam Fishing Co Ltd Hull
May 1915 Rqd by the Royal Navy as a minesweeper No. FY 1767 renamed CASSANDRA II. 1919 returned and reverted. 1920 to Alliance Steam Trawling Co Ltd, Hull. 1922 to J Ellis & Co, Grimsby (GY106). 1925 to John Robinson Ltd, Grimsby. 1927 to B Allenby, Aberdeen (A236). 1932 to G W Fowler, Aberdeen. 26.08.1935 Vessel foundered in the North Sea after springing a leak 46 miles east north-east of Aberdeen. All crew rescued by the Peterhead drifter HOPEFUL PD504 (94 gt/ b 1907).					
OBERON 121100 H851 Steam Trawler	93 31.10.1905 14.12.1905	174 55	108.5 21.5	Amos & Smith 45 NHP 9.5 knots	Hellyer Steam Fishing Co Ltd Hull
18.03.1913 Vessel posted missing:- lost with all nine crew whilst fishing in the North Sea.					
BELOVAR 122715 GY109 Steam Trawler	94 29.11.1905 01.02.1906	242 93	125.0 22.0	C.D. Holmes 65 NHP 10.5 knots	Alec Black Grimsby
31.01.1913 Sailed from Fleetwood on a 12 day fishing trip. Last reported off the west coast of Scotland. 06.02.1913 Vessel posted missing:- lost with all ten crew.					
ANTONIO 123216 H857 Steam Trawler	95 29.11.1905 01.01.1906	174 55	108.5 21.5	Amos & Smith 45 NHP 9.5 knots	Hellyer Steam Fishing Co Ltd Hull
12.03.1906 Vessel posted missing:- lost with all hands whilst fishing in the North Sea on her second voyage.					
VIOLA 123229 H868 Steam Trawler	96 17.01.1906 14.02.1906	174 55	108.5 21.5	Amos & Smith 45 NHP 9.5 knots	Hellyer Steam Fishing Co Ltd Hull
Sep 1914 Rqd by the Royal Navy as a minesweeper No. FY 614 renamed VIOLA III. 1919 returned. 1919 Sold to A/S Sandsfjord Trawlfiskeselskap, Sandsfjord, Norway renamed KAPSDUEN. 1926 to Cia Argentina de Pesca SA, Buenos Aires, Argentina renamed DIAS. *(Converted to whaling vessel).* 1974 Vessel scuttled at its moorings in Grytuiken, South Georgia Falkland Islands. 1999 Still intact.					
JESSICA 123232 H870 Steam Trawler	97 17.01.1906 01.03.1906	174 55	108.5 21.5	Amos & Smith 45 NHP 9.5 knots	Hellyer Steam Fishing Co Ltd Hull
Aug 1914 Rqd by the Royal Navy as a minesweeper No. FY 13. 1919 returned. 31.07.1917 Sold to D Curzon, Milford Haven. Nov 1919 to Dobson Steam Fishing Co Ltd, Grimsby (GY674). 1923 to Kelsall Bros & Beeching Ltd, Hull (H895). 1936 Vessel sold to shipbreakers and broken up.					
MIRANDA 123237 H875 Steam Trawler	98 13.02.1906 15.03.1906	174 55	108.5 21.5	Amos & Smith 45 NHP 9.5 knots	Hellyer Steam Fishing Co Ltd Hull
Sep 1914 Rqd by the Royal Navy as a minesweeper No. FY 601 renamed MIRANDA III. 1918 returned and reverted. 1918 Sold to C Curzon, Milford Haven. 14.01.1918 Vessel wrecked in Pelwick Bay.					

Rosalind – Ariel – Bianca – Cassandra –
Oberon – Belovar – Antonio – Viola – Jessica –

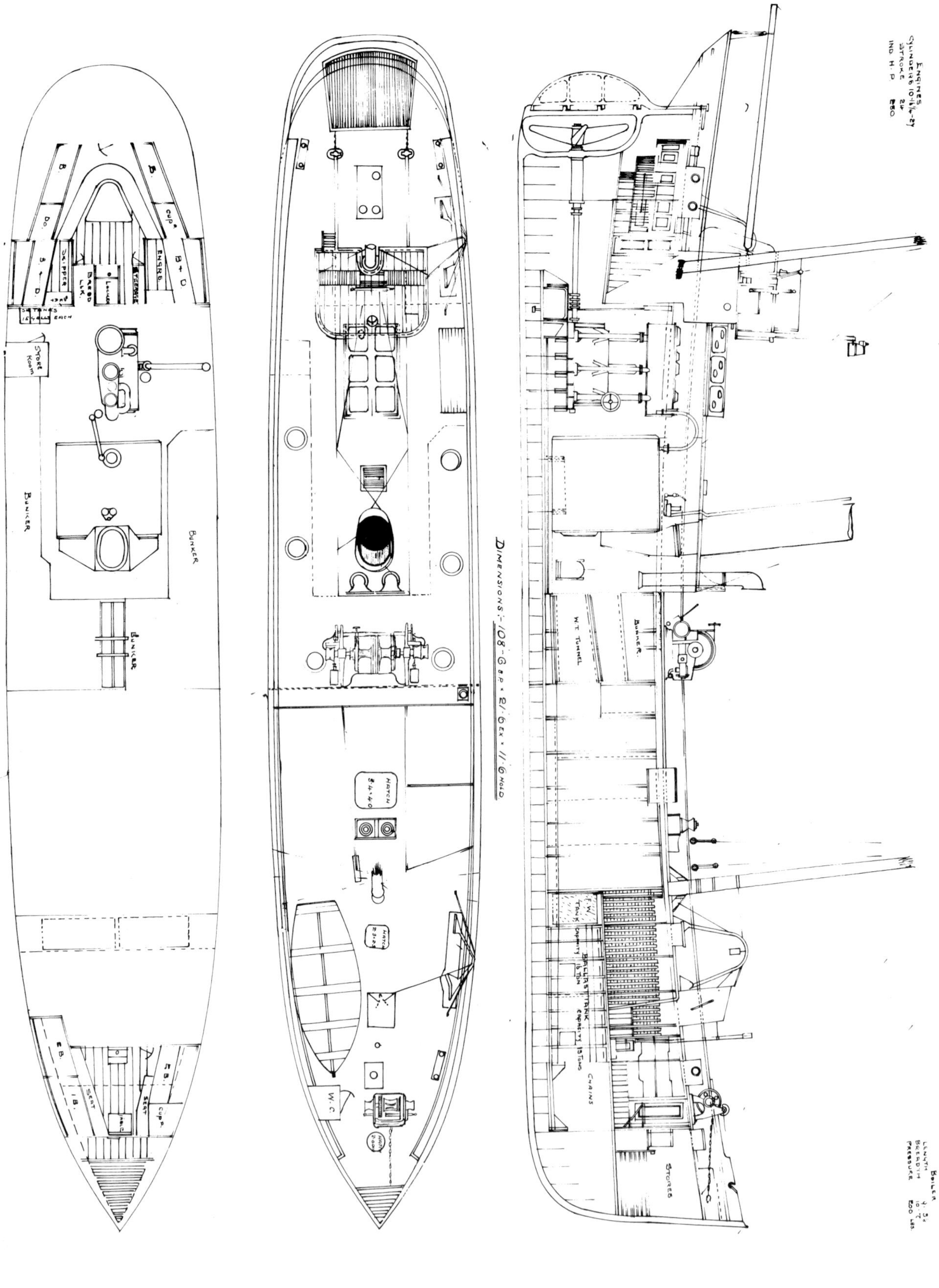

<table>
<tr><th rowspan="2">NAME
Official No.
Port Letters Numbers</th><th rowspan="2">Yard No.
Launched
Registered</th><th colspan="2">Registered</th><th rowspan="2">Engine Builder
Horse Power
Reg'd Speed</th><th rowspan="2">OWNER
(Built for)</th></tr>
<tr><th>G Ton
N Ton</th><th>L Ft
B Ft</th></tr>
<tr><td>OCTAVIA
123238
H876 Steam Trawler</td><td>99
13.02.1906
22.03.1906</td><td>174
55</td><td>108.5
21.5</td><td>Amos & Smith
45 NHP
9.5 knots</td><td>Hellyer Steam
Fishing Co Ltd
Hull</td></tr>
<tr><td colspan="6">1917 Rqd by the Royal Navy as a fishing trawler (Fishery Reserve). 1919 returned.
09.11.1919 Sold to C Dobson, Grimsby.(GY102). 1920 to Home & Colonial Steam Fishing Co Ltd, Yarmouth.
Oct 1925 to F Parkes, Grimsby. 1926 to W C Farrow, Hull (H274). 1927 to Ocean Steam Fishing Co Ltd, Hull.
06.11.1929 to Holderness Steam Trawling Co Ltd, Hull. 1936 to R Hudson, (Managers), Fleetwood.
13.02.1937 Vessel sank following a collision with the Fleetwood trawler GEORGE COUSINS LO66 (276 gt/ b 1919) off Ramsey, Isle of Man. All crew rescued.</td></tr>
<tr><td>BORNEO
122719
GY115 Steam Trawler</td><td>100
28.12.1905
16.02.1906</td><td>211
76</td><td>115.33
21.5</td><td>C.D. Holmes
60 NHP
10 knots</td><td>Grant & Robinson
Grimsby</td></tr>
<tr><td colspan="6">Nov 1914 Rqd by the Royal Navy as a minesweeper No. FY 1809.
18.06.1917 Vessel sunk by mine off Beachy Head. Mine laid by UC17 on the same day.</td></tr>
<tr><td>AUCUBA
123561
GY117 Steam Trawler</td><td>101
13.01.1906
09.03.1906</td><td>211
76</td><td>115.33
21.5</td><td>C.D. Holmes
60 NHP
10 knots</td><td>Grant & Robinson
Grimsby</td></tr>
<tr><td colspan="6">Dec 1914 Rqd by the Royal Navy as a boom defence vessel. 1919 returned.
01.06.1927 Sold to Arthur Grant & Sons, Grimsby. 07.03.1930 to Rugby Steam Fishing Co Ltd, Grimsby.
29.04.1933 to Filey United Steam Trawling Co Ltd, Scarborough. 07.10.1942 to Parkholme Trawlers Ltd, Grimsby.
01.11.1944 to Rushcliffe Trawlers Ltd, Hull. 08.04.1948 to Derwent Trawlers Ltd, Grimsby.
05.09.1951 Vessel sank following a collision with the Italian ss MARIA BIBOLINI (7167 gt/ b 1943) while trawling in darkness off Robin Hoods Bay Yorkshire. Unable to launch the lifeboat all ten crew were rescued by a boat from the MARIA BILOLINI and subsequently landed at Rotterdam.</td></tr>
<tr><td>NERISSA
123245
H879 Steam Trawler</td><td>102
27.02.1906
04.04.1906</td><td>173
53</td><td>108.5
21.5</td><td>Amos & Smith
45 NHP
9.5 knots</td><td>Hellyer Steam
Fishing Co Ltd
Hull</td></tr>
<tr><td colspan="6">Aug 1915 Rqd by the Royal Navy as a minesweeper renamed NERISSA II No. FY 1793.
01.07.1917 Sold to W A Massey & Sons Ltd, Hull.
28.02.1918 Vessel wrecked off the island of Lemnos, Greece at the end of Valanidhi Shoal whilst still on Admiralty service.</td></tr>
<tr><td>JULIET
123246
H880 Steam Trawler</td><td>103
27.02.1906
04.04.1906</td><td>173
53</td><td>108.5
21.5</td><td>Amos & Smith
45 NHP
9.5 knots</td><td>Hellyer Steam
Fishing Co Ltd
Hull</td></tr>
<tr><td colspan="6">Sep 1914 Rqd by the Royal Navy as a minesweeper No. FY 45. 1919 returned.
04.09.1917 Sold to Lady Beardmore / C Curzon, Milford Haven. 1919 to Dobson Steam Fishing Co Ltd, Grimsby (GY660).
1923 to Kelsall Bros & Beeching Ltd, Hull (H902). 06.03.1936 to Crescent Trawlers Co Ltd, Hull.
20.08.1941 Vessel sunk by German aircraft 30 miles south of Old Head of Kinsale. All eleven crew rescued.</td></tr>
<tr><td>PHOEBE
123253
H881 Steam Trawler</td><td>104
12.04.1906
08.05.1906</td><td>178
53</td><td>108.5
21.5</td><td>Amos & Smith
45 NHP
9.5 knots</td><td>Hellyer Steam Fishing
Co Ltd
Hull</td></tr>
<tr><td colspan="6">Sep 1914 Rqd by the Royal Navy as a minesweeper/bomb thrower No. FY 44 renamed (1915) PHOEBE II.
1919 returned and reverted. 04.09.1917 Sold to Mrs H D Hordern & C Curzon, Milford Haven.
1919 to Dobson Steam Fishing Co Ltd, Grimsby (GY665). 1923 to Hull Steam Fishing & Ice Co Ltd, Hull (H901).
1936 to Crescent Trawlers Co Ltd, Milford Haven. 1948 to N G Chamberlain, Milford Haven.
21.01.1952 Vessel sold to shipbreakers. May 1952 Broken up at Milford Haven.</td></tr>
<tr><td>HERO
123259
H886 Steam Trawler</td><td>105
10.05.1906
12.06.1906</td><td>173
53</td><td>108.5
21.5</td><td>Amos & Smith
45 NHP
9.5 knots</td><td>Hellyer Steam
Fishing Co Ltd
Hull</td></tr>
<tr><td colspan="6">03.05.1915 Vessel captured by U-boat in the North Sea and sunk by time bombs 150 miles off Hornsea, Yorkshire.</td></tr>
<tr><td>ANGELO
123263
H890 Steam Trawler</td><td>106
24.05.1906
26.06.1906</td><td>173
53</td><td>108.5
21.5</td><td>Amos & Smith
45 NHP
9.5 knots</td><td>Hellyer Steam
Fishing Co Ltd
Hull</td></tr>
<tr><td colspan="6">21.05.1915 Vessel sunk by mine in the North Sea on the Dogger Bank.</td></tr>
<tr><td>GONZALO
123265
H892 Steam Trawler</td><td>107
09.06.1906
09.07.1906</td><td>173
53</td><td>108.5
21.5</td><td>Amos & Smith
45 NHP
9.5 knots</td><td>Hellyer Steam
Fishing Co Ltd
Hull</td></tr>
<tr><td colspan="6">Jun 1915 Rqd by the Royal Navy as a minesweeper No. FY 2578. 1919 returned.
31.07.1917 Sold to W A Massey & Sons Ltd, Hull. 1920 to Isaac Bunch, Grimsby renamed HONORIA (GY1403).
Nov 1938 Vessel sold to shipbreakers and broken up.</td></tr>
</table>

<table>
<tr><th rowspan="2">NAME
Official No.
Port Letters Numbers</th><th rowspan="2">Yard No.
Launched
Registered</th><th colspan="2">Registered</th><th rowspan="2">Engine Builder
Horse Power
Reg'd Speed</th><th rowspan="2">OWNER
(Built for)</th></tr>
<tr><th>G Ton
N Ton</th><th>L Ft
B Ft</th></tr>
<tr><td>FORTUNA
123567
GY140 Steam Trawler</td><td>108
14.03.1906
08.05.1906</td><td>259
111</td><td>128.33
22.0</td><td>C.D. Holmes
63 NHP
10.75 knots</td><td>Alec L Black
Grimsby</td></tr>
<tr><td colspan="6">16.06.1909 Sold to South Western Steam Fishing Co Ltd, Grimsby. 05.05.1913 to Thomas W Baskcomb, Grimsby.
27.09.1915 to Spurn Steam Trawling Co, Grimsby. 29.11.1916 to George F Sleight, Grimsby.
1917 Rqd by the Royal Navy as a fishing trawler (Fishery Reserve). 1919 returned.
28.11.1933 to Dobson Ship Repair Co Ltd, Grimsby. 11.06.1940 Rqd by the Royal Navy as an auxiliary patrol vessel.
03.04.1941 Vessel sunk by German aircraft off St Abb's Head. All crew lost.</td></tr>
<tr><td>INVICTA
123568
GY146 Steam Trawler</td><td>109
10.04.1906
26.05.1906</td><td>259
111</td><td>128.33
22.0</td><td>C.D. Holmes
63 NHP
10.75 knots</td><td>Alec L Black
Grimsby</td></tr>
<tr><td colspan="6">11.06.1909 Sold to South Western Steam Fishing Co Ltd, Grimsby.
17.12.1911 to P A Olafsson, Patriksfjord, Iceland renamed EGGERT OLAFSSON (RE156).
31.01.1913 to Aakties Eggert Olafsson (Elias Stefonsson) Patriksfjord (BA127).
15.12.1917 to Marine Nationale Francaise (French Navy) renamed GORILLE.
1919 to Maurice Bernard, Boulogne renamed CYCLONE. (B778). 1927 to Mre Wattare Boulogne.
1929 to Victor Fourny Boulogne. 1932 to Commandant Baule, Boulogne.
1933 to Mre Wattiau Boulogne renamed SAINTE THERESE DE LISIEUX .
1936 Vessel sold to shipbreakers and broken up.</td></tr>
<tr><td>EARL HEREFORD
123569
GY147 Steam Trawler</td><td>110
10.04.1906
18.06.1906</td><td>259
111</td><td>128.33
22.0</td><td>C.D. Holmes
63 NHP
10.75 knots</td><td>Earl Steam Fishing Co Ltd
Grimsby</td></tr>
<tr><td colspan="6">21.12.1912 Sold to Christian M Evensen, Thorshaven , Færoe Islands.
1917 to French Navy as an auxiliary patrol vessel renamed GUENON.
1919 to F Evan, L`Orient France renamed PEN-ER-VRO.1933 to L Ballias renamed RAUZAN.
1942 Rqd by the German Navy No. V421. 04.06.1944. Lost during the invasion of Europe. 1951 Vessel raised and scrapped.</td></tr>
<tr><td>Not Built</td><td>111</td><td colspan="4">Ordered by Alec L Black Grimsby but cancelled</td></tr>
<tr><td>REGAL
123573
GY158 Steam Trawler</td><td>112
10.05.1906
07.07.1906</td><td>212
77</td><td>116.0
21.5</td><td>Amos & Smith
63 NHP
10 knots</td><td>Loyal Steam Fishing Co Ltd
Grimsby</td></tr>
<tr><td colspan="6">Jun 1915 Rqd by the Royal Navy as a minesweeper No. FY 1539. 1919 returned.
04.07.1923 Vessel wrecked off Aveiro, Portugal after being abandoned.
The skipper and crew succeeded in getting ashore safely and made their way to Oporto.</td></tr>
<tr><td>SICYON
123575
GY163 Steam Trawler</td><td>113
24.05.1906
01.08.1906</td><td>282
120</td><td>130.0
22.25</td><td>Amos & Smith
92 NHP
10.5 knots</td><td>Standard Steam
Fishing Co Ltd
Grimsby</td></tr>
<tr><td colspan="6">Sep 1914 Rqd by the Royal Navy as a minesweeper No. FY 30. 1919 returned.
15.01.1933 Vessel wrecked after running aground in a blizzard off Heirakkasletta, north-east Iceland. All twelve crew saved.</td></tr>
<tr><td>PRETORIA
123579
GY180 Steam Trawler</td><td>114
23.06.1906
27.08.1906</td><td>282
120</td><td>130.0
22.25</td><td>Amos & Smith
92 NHP
10.5 knots</td><td>Great Grimsby & East Coast
Steam Fishing Co Ltd
Grimsby</td></tr>
<tr><td colspan="6">Mar 1915 Rqd by the Royal Navy as a minesweeper No. FY 32 renamed PRETORIA II .Sep 1915 returned and reverted.
10.07.1917 Vessel captured by U-boat and sunk by gunfire 60 miles south by east of Sydero Færoe Islands.</td></tr>
<tr><td>SHERATON
125043
GY230 Steam Trawler</td><td>115
19.11.1906
15.01.1907</td><td>282
120</td><td>130.0
22.25</td><td>Amos & Smith
92 NHP
10.5 knots</td><td>Standard Steam Fishing Co
Grimsby</td></tr>
<tr><td colspan="6">Jun 1916 Rqd by the Royal Navy as a boom defence vessel No. FY 1659. 1919 returned.
05.06.1940 Rqd by the Royal Navy as an auxiliary patrol vessel / minesweeper No. FY 1788. Sep 1944 returned.
17.05.1946 Vessel sold to the RAF and used as a target vessel. 23.04.1947 Vessel wrecked near Hunstanton Lighthouse.</td></tr>
<tr><td>NORTHUMBRIA
123580
GY169 Steam Trawler</td><td>116
23.06.1906
29.08.1906</td><td>211
76</td><td>115.33
21.5</td><td>C.D. Holmes
60 NHP
10 knots</td><td>East Anglia Steam
Fishing Co Ltd
Grimsby</td></tr>
<tr><td colspan="6">Sep 1914 Rqd by the Royal Navy as a minesweeper No. FY 623.
03.03.1917 Vessel sunk by mine near May Island. The mine was laid by UC29 on same day.</td></tr>
</table>

Yard No.118
1906 RIGOLETTO
Photo by courtesy of The Grimsby Evening Telegraph

Yard No.119
1906 BRITISH EMPIRE
Photo:- Barnard and Straker Collection

Yard No.131
1906 VIRGINIAN
Photo by courtesy of Steve Pulfrey

NAME Official No. Port Letters Numbers	Yard No. Launched Registered	Registered G Ton N Ton	 L Ft B Ft	Engine Builder Horse Power Reg'd Speed	OWNER (Built for)
RIANO 123583 GY181 Steam Trawler	117 25.06.1906 05.09.1906	212 79	117.0 22.0	C.D. Holmes 63 NHP 10.5 knots	George F Sleight Grimsby
Nov 1914 Rqd by the Royal Navy as a minesweeper No. FY 671. 1919 returned. 01.10.1933 Sold to Sleight & Humphrey, Grimsby. 19.05.1949 to George F Sleight & Sons Ltd, Grimsby. 15.10.1956 to Derwent Trawlers Ltd, Grimsby. 25.07.1960 to T C & F Moss, Grimsby. 28.07.1960 Vessel sold for scrap to Jacques Bakker en Zonen, Belgium. 01.08.1960 Arrived Bruges for breaking up.					
RIGOLETTO 123584 GY185 Steam Trawler	118 25.07.1906 13.09.1906	212 79	117.0 22.0	C.D. Holmes 63 NHP 10.5 knots	George F Sleight Grimsby
Dec 1914 Rqd by the Royal Navy as a minesweeper No. FY 726. 1919 returned. 17.11.1933 Sold to Sleight & Humphrey, Grimsby. 18.04.1940 Rqd by the Royal Navy as a boom defence vessel No. FY 4.451. 09.07.1945 returned. 19.05.1949 to George F Sleight & Sons Ltd, Grimsby. 15.10.1956 to Derwent Trawlers Ltd, Grimsby. 1956 Vessel sold to BISCO and allocated to J J King & Co Ltd. 23.10.1956 Arrived Gateshead for breaking up.					
BRITISH EMPIRE 123285 H908 Steam Trawler	119 23.08.1906 15.10.1906	278 101	135.0 22.25	C.D. Holmes 70 NHP 11 knots	Cargill Steam Fishing Co Ltd Hull
30.12.1913 Vessel wrecked 1.5 miles south-west of Kolsvig, Northwest Fjords, Iceland in darkness and heavy rain. The trawler's engine room rapidly flooded so distress rockets were fired. At first light the twelve crew were able to make their way ashore and were escorted to safety by an Icelandic rescue party.					
QUAIL 123593 GY215 Steam Trawler	120 02.10.1906 30.11.1906	265 108	130.0 22.5	C.D. Holmes 70 NHP 11 knots	Thomas Baskcomb Grimsby
1917 Rqd by the Royal Navy as a fishing trawler (Fishery Reserve). 1919 returned. 1933 Sold to Amalgamated Steam Fishing Co Ltd, Grimsby. 18.10.1935 Vessel sold to Dutch shipbreakers and broken up.					
GREBE 123597 GY219 Steam Trawler	121 02.10.1906 13.12.1906	265 108	130.0 22.5	C.D. Holmes 70 NHP 11 knots	Thomas Baskcomb Grimsby
1917 Rqd by the Royal Navy as a fishing trawler (Fishery Reserve). 1919 returned. 1933 Sold to Amalgamated Steam Fishing Co Ltd, Grimsby. 18.10.1935 Vessel sold to Dutch shipbreakers and broken up.					
TUNISIAN 123589 GY205 Steam Trawler	122 06.09.1906 06.11.1906	221 76	115.33 21.5	C.D. Holmes 76 NHP 10 knots	Thomas Robinson Grimsby
09.06.1915 Vessel captured by U-boat in the North Sea and sunk by gunfire 95 miles north-east by north of Spurn Point.					
RUSSELL 123585 GY192 Steam Trawler	123 25.07.1906 29.09.1906	246 100	125.0 22.0	C.D. Holmes 63 NHP 10.5 knots	William Garrett Grimsby
May 1915 Rqd by the Royal Navy as a minelayer (24 mines) No. N3A and N87 renamed RUSSELL II. 1920 returned. 01.06.1927 to Arthur Grant, Grimsby. 28.02.1930 to Rugby Steam Fishing Co Ltd, Grimsby renamed RUSSELL. 28.02.1934 to Taylor Steam Fishing Co Ltd, Grimsby. 1956 Vessel sold to BISCO and allocated to C W Dorkin & Co Ltd. 02.06.1956 Arrived Gateshead for breaking up.					
RODNEY 123587 GY195 Steam Trawler	124 22.08.1906 22.10.1906	246 100	125.0 22.0	C.D. Holmes 63 NHP 10.5 knots	William Grant Grimsby
May 1915 Rqd by the Royal Navy as a minesweeper No. FY 953 renamed (1917) RODNEY III. 1919 returned and reverted. 22.09.1918 Sold to Smith & Peacock, Grimsby. 16.01.1921 to Sylvia Steam Fishing Co Ltd, Grimsby. 30.08.1922 to Dobson Steam Fishing Co Ltd, Grimsby. 25.02.1931 to Charles Dobson, Grimsby. 02.10.1940 to Consolidated Fisheries, Grimsby. 03.03.1941 Vessel sank following a collision with the Grimsby trawler CARIEDA GY908 *(see Yard No. 275).*					
FALSTAFF 123292 H917 Steam Trawler	125 04.10.1906 12.11.1906	173 53	108.5 21.5	Amos & Smith 45 NHP 9.5 knots	Hellyer Steam Fishing Co Ltd Hull
Oct 1915 Rqd by the Royal Navy as a minesweeper No. FY 1795. 1917 returned. 31.07.1917 Sold to C Curzon, Milford Haven. 1920 to T Lerchundi & Hijos, San Sabastian, Spain renamed PASAYA. 16.03.1971 Vessel foundered 30 miles off Pasages following leak in the engine room.					

NAME Official No. Port Letters Numbers	Yard No. Launched Registered	Registered G Ton N Ton	 L Ft B Ft	Engine Builder Horse Power Reg'd Speed	OWNER (Built for)
BEATRICE 123298 H922 Steam Trawler	126 22.10.1906 03.12.1906	173 53	108.5 21.5	Amos & Smith 45 NHP 9.5 knots	Hellyer Steam Fishing Co Ltd Hull
Sep 1914 Rqd by the Royal Navy as a minesweeper No. FY 621. 1919 returned. 31.07.1917 Sold to C Curzon, Milford Haven. 1919 to J McKechnie / Curzon, Hull. 1919 to C Dobson, Grimsby (GY637). 1920 to Dobson Steam Fishing Co Ltd, Grimsby. 1923 to Hull Steam Fishing & Ice Co, Hull (H906). 1936 Vessel sold to shipbreakers and broken up.					
DORCAS 124731 H925 Steam Trawler	127 17.11.1906 17.12.1906	173 53	108.5 21.5	Amos & Smith 45 NHP 9.5 knots	Hellyer Steam Fishing Co Ltd Hull
Aug 1914 Rqd by the Royal Navy as a minesweeper No. FY 14. 1919 returned. 31.07.1917 Sold to C Curzon, Milford Haven. 1920 to T Lerchundi & Hijos, San Sabastian , Spain renamed DONOSTIA. 1945 to Soc R C Hijos & TL, San Sabastian. 1958 to Luis Perez Sanchez, San Sabastian. 1973 Vessel sold to shipbreakers in Spain and broken up.					
BLANCHE 124735 H928 Steam Trawler	128 18.12.1906 21.01.1907	173 53	108.5 21.5	Amos & Smith 45 NHP 9.5 knots	Hellyer Steam Fishing Co Ltd Hull
May 1915 Rqd by the Royal Navy as a minesweeper No. FY 1768. 1919 returned. 31.07.1917 Sold to Capt Q Dick / Curzon, Milford Haven.1929 to Countess Howe / Curzon, Hull. 1938 to J W Hates, Hull. 1945 to Wendover Fishing Co Ltd, Grimsby (GY133). 1946 to St Christopher Steam Fishing Co Ltd, Grimsby. 1952 Vessel sold to shipbreakers. 26.09.1952 Registration closed on advice that the vessel was broken up.					
CICERO 124742 H931 Steam Trawler	129 18.12.1906 11.02.1907	173 53	108.5 21.5	Amos & Smith 45 NHP 9.5 knots	Hellyer Steam Fishing Co Ltd Hull
Sep 1914 Rqd by the Royal Navy as a minesweeper No. FY 149 renamed (1917) CICERO II. 1919 returned and reverted. 31.07.1917 Sold to C Curzon, Milford Haven. 1926 to Brand & Curzon Ltd, Milford Haven. 16.11.1929 to Trident Steam Fishing Co Ltd, Hull renamed BARNSNESS. 16.10.1934 to A Robertson, Aberdeen (A146). 1938 to A King, Aberdeen. 1940 G Robb & Sons Ltd, Aberdeen. 27.02.1940 Rqd by the Royal Navy as a barrage balloon vessel No. FY 4.443. 30.12.1944 returned. 1952 Vessel sold to BISCO and allocated to shipbreakers. Mar 1952 Broken up at Bo' ness.					
TOUCHSTONE 124747 H934 Steam Trawler	130 18.01.1907 01.03.1907	173 53	108.5 21.5	Amos & Smith 45 NHP 9.5 knots	Hellyer Steam Fishing Co Ltd Hull
Sep 1914 Rqd by the Royal Navy as a minesweeper No. FY 46. Nov 1918 returned. 31.07.1917 Sold to C Curzon, Milford Haven. 13.05.1919 to Mons Steam Fishing Co Ltd, Hull. 02.02.1934 to J C Douglas Johnstone, Aberdeen (A229). 1938 to D Wood, Aberdeen. 19.02.1940 Rqd by the Royal Navy as a minesweeper No. FY 1610. 05.12.1941 returned. 1943 to P & J Johnstone, Aberdeen. 1947 to J Brown, Aberdeen. 1956 Vessel sold to BISCO and allocated to Malcolm Brechin. Jun 1956 Broken up at Granton.					
VIRGINIAN 123600 GY211 Steam Trawler	131 22.10.1906 20.12.1906	211 76	115.33 21.5	C.D. Holmes 60 NHP 10 knots	Onward Steam Fishing Co Ltd Grimsby
Sep 1914 Rqd by the Royal Navy as a minesweeper No. FY 618 renamed VIRGINIAN II. 1919 returned and reverted. 05.11.1946 Vessel sank following a collision in the North Sea with the troopship EMPIRE RAPIER (7177 gt/ b 1943) 30 miles north north-east of the Humber. After anchoring alongside the stricken trawler an attempt was made take the VIRGINIAN in tow, but she sank. The eleven crew were taken aboard the EMPIRE RAPIER and were landed at Hull.					
AGILE 125056 GY263 Steam Trawler	132 17.01.1907 22.04.1907	246 100	125.0 22.0	C.D. Holmes 63 NHP 10.5 knots	William Grant Grimsby
Dec 1914 Rqd by the Royal Navy as a minesweeper No. FY 697. 27.04.1917 Vessel sunk by mine off Sunk Head light-vessel Harwich. Mines laid by UC 11 on 25.04.1917.					
ST. VINCENT 124743 H933 Steam Trawler	133 03.01.1907 12.02.1907	185 67	110.5 21.5	Amos & Smith 50 NHP 10 knots	Hull Steam Fishing & Ice Co Ltd Hull
Oct 1914 Rqd by the Royal Navy as a minesweeper No. FY 369 renamed (1915) ST. VINCENT II. 1919 returned and reverted. 1936 Sold to R P Lewis, Milford Haven. 1945 to Ritchie & Davis Ltd, Milford Haven. 1951 Vessel sold for scrap to Thos W Ward Ltd, Milford Haven. 21.01.1952 Registration closed on advice that breaking up was completed.					

Yard No.138
1907 PRINCESSE MARIE - JOSÉ
Photo:- Barnard and Straker Collection

Yard No.144
1913 THURINGIA
Photo:- Barnard and Straker Collection

Yard No.148
1907 CLAIRE
Photo by courtesy of The Grimsby Evening Telegraph

NAME Official No. Port Letters Numbers	Yard No. Launched Registered	Registered G Ton N Ton	 L Ft B Ft	Engine Builder Horse Power Reg'd Speed	OWNER (Built for)
ST. LUCIA 124749 H937 Steam Trawler	134 03.01.1907 15.03.1907	185 67	110.5 21.5	Amos & Smith 50 NHP 10 knots	Hull Steam Fishing & Ice Co Ltd Hull
1917 Rqd by the Royal Navy as a fishing trawler (Fishery Reserve). 1919 returned. 1936 Sold to Colin H Brand, Milford Haven. 1938 to R P Lewis, Aberdeen. 1947 to R Lewis, F Nelson, L McKinnon and others Castlebay. 1952 Vessel sold for scrap to Thos W Ward Ltd. 12.02.1952 Arrived Preston for breaking up.					
FRASER 124778 H951 Steam Trawler	135 18.03.1907 12.07.1907	310 123	137 22.75	C.D. Holmes 84 NHP 11 knots	Neptune Steam Fishing Co Ltd Hull
Apr 1915 Rqd by the Royal Navy as a minesweeper No. FY 1379. 17.06.1917 Vessel sunk by mine off Boulogne. Mines laid the same day by UC65.					
FEDERAL 125058 GY272 Steam Trawler	136 14.02.1907 08.05.1907	243 84	120.5 22.0	C.D. Holmes 63 NHP 10.5 knots	Pelham Steam Fishing Co Ltd Grimsby
14.01.1911 Sold to Thomas Baskcomb, Grimsby renamed ROSELLA. 29.10.1914 Vessel sunk by mine in the North Sea 25 miles south east of the Tynemouth.					
RENOWN 125060 GY281 Steam Trawler	137 14.02.1907 29.05.1907	243 84	120.5 22.0	C.D. Holmes 63 NHP 10.5 knots	Marshall Line Steam Fishing Co Ltd Grimsby
20.01.1911 Sold to Thomas Baskcomb, Grimsby renamed CORELLA. Dec 1914 Rqd by the Royal Navy as a minesweeper No. FY 952. 1919 returned. 22.09.1919 Vessel posted missing:- lost with all hands.					
PRINCESSE MARIE-JOSE O60 Steam Trawler	138 15.04.1907 18.07.1907	270 152	125.0 22.0	C.D. Holmes 63 NHP 10.5 knots	A T Golder Ostend Belgium
21.03.1912 Vessel sank following a collision off the coast of Iceland.					
EROS 125064 GY284 Steam Trawler	139 15.04.1907 15.07.1907	286 122	135.0 22.5	C.D. Holmes 70 NHP 11 knots	Roberts & Ruthven Ltd Grimsby
Dec 1914 Rqd by the Royal Navy as a minesweeper No. FY 698. 05.09.1917 Vessel sunk by mine off Folkestone.					
SANSON 125065 GY295 Steam Trawler	140 25.06.1907 07.08.1907	231 90	120.0 22.0	Amos & Smith 69 NHP 10 knots	Standard Steam Fishing Co Ltd Grimsby
Sep 1915 Rqd by the Royal Navy as a minesweeper / bomb thrower No. FY 1863. 1919 returned. 15.02.1937 Sold to Hopewell & Taylor, Grimsby. 26.05.1937 to Japan Fishing Co Ltd, Grimsby. 29.11.1939 Rqd by the Royal Navy as a minesweeper No. FY 901 (1943) fuel supply vessel No. Y7.31. 24.09.1946 returned. 1951 Vessel sold to shipbreakers for scrap and broken up.					
ROMAN 124774 H948 Steam Trawler	141 16.03.1907 13.06.1907	357 149	145.0 24.0	C.D. Holmes 113 NHP 11 knots	Imperial Steam Fishing Co Ltd Hull
1911 Sold to Packers Steam Ship Co Ltd, Vancouver, Canada. 24.11.1916 Vessel wrecked on Key Reef, Snow Pass, Alaska.					
STAUNTON 127821 GY350 Steam Trawler	142 21.10.1907 22.01.1908	282 120	130.0 22.25	Amos & Smith 90 NHP 10.75 knots	Standard Steam Fishing Co Ltd Grimsby
Nov 1914 Rqd by the Royal Navy as a minesweeper No. FY 710. 1920 returned. June 1940 - 26.07.1940 Rqd by the Royal Navy as an auxiliary patrol vessel. 28.7.1940 Vessel lost with all thirteen crew presumed to have been blown up by mine 8 cables from Knoll Buoy in the Thames Estuary on return voyage to owners.					
ROYALLIEU 125072 GY313 Steam Trawler	143 14.05.1907 27.08.1907	211 76	115.33 21.5	C.D. Holmes 70 NHP 10.5 knots	Alec Black Grimsby
14.09.1910 Sold to Thomas W Baskcomb, Grimsby. Feb 1915 Rqd b0y the Royal Navy as a minesweeper No. FY 1145. 1919 returned. 07.05.1919 to Overseas Steam Fishing Co Ltd, Grimsby. 25.11.1940 Rqd by the Royal Navy as a minesweeper No. FY 835. 22.11.1945 returned. 14.02.1942 to Beeley & Sleight Ltd, Grimsby. 24.06.1946 to Grimsby Merchants Amalgamated Fishing Co Ltd, Grimsby. 26.08.1953 to George F Sleight & Sons Ltd, Grimsby renamed RIZZIO. 15.10.1956 to Derwent Trawlers Ltd, Grimsby. 24.01.1959 to Ross Trawlers Ltd, Grimsby. 1961 Vessel sold for scrap to Jacques Bakker en Zonen, Belgium. 28.01.1961 Arrived Bruges for breaking up.					

NAME Official No. Port Letters Numbers	Yard No. Launched Registered	Registered G Ton N Ton	 L Ft B Ft	Engine Builder Horse Power Reg'd Speed	OWNER (Built for)
THURINGIA 134774 GY855 Steam Trawler	144 08.04.1913 04.06.1913	296 121	130.0 23.0	Amos & Smith 68 NHP 10.5 knots	Great Grimsby & East Coast Steam Fishing Co Ltd Grimsby
Apr 1915 Rqd by the Royal Navy as an auxiliary patrol vessel No. FY 1624. 11.11.1917 Vessel captured by U-95 and sunk by torpedo off Youghal Ireland.					
REVIGO 125068 GY296 Steam Trawler	145 15.04.1907 10.08.1907	230 82	117.0 22.0	C.D. Holmes 63 NHP 10.5 knots	George F Sleight Ltd Grimsby
07.09.1914 Vessel sunk by mine in the North Sea 25 miles east ½ north of Spurn Point.					
SARGON 134776 GY858 Steam Trawler	146 08.04.1913 04.06.1913	296 121	130.0 23.0	Amos & Smith 68 NHP 10.5 knots	Standard Steam Fishing Co Ltd Grimsby
Dec 1914 Rqd by the Royal Navy as a minesweeper No. FY 702. 1919 returned. Aug 1939 Rqd by the Royal Navy as a minesweeper No. FY 572. 03.07.1945 reverted. 20.01.1942 Sold to St Andrews Steam Fishing Co Ltd, Hull. 06.12.1945 to Adam Steam Fishing Co Ltd, Grimsby. 01.12.1948 Vessel wrecked off Patreksfjördur, Iceland whilst seeking shelter during a blizzard. Eleven crew lost and six rescued.					
REPERIO 125069 GY298 Steam Trawler	147 14.05.1907 15.08.1907	230 82	117.0 22.0	C.D. Holmes 63 NHP 10.5 knots	George F Sleight Grimsby
28.12.1908 Vessel stranded Robin Hoods Bay, Yorkshire. 01.01.1909 re-floated. Jan 1915 Rqd by the Royal Navy as a boom defence vessel. Dec 1918 returned. 20.10.1931 The trawler LUCERNE GY1202 (198 gt/ b 1900) sank in the North Sea following a collision with the REPERIO off Spurn Point. 17.11.1933 Sold to George F Sleight & Raymond L Humphrey, Grimsby. 19.05.1949 to George F Sleight & Sons Ltd, Grimsby. 15.10.1956 to Derwent Trawlers Ltd, Grimsby. 24.01.1959 to Ross Trawlers Ltd, Grimsby. 1962 Vessel sold for scrap to Van Heyghen Freres, Belgium. 11.03.1962 Arrived Ghent for breaking up.					
CLAIRE 125073 GY318 Steam Trawler	148 29.06.1907 28.09.1907	219 111	117.0 21.5	C.D. Holmes 60 NHP 10 knots	William Grant Grimsby
Apr 1915 Rqd by the Royal Navy as a minesweeper No. FY 1466. 1919 returned. 01.06.1927 to Arthur Grant, Grimsby.25.11.1939 Rqd by the Royal Navy as a minesweeper. 06.02. 1940 returned. 1958 Vessel sold for scrap to Jacques Bakker en Zonen, Belgium. 10.03.1958 Arrived Bruges for breaking up.					
RIDEO 125071 GY314 Steam Trawler	149 25.06.1907 11.09.1907	230 82	117.0 22.0	C.D. Holmes 63 NHP 10.5 knots	George F Sleight Grimsby
24/26.8.1914 Vessel captured and sunk by German Torpedo boats in the North Sea.					
VERA 124791 H960 Steam Trawler	150 27.07.1907 27.09.1907	333 149	140.0 23.75	Amos & Smith 87 NHP 10.5 knots	Humber Steam Trawling Co Ltd Hull
May 1915 Rqd by the Royal Navy as a minesweeper No. FY 1569. 1919 returned. 1920 Sold to Fresh Fish Supplies Ltd, Hull. 1923 Lancashire Fishing Co, Fleetwood. 05.03.1925 Vessel wrecked at Myrdalssandur, south Iceland.					
GRENADA 125077 GY323 Steam Trawler	151 29.06.1907 14.10.1907	219 111	117.0 21.5	C.D. Holmes 60 NHP 10 knots	Grant & Baker Steam Fishing Co Ltd Grimsby
Dec 1914 Rqd by the Royal Navy as a minesweeper No. FY 714 renamed GRENADIER. 1919 returned and reverted. 24.06.1932 Sold to Howe Steam Fishing Co, Grimsby. 03.04.1933 to James Porter, Aberdeen (A528). 1951 Vessel sold to BISCO and allocated to Metal Industries, Fife. 28.04.1951 Arrived Charlestown for breaking up.					
OTHELLO 124786 H956 Steam Trawler	152 13.07.1907 03.09.1907	206 64	110.5 22.25	Amos & Smith 50 NHP 10 knots	Hellyer Steam Fishing Co Ltd Hull
Mar 1915 Rqd by the Royal Navy as a minesweeper No. FY 1193 renamed OTHELLO II. 31.10.1915 Vessel sunk by mine off Leathercoat. Only one crewman rescued.					

<table>
<tr><th rowspan="2">NAME
Official No.
Port Letters Numbers</th><th rowspan="2">Yard No.
Launched
Registered</th><th colspan="2">Registered</th><th rowspan="2">Engine Builder
Horse Power
Reg'd Speed</th><th rowspan="2">OWNER
(Built for)</th></tr>
<tr><th>G Ton
N Ton</th><th>L Ft
B Ft</th></tr>
<tr><td>IAGO
124794
H963 Steam Trawler</td><td>153
25.07.1907
09.10.1907</td><td>206
64</td><td>110.5
22.25</td><td>Amos & Smith
50 NHP
10 knots</td><td>Hellyer Steam
Fishing Co Ltd
Hull</td></tr>
<tr><td colspan="6">Mar 1915 Rqd by the Royal Navy as a minesweeper No. FY 1364. 1919 returned.
11.07.1918 Sold to Mrs E M Lawford & C Curzon, Milford Haven. 1920 to Iago Steam Trawling Co Ltd, Milford Haven .
1928 to Ocean Steam Fishing Co Ltd, Hull. 1936 to Torbay Trawlers Ltd, Brixham. 1940 to J S Ellis, Scarborough.
16.09.1940 Vessel foundered off the Hebrides.</td></tr>
<tr><td>SAXON
124803
H970 Steam Trawler</td><td>154
11.09.1907
24.11.1907</td><td>347
135</td><td>140.0
23.5</td><td>Amos & Smith
87 NHP
10.5 knots</td><td>Imperial Steam
Fishing Co Ltd
Hull</td></tr>
<tr><td colspan="6">02.12.1913 Sold to P Feixas, Barcelona, Spain. 1919 to Cia Maritima 'Iberia' San Sabastian renamed MARIA.
1927 to F Freixas, San Sabastian. 1931 Freixas Hermanos SA, Barcelona.
1936 Rqd by the Spanish Navy as a patrol boat No. GVC16.
Jan 1939 Sank at Barcelona. 20.06.1939 Salved and returned to Freixas Hermanos.
1956 to Antonio Aguirrego - Mezcorja Mendizabal, Barcelona. 1968 Vessel sold to shipbreakers and broken up.</td></tr>
<tr><td>SEMIRAMIS
125079
GY324 Steam Trawler</td><td>155
26.08.1907
24.10.1907</td><td>246
126</td><td>125.0
22.0</td><td>C.D. Holmes
70 NHP
10.5 knots</td><td>Roberts & Ruthven Ltd
Grimsby</td></tr>
<tr><td colspan="6">Aug 1914 Rqd by the Royal Navy as a minesweeper No. FY 358. 1919 returned.
06.11.1925 Sold to Tvala A/B Noprdsjon, Gothenburg, Sweden renamed GORAN.
1953 to Cia Societa Maritanos Urmas, Honduras. 1964 Vessel sold to shipbreakers and broken up.</td></tr>
<tr><td>MOPSA
124796
H966 Steam Trawler</td><td>156
13.08.1907
29.10.1907</td><td>206
64</td><td>110.5
22.25</td><td>Amos & Smith
50 NHP
10 knots</td><td>Hellyer Steam
Fishing Co Ltd
Hull</td></tr>
<tr><td colspan="6">Mar 1915 Rqd by the Royal Navy as a minesweeper No. FY 1606. 1919 returned.
03.07.1918 Sold to Iago Steam Trawling Co Ltd, Hull.
28.02.1928 to Trident Steam Fishing Co Ltd, Hull renamed STROMNESS.
25.09.1935 to J T Stewart, Aberdeen (A380). 04.10.1939 Vessel wrecked north of Aberdeen.</td></tr>
<tr><td>HATFIELD

Water Boat</td><td>157
10.10.1907
00.00.1907</td><td>26</td><td>51.0
14.0</td><td>N/A</td><td>Mr Leggott
Hull</td></tr>
<tr><td colspan="6">Used for bunkering fresh water to vessels in and around the port of Hull.</td></tr>
<tr><td>TOURACO
125090
GY347 Steam Trawler</td><td>158
07.11.1907
17.01.1908</td><td>245
113</td><td>120.5
22.0</td><td>Amos & Smith
76 NHP
10.5 knots</td><td>Cleethorpes Steam
Trawling Co Ltd
Grimsby</td></tr>
<tr><td colspan="6">Laid down as PENGUIN. Sep 1914 Rqd by the Royal Navy as a minesweeper No. FY 609. 1920 returned.
16.04.1918 Sold to Walter H Beeley, Grimsby. 20.06.1919 to Talbot Steam Trawling Co Ltd, Fleetwood (FD219).
1926 to R W Lewis, Aberdeen (A134) renamed JEAN HAY. 1930 to J J Walker, Aberdeen.
1937 Vessel sold to shipbreakers and broken up.</td></tr>
<tr><td>ARACARI
127824
GY355 Steam Trawler</td><td>159
07.11.1907
06.02.1908</td><td>245
113</td><td>120.5
22.0</td><td>Amos & Smith
76 NHP
10.5 knots</td><td>Cleethorpes Steam
Trawling Co Ltd
Grimsby</td></tr>
<tr><td colspan="6">Laid down as SEAGULL. Sep 1914 Rqd by the Royal Navy as a minesweeper No. FY 514. 1919 returned.
16.04.1918 Sold to Walter H Beeley, Grimsby. 21.05.1918 to Ernest Taylor, Grimsby.
07.07.1919 to Taylor & Ashworth, Fleetwood . 1920 to Talbot Steam Trawling Co Ltd, Fleetwood (FD218).
1926 to R W Lewis, Aberdeen (A155). 1932 to Mrs M Laycock, Milford Haven (M101).
1938 to Pettit & Younds, Milford Haven. 1939 Rqd by the Royal Navy as a minesweeper.
1940 returned. 1943 Rqd by the Royal Navy as a fuel carrier No. Y7.2.
03.10.1943 Grounded and declared a total loss on Filicudi Island north of Sicily.</td></tr>
<tr><td>GREAT ADMIRAL
127825
GY361 Steam Trawler</td><td>160
07.12.1907
12.02.1908</td><td>284
117</td><td>135.0
22.5</td><td>C.D. Holmes
70 NHP
11 knots</td><td>Edward C Grant
Grimsby</td></tr>
<tr><td colspan="6">04.10.1912 Registry transferred to Denmark. (For fishing in the Moray Firth as British flag vessels were banned).
28.10.1915 to Edward C Grant, Grimsby. 30.10.1915 to A & M Smith Ltd, Grimsby.
1917 Rqd by the Royal Navy as a fishing trawler. 1919 returned. 27.01.1920 to Direct Fish Supplies Ltd, Grimsby.
06.09.1922 to Thomas W Baskcomb, Grimsby. 25.11.1935 to Boston Deep Sea Fishing Co Ltd, Grimsby.
17.10.1942 to Northern Trawlers Ltd, Grimsby. May 1940 Rqd by the Royal Navy as an auxiliary patrol vessel No. 4.146.
Jun 1945 returned. 05.06.1947 Vessel sold to West of Scotland Shipbreakers and broken up at Troon.</td></tr>
</table>

Yard No.163
1908 REVELLO
Photo by courtesy of George Scales

Yard No.171
1908 MACFARLANE
Photo:- Barnard and Straker Collection

Yard No.179
1909 DOGBERRY
Photo:- Barnard and Straker Collection

<table>
<tr><th rowspan="2">NAME
Official No.
Port Letters Numbers</th><th rowspan="2">Yard No.
Launched
Registered</th><th colspan="2">Registered</th><th rowspan="2">Engine Builder
Horse Power
Reg'd Speed</th><th rowspan="2">OWNER
(Built for)</th></tr>
<tr><th>G Ton
N Ton</th><th>L Ft
B Ft</th></tr>
<tr><td>**KINSMAN**
124821
Steam Tug</td><td>161
22.02.1908
08.04.1908</td><td>119
6</td><td>95.0
19.0
-</td><td>Vauxhall & West
53 NHP
11.5 knots</td><td>Thomas Gray & Co Ltd
Hull</td></tr>
<tr><td colspan="6">03.01.1917 Hired by the Royal Navy for harbour duties. 09.05.1919 returned. 15.03.1921 Sold to United Towing, Hull.
14.07.1930 to J P Knight Rochester renamed KEVERNE. 1947 to Dimitri Vernicos, Greece renamed ELENI II.
1954 to Nicolaos Vernicca Shipping Co, Piræus renamed NICOLAOS. 1958 to Mich. Bias & Co Piræus.
1978 to G & J Xindaralos & Evezos, Piræus. 1979 Vessel deleted from Lloyds Register of Shipping.</td></tr>
<tr><td>**ORIZABA**
127827
GY356 Steam Trawler</td><td>162
21.01.1908
03.04.1908</td><td>233
90</td><td>120.0
22.0</td><td>C.D. Holmes
70 NHP
10.5 knots</td><td>Alfred Bannister
Grimsby</td></tr>
<tr><td colspan="6">Dec 1914 Rqd by the Royal Navy as a boom defence vessel. 1919 returned.
15.04.1919 Sold to Forward Steam Fishing Co Ltd, Grimsby.
17.08.1940 Rqd by the Royal Navy minesweeper No. FY 1897 (Jan 1944) fuel trawler No. Y7.23.
10.12.1944 returned. 11.04.1946 Laid up at Alexandra Dock Grimsby.
1949 Vessel sold to BISCO and allocated to J J King & Co Ltd 06.06.1949 Left Grimsby to be broken up at Gateshead.</td></tr>
<tr><td>**REVELLO**
127830
GY373 Steam Trawler</td><td>163
02.04.1908
11.06.1908</td><td>230
107</td><td>117.0
22.0</td><td>C.D. Holmes
63 NHP
10.5 knots</td><td>George F Sleight
Grimsby</td></tr>
<tr><td colspan="6">Nov 1914 Rqd by the Royal Navy as a minesweeper No. FY 673. 1919 returned.
17.11.1933 Sold to George F Sleight & Raymond L Humphrey, Grimsby.
29.11.1939 Rqd by the Royal Navy as a minesweeper No. FY 778. 10.03.1941 Vessel sank. Aug 1941 Salved.
1943 Rqd by the Min of Ag, Fish & Food.17.06.1946 returned.17.05.1949 to George F Sleight & Sons, Grimsby.
15.10.1956 to Derwent Trawlers Ltd, Grimsby. 24.01.1959 to Ross Trawlers Ltd, Grimsby. 07.12.1959 Vessel foundered 18 miles off Spurn Light-vessel after springing a leak in heavy weather. The eleven crew took to life-rafts and were picked up by the Newcastle cargo vessel BALUCHISTAN (8370 gt/ b 1956) which had responded to the trawler's call for assistance.</td></tr>
<tr><td>**REPORTO**
127831
GY380 Steam Trawler</td><td>164
16.04.1908
30.06.1908</td><td>230
107</td><td>117.0
22.0</td><td>C.D. Holmes
63 NHP
10.5 knots</td><td>George F Sleight
Grimsby</td></tr>
<tr><td colspan="6">Feb 1915 Rqd by the Royal Navy as a minesweeper No. FY 455. 1919 returned.
17.11.1933 Sold to George F Sleight & Raymond L Humphrey, Grimsby.
27.11.1939 Rqd by the Royal Navy as an auxiliary patrol vessel . 03.02.1948 returned.
17.05.1949 to George F Sleight & Sons, Grimsby.
1956 Vessel sold for scrap to Jacques Bakker en Zonen, Belgium. 14.03.1956 Arrived Bruges for breaking up.</td></tr>
<tr><td>**MEDIAN**
127833
GY384 Steam Trawler</td><td>165
30.04.1908
15.07.1908</td><td>214
104</td><td>117.0
21.5</td><td>C.D. Holmes
60 NHP
10 knots</td><td>Onward Steam Fishing Co Ltd
Grimsby</td></tr>
<tr><td colspan="6">25.03.1917 Vessel captured by U-boat 30 miles east by south of Aberdeen and sunk by time bombs. All crew rescued.</td></tr>
<tr><td>**ALFRED-EDITH**

O35 Steam Trawler</td><td>166
15.06.1908
05.08.1908</td><td>261
141</td><td>125.0
22.0</td><td>C.D. Holmes
63 NHP
10.5 knots</td><td>Alfred T Golder
Ostend
Belgium</td></tr>
<tr><td colspan="6">1917 Rqd by the Royal Navy as a fishing trawler (Fishery Reserve). 1919 returned.
1933 Sold to Dobson Ship Repairing Co, Grimsby (GY510) renamed LUCERNE Official No. 162870.
1937 Vessel sold to shipbreakers and broken up.</td></tr>
<tr><td>**TRYGON**
127566
FD221 Steam Trawler</td><td>167
30.06.1908
28.08.1908</td><td>289
112</td><td>130.0
23.0</td><td>Amos & Smith
88 NHP
11 knots</td><td>Mount Steam Fishing Co Ltd
Fleetwood</td></tr>
<tr><td colspan="6">Feb 1915 Rqd by the Royal Navy as an auxiliary patrol vessel No. FY 978.
30.03.1915 Vessel sunk following a collision in the Clyde.</td></tr>
<tr><td>**LUNDY**
128111
H993 Steam Trawler</td><td>168
16.06.1908
16.09.1908</td><td>188
73</td><td>110.5
22.2</td><td>Amos & Smith
49 NHP
10 knots</td><td>Hull Steam Fishing
& Ice Co Ltd
Hull</td></tr>
<tr><td colspan="6">May 1915 Rqd by the Royal Navy as a minesweeper No. FY 1791.
16.08.1915 Vessel sank following a collision in Sulva Bay, Turkey. (Dardanelles campaign).</td></tr>
</table>

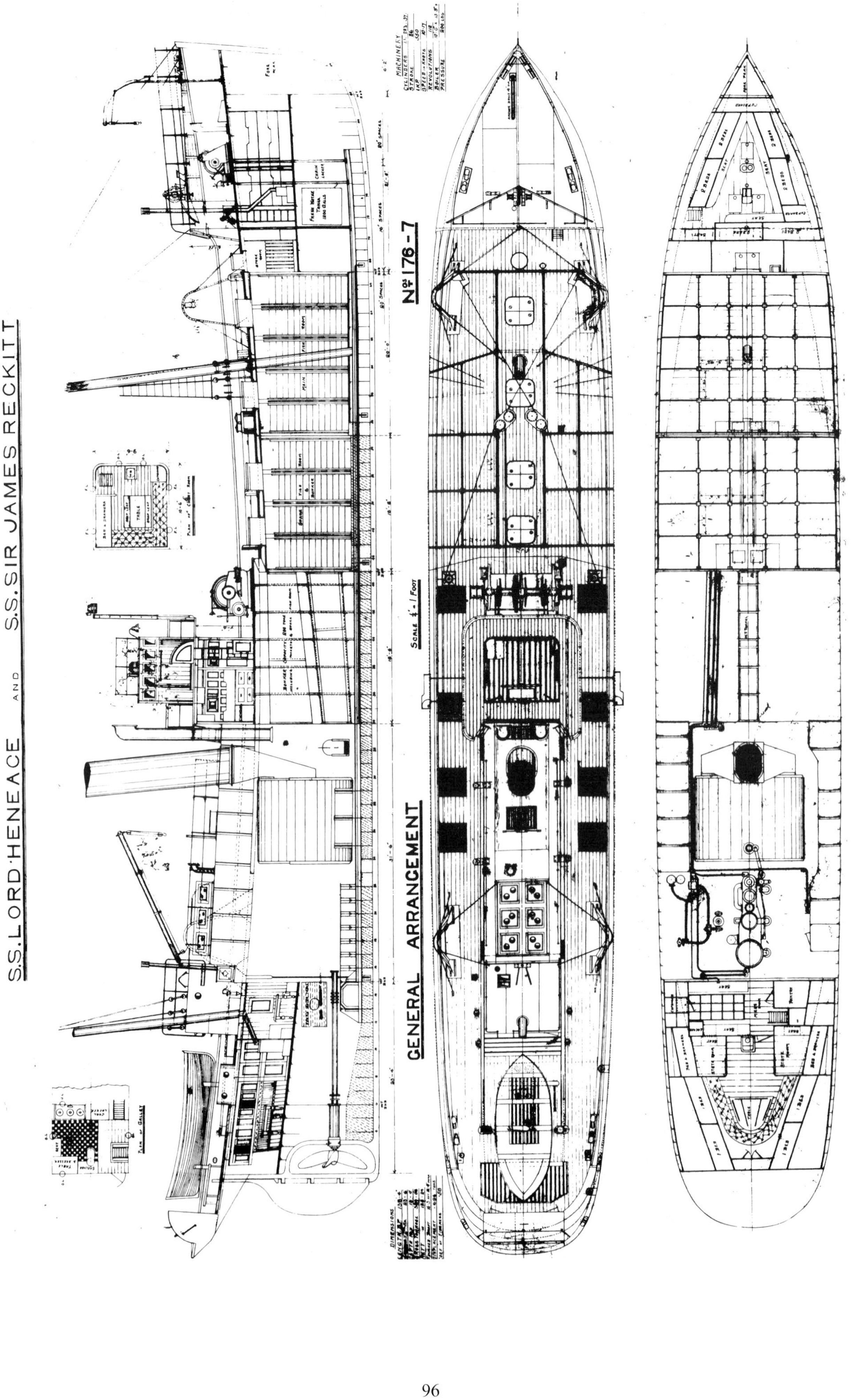
S.S. LORD HENEAGE AND S.S. SIR JAMES RECKITT
GENERAL ARRANGEMENT
No 176-7
SCALE 1/4" = 1 FOOT

NAME Official No. Port Letters Numbers	Yard No. Launched Registered	Registered G Ton N Ton	 L Ft B Ft	Engine Builder Horse Power Reg'd Speed	OWNER (Built for)
CAPE TOWN 128121 H998 Steam Trawler	169 15.08.1908 16.10.1908	188 73	110.5 22.2	Amos & Smith 49 NHP 10 knots	Hull Steam Fishing & Ice Co Ltd Hull
1917 Rqd by the Royal Navy as a fishing trawler (Fishery Reserve) renamed CAPE TOWN II. 1919 returned and reverted. 1937 Sold to R P Lewis, Milford Haven. 03.12.1939 Rqd by the Royal Navy as a minesweeper renamed STORMCOCK. 1940 returned and reverted. 1945 to Pair Fishing Co Ltd, Milford Haven. 1948 to Cranbrook Shipping Co Ltd, London (based at Lowestoft). 1956 Vessel sold for scrap to Jacques Bakker en Zonen, Belgium. 15.03.1956 Arrived Bruges for breaking up.					
GIBRALTAR 128122 H1000 Steam Trawler	170 15.08.1908 27.10.1908	188 73	110.5 22.2	Amos & Smith 49 NHP 10 knots	Hull Steam Fishing & Ice Co Ltd Hull
04.04.1917 Vessel captured by U-boat and sunk by time-bombs 20 miles ENE of Rattray Head Scotland. All crew rescued.					
MACFARLANE 128120 H997 Steam Trawler	171 29.08.1908 14.10.1908	284 116	135.0 22.5	C.D. Holmes 86 NHP 11 knots	Neptune Steam Fishing Co Ltd Hull
Feb 1915 Rqd by the Royal Navy as a minesweeper No. FY 1220. 1919 returned. 1918 Sold to W Allnut, Grimsby (GY1119). 09.02.1920 to H/F Draupnir Vestmanaeyjar, Iceland renamed DRAUPNIR (VE230). 1925 to H/F Draupnir, Reykjavik (RE258). 11.10.1932 to Samuinnufelaginu Bjargi, Reykyavik renamed GEYSIR. 19.11.1933 Vessel stranded Torness, Pentland Firth. The trawler was re-floated but foundered.					
ST. IVES 128129 H11 Steam Trawler	172 10.12.1908 16.02.1909	325 145	140.0 23.75	C.D. Holmes 86 NHP 11 knots	Thomas Hamling & Co Ltd Hull
Mar 1915 Rqd by the Royal Navy as an auxiliary patrol vessel No. FY 1192. 21.12.1916 Vessel sunk by mine off St Anthony, Falmouth. One officer and ten ratings lost.					
ROLULO 127838 GY399 Steam Trawler	173 06.02.1909 23.03.1909	170 69	105.0 21.0	C.D. Holmes 59 NHP 9 knots	George F Sleight Grimsby
Apr 1915 Rqd by the Royal Navy as an auxiliary patrol vessel No. FY 1468. 27.05.1915 Vessel wrecked on Obb Rock, Isle of Lewis.					
RAPIO 127839 GY400 Steam Trawler	174 24.02.1909 03.04.1909	170 69	105.0 21.0	C.D. Holmes 59 NHP 9 knots	George F Sleight Grimsby
Feb 1915 Vessel posted missing:- Lost with all hands. 08.02.1915 Left Grimsby for a fishing trip in the North Sea, not heard of again.					
HANDYMAN 128136 Steam Tug	175 22.02.1909 00.03.1909	86	85.0 17.0	Vauxhall & West 42 NHP 11.5 knots	Thomas Gray & Co Ltd Hull
15.04.1921 Sold to United Towing Co Hull. 1936 Vessel sold to shipbreakers and broken up.					
LORD HENEAGE 128173 H27 Steam Trawler	176 10.03.1909 19.05.1909	324 125	138.33 23.5	Amos & Smith 93 NHP 11 knots	Yorkshire Steam Fishing Co Ltd Hull
Feb 1915 Rqd by the Royal Navy as a minesweeper / bomb thrower No. FY 1140. 1919 returned. 26.09.1918 Sold to W Would, Grimsby (GY1211). 01.04.1920 to Woodbury Steam Fishing Co Ltd, Grimsby. 14.07.1924 to Soc De Pesca 'Golfinho' Ltd, Lisbon, Portugal renamed GOLFINHO. 1929 to Soc Maritima Treve Ltda, Lisbon renamed MARIA RAQUEL PRIMEIRO. 1930 to A Cilia, Lisbon renamed PRAIA de VICTORIA. 29.11.1935 Vessel sank following a collision in the River Tagus.					
SIR JAMES RECKITT 128177 H32 Steam Trawler	177 22.04.1909 03.06.1909	324 125	138.33 23.5	Amos & Smith 93 NHP 11 knots	Pickering & Haldane's Steam Trawling Co Ltd Hull
Sep 1915 Rqd by the Royal Navy as a minesweeper with hydrophonic listening equipment No. FY 1887. 1919 returned. 26.09.1918 Sold to A Bannister, Grimsby (GY1203). 23.08.1922 to Estrella D'Alva Ltda Empreza De Pesca A Vap, Lisbon, Portugal renamed ESTRELLA D'ALVA. 1941 Sold to the Royal Navy as a minesweeper No. FY 1927 renamed SUNBURST. 1946 Returned to Portuguese owners at Kilindina renamed ESTRELLA D'ALVA. 1956 Vessel sold to shipbreakers and broken up.					

<table>
<tr><th rowspan="2">NAME
Official No.
Port Letters Numbers</th><th rowspan="2">Yard No.
Launched
Registered</th><th colspan="2">Registered</th><th rowspan="2">Engine Builder
Horse Power
Reg'd Speed</th><th rowspan="2">OWNER
(Built for)</th></tr>
<tr><th>G Ton
N Ton</th><th>L Ft
B Ft</th></tr>
<tr><td>LEONATO
129208
H41 Steam Trawler</td><td>178
08.05.1909
15.06.1909</td><td>213
78</td><td>111.25
22.5</td><td>Amos & Smith
45 NHP
10 knots</td><td>Hellyer Steam
Fishing Co Ltd
Hull</td></tr>
<tr><td colspan="6">1917 Rqd by the Royal Navy as a fishing trawler (Fishery Reserve). 1919 returned.
1920 Sold to Jutland Steam Trawling Co Ltd, renamed NAVAL ESCORT.
1925 to Walker Steam Fishing Co, Aberdeen (A122). 1926 to Regent Fishing Co Ltd, Aberdeen renamed DANDARA.
1929 to Brand & Curzon Ltd, Milford Haven. 1938 to Milford Fishing Ltd, Milford Haven (M279).
1939 Rqd by the Royal Navy as a minesweeper . 1940 returned.
24.04.1941 to Hull Northern Steam Fishing Co Ltd, Hull (H417). 1943 to Hellyer Bros Ltd, Hull.
1944 to Kingston Steam Trawling Co Ltd, Hull. 1945 to Standard Steam Fishing Co Ltd, Grimsby (GY34).
1951 to Nigg Fishing Co Ltd, Aberdeen (A671).
1959 Vessel sold for scrap to Atlantic Reed F W Joch, Germany. 16.01.1959 Arrived Hamburg for breaking up.</td></tr>
<tr><td>DOGBERRY
129222
H46 Steam Trawler</td><td>179
22.05.1909
08.07.1909</td><td>213
78</td><td>111.25
22.5</td><td>Amos & Smith
45 NHP
10 knots</td><td>Hellyer Steam
Fishing Co Ltd
Hull</td></tr>
<tr><td colspan="6">03.06.1915 Vessel captured by U-boat in the North Sea and sunk by time bombs 120 miles north north-east of Aberdeen.</td></tr>
<tr><td>YORICK
129236
H49 Steam Trawler</td><td>180
05.06.1909
28.07.1909</td><td>213
78</td><td>111.25
22.5</td><td>Amos & Smith
45 NHP
10 knots</td><td>Hellyer Steam
Fishing Co Ltd
Hull</td></tr>
<tr><td colspan="6">1918 Rqd by the Royal Navy as a fishing trawler (Fishery Reserve). 1919 returned.
27.11.1919 Sold to Northern Steam Fishing Co Ltd, Hull. 03.01.1930 to Hellyer Steam Fishing Co Ltd, Hull.
1931 to Jenkerson & Jones, Milford Haven. 14.11.1935 to A Hay, Aberdeen (A382). 1941 to Hellyer Bros Ltd, Hull (H410).
05.07.1944 to Ocean Steam Fishing Co Ltd, Hull. 27.06.1945 to Eton Steam Fishing Co, Hull.
05.02.1946 to Dagger Line, Hull. 1948 to Grateful Steam Fishing Co Ltd, Aberdeen (A247).
1955 Vessel sold (£2525) to BISCO and allocated to Metal Industries. 02.08.1955 Arrived Charlestown for breaking up.</td></tr>
<tr><td>KONG FREDERIK III

F145 Steam Trawler</td><td>181
07.06.1909
27.07.1909</td><td>260
105</td><td>125.0
22.0</td><td>Gt.Central Eng.
76 NHP
11 knots</td><td>G E Forum
Esbjerg
Denmark</td></tr>
<tr><td colspan="6">15.04.1915 Sold to Frank Barrett, Grimsby GY482 Official No. 137026 renamed (1919) KING FREDERIK.
May 1915 Rqd by the Royal Navy as a minesweeper No. FY 2659. 1919 returned.
21.01.1920 to Direct Fish Supplies Ltd, Grimsby.
06.09.1922 to T W Baskcomb, Grimsby renamed (22.03.1928) MAGNOLIA. 28.10.1935 to Henry Franklin Ltd, Grimsby.
31.05.1940 Rqd by the Royal Navy as an auxiliary patrol vessel No. FY 4.257 renamed GLACIER.
28.06.1944 returned and reverted.
19.08.1952 Whilst fishing in the North Sea the MAGNOLIA sprang a leak. The trawler was taken in tow by ROSE OF ENGLAND GY236 (222gt/ b 1909). 20.08.1952 A nineteen hour struggle to save the stricken trawler ended when she sank. The crew jumped into the sea and the ROSE OF ENGALAND picked up the survivors but three crew were lost.</td></tr>
<tr><td>CEDAR
127843
GY480 Steam Trawler</td><td>182
19.06.1909
18.09.1909</td><td>219
106</td><td>117.0
21.5</td><td>Gt.Central Eng.
60 NHP
10.25 knots</td><td>William Grant
Grimsby</td></tr>
<tr><td colspan="6">Mar 1915 Rqd by the Royal Navy as a minesweeper No. FY 1229. 1919 returned.
1924 to J Arcelus, San Sabastian, Spain renamed NERE FEDEA. 1931 Sold to V Trullerque Montoro, Valencia.
1969 Vessel sold to Spanish shipbreakers and broken up.</td></tr>
<tr><td>GADRA
127847
GY485 Steam Trawler</td><td>183
05.08.1909
28.09.1909</td><td>219
106</td><td>117.0
21.5</td><td>Gt.Central Eng.
60 NHP
10.25 knots</td><td>Grant & Baker Steam
Fishing Co Ltd
Grimsby</td></tr>
<tr><td colspan="6">Apr 1915 Rqd by the Royal Navy as a minesweeper No. FY 1467. 1919 returned.
24.07.1932 Sold to Howe Steam Fishing Co Ltd, Grimsby. 05.03.1934 to Diamonds Steam Fishing Co Ltd, Grimsby.
29.11.1939 Rqd by the Royal Navy as a minesweeper. 02.03.1940 returned.
06.01.1941 Vessel sunk by mine 1½ miles off Myling Head, Færoe Islands. Seven crew lost three rescued.</td></tr>
<tr><td>MINORU
127845
GY484 Steam Trawler</td><td>184
05.08.1909
24.09.1909</td><td>260
105</td><td>125.0
22.0</td><td>Gt.Central Eng.
76 NHP
10.5 knots</td><td>Orient Steam Fishing Co Ltd
Grimsby</td></tr>
<tr><td colspan="6">Aug 1914 Rqd by the Royal Navy as a minesweeper No. FY 348 renamed (1917) MINORU II. 1920 returned and reverted.
10.06.1920 Sold to British Fish Supplies, Grimsby. 06.09.1922 to Thomas W Baskcomb, Grimsby.
22.10.1935 to Fred Parkes, Grimsby. 24.10.1935 to Dobson Ship Repair Co, Grimsby.
1937 Vessel sold to shipbreakers. 20.04.1937 Registration closed on advice that breaking up was completed.</td></tr>
</table>

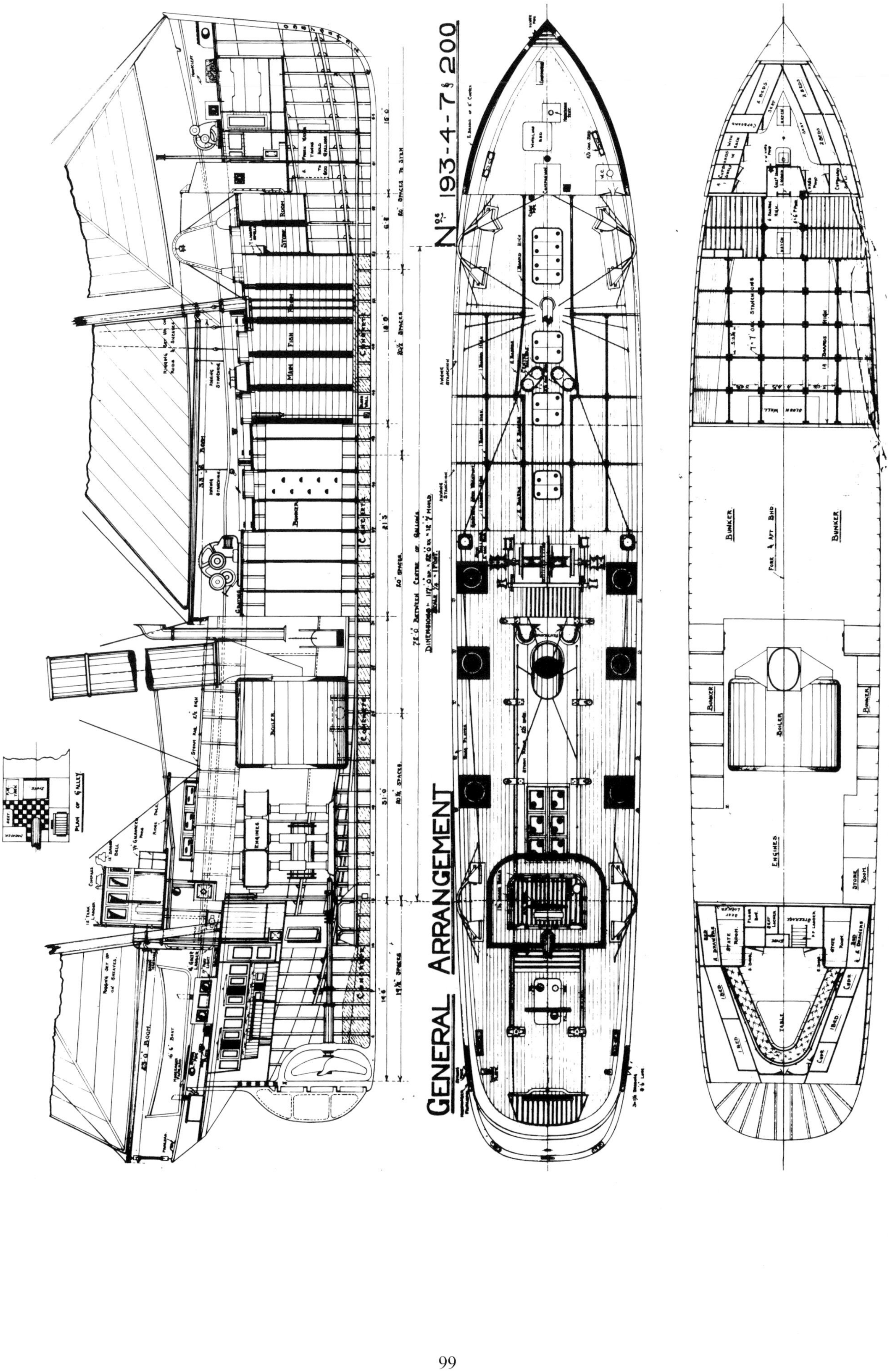

GENERAL ARRANGEMENT
Nos 193-4-7 & 200
72'0" Between Centre of Gallows
Dimensions - 117'0" BP x 22'0" EX x 12'7" Mould
Scale 1/8" = 1 Foot
BUNKER
FORE & AFT BHD
BOILER
ENGINES
STORE ROOM
MAIN FISH ROOM
STORE ROOM
PLAN OF GALLEY

NAME Official No. Port Letters Numbers	Yard No. Launched Registered	Registered G Ton N Ton	 L Ft B Ft	Engine Builder Horse Power Reg'd Speed	OWNER (Built for)
CONSORT 127850 GY498 Steam Trawler	185 02.09.1909 11.11.1909	181 80	110.0 21.0	Gt.Central Eng. 60 NHP 10 knots	Queen Steam Fishing Co Ltd Grimsby
Apr 1915 Rqd by the Royal Navy as a minesweeper No. FY 1612. 1919 returned. 03.02.1953 to James Mowatt, Aberdeen. Aug 1954 Vessel sold to Belgium shipbreakers and broken at Antwerp.					
GABIR 127848 GY497 Steam Trawler	186 02.09.1909 15.11.1909	219 106	117.0 21.5	Gt.Central Eng. 60 NHP 10.5 knots	Grant & Baker Steam Fishing Co Ltd Grimsby
May 1915 Rqd by the Royal Navy as a minesweeper No. FY 1486. 17.12.1917 Alec Black, Grimsby. 01.01.1918 John L Green, Grimsby. 24.05.1918 Vessel sunk by mine in the North Sea off Lowestoft. Mines laid by UC17 on 23.05.1918.					
CALPHURNIA 127849 GY495 Steam Trawler	187 16.09.1909 03.11.1909	284 112	135.0 22.5	C.D. Holmes 70 NHP 10 knots	Grimsby Alliance Steam Fishing Co Ltd Grimsby
12.09.1913 Vessel stranded in a Norwegian Fjord on passage from White Sea to Hull. Was later salved. 14.09.1914 Vessel posted missing:- Lost with all hands.					
TETNEY 127844 Steam Lighter	188 16.08.1909 13.09.1909	47 32	60.0 15.0	Dixon & Hutchinson 42 NHP 7 knots	The Tetney Oil & Manure Co Grimsby
15.02.1917 Sold to Anglo - American Oil Co Ltd, London. 1922 Diesel engine fitted. 22.08.1956 Vessel sold to BISCO and broken up.					
SERIEMA 127851 GY504 Steam Trawler	189 02.10.1909 30.11.1909	279 115	135.0 22.75	C.D. Holmes 70 NHP 10.5 knots	Thomas W Baskcomb Grimsby
Jun 1916 Rqd by the Royal Navy as a boom defence vessel. 1919 returned. 1933 Sold to Amalgamated Steam Fishing Co Ltd, Grimsby. 22.02.1935 Mayfair Fishing Co Ltd, Grimsby renamed MAYFAIR. 06.03.1939 Vessel sold to Dutch shipbreakers and broken up.					
MARTINETA 127852 GY505 Steam Trawler	190 16.10.1909 14.12.1909	279 115	135.0 22.75	C.D. Holmes 70 NHP 10.5 knots	Thomas W Baskcomb Grimsby
Oct 1916 Rqd by the Royal Navy as a boom defence vessel. 1920 returned. 07.05.1920 Sold to J Arcelus, San Sebastian, Spain renamed TITO. 1925 to Pescaderias Corunesas SA, San Sebastian. 1936 Rqd by the Nationalist Navy. 1939 returned. 1942 José DoCampo Prado, San Sabastian. 1967 Vessel sold to Spanish shipbreakers and broken up.					
NEMROD O125 Steam Trawler	191 29.11.1909 18.01.1910	215 99	116.5 21.75	C.D. Holmes 60 NHP 10 knots	H.P. Aspeslagh Ostend Belgium
06.02.1910 Vessel wrecked in Chale Bay Isle of Wight.					
ALBERIA 127854 GY506 Steam Trawler	192 15.01.1910 17.03.1910	318 125	135.0 24.0	C.D. Holmes 84 NHP 10.5 knots	Crown Steam Fishing Co Ltd Grimsby
11.05.1910 Sold to Empreza Central De Pesca A Vapor Ltda, Lisbon, Portugal renamed RIO TEJO. Sep 1915 Sold to Royal Navy as an auxiliary patrol vessel No. FY 175. renamed ARCTURUS (1918) ARCTURUS II. 17.05.1919 to Cruz Bros, Gibraltar renamed ALBERIA. 1920 to Empreza Central De Pesca A Vapor Ltda, Lisbon, Portugal. 1928 to Cia Portuguesa de Pesca, Lisbon. 1978 Vessel sold to shipbreakers and broken up.					
RECORDO 127855 GY507 Steam Trawler	193 14.02.1910 04.04.1910	230 105	117.0 22.0	C.D. Holmes 63 NHP 10 knots	George F Sleight Grimsby
Feb 1915 Rqd by the Royal Navy as a minesweeper . 1920 returned. 17.11.1933 to Sleight & Humphreys, Grimsby. 27.11.1939 Rqd by the Royal Navy as a minesweeper . 08.02.1940 returned. 17.05.1949 to George F Sleight, Grimsby. 1955 Vessel sold for scrap to Jacques Bakker en Zonen, Belgium. 17.07.1955 Arrived Bruges for breaking up.					
RESONO 127856 GY508 Steam Trawler	194 12.03.1910 23.04.1910	230 105	117.0 22.0	C.D. Holmes 63 NHP 10 knots	George F Sleight Grimsby
Jan 1915 Rqd by the Royal Navy as a minesweeper No. FY 1042. 26.12.1915 Vessel sunk by mine near Sunk Light Vessel Thames Estuary. Mines laid by UC5 on 17.12.1915.					

<table>
<tr><th rowspan="2">NAME
Official No.
Port Letters Numbers</th><th rowspan="2">Yard No.
Launched
Registered</th><th colspan="2">Registered</th><th rowspan="2">Engine Builder
Horse Power
Reg'd Speed</th><th rowspan="2">OWNER
(Built for)</th></tr>
<tr><th>G Ton
N Ton</th><th>L Ft
B Ft</th></tr>
<tr><td>DROMIO
129278
H102 Steam Trawler</td><td>195
09.06.1910
20.07.1910</td><td>207
82</td><td>112.0
22.5</td><td>Amos & Smith
45 NHP
10 knots</td><td>Hellyer Steam
Fishing Co Ltd
Hull</td></tr>
<tr><td colspan="6">06.06.1915 Vessel captured by U-boat and sunk by gunfire 35 miles north-east by east of Buchan Ness near Peterhead Scotland.</td></tr>
<tr><td>PERICLES
129283
H131 Steam Trawler</td><td>196
25.06.1910
17.08.1910</td><td>207
82</td><td>112.0
22.5</td><td>Amos & Smith
45 NHP
10 knots</td><td>Hellyer Steam
Fishing Co Ltd
Hull</td></tr>
<tr><td colspan="6">1917 Rqd by the Royal Navy as a fishing trawler (Fishery Reserve). 1919 returned.
1920 Sold to Hull Northern Fishing Co Ltd, Hull. 06.03.1929 to Ocean Steam Fishing Co Ltd, Hull.
16.12.1935 to A R Buthley, Aberdeen renamed MARY BRUCE (A393).
1943 to Fort Rona Trawling Co Ltd, Milford Haven (M147).
1947 to United Trawlers Ltd, Milford Haven. 1948 to Shoals Fishing Co Ltd, Lowestoft (LT368).
1953 Vessel sold for scrap and allocated to C W Dorkin & Co Ltd . 12.03.1953 Arrived Gateshead for breaking up.</td></tr>
<tr><td>REPRO
127857
GY510 Steam Trawler</td><td>197
13.04.1910
09.06.1910</td><td>230
105</td><td>117.0
22.0</td><td>C.D. Holmes
63 NHP
10 knots</td><td>George F Sleight
Grimsby</td></tr>
<tr><td colspan="6">Feb 1915 Rqd by the Royal Navy as a minesweeper No. FY 1138.
26.04.1917 Vessel sunk by mine off Tod Point Tees Estuary mine laid by UC41 on 19.04.1917.</td></tr>
<tr><td>ST. JOHNS
129270
H81 Steam Trawler</td><td>198
12.05.1910
20.06.1910</td><td>208
80</td><td>112.0
22.3</td><td>Amos & Smith
50 NHP
10 knots</td><td>Hull Steam Fishing
& Ice Co Ltd
Hull</td></tr>
<tr><td colspan="6">The ST. JOHNS was one of the first trawlers built with electric lighting.
Oct 1915 Rqd by the Royal Navy as a minesweeper No. FY 1906.
03.06.1918 Vessel captured by U-boat No.UB105 and sunk by gunfire 45 miles north of Tory Island.</td></tr>
<tr><td>STORNOWAY
129275
H83 Steam Trawler</td><td>199
25.05.1910
04.07.1910</td><td>208
80</td><td>112.0
22.3</td><td>Amos & Smith
50 NHP
10 knots</td><td>Hull Steam Fishing
& Ice Co Ltd
Hull</td></tr>
<tr><td colspan="6">The STORNOWAY was one of the first trawlers built with electric lighting.
Jun 1915 Rqd by the Royal Navy as a minesweeper No. FY 1792. 1919 returned.
06.03.1936 Vessel sold to shipbreakers and broken up.</td></tr>
<tr><td>RENCO
127862
GY512 Steam Trawler</td><td>200
09.06.1910
20.07.1910</td><td>230
105</td><td>117.0
22.0</td><td>C.D. Holmes
63 NHP
10 knots</td><td>George F Sleight
Grimsby</td></tr>
<tr><td colspan="6">Feb 1915 Rqd by the Royal Navy as a minesweeper No. FY 1130. 1919 returned.
17.11.1933 to Sleight & Humphreys, Grimsby. 29.11.1939 Rqd by the Royal Navy as a minesweeper. 23.01.1940 returned.
17.05.1949 to George F Sleight, Grimsby. 15.10.1956 Sold to Derwent Trawlers Ltd, Grimsby.
1956 Vessel sold to BISCO and allocated to C W Dorkin & Co Ltd, . 12.11.1956 Arrived Gateshead for breaking up.</td></tr>
<tr><td>CORIENTES
127867
GY552 Steam Trawler</td><td>201
09.06.1910
08.09.1910</td><td>280
119</td><td>131.5
22.5</td><td>C.D. Holmes
80 NHP
10.25 knots</td><td>Thomas Baskcomb
Grimsby</td></tr>
<tr><td colspan="6">Feb 1915 Rqd by the Royal Navy as a minesweeper No. FY 1149.
23.06.1917 Vessel sunk by mine off Malin Head. Mine laid by UC79 on 14.06.1917.</td></tr>
<tr><td>CORYTHAIX
127869
GY553 Steam Trawler</td><td>202
24.08.1910
10.09.1910</td><td>280
119</td><td>131.5
22.5</td><td>C.D. Holmes
80 NHP
10.25 knots</td><td>Thomas Baskcomb
Grimsby</td></tr>
<tr><td colspan="6">Feb 1915 Rqd by the Royal Navy as a minesweeper/boom defence vessel No. FY 456. 1920 returned.
07.05.1920 Sold to Soc Anon Pesca Y Nav, San Sebastian, Spain renamed JOSE MARIA.
1931 to Guzman Rodriguez Rincun, San Sabastian. 1961 to Guzman Rodriguez Rincun & Hijos, Corunna.
1970 Vessel sold to Spanish shipbreakers and broken up.</td></tr>
<tr><td>COURTIER
127864
GY564 Steam Trawler</td><td>203
25.06.1910
08.08.1910</td><td>181
80</td><td>110.0
21.0</td><td>C.D. Holmes
55 NHP
10 knots</td><td>Queen Steam Fishing Co Ltd
Grimsby</td></tr>
<tr><td colspan="6">Jan 1915 Rqd by the Royal Navy as a minesweeper No. FY 449.
06.01.1916 Vessel sunk by mine in the North Sea off Kilnsea, Yorkshire.</td></tr>
</table>

Yard No.185
1909 CONSORT
Photo by courtesy of George Scales

Yard No.206
1910 RIBY
Photo by courtesy of George Scales

Yard No.211
1911 DANE
Photo:- Barnard and Straker Collection

<table>
<tr><th>NAME
Official No.
Port Letters Numbers</th><th>Yard No.
Launched
Registered</th><th colspan="2">Registered</th><th>Engine Builder
Horse Power
Reg'd Speed</th><th>OWNER
(Built for)</th></tr>
<tr><th></th><th></th><th>G Ton
N Ton</th><th>L Ft
B Ft</th><th></th><th></th></tr>
<tr><td>TRIER
129293
H153 Steam Trawler</td><td>204
08.08.1910
28.09.1910</td><td>324
141</td><td>138.33
23.5</td><td>C.D. Holmes
82 NHP
10.5 knots</td><td>John Hollingsworth
Hull</td></tr>
<tr><td colspan="6">Apr 1915 Rqd by the Royal Navy as a minesweeper No. FY 1377. 1919 returned.
11.05.1918 Sold to Henry Burns, Grimsby (GY1117). 1919 to Progressive Trawlers Ltd, Grimsby.
28.06.1921 to Marles Y Serra S.En.C, Barcelona, Spain renamed SANTA CRISTINA.
25.12.1935 Vessel wrecked off Zahara near Conil.</td></tr>
<tr><td>NARVAL

O141 Steam Trawler</td><td>205
23.07.1910
00.10.1910</td><td>214
99</td><td>116.5
21.75</td><td>C.D. Holmes
60 NHP
10 knots</td><td>H. P.Aspeslagh
Ostend
Belgium</td></tr>
<tr><td colspan="6">Mar 1916 Rqd by the Royal Navy as a minesweeper No. FY 3268.
26.11.1916 Vessel lost with all hands on passage from Harwich to Grimsby.</td></tr>
<tr><td>RIBY
132092
GY594 Steam Trawler</td><td>206
06.09.1910
15.12.1910</td><td>214
98</td><td>118.66
21.5</td><td>C.D. Holmes
63 NHP
10.5 knots</td><td>William Grant
Grimsby</td></tr>
<tr><td colspan="6">Jun 1915 Rqd by the Royal Navy as a boom defence vessel. 1919 returned.
13.03.1930 Sold to Rugby Steam Fishing Co Ltd, Grimsby.02.05.1933 to The Connie Steam Trawling Co Ltd, Scarborough.
12.10.1939 to Filey United Trawlers Ltd, Scarborough. 23.12.1941 to J Bennett, Grimsby.
02.11.1944 to Pickering & Haldane's Steam Trawling Co Ltd, Hull. 19.06.1945 to H B Ingram, Fleetwood.
06.01.1951 Vessel sold for scrap to Thos W Ward Ltd, Preston. 15.03.1951 Registration closed vessel broken up.</td></tr>
<tr><td>CAMBODIA
132094
GY597 Steam Trawler</td><td>207
04.01.1911
13.02.1911</td><td>284
115</td><td>135.0
22.5</td><td>Gt.Central Eng.
80 NHP
10.5 knots</td><td>Grimsby Alliance Steam
Fishing Co Ltd
Grimsby</td></tr>
<tr><td colspan="6">May 1915 Rqd by the Royal Navy as a minesweeper No. FY 1521. 1919 returned.
28.03.1918 Sold to Savoy Steam Fishing Co Ltd, Grimsby.
17.08.1928 to Forward Steam Fishing Co Ltd, Grimsby .renamed NAPIER.
23.02.1933 to Benjamin H O Nicholson, Aberdeen (A244). 1935 to W Jamison Aberdeen.
1937 Vessel sold (£720) to Metal Industries. 18.12.1937 Arrived Charlestown Fife for breaking up.</td></tr>
<tr><td>CHRISTOPHER
132224
H207 Steam Trawler</td><td>208
17.01.1911
00.03.1911</td><td>316
135</td><td>138.33
23.5</td><td>Amos & Smith
93 NHP
11 knots</td><td>Pickering & Haldane's Steam
Trawling Co Ltd
Hull</td></tr>
<tr><td colspan="6">May 1915 Rqd by the Royal Navy as an auxiliary patrol vessel No. FY 1502.
30.03.1917 Vessel sunk by mine off Southwold near Lowestoft. Mines laid by UC14 on 24.03.1917.</td></tr>
<tr><td>ESCALLONIA
132101
GY631 Steam Trawler</td><td>209
16.03.1911
16.05.1911</td><td>285
123</td><td>132.0
22.5</td><td>C.D. Holmes
80 NHP
10.5 knots</td><td>North Eastern Steam
Fishing Co Ltd
Grimsby</td></tr>
<tr><td colspan="6">Mar 1915 Rqd by the Royal Navy as a minesweeper No. FY 43. 1919 returned.
02.12.1919 Sold to Thomas W Baskcomb, Grimsby. 22.10.1935 to Fred Parkes, Grimsby.
1937 Vessel sold for scrap to Thos W Ward Ltd, Preston.
26.01.1938 Registration closed on advice that breaking up was completed.</td></tr>
<tr><td>FREESIA
132102
GY633 Steam Trawler</td><td>210
03.04.1911
17.05.1911</td><td>285
123</td><td>132.0
22.5</td><td>C.D. Holmes
80 NHP
10.5 knots</td><td>North Eastern Steam
Fishing Co Ltd
Grimsby</td></tr>
<tr><td colspan="6">Dec 1914 Rqd by the Royal Navy as a minesweeper No. FY 716. 1919 returned.
02.12.1919 Sold to Thomas W Baskcomb, Grimsby.
01.01.1922 Whilst homeward bound from the Færoes the FREESIA stranded at Skippigee Birsay, Orkney Islands. She was re-floated but was driven towards Costa Head and foundered. The Stromness lifeboat rescued two crew but nine were lost.</td></tr>
<tr><td>DANE
132235
H227 Steam Trawler</td><td>211
02.02.1911
28.03.1911</td><td>346
135</td><td>140.0
24.0</td><td>Amos & Smith
87 NHP
11 knots</td><td>Imperial Steam
Fishing Co Ltd
Hull</td></tr>
<tr><td colspan="6">Apr 1915 Rqd by the Royal Navy as a minesweeper No. FY 1370 renamed DANE II. 1919 returned and reverted.
1920 Sold to Hellyer Bros Ltd, Hull. 06,01.1928 to Christenson & Co Ltd, Hull.
1931 to Dane Fishing Co Ltd, Hull. 1934 to H Elliott & Sons Ltd, Fleetwood. 1939 to Prince Fishing Co Ltd, Fleetwood.
Jan 1940 Rqd by the Royal Navy as a minesweeper No. FY 554. Jan 1946 returned.
1943 to H Markham Cook Ltd, Grimsby. 1946 (GY417). 10.09.1946 Laid up at Alexandra Dock Grimsby.
1947 to Drum Fishing Co Ltd, Granton renamed DRUMSKEUGH (GN37). 16.06.1947 Left Grimsby for Granton.
Feb 1954 Vessel sold to BISCO and allocated to Malcolm Brechin and broken up at Granton.</td></tr>
</table>

NAME **Official No.** **Port Letters Numbers**	**Yard No.** **Launched** **Registered**	**Registered** **G Ton** **N Ton**	 **L Ft** **B Ft**	**Engine Builder** **Horse Power** **Reg'd Speed**	**OWNER** **(Built for)**
NORMAN 132241 H249 Steam Trawler	212 15.02.1911 24.04.1911	346 135	140.0 24.0	Amos & Smith 87 NHP 11 knots	Imperial Steam Fishing Co Ltd Hull
May 1915 Rqd by the Royal Navy as a minesweeper No. FY 1575 renamed NORMAN II. 1919 returned and reverted. 27.10.1919 Sold to Hellyer Bros Ltd, Hull renamed (1938) DERVISH. June 1940 Rqd by the Royal Navy as an auxiliary patrol vessel . 09.09.1940 Vessel sunk by mine 2.6 miles x 156° from the Humber Light-vessel. Three crew lost eleven rescued.					
IMPERIALIST 132242 H250 Steam Trawler	213 04.03.1911 02.05.1911	346 135	140.0 24.0	Amos & Smith 87 NHP 11 knots	Imperial Steam Fishing Co Ltd Hull
06.09.1914 Vessel sunk by mine 40 miles E N E of Tynemouth. Two crew lost.					
CROXBY 132105 GY642 Steam Trawler	214 01.05.1911 19.06.1911	215 104	118.66 21.5	C.D. Holmes 67 NHP 10.5 knots	William Grant Grimsby
May 1915 Rqd by the Royal Navy as a minesweeper No. FY 1632. 1919 returned. 07.03.1930 Sold to Rugby Steam Fishing Co Ltd, Grimsby. 09.02.1934 to H Robinson, Grimsby. 25.06.1935 Vessel sank following a collision with the trawler EBOR BELLE GY101 (174 gt/ b 1909) off Aberdeen. Later salved. 13.05.1940 to Supreme Fishing Co Ltd, Grimsby. 05.07.1943 to John Carl Ross, Grimsby. 23.07.1946 to Grimsby Amalgamated Trawlers Ltd, Grimsby. 13.05.1952 to Alfred Bannister (Trawlers) Ltd, Grimsby. 27.03.1960 Vessel sold for scrap to Heuvelman Metaalhandel Sloopwerken and broken up at Krimpen Ijssel, Holland.					
GARU 132108 GY644 Steam Trawler	215 01.05.1911 13.07.1911	215 104	118.66 21.5	C.D. Holmes 67 NHP 10.5 knots	Grant & Baker Steam Fishing Co Ltd Grimsby
Mar 1915 Rqd by the Royal Navy as a minesweeper No. FY 1601. 1919 returned. 23.12.1928 Vessel wrecked 8 miles off Boubjerg Lighthouse, Jutland, Denmark. All eight crew rescued.					
NIGHT-HAWK 132107 GY643 Steam Trawler	216 29.04.1911 21.06.1911	287 112	130.0 23.0	C.D. Holmes 88 NHP 10.5 knots	Pioneer Steam Fishing Co Ltd Grimsby
Aug 1914 Rqd by the Royal Navy as a minesweeper No. FY 57. 25.12.1914 Vessel sunk by mine laid by German cruiser KOLBERG (b 1909) in the North Sea off Scarborough. Six crew lost seven rescued.					
BARDOLPH 132258 H296 Steam Trawler	217 29.06.1911 29.07.1911	215 87	112.0 22.5	Amos & Smith 46 NHP 9.5 knots	Hellyer Steam Fishing Co Ltd Hull
1913 One of the first trawlers fitted with wireless. 05.06.1915 Vessel captured by U-boat and sunk by gunfire 115 miles southwest of Sumburgh Head , Shetlands.					
CALIBAN 132260 H313 Steam Trawler	218 15.07.1911 31.07.1911	215 87	112.0 22.5	Amos & Smith 46 NHP 9.5 knots	Hellyer Steam Fishing Co Ltd Hull
1913 One of the first trawlers fitted with wireless. 12.04.1917 Vessel captured by U-boat and sunk by gunfire 45 miles NE by N of Rattray Head Scotland.					
PAMELA 132257 H283 Steam Trawler	219 30.05.1911 27.07.1911	331 142	140.0 23.75	Amos & Smith 84 NHP 10.5 knots	Humber Steam Trawling Co Ltd Hull
18.01.1915 Vessel wrecked in Falkknar Fjord, west coast of Iceland. All crew rescued.					
JACAMAR 132112 GY649 Steam Trawler	220 15.07.1911 08.09.1911	293 128	135.0 22.75	C.D. Holmes 80 NHP 10.5 knots	Thomas Baskcomb Grimsby
May 1915 Rqd by the Royal Navy as a minesweeper No. FY 1207. 28.01.1917 Vessel sank following a collision off Folkestone Light Vessel.					
HOUBARA 132113 GY650 Steam Trawler	221 29.07.1911 08.09.1911	293 128	135.0 22.75	C.D. Holmes 80 NHP 10.5 knots	Thomas Baskcomb Grimsby
Apr 1915 Rqd by the Royal Navy as a minesweeper No. FY 1618. 1919 returned. 19.10.1915 Sold to Thomas Baskcomb Ltd, Grimsby. 12.07.1933 to Amalgamated Steam Fishing, Grimsby 22.02.1935 Holborn Fishing Co Ltd, Grimsby renamed (08.03.1935) HOLBORN. 1939 Vessel sold to shipbreakers. 06.03.1939 Registration closed on advice that breaking up was completed.					

Yard No.219
1911 PAMELA
Photo:- Barnard and Straker Collection

Yard No.221
1911 HOUBARA as HOLBORN
Photo by courtesy of George Scales

Yard No.228
1911 DE LA POLE
Photo:- Barnard and Straker Collection

NAME Official No. Port Letters Numbers	Yard No. Launched Registered	Registered G Ton N Ton	 L Ft B Ft	Engine Builder Horse Power Reg'd Speed	OWNER (Built for)
ATHELSTAN 132114 GY648 Steam Trawler	222 15.08.1911 04.10.1911	202 90	115.33 21.5	C.D. Holmes 67 NHP 10 knots	Onward Steam Fishing Co Ltd Grimsby
Aug 1914 Rqd by the Royal Navy as a minesweeper No. FY 343. 1919 returned. 17.09.1927 Sold to Sir Thomas Robinson & Sons, Grimsby. 29.11.1939 Rqd by the Royal Navy as an auxiliary patrol vessel . Jan 1940 returned. 26.04.1940 Departed Grimsby for the fishing grounds 50-60 miles east of Whitby and was last seen in Pos'n Lat 54° 00' N Long 001° 55'E by the trawler CLARE GY318 on the 27.04.1940. Apr 1940 Vessel posted missing:-Lost with all nine crew.					
PARTHIAN 132115 GY646 Steam Trawler	223 15.08.1911 17.10.1911	202 90	115.33 21.5	C.D. Holmes 67 NHP 10 knots	Onward Steam Fishing Co Ltd Grimsby
Aug 1914 Rqd by the Royal Navy as a minesweeper No. FY 328 renamed PARTHIAN II. 1919 returned and reverted. 17.09.1927 Sold to Sir Thomas Robinson & Sons, Grimsby. Nov 1939 Rqd by the Royal Navy as an auxiliary patrol vessel . Dec 1939 returned. 16.12.1941 Vessel lost following a collision off the Isle of Lewis with the Greek ship ATLANTICOS (5446 gt/ b 1919) . All the crew of the trawler were rescued.					
IRANIAN 134756 GY728 Steam Trawler	224 13.11.1911 30.12.1911	202 90	115.33 21.5	C.D. Holmes 67 NHP 10 knots	Thomas Robinson Grimsby
Mar 1915 Rqd by the Royal Navy as a minesweeper No. FY 1604. 1919 returned. 17.09.1927 Sold to Sir Thomas Robinson & Sons, Grimsby. 27.11.1939 Rqd by the Royal Navy as an auxiliary patrol vessel . 15.12.1939 returned. 24.12.1941 to J Bennett, Grimsby. 12.01.1944 Departed Grimsby for fishing grounds off Hornsea . 13.01.1944 Vessel posted missing (War Loss). All twelve crew lost.					
SCHIPPERKE 132259 H308 Steam Trawler	225 12.06.1911 31.07.1911	331 142	140.0 23.75	Amos & Smith 84 NHP 10.5 knots	Humber Steam Trawling Co Ltd Hull
Aug 1915 Rqd by the Royal Navy as a minesweeper / bomb thrower No. FY 1749. 1919 returned. 1919 Sold to Fresh Fish Supplies Ltd, Grimsby. 1923 to Ramon Feixas, Barcelona, Spain renamed PEDRO. 1936 Rqd by the Spanish Navy renamed PEDRO I . 1939 to V Larrañago Ortuzar, Barcelona. 10.03.1942 Vessel stranded on the coast of Rio de Oro Morocco. 15.04.1942 Vessel sank whilst being towed towards the Canary Islands.					
MACKENZIE 132275 H349 Steam Trawler	226 12.09.1911 01.11.1911	335 136	140.0 23.75	C.D. Holmes 86 NHP 10.5 knots	Neptune Steam Fishing Co Ltd Hull
Aug 1914 Rqd by the Royal Navy as a minesweeper No. FY 336. 1918 returned. 1919 Sold to Yarborough Steam Fishing Co Ltd, Grimsby (GY99). 25.01.1920 Sold to Fiskiveidahlutafelagid Kari, Reykjavik, Iceland renamed AUSTRI (RE238). 04.11.1924 to H/F Kara Videy, Gullbringusyslu, (GK238). 07.09.1927 Vessel wrecked at Vatnsnes, west coast of Iceland.					
SAINT MALO 132278 H371 Steam Trawler	227 08.09.1911 08.11.1911	335 136	140.0 23.75	C.D. Holmes 86 NHP 10.5 knots	Thomas Hamling & Co Ltd Hull
Apr 1914 Rqd by the Royal Navy as a minesweeper No. FY 1375. 1919 returned. 06.12.1918 Sold to St. Malo Steam Fishing Co Ltd, Grimsby (GY523). 1930 W Garratt, Grimsby renamed CARFAX. 1932 to Edward C Grant, Grimsby renamed WARDOUR. 1935 Clan Steam Fishing (Grimsby) Co Ltd, Grimsby. 28.08.1939 Rqd by the Royal Navy as a minesweeper No. FY 581. 16.04.1946 returned. 1947 transferred to Fleetwood. 1951 to Fern Leaf Co Ltd, Fleetwood. 1953 (FD146). 1954 Vessel sold for scrap to Haulbowline Ind Ltd 29.07.1954 Arrived Passage West Co Cork for breaking up.					
DE LA POLE 132285 H377 Steam Trawler	228 11.10.1911 01.12.1911	255 107	120.5 23.0	Amos & Smith 72 NHP 10.5 knots	National Steam Fishing Co Ltd Hull
May 1915 Rqd by the Royal Navy as a minesweeper No. FY 1636. 04.02.1916 Vessel wrecked on the Goodwin Sands.					

<table>
<tr><th>NAME
Official No.
Port Letters Numbers</th><th>Yard No.
Launched
Registered</th><th colspan="2">Registered</th><th>Engine Builder
Horse Power
Reg'd Speed</th><th>OWNER
(Built for)</th></tr>
<tr><th></th><th></th><th>G Ton
N Ton</th><th>L Ft
B Ft</th><th></th><th></th></tr>
<tr><td>MYNA
132288
H379 Steam Trawler</td><td>229
24.10.1911
11.12.1911</td><td>333
134</td><td>140.0
23.75</td><td>C.D. Holmes
86 NHP
10.5 knots</td><td>St Andrews Steam
Fishing Co Ltd
Hull</td></tr>
<tr><td colspan="6">Feb 1915 Rqd by the Royal Navy as a minesweeper No. FY 1174. 1919 returned.
10.10.1932 Sold to Pickering & Haldane's Steam Trawling Co Ltd, Hull.
26.05.1934 to John McCann, Hull renamed MEROK.1935 to Charleson Fishing Co Ltd, Hull renamed CAPE ROYDS.
28.11.1935 to A/S Nordlands Fiskeeksport, Tromso, Norway renamed BORTIND.
14.06.1940 Arrived Torshaven, Færoe Island.
1940 Rqd by the Royal Navy as an auxiliary patrol vessel / minesweeper No. J.394. 1946 returned.
1958 to A/S Nordlands Fiskeeksport, Tromso (7 cyl Alpha Diesel D/S diesel engine fitted).
1962 to A/S Tromso Tralfiske, Tromso renamed TROMSOY IV.
1965 to Kyrre Bogstrand Partrederi, Tromso renamed LENVIKTRAL.1976 to A/S Havfiskeselskap, Tromso.
1977 Vessel deleted from Lloyds Register of Shipping.</td></tr>
<tr><td>RALCO
132116
GY663 Steam Trawler</td><td>230
09.11.1911
05.01.1912</td><td>228
107</td><td>117.0
22.0</td><td>C.D. Holmes
70 NHP
10 knots</td><td>George F Sleight
Grimsby</td></tr>
<tr><td colspan="6">Nov 1914 Rqd by the Royal Navy as a minesweeper No. FY 672. 1919 returned.
17.11.1933 to Sleight & Humphreys, Grimsby.
29.11.1939 Rqd by the Royal Navy as an auxiliary patrol vessel . 22.01.1940 returned.
17.05.1949 Sold to George F Sleight & Sons, Grimsby.
1955 Vessel sold for scrap to Jacques Bakker en Zonen, Belgium. 17.07.1955 Arrived Bruges for breaking up.</td></tr>
<tr><td>RESPONSO
132118
GY666 Steam Trawler</td><td>231
09.11.1911
15.01.1912</td><td>228
107</td><td>117.0
22.0</td><td>C.D. Holmes
70 NHP
10 knots</td><td>George F Sleight
Grimsby</td></tr>
<tr><td colspan="6">Jan 1914 Rqd by the Royal Navy as a minesweeper No. FY 196. 31.12.1915 Vessel stranded Sanday Island.</td></tr>
<tr><td>STRONSAY
132299
H387 Steam Trawler</td><td>232
21.11.1911
15.01.1912</td><td>207
81</td><td>112.0
22.5</td><td>Amos & Smith
49 NHP
9.5 knots</td><td>Hull Steam Fishing
& Ice Co Ltd
Hull</td></tr>
<tr><td colspan="6">Sep 1915 Rqd by the Royal Navy as a minesweeper No. FY 1969. 1919 returned.
1937/38 Vessel sold to shipbreakers and broken up.</td></tr>
<tr><td>WESTRAY
132300
H390 Steam Trawler</td><td>233
07.12.1911
29.01.1912</td><td>207
81</td><td>112.0
22.5</td><td>Amos & Smith
49 NHP
9.5 knots</td><td>Hull Steam Fishing
& Ice Co Ltd
Hull</td></tr>
<tr><td colspan="6">Feb 1917 Rqd by the Royal Navy as a minesweeper No. FY 1277. 1919 returned.
1937/38 Vessel sold to shipbreakers and broken up.</td></tr>
<tr><td>RECOLO
132120
GY668 Steam Trawler</td><td>234
23.12.1911
20.02.1912</td><td>176
67</td><td>105.0
21.0</td><td>C.D. Holmes
60 NHP
10 knots</td><td>George F Sleight
Grimsby</td></tr>
<tr><td colspan="6">26.04.1915 Vessel sunk by mine in the North Sea 60 miles east by north of Spurn Point.</td></tr>
<tr><td>RELEVO
132121
GY670 Steam Trawler</td><td>235
23.01.1912
04.03.1912</td><td>176
67</td><td>105.0
21.0</td><td>C.D. Holmes
60 NHP
10 knots</td><td>George F Sleight
Grimsby</td></tr>
<tr><td colspan="6">Apr 1915 Rqd by the Royal Navy as a minesweeper No. FY 1615. 30.12.1916 Vessel wrecked off El Arish, Egypt.</td></tr>
<tr><td>BIRCH
132125
GY677 Steam Trawler</td><td>236
23.01.1912
20.03.1912</td><td>215
106</td><td>118.66
21.5</td><td>C.D. Holmes
67 NHP
10.5 knots</td><td>William Grant
Grimsby</td></tr>
<tr><td colspan="6">Feb 1915 Rqd by the Royal Navy as a minesweeper No. FY 1129.
23.08.1916 Vessel sunk by mine in the North Sea off Yarmouth. Mine laid by UC1 on 20.08.1916.</td></tr>
<tr><td>ROWSAY
133372
H410 Steam Trawler</td><td>237
23.12.1911
05.02.1912</td><td>207
81</td><td>112.0
22.5</td><td>Amos & Smith
49 NHP
9.5 knots</td><td>Hull Steam Fishing
& Ice Co Ltd
Hull</td></tr>
<tr><td colspan="6">Feb 1917 Rqd by the Royal Navy anti-submarine vessel with Hydrophonic listening equipment No. FY 1665.1919 returned.
12.06.1932 Vessel sank following a collision with ss VARG (5702 gt/ b 1928) in the North Sea.</td></tr>
</table>

Yard No.229
1911 MYNA
Photo:- Barnard and Straker Collection

Yard No.240
1912 NINUS as LOVINIA
Photo by courtesy of George Scales

Yard No.249
1912 GOOD LUCK
Photo:- Barnard and Straker Collection

NAME Official No. Port Letters Numbers	Yard No. Launched Registered	Registered G Ton N Ton	 L Ft B Ft	Engine Builder Horse Power Reg'd Speed	OWNER (Built for)
QUERCIA 132126 GY680 Steam Trawler	238 07.02.1912 10.04.1912	288 144	130.0 22.25	Amos & Smith 89 NHP 10.5 knots	Great Grimsby & East Coast Steam Fishing Co Ltd Grimsby
Dec 1914 Rqd by the Royal Navy as a minesweeper / escort vessel No. FY 446. 1919 returned. 18.10.1941 Sold to J Bennett, Grimsby. 28.08.1942 Rqd by the Royal Navy as a fuel carrier No. Y7.43(Apr 1944) port defence vessel No. 4.336. Jan 1946 returned. 1950 Vessel sold for scrap to Henry Scarr Hessle. 11.05.1950 Breaking up completed.					
SHELDON 132128 GY696 Steam Trawler	239 23.02.1912 23.04.1912	288 144	130.0 22.25	Amos & Smith 89 NHP 10.5 knots	Standard Steam Fishing Co Ltd Grimsby
Mar 1915 Rqd by the Royal Navy as a minesweeper / bomb thrower No. FY 1407. 1919 returned. 01.01.1940 Sold to Sir Thomas Robinson & Son, Grimsby. 28.05.1940 Rqd by the Royal Navy as an auxiliary patrol vessel No. FY 4.143. Sep 1941 as a minesweeper / fuel carrier No. Y 7.38. Jan 1945 returned. 30.01.1953 Vessel left Kirkwall for the Færoese fishing grounds. 31.01.1953 Presumed to have sunk in storm force conditions 60 miles north west of Dennis Head. Vessel posted missing:- Lost with all hands.					
NINUS 132131 GY700 Steam Trawler	240 06.03.1912 23.04.1912	292 124	130.0 23.0	C.D. Holmes 80 NHP 10 knots	Roberts & Ruthven Ltd Grimsby
Jun 1915 Rqd by the Royal Navy anti-submarine vessel with Hydrophonic listening equipment No. FY 1536.1919 returned. 18.10.1927 Sold to Earl Steam Fishing Co Ltd, Grimsby renamed (31.10.1927) LOVANIA. 12.06.1940 Rqd by the Royal Navy as an auxiliary patrol vessel (1941) minesweeper No. FY 942. 21.02.1946 returned. 10.12.1949 to Sir Alec Black, Grimsby. 05.06.1942 to J Bennett, Grimsby. 30.01.1947 to Inch Fishing Co Ltd, Granton renamed INCHGARVIE (GN30). Jul 1953 Vessel sold for scrap to Contieri Navali del Golfo, Genoa, Italy and broken up at Spezia.					
EDWARDIAN 132135 GY704 Steam Trawler	241 23.03.1912 14.05.1912	295 120	130.0 23.0	Amos & Smith 89 NHP 10.5 knots	Loyal Steam Fishing Co Ltd Grimsby
Apr 1915 Rqd by the Royal Navy as a minesweeper / bomb thrower No. FY 1453. 1919 returned. 21.03.1930 Driven ashore in a blizzard and stranded near Myrar Dyra Fjord, north Iceland. All twelve crew took to the lifeboat and drifted some 50 miles before landing at Sandgerdi southern Faxafloi. One crewman died of exposure. The Danish gunboat ÆGIR (162 gt/ b 1906) came to her assistance and searched for the crew but they had already reached safety.					
RAETIA 132138 GY707 Steam Trawler	242 23.03.1912 24.05.1912	295 120	130.0 23.0	Amos & Smith 89 NHP 10.5 knots	Great Grimsby & East Coast Steam Fishing Co Ltd Grimsby
Mar 1915 Rqd by the Royal Navy as a minesweeper No. FY 1232. 1919 returned. 28.08.1939 Rqd by the Royal Navy as an auxiliary patrol vessel No. FY 571 / minesweeper No. FY 4.142 1944 Fuel carrier No. Y7.26. 25.02.1946 returned. 14.01.1942 Sold to Boston Deep Sea Fishing Co Ltd, Grimsby. 1946 Vessel sold to shipbreakers. 15.11.1946 Registration closed on advice that breaking up was completed.					
SOLON 132139 GY714 Steam Trawler	243 20.04.1912 13.06.1912	295 120	130.0 23.0	Amos & Smith 89 NHP 10.5 knots	Standard Steam Fishing Co Ltd Grimsby
Aug 1914 Rqd by the Royal Navy as a minesweeper No. FY 55. 1919 returned. 11.11.1928 Vessel stranded near Myrdals-jökull (sand), south Iceland in a heavy gale. All twelve crew landed ashore but suffered terrible hardships before reaching the safety of an isolated farmhouse. One crewman died of exposure.					
PAVLOVA 134736 GY716 Steam Trawler	244 20.04.1912 09.07.1912	342 190	140.0 24.0	Amos & Smith 68 NHP 10.5 knots	South Western Steam Fishing Co Ltd Grimsby
Aug 1914 Rqd by the Royal Navy as a minesweeper No. FY 56. 1919 returned. 11.10.1915 Sold to Thomas W Baskcomb, Grimsby renamed (10.12.1931) EUTHAMIA. 22.10.1935 to Fred Parkes, Grimsby. 14.02.1936 to Park Holme Trawlers, Fleetwood. 03.06.1936 to Mar Rose Ltd, Fleetwood renamed MARGARET ROSE. 19.03.1940 to Loch Fishing Co, Hull. Mar 1940 Sold to the Royal Navy as a minesweeper No. FY 802. 29.04.1946 to O/S A/S Anglo, Haugesund, Norway renamed MORNA. 1951 Vessel sold for scrap to Soc Anon Elbros, Belgium. 02.11.1951 Arrived Antwerp for breaking up.					

<table>
<tr><th rowspan="2">NAME
Official No.
Port Letters Numbers</th><th rowspan="2">Yard No.
Launched
Registered</th><th colspan="2">Registered</th><th rowspan="2">Engine Builder
Horse Power
Reg'd Speed</th><th rowspan="2">OWNER
(Built for)</th></tr>
<tr><th>G Ton
N Ton</th><th>L Ft
B Ft</th></tr>
<tr><td>RAYON D'OR
134738
GY719 Steam Trawler</td><td>245
15.06.1912
25.07.1912</td><td>342
190</td><td>140.0
24.0</td><td>Amos & Smith
68 NHP
10.5knots</td><td>South Western Steam
Fishing Co Ltd
Grimsby</td></tr>
<tr><td colspan="6">06.07.914 Sold to Martinus A Olesen & Christian P Jensen, Grimsby.
27.12.1916 to Golden Ray Fishing Co Ltd, Halifax, Nova Scotia, Canada.
1939 Rqd by the Royal Canadian Navy as a minesweeper. 1945 returned. 1945 to Emil Pawlite, Halifax, Nova Scotia.
Feb 1954 Vessel sold to shipbreakers in Canada and broken up.</td></tr>
<tr><td>REMEXO
134738
GY721 Steam Trawler</td><td>246
18.06.1912
16.08.1912</td><td>230
108</td><td>117.0
22.0</td><td>C.D. Holmes
63 NHP
10 knots</td><td>George F Sleight
Grimsby</td></tr>
<tr><td colspan="6">Feb 1915 Rqd by the Royal Navy as a minesweeper No. FY 1136. 1920 returned.
17.11.1933 Sold to Sleight & Humphreys, Grimsby.
Nov 1939 Rqd by the Royal Navy as an auxiliary patrol vessel / minesweeper No. FY 875. 17.12.1945 returned.
17.05.1949 to George F Sleight & Sons, Grimsby.
1959 Vessel sold for scrap to Sormema, Belgium . 14.04.1959 Arrived Hemixen for breaking up.</td></tr>
<tr><td>REBONO
134739
GY731 Steam Trawler</td><td>247
18.07.1912
23.08.1912</td><td>175
68</td><td>105.0
21.0</td><td>C.D. Holmes
60 NHP
10 knots</td><td>George F Sleight
Grimsby</td></tr>
<tr><td colspan="6">23.09.1914 Vessel sunk by mine in the North Sea 25 miles east by north of Spurn Lightship.</td></tr>
<tr><td>MONIMIA
134740
GY734 Steam Trawler</td><td>248
15.06.1912
26.081912</td><td>342
190</td><td>140.0
24.0</td><td>Amos & Smith
68 NHP
10.5 knots</td><td>South Western Steam
Fishing Co Ltd
Grimsby</td></tr>
<tr><td colspan="6">10.07.1914 Vessel sank following a collision with the ss JERVAULX ABBEY (1188 gt/ b 1908), (Hull & Netherlands Steamship Co Ltd) , near Bull Buoy in the River Humber. The JERVAULX ABBEY picked up all the crew of the trawler.</td></tr>
<tr><td>GOOD LUCK
133404
H497 Steam Trawler</td><td>249
18.07.1912
1912</td><td>294
131</td><td>130.0
23.5</td><td>Amos & Smith
87 NHP
10.5 knots</td><td>Humber Steam
Trawling Co Ltd
Hull</td></tr>
<tr><td colspan="6">Apr 1915 Rqd by the Royal Navy as a minesweeper escort vessel No. FY 1342. 1919 returned.
1920 Sold to Fresh Fish Supplies Ltd, Hull. 1922 to Ashton & Welsh Ltd, Fleetwood renamed TRANQUIL (FD425).
1933 to Endeavour Trawlers Ltd, Fleetwood. 1937 to Cevic Steam Fishing Co Ltd, Fleetwood.
28.04.1940 Rqd by the Royal Navy as a minesweeper No. FY 920.
14.06.1942 Left Tilbury Docks after undergoing repairs. 16.06.1942 Vessel sank following a collision off Deal, Kent.</td></tr>
<tr><td>TARTAN
134743
GY723 Steam Trawler</td><td>250
12.08.1912
17.09.1912</td><td>202
89</td><td>115.33
21.5</td><td>C.D. Holmes
67 NHP
10 knots</td><td>Thomas Robinson
Grimsby</td></tr>
<tr><td colspan="6">Apr 1915 Rqd by the Royal Navy as a minesweeper No. FY 1607. 1919 returned.
17.09.1927 Sold to Sir Thomas Robinson & Sons, Grimsby.
29.11.1939 Rqd by the Royal Navy as a minesweeper No. FY 915.
15.04.1940 as an auxiliary patrol vessel No. FY 4.45. 06.03.1946 returned.
1963 Vessel sold for scrap to Thomas Young & Sons Ltd. 11.01.1963 Breaking up commenced at Sunderland.</td></tr>
<tr><td>ROWSLEY
134746
GY751 Steam Trawler</td><td>251
17.08.1912
05.12.1912</td><td>213
89</td><td>117.0
21.5</td><td>Amos & Smith
67 NHP
10 knots</td><td>John L Green
Grimsby</td></tr>
<tr><td colspan="6">11.12.1914 Sold to Walter H Beeley, Grimsby.
Apr 1915 Rqd by the Royal Navy as a minesweeper No. FY 1610. 1919 returned.
01.04.1923 to Walter H Beeley & George F Sleight Ltd, Grimsby.
05.06.1941 to Basil A Parkes, Grimsby. 07.10.1941 to Great Western Steam Fishing Co Ltd, Grimsby.
26.10.1944 to Wyre Steam Trawling Co Ltd, Fleetwood. 29.11.1944 to Ribble Trawlers Ltd, Grimsby.
Mar 1954 Vessel sold to BISCO and allocated to Edgar G Rees and broken up at Llanelly.</td></tr>
<tr><td>SUNCLOUD
134747
GY753 Steam Trawler</td><td>252
31.08.1912
21.10.1912</td><td>213
89</td><td>117.0
21.5</td><td>Amos & Smith
67 NHP
10 knots</td><td>Pelham Steam Fishing Co Ltd
Grimsby</td></tr>
<tr><td colspan="6">12.03.1913 Sold to North Western Steam Fishing Co, Grimsby.
20.03.1914 Sold to Grimsby & North Sea Steam Fishing Co Ltd, Grimsby.
Sep 1914 Rqd by the Royal Navy as a minesweeper No. FY 611. 1919 returned.
03.07.1919 Left Grimsby for North Sea fishing grounds. 08.07.1919 Last heard of. Posted missing :- Lost with all hands.</td></tr>
</table>

<table>
<tr><th>NAME
Official No.
Port Letters Numbers</th><th>Yard No.
Launched
Registered</th><th colspan="2">Registered
G Ton / L Ft
N Ton / B Ft</th><th>Engine Builder
Horse Power
Reg'd Speed</th><th>OWNER
(Built for)</th></tr>
<tr><td>SIALKOT
134751
GY780 Steam Trawler</td><td>253
28.09.1912
16.11.1912</td><td>308
138</td><td>135.0
23.5</td><td>C.D. Holmes
84 NHP
10.5 knots</td><td>Edgar C Grant &
Joseph W Little
Grimsby</td></tr>
<tr><td colspan="6">Dec 1914 Rqd by the Royal Navy as a boom defence vessel / minesweeper No. FY 1660. 1919 returned
15.03.1920 Sold to Hlutafelelagid Geir, Reykjavik, Iceland renamed GEIR (RE241).
31.03.1924 to Hlutafelagid Hronn, Reykjavik. 28.11.1946 to P/F Atlantis, Fuglejord, Færoe Islands renamed VITIN.
1952 Vessel sold to BISCO (for £5750) and allocated to Metal Industries. 15.02.1952 Arrived at Rosyth for breaking up.</td></tr>
<tr><td>IMPERIA
134749
GY758 Steam Trawler</td><td>254
14.09.1912
31.10.1912</td><td>213
89</td><td>117.0
21.5</td><td>Amos & Smith
58 NHP
10 knots</td><td>Pelham Steam Fishing Co Ltd
Grimsby</td></tr>
<tr><td colspan="6">28.06.1913 Sold to North Western Steam Fishing Co, Grimsby.
20.03.1914 to Grimsby and North Sea Steam Trawling Co Ltd, Grimsby.
Sep 1914 Rqd by the Royal Navy No. FY 620. 1919 returned. 05.08.1921 to Trawlers White Sea & Grimsby Ltd, Grimsby.
25.01.1939 Rqd by the Royal Navy as an auxiliary patrol vessel No. FY 813 (1940) boom defence vessel.
16.11.1945 returned. 15.01.1942 to Trawlers, Grimsby Ltd, Grimsby. 03.01.1946 to T C & F Moss Ltd, Grimsby.
1957 Vessel sold (£5357) to Shipbreaking Industries Ltd, Fife. 30.01.1957 Arrived Charlestown for breaking up.</td></tr>
<tr><td>CARDINAL
133418
H584 Steam Trawler</td><td>255
26.10.1912
10.12.1912</td><td>309
133</td><td>136.0
23.5</td><td>C.D. Holmes
80 NHP
10.5 knots</td><td>Marine Steam Fishing Co Ltd
Hull</td></tr>
<tr><td colspan="6">May 1915 Rqd by the Royal Navy No. FY 1576. 1920 returned.
27.11.1918 Sold to East Riding Steam Fishing Co Ltd, Hull. 1925 to Storrs Steam Trawling Co Ltd, Hull.
11.12.1925 Vessel wrecked near the wireless station at Injoy, Rolvsoeyhavn, Norway in a severe gale and blizzard.
In atrocious conditions a Norwegian rescue party brought ashore all twelve crew and the pilot by breeches buoy.</td></tr>
<tr><td>JAMES CARRUTHERS
134748
GY762 Steam Trawler</td><td>256
09.09.1912
30.10.1912</td><td>233
97</td><td>118.0
22.0</td><td>C.D. Holmes
58 NHP
10 knots</td><td>Atlin Construction Co Ltd
British Columbia
Canada</td></tr>
<tr><td colspan="6">Vessel Canadian owned but registered at Grimsby Thomas Robinson agent.
24.03.1918 Sold to Canadian Fish & Cold Storage Co Ltd, Grimsby.
25.01.1930 Registration transferred to Port of Prince Rupert, British Columbia, Canada, (converted to a Tug).
1934 to White Rock Tug Co, Prince Rupert, British Columbia.
1938 Northwest Towing Co, Vancouver. 1943 W C Gibson, Vancouver renamed (1956) NSP No. 14.
1974 Vessel deleted from Lloyds Register of Shipping.</td></tr>
<tr><td>DESIREE
134753
GY788 Steam Trawler</td><td>257
29.10.1912
04.12.1912</td><td>213
88</td><td>117.0
21.5</td><td>Amos & Smith
58 NHP
10 knots</td><td>Pelham Steam Fishing Co Ltd
Grimsby</td></tr>
<tr><td colspan="6">Aug 1914 Rqd by the Royal Navy as a minesweeper No. FY 251. 1919 returned.
06.05.1914 Sold to Neal Green, Grimsby. 10.02.1920 to Harold Bacon, Grimsby.
26.03.1920 to Trawlers White Sea & Grimsby Ltd, Grimsby.
29.11.1939 Rqd by the Royal Navy as a minesweeper . 16.01.1941 Vessel sunk by mine in the Thames Estuary.</td></tr>
<tr><td>SILICIA
134758
GY809 Steam Trawler</td><td>258
27.11.1912
14.01.1913</td><td>249
98</td><td>120.0
22.5</td><td>Amos & Smith
62 NHP
10 knots</td><td>Great Grimsby & East Coast
Steam Fishing Co Ltd
Grimsby</td></tr>
<tr><td colspan="6">Sep 1914 Rqd by the Royal Navy as a minesweeper No. FY 60. 1919 returned.
15.02.1937 Sold to Hopwood & Taylor, Grimsby. 24.05.1937 to Japan Fishing Co Ltd, Grimsby.
29.08.1939 Rqd by the Royal Navy as a minesweeper .
08.05.1941 Vessel sunk by mine off the Albert Dock, Hull Roads, River Humber.</td></tr>
<tr><td>STREPHON
134760
GY810 Steam Trawler</td><td>259
27.11.1912
28.01.1913</td><td>249
98</td><td>120.0
22.5</td><td>Amos & Smith
62 NHP
10 knots</td><td>Standard Steam
Fishing Co Ltd
Grimsby</td></tr>
<tr><td colspan="6">Mar 1915 Rqd by the Royal Navy as an anti-submarine vessel with Hydrophonic listening equipment No. FY 1233.
1919 returned. 15.02.1937 Sold to Hopwood & Taylor, Grimsby. 09.06.1937 to Japan Fishing Co Ltd, Grimsby.
25.08.1940 Rqd by the Royal Navy as a minesweeper No. FY 1829. 12.02.1946 returned.
10.01.1961 Vessel sold for scrap to Verrenigde Utrechte, Izjerhandel, Holland and broken up at Utrecht.</td></tr>
<tr><td>WORSLEY
134761
GY814 Steam Trawler</td><td>260
09.12.1912
10.02.1913</td><td>309
138</td><td>135.0
23.5</td><td>C.D. Holmes
84 NHP
10.5 knots</td><td>Edward C Grant
Grimsby</td></tr>
<tr><td colspan="6">Jul 1915 Rqd by the Royal Navy as an auxiliary patrol vessel.
14.08.1915 Vessel sunk by mine off Aldeburgh. Mine laid by UC6 on 13.08.1915.</td></tr>
</table>

Yard No.255
1912 CARDINAL
Photo:- Barnard and Straker Collection

Yard No.258
1912 SILICIA
Photo by courtesy of George Scales

Yard No.261
1913 PASSING
Photo:- Author's Collection

NAME Official No. Port Letters Numbers	Yard No. Launched Registered	Registered G Ton N Ton	 L Ft B Ft	Engine Builder Horse Power Reg'd Speed	OWNER (Built for)
PASSING 135966 GY877 Steam Trawler	261 05.06.1913 21.08.1913	459 291	160.0 26.0	Amos & Smith 68 NHP 10 knots	South Western Steam Fishing Co Ltd Grimsby
06.11.1913 Sold to Alec Black, Grimsby. 14.10.1914 to South Western Steam Fishing Co Ltd, Grimsby. Aug 1914 Rqd by the Royal Navy as a minesweeper No. FY 58. Dec 1914 Vessel damaged by mine off Bridlington and towed into Scarborough Harbour by the paddle steamer BRIGHTON QUEEN (553 gt/ b 1897) for repairs. 1915 Returned to the Royal Navy No. FY 1542. 1920 returned. 19.06.1917 to North Western Steam Fishing Co Ltd, Grimsby. 17.06.1920 to Pecheries A Vap Congo, Bonaire, Belgium renamed BOULA MATARI (O130). 14.02.1925 to La Morue Francaise Et Secheries, De Fecamp, France renamed PACIFIQUE (SPM121). 14.12.1928 Whilst fishing off Newfoundland the French trawlers COMMANDANT EMAILLE, MOUNT KEMMEL and ASIE picked up a faint distress radio signal from the PACIFIQUE. However no trace of the vessel was found. Jan 1929 Vessel posted missing :-Lost with all hands.					
WALLENA 135998 GY12 Steam Trawler	261A 17.12.1913 03.03.1914	225 111	117.0 22.0	C.D. Holmes 66 NHP 10 knots	Walter Olney Grimsby
Jan 1915 Rqd by the Royal Navy as a minesweeper No. FY 907. 1919 returned. 04.10.1915 Sold to Neva Steam Trawlers Ltd, Fleetwood (FD82). 1924 to J N & Bacon, Grimsby (GY132). 1930 Kottingham Trawling Co Ltd, Grimsby. Nov 1939 Rqd by the Royal Navy as a minesweeper No. FY 832. Apr 1945 boom gate defence vessel. Nov 1945 returned. 1944 to Parkholme Trawlers Ltd, Grimsby. 11.09.1946 Laid up at Alexandra Dock Grimsby. 1949 Vessel sold to John R Hepworth, Hull. 27.07.1949 Left Grimsby to be broken up at Paull.					
KENNYMORE 136000 GY38 Steam Trawler	261B 14.01.1914 06.03.1914	225 111	117.0 22.0	C.D. Holmes 66 NHP 10 knots	South Western Steam Fishing Co Ltd Grimsby
Apr 1914 Rqd by the Royal Navy as a minesweeper / bomb thrower No. FY 1373. 1919 returned. 11.10.1915 Sold to Thomas W Baskcomb, Grimsby. 24.10.1935 to Dobson Ship Repair Co Ltd, Grimsby. 27.11.1939 Rqd by the Royal Navy as a minesweeper No. FY 857. 25.11.1940 Vessel sunk by mine off the Thames Estuary.					
SWEEPER 134771 GY853 Steam Trawler	262 24.02.1914 08.05.1914	395 235	150.0 25.0	Amos & Smith 68 NHP 10 knots	South Western Steam Fishing Co Ltd Grimsby
Aug 1914 Rqd by the Royal Navy as a bomb thrower / minesweeper No. FY 54. 1919 returned. 11.10.1915 Sold to Thomas W Baskcomb, Grimsby. 25.11.1935 to Boston Deep Sea Fishing Co Ltd, Grimsby. 1936 to A/S Norrdhavet, Kristiansnd, Norway. 1939 Rqd by the Royal Norwegian Navy renamed NORDHAV II. 15.06.1940 Arrived at Torshaven, Færoe Islands / served as a minesweeper with the Royal Navy No. FY 1906. 10.03.1945 Vessel torpedoed and sunk by U-boat No. U714 commanded by Capt Schwebke off Dundee. Whilst serving with the 71 minesweeper group based at Dundee.					
RENZO 134765 GY826 Steam Trawler	263 11.01.1913 12.03.1913	230 107	117.0 22.0	C.D. Holmes 70 NHP 10 knots	George F Sleight Grimsby
Nov 1914 Rqd by the Royal Navy as a minesweeper No. FY 198. 1919 returned. 17.11.1933 Sold to Sleight & Humphrey, Grimsby. Nov 1939 Rqd by the Royal Navy as a minesweeper No. FY 893. Oct 1945 returned. 17.05.1949 to George F Sleight & Sons Ltd, Grimsby. 1955 Vessel sold for scrap to Jacques Bakker en Zonen, Belgium. 13.11.1955 Arrived Bruges for breaking up.					
RODINO 134766 GY836 Steam Trawler	264 25.01.1913 17.03.1913	230 107	117.0 22.0	C.D. Holmes 70 NHP 10 knots	George F Sleight Grimsby
Mar 1915 Rqd by the Royal Navy as a minesweeper No. FY 1230. 1919 returned. 17.11.1933 Sold to Sleight & Humphrey, Grimsby. 25.11.1939 Rqd by the Royal Navy as a minesweeper No. FY 840. 24.07.1940 Vessel sunk by German aircraft off Dover.					

<table>
<tr><th rowspan="2">NAME
Official No.
Port Letters Numbers</th><th rowspan="2">Yard No.
Launched
Registered</th><th colspan="2">Registered</th><th rowspan="2">Engine Builder
Horse Power
Reg'd Speed</th><th rowspan="2">OWNER
(Built for)</th></tr>
<tr><th>G Ton
N Ton</th><th>L Ft
B Ft</th></tr>
<tr><td>WARLAND
134762
GY819 Steam Trawler</td><td>265
11.12.1912
25.02.1913</td><td>214
88</td><td>117.0
21.5</td><td>Amos & Smith
58 NHP
10 knots</td><td>Alec Black
Grimsby</td></tr>
<tr><td colspan="6">25.03.1915 Sold to Alfred W Baxter, Grimsby.
May 1915 Rqd by the Royal Navy as a bomb thrower / minesweeper No. FY 1626. 1919 returned.
25.09.1917 to Sleights Steam Fishing Co, Grimsby. 07.11.1917 to Walter H Beeley, Grimsby.
30.03.1919 to Thorganby Steam Fishing Co, Grimsby. 02.05.1919 to Leopold D Napier, Grimsby.
11.02.1920 to Smithfield Trawlers Ltd, London. 21.08.1922 to Marshall Line Steam Fishing Co Ltd, Grimsby (GY299).
20.07.1926 to Pelham Steam Fishing Co Ltd, Grimsby. 19.09.1928 to Earl Steam Fishing Co Ltd, Grimsby.
16.09.1931 to Matthew J McCabe, Dublin. (D125).
Apr 1940 Rqd by the Royal Navy as an auxiliary patrol vessel.
18.02.1942 Vessel sunk by German Aircraft in the North Sea.</td></tr>
<tr><td>LOROONE
134764
GY830 Steam Trawler</td><td>266
11.01.1913
11.03.1913</td><td>214
88</td><td>117.0
21.5</td><td>Amos & Smith
58 NHP
10 knots</td><td>Pelham Steam Fishing Co Ltd
Grimsby</td></tr>
<tr><td colspan="6">24.09.1915 Sold to Rushworth Steam Fishing Co Ltd, Grimsby.
Jun 1915 Rqd by the Royal Navy as a minesweeper No. FY 1588. 1919 returned.
22.03.1918 to Yarborough Steam Fishing Co, Grimsby. 20.02.1919 to Thorganby Steam Fishing Co Ltd, Grimsby.
08.03.1926 to T C & F Moss, Grimsby renamed (17.04.1926) CALVERTON.
27.11.1939 Rqd by the Royal Navy as a minesweeper No. FY 775.
29.11.1940 Vessel sunk by mine in the Humber Estuary. Whilst serving with the 110 minesweeper group based at Grimsby.</td></tr>
<tr><td>RODOSTO
134769
GY839 Steam Trawler</td><td>267
11.02.1913
15.04.1913</td><td>173
76</td><td>106.66
21.0</td><td>C.D. Holmes
62 NHP
10 knots</td><td>George F Sleight
Grimsby</td></tr>
<tr><td colspan="6">May 1915 Rqd by the Royal Navy No. FY 1490. 1920 returned.
17.11.1933 Sold to Sleight & Humphrey, Grimsby. 17.05.1949 to George F Sleight & Sons Ltd, Grimsby.
1956 Vessel sold for scrap to Jacques Bakker en Zonen, Belgium. 28.03.1956 Arrived Bruges for breaking up.</td></tr>
<tr><td>MARTHE

O43 Steam Trawler</td><td>268
10.02.1913
16.04.1913</td><td>243
123</td><td>120.0
22.0</td><td>C.D. Holmes
71 NHP
10.5 knots</td><td>A T Golder & Co
Ostend
Belgium.</td></tr>
<tr><td colspan="6">1917 Rqd by the Royal Navy as a fishing trawler (Fishery Reserve). 1919 returned.
1929 Sold to Pecheries Nationales Belges S/A, Ostend, Belgium.
1934 to T H Scales & Sons Leith renamed CRAIG ISLAND (LH141) Official No. 161838.
27.11.1939 - 1944 Rqd by the Royal Navy as a boom defence vessel No. Z.157. 23.02.1946 returned.
31.09.1942 to J Marr & Sons Ltd, Hull.
08.03.1946 Vessel sold for scrap to J Cameron, Peterhead. 06.05.1946 Commenced breaking up.</td></tr>
<tr><td>REMAGIO
134770
GY843 Steam Trawler</td><td>269
08.03.1913
20.04.1913</td><td>173
76</td><td>106.66
21.0</td><td>C.D. Holmes
62 NHP
10 knots</td><td>George F Sleight
Grimsby</td></tr>
<tr><td colspan="6">May 1915 Rqd by the Royal Navy as a minesweeper No. FY 1487. 1919 returned.
17.11.1933 Sold to Sleight & Humphrey, Grimsby.
08/09.06.1941 Damaged by aircraft bombs near Bamburgh Northumberland.
17.05.1949 to George F Sleight & Sons Ltd, Grimsby.
1956 Vessel sold for scrap to Jacques Bakker en Zonen, Belgium. 28.03.1956 Arrived Bruges for breaking up.</td></tr>
<tr><td>UNITIA
135970
GY924 Steam Trawler</td><td>269A
19.07.1913
17.09.1913</td><td>296
122</td><td>130.0
23.0</td><td>Amos & Smith
68 NHP
10 knots</td><td>Great Grimsby & East Coast
Steam Fishing Co Ltd
Grimsby</td></tr>
<tr><td colspan="6">Dec 1914 Rqd by the Royal Navy as a minesweeper No. FY 699. 1919 returned.
1940 Rqd by the Royal Navy as a minesweeper No. FY 1852. renamed PORTIA.
28.05.1940 as an auxiliary patrol vessel. Feb 1941 as a minesweeper. 27.01.1946 returned and reverted.
14.01.1942 Sold to Boston Deep Sea Fishing Co Ltd, Grimsby. 25.03.1946 to Nordic Fishing Co Ltd, London.
28.07.1947 to Edna Deep Sea Fishing Co Ltd, Grimsby. 25.11.1950 to Kimbrace Fishing Ltd, Aberdeen (A663).
24.05.1952 Vessel stranded on rocks between Rowsay and Egilsay. 09.06.1952 Re-floated and towed to Kirkwall.
1954 Vessel sold for scrap to Belgian shipbreakers and broken up.</td></tr>
</table>

NAME Official No. Port Letters Numbers	Yard No. Launched Registered	Registered G Ton N Ton	 L Ft B Ft	Engine Builder Horse Power Reg'd Speed	OWNER (Built for)
CORTINA 134775 GY862 Steam Trawler	270 24.04.1913 16.06.1913	214 89	117.0 21.5	C.D. Holmes 66 NHP 10 knots	Neal Green Grimsby
Apr 1915 Rqd by the Royal Navy as a minesweeper No. FY 1621. 1919 returned. 10.02.1929 Sold to Harold Bacon, Grimsby. 26.03. 1920 to Trawlers White Sea & Grimsby Ltd, Grimsby. 1939 Rqd by the Royal Navy as an auxiliary patrol vessel / minesweeper. 07.12.1940 Vessel lost following a collision off the River Humber. Whilst serving with the 111 minesweeper group based at Grimsby.					
RONONIA 134777 GY865 Steam Trawler	271 24.04.1913 28.06.1913	214 89	117.0 21.5	C.D. Holmes 66 NHP 10 knots	Pelham Steam Fishing Co Ltd Grimsby
30.08.1913 Sold to Walter Olney, Fleetwood (FD88). 04.10.1915 to Neva Steam Trawling Co Ltd, Fleetwood. Jun 1915 Rqd by the Royal Navy as a minesweeper No. FY 1594. 1919 returned. 1924 to J N & H Bacon, Grimsby (GY134). 1930 to Kottingham Trawling Co Ltd, Grimsby. 05.03.1942 Vessel posted missing:- Lost with all hands.					
SCARRON 135973 GY935 Steam Trawler	271A 19.07.1913 07.10.1913	296 122	130.0 23.0	Amos & Smith 68 NHP 10 knots	Standard Steam Fishing Co Ltd Grimsby
Sep 1915 Rqd by the Royal Navy as a bomb thrower / minesweeper No. FY 1864. 1919 returned. 1940 Rqd by the Royal Navy as a minesweeper No. FY 1913. 1945 returned. 14.01.1942 Sold to St Andrews Steam Fishing Co Ltd, Hull. 1946 Vessel sold for scrap to Edgar G Rees. 07.07.1946 Breaking up commenced at Llanelly.					
RENARRO 134780 GY868 Steam Trawler	272 08.05.1913 15.07.1913	230 107	117.0 22.0	C.D. Holmes 70 NHP 10.5 knots	George F Sleight Grimsby
Feb 1915 Rqd by the Royal Navy as a minesweeper No. FY 1043. 10.11.1918 Vessel sunk by mine in the Dardanelles.					
RIPARVO 134782 GY870 Steam Trawler	273 07.06.1913 29.07.1913	230 107	117.0 22.0	C.D. Holmes 70 NHP 10.5 knots	George F Sleight Grimsby
Mar 1915 Rqd by the Royal Navy as a minesweeper No. FY 1236. 02.11.1918 Vessel sank following a collision north of Benghazi in the Mediterranean Sea.					
AMPULLA 135978 GY949 Steam Trawler	273A 20.08.1913 24.10.1913	248 99	120.0 22.5	Amos & Smith 62 NHP 10 knots	Loyal Steam Fishing Co Ltd Grimsby
Sep 1914 Rqd by the Royal Navy as a minesweeper No. FY 59. 1919 returned. 22.05.1940 Sold to Sir Alec Black, Grimsby. 1940 Rqd by the Royal Navy as an auxiliary patrol vessel / minesweeper No. FY 4.119. 1946 returned. 08.04.1943 to Grimsby Motor Trawlers Ltd, Grimsby. 30.07.1949 to Trawlers, Grimsby Ltd, Grimsby. 10.04.1953 to Derwent Trawlers Ltd, Grimsby. 29.01.1959 to Ross Trawlers Ltd, Grimsby. 1962 Vessel sold for scrap to Van Heyghen Freres, Belgium. 23.02.1962 Arrived Ghent for breaking up.					
VINDELECIA 135981 GY954 Steam Trawler	274 17.09.1913 10.11.1913	248 99	120.0 22.5	Amos & Smith 62 NHP 10 knots	Great Grimsby & East Coast Steam Fishing Co Ltd Grimsby
Sep 1914 Rqd by the Royal Navy as a minesweeper No. FY 452. 1919 returned. 15.02.1937 Sold to Hopwood & Taylor, Grimsby. 02.06.1937 to Japan Fishing Co Ltd, Grimsby. 08.06.1940 Rqd by the Royal Navy as an auxiliary patrol vessel No. FY 1711. 12.01.1942 returned. 12.03.1943 Rqd by the Royal Navy as a fuel carrier No. Y7.5. Served at Normandy in the 35th landing barge - supply and repair Flotilla. 07.12.1945 returned. 04.12.1960 Vessel sprang a leak in heavy weather and foundered approx 90 miles off Spurn Point.					
SIMERSON 135982 GY960 Steam Trawler	274A 30.09.1913 02.12.1913	248 99	120.0 22.5	Amos & Smith 62 NHP 10 knots	Standard Steam Fishing Co Ltd Grimsby
May 1915 Rqd by the Royal Navy as a minesweeper No. FY 1447. 1919 returned. 15.02.1937 Sold to Hopwood & Taylor, Grimsby. 21.05.1937 to Japan Fishing Co Ltd, Grimsby. 1940 Rqd by the Royal Navy as an auxiliary patrol vessel No. FY 4.278. 14.06.1946 returned. 28.07.1956 Vessel sold for scrap to B J Nijkerk, Belgium and broken up at Antwerp.					

Yard No.267
1913 RODOSTO
Photo by courtesy of The Grimsby Evening Telegraph

Yard No.277
1913 THE TETRARCH
Photo by courtesy of George Scales

Yard No.285
1913 BEMPTON (At Aberdeen)
Photo:- Author's Collection

<table>
<tr><th rowspan="2">NAME
Official No.
Port Letters Numbers</th><th rowspan="2">Yard No.
Launched
Registered</th><th colspan="2">Registered</th><th rowspan="2">Engine Builder
Horse Power
Reg'd Speed</th><th rowspan="2">OWNER
(Built for)</th></tr>
<tr><th>G Ton
N Ton</th><th>L Ft
B Ft</th></tr>
<tr><td>CARIEDA
135968
GY908 Steam Trawler</td><td>275
21.06.1913
25.08.1913</td><td>225
112</td><td>117.0
22.0</td><td>C.D. Holmes
66 NHP
10 knots</td><td>Pelham Steam Fishing Co Ltd
Grimsby</td></tr>
<tr><td colspan="6">Apr 1915 Rqd by the Royal Navy as a minesweeper No. FY 1751. 1919 returned.
24.09.1915 Sold to Rushworth Steam Fishing Co Ltd, Grimsby. 22.03.1918 to Yarborough Steam Fishing Co Ltd, Grimsby.
25.07.1924 to Harold Bacon, Grimsby. 05.09.1930 to Kottingham Trawling Co, Grimsby.
18.04.1940 Rqd by the Royal Navy as a balloon barrage vessel. 24.04.1940 returned.
03.01.1944 to Parkholme Trawling Co, Grimsby. 30.07.1949 to Trawlers Grimsby Ltd, Grimsby.
10.04.1953 to Derwent Trawlers Ltd, Grimsby. 1958 Vessel sold for scrap to Arie Rijsdijk Boss & Zonen, Holland.
24.07.1958 Arrived Hendrik-Ido-Ambracht for breaking up.</td></tr>
<tr><td>THUNDERSTONE
135967
GY907 Steam Trawler</td><td>276
21.06.1913
23.08.1913</td><td>225
112</td><td>117.0
22.0</td><td>C.D. Holmes
66 NHP
10 knots</td><td>North Western Steam
Fishing Co Ltd
Grimsby</td></tr>
<tr><td colspan="6">Apr 1915 Rqd by the Royal Navy as a minesweeper No. FY 1755. 1919 returned.
11.10.1915 Sold to Thomas W Baskcomb, Grimsby. 10.07.1919 to Harry Wood & Co, Grimsby.
11.08.1923 to Pelham Steam Fishing Co Ltd, Grimsby. 19.09.1928 to Earl Steam Fishing Co Ltd, Grimsby .
24.04.1940 Rqd by the Royal Navy as a barrage balloon vessel. 24.08.1943 returned.
10.12.1940 to Sir Alec Black, Grimsby. 08.02.1943 to Shire Trawlers Ltd, Grimsby.
25.05.1944 to Parkholme Trawlers Ltd, Grimsby. 30.07.1949 to Trawlers, Grimsby Ltd, Grimsby.
10.04.1953 to Derwent Trawlers Ltd, Grimsby. 14.11.1958 to Forward Steam Fishing Co Ltd, Grimsby.
29.10.1962 Vessel sold for scrap to Van Den Bossche & Co, Belgium. 17.11.1962 Arrived Boom for breaking up.</td></tr>
<tr><td>THE TETRARCH
135975
GY945 Steam Trawler</td><td>277
22.07.1913
14.10.1913</td><td>225
112</td><td>117.0
22.0</td><td>C.D. Holmes
58 NHP
10 knots</td><td>North Western Steam
Fishing Co Ltd
Grimsby</td></tr>
<tr><td colspan="6">Aug 1914 Rqd by the Royal Navy as a minesweeper No. FY 254. 1919 returned.
11.10.1915 Sold to Thomas W Baskcomb, Grimsby. 24.10.1935 to Dobson Ship Repair Co Ltd, Grimsby.
24.12.1940 to Perihelion Steam Fishing Co Ltd, Grimsby. 30.11.1941 Vessel sank following a collision with the ss KOOLGA (1110 gt/ b 1910) near 20 T buoy off Coquet Island. Nine crew lost.</td></tr>
<tr><td>RESOLVO
135974
GY942 Steam Trawler</td><td>278
20.08.1913
06.10.1913</td><td>231
108</td><td>117.4
22.0</td><td>C.D. Holmes
70 NHP
10.5 knots</td><td>George F Sleight
Grimsby</td></tr>
<tr><td colspan="6">Feb 1915 Rqd by the Royal Navy as a minesweeper No. FY 459. 1920 returned.
17.11.1933 Sold to Sleight & Humphrey, Grimsby. 1939 Rqd by the Royal Navy as a minesweeper No. FY 821.
12.10.1940 Vessel beached after being badly damaged by a mine in the Thames Estuary and sold for breaking up.</td></tr>
<tr><td>RISTANGO
135976
GY946 Steam Trawler</td><td>279
02.09.1913
17.10.1913</td><td>178
68</td><td>106.7
21.0</td><td>C.D. Holmes
61 NHP
10 knots</td><td>George F Sleight
Grimsby</td></tr>
<tr><td colspan="6">Nov 1914 Rqd by the Royal Navy as a minesweeper No. FY 819. 1919 returned.
17.11.1933 Sold to Sleight & Humphrey, Grimsby. 1940 Rqd by the Royal Navy as a boom gate vessel at Sheerness.
14.11.1940 Vessel capsized and sank after fouling the Medway boom at Sheerness.</td></tr>
<tr><td>RETRUDO
135980
GY952 Steam Trawler</td><td>280
02.09.1913
31.10.1913</td><td>178
68</td><td>106.7
21.0</td><td>C.D. Holmes
61 NHP
10 knots</td><td>George F Sleight
Grimsby</td></tr>
<tr><td colspan="6">Apr 1915 Rqd by the Royal Navy as a minesweeper No. FY 1623. 1920 returned.
17.11.1933 Sold to Sleight & Humphrey, Grimsby. 17.05.1949 to George F Sleight & Sons Ltd, Grimsby.
1956 Vessel sold for scrap to B J Nijkerk S/A, Belgium. 15.03.1956 Arrived Boom for breaking up.</td></tr>
<tr><td>THEBAN
135985
GY937 Steam Trawler</td><td>281
30.09.1913
02.12.1913</td><td>202
90</td><td>115.4
21.5</td><td>C.D. Holmes
67 NHP
10 knots</td><td>Thomas Robinson
Grimsby</td></tr>
<tr><td colspan="6">Sep 1914 Rqd by the Royal Navy as an auxiliary patrol vessel No. FY 617. Dec 1918 returned.
07.11.1919 Vessel posted missing:- lost with all hands.</td></tr>
<tr><td>LIBYAN
135987
GY938 Steam Trawler</td><td>282
18.10.1913
05.12.1913</td><td>202
90</td><td>115.4
21.5</td><td>C.D. Holmes
67 NHP
10 knots</td><td>Onward Steam Fishing Co Ltd
Grimsby</td></tr>
<tr><td colspan="6">Feb 1915 Rqd by the Royal Navy as a minesweeper No. FY 1127. 1919 returned.
1940 Rqd by the Royal Navy as a minesweeper No. FY 1800 / fuel carrier No. Y7.18 (1944) target towing vessel.
16.08.1946 returned. 1957 Vessel sold for scrap to F & W Joch, Germany. 14.04.1957 Arrived Hamburg for breaking up.</td></tr>
</table>

<table>
<tr><th rowspan="2">NAME
Official No.
Port Letters Numbers</th><th rowspan="2">Yard No.
Launched
Registered</th><th colspan="2">Registered</th><th rowspan="2">Engine Builder
Horse Power
Reg'd Speed</th><th rowspan="2">OWNER
(Built for)</th></tr>
<tr><th>G Ton
N Ton</th><th>L Ft
B Ft</th></tr>
<tr><td>ETRUSCAN
135990
GY939 Steam Trawler</td><td>283
18.10.1913
01.01.1914</td><td>202
90</td><td>115.4
21.5</td><td>C.D. Holmes
67 NHP
10 knots</td><td>Thomas Robinson
Grimsby</td></tr>
<tr><td colspan="6">Sep 1915 Rqd by the Royal Navy as a minesweeper No. FY 1882. 1919 returned.
Nov 1939 Rqd by the Royal Navy as a minesweeper / auxiliary patrol vessel (1944) fuel carrier No. FY 854.
28.11.1944 returned. 28.11.1945 Vessel last seen leaving the fishing grounds.
Dec 1945 Vessel posted missing:- Lost with all eleven crew.</td></tr>
<tr><td>FILEY
136171
H8 Steam Trawler</td><td>284
29.11.1913
00.01.1914</td><td>226
87</td><td>115.5
22.5</td><td>Amos & Smith
94 NHP
11 knots</td><td>Hull Steam Fishing &
Ice Co Ltd
Hull</td></tr>
<tr><td colspan="6">Mar 1915 Sold to the Admiralty No. 1363. Vessel wrecked 02.10.1916 in Camusmore Bay Tory Island.
1917 Salvaged and returned to the Royal Navy No. FY 3826. 01.06.1920 to Hull Steam Fishing & Ice Co Ltd, Hull (H191).
06.03.1936 to Heward Trawlers Ltd, London (LO189). 27.04.1943 to Kingston Steam Trawling Co Ltd, Hull (H547).
15.11.1944 to Iago Steam Trawlers Ltd, London. 1948 to A Hay Aberdeen (A232).
15.06.1959 Vessel sold for scrap to Scherpswerf De Beer Zaandam, Belgium. 25.06.1959 Arrived Antwerp for breaking up.</td></tr>
<tr><td>BEMPTON
136174
H19 Steam Trawler</td><td>285
29.11.1913
00.02.1914</td><td>226
87</td><td>115.5
22.5</td><td>Amos & Smith
94 NHP
11 knots</td><td>Hull Steam Fishing
& Ice Co Ltd
Hull</td></tr>
<tr><td colspan="6">Apr 1915 Rqd by the Royal Navy as a minesweeper No. FY 1369. 1919 returned.
06.03.1936 Sold to Heward Trawlers Ltd, London (LO192). 27.04.1943 to Kingston Steam Trawling Co Ltd, Hull (H546).
07.03.1957 to Loyal Steam Fishing Co Ltd, Grimsby (GY29). 1951 to A Hay Aberdeen (A673).
1958 Vessel sold for scrap to F & W Joch, Germany. 07.05.1958 Arrived Hamburg for breaking up.</td></tr>
<tr><td>ST. ELMO
136170
H3 Steam Trawler</td><td>286
15.11.1913
00.03.1914</td><td>314
125</td><td>136.0
23.5</td><td>C.D. Holmes
86 NHP
11 knots</td><td>St Andrews Steam
Fishing Co Ltd
Hull</td></tr>
<tr><td colspan="6">May 1915 Rqd by the Royal Navy as a bomb thrower / minesweeper No. FY 1583. 1919 returned.
06.03.1921 Vessel wrecked 23 miles west of Portland on the south coast of Iceland. All twelve crew rescued.</td></tr>
<tr><td>TERVANI
135999
GY10 Steam Trawler</td><td>287
18.10.1913
02.03.1914</td><td>457
301</td><td>160.0
26.0</td><td>C.D. Holmes
89 NHP
11 knots</td><td>Alec Black
Grimsby</td></tr>
<tr><td colspan="6">14.10.1914 Sold to South Western Steam Fishing Co Ltd, Grimsby. 11.10.1915 to Thomas W Baskcomb, Grimsby.
May 1915 Rqd by the Royal Navy as an auxiliary patrol vessel No. FY 3204.
21.11.1916 Vessel sunk by mine off Orford Ness. Mine laid by UC 4.</td></tr>
<tr><td>EROICAN
136001
GY35 Steam Trawler</td><td>288
15.01.1914
07.03.1914</td><td>225
112</td><td>117.0
22.0</td><td>Amos & Smith
68 NHP
9.5 knots</td><td>North Western Steam
Fishing Co Ltd
Grimsby</td></tr>
<tr><td colspan="6">Aug 1914 Rqd by the Royal Navy as a minesweeper No. FY 294. 1920 returned.
02.11.1915 Sold to Harold Croft Baker, Grimsby. 20.04.1920 to Savoy Steam Fishing Co Ltd, Grimsby.
24.05.1928 to Harold Croft Baker & Sons Ltd, Grimsby. 09.02.1937 to Dominion Steam Fishing Co Ltd, Grimsby.
1940 Rqd by the Royal Navy as a minesweeper No. FY 518 / fuel carrier No. FY 4.144. 1949 returned.
1961 Vessel sold for scrap to H.P. Heuvelman NV, Holland. 15.06.1961 Arrived New Waterway for breaking up.</td></tr>
<tr><td>CORCYRA
136003
GY63 Steam Trawler</td><td>288A
12.02.1914
17.04.1914</td><td>225
112</td><td>117.0
22.0</td><td>Amos & Smith
68 NHP
9.5 knots</td><td>South Western Steam
Fishing Co Ltd
Grimsby</td></tr>
<tr><td colspan="6">Aug 1914 Rqd by the Royal Navy as a minesweeper No. FY 278.
20.02.1915 Vessel stranded off Bacton. Dec 1916 Salvaged and returned to service.
10.02.1917 Sold to George W White & John W Willows, Grimsby (GY104).
06.07.1918 to Stringer's Steam Fishing Co Ltd, Boston (BN142).
1922 to South Western Steam Fishing Co, Grimsby (GY1021).
1925 to Earl Steam Fishing Co Ltd, Grimsby. 1938 to McCabe & Curtis Dublin (D120).
1940 Sold to the Royal Navy as an auxiliary patrol vessel (21.05.1943) water carrier No. FY 293.
1946 to Earl Steam Fishing Co, Grimsby (GY281) .27.08.1947 to W & J Wood Aberdeen (A307).
1960 to Devanha Fishing Co Ltd, Aberdeen.
1961 Vessel sold for scrap to Van den Marel de Korte, Holland. 05.08.1961 Arrived Krimpen A/D Ijssel for breaking up.</td></tr>
</table>

<table>
<tr><th rowspan="2">NAME
Official No.
Port Letters Numbers</th><th rowspan="2">Yard No.
Launched
Registered</th><th colspan="2">Registered</th><th rowspan="2">Engine Builder
Horse Power
Reg'd Speed</th><th rowspan="2">OWNER
(Built for)</th></tr>
<tr><th>G Ton
N Ton</th><th>L Ft
B Ft</th></tr>
<tr><td>WARSTAR
136005
GY73 Steam Trawler</td><td>289
12.02.1914
14.05.1914</td><td>225
112</td><td>117.0
22.0</td><td>Amos & Smith
68 NHP
9.5 knots</td><td>Pelham Steam Fishing Co Ltd
Grimsby</td></tr>
<tr><td colspan="6">Aug 1915 Rqd by the Royal Navy as a minesweeper No. FY 1633. 1919 returned.
29.02.1916 Sold to Harold Croft Baker, Grimsby. 07.10.1918 to Harry Wood & Others, Grimsby.
13.12.1919 to Harry Wood, Grimsby. 26.01.1920 to Lewis Steam Trawling Co, Grimsby.
16.09.1938 to M J McCabe & W M Curtis, Dublin. 1940 to Earl Steam Fishing Co Ltd, Grimsby (GY294).
1946 to W Wood, Aberdeen (A130).
1959 Vessel sold to BISCO for £2050 allocated to Shipbreaking Industries. 07.11.1959 Arrived Charlestown for breaking up.</td></tr>
<tr><td>EARL ESSEX
136002
GY48 Steam Trawler</td><td>290
07.01.1914
01.04.1914</td><td>225
112</td><td>117.0
22.0</td><td>Amos & Smith
68 NHP
9.5 knots</td><td>Earl Steam Fishing Co Ltd
Grimsby</td></tr>
<tr><td colspan="6">Aug 1914 Rqd by the Royal Navy as a minesweeper No. FY 292. 1920 returned.
02.11.1915 Sold to Harold Croft Baker, Grimsby. 08.01.1923 to Strand Steam Fishing Co Ltd, Grimsby.
06.02.1937 to Sir Thomas Robinson & Sons Ltd, Grimsby.
Nov 1939 Rqd by the Royal Navy as a minesweeper No. FY 852. 29.02.1946 returned.
24.04.1946 Vessel sank in the North Sea when a mine that had been trawled up exploded, one survivor was picked up by the trawler VERA GRACE FD211 (232 gt/ b 1908) which was fishing near by and had seen the explosion. Ten crew were lost.</td></tr>
<tr><td>BY GEORGE
136004
GY69 Steam Trawler</td><td>291
17.01.1914
18.04.1914</td><td>225
112</td><td>117.0
22.0</td><td>Amos & Smith
68 NHP
9.5 knots</td><td>North Western Steam
Fishing Co Ltd
Grimsby</td></tr>
<tr><td colspan="6">Aug 1914 Rqd by the Royal Navy as a minesweeper No. FY 253. 02.11.1915 Sold to Harold Croft Baker, Grimsby.
07.09.1917 Vessel sunk by mine in the Aegean Sea Gulf of Ruphani. Mine laid by UC23 on 11.07.1917.</td></tr>
<tr><td>FEZENTA
137019
GY444 Steam Trawler</td><td>292
12.03.1914
00.06.1914</td><td>228
95</td><td>117.0
22.0</td><td>Amos & Smith
68 NHP
9.5 knots</td><td>Alec Black
Grimsby</td></tr>
<tr><td colspan="6">1914 Vessel registered at Thorshaven, Færoe Island (TN216).
Mar 1915 Rqd by the Royal Navy as a minesweeper No. FY 1362. 1919 returned.
10.03.1915 to Reunion Steam Fishing Co Ltd, Grimsby. 02.11.1915 to Savoy Steam Fishing Co Ltd, Grimsby.
14.06.1918 to John L Green, Grimsby. 09.02.1923 to Strand Steam Fishing Co Ltd, Grimsby.
11.09.1933 to Harold Croft Baker, Grimsby. 09.02.1937 to Onward Steam Fishing Co Ltd, Grimsby.
15.11.1939 Rqd by the Royal Navy as a minesweeper / auxiliary patrol vessel No. FY 587. 15.11.1945 returned.
1961 Vessel sold for scrap to Van Heyghen Freres, Belgium. 15.10.1961 Arrived Bruges for breaking up.</td></tr>
<tr><td>EXYAHNE
136012
GY150 Steam Trawler</td><td>293
12.03.1914
16.06.1914</td><td>226
113</td><td>117.0
22.0</td><td>Amos & Smith
68 NHP
9.5 knots</td><td>Marshall Line Steam
Fishing Co Ltd
Grimsby</td></tr>
<tr><td colspan="6">Sep 1914 Rqd by the Royal Navy as a minesweeper No. FY 264. 1919 returned.
02.11.1915 Sold to Savoy Steam Fishing Co Ltd, Grimsby. 24.05.1928 to Harold Croft Baker & Sons Ltd, Grimsby.
06.02.1937 to Sir Thomas Robinson & Sons Ltd, Grimsby.
Nov 1939 Rqd by the Royal Navy as a minesweeper / auxiliary patrol vessel No. FY 878. 13.12.1945 returned.
1961 Vessel sold for scrap to H.P. Heavelman N V Krimpen. 09.04.1961 Arrived A/D Ijssel, Holland for breaking up.</td></tr>
<tr><td>OTTILIE
136010
GY144 Steam Trawler</td><td>294
12.03.1914
15.06.1914</td><td>226
113</td><td>117.0
22.0</td><td>Amos & Smith
68 NHP
9.5 knots</td><td>Marshall Line Steam
Fishing Co Ltd
Grimsby</td></tr>
<tr><td colspan="6">May 1915 Rqd by the Royal Navy as a minesweeper No. FY 1757. 1919 returned.
06.01.1916 Sold to Alfred W Baxter, Grimsby. 22.04.1919 to Neal Green, Grimsby.
10.02.1920 to Harold Bacon, Grimsby. 26.03.1920 to Trawlers White Sea & Grimsby Ltd, Grimsby.
15.01.1942 to Trawlers Grimsby Ltd, Grimsby. 15.01.1946 to Derwent Trawlers Ltd, Grimsby.
1955 Vessel sold for scrap to Van Heyghen Freres, Belgium. 16.12.1955 Arrived Ghent for breaking up.</td></tr>
<tr><td>ILUSTRA
136008
GY127 Steam Trawler</td><td>295
14.03.1914
09.06.1914</td><td>448
281</td><td>160.0
26.0</td><td>C.D. Holmes
89 NHP
11 knots</td><td>South Western Fishing Co,
Grimsby.</td></tr>
<tr><td colspan="6">Aug 1914 Rqd by the Royal Navy as a minesweeper No. FY 53. 1919 returned.
27.12.1916 Sold to Thomas W Baskcomb, Grimsby.
21.01.1920 Vessel wrecked at Gardatauger in Paroe Bay, east of Kevalik, Iceland.</td></tr>
<tr><td>THE BANYERS
136009
GY128 Steam Trawler</td><td>296
09.04.1914
09.06.1914</td><td>448
281</td><td>160.0
26.0</td><td>C.D. Holmes
89 NHP
11 knots</td><td>South Western Fishing Co,
Grimsby.</td></tr>
<tr><td colspan="6">Dec 1914 Rqd by the Royal Navy as a minesweeper No. FY 450.
06.01.1915 Vessel sunk by mine whilst sweeping in Cayton Bay near Scarborough.</td></tr>
</table>

Yard No.300B
1914 RESTRIVO (At Scarborough)
Photo by courtesy of George Scales

Yard No.301
1914 DONALDA
Photo:- Barnard and Straker Collection

Yard No.303
1914 FORWARD HO
Photo:- Barnard and Straker Collection

NAME Official No. Port Letters Numbers	Yard No. Launched Registered	Registered G Ton N Ton	 L Ft B Ft	Engine Builder Horse Power Reg'd Speed	OWNER (Built for)
REMARKO 136987 GY228 Steam Trawler	297 27.04.1914 09.07.1914	245 107	120.5 22.0	C.D. Holmes 80 NHP 10.5 knots	George F Sleight Grimsby
May 1915 Rqd by the Royal Navy as a minesweeper No. FY 1489. 03.12.1916 Vessel sunk by mine in the North Sea off Lowestoft. Mine laid by UC4 on 07.11.1916. Skipper lost.					
RELONZO 136988 GY229 Steam Trawler	298 11.05.1914 09.07.1914	245 107	120.5 22.0	C.D. Holmes 80 NHP 10.5 knots	George F Sleight Grimsby
Apr 1915 Rqd by the Royal Navy as an anti-submarine vessel with Hydrophonic listening equipment No. FY 1614. 1920 returned. 17.11.1933 Sold to Sleight & Humphrey, Grimsby. 1939 Rqd by the Royal Navy as a minesweeper No. FY 843. 20.01.1941 Vessel sunk by mine in the River Mersey in Crosby Channel, off C 10 Red buoy. Whilst serving with the 136 minesweeper group based at Birkenhead.					
RECEPTO 136991 GY254 Steam Trawler	299 06.06.1914 23.07.1914	245 107	120.5 22.0	C.D. Holmes 80 NHP 10.5 knots	George F Sleight Grimsby
Nov 1914 Rqd by the Royal Navy as a minesweeper No. FY 47. 16.02.1917 Vessel sunk by mine in the North Sea off Longscar buoy in Tees Bay. Mine laid by UC30 on 12.02.1917					
RETAKO 136990 GY253 Steam Trawler	300 06.06.1914 23.07.1914	245 107	120.5 22.0	C.D. Holmes 80 NHP 10.5 knots	George F Sleight Grimsby
Apr 1915 Rqd by the Royal Navy as a minesweeper No. FY 1608. 1919 returned. 17.11.1933 Sold to Sleight & Humphrey, Grimsby. Nov 1939 Rqd by the Royal Navy as an auxiliary patrol vessel / minesweeper No. FY 838. 16.02.1945 returned. 01.10.1940 Vessel damaged following a collision with the minesweeper BRITOMART (b 1938) in the Firth of Forth. 17.05.1949 to George F Sleight & Sons Ltd, Grimsby. 06.07.1960 to T C & F Moss, Grimsby. 1962 Vessel sold for scrap to Van Heyghen Freres, Belgium. 08.03.1962 Arrived Ghent for breaking up.					
RETURNO 136989 GY264 Steam Trawler	300A 10.06.1914 23.07.1914	245 107	120.5 22.0	C.D. Holmes 80 NHP 10.5 knots	George F Sleight Grimsby
Mar 1915 Rqd by the Royal Navy as a minesweeper No. FY 1602. 1919 returned. 17.11.1933 Sold to Sleight & Humphrey, Grimsby. 1939 Rqd by the Royal Navy as a minesweeper No. FY 839 / fuel carrier No. Y7.27. 1945 returned. 17.05.1949 to George F Sleight & Sons Ltd, Grimsby. 09.10.1956 to Ross Trawlers Ltd, Grimsby. 1962 Vessel sold for scrap to Van Heyghen Freres, Belgium. 30.03.1962 Arrived Ghent for breaking up.					
RESTRIVO 136992 GY265 Steam Trawler	300B 10.06.1914 27.07.1914	245 107	120.5 22.0	C.D. Holmes 80 NHP 10.5knots	George F Sleight Grimsby
Nov 1914 Rqd by the Royal Navy as a minesweeper No. FY 48. 1919 returned. 17.11.1933 Sold to Sleight & Humphrey, Grimsby. Nov 1939 Rqd by the Royal Navy as a minesweeper No. FY 834. 17.01.1945 returned. 17.05.1949 to George F Sleight & Sons Ltd, Grimsby. 1962 Vessel sold for scrap to Van Heyghen Freres, Belgium. 21.03.1962 Arrived Ghent for breaking up.					
DONALDA 136011 GY149 Steam Trawler	301 28.03.1914 15.06.1914	226 113	117.0 22.0	Amos & Smith 68 NHP 9.5 knots	Alec Black Grimsby
May 1915 Rqd by the Royal Navy as a minesweeper No. FY 1760. 1919 returned. 06.01.1916 Sold to Alfred M Baxter, Grimsby. 25.01.1918 to William Hill, Grimsby. 12.04.1918 to Victoria Steam Fishing Co Ltd, Grimsby. 19.12.1929 to Lindsey Steam Fishing Co Ltd, Grimsby. 24.12.1941 to Active Fishing Co, Fleetwood. 08.07.1942 to Hudson Bros (Trawlers) Ltd, Hull (H12). 1945 to Grimsby Motor Trawlers Ltd, Grimsby (GY78). 30.07.1949 to Trawlers Grimsby Ltd, Grimsby. 10.04.1953 to Derwent Trawlers Ltd, Grimsby. 1957 Vessel sold to BISCO and allocated to C W Dorkin & Co Ltd. 31.01.1957 Arrived Gateshead for breaking up.					

NAME Official No. Port Letters Numbers	Yard No. Launched Registered	Registered G Ton N Ton	 L Ft B Ft	Engine Builder Horse Power Reg'd Speed	OWNER (Built for)
DESTINN 137005 GY307 Steam Trawler	302 27.06.1914 30.09.1914	226 113	117.0 22.0	Amos & Smith 74 NHP 10 knots	Marshall Line Steam Fishing Co Grimsby
May 1915 Rqd by the Royal Navy as a minesweeper No. FY 1587. 1919 returned. 06.01.1916 Sold to Alfred W Baxter, Grimsby. 04.04.1917 to Joseph Harris, Grimsby. 21.08.1922 to Reunion Steam Fishing Co Ltd, Grimsby. 17.11.1926 to Pelham Steam Fishing Co Ltd, Grimsby. 19.09.1928 to Earl Steam Fishing Co Ltd, Grimsby. 16.09.1938 to McCabe & Curtis, Dublin (D124). 1940 to Earl Steam Fishing Co Ltd, Grimsby. Sep 1940 Sold to the Royal Navy as an auxiliary patrol vessel No. FY 1719. 1943 Water boat. Sep 1946 to War Department. 1947 Vessel sold for scrap to Thos W Ward Ltd, and broken up at Preston.					
MORVINA 137004 GY300 Steam Trawler	303 27.06.1914 30.09.1914	226 113	117.0 22.0	C.D. Holmes 75 NHP 10 knots	John L Green Ltd Grimsby
Apr 1915 Rqd by the Royal Navy as a minesweeper No. FY 1439. 1919 returned. 19.10.1915 Sold to Harold Croft Baker, Grimsby. 04.12.1916 to Savoy Steam Fishing Co Ltd, Grimsby. 05.12.1919 to John L Green Ltd, Grimsby. 16.11.1925 to Harold Bacon, Grimsby. 05.09.1930 to Kottingham Trawling Co, Grimsby. 13.05.1936 Whilst homeward for Grimsby the MORVINA stranded in thick fog on a holm, near the north coast of Egilsay, Orkney Islands. The steamer EARL SIGURD (221 gt/ b 1931) observed the MORVINA's plight and stood by her until high tide when she towed the trawler off, but she heeled over and sank. All the crew were rescued by the EARL SIGURD.					
WARLORD 137010 GY341 Steam Trawler	304 27.07.1914 23.10.1914	226 113	117.0 22.0	C.D. Holmes 75 NHP 10 knots	Alec Black Grimsby
Apr 1915 Rqd by the Royal Navy as a minesweeper No. FY 1444. 1919 returned. 01.03.1926 Sold to J E Harrison, Grimsby. 08.11.1938 to Earl Steam Fishing Co Ltd, Grimsby. 1940 to Sir Alec Black, Grimsby. 10.07.1941 to Neale & West Ltd, Cardiff (CF36). 23.01.1950 Vessel sold for scrap to Thos W Ward Ltd, and broken up at Milford Haven.					
EARL HOWARD 137009 GY332 Steam Trawler	305 27.07.1914 22.10.1914	226 113	117.0 22.0	C.D. Holmes 75 NHP 10 knots	Earl Steam Fishing Co Ltd Grimsby
11.12.1914 Vessel posted missing:- Lost with all hands - presumed mined in the North Sea north east of Spurn Head.					
EARL LENNOX 137014 GY367 Steam Trawler	306 25.08.1914 24.11.1914	226 113	117.0 22.0	C.D. Holmes 75 NHP 10 knots	Earl Steam Fishing Co Ltd Grimsby
1915 Sold to Strand Steam Fishing Co Ltd, Grimsby. Apr 1915 Rqd by the Royal Navy as a minesweeper No. FY 1441 renamed ERLING (TN258) then EARL LENNOX. 23.10.1917 Vessel sunk by mine in Sound of Islay.					
STALWART 136219 H213 Steam Trawler	307 24.08.1914 10.11.1914	333 136	138.7 23.5	C.D. Holmes 82 NHP 10.5 knots	John Hollingworth Hull
Mar 1917 Rqd by the Royal Navy as a bomb thrower / minesweeper No. FY 2999 renamed (1918) STALWART II. 1919 returned and reverted.26.04.1918 Sold to H Burns, Grimsby (GY1116). 11.05.1918 to Faeroe Steam Fishing Co Ltd, Grimsby. 22.10.1919 to Progressive Trawlers Ltd, Grimsby. 17.11.1921 to Marles Y Serra S.En.C. Barcelona, Spain renamed (1927) SANTA ROSA. 1935 to E Gonzalez, Barcelona. 1936 to The Basque Navy renamed GAZ TEIZ. Jun 1937 Captured at Santander by the Nationalist Navy and renamed VIRGEN DEL CARMEN. 1939 returned and reverted. 1963 to Fidel G R & José & Julio Gonzales, Corunna. 14.06.1985 Vessel sold to Spanish shipbreakers and broken up.					
CADET 136218 H210 Steam Trawler	308 07.09.1914 19.12.1914	323 134	136.0 23.5	C.D. Holmes 87 NHP 10.5 knots	Marine Steam Fishing Co Ltd Hull
1917 Rqd by the Royal Navy as a fishing trawler (Fishery Reserve). 1919 returned. 1926 Sold to Storr's Steam Trawling Co Ltd, Hull renamed SAIPH. 28.03.1929 to Trident Steam Fishing Co Ltd, Hull renamed (15.05.1929) ROSENESS. 31.12.1938 to Jutland Amalgamated Trawlers Ltd, Hull renamed LADY ESTELLE. 02.06.1940 Rqd by the Royal Navy as an anti-submarine vessel No. FY 176. 16.09.1946 returned. 01.10.1942 to J Marr & Son Ltd, Hull. 1943 to Thornton Trawlers Ltd, Hull. Jun 1945 to Parkholme Trawlers, Grimsby (GY52). Sep 1945 to Trawlers, Grimsby. 1947 to NV Vissch. Maats "Pettin", Ijmuiden, Holland renamed SCHOORL.1955 Vessel sold to shipbreakers and broken up.					

<table>
<tr><th rowspan="2">NAME
Official No.
Port Letters Numbers</th><th rowspan="2">Yard No.
Launched
Registered</th><th colspan="2">Registered</th><th rowspan="2">Engine Builder
Horse Power
Reg'd Speed</th><th rowspan="2">OWNER
(Built for)</th></tr>
<tr><th>G Ton
N Ton</th><th>L Ft
B Ft</th></tr>
<tr><td>SIR JOHN JELLICOE
136245
H310 Steam Trawler</td><td>309
22.09.1914
18.12.1914</td><td>351
165</td><td>140.0
24.0</td><td>Amos & Smith
100 NHP
11 knots</td><td>Imperial Steam Fishing Co Ltd
Hull</td></tr>
<tr><td colspan="6">May 1915 Rqd by the Royal Navy as a minesweeper No. FY 1577 renamed JERICHO. 1920 returned.
20.11.1918 to "D" Line Steam Fishing Co Ltd, Grimsby renamed DARGLE (GY1170).
1928 to W Garrat, Grimsby. 1932 to T Fisher, Grimsby. Nov 1933 to J Little Grimsby.
Dec 1933 to Kopanes Steam Fishing Co Ltd, Grimsby renamed KOPANES.
02.06.1940 Rqd by the Royal Navy as an auxiliary patrol vessel.
19.04.1941 Vessel sunk in the North Sea by German aircraft off the River Tyne.</td></tr>
<tr><td>SIR JOHN FRENCH
136236
H262 Steam Trawler</td><td>310
06.10.1914
18.12.1914</td><td>351
165</td><td>140.0
24.0</td><td>Amos & Smith
100 NHP
11 knots</td><td>Imperial Steam Fishing Co Ltd
Hull</td></tr>
<tr><td colspan="6">May 1915 Rqd by the Royal Navy as an anti-submarine with Hydrophonic listening equipment No. FY 1501.1919 returned.
26.04.1918 Sold to John Willows, Grimsby (GY1152). 17.05.1919 to Alfred Grant, Grimsby.
09.04.1920 to Sir John French Steam Fishing Co Ltd, Halifax, Nova Scotia, Canada.
23.07.1923 Vessel wrecked at Dantyic in Fortune Bay, Newfoundland.</td></tr>
<tr><td>LORD FISHER
136247
H264 Steam Trawler</td><td>311
06.10.1914
00.03.1915</td><td>351
165</td><td>140.0
24.0</td><td>Amos & Smith
100 NHP
11 knots</td><td>Imperial Steam Fishing Co Ltd
Hull</td></tr>
<tr><td colspan="6">May 1915 Rqd by the Royal Navy as a minesweeper No. FY 1519 renamed LORDSHIP. 1919 returned and reverted.
1920 Sold to Hellyer Bros Ltd, Hull. 27.01.1927 to John Oddsson & Co Ltd, Hull (ex Hellyer skipper).
18.12.1930 Vessel wrecked on the Hraun Hafu line of reefs near Hraunhafnartangi Point, north coast of Iceland .
All thirteen crew taken off by the Grimsby trawler LOYAL GY501 (see Yard No.509).</td></tr>
<tr><td>SEAWARD HO
136247
H312 Steam Trawler</td><td>312
19.11.1914
00.00.1915</td><td>331
138</td><td>137.0
23.7</td><td>Amos & Smith
84 NHP
10.5 knots</td><td>S T White & Co Ltd
Hull</td></tr>
<tr><td colspan="6">May 1915 Rqd by the Royal Navy as a bomb thrower / minesweeper No. FY 1512 renamed (1918) ATTENTIVE III.
1919 returned and reverted. 1920 Sold to Newington Steam Trawling Co Ltd, Hull renamed GUY THORNE.
07.03.1927 Vessel stranded on the north-west coast of Norway at Mefjordboen, Vestfjorder and later salved.
1928 to J E Rushworth, Grimsby (GY465). 1930 to Dale Steam Fishing Co Ltd, Grimsby.
1933 to J E Rushworth, Grimsby renamed (1934) WINOOKA. 1935 to Boston Deep Sea Fishing Co Ltd, Fleetwood.
15.03.1936 Vessel sank following a collision with the Fleetwood trawler ETHEL TAYLOR FD363 (276 gt/ b 1917),
off the west coast of Scotland.</td></tr>
<tr><td>FORWARD HO
136250
H331 Steam Trawler</td><td>313
19.11.1914
04.05.1915</td><td>268
107</td><td>123.8
22.7</td><td>Amos & Smith
78 NHP
10.5 knots</td><td>S T White & Co Ltd
Hull</td></tr>
<tr><td colspan="6">Jul 1915 Rqd by the Royal Navy as a minesweeper No. FY 1560. 1919 returned.
1926 Sold to Thomas W Baskcomb, Grimsby. 16.04.1926 to Seaward Fishing Co Ltd, Hull.
1927 to Hudson Steam Fishing Co Ltd, Hull. 06.11.1929 to Herbert Field, Hull.
13.10.1933 to Trident Steam Fishing Co Ltd, Hull renamed (02.11.1933) SUTHERNESS.
02.06.1940 Rqd by the Royal Navy as an auxiliary patrol vessel No. FY 4.174 (1941) minesweeper No. FY 1563.
04.09.1945 returned. 02.01.1945 to Westward Trawlers Ltd, Milford Haven (M97).
10.06.1961 Vessel sank after springing a leak in the engine-room. 15 miles from Islay Pos'n Lat 55° 48'N Long 006° 43'W.</td></tr>
<tr><td>PRINCESS MARIE JOSÉ
136234
H242 Steam Trawler</td><td>314
17.12.1914
12.02.1915</td><td>274
109</td><td>125.0
22.7</td><td>C.D. Holmes
80 NHP
10.5 knots</td><td>Armitage's Steam
Trawling Co Ltd
Hull</td></tr>
<tr><td colspan="6">1915 Rqd by the Royal Navy as a bomb thrower / minesweeper No. FY 1770. 1919 returned.
1920 Sold to Sun Steam Trawling Co, Fleetwood (FD12).
1934 to Robertson & Wood, Aberdeen renamed FEUGHSIDE (A114).
06.10.1939 to Loch Fishing Co Ltd, Hull renamed (29.11.1939) LOCH HOPE. (H220).
1940 Rqd by the Royal Navy as an auxiliary patrol vessel No. FY 4.97. 1945 returned. 10.08.1945 to A & M Smith, Hull.
11.06.1947 Vessel sank off the east coast of Iceland when a mine that had been trawled up exploded. One crewman was lost,
seventeen survivors were picked up by the Fleetwood trawler URKA FD289 (249 gt/ b 1917) and landed at Seydisfjord.</td></tr>
</table>

<table>
<tr><th rowspan="2">NAME
Official No.
Port Letters Numbers</th><th rowspan="2">Yard No.
Launched
Registered</th><th colspan="2">Registered</th><th rowspan="2">Engine Builder
Horse Power
Reg'd Speed</th><th rowspan="2">OWNER
(Built for)</th></tr>
<tr><th>G Ton
N Ton</th><th>L Ft
B Ft</th></tr>
<tr><td>EARL KITCHENER
136258
H345 Steam Trawler</td><td>315
02.02.1915
15.06.1915</td><td>348
162</td><td>140.0
24.0</td><td>Amos & Smith
87 NHP
10.5 knots</td><td>Imperial Steam Fishing Co Ltd
Hull</td></tr>
<tr><td colspan="6">Oct 1915 Rqd by the Royal Navy as a minesweeper No. FY 1907. 1920 returned.
27.10.1919 Sold to Hellyer Bros Ltd, Hull. 29.08.1939 Rqd by the Royal Navy as a minesweeper No. FY 1633.
1946 returned. 30.07.1945 to Lord Line Ltd, Hull. 04.04.1950 to Associated Fisheries Ltd, Hull.
1953 Vessel sold to BISCO and allocated to Thomas Young & Sons Ltd. 06.02.1953 Arrived Sunderland for breaking up.
03.07.1953 Vessel re-allocated to Stockton Shipping & Salvage Co and broken up at Thornaby on Tees.</td></tr>
<tr><td>COMMANDER BOYLE
139261
H353 Steam Trawler</td><td>316 (1)
17.02.1915
13.07.1915</td><td>243
96</td><td>115.5
22.5</td><td>Amos & Smith
80 NHP
10.5 knots</td><td>Hellyer Steam Fishing Co Ltd
Hull</td></tr>
<tr><td colspan="6">23.08.1915 Vessel sunk by mine 40 miles north by west of Rattray Head whilst fishing from Fleetwood. Three crew lost.</td></tr>
<tr><td>COMMANDER NASMITH
139266
H385 Steam Trawler</td><td>316 (2)
17.02.1915
00.08.1915</td><td>243
96</td><td>115.5
22.5</td><td>Amos & Smith
80 NHP
10.5 knots</td><td>Hellyer Steam Fishing Co Ltd
Hull</td></tr>
<tr><td colspan="6">Sep 1915 Rqd by the Royal Navy as a bomb thrower / minesweeper No. FY 1968. 1919 returned.
30.10.1923 Sold to Eastern Fishing Co Ltd, Hull.
12.06.1940 Rqd by the Royal Navy as an auxiliary patrol vessel / minesweeper No. FY 516. 10.05.1945 returned.
14.03.1946 to Lindern Fishing Co Ltd, Grimsby (GY241). 1951 to J Mowatt, Aberdeen renamed ELMO (A668).
Mar 1953 Vessel sold for scrap to Malcolm Brechin and broken up at Granton.</td></tr>
<tr><td>CANTATRICE
137022
GY469 Steam Trawler</td><td>317
04.02.1915
30.03.1915</td><td>302
152</td><td>130.0
23.3</td><td>C.D. Holmes
82 NHP
10.5 knots</td><td>William J Barrett
Grimsby</td></tr>
<tr><td colspan="6">Jul 1915 Rqd by the Royal Navy as a minesweeper No. FY 3205.
05.11.1916 Vessel sunk by mine near Yarmouth. Mines laid by UC18 on 25.10.1916.</td></tr>
<tr><td>KINGS GREY
137028
GY486 Steam Trawler</td><td>318
19.12.1914
22.04.1915</td><td>338
189</td><td>140.3
25.0</td><td>C.D. Holmes
82 NHP
11 knots</td><td>Earl Steam Fishing Co Ltd
Grimsby</td></tr>
<tr><td colspan="6">May 1915 Rqd by the Royal Navy as a minesweeper No. FY 1628. 1919 returned.
19.04.1920 Sold to South Western Steam Fishing Co Ltd, Grimsby. 02.07.1920 to Sir Alec Black, Grimsby.
20.01.1922 to Hellyer Bros Ltd, Hull (H402).
31.08.1939 Rqd by the Royal Navy as an auxiliary patrol vessel No. 4.87. 16.10.1939 returned.
31.05.1940 Rqd by the Royal Navy as a minesweeper No. FY 502. 26.09.1946 returned.
30.07.1945 to Lord Line Ltd, Hull (H402). 20.10.1947 to Yorkshire Trawlers Ltd, Hull.
04.08.1950 to Boyd Line Ltd, Hull renamed (11.09.1950) ARCTIC ROVER.
05.03.1952 to Percival Steam Fishing Co Ltd, Hull renamed (14.07.1952) SWANLAND.
1953 to St Andrews Steam Fishing Co Ltd, Hull. 23.03.1954 to Boyd Line Ltd, Hull.
24.04.1954 Vessel sold for scrap to Van Heyghen Freres, Belgium and broken up at Ghent.</td></tr>
<tr><td>JELLICOE
137030
GY522 Steam Trawler</td><td>319
19.12.1914
23.06.1915</td><td>338
189</td><td>140.0
25.0</td><td>C.D. Holmes
88 NHP
10 knots</td><td>Earl Steam Fishing Co Ltd
Grimsby</td></tr>
<tr><td colspan="6">04.07.1917 Sold to Neal Green, Grimsby renamed (26.06.1919) CERESIO.
Jul 1915 Rqd by the Royal Navy as a minesweeper No. FY 1546 renamed RUSHCOE. 1919 returned and reverted.
10.02.1920 to Harold Bacon, Grimsby. 26.03.1920 to Trawlers White Sea & Grimsby Ltd, Grimsby.
21.03.1922 to Hellyer Bros Ltd, Hull (H447).
05.09.1939 Rqd by the Royal Navy as a minesweeper No. FY 524. 1945 returned.
08.05.1947 to Lord Line Ltd, Hull. 1948 to Jens P Bager, Marstal, Denmark, (converted to a cargo vessel).
(Lengthened to 156.3 ft 360 Gross Tons) (4 cyl Burmeister & Wain diesel engine fitted)
1960 to I/S Bothe & Hermansen, Marstal. 1973 to Gunnar Jensen Partrederi, Marstal.
1976 to I M Jann, Kingstown, St Vincent, West Indies renamed KELVIN AND CLIDE.
31.10.1983 Vessel (converted to a storage Hulk), Port of Spain, Trinidad.</td></tr>
</table>

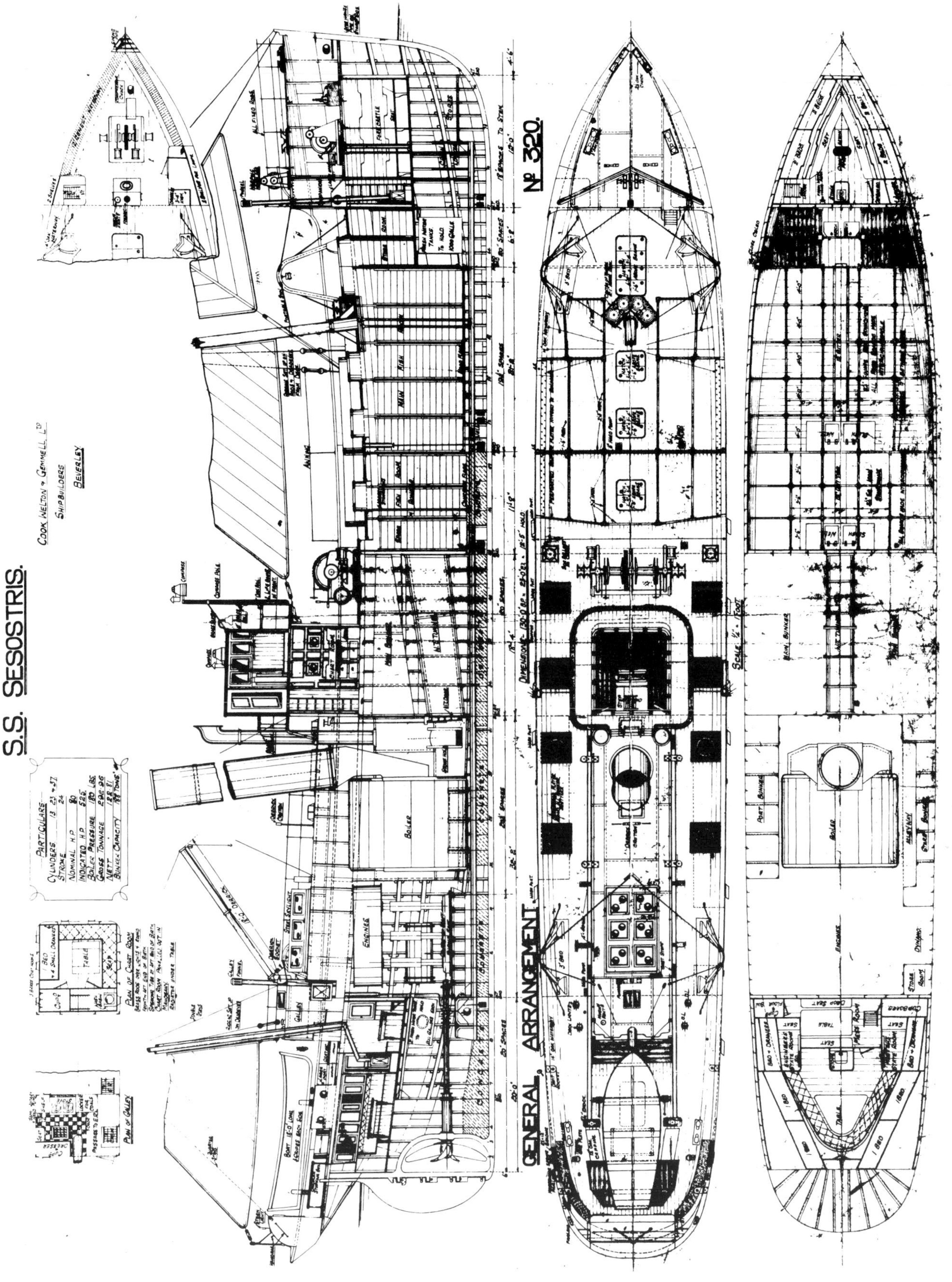
S.S. SESOSTRIS.
COOK, WELTON & GEMMELL, LTD
SHIPBUILDERS
BEVERLEY
No 320.
GENERAL ARRANGEMENT
PARTICULARS
BOILER
ENGINES

<table>
<tr><th rowspan="2">NAME
Official No.
Port Letters Numbers</th><th rowspan="2">Yard No.
Launched
Registered</th><th colspan="2">Registered</th><th rowspan="2">Engine Builder
Horse Power
Reg'd Speed</th><th rowspan="2">OWNER
(Built for)</th></tr>
<tr><th>G Ton
N Ton</th><th>L Ft
B Ft</th></tr>
<tr><td>SESOSTRIS
138957
GY894 Steam Trawler</td><td>320
14.09.1915
04.04.1916</td><td>293
123</td><td>130.3
23.0</td><td>C.D. Holmes
89 NHP
10.5 knots</td><td>Roberts & Ruthven Ltd
Grimsby</td></tr>
<tr><td colspan="6">May 1916 Rqd by the Royal Navy as a bomb thrower / minesweeper with Hydrophonic listening No. FY 1998.
1919 returned. 18.10.1927 Sold to Earl Steam Fishing Co, Grimsby. 04.11.1927 to Joseph Little Grimsby.
08.05.1929 to Rinovia Steam Fishing Co Ltd, Grimsby renamed (02.11.1927) RINOVIA.
16.04.1931 to the Turkish Government Fisheries Institute renamed BALIK (1955) renamed HAMIT NACI.
1955 to Ziya Ve Kalkavan Kollectif Sirketi, Istanbul, Turkey renamed ZIYA KALKAVAN (5 cyl Atlas-diesel engine fitted).
30.07.1959 Vessel capsized at Haskoy slipway Istanbul after being incorrectly ballasted. 30.08.1959 re-floated.
1990 to Surkrudurmus Ortakiari, Istanbul renamed EKINLIK II.
1992 toDurmu Saglu Denizcicik, Istanbul renamed VAKFIK EBIR-I.
29.05.1997 Vessel stranded off Catanzaro, southern Italy with 215 illegal immigrants on board re-floated
and towed to Catanzaro. 1999 Vessel still in Service.</td></tr>
<tr><td>SEA SWEEPER
139276
H409 Steam Trawler</td><td>321
31.05.1915
09.12.1915</td><td>329
138</td><td>136.0
24.0</td><td>Amos & Smith
100 NHP
11 knots</td><td>Humber Steam
Trawling Co Ltd
Hull</td></tr>
<tr><td colspan="6">Jan 1916 Rqd by the Royal Navy as a minesweeper with Hydrophonic listening equipment No. FY 1979. 1919 returned.
1920 Sold to Fresh Fish Supplies Ltd, Hull. 1923 to Thomas Hamling & Co Ltd, Hull.
1928 to Dinas Steam Trawling Co Ltd, Fleetwood (FD171).
20.11.1939 Vessel captured and sunk by gunfire by U-33 Commander Von Dresky 25 miles north-west by west of Tory Island</td></tr>
<tr><td>SEA MONARCH
139277
H411 Steam Trawler</td><td>322
31.05.1915
17.08.1915</td><td>329
138</td><td>136.0
24.0</td><td>Amos & Smith
100 NHP
11 knots</td><td>Humber Steam
Trawling Co Ltd
Hull</td></tr>
<tr><td colspan="6">Feb 1916 Rqd by the Royal Navy as a bomb thrower/minesweeper No. FY 1983. 1919 returned.
1920 Sold to Fresh Fish Supplies Ltd, Hull. 1923 to Thomas Hamling & Co Ltd, Hull.
1928 to Dinas Steam Trawling Co Ltd, Fleetwood (FD169).
30.11.1940 Rqd by the Royal Navy as a boom defence vessel No. Z.115. 23.11.1943 Sold to the Royal Navy.
31.01.1947 Vessel sold for scrap to James N Connell. 28.02.1947 Arrived Glasgow for breaking up.</td></tr>
<tr><td>FLANDRE
137033
GY598 Steam Trawler</td><td>323
30.04.1915
13.08.1915</td><td>226
109</td><td>117.0
22.0</td><td>Amos & Smith
70 NHP
9 knots</td><td>Reunion Steam Fishing Co Ltd
Grimsby</td></tr>
<tr><td colspan="6">Sep 1915 Rqd by the Royal Navy as a minesweeper No. FY 853. 1918 returned.
19.07.1917 Sold to North Western Steam Fishing Co Ltd, Grimsby.
27.02.1918 to Rushworth Steam Fishing Co Ltd, Grimsby. 26.06.1919 to Yarborough Steam Fishing Co Ltd, Grimsby.
31.07.1924 to South Western Steam Fishing Co Ltd, Grimsby. 02.11.1925 to Earl Steam Fishing Co Ltd, Grimsby.
06.06.1940 Rqd by the Royal Navy as an auxiliary patrol vessel (Nov 1941) minesweeper No. FY 1715.
13.03.1945 returned. 08.02.1943 to Shire Trawlers Ltd, Grimsby. 06.12.1944 to Parkholme Trawlers Ltd, Grimsby.
30.07.1949 to Trawlers Grimsby Ltd, Grimsby. 10.04.1953 to Derwent Trawlers Ltd, Grimsby.
1958 Vessel sold for scrap to Atlantic Rhederei F & W Joch, Germany. 11.04.1958 Arrived Hamburg for breaking up.</td></tr>
<tr><td>FLYING WING
138939
GY690 Steam Trawler</td><td>324
30.04.1915
05.10.1915</td><td>226
109</td><td>117.0
22.0</td><td>Amos & Smith
70 NHP
9 knots</td><td>Marshall Line Steam
Fishing Co Ltd
Grimsby</td></tr>
<tr><td colspan="6">Nov 1915 Rqd by the Royal Navy as minesweeper No. FY 1958. 1919 returned.
29.02.1917 Sold to Henry C Baker, Grimsby. 26.03.1918 to William Baynton, Grimsby.
23.03.1920 to Headway Steam Fishing Co Ltd, Grimsby. 26.01.1922 to Sir Thomas Robinson, Grimsby.
17.09.1927 to Sir Thomas Robinson & Sons Ltd, Grimsby.
27.11.1939 Rqd by the Royal Navy as a minesweeper. 08.04.1940 returned.
28.05.1940 Rqd by the Royal Navy anti - submarine vessel (1941) minesweeper No. FY 880. 07.08.1946 returned.
1962 Vessel sold for scrap to Van Den Bossche & Co, Belgium. 19.03.1962 Arrived Boom for breaking up.</td></tr>
<tr><td>CARILON
138940
GY692 Steam Trawler</td><td>325
28.04.1915
05.10.1915</td><td>226
109</td><td>117.0
22.0</td><td>Amos & Smith
75 NHP
9 knots</td><td>Marshall Line Steam
Fishing Co Ltd
Grimsby</td></tr>
<tr><td colspan="6">24.12.1915 Vessel sunk by mine off Margate. Mine laid by UC1 on 23.12.1915.</td></tr>
</table>

NAME Official No. Port Letters Numbers	Yard No. Launched Registered	Registered G Ton N Ton	 L Ft B Ft	Engine Builder Horse Power Reg'd Speed	OWNER (Built for)
WAR WING 138945 GY857 Steam Trawler	326 29.04.1915 03.02.1916	226 109	117.0 22.0	Amos & Smith 75 NHP 9 knots	Pelham Steam Fishing Co Ltd Grimsby
Jun 1916 Rqd by the Royal Navy as a minesweeper No. FY 3286. 1919 returned. 27.12.1916 Sold to Thomas W Baskcomb, Grimsby. 24.10.1935 to Dobson Ship Repair Co Ltd, Grimsby. 29.11.1939 Rqd by the Royal Navy as a minesweeper No. FY 906 (1944) store carrier. 1946 returned. 26.03.1945 to Wembley Steam Fishing Co Ltd, Grimsby. 29.09.1948 to Wharfedale Trawlers Ltd, Grimsby. 10.12.1948 to Cramond Fishing Co Ltd, Leith renamed CRAMOND ISLAND (LH26). 1953 to Sir Thomas Robinson, Grimsby renamed SARDINION (GY251). 1964 Vessel sold for scrap to Scrapping Co SRL of Brussels. 07.11.1964 Arrived Antwerp for breaking up.					
GELSINA 138946 GY869 Steam Trawler	327 12.10.1915 18.02.1916	226 109	117.0 22.0	Amos & Smith 75 NHP 9 knots	Walter Olney Grimsby
Feb 1916 Rqd by the Royal Navy as a minesweeper No. FY 3258. 25.06.1917 Vessel sunk by mine off Girdleness. Mine laid by UC40 on the same day.					
VIVANTI 138951 GY878 Steam Trawler	328 12.10.1915 08.03.1916	226 109	117.0 22.0	Amos & Smith 75 NHP 9 knots	North Western Steam Fishing Co Ltd Grimsby
Mar 1916 Rqd by the Royal Navy as a minesweeper No. FY 3264. 07.03.1917 Vessel foundered off Fairlight Hastings.					
RONSO 137034 GY605 Steam Trawler	329 01.07.1915 00.11.1915	248 108	120.5 22.0	C.D. Holmes 80 NHP 10.5 knots	George F Sleight Grimsby
Jan 1916 Rqd by the Royal Navy as a minesweeper No. FY 862. 1920 returned. 17.11.1933 Sold to Sleight and Humphrey, Grimsby. Nov 1939 Rqd by the Royal Navy as a minesweeper No. FY 841 / fuel carrier No. Y7.29. 11.01.1946 returned. 17.05.1949 to George F Sleight, Grimsby. 1962 Vessel sold for scrap to Van Heyghen Freres, Belgium. 17.03.1962 Arrived Ghent for breaking up.					
REGARDO 137035 GY623 Steam Trawler	330 01.07.1915 11.12.1915	248 108	120.5 22.0	C.D. Holmes 80 NHP 10.5 knots	George F Sleight Grimsby
Dec 1915 Rqd by the Royal Navy as a minesweeper No. FY 1963. 1919 returned. 17.11.1933 Sold to Sleight and Humphrey, Grimsby. Nov 1939 Rqd by the Royal Navy as a minesweeper No. FY 831 / fuel carrier No. Y7.33. 17.12.1945 returned. 17.05.1949 to George F Sleight, Grimsby.15.10.1956 Sold to Derwent Trawlers, Grimsby. 26.07.1960 to Yorkshire Trawlers, Grimsby. 1962 Vessel sold for scrap to Van Heyghen Freres, Belgium. 08.05.1962 Arrived Bruges for breaking up.					
RECONO 138936 GY625 Steam Trawler	331 14.08.1915 06.09.1916	248 108	120.33 22.0	C.D. Holmes 80 NHP 10.5 knots	George F Sleight Grimsby
Mar 1916 Rqd by the Royal Navy as a minesweeper / escort vessel No. FY 1988. 1920 returned. 17.11.1933 Sold to Sleight and Humphrey, Grimsby. Nov 1939 Rqd by the Royal Navy as a minesweeper / 23.11.1944 boom defence vessel No. FY 786. 05.07.1945 returned. 17.05.1949 to George F Sleight, Grimsby. .10.1956 Sold to Derwent Trawlers, Grimsby. 1962 Vessel sold for scrap to Van Heyghen Freres, Belgium. 03.03.1962 Arrived Ghent for breaking up.					
RISKATO 138969 GY914 Steam Trawler	332 09.11.1915 29.05.1916	248 108	120.33 22.0	C.D. Holmes 80 NHP 10.5 knots	George F Sleight Grimsby
May 1916 Rqd by the Royal Navy as a minesweeper No. FY 3281. 1919 returned. 17.11.1933 Sold to Sleight and Humphrey, Grimsby. 25.06.1940 Rqd by the Royal Navy as an auxiliary patrol vessel No. FY 4.302. 1946 returned. 17.05.1949 to George F Sleight, Grimsby. 15.10.1956 Sold to Derwent Trawlers, Grimsby. 1956 Vessel sold to BISCO and allocated to C W Dorkin & Co Ltd. 23.10.1956 Arrived Gateshead for breaking up.					
RESPARKO 138973 GY926 Steam Trawler	333 06.12.1915 07.07.1916	248 108	120.33 22.0	C.D. Holmes 80 NHP 10.5 knots	George F Sleight Grimsby
Sep 1916 Rqd by the Royal Navy as a minesweeper No. FY 2958. 1919 returned. 17.11.1933 Sold to Sleight and Humphrey, Grimsby. 1939 Rqd by the Royal Navy as a minesweeper No. FY 822 based at Portsmouth. 20.08.1940 Vessel sunk by German aircraft at Falmouth. All crew rescued.					

Yard No.330
1915 REGARDO
Photo by courtesy of The Grimsby Evening Telegraph

Yard No.340
1916 VALMONT
Photo by courtesy of The Grimsby Evening Telegraph

Yard No.340E
1917 WAR DUKE
Photo by courtesy of The Grimsby Evening Telegraph

NAME Official No. Port Letters Numbers	Yard No. Launched Registered	Registered G Ton N Ton	 L Ft B Ft	Engine Builder Horse Power Reg'd Speed	OWNER (Built for)
ROYALO 138977 GY941 Steam Trawler	334 06.12.1915 11.08.1916	248 108	120.33 22.0	C.D. Holmes 80 NHP 10.5 knots	George F Sleight Grimsby

Aug 1916 Rqd by the Royal Navy as a minesweeper No. FY 2995. 1919 returned.
17.11.1933 Sold to Sleight and Humphrey, Grimsby.
1939 Rqd by the Royal Navy as a minesweeper No. FY 825 based at Lowestoft.
01.09.1940 Vessel sunk by mine during mine-sweeping operations in Mounts Bay Cornwall 1 mile off Penzance Pier. Eight crew lost.

RIVIERE 138956 GY893 Steam Trawler	335 09.11.1915 06.05.1916	226 109	117.0 22.0	Amos & Smith 74 NHP 9.5 knots	Alec Black Grimsby

May 1916 Rqd by the Royal Navy as a minesweeper No. FY 1261. 1919 returned.
06.11.1917 Sold to Yarborough Steam Fishing Co Ltd, Grimsby.
19.02.1918 to Great Northern Steam Ship Fishing Co Ltd, Hull (H596).
1919 to J Coombes, Grimsby (GY14). 1926 to Earl Steam Fishing Co Ltd, Grimsby.
21.04.1940 Rqd by the Royal Navy as a barrage balloon vessel. 02.11.1944 returned.
08.02.1943 to Shire Trawlers Ltd, Grimsby. 02.11.1944 to Pickering & Haldane, Hull.
22.01.1945 to Parkholme Trawlers Ltd, Grimsby. 10.04.1953 to Derwent Trawlers Ltd, Grimsby.
10.06.1953 Vessel sank following a collision with the ss FIRELIGHT (2841 gt/ b 1943) in thick fog whilst homeward bound to Grimsby from the West of Scotland fishing grounds. The RIVIERE sank rapidly with only three survivors picked up by the FIRELIGHT despite an extensive search of the area by the coaster and the Flamborough lifeboat. Ten crew lost.

NOVELLI 138954 GY889 Steam Trawler	336 09.12.1915 18.05.1916	226 109	117.0 22.0	Amos & Smith 74 NHP 9.5 knots	North Western Steam Fishing Co Ltd Grimsby

May 1916 Rqd by the Royal Navy as a bomb thrower / minesweeper No. FY 3279. 1919 returned.
05.02.1917 Sold to Rowland Hill, Grimsby. 17.09.1917 to Walter H Beeley, Grimsby.
20.02.1918 to Great Northern Steam Fishing Co Ltd, Hull (H592).
1919 to Shaftesbury Steam Fishing Co Ltd, Grimsby (GY361). 1926 to Kottingham Trawlers Co Ltd, Grimsby.
1944 to Parkholme Trawlers Ltd, Grimsby. 1945 to Trawlers, Grimsby Ltd, Grimsby.
10.04.1953 to Derwent Trawlers Ltd, Grimsby. 1956 to Yorkshire Trawlers Ltd, Grimsby.
05.03.1959 Vessel sold for scrap to Van Den Bossche & Co, Belgium. 08.03.1959 Arrived Boom for breaking up.

SALVINI 138955 GY892 Steam Trawler	337 09.12.1915 06.06.1916	226 109	117.0 22.0	Amos & Smith 74 NHP 9.5 knots	Alec Black Grimsby

Jun 1916 Rqd by the Royal Navy as a minesweeper No. FY 3283. 1919 returned.
05.02.1917 Sold to Roland Hill, Grimsby. 20.02.1918 to Great Northern Steam Fishing Co Ltd, Hull (H593).
1919 to Coombes Ltd, Grimsby (GY70). 1925 to Earl Steam Fishing Co Ltd, Grimsby.
19.04.1940 Rqd by the Royal Navy as a barrage balloon vessel / fuel carrier No. FY 4.457. 21.11.1944 returned.
10.12.1940 to Sir Alec Black, Grimsby. 08.02.1943 to Shire Trawlers Ltd, Grimsby.
1947 to Alfred Bannister Trawlers Ltd, Grimsby.
15.12.1959 Vessel sold for scrap to A C Slooten, Holland and broken up at Wormer.

LOUIS BOTHA 138961 GY896 Steam Trawler	338 05.02.1916 24.06.1916	226 109	117.0 22.0	Amos & Smith 74 NHP 9.5 knots	Pelham Steam Fishing Co Ltd Grimsby

Jun 1916 Rqd by the Royal Navy as a minesweeper No. FY 3289. 1919 returned.
08.01.1917 Sold to Aldersyde Steam Fishing Co Ltd, Grimsby.
19.02.1918 to Great Northern Steam Ship Fishing Co Ltd, Hull (H601). 1919 to J W Smethurst, Grimsby (GY305).
1924 to Pelham Steam Fishing Co Ltd, Grimsby.
1928 to Earl Steam Fishing Co Ltd, Grimsby.1940 to Sir Alec Black, Grimsby.
11.06.1940 Rqd by the Royal Navy as an auxiliary patrol vessel No. FY 4.207. 11.12.1941 returned.
16.09.1942 to Hudson Bros (Trawlers) Ltd, Hull. (H300).
07.03.1944 Vessel wrecked after stranding in fog at Veidos off the south coast of Iceland during wartime fishing operations. Four crew lost eleven rescued. See also WAR GREY *(Yard No. 340D)* and LIMESLADE *(Yard No.409)*.

<table>
<tr><th rowspan="3">NAME
Official No.
Port Letters Numbers</th><th rowspan="3">Yard No.
Launched
Registered</th><th colspan="2">Registered</th><th rowspan="3">Engine Builder
Horse Power
Reg'd Speed</th><th rowspan="3">OWNER
(Built for)</th></tr>
<tr><th>G Ton</th><th>L Ft</th></tr>
<tr><th>N Ton</th><th>B Ft</th></tr>
<tr><td>ORVICTO
138962
GY897 Steam Trawler</td><td>339
05.02.1916
13.07.1916</td><td>226
109</td><td>117.0
22.0</td><td>Amos & Smith
74 NHP
9.5 knots</td><td>South Western Steam
Fishing Co Ltd
Grimsby</td></tr>
<tr><td colspan="6">Sep 1916 Rqd by the Royal Navy as a bomb thrower / minesweeper No. FY 2962. 1919 returned.
08.01.1917 Sold to Aldersyde Steam Fishing Co Ltd, Grimsby.
19.02.1918 to Great Northern Steam Ship Fishing Co Ltd, Hull (H603). 26.08.1918 to William Hill Grimsby (GY1179).
12.12.1918 to Northern Steam Fishing Co Ltd, Grimsby. 27.12.1933 to Sir Thomas Robinson & Sons Ltd, Grimsby.
19.04.1940 Rqd by the Royal Navy as a danlayer / auxiliary patrol vessel No. FY 909. 31.10.1945 returned.
1961 Vessel sold for scrap to A C Slooten, Holland. 03.05.1961 Arrived Wormer for breaking up.</td></tr>
<tr><td>VALMONT
138956
GY885 Steam Trawler</td><td>340
08.01.1916
04.04.1916</td><td>226
109</td><td>117.0
22.0</td><td>Amos & Smith
92 NHP
11 knots</td><td>South Western Steam
Fishing Co Ltd
Grimsby</td></tr>
<tr><td colspan="6">May 1916 Rqd by the Royal Navy as a minesweeper No. FY 864. 1918 returned.
27.02.1917 Sold to Neal Green, Grimsby. 04.06.1917 to Cleethorpes Steam Trawling Co Ltd, Grimsby.
25.02.1919 to Victoria Steam Fishing Co Ltd, Grimsby. 19.12.1929 to Lindsey Steam Fishing Co Ltd, Grimsby.
29.11.1939 Rqd by the Royal Navy as a minesweeper No. FY 872. 1945 returned.
1961 Vessel sold for scrap to Vereenigde Utrechtse Ijzerhandel, Utrecht, Holland.
31.10.1961 Registration closed on advice that the vessel was broken up.</td></tr>
<tr><td>CARENCY
138981
GY956 Steam Trawler</td><td>340A
20.04.1916
00.12.1916</td><td>233
108</td><td>117.0
22.0</td><td>Gt. Central Eng
70 NHP
10.25 knots</td><td>Earl Steam Fishing Co Ltd
Grimsby</td></tr>
<tr><td colspan="6">16.08.1916 Left Hull in tow for Grimsby for machinery to be fitted.
Dec 1916 Rqd by the Royal Navy as a minesweeper No. FY 2984. 1919 returned.
14.12.1916 Sold to The Beacon Steam Fishing Co Ltd, Grimsby.
19.02.1918 to Great Northern Steam Ship Fishing Co Ltd, Hull (H611).
1918 to Star Steam Trawling Co Ltd, Hull. 1921 to South Western Steam Fishing Co Ltd, Grimsby (GY46).
1924 to Earl Steam Fishing Co Ltd, Grimsby. 1938 to W M M Curtis & McCabe, Dublin (D119).
Aug 1939 Sold to the Royal Navy as an anti-submarine trawler and examination vessel No. FY 295. 1947 returned.
1947 to W Wood, Aberdeen (A129).
28.06.1957 Vessel stranded in thick fog at Greenigoe one mile north of Wick the crew transferred to the GILMAR A300 (218 gt/ b 1915). The GILMAR tried to pull the CARENCY free but after moving twenty feet she stuck fast again. Two hours later she slid off the rocks and sank.</td></tr>
<tr><td>VALESCA
138970
GY915 Steam Trawler</td><td>340B
02.05.1916
00.08.1916</td><td>188
82</td><td>110.33
21.0</td><td>Shields Eng Co
69 NHP
10 knots</td><td>South Western Steam
Fishing Co Ltd
Grimsby</td></tr>
<tr><td colspan="6">17.06.1916 Left Hull in tow for South Shields for machinery to be fitted.
Sep 1916 Rqd by the Royal Navy as a bomb thrower / minesweeper No. FY 2963. 1919 returned.
01.01.1918 Sold to John L Green, Grimsby. 17.05.1922 to North Western Steam Fishing Co Ltd, Grimsby.
20.02.1926 to Pelham Steam Fishing Co Ltd, Grimsby. 19.09.1928 to Earl Steam Fishing Co Ltd, Grimsby.
29.11.1939 Rqd by the Royal Navy as a minesweeper / wreck dispersal vessel No. FY 814. 1945 returned.
10.12.1940 to Sir Alec Black, Grimsby. 08.02.1943 to Shire Trawlers Ltd, Grimsby.
06.03.1948 to Alexander Hay & William Brebner Aberdeen (A536). 1950 to Ch & Arm A Seghers, Ostend, Belgium renamed CHARVIC (O335). (6 cyl Motoren Werke Mannheim A. G. diesel engine fitted).
1972 to Rederij Java, Ostend, renamed JAVA IV. 1991 Vessel deleted from Lloyds Register of Shipping.</td></tr>
<tr><td>SABREUR
138976
GY932 Steam Trawler</td><td>340C
22.05.1916
28.07.1916</td><td>188
82</td><td>110.33
21.0</td><td>Shield Eng Co
69NHP
10 knots</td><td>Alec Black
Grimsby</td></tr>
<tr><td colspan="6">Sep 1916 Rqd by the Royal Navy as a minesweeper No. FY 2964. 1919 returned.
01.01.1918 Sold to Strand Steam Fishing Co Ltd, Grimsby. 09.02.1937 to Sir Thomas Robinson & Sons Ltd, Grimsby.
1939 Rqd by the Royal Navy as a minesweeper / auxiliary patrol vessel No. FY 824 renamed BADINAGE.
1945 returned and reverted.
1960 Vessel sold to BISCO and allocated to C W Dorkin & Co Ltd. 20.04.1960 Arrived Gateshead for breaking up.</td></tr>
</table>

<table>
<tr><th rowspan="2">NAME
Official No.
Port Letters Numbers</th><th rowspan="2">Yard No.
Launched
Registered</th><th colspan="2">Registered</th><th rowspan="2">Engine Builder
Horse Power
Reg'd Speed</th><th rowspan="2">OWNER
(Built for)</th></tr>
<tr><th>G Ton
N Ton</th><th>L Ft
B Ft</th></tr>
<tr><td>WAR GREY
139940
GY1033 Steam Trawler</td><td>340D
28.12.1916
24.03.1917</td><td>246
98</td><td>117.0
22.0</td><td>Amos & Smith
74 NHP
9.5 knots</td><td>South Western Steam
Fishing Co Ltd
Grimsby</td></tr>
<tr><td colspan="6">Jul 1917 Rqd by the Royal Navy as a minesweeper fitted with Hydrophonic listening equipment No. FY 3342.
1919 returned. 19.02.1918 Sold to Great Northern Steam Ship Fishing Co Ltd, Hull (H612).
1919 to E E Cox, Grimsby (GY516). 1933 to Arctic Steam Fishing Co Ltd, Grimsby.
1941 to City Steam Fishing Co Ltd, Hull. 11.09.1941 Vessel damaged by aircraft bombs off Sunderland.
19.01.1942 to Hudson Bros (Trawlers) Ltd, Hull.
07.03.1944 Vessel stranded in fog at Veido off the south coast of Iceland during wartime fishing operations along with the LIMESLADE (see Yard No.409) and LOUIS BOTHA (see Yard No.338). Re-floated and returned to Hull for repairs.
12.01.1945 to Hull Merchants Amalgamated Trawlers Ltd, Hull renamed TOBRUK (H14).
14.02.1947 to G Sanger, Grimsby. 1950 to Alex Hay, Aberdeen renamed G D TAYLOR (A644).
1955 Vessel sold to BISCO and allocated to Malcolm Brechin and broken up at Granton.</td></tr>
<tr><td>WAR DUKE
139949
GY1037 Steam Trawler</td><td>340E
11.01.1917
21.04.1917</td><td>246
98</td><td>117.0
22.0</td><td>Gt. Central Eng
74 NHP
10.25 knots</td><td>George W White &
John N Willows
Grimsby</td></tr>
<tr><td colspan="6">21.03.1917 Left Hull in tow for Grimsby for machinery to be fitted.
May 1917 Rqd by the Royal Navy as a minesweeper No. FY 1268. 1919 returned.
30.07.1919 Sold to Yarborough Steam Fishing Co Ltd, Grimsby. 25.07.1924 to Harold Bacon, Grimsby.
05.08.1930 to Kottingham Trawling Co Ltd, Grimsby.
21.04.1939 Rqd by the Royal Navy as a minesweeper No. FY 582. 25.04.1946 returned.
03.01.1944 to Parkholme Trawlers Ltd, Grimsby. 30.07.1949 to Trawlers, Grimsby Ltd, Grimsby.
10.04.1953 to Derwent Trawlers Ltd, Grimsby. 11.01.1956 to Alfred Bannister Trawlers Ltd, Grimsby.
1963 Vessel sold for scrap to J J King & Co Ltd. 26.04.1963 Arrived Gateshead for breaking up.</td></tr>
<tr><td>LORD SELBOURNE
139949
GY1058 Steam Trawler</td><td>340F
27.04.1917
00.09.1917</td><td>246
98</td><td>117.0
22.0</td><td>Gt. Central Eng
76 NHP
10 knots</td><td>Pelham Steam Fishing Co Ltd
Grimsby</td></tr>
<tr><td colspan="6">00.09.1917 Left Hull in tow for Grimsby for machinery to be fitted. 22.08.1917 Sold to Beacon Steam Fishing Co, Grimsby.
Oct 1917 Rqd by the Royal Navy as a minesweeper and escort vessel No. FY 1652. 1919 returned.
19.02.1918 to Great Northern Steam Ship Fishing Co Ltd, Hull (H615). Sep 1919 to I Abrahams, Grimsby (GY509).
Nov 1919 to St Vincent Steam Fishing Co Ltd, Grimsby. 1923 to North Western Steam Fishing Co Ltd, Grimsby.
1926 to Pelham Steam Fishing Co Ltd, Grimsby. 1928 to Earl Steam Fishing Co Ltd, Grimsby.
1940 Rqd by the Royal Navy as an auxiliary patrol vessel No. FY 2964 based at Grimsby.
31.03.1941 Vessel sunk by mine in the Humber Estuary 3 miles off Spurn Head.</td></tr>
<tr><td>LORD ALVERSTONE
139950
GY1059 Steam Trawler</td><td>340G
27.04.1917
25.06.1917</td><td>246
98</td><td>117.0
22.0</td><td>Shields Eng Co
69 NHP
10 knots</td><td>North Western Steam
Fishing Co Ltd
Grimsby</td></tr>
<tr><td colspan="6">07.08.1917 Sold to Beacon Steam Fishing Co, Grimsby.
Jun 1917 Rqd by the Royal Navy as a minesweeper No. FY 3047.
12.12.1917 Vessel sunk by the German cruiser EMDEN (b 1909) and destroyers in the North Sea.</td></tr>
<tr><td>HUGH BLACK
FY 3602
Non-Standard Castle Class</td><td>340J
09.05.1917
22.08.1917</td><td>265
107</td><td>125.0
22.0</td><td>Amos & Smith
480 IHP
10.5 knots</td><td>The Admiralty
Whitehall
London</td></tr>
<tr><td colspan="6">Originally ordered by Hull Northern Fishing Co Ltd, Hull but purchased by the Admiralty on the stocks.
1919 Registered by the Admiralty as a trawler LO460 Official No. 144294.
1923 Sold to Hull Northern Fishing Co Ltd, Hull renamed MACBETH (H827).
06.04.1929 to Diamonds Steam Fishing Co Ltd, Grimsby renamed OGANO (GY69).
28.05.1940 Rqd by the Royal Navy as a minesweeper No. FY 803. 24.11.1944 returned.
1939 to St Andrews Steam Fishing Co Ltd, Hull. 26.01.1945 to Ogano Steam Fishing Co Ltd, Grimsby.
24.04.1950 Whilst steaming towards Sydisfjord to land an injured crewman the OGANO stranded on Brokur Reef, near Eystrahorn south east coast of Iceland. Re-floated but leaking heavily she was beached and abandoned at Stodvarfjordr. During the incident the trawler LOMBARD GY478 (272 gt/ b 1909) stood by her. All the crew were rescued.</td></tr>
</table>

<table>
<tr><th rowspan="2">NAME
Official No.
Port Letters Numbers</th><th rowspan="2">Yard No.
Launched
Registered</th><th colspan="2">Registered</th><th rowspan="2">Engine Builder
Horse Power
Reg'd Speed</th><th rowspan="2">OWNER
(Built for)</th></tr>
<tr><th>G Ton
N Ton</th><th>L Ft
B Ft</th></tr>
<tr><td>JAMES BERRY
FY 3603
Non-Standard Castle Class</td><td>340K
09.05.1917
30.08.1917</td><td>249
109</td><td>125.4
22.6</td><td>Amos & Smith
480 IHP
10.5 knots</td><td>The Admiralty
Whitehall
London</td></tr>
<tr><td colspan="6">Originally ordered by Hull Northern Fishing Co Ltd, Hull but purchased by the Admiralty on the stocks.
1919 Registered by the Admiralty as a trawler LO478 Official No. 145066.
1922 Sold to Hull Northern Fishing Co Ltd, Hull renamed MONTANO (H818).
01.05.1929 to Orontes Steam Fishing Co Ltd, Grimsby (GY83). 1932 to Southampton Steam Fishing Co Ltd, Grimsby.
31.05.1940 Rqd by the Royal Navy as a minesweeper / auxiliary patrol vessel No. FY 803. 02.01.1946 returned.
1944 to J C Llewellin Swansea. 1945 to Yolland Bros Ltd, Milford Haven (M53).
17.03.1953 Vessel sold to BISCO and allocated to Malcolm Brechin and broken up at Granton.</td></tr>
<tr><td>RICHARD BAGLEY
FY 3604
Non-Standard Castle Class</td><td>340L
09.06.1917
20.09.1917</td><td>249
109</td><td>125.4
22.6</td><td>Amos & Smith
480 IHP
10.5 knots</td><td>The Admiralty
Whitehall
London</td></tr>
<tr><td colspan="6">Originally ordered by Kingston Steam Trawling Co Ltd, Hull but purchased by the Admiralty on the stocks.
1919 Registered by the Admiralty as a trawler Official No. 143766.
1921 Sold to Kingston Steam Trawling Co Ltd, Hull renamed MALACOLITE (H574).
25.10.1928 to J Stewart Ltd, Hull. 20.01.1931 to W Beeley, Grimsby (GY342).
Feb 1931 to Princess Steam Fishing Co Ltd, Grimsby.
28.08.1939 Rqd by the Royal Navy as a minesweeper. 19.01.1940 returned.
19.03.1940 Rqd by the Royal Navy as a minesweeper No. FY 796. 17.09.1945 returned.
1946 to Grimsby Merchants Amalgamated Trawlers Ltd, Grimsby.
1950 to D Wood Aberdeen renamed STRATHALLEN (A650).
21.06.1954 Vessel sold for scrap to Van Heyghen Freres, Belgium and broken up at Ghent.</td></tr>
<tr><td>JOHN BROOKER
FY 3605
Non-Standard Castle Class</td><td>340M
09.06.1917
01.12.1917</td><td>249
109</td><td>125.4
22.6</td><td>Amos & Smith
480 IHP
10.5 knots</td><td>The Admiralty
Whitehall
London</td></tr>
<tr><td colspan="6">Originally ordered by Kingston Steam Trawling Co Ltd, Hull but purchased by the Admiralty on the stocks.
1919 Registered by the Admiralty as a trawler Official No. 146195.
1921 Sold to Kingston Steam Trawling Co Ltd, Hull renamed OBSIDIAN (H333).
12.11.1934 to Ocean Steam Fishing Co Ltd, Hull. 24.04.1935 to Lander & Paterson, Aberdeen (A301).
12.10.1939 to Loch Fishing Co Ltd, Hull renamed LOCH PARK (H219).
1940 Rqd by the Royal Navy as a minesweeper No. FY 1835. 1945 returned.
16.03.1946 to Anglo Steam Fishing Co Ltd, Grimsby (GY259). 1952 to United Steam Fishing Co Ltd, Grimsby.
24.01.1957 to Derwent Trawlers Ltd, Grimsby. 06.01.1958 to A Bannister Trawlers Ltd, Grimsby.
15.07.1962 Vessel sold for scrap to Paul Bergsoe & Son Jernhavnen, Masnedo, Denmark and broken up at Copenhagen.</td></tr>
<tr><td>THOMAS BLACKHORN
FY3606
Non-Standard Castle Class</td><td>340N
07.07.1917
17.12.1917</td><td>249
109</td><td>125.4
22.5</td><td>Amos & Smith
480 IHP
10.5 knots</td><td>The Admiralty
Whitehall
London</td></tr>
<tr><td colspan="6">Originally ordered by Kingston Steam Trawling Co Ltd, Hull but purchased by the Admiralty on the stocks.
16.05.1919 Loaned to the United States Navy for mine-sweeping duties in the North Sea. 05.10.1919 returned.
1919 Registered by the Admiralty as a trawler LO275 Official No. 143881.
1922 Sold to Kingston Steam Trawling Co Ltd, Hull renamed ALEXANDRITE (H726).
11.10.1923 Vessel wrecked at Artley Shoot, Buckton Cliff Yorkshire. In dense fog whilst homeward bound for Hull from the Scottish fishing grounds. All the crew were rescued by a Filey motor coble and landed at Filey.</td></tr>
<tr><td>THOMAS BUCKLEY
FY 3607
Non-Standard Castle Class</td><td>340P
07.07.1917
20.12.1917</td><td>249
109</td><td>125.4
22.5</td><td>Amos & Smith
480 IHP
10.5 knots</td><td>The Admiralty
Whitehall
London</td></tr>
<tr><td colspan="6">Originally ordered by Kingston Steam Trawling Co Ltd, Hull but purchased by the Admiralty on the stocks.
28.05.1919 Loaned to the United States for mine-sweeping duties in the North Sea. 03.10.1919 returned.
1919 Registered by the Admiralty as a trawler LO276 Official No. 144317.
1922 Sold to Kingston Steam Trawling Co Ltd, Hull renamed CEYLONITE (H724).
29.01.1930 to Taylor Steam Fishing Co Ltd, Grimsby (GY170).
09.04.1940 Rqd by the Royal Navy as a minesweeper No. FY 1853. 22.05.1946 returned.
1939 to St Andrews Steam Fishing Co Ltd, Grimsby. 1947 to Joe Croan Newhaven Edinburgh (LH246).
1960 Vessel sold to BISCO for £2750 and allocated to Metal Industries. 14.06.1960 Arrived Charlestown for breaking up.</td></tr>
</table>

Yard No.340K
1917 JAMES BERRY as MONTANO
Photo by courtesy of George Scales

Yard No.341
1916 LAPAGERIA as MARY CROAN
Photo:- Author's Collection

Yard No.346
1916 SEDDON
Photo:- Author's Collection

<table>
<tr><th rowspan="2">NAME
Official No.
Port Letters Numbers</th><th rowspan="2">Yard No.
Launched
Registered</th><th colspan="2">Registered</th><th rowspan="2">Engine Builder
Horse Power
Reg'd Speed</th><th rowspan="2">OWNER
(Built for)</th></tr>
<tr><th>G Ton
N Ton</th><th>L Ft
B Ft</th></tr>
<tr><td>LAPAGERIA
139919
GY890 Steam Trawler</td><td>341
08.02.1916
08.10.1916</td><td>263
119</td><td>125.3
22.5</td><td>C.D. Holmes
79 NHP
10.5 knots</td><td>Dawson Robinson
Grimsby</td></tr>
<tr><td colspan="6">Oct 1916 Rqd by the Royal Navy as a minesweeper No. FY 3311. 1919 returned.
15.02.1924 Sold to Harry Robinson, Grimsby. 07.05.1929 to Fred Dawson Robinson.
Sep 1940 Rqd by the Royal Navy as an auxiliary patrol vessel / 13.08.1942 fuel carrier No. FY 4.315. 05.02.1946 returned.
26.04.1951 to Joseph Croan, Newhaven, Edinburgh renamed MARY CROAN (LH99).
02.09.1957 Vessel sold to BISCO and allocated to Malcolm Brechin and broken up at Granton.</td></tr>
<tr><td>RUGBY
139924
GY994 Steam Trawler</td><td>342
20.07.1916
16.08.1916</td><td>274
123</td><td>125.3
22.5</td><td>C.D. Holmes
79 NHP
10.5 knots</td><td>William Grant
Grimsby</td></tr>
<tr><td colspan="6">Nov 1916 Rqd by the Royal Navy as a bomb thrower / minesweeper No. FY 2979 renamed RUGBY II.
1919 returned and reverted. 11.03.1938 Sold to Harry Robinson, Grimsby.
14.08.1939 to Earl Steam Fishing Co Ltd, Grimsby.
30.05.1940 Rqd by the Royal Navy as a minesweeper / auxiliary patrol vessel No. FY 4.162
1943 Fuel carrier No. Y7.30. 22.05.1946 returned.
10.09.1941 to North Star Steam Fishing Co Ltd, Aberdeen. 1944 to Parkholme Trawlers Ltd, Grimsby. 1946 (GY18).
29.07.1948 to Tilbrook Trawlers Ltd, Grimsby. 1953 to Joseph Croan Granton Edinburgh (LH92).
1955 Vessel sold to BISCO (£2400) allocated to Shipbreaking Industries Ltd.
24.03.1955 Arrived Inverkeithing for breaking up.</td></tr>
<tr><td>GAMBRI
139923
GY992 Steam Trawler</td><td>343
16.09.1916
29.03.1917</td><td>274
123</td><td>125.3
22.5</td><td>C.D. Holmes
79 NHP
10.5 knots</td><td>Grant & Baker Steam
Fishing Co Ltd
Grimsby</td></tr>
<tr><td colspan="6">Apr 1917 Rqd by the Royal Navy as a minesweeper No. FY 1263.
18.01.1918 Vessel sunk by mine near the Royal Sovereign Light Vessel. Mine laid by UC71 on the same day.</td></tr>
<tr><td>ST. HUBERT
138298
H493 Steam Trawler</td><td>344
19.06.1916
14.09.1916</td><td>349
140</td><td>140.0
24.0</td><td>C.D. Holmes
86 NHP
10.5 knots</td><td>St Andrews Steam
Fishing Co Ltd
Hull</td></tr>
<tr><td colspan="6">Sep 1916 Rqd by the Royal Navy as a minesweeper No. FY 3306. 1919 returned.
18.03.1922 Vessel seized by USSR Navy off Russian coast crew sent home in an Icebreaker.
30.10.1923 Vessel returned to Hull.
20.02.1939 Sold to S J Ellefen & MJ Mortensen, Midvaag, Færoes renamed NYGGJABERG.
15.02.1942 Vessel left Færoes for the Icelandic fishing grounds. 06.03.1942 Last seen steaming eastwards after being
at anchor off the Vestman Islands with the Færoese trawler STELLA ARGOS. Not heard of again.</td></tr>
<tr><td>SETHON
138974
GY928 Steam Trawler</td><td>345
22.04.1916
16.10.1916</td><td>295
114</td><td>130.2
23.0</td><td>Amos & Smith
89 NHP
9.5 knots</td><td>Standard Steam Fishing Co Ltd
Grimsby</td></tr>
<tr><td colspan="6">Oct 1916 Rqd by the Royal Navy as a bomb thrower / minesweeper No. FY 3310. 1919 returned.
05.06.1940 Rqd by the Royal Navy as a minesweeper / auxiliary patrol vessel No. FY 883. 02.10.1945 returned.
14.01.1942 Sold To St Andrews Fishing Co Ltd, Hull. 03.12.1945 to Mason Trawlers Ltd, Fleetwood (FD166).
1959 Vessel sold for scrap to Scrapping Co SRL, Belgium. 16.07.1959 Left Fleetwood for Boom for breaking up.</td></tr>
<tr><td>SEDDON
139922
GY991 Steam Trawler</td><td>346
20.05.1916
03.11.1916</td><td>296
115</td><td>130.2
23.0</td><td>Amos & Smith
89 NHP
9.5 knots</td><td>Standard Steam Fishing Co Ltd
Grimsby</td></tr>
<tr><td colspan="6">Nov 1916 Rqd by the Royal Navy as minesweeper No. FY 3313. 1919 returned.
02.06.1940 Rqd by the Royal Navy as a minesweeper No. FY 1993 / auxiliary patrol vessel No. FY 4.166.
07.02.1946 returned. 14.01.1942 Sold to St Andrews Fishing Co Ltd, Hull. 12.08.1947 to Dagon Fishing Co, Grimsby.
29.03.1948 to Seddon Fishing Co Ltd, London. 16.04.1951 to J Craig Stores, Aberdeen (A684).
1960 Vessel sold for scrap to James A White & Co Ltd, . 22.04.1960 Arrived St Davids on the River Forth for breaking up.</td></tr>
<tr><td>SARPEDON
139920
GY984 Steam Trawler</td><td>347
18.04.1916
22.11.1916</td><td>344
138</td><td>135.4
23.5</td><td>Amos & Smith
89 NHP
10 knots</td><td>Standard Steam Fishing Co Ltd
Grimsby</td></tr>
<tr><td colspan="6">Jan 1917 Rqd by the Royal Navy as a minesweeper No. FY 2998 renamed SARPEDON II. 1919 returned and reverted.
08.06.1940 Rqd by the Royal Navy as an auxiliary patrol vessel / minesweeper No. FY 4.05. 25.07.1945 returned.
14.01.1942 Sold to St Andrews Fishing Co Ltd, Hull. 25.10.1945 to Kenneth Persival (Trawlers) Hull (H142).
10.03.1947 to Anglo Steam Fishing Co Ltd, Grimsby (GY466).
06.10.1952 Vessel sold to BISCO allocated to Stockton Shipping & Salvage Co Ltd, and broken up at Thornaby on Tees.</td></tr>
</table>

<table>
<tr><th rowspan="2">NAME
Official No.
Port Letters Numbers</th><th rowspan="2">Yard No.
Launched
Registered</th><th colspan="2">Registered</th><th rowspan="2">Engine Builder
Horse Power
Reg'd Speed</th><th rowspan="2">OWNER
(Built for)</th></tr>
<tr><th>G Ton
N Ton</th><th>L Ft
B Ft</th></tr>
<tr><td>JERIA
139921
GY985 Steam Trawler</td><td>348
17.07.1916
16.12.1916</td><td>344
138</td><td>135.0
23.5</td><td>Amos & Smith
89 NHP
10 knots</td><td>Great Grimsby & East Coast
Steam Fishing Co Ltd
Grimsby</td></tr>
<tr><td colspan="6">Dec 1916 Rqd by the Royal Navy as a minesweeper No. FY 3319. 1917 returned.
07.09.1929 Vessel wrecked after running aground in thick fog on St Johns Head, Hoy, Orkney Islands whilst homeward bound to Grimsby from the Icelandic fishing grounds. The crew fired distress flares which were seen by the Aberdeen fishing liner CURLEW A906 (180 gt/ b1912) which came to the assistance. All twelve crew of the JERIA launched the ship's boat and were taken in tow by the CURLEW into the harbour at Stromness and all landed safely.</td></tr>
<tr><td>KASTORIA
139930
GY1017 Steam Trawler</td><td>349
28.10.1916
15.01.1917</td><td>307
121</td><td>130.2
23.0</td><td>Amos & Smith
89 NHP
10 knots</td><td>Great Grimsby & East Coast
Steam Fishing Co Ltd
Grimsby</td></tr>
<tr><td colspan="6">Jan 1917 Rqd by the Royal Navy as a minesweeper / escort vessel No. FY 3324. 1919 returned.
02.06.1940 Rqd by the Royal Navy as an auxiliary patrol vessel / minesweeper No. FY 4.148. 1946 returned.
14.01.1942 Sold to Boston Deep Sea Fishing Co Ltd, Grimsby.
15.04.1947 to Dalmor Przedsiebjorstwo Polowow Dalekomorskich, Gdynia, Poland.
1959 Vessel sold to shipbreakers and broken up.</td></tr>
<tr><td>MORAVIA
139931
GY1018 Steam Trawler</td><td>350
28.10.1916
13.01.1917</td><td>307
121</td><td>130.2
23.0</td><td>Amos & Smith
89 NHP
10 knots</td><td>Great Grimsby & East Coast
Steam Fishing Co Ltd
Grimsby</td></tr>
<tr><td colspan="6">Jun 1917 Rqd by the Royal Navy as a minesweeper No. FY 1272. 1919 returned.
09.01.1932 Whilst off Iceland the vessel was severely damaged when struck by a mountainous sea. The wheelhouse was wrecked the funnel and mizzen mast were swept away. The skipper and one crewman were washed overboard and lost. After thirty-six hours the Hull trawler CAPE GRISNEZ H84 (325 gt/ b 1919) found the MORAVIA with the ten surviving crew members and towed her to Grimsby (approx 900 miles)
06.06.1940 Rqd by the Royal Navy as an auxiliary patrol vessel / minesweeper No. FY 1819.
14.01.1942 Sold to Boston Deep Sea Fishing Co Ltd, Grimsby.
14.03.1943 Vessel sunk by mine in the North Sea reported position 52° 15'N 001° 48.3'E.</td></tr>
<tr><td>SUSARION
139928
GY1012 Steam Trawler</td><td>351
30.08.1916
20.02.1917</td><td>261
102</td><td>120.0
22.5</td><td>Amos & Smith
74 NHP
9.5 knots</td><td>Standard Steam Fishing Co Ltd
Grimsby</td></tr>
<tr><td colspan="6">Feb 1917 Rqd by the Royal Navy as a minesweeper No. FY 3002. 1919 returned.
22.05.1940 Sold to Sir Alec Black, Grimsby. 02.06.1940 Rqd by the Royal Navy as an auxiliary patrol vessel .
07.05.1941 Vessel sunk by German Aircraft off the River Humber 3 miles south by east of the Humber Light-vessel.</td></tr>
<tr><td>SIMPSON
139933
GY1024 Steam Trawler</td><td>352
02.09.1916
21.02.1917</td><td>261
102</td><td>120.0
22.5</td><td>Amos & Smith
74 NHP
9.5 knots</td><td>Standard Steam Fishing Co Ltd
Grimsby</td></tr>
<tr><td colspan="6">May 1917 Rqd by the Royal Navy as a minesweeper No. FY 1269. 1919 returned.
22.05.1940 Sold to Sir Alec Black, Grimsby.
08.06.1940 Rqd by the Royal Navy as a minesweeper No. FY 545. 06.08.1946 returned.
08.04.1943 to Grimsby Motor Trawlers Ltd, Grimsby. 30.07.1949 to Trawlers Grimsby Ltd, Grimsby.
10.04.1953 Derwent Trawlers Ltd, Grimsby.
1956 Vessel sold to BISCO and allocated to J J King & Co Ltd. 25.04.1956 Arrived Gateshead for breaking up.</td></tr>
<tr><td>HELVETIA
139934
GY1026 Steam Trawler</td><td>353
30.09.1916
26.02.1917</td><td>261
102</td><td>120.0
22.5</td><td>Amos & Smith
74 NHP
9.5 knots</td><td>Great Grimsby & East Coast
Steam Fishing Co Ltd
Grimsby</td></tr>
<tr><td colspan="6">Vessel originally to have been named ANDRIA.
Apr 1917 Rqd by the Royal Navy as an anti-submarine vessel with Hydro listening equipment No. FY 1266. 1919 returned.
22.05.1940 Sold to Sir Alec Black, Grimsby.
10.06.1940 Rqd by the Royal Navy as an auxiliary patrol vessel / minesweeper No. FY 4.86. 30.09.1946 returned
1943 Sold to J E Harrison, Grimsby. 08.04.1943 to Grimsby Motor Trawlers Ltd, Grimsby.
30.07.1949 to Trawlers Grimsby Ltd, Grimsby. 10.04.1953 to Derwent Trawlers Ltd, Grimsby.
1958 Vessel sold for scrap to Jacques Bakker en Zonen, Belgium. 12.02.1958 Arrived Bruges for breaking up.</td></tr>
<tr><td>OLYMPIA
139955
GY1080 Steam Trawler</td><td>354
22.05.1917
26.07.1917</td><td>261
102</td><td>120.0
22.5</td><td>Amos & Smith
74 NHP
9.5 knots</td><td>Great Grimsby & East Coast
Steam Fishing Co Ltd
Grimsby</td></tr>
<tr><td colspan="6">Vessel originally to have been named BISACCIA. Sep 1917 Rqd by the Royal Navy as an anti-submarine vessel fitted with Hydrophonic listening equipment No. FY 3064. 1919 returned. Dec 1939 Rqd by the Royal Navy as a minesweeper No. FY 1586. 30.10.1945 returned . 14.01.1942 Sold to Boston Deep Sea Fishing Co Ltd, Grimsby.
09.05.1946 to Channel Trawling Co Ltd, Grimsby. 21.02.1949 to Taylor Steam Fishing Co Ltd, Grimsby.
02.07.1962 Vessel sold to N V Machinehandel & Sheepssloperij, Holland and broken up at Niew Lekkerland.</td></tr>
</table>

<table>
<tr><th rowspan="2">NAME
Official No.
Port Letters Numbers</th><th rowspan="2">Yard No.
Launched
Registered</th><th colspan="2">Registered</th><th rowspan="2">Engine Builder
Horse Power
Reg'd Speed</th><th rowspan="2">OWNER
(Built for)</th></tr>
<tr><th>G Ton
N Ton</th><th>L Ft
B Ft</th></tr>
<tr><td>OSWALDIAN
139962
GY1104 Steam Trawler</td><td>355
24.07.1917
05.10.1917</td><td>261
102</td><td>120.0
22.5</td><td>Amos & Smith
74 NHP
9.5 knots</td><td>Loyal Steam Fishing Co Ltd
Grimsby</td></tr>
<tr><td colspan="6">Sep 1917 Rqd by the Royal Navy as a minesweeper No. FY 1651. 1919 returned
22.05.1940 Sold to Sir Alec Black, Grimsby.
May1940 Rqd by the Royal Navy as a minesweeper / auxiliary patrol vessel based at Milford Haven.
04.08.1940 Vessel sunk by mine off Breaksea Light-vessel in the Bristol Channel.
Seven survivors picked up and landed at Barry.</td></tr>
<tr><td>MITRES
139963
GY1105 Steam Trawler</td><td>356
24.07.1917
08.10.1917</td><td>261
102</td><td>120.0
22.5</td><td>Amos & Smith
74 NHP
9.5 knots</td><td>Loyal Steam Fishing Co Ltd
Grimsby</td></tr>
<tr><td colspan="6">Dec 1917 Rqd by the Royal Navy as an auxiliary patrol vessel No. FY 3078. 1919 returned.
22.05.1940 Sold to Sir Alec Black, Grimsby.
09.06.1940 Rqd by the Royal Navy as an auxiliary patrol vessel / salvage vessel No. 4.04. 30.11.1945 returned.
1943 Sold to J E Harrison, Grimsby. 08.03.1943 to Grimsby Motor Trawlers Ltd, Grimsby.
30.07.1949 to Trawlers Grimsby Ltd, Grimsby. 10.04.1953 to Derwent Trawlers Ltd, Grimsby.
24.01.1959 to Ross Trawlers Ltd, Grimsby.
30.07.1959 Vessel sold for scrap to Scrapping Co S P T, Belgium and broken up at Antwerp.</td></tr>
<tr><td>JOHN APPELBY
FY 3612
Non-Standard Mersey Class</td><td>357
30.01.1917
25.05.1917</td><td>286
112</td><td>130.0
23.0</td><td>Amos & Smith
89 NHP
10.5 knots</td><td>The Admiralty
Whitehall
London</td></tr>
<tr><td colspan="6">Ordered by Great Grimsby & East Coast Steam Fishing Co Ltd, Grimsby as the CORINTHIA
but purchased by the Admiralty on the stocks. 1919 Registered by the Admiralty as a trawler LO286 Official No. 143469.
1922 Sold to the Fleetwood Steam Fishing Co Ltd, Fleetwood renamed LOIS (FD424).
27.02.1940 Rqd by the Royal Navy as a minesweeper No. FY 781. 31.11.1944 returned.
05.01.1947 Vessel wrecked at Grindavik off the south-west coast of Iceland in a blizzard and rough seas. Fifteen crew were rescued by breeches buoy but the skipper who was the last to leave the stricken vessel was swept away by the raging sea.</td></tr>
<tr><td>JOHN ARTHUR
FY 3613
Non-Standard Mersey Class</td><td>358
10.02.1917
15.06.1917</td><td>306
121</td><td>130.0
23.0</td><td>Amos & Smith
89 NHP
10.5 knots</td><td>The Admiralty
Whitehall
London</td></tr>
<tr><td colspan="6">Ordered by Standard Steam Fishing Co Ltd, Grimsby as the SANNYRION but purchased by the Admiralty on the stocks.
1919 Registered by the Admiralty as a trawler LO299 Official No. 143963.
1922 Sold to the Fleetwood Steam Fishing Co Ltd, Fleetwood renamed GLADYS (FD423).
29.11.1939 Rqd by the Royal Navy as a boom defence vessel . 23.11.1943 Sold to The Admiralty.
1947 to James Buckie Ship & Shipyard Co Ltd, Leith renamed THE BRUCE (LH21). 1949 to Joseph Croan, Leith.
1961 Vessel sold for scrap to G & W Brunton, Grangemouth. 28.06.1961 Breaking up commenced.</td></tr>
<tr><td>RESMILO
139938
GY1029 Steam Trawler</td><td>359
27.11.1916
14.03.1916</td><td>258
113</td><td>120.4
22.0</td><td>C.D. Holmes
80 NHP
10.5 knots</td><td>George F Sleight
Grimsby</td></tr>
<tr><td colspan="6">Mar 1917 Rqd by the Royal Navy a bomb thrower / anti-submarine vessel
with Hydrophonic listening equipment also served as a minesweeper No. FY 3021. 1920 returned.
17.11.1933 Sold to Sleight and Humphrey, Grimsby.
09.09.1940 Rqd by the Royal Navy as a minesweeper. 20.06.1941 Vessel sunk by German Aircraft off the end of the south Breakwater at Peterhead. Bomb burst under the trawler splitting her plates All crew rescued. Whilst serving with the 70 minesweeper group based at, Aberdeen. 1946 Vessel raised and scrapped.</td></tr>
<tr><td>REFUNDO
139953
GY1063 Steam Trawler</td><td>360
27.11.1916
20.06.1916</td><td>258
113</td><td>120.5
22.0</td><td>C.D. Holmes
80 NHP
10.5 knots</td><td>George F Sleight
Grimsby</td></tr>
<tr><td colspan="6">Jul 1917 Rqd by the Royal Navy a bomb thrower / anti-submarine vessel
with Hydrophonic listening equipment also served as a minesweeper No. FY 3053. 1919 returned.
01.06.1927 Sold to Raymond L Humphrey, Grimsby. 01.10.1933 to George F Sleight.
Nov 1939 Rqd by the Royal Navy as a minesweeper No. FY 830.
18.12.1940 Vessel mined off Harwich taken in tow but sank west of the Beach End Buoy. Two crew lost.
Whilst serving with the 117 minesweeper group based at Harwich.</td></tr>
<tr><td>REMINDO
139957
GY1089 Steam Trawler</td><td>361
26.02.1917
02.10.1917</td><td>258
113</td><td>120.5
22.0</td><td>C.D. Holmes
80 NHP
10.5 knots</td><td>George F Sleight
Grimsby</td></tr>
<tr><td colspan="6">Sep 1917 Rqd by the Royal Navy as an anti-submarine vessel with Hydrophonic listening equipment No. FY 3065.
02.02.1918 Vessel sunk by UC 79 off Portland.</td></tr>
</table>

Yard No.357
1917 JOHN APPLEBY as LOIS
Photo:- Author's Collection

Yard No.365
1919 ATHENIAN
Photo by courtesy of Steve Pulfrey

Yard No.368
1919 SKÚLI FÓGETI
Photo by courtesy of The Icelandic Maritime Museum, Hafnarfjördur

NAME Official No. Port Letters Numbers	Yard No. Launched Registered	Registered G Ton N Ton	 L Ft B Ft	Engine Builder Horse Power Reg'd Speed	OWNER (Built for)
RESERCHO 139961 GY1103 Steam Trawler	362 26.02.1917 02.10.1917	258 113	120.5 22.0	C.D. Holmes 80 NHP 10.5 knots	George F Sleight Grimsby
Jan 1918 Rqd by the Royal Navy a minesweeper No. FY 3081. 1919 returned. 17.11.1933 Sold to Sleight and Humphrey, Grimsby. 28.12.1939 Vessel sunk by mine 6 miles south-east by east of Flamborough Head, all ten crew rescued. Mine laid by U15.					
JOHN BURLINGHAM FY3600 Non-Standard Castle Class	363 21.04.1917 13.07.1917	266 105	125.0 22.0	Amos & Smith 80 NHP 10.5 knots	The Admiralty Whitehall London
Originally ordered by George F Sleight as the REHEARO but purchased by the Admiralty on the stocks. 1919 Registered by the Admiralty as a trawler Official No. 143801. 1920 to George F Sleight, Grimsby renamed REHEARO GY829. 03.09.1940 Rqd by the Royal Navy as a minesweeper No. FY 1791. Jan 1946 returned. 15.10.1956 to Derwent Trawlers, Grimsby. 24.01.1959 to Ross Trawlers Ltd, Grimsby. 1961 Vessel sold for scrap to H.P. Heavelman N V Krimpen. 27.04.1961 Arrived A/D Ijssel, Holland for breaking up.					
ROBERT BETSON FY 3601 Non-Standard Castle Class	364 21.04.1917 27.07.1917	266 105	125.0 22.0	Amos & Smith 80 NHP 10.5 knots	The Admiralty Whitehall London
Originally ordered by George F Sleight as the REMILLO but purchased by the Admiralty on the stocks. 1919 Registered by the Admiralty as a trawler Official No. 143803. Jan 1920 to George F Sleight, Grimsby GY13 (Apr 1920) renamed REMILLO (GY852). Apr 1940 Rqd by the Royal Navy as a danlayer / auxiliary patrol vessel based at Grimsby . 27.02.1941 Vessel sunk by mine in the River Humber 1.76 miles west ½ north of Spurn Point Lighthouse.					
ATHENIAN 140789 GY357 Steam Trawler	365 17.04.1919 00.06.1919	218 96	117.0 21.6	C.D. Holmes 67 NHP 10 knots	Onward Steam Fishing Co Ltd Grimsby
Last coal powered Steam Trawler in service, based at Grimsby. 25.11.1939 Rqd by the Royal Navy as a minesweeper No. FY 757 / fuel carrier No. Y7.1. Aug 1946 returned. 05.11.1946 The SERAPION GY1154 *(see Hull Yard No. 256)* sank in the North Sea following a collision with the ATHENIAN 6 miles off the River Humber. 04.10.1960 The ZEFYR GY351 sank in the North Sea following a collision with the ATHENIAN 47 miles east north-east of Spurn Point. 1964 Vessel sold for scrap to Scrapping Co S.R.L, Brussels. 07.11.1964 Arrived Antwerp for breaking up.					
MEDIAN 140792 GY430 Steam Trawler	365A 17.05.1919 21.07.1919	216 96	117.0 21.6	C.D. Holmes 67 NHP 10 knots	Onward Steam Fishing Co Ltd Grimsby
25.11.1939 Rqd by the Royal Navy as an auxiliary patrol vessel 08.02.1940 returned. 1962 Vessel sold for scrap to Van Den Bossche & Co, Belgium. 13.05.1962 Arrived Boom for breaking up.					
Not Built	366A	Ordered by Thomas Robinson, Grimsby			
CHAMONIX 140801 GY717 Steam Trawler	367 28.08.1919 24.12.1919	226 87	117.0 22.0	C.D. Holmes 67 NHP 10 knots	Neale Green Grimsby
1919 Sold to E Cox Grimsby . 21.07.1921 Left Grimsby for a North Sea fishing trip 25.07.1921 Vessel last sighted Posted missing:- Lost with all nine crew.					
SKÚLI FÓGETI RE144 Steam Trawler	368 25.10.1919 25.03.1920	348 142	140.0 25.0	C.D. Holmes 86 NHP 10.5 knots	Fiskiveidafelagid Alliance Reykjavik Iceland
10.04.1933 Vessel wrecked at Reykjanes.					
HATSUSE 143502 CF61 Steam Trawler	369 13.09.1919 04.03.1920	282 110	128.5 23.6	C.D. Holmes 85 NHP 10.5 knots	Neale & West Ltd Cardiff
1927 Sold to Consolidated Fisheries Ltd, Grimsby renamed DAGON (GY438). 26.08.1939 Rqd by the Royal Navy as a minesweeper . 13.10.1939 returned. 31.10.1941 to Marr & Son Ltd, Fleetwood . 25.09.1945 to A G Tilbrook, Milford Haven. 1952 to Devanha Fishing Co Ltd, Aberdeen renamed CASIMIR (A710). 1955 Vessel sold to BISCO and allocated to Metal Industries. 28.11.1955 Arrived Charlestown for breaking up.					
APRIL RE151 Steam Trawler	370 24.11.1919 00.02.1920	343 177	140.0 25.0	C.D. Holmes 86 NHP 10.5 knots	Fiskiveidafelagid Alliance Reykjavik Iceland
01.12.1930 Vessel sank off Vestmann Islands whilst on passage from England to Iceland. All eighteen crew lost.					

<table>
<tr><th rowspan="2">NAME
Official No.
Port Letters Numbers</th><th rowspan="2">Yard No.
Launehed
Registered</th><th colspan="2">Registered</th><th rowspan="2">Engine Builder
Horse Power
Reg'd Speed</th><th rowspan="2">OWNER
(Built for)</th></tr>
<tr><th>G Ton
N Ton</th><th>L Ft
B Ft</th></tr>
<tr><td>ASAMA
143501
CF62 Steam Trawler</td><td>371
13.09.1919
10.02.1920</td><td>282
110</td><td>128.5
23.6</td><td>C.D. Holmes
85 NHP
10.5 knots</td><td>Neale & West Ltd
Cardiff</td></tr>
<tr><td colspan="6">1929 Sold to Cam & Sons, Sydney New South Wales, Australia renamed ALFIE CAM.
22.06.1940 Rqd by the Royal Australian Navy as a minesweeper No. FY 97.
29.06.1943 Sold to the Royal Australian Navy. 27.09.1944 to Cam & Sons, Sydney.
10.07.1953 Vessel wrecked near Eden, New South Wales.</td></tr>
<tr><td>RAYMONT
138959
GY895 Steam Trawler</td><td>372
05.03.1916
26.07.1916</td><td>226
108</td><td>117.0
22.0</td><td>Amos & Smith
74 NHP
9.5 knots</td><td>South Western Steam
Fishing Co Ltd
Grimsby</td></tr>
<tr><td colspan="6">Ordered by George W White & John N Willows, Grimsby but sold on the stocks.
08.01.1917 to Aldersyde Steam Fishing Co, Grimsby.
Sep 1916 Rqd by the Royal Navy as a minesweeper No. FY 2967. 1919 returned.
29.04.1918 to Great Northern Steam Ship Fishing Co Ltd, Hull (H599). 1919 to J W Smethurst, Grimsby (GY304).
1920 to H Smethurst, Grimsby. 1926 to Trawlers White Sea & Grimsby Ltd, Grimsby.
27.11.1939 Rqd by the Royal Navy as a minesweeper. No. FY 785 (1944) Store carrier. 19.03.1946 returned and laid up.
1942 to Trawlers Grimsby Ltd, Grimsby.
1949 Vessel sold to BISCO and allocated to J J King & Co Ltd. 06.06.1949 Arrived Gateshead for breaking up.</td></tr>
<tr><td>JOHN BRICE
FY 3608
Non-Standard Castle Class</td><td>373
22.08.1917
04.01.1918</td><td>260
112</td><td>125.1
22.9</td><td>Amos & Smith
480 IHP
10.5 knots</td><td>The Admiralty
Whitehall
London</td></tr>
<tr><td colspan="6">1917 Sold to the Admiralty on the stocks and completed as a Non-Standard Castle Class bomb thrower / minesweeper.
1919 Registered by the Admiralty as a trawler (1920) renamed DERWENT.
1923 to R Maubaillarca & Cie, Belgium renamed BEAULNE-VERNEUIL.
1939 to F E Menu (Association Rochelaise De Peche A Vapeur), La Rochelle, France.
1939 Rqd by the French Navy as a minesweeper No.AD100. 03.07.1940 Commandeered at Plymouth by the Royal Navy and used as a boom defence vessel No. Z.247. 30.03.1946 returned.
1952 Vessel sold for scrap to Thos W Ward Ltd. 09.12.1952 Arrived Grays River Thames for breaking up.</td></tr>
<tr><td>JOHN BRENNAN
FY 3609
Non-Standard Castle Class</td><td>374
04.09.1917
12.01.1918</td><td>273
112</td><td>125.4
22.7</td><td>Amos & Smith
480 IHP
10.5 knots</td><td>The Admiralty
Whitehall
London</td></tr>
<tr><td colspan="6">1917 Sold to the Admiralty on the stocks and completed as a Non-Standard Castle Class bomb thrower / minesweeper.
1919 Registered by the Admiralty as a trawler LO484 Official No. 145080.
1922 to Kingston Steam Trawling Co Ltd, Hull renamed IOLITE (H576).
08.11.1934 to Diamonds Steam Fishing Co Ltd, Grimsby renamed OSAKO (GY100).
11.02.1940 Rqd by the Royal Navy as a minesweeper No. FY 580. 15.12.1945 returned.
21.04.1956 Vessel sank off the Færoes after springing a leak in the fish room in rough weather.
The Grimsby trawler THESSALONIAN GY112 which was fishing nearby immediately responded to the call for assistance. The skipper realising he could not get close because of the state of the sea launched life-saving dinghies and in a dramatic shuttle service floated the dinghies on a line back and forth until all thirteen crew were rescued.</td></tr>
<tr><td>JOHN ANDERSON
FY 3610
Non-Standard Castle Class</td><td>375
20.09.1917
19.12.1917</td><td>260
112</td><td>125.4
22.7</td><td>Amos & Smith
480 IHP
10.5 knots</td><td>The Admiralty
Whitehall
London</td></tr>
<tr><td colspan="6">1917 Sold to the Admiralty on the stocks and completed as a Non-Standard Castle Class anti-submarine vessel .
1919 Registered by the Admiralty as a trawler LO480 Official No. 145074 renamed CHARLES DORAN.
1922 to St Andrews Steam Fishing Co Ltd, Hull (H760).
07.12.1937 to A M Morrice Aberdeen (A460). 1940 to St Andrews Steam Fishing Co Ltd, Aberdeen.
05.02.1940 Rqd by the Royal Navy as a minesweeper No. FY 597. 16.11.1945 returned.
1948 to A J Tilbrook Aberdeen. 1953 to Medway Fishing Co Ltd, Fleetwood (FD275).
1957 Vessel sold to BISCO and allocated to Thos W Ward Ltd . 25.03.1957 Arrived Barrow for breaking up.</td></tr>
<tr><td>GEORGE AUNGER
FY 3611
Non-Standard Castle Class</td><td>376
20.09.1917
02.01.1918</td><td>260
112</td><td>125.4
22.7</td><td>Amos & Smith
480 IHP
10.5 knots</td><td>The Admiralty
Whitehall
London</td></tr>
<tr><td colspan="6">1917 Sold to the Admiralty on the stocks and completed as a Non-Standard Castle Class bomb thrower / minesweeper.
1919 Registered by the Admiralty as a trawler LO403 Official No. 145079.
1922 to Bunch Steam Fishing Co Ltd, Grimsby (GY325). 1929 to G Leiper Aberdeen (A37).
25.04.1930 Vessel wrecked after running ashore in thick fog on May Island, Firth of Forth whilst on a coaling trip.
Two crew lost four rescued.</td></tr>
</table>

NAME Official No. Port Letters Numbers	Yard No. Launched Registered	Registered G Ton N Ton	 L Ft B Ft	Engine Builder Horse Power Reg'd Speed	OWNER (Built for)
WILLIAM BROWIS FY 3582 Castle Class	377 18.10.1917 26.01.1918	275 119	125.5 23.6	Amos & Smith 480 IHP 10.5 knots	The Admiralty Whitehall London

1919 Registered by the Admiralty as a trawler LO452 Official No. 143932.
1922 Sold to Boston Deep Sea Fishing Co Ltd, Boston renamed GONERBY (BN166).
1923 to Pecheries A Vapeur Soc. Anon, Ostend, Belgium renamed JOHN.
1933 to Hellyer Bros Ltd, Hull renamed SPANIARD (H530).
19.06.1936 to Milford Steam Fishing Co Ltd, Milford Haven renamed MILFORD QUEEN (M225).
31.08.1939 Rqd by the Royal Navy as a minesweeper No. FY 615. Dec1945 returned
1948 to J Craig, Aberdeen renamed MILBURN (A4920).
1960 Vessel sold for scrap and allocated to James A White & Co Ltd. 16.04.1960 Arrived St Davids on Forth for breaking up

NAME Official No. Port Letters Numbers	Yard No. Launched Registered	G Ton N Ton	L Ft B Ft	Engine Builder Horse Power Reg'd Speed	OWNER (Built for)
PETER BLUMBERRY FY 3583 Castle Class	378 18.10.1917 06.02.1918	290 119	125.5 23.6	Amos & Smith 480 IHP 10.5 knots	The Admiralty Whitehall London

1919 Registered by the Admiralty as a trawler LO346 Official No. 144507.
1921 Sold to Soc De Pecheries De Havre, La Havre, France renamed INGOUVILLE .
1926 to Charpin Del Pierre & Co, Boulogne, France renamed St PIERRE-St PAUL.
1930 to J H Dove Milford Haven renamed STANFREL (M69).
15.05.1933 Vessel foundered after being abandoned due to a burst steam pipe 45 miles off the Dingle coast at approx 1520 hr

NAME Official No. Port Letters Numbers	Yard No. Launched Registered	G Ton N Ton	L Ft B Ft	Engine Builder Horse Power Reg'd Speed	OWNER (Built for)
JOSEPH BUTTON FY 3584 Castle Class	379 17.12.1917 24.04.1918	290 119	125.5 23.6	Amos & Smith 480 IHP 10.5 knots	The Admiralty Whitehall London

1919 Registered by the Admiralty as a trawler LO241 Official No. 143829.
1920 Sold to Skomer Steam Ship Co Ltd, Cardiff. 1923 to Brand & Curzon Ltd, London .
1938 to Milford Fishing Co Ltd, London (M272). 31.07.1939 J Marr & Son Ltd, Fleetwood.
29.08.1939 Rqd by the Royal Navy as a minesweeper . 22.10.1940 Vessel sunk by mine in the North Sea off Aldeburgh.
Whilst serving with the 56 minesweeper group based at Harwich.

NAME Official No. Port Letters Numbers	Yard No. Launched Registered	G Ton N Ton	L Ft B Ft	Engine Builder Horse Power Reg'd Speed	OWNER (Built for)
WILLIAM BRADY FY 3585 Castle Class	380 17.12.1917 04.05.1918	290 119	125.5 23.6	Amos & Smith 480 IHP 10.5 knots	The Admiralty Whitehall London

1919 Registered by the Admiralty as a trawler LO347 Official No. 143812.
1920 to Quinton Dick, London. 1929 to Countess Howe, London. 01.11.1930 to Brand & Curzon, Milford Haven.
04.11.1932 to Mills Steam Ship Co Ltd, London. 1938 to Mrs Curzon London.
Aug 1939 Rqd by the Royal Navy as an auxiliary patrol vessel No. FY 4.112. Feb 1946 returned.
11.11.1942 to Aldred Fishing Co Ltd, Grimsby. 1946 to Milford Fishing Ltd, London.
1951 to Japan Fishing Co Ltd, Grimsby renamed TOKIO (GY167).
1960 Vessel sold for scrap and allocated to C W Dorkin & Co Ltd. 10.06.1960 Arrived Gateshead for Breaking up.

NAME Official No. Port Letters Numbers	Yard No. Launched Registered	G Ton N Ton	L Ft B Ft	Engine Builder Horse Power Reg'd Speed	OWNER (Built for)
JOSEPH BARRATT FY 3586 Castle Class	381 02.11.1917 01.03.1918	290 119	125.5 23.6	Amos & Smith 480 IHP 10.5 knots	The Admiralty Whitehall London

1919 Registered by the Admiralty as a trawler LO252 Official No. 143800.
1919 Sold to Skomer Steam Ship Co Ltd, Cardiff renamed LOCH MORAR. 1920 to Brand & Curzon Ltd, London.
1929 to A S Bowlby, London. 1929 to Vanessa Fishing Co Ltd, London.
1933 to P Fischeaux, Bordeaux, France renamed SAINT BARNABE.
1934 to Boston Deep Sea Fishing Co Ltd, Fleetwood renamed HARRY HAWKE.
19.08.1935 to Caledonian Fishing Co Ltd, Hull renamed LOCH KINNORD (H204).
06.04.1939 to Trident Steam Fishing Co Ltd, Hull renamed TILBURY NESS.
03.09.1939 Rqd by the Royal Navy as a minesweeper. 01.11.1940 Vessel sunk by German aircraft in the Thames estuary.

NAME Official No. Port Letters Numbers	Yard No. Launched Registered	G Ton N Ton	L Ft B Ft	Engine Builder Horse Power Reg'd Speed	OWNER (Built for)
RICHARD BACON FY 3587 Castle Class	382 02.11.1917 12.03.1918	290 119	125.5 23.6	Amos & Smith 480 IHP 10.5 knots	The Admiralty Whitehall London

1919 Registered by the Admiralty as a trawler LO438 Official No. 143809.
1922 Sold to Boston Deep Sea Fishing Co Ltd, Fleetwood renamed HAGNABY (BN179).
1926 to V Fourny, Boulogne, France renamed PROFESSEUR BERGONIE.
1930 to Boston Deep Sea Fishing Co Ltd, Fleetwood renamed DAILY CRONICLE (FD69).
1934 to T L Devlin Granton renamed COMMODATOR (GN6).
29.08.1939 Rqd by the Royal Navy as a minesweeper No. FY 634. 04.10.1945 returned.
1943 to Mrs Breen Granton. 1945 to Grimsby Merchants Amalgamated Fishing Co Ltd, Grimsby (GY57).
1948 to R G Parsley, Milford Haven renamed LYNANDI.
1954 Vessel sold for scrap to Thos W Ward Ltd. 27.08.1954 Arrived Milford Haven for breaking up.

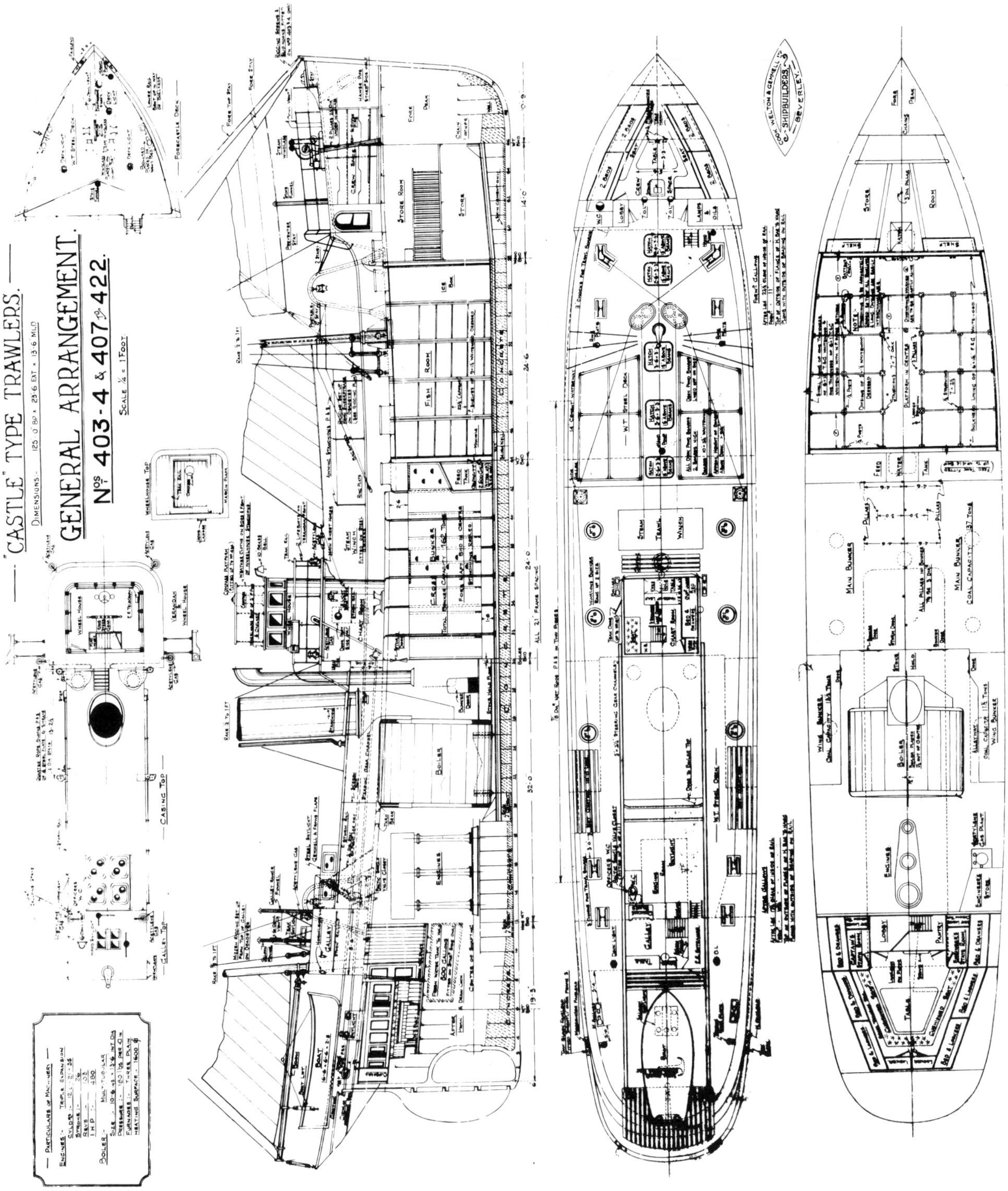

"CASTLE" TYPE TRAWLERS.
DIMENSIONS:- 125'-0" BP × 23'-6" EXT × 13'-6" MLD
GENERAL ARRANGEMENT.
NOS 403-4 & 407 TO 422.
SCALE ¼" = 1 FOOT
PARTICULARS OF MACHINERY
ENGINES:- TRIPLE EXPANSION
CYLDRS:- 12½ - 21 - 35
STROKE:- 26
REVS:- 103
I.H.P.:- 480
BOILER:- MULTITUBULAR
SIZE:- 10'-6" × 13'-6" INT. DIA
PRESSURE:- 180 LBS PER O"
FURNACES:- THREE PLAIN
HEATING SURFACE:- 1600 □'
GALLEY TOP
CASING TOP
WHEELHOUSE TOP
VERANDAH WHEEL HOUSE
FORECASTLE DECK
BOAT
GALLEY
ENGINES
BOILER
CROSS BUNKER
FISH ROOM
STORE ROOM
STORE
FORE PEAK
ICE BOX
CHART ROOM
STEAM WINCH
CONCRETE
ALL 21" FRAME SPACING
W.T. STEEL DECK
STEAM TRAWL WINCH
MAIN BUNKER
WING BUNKER
COAL CAPACITY 137 TONS
FEED WATER TANK
COOK, WELTON & GEMMELL LTD
SHIPBUILDERS
BEVERLEY.

<table>
<tr><th rowspan="2">NAME
Official No.
Port Letters Numbers</th><th rowspan="2">Yard No.
Launched
Registered</th><th colspan="2">Registered</th><th rowspan="2">Engine Builder
Horse Power
Reg'd Speed</th><th rowspan="2">OWNER
(Built for)</th></tr>
<tr><th>G Ton
N Ton</th><th>L Ft
B Ft</th></tr>
<tr><td>PHINEAS BEARD
FY 3588
Castle Class</td><td>383
24.11.1917
22.03.1918</td><td>290
119</td><td>125.5
23.6</td><td>Amos & Smith
480 IHP
10.5 knots</td><td>The Admiralty
Whitehall
London</td></tr>
<tr><td colspan="6">1919 Registered by the Admiralty as a trawler LO283 Official No. 143773.
1920 Sold to Brand & Curzon Ltd, Milford Haven. 1925 to A G Hordern, Milford Haven.
1938 Milford Fishing Ltd, Milford Haven (M271). 29.08.1939 Rqd by the Royal Navy as a minesweeper.
08.12.1941 Vessel sunk by German aircraft off the east coast of Scotland.</td></tr>
<tr><td>THOMAS CONNOLLY
FY 3589
Castle Class</td><td>384
29.11.1917
10.04.1918</td><td>290
119</td><td>125.5
23.6</td><td>Amos & Smith
480 IHP
10.5 knots</td><td>The Admiralty
Whitehall
London</td></tr>
<tr><td colspan="6">1919 Registered by the Admiralty as a trawler LO285 Official No. 143861.
1923 Sold to A G Horden managed by Brand & Curzon Ltd, London. 1938 to Milford Fishing Ltd, London (M270).
30.11.1939 Rqd by the Royal Navy as a boom defence vessel based at Sheerness.
17.12.1940 Vessel sunk by mine off Sheerness.</td></tr>
<tr><td>WILLIAM BELL
FY 3590
Castle Class</td><td>385
17.01.1918
15.05.1918</td><td>290
119</td><td>125.5
23.6</td><td>Amos & Smith
480 IHP
10.5 knots</td><td>The Admiralty
Whitehall
London</td></tr>
<tr><td colspan="6">1919 Registered by the Admiralty as a trawler LO201 Official No. 143811.
1919 to Mills Steam Ship Co Ltd, London. 29.01.1931 to Brand & Curzon Ltd, London.
09.06.1940 Rqd by the Royal Navy as a minesweeper No. FY 1727. 23.02.1946 returned.
15.01.1942 to J Marr & Son Ltd, Fleetwood.
1946 Vessel sold for scrap to W H Arnott Shipbreakers. 11.03.1946 Arrived Troon for breaking up.</td></tr>
<tr><td>PATRICK BOWE
FY 3591
Castle Class</td><td>386
17.01.1918
25.05.1918</td><td>290
119</td><td>125.5
23.6</td><td>Amos & Smith
480 IHP
10.5 knots</td><td>The Admiralty
Whitehall
London</td></tr>
<tr><td colspan="6">1919 Registered by the Admiralty as a trawler (1920) renamed TEST. 1922 Sold to Spanish Navy renamed UAD TARGA.
01.09.1931 Vessel wrecked in Arosa Bay.</td></tr>
<tr><td>THOMAS BOOTH
FY 3592
Castle Class</td><td>387
14.02.1918
06.06.1918</td><td>290
126</td><td>125.5
23.6</td><td>Amos & Smith
480 IHP
10.5 knots</td><td>The Admiralty
Whitehall
London</td></tr>
<tr><td colspan="6">1919 Registered by the Admiralty as a trawler LO227 Official No. 143767.
1920 Sold to Skomer Steam Shipping Co Ltd, London.
1923 to Brand & Curzon Ltd, London. 1938 Milford Fishing Ltd, Milford Haven (M274).
28.08.1939 Rqd by the Royal Navy as a minesweeper . 24.10.1939 returned.
1955 Vessel sold for scrap to Thos W Ward Ltd. 12.01.1955 Arrived Milford Haven for breaking up.</td></tr>
<tr><td>CHARLES BOYES
FY 3593
Castle Class</td><td>388
14.02.1918
15.06.1918</td><td>290
126</td><td>125.5
23.6</td><td>Amos & Smith
480 IHP
10.5 knots</td><td>The Admiralty
Whitehall
London</td></tr>
<tr><td colspan="6">1919 Registered by the Admiralty as a trawler LO334 Official No. 143886.
1920 Sold to Elspeth Lady Beardmore managed by Brand & Curzon Ltd, London.
14.06.1932 to Brand & Curzon Ltd, London. 04.10.1932 to Mills Steam Ship Co Ltd, London.
06.08.1936 to Mrs Fraser, Aberdeen. 1938 to Brand & Curzon Ltd, London.
22.07.1938 to St Andrews Steam Fishing Co Ltd, Hull (H526).
01.09.1939 Rqd by the Royal Navy as a minesweeper .
25.05.1940 Vessel sunk by mine in the North Sea. Nineteen crew lost three rescued.
Whilst serving with the 40 minesweeper group based at Yarmouth.</td></tr>
<tr><td>FREDRICK BUSH
FY 3594
Castle Class</td><td>389
14.03.1918
27.06.1918</td><td>290
126</td><td>125.5
23.6</td><td>Amos & Smith
480 IHP
10.5 knots</td><td>The Admiralty
Whitehall
London</td></tr>
<tr><td colspan="6">1919 Registered by the Admiralty as a trawler LO249 Official No. 145174.
1922 Sold to D Pettit Ltd, Milford Haven renamed CAWDOR (M249).
01.11.1928 Vessel foundered in Position Lat 53° 25'N 012° 30'W.</td></tr>
<tr><td>ROBERT BOWEN
FY 3595
Castle Class</td><td>390
14.03.1918
06.07.1918</td><td>290
126</td><td>125.5
23.6</td><td>Amos & Smith
480 IHP
10.5 knots</td><td>The Admiralty
Whitehall
London</td></tr>
<tr><td colspan="6">1919 Registered by the Admiralty as a trawler LO254 Official No. 143810.
1920 Sold to Britannic Trawling Co Ltd, London. 1926 to Brand & Curzon Ltd, London.
1938 to Milford Fishing Ltd, Milford Haven (M269). 31.07.1939 to J Marr & Son Ltd, Fleetwood.
31.08.1939 Rqd by the Royal Navy as a minesweeper .
09.02.1940 Vessel sunk by German aircraft off Aberdeen. Whilst serving with minesweeper group based at Aberdeen.</td></tr>
</table>

<table>
<tr><th rowspan="2">NAME
Official No.
Port Letters Numbers</th><th rowspan="2">Yard No.
Launched
Registered</th><th colspan="2">Registered</th><th rowspan="2">Engine Builder
Horse Power
Reg'd Speed</th><th rowspan="2">OWNER
(Built for)</th></tr>
<tr><th>G Ton
N Ton</th><th>L Ft
B Ft</th></tr>
<tr><td>JOHN BAPTISH
FY3596
Castle Class</td><td>391
29.04.1918
16.07.1918</td><td>290
126</td><td>125.5
23.6</td><td>Amos & Smith
480 IHP
10.5 knots</td><td>The Admiralty
Whitehall
London</td></tr>
<tr><td colspan="6">1919 Registered by the Admiralty as a trawler LO234 Official No. 143835.
1920 Sold to Skomer Steam Shipping Co Ltd, London. 1921 to Brand & Curzon Ltd, London.
1938 to Milford Fishing Ltd, Milford Haven (M275).
28.08.1939 Rqd by the Royal Navy as a minesweeper . 11.10.1939 returned.
07.09.1940 Vessel last reported leaving the fishing grounds off The Old Head of Kinsale.
09.09.1940 Declared sunk by mine south of the Coningbeg Light-vessel lost with all hands.</td></tr>
<tr><td>JOHN BOMKWORTH
FY 3597
Castle Class</td><td>392
29.04.1918
26.07.1918</td><td>290
126</td><td>125.5
23.6</td><td>Amos & Smith
480 IHP
10.5 knots</td><td>The Admiralty
Whitehall
London</td></tr>
<tr><td colspan="6">1919 Registered by the Admiralty as a trawler Official No. 143816. (Sep 1920) renamed WEAR.
1922 Sold to Spanish Navy renamed UAD RAS. 1933 Vessel reported lost:- no details.</td></tr>
<tr><td>THOMAS BARTLETT
FY3598
Castle Class</td><td>393
29.05.1918
08.08.1918</td><td>290
126</td><td>125.5
23.6</td><td>Amos & Smith
480 IHP
10.5 knots</td><td>The Admiralty
Whitehall
London</td></tr>
<tr><td colspan="6">1919 Registered by the Admiralty as a trawler LO373 Official No. 143879.
11.05.1920 Sold to Brand & Curzon Ltd, London. 1920 to A S Hordern, London.
1938 to Milford Fishing Ltd, Milford Haven renamed HORDERN (M273).
27.11.1939 Rqd by the Royal Navy as a minesweeper No. FY 553. 28.05.1940 Vessel sunk by British mine off Calais.</td></tr>
<tr><td>JOHN BATEMAN
FY3599
Castle Class</td><td>394
29.04.1918
27.08.1918</td><td>290
108</td><td>125.5
23.6</td><td>Amos & Smith
480 IHP
10.5 knots</td><td>The Admiralty
Whitehall
London</td></tr>
<tr><td colspan="6">1919 Registered by the Admiralty as a fishing trawler LO45 Official No. 145061.
1922 Sold to Boston Deep Sea Fishing Co Ltd, Boston renamed ANDERBY (BN176).
1926 to Pasqueriascant, Spain renamed PESQUERIAS CANTABRICAS No. 1.
1936 Rqd by the Spanish Nationalist Navy renamed CANTABRICO. 1939 returned and reverted.
1964 Vessel sold to shipbreakers and broken up in Spain.</td></tr>
<tr><td>WILLIAM CALDWELL
FY3719
Castle Class</td><td>395
12.06.1918
16.11.1918</td><td>290
126</td><td>125.5
23.6</td><td>Amos & Smith
480 IHP
10.5 knots</td><td>The Admiralty
Whitehall
London</td></tr>
<tr><td colspan="6">1919 Registered by the Admiralty as a trawler LO374 Official No. 143882.
28.05.1919 Loaned to the United States Navy. 06.10.1919 returned to Royal Navy.
11.05.1920 Sold to E Brand & J H Dove, London. 1923 Sold to J H Dove, London.
1937 to Pembroke Hake Fishing Co Ltd, London. 1939 to Boston Deep Sea Fishing Co Ltd, London.
Jan 1940 Rqd by the Royal Navy as a boom defence vessel No. Z142. 1946 returned.
1946 to Inch Fishing Co Ltd, Glasgow. 1949 to Clyde Fishing Co Ltd, Granton (GN56).
1957 Vessel sold to BISCO and allocated to Malcolm Brechin. 30.07.1957 Arrived Granton for breaking up.</td></tr>
<tr><td>RICHARD CROFTS
FY3720
Castle Class</td><td>396
13.06.1918
03.12.1918</td><td>290
126</td><td>125.5
23.6</td><td>Amos & Smith
480 IHP
10.5 knots</td><td>The Admiralty
Whitehall
London</td></tr>
<tr><td colspan="6">1919 Registered by the Admiralty as a trawler LO365 Official No. 143931.
1921 Sold to Iago Steam Trawling Co Ltd, Milford Haven.
Aug 1939 Rqd by the Royal Navy as a minesweeper No. FY 530. 1940 returned.
15.07.1941 Rqd by the Royal Navy as a minesweeper No. FY 530. 06.08.1945 returned.
1945 to Lewis Wilcox & Co Ltd, London.
20.02.1953 Vessel struck a reef and foundered near Cornaig Beg on the west side of the Island of Coll, Inner Hebrides in fog. A distress message was sent and the crew put on their life jackets, they just had time to launch a dingy float as the trawler rolled over and sank. Four crew managed to reach the shore assisted by the Coll lifesaving crew, but eight men including the skipper perished in the icy cold seas.</td></tr>
<tr><td>GEORGE COCHRAN
FY3721
Castle Class</td><td>397
28.06.1918
14.12.1918</td><td>290
126</td><td>125.5
23.6</td><td>Amos & Smith
480 IHP
10.5 knots</td><td>The Admiralty
Whitehall
London</td></tr>
<tr><td colspan="6">28.05.1919 Loaned to the United States Navy. 11.08.1919 returned to Royal Navy.
1919 Registered by the Admiralty as a trawler LO557 Official No. 144314.
1920 Sold to Phillips Mills & Co London. 1923 to Ontario Fishing Ltd, London.
1927 to Newfoundland Transport Co Ltd, Halifax, Nova Scotia, Canada.
20.01.1929 Vessel left Sydney, Cape Breton, Canada and not heard of again. Jan 1929 Posted missing:- Lost with all hands.</td></tr>
</table>

<table>
<tr><th rowspan="2">NAME
Official No.
Port Letters Numbers</th><th rowspan="2">Yard No.
Launched
Registered</th><th colspan="2">Registered</th><th rowspan="2">Engine Builder
Horse Power
Reg'd Speed</th><th rowspan="2">OWNER
(Built for)</th></tr>
<tr><th>G Ton
N Ton</th><th>L Ft
B Ft</th></tr>
<tr><td>WILLIAM DARNOLD
FY3722
Castle Class</td><td>398
11.07.1918
23.12.1918</td><td>290
126</td><td>125.5
23.6</td><td>Amos & Smith
480 IHP
10.5 knots</td><td>The Admiralty
Whitehall
London</td></tr>
<tr><td colspan="6">30.05.1919 Loaned to the United States Navy. 11.08.1919 returned to Royal Navy.
09.07.1919 Damaged by mine between the north of Scotland and the south of Iceland.
1919 Registered by the Admiralty as a trawler Official No. 143883.
11.05.1920 Sold to West Riding Steam Trawling Co Ltd, Hull renamed CAPE HATTERAS (H222).
1923 to Kingston Steam Trawling Co Ltd, Hull renamed HESSONITE.
04.10.1924 Vessel wrecked 2 miles from Birsay, Orkney Islands in darkness and fog whilst homeward bound from the North Færoese fishing grounds. The Sromness lifeboat managed to rescue all twelve crew despite the heavy seas.</td></tr>
<tr><td>JOHN GRAHAM
FY3778
Castle Class</td><td>399
27.07.1918
09.01.1919</td><td>290
108</td><td>125.5
23.6</td><td>Amos & Smith
480 IHP
10.5 knots</td><td>The Admiralty
Whitehall
London</td></tr>
<tr><td colspan="6">30.05.1919 Loaned to the United States Navy to assist in the sweeping of the North Sea Mine Barrage. 12.08.1919 returned.
1919 Registered by the Admiralty as a trawler LO268 Official No. 143925.
1921 Sold to Kingston Steam Trawling Co Ltd, Hull renamed RUBY (H393).
18.02.1935 to The City Steam Fishing Co Ltd, Hull renamed (11.11.1935) EASTCOATES.
07.02.1937 Vessel transferred to Fleetwood. 19.08.1939 Returned to Hull.
28.08.1939 Rqd by the Royal Navy as a minesweeper No. FY 1771. 26.10.1939 returned.
28.08.1940 Rqd by the Royal Navy as a minesweeper No. FY 1771. 27.04.1945 returned.
28.04.1947 to Odafoam Ltd, London. 03.08.1950 to J Marr & Son Ltd, Fleetwood.
1955 Vessel sold for scrap to The West of Scotland Shipbreaking Co Ltd. 23.07.1955 Arrived Troon for breaking up.</td></tr>
<tr><td>JOHN GAUNTLET
FY3779
Castle Class</td><td>400
12.08.1918
18.03.1919</td><td>290
126</td><td>125.5
23.6</td><td>Amos & Smith
480 IHP
10.5 knots</td><td>The Admiralty
Whitehall
London</td></tr>
<tr><td colspan="6">1919 Registered by the Admiralty as a trawler Official No. 143960.
11.05.1920 Sold to A M Jeevanjee, Bombay, India renamed NAIROBI.
02.12.1922 Vessel wrecked at Malindi.</td></tr>
<tr><td>GRIFFITH GRIFFITH
FY3780
Castle Class</td><td>401
27.08.1918
22.03.1919</td><td>290
126</td><td>125.5
23.6</td><td>Amos & Smith
480 IHP
10.5 knots</td><td>The Admiralty
Whitehall
London</td></tr>
<tr><td colspan="6">1919 Registered by the Admiralty as a trawler Official No. 143958.
11.05.1920 Sold to A M Jeevanjee Bombay India renamed KILINDINI.
1923 to The Sheikh of Kuwait. 1924 to Murjee Ratanshik Co, Bombay, India.
06.02.1925 Vessel sank near Badagara on passage from Badagara towards Bombay with a cargo of copra and ginger.</td></tr>
<tr><td>MICHAEL GRIFFITH
FY3781
Castle Class</td><td>402
05.09.1918
05.04.1919</td><td>290
126</td><td>125.5
23.6</td><td>Amos & Smith
480 IHP
10.5 knots</td><td>The Admiralty
Whitehall
London</td></tr>
<tr><td colspan="6">1919 Registered by the Admiralty as a trawler LO529 Official No. 145118.
1923 Sold to H Leetham & Sons Ltd, Hull. 1926 to Phoenix Trawling Co Ltd, London. 1930 Ritchie & Davis Ltd, London.
30.08.1939 Rqd by the Royal Navy as a minesweeper No. FY 567 (1943) boom defence vessel. Jan 1945 returned.
1945 to Clifton Steam Trawlers Ltd, Fleetwood (FD249).
31.01.1953 Vessel wrecked 7 miles south of Barra Head. One distress message was received reporting that the trawler was helpless, full of water, and out of steam. All thirteen crew lost.</td></tr>
<tr><td>JOHN GULIPSTER
FY3782
Castle Class</td><td>403
24.09.1918
17.04.1919</td><td>290
126</td><td>125.5
23.6</td><td>Amos & Smith
480 IHP
10.5 knots</td><td>The Admiralty
Whitehall
London</td></tr>
<tr><td colspan="6">Royal Navy Castle Class completed as a fishing trawler.
1919 Sold to J Johnson Scarborough renamed BETTY JOHNSON (SH50) Official No. 143256.
1922 to Prince Fletcher Trawlers Ltd, Fleetwood (FD168).
1928 to Melling Trawlers Ltd, Fleetwood renamed ANNIE MELLING.
18.01.1932 to Farrows Steam Fishing Co Ltd, Hull renamed ANDREW MARVEL (H399).
23.03.1933 to Hudson Bros (Trawlers) Ltd, Hull. 19.12.1935 to Thos L Devlin Leith renamed COMITATUS (GN39).
28.08.1939 Rqd by the Royal Navy as a minesweeper No. FY 633. 09.10.1945 returned.
09.10.1945 to Dinas Steam Trawling Co Ltd, Fleetwood. 1952 to Queen Steam Fishing Co Ltd, Grimsby (GY228).
19.06.1956 Vessel sold for scrap to Van Heyghen Freres, Belgium and broken up at Ghent.</td></tr>
</table>

NAME Official No. Port Letters Numbers	Yard No. Launched Registered	Registered G Ton N Ton	 L Ft B Ft	Engine Builder Horse Power Reg'd Speed	OWNER (Built for)
PHILIP GODBY FY3783 Castle Class	404 24.09.1918 06.05.1919	290 126	125.5 23.6	Amos & Smith 480 IHP 10.5 knots	The Admiralty Whitehall London
Royal Navy Castle Class completed as a fishing trawler. 1919 Sold to H Smethurst, Grimsby (GY309) Official No. 143785. 1920 to Derby Steam Trawling Co Ltd, Grimsby. 1923 to Godby Steam Fishing Co Ltd, Fleetwood (FD407). 1924 to Neva Steam Trawlers Ltd, Fleetwood renamed CISNELL. 1926 to Jenkerson & Jones, London renamed TOGIMO (LO122). 02.09.1939 Rqd by the Royal Navy as a minesweeper. 13.11.1939 returned. 11.02.1940 Vessel captured by U37 and sunk by gunfire commanded by Werner Hartmann off the west coast of Ireland in approx position 50° 40'N 011° 02'W.					
KILCHATTAN FY4013 Kil Class Patrol Gunboat	405 13.04.1918 29.11.1918	522 244	170.0 30.0	Amos & Smith 1400 IHP 13 knots	The Admiralty Whitehall London
14.02.1920 Sold to Robinson Brown Joplin, Newcastle renamed BENTON Official No.144890 *(converted to a cargo vessel), (Lengthened to 174.9 ft 628 Gross Tons).* 1922 to Reed Johan Ick GMBU, Hamburg, Germany renamed FUNDUS. 1925 to Skibs A/S Motor, Kragerö, Norway renamed STEINMANN. 1935 to A/S Ryvarden, Haugesund renamed ISLAND. 08.12.1941 Vessel sunk in Vestifjord by Royal Navy submarine HMS SEALION No. N72 (b 1934).					
KILCHVAN FY4014 Kil Class Patrol Gunboat	406 13.04.1918 29.11.1918	522 244	170.0 30.0	Amos & Smith 1400 IHP 13 knots	The Admiralty Whitehall London
14.02.1920 Sold to Robinson Brown Joplin, Newcastle renamed BELSAY Official No. 144889 *(converted to a cargo vessel), (Lengthened to 174.9 ft 629 Gross Tons).* 1922 Reed Johan Ick GMBU, Hamburg, Germany renamed DISKUS. 1925 to Nordische GMB, Hamburg. 1926 to Zeevaart Maats "Scheldestroon", Ghent, Belgium renamed SCHELDEDAM. 1933 to Soc Anon Mait et Commerciale "Semarco", Antwerp. 15.03.1934 Vessel sank in Pos'n 50° 50'N 008° 25'W on passage from Antwerp towards Galway with a cargo of cement.					
GEORGE AIKEN FY4291. Castle Class	407 19.12.1918 23.08.1919	290 126	125.5 23.6	Amos & Smith 480 IHP 10.5 knots	The Admiralty Whitehall London
Royal Navy Castle Class completed as a fishing trawler. 1919 Sold to J Coombes, Grimsby renamed CECIL COOMBES (GY487) Official No. 140796 (1922) renamed HIGHBRIDGE. 1925 to M.F Pujol, Cadiz, Spain renamed SANTA URBANA. 1931 to L Carranza, Cadiz. 1936 to Anselmo Cea Garcia, Cadiz. 1936 Rqd by the Nationalist Spanish Navy. 1939 returned. 1971 Vessel sold to shipbreakers and broken up in Spain.					
KILCLIEF FY4015 Kil Class Patrol Gunboat	407A 08.09.1918 01.08.1919	522 244	170.0 30.0	Amos & Smith 1400 IHP 13 knots	The Admiralty Whitehall London
14.02.1920 Sold to Holme Line, Newcastle renamed TYNEHOLME Official No. 142870, *(converted to a cargo vessel). (Lengthened to 174.9 ft 628 Gross Tons).* 08.01.1940 Vessel sank in the North Sea following a collision with the ss GITANO (3956 gt/ b 1921) whilst on passage from Sunderland towards Rotterdam with a cargo of coal. Fourteen crew lost four rescued.					
JOHN AIKENHEAD FY4292 Castle Class	408 19.12.1918 14.11.1919	290 126	125.5 23.6	Amos & Smith 480 IHP 10.5 knots	The Admiralty Whitehall London
Royal Navy Castle Class completed as a fishing trawler. 1919 Sold to J Johnson Scarborough renamed POLLY JOHNSON (SH171) Official No. 143267. 31.01.1922 to W A Massey & Sons Ltd, Hull (H322). 1932 Managed by Kingston Steam Trawling Co Ltd, Hull for W A Massey & Sons Ltd, Hull. 31.08.1939 Rqd by the Royal Navy as a minesweeper, based at Dover. 29.05.1940 Vessel sunk by German aircraft off Dunkirk whilst evacuating Allied forces. Hit by bombs she broke adrift and sank near the harbour entrance. One gunner killed.					
KILCLOGHER FY4016 Kil Class Patrol Gunboat	408A 24.11.1918 00.00.1919	522 244	170.0 30.0	Amos & Smith 1400 IHP 13 knots	The Admiralty Whitehall London
14.02.1920 Sold to Robinson Brown Joplin, Newcastle renamed NORTHENER Official No. 142364 *(converted to a cargo vessel).(Lengthened to 174.9 ft 628 Gross Tons).* 1929 to Africa Occidental SA, Fernando Po, Spain renamed REGINA . 1933 to The Government of Nigeria renamed LAGOS REGINA. 1938 Vessel deleted from Lloyds Register of Shipping on advice that the vessel had sunk and had been broken up.					

Yard No.396
1918 RICHARD CROFTS
Photo:- Author's Collection

Yard No.409
1919 JOHN ASHLEY as LIMESLADE
Photo by courtesy of George Scales

Yard No.416
1919 THOMAS ALTOFT
Photo:- Author's Collection

<table>
<tr><th rowspan="2">NAME
Official No.
Port Letters Numbers</th><th rowspan="2">Yard No.
Launched
Registered</th><th colspan="2">Registered</th><th rowspan="2">Engine Builder
Horse Power
Reg'd Speed</th><th rowspan="2">OWNER
(Built for)</th></tr>
<tr><th>G Ton
N Ton</th><th>L Ft
B Ft</th></tr>
<tr><td>JOHN ASHLEY
FY 4293
Castle Class</td><td>409
18.03.1919
13.10.1919</td><td>290
126</td><td>125.5
23.6</td><td>Amos & Smith
480 IHP
10.5 knots</td><td>The Admiralty
Whitehall
London</td></tr>
<tr><td colspan="6">Royal Navy Castle Class completed as a fishing trawler.
1920 Sold to Rhondda Fishing Co Ltd Swansea renamed LIMESLADE SA10 Official No. 136155.
1939 to 1945 Not requisitioned by the Royal Navy but retained as a fishing trawler.
16.09.1942 to A & M Smith Ltd, Hull (H548).
07.03.1944 Stranded at Veidios south coast of Iceland along with the Hull trawlers WAR GREY (see Yard No.340D) and LOUIS BOTHA (see Yard No.338) re-floated and returned to Hull. 27.10.1945 to St Andrew's Steam Fishing Co Ltd, Hull.
31.07.1946 to Grimsby Lining & Trawlers Co Ltd, Grimsby (GY239).
1952 Vessel sold to BISCO for scrap and allocated to J J King & Co Ltd. 22.02.1952 Arrived Gateshead for breaking up.</td></tr>
<tr><td>EGILIAS AKERMAN
FY 4294
Castle Class</td><td>410
18.03.1919
13.11.1919</td><td>290
126</td><td>125.5
23.6</td><td>Amos & Smith
86 NHP
10.5 knots</td><td>The Admiralty
Whitehall
London</td></tr>
<tr><td colspan="6">Royal Navy Castle Class completed as a fishing trawler.
1919 Sold to Boston Deep Sea Fishing Co Ltd, Boston renamed KESTEVEN BN146 Official No. 143471.
1926 to V Fourny, Boulogne, France renamed IMPREVU.
1930 to Boston Deep Sea Fishing Co Ltd, Fleetwood renamed DAILY MIRROR (FD71).
1935 to J L Devlin Granton renamed COMPUTATOR (GN42).
1939 Rqd by the Royal Navy as a minesweeper No. FY 635.
21.01.1945 Vessel sank following a collision with Royal Navy Destroyer HMS VANOC (b 1917) in Seine Bay Normandy.</td></tr>
<tr><td>THOMAS ADNEY
FY 4295
Castle Class</td><td>411
02.04.1919
06.11.1919</td><td>290
126</td><td>125.5
23.6</td><td>Amos & Smith
86 NHP
10.5 knots</td><td>The Admiralty
Whitehall
London</td></tr>
<tr><td colspan="6">Royal Navy Castle Class completed as a fishing trawler.
1919 Sold to Boston Deep Sea Fishing Co Ltd, Boston renamed LINDSEY BN150 Official No. 143472.
03.09.1920 Departed Boston for fishing grounds, not seen or heard of again.
08.09.1920 Vessel posted missing:- lost with all hands.</td></tr>
<tr><td>DOMINICK ADDISON
FY 4296
Castle Class</td><td>412
02.04.1919
18.11.1919</td><td>290
126</td><td>125.5
23.6</td><td>Amos & Smith
86 NHP
10.5 knots</td><td>The Admiralty
Whitehall
London</td></tr>
<tr><td colspan="6">Royal Navy Castle Class completed as a fishing trawler.
1919 Sold to Tucker Tippett & Co Ltd Cardiff renamed TENEDOS CF64 Official No. 139639.
1929 to H E Rees, Milford Haven (M24).1933 to M W Howell, Milford Haven.
28.08.1939 Rqd by the Royal Navy as a minesweeper No. FY 517 renamed GADFLY. 03.09.1945 returned and reverted.
1948 to Yolland Bros Ltd, Milford Haven. 1952 to Japan Fishing Co Ltd, Grimsby renamed HONDO (GY195).
24.11.1960 Vessel sold for scrap to Van Den Bossche, Belgium. 01.12.1960 Breaking up commenced at Boom..</td></tr>
<tr><td>ISAAC ARTHAN
FY 4297
Castle Class</td><td>413
01.05.1919
10.01.1920</td><td>290
126</td><td>125.5
23.6</td><td>Amos & Smith
86 NHP
10.5 knots</td><td>The Admiralty
Whitehall
London</td></tr>
<tr><td colspan="6">Royal Navy Castle Class completed as a fishing trawler.
1921 Sold to Kingston Steam Trawling Co Ltd, Hull renamed AMBER H359 Official No. 144282.
17.11.1934 to Ocean Steam Fishing Co Ltd, Hull renamed OCEAN HARRIER.
24.01.1936 to Malcolm Smith Ltd, Aberdeen renamed LOCH BUIE (A401).
29.08.1939 Rqd by the Royal Navy as a minesweeper No. FY 688. 11.03.1946 returned.
1959 Vessel sold for scrap to Van Den Bossche, Belgium. 01.11.1959 Arrived Boom for breaking up.</td></tr>
<tr><td>ANDREW APSLEY
FY 4298
Castle Class</td><td>414
02.06.1919
09.12.1919</td><td>290
126</td><td>125.5
23.6</td><td>Amos & Smith
86 NHP
10.5 knots</td><td>The Admiralty
Whitehall
London</td></tr>
<tr><td colspan="6">Royal Navy Castle Class completed as a fishing trawler.
13.10.1919 Sold to H E Rees, Swansea renamed CALLANCROFT SA32 Official No. 136159.
1922 to Fred Parkes, Boston. 03.05.1925 to Hull Northern Fishing Co Ltd, Hull (H164).
1929 to H Westernborg, Milford Haven (M254).
15.01.1930 to McRae Steam Trawling Co Ltd, Milford Haven renamed DUNCAN McRAE.
1936 to Milford Steam Trawling Co Ltd, Milford Haven renamed MILFORD EARL.
30.08.1939 Rqd by the Royal Navy as a minesweeper.
08.04.1941 Vessel sunk by German aircraft off Lunan Bay east coast of Scotland five crew lost five rescued.</td></tr>
</table>

<table>
<tr><th rowspan="2">NAME
Official No.
Port Letters Numbers</th><th rowspan="2">Yard No.
Launched
Registered</th><th colspan="2">Registered</th><th rowspan="2">Engine Builder
Horse Power
Reg'd Speed</th><th rowspan="2">OWNER
(Built for)</th></tr>
<tr><th>G Ton
N Ton</th><th>L Ft
B Ft</th></tr>
<tr><td>JOSHUA ARABIN
FY 4299
Castle Class</td><td>415
01.05.1919
09.10.1919</td><td>290
126</td><td>125.5
23.6</td><td>Amos & Smith
86 NHP
10.5 knots</td><td>The Admiralty
Whitehall
London</td></tr>
<tr><td colspan="6">Royal Navy Castle Class completed as a fishing trawler.
1920 Sold to Montrose Fishing Co Ltd Montrose renamed RIVER FORTH ME67 Official No. 144161.
1923 to Melling Trawlers Ltd, Fleetwood renamed LENA MELLING (FD417).
18.01.1932 to Farrows Steam Fishing Co Ltd, Hull renamed DE LA POLE (H395).
23.08.1933 to Hudson Steam Fishing Co Ltd, Hull. 12.11.1935 to H E Rees, Milford Haven (M195).
01.09.1939 to Henrikson & Co Ltd, Hull (H234).
28.05.1940 Rqd by the Royal Navy as an auxiliary patrol vessel No. FY 4.129.
Jun 1941 as a minesweeper No. FY 558. 19.12.1945 returned.
13.02.1944 to Clifton Steam Trawling Co Ltd, Fleetwood (1946) (FD144).
1957 Vessel sold for scrap to Thos W Ward Ltd. 02.07.1957 Delivered to Milford Haven for breaking up.</td></tr>
<tr><td>THOMAS ALTOFT
FY 4300
Castle Class</td><td>416
02.06.1919
01.07.1920</td><td>290
126</td><td>125.5
23.6</td><td>Amos & Smith
86 NHP
10.5 knots</td><td>The Admiralty
Whitehall
London</td></tr>
<tr><td colspan="6">Royal Navy Castle Class completed as a fishing trawler.
1920 Sold to Iago Steam Trawlers Ltd, London H132 Official No. 144027.
28.11.1922 to Albion Steam Fishing Co Ltd, Hull. 07.02.1939 to Mills Steam-Ship Co Ltd, Hull.
30.08.1939 Rqd by the Royal Navy as a minesweeper No. FY 552. 22.04.1946 returned.
15.01.1942 to J Marr & Son Ltd, Fleetwood. 08.11.1947 Vessel wrecked on rocks off Glas Island, Scalpay, Harris.
The Fleetwood trawler FLANDERS FD165 (see Yard No.417) responded to the distress message and with great skill the skipper steamed close enough to the bow of the stricken trawler to allow a few of the crew to jump aboard the FLANDERS. This manoeuvre was repeated several times until all fifteen crewmen were rescued.</td></tr>
<tr><td>CHARLES ANTRAM
FY 4401
Castle Class</td><td>417
18.06.1919
13.02.1920</td><td>290
126</td><td>125.5
23.6</td><td>Amos & Smith
86 NHP
10.5 knots</td><td>The Admiralty
Whitehall
London</td></tr>
<tr><td colspan="6">Royal Navy Castle Class completed as a fishing trawler.
13.02.1920 Sold to Soc. Anon Armement Ostendais, Ostend, Belgium renamed EDMOND VAN BEVEREN.
1938 to Rhondda Fishing Co Ltd, Grimsby renamed FLANDERS (GY10) Official No. 144391.
30.08.1939 Rqd by the Royal Navy as a minesweeper No. FY 600. 23.04.1946 returned.
1943 to Mason Trawlers Ltd, Fleetwood (FD165).
1959 Vessel sold to BISCO, allocated to West of Scotland Ship Breaking Co Ltd. 17.11.1959 Arrived Troon for breaking up.</td></tr>
<tr><td>GEORGE ADGELL
FY 4402
Castle Class</td><td>418
18.06.1919
10.01.1920</td><td>290
126</td><td>125.5
23.6</td><td>Amos & Smith
86 NHP
10.5 knots</td><td>The Admiralty
Whitehall
London</td></tr>
<tr><td colspan="6">Royal Navy Castle Class completed as a fishing trawler.
1920 Sold to Blackburn Trawlers Ltd, Fleetwood (FD368) Official No. 141953.
1938 to Parkholme Trawlers Ltd, Fleetwood. 14.03.1939 to St Andrew's Steam Fishing Co Ltd, Hull.
12.06.1940 Rqd by the Royal Navy an auxiliary patrol vessel No. FY 1926. 1941 minesweeper.17.01.1946 returned.
07.02.1946 to Yolland Bros Ltd, Milford Haven. 08.07.1948 J Marr & Son Ltd, Fleetwood.
1953 Vessel sold to BISCO and allocated to Thos W Ward Ltd. 03.07.1953 Arrived Preston for breaking up.</td></tr>
<tr><td>THOMAS ALLEN
FY 4403
Castle Class</td><td>419
18.07.1919
17.03.1920</td><td>278
115</td><td>125.5
23.6</td><td>Amos & Smith
86 NHP
10.5 knots</td><td>The Admiralty
Whitehall
London</td></tr>
<tr><td colspan="6">Royal Navy Castle Class completed as a fishing trawler.
1920 Sold to Soc. Anon Armement Ostendais, Ostend, Belgium renamed THEOPHILE MASSART.
09.12.1933 to Hellyer Bros Ltd, Hull renamed BENGALI (H533) Official No. 144394.
19.03.1936 to Milford Steam Trawling Co Ltd, Milford Haven renamed MILFORD PRINCE (M224).
Aug 1939 Rqd by the Royal Navy as a minesweeper No. FY 614. Dec 1945 returned.
1951 to Onward Steam Fishing Co Ltd, Grimsby renamed PHILIPPIAN (GY164).
1960 Vessel sold to BISCO and allocated to J J King & Co Ltd. 20.04.1960 Arrived Gateshead for breaking up.</td></tr>
</table>

<table>
<tr><th rowspan="2">NAME
Official No.
Port Letters Numbers</th><th rowspan="2">Yard No.
Launched
Registered</th><th colspan="2">Registered</th><th rowspan="2">Engine Builder
Horse Power
Reg'd Speed</th><th rowspan="2">OWNER
(Built for)</th></tr>
<tr><th>G Ton
N Ton</th><th>L Ft
B Ft</th></tr>
<tr><td>THOMAS ALEXANDER
FY 4404
Castle Class</td><td>420
18.07.1919
04.06.1920</td><td>290
126</td><td>125.5
23.6</td><td>Amos & Smith
86 NHP
10.5 knots</td><td>The Admiralty
Whitehall
London</td></tr>
<tr><td colspan="6">Royal Navy Castle Class completed as a fishing trawler.
22.04.1920 Sold to Remy & Huret, Boulogne, France renamed ETOILE POLAIRE II.
1930 Boston Deep Sea Fishing Co Ltd, Fleetwood renamed DAILY EXPRESS (FD68) Official No. 144518.
13.12.1933 to Hellyer Bros Ltd, Hull renamed TURCOMAN (H523).
21.09.1936 to R Irvin & Sons Ltd, Aberdeen renamed BEN DEARG (A416).
28.08.1939 Rqd by the Royal Navy as a minesweeper No. FY 690. 06.06.1946 returned.
06.03.1942 to J Marr & Son Ltd, Fleetwood (1946) (FD286).
01.07.1949 to Anglo Australian Fishing Co Port of Albany, Western Australia.
1953 Vessel used as a target vessel and sunk by the Australian Navy.</td></tr>
<tr><td>ANDREW ANDERSON
FY 4405
Castle Class</td><td>421
15.08.1919
30.04.1920</td><td>290
126</td><td>125.5
23.6</td><td>Amos & Smith
86 NHP
10.5 knots</td><td>The Admiralty
Whitehall
London</td></tr>
<tr><td colspan="6">Royal Navy Castle Class completed as a fishing trawler.
13.02.1922 Sold to Boston Deep Sea Fishing Co Ltd, Boston renamed NORMANBY (BN179). Official No. 144517.
1929 to Pesquerias Cantrabricas S.A Empresa DeVap San Sebastian, Spain renamed PESQUERIAS CANTRABRICAS No2.
02.04.1949 Vessel wrecked near Castillo de San Sebastian Lighthouse.</td></tr>
<tr><td>THOMAS BOUDIGE
FY 4406
Castle Class</td><td>422
15.08.1919
17.08.1920</td><td>277
109</td><td>125.5
23.6</td><td>Amos & Smith
86 NHP
10.5 knots</td><td>The Admiralty
Whitehall
London</td></tr>
<tr><td colspan="6">Royal Navy Castle Class completed as a fishing trawler.
1921 Sold to Kingston Steam Trawling Co Ltd, Hull renamed JADE (H340) Official No. 144519.
19.10.1934 to Trident Steam Fishing Co Ltd, Hull renamed DARNETT NESS.
26.08.1939 Rqd by the Royal Navy as a minesweeper No. FY 542. 03.09.1945 returned.
25.10.1944 to J Marr & Son Ltd, Fleetwood.
1956 Vessel sold for scrap to Hammond Lane Foundry Dublin. 29.06.1956 Arrived Dublin for breaking up.</td></tr>
</table>

Yard No.422
1919 THOMAS BOUDIGE as H.M.T. DARNETT NESS
Photo by courtesy of Hull Maritime Museum

Vessels built at Beverley 1920 to 1939.

NAME Official No. Port Letters Numbers	Yard No. Launched Registered	Registered G Ton N Ton	 L Ft B Ft	Engine Builder Horse Power Reg'd Speed	OWNER (Built for)
MAI RE155 Steam Trawler	423 20.02.1920 00.06.1920	336 169	140.0 25.0	C.D.Holmes NHP 10.5 knots	Fiskeriselskabet Reykjavik Iceland
Ordered as Castle Class EPHRAIM BRIGHT No. FY 4407 but cancelled by Admiralty. 04.01.1926 Sold to Fiskiveidahlutafelagid Reykjavik.12.02.1930 to Baejarutgerd Hafnarfjardor Hafnarfjord (GK346). 23.06.1955 Vessel sold for scrap to G P Kolka, Odense, Denmark and broken up.					
NJORDUR RE36 Steam Trawler	424 20.02.1920 00.07.1920	343 142	140.0 25.0	C.D.Holmes 91 NHP 10.5 knots	Fiskiveidahlutafelagid Njordur Reykjavik Iceland
Ordered as Castle Class WILLIAM BENNETT No. FY 4408 but cancelled by Admiralty. 29.06.1932 Sold to Samvinnufelaginu Haukanesi, Hafnafjord, Iceland renamed HAUKANES (GK347). 23.06.1939 to Utvegsbanki Islands H/F, Reykjavik. 05.10.1940 to H/F Vifli, Hafnafjord. 22.02.1952 Vessel removed from the Icelandic Register sold for scrap to Belgium shipbreakers. 22.03.1952 Arrived Antwerp for breaking up.					
KARI SOLMUNDARSON GK153 Steam Trawler	425 05.03.1920 00.07.1920	341 144	140.0 25.0	C.D.Holmes 92 NHP 10.5 knots	Fiskiveidahlutafelagid Kari, Videy, Gullbringusyslu Reykjavik Iceland
Ordered as Castle Class JOHN BENSON No. FY 4409 but cancelled by Admiralty. 12.01.1932 Sold to Utvegsbanki Islands H/F, Reykjavik. 19.11.1932 to Fiskiveidahlutafelaginu Alliance, Reykjavik renamed KARI (RE111). 03.08.1946 to Klakksvikar Fiskivinnufelag, Færoe Islands renamed BARMUR. 14.10.1955 Vessel sold for scrap to Gunner Hansen, Odense, Denmark and broken up.					
KYOTO 143516 CF65 Steam Trawler	426 23.03.1920 00.09.1920	281 110	128.6 23.6	C.D.Holmes 85 NHP 10.5 knots	Neale & West Ltd Cardiff
Ordered as Castle Class RICHARD BANE No. FY 4410 but cancelled by Admiralty. 1930 Sold to Hakin Trawling Co Ltd, Milford Haven (M5). 1938 to Westward Trawlers Ltd, Milford Haven renamed RUDILAIS. 01.09.1939 Rqd by the Royal Navy as a minesweeper No. FY 528. Jan 1946 returned (M50). 1948 to Wyre Steam Trawling Co Ltd, Fleetwood renamed WYRE CORSAIR (FD287). 1956 Vessel sold for scrap to B J Nijkerk S/A, Belgium. 19.04.1956 Left Fleetwood for Antwerp for breaking up.					
IJIUN 143517 CF66 Steam Trawler	427 23.03.1920 00.09.1920	281 110	128.6 23.6	C.D.Holmes 85 NHP 10.5 knots	Neale & West Ltd Cardiff
Ordered as Castle Class JAMES BAIRD No. FY 4411 but cancelled by Admiralty. 1930 Sold to Pettit & Youds, Milford Haven (M39). 30.08.1939 Rqd by the Royal Navy as a minesweeper No. FY 612/ (1944) danlayer. 15.01.1946 returned 1948 to Pair Fishing Co Ltd, Milford Haven. 1952 to J Craig, Aberdeen renamed WOODBURN (A711). 1959 Vessel sold for scrap to Van Den Bossche, Belgium 19.11.1959 Arrived Boom for breaking up.					
RIGHTO 140816 GY1267 Steam Trawler	428 09.02.1920 00.09.1920	278 122	125.0 22.8	C.D.Holmes 91 NHP 10.5 knots	G F Sleight Grimsby
Ordered as Castle Class MATHEW BERRYMAN No. FY 4412 but cancelled by Admiralty. 11.09.1939 Rqd by the Royal Navy as a mine-sweeper / danlayer No. FY 604. 27.11.1944 returned. 15.10.1956 Sold to Derwent Trawlers Ltd, Grimsby. 24.01.1959 to Ross Trawlers Ltd, Grimsby. 1962 Vessel sold for scrap to Van Heyghen Freres, Belgium. 04.03.1962 Arrived Ghent for breaking up.					
REBOUNDO 140817 GY1268 Steam Trawler	429 20.04.1920 00.10.1920	278 122	125.0 22.8	C.D.Holmes 91 NHP 10.5 knots	G F Sleight Grimsby
Ordered as Castle Class WILLIAM BURTE No. FY 4413 but cancelled by Admiralty. 11.09.1939 Rqd by the Royal Navy as minesweeper No. FY 602. 17.12.1945 returned. 15.10.1956 Sold to Derwent Trawlers Ltd, Grimsby. 24.01.1959 to Ross Trawlers Ltd, Grimsby. 1962 Vessel sold for scrap to Van Heyghen Freres, Belgium. 13.03.1962 Arrived Ghent for breaking up.					
Not Built	430 - 431 - 432 - 433 Trawlers ordered by G F Sleight, Grimsby but order cancelled.				

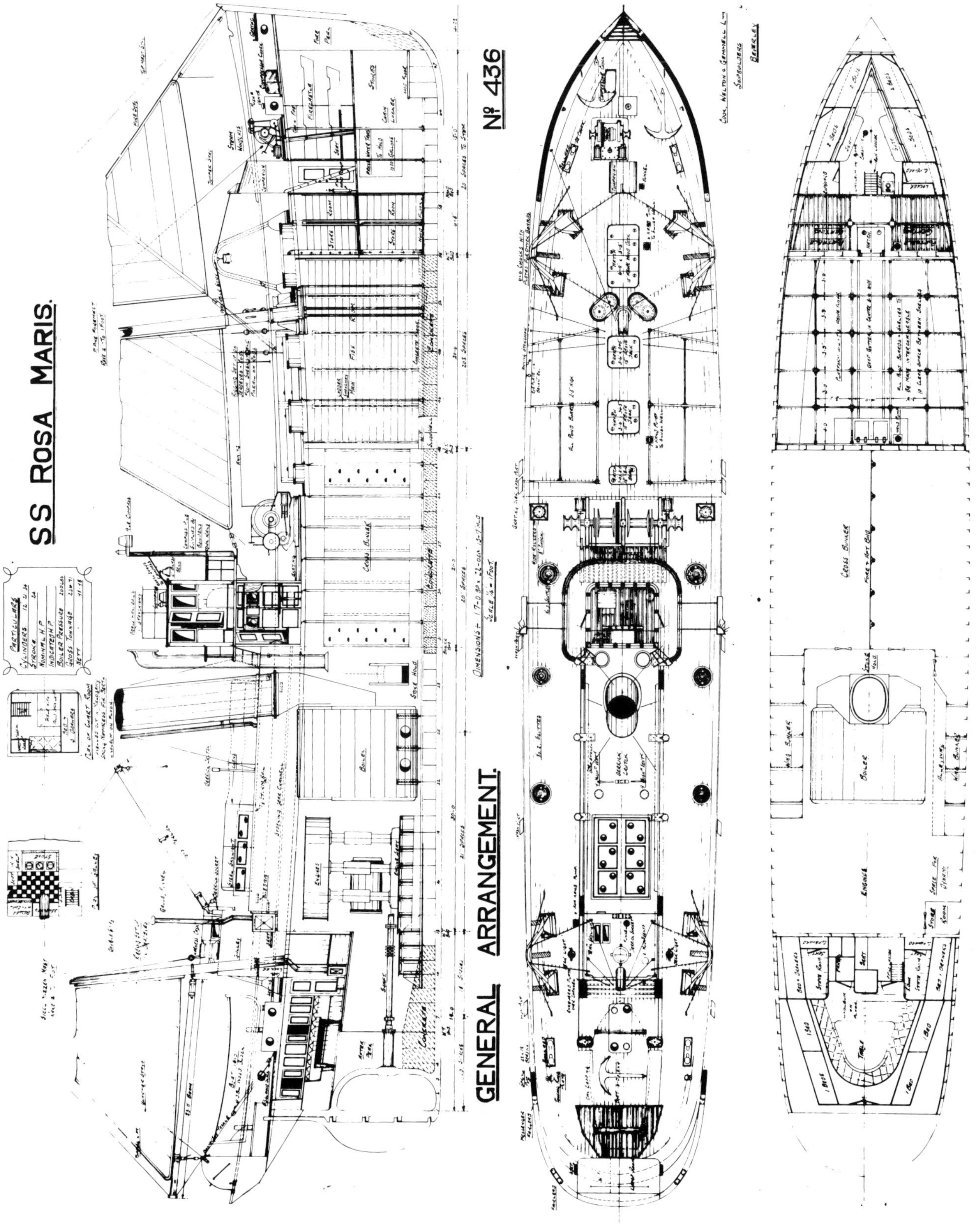
SS ROSA MARIS.
GENERAL ARRANGEMENT.
Nº 436

NAME Official No. Port Letters Numbers	Yard No. Launched Registered	Registered G Ton N Ton	 L Ft B Ft	Engine Builder Horse Power Reg'd Speed	OWNER (Built for)
STURTON 140815 GY1241 Steam Trawler	434 20.04.1920 00.10.1920	251 124	120.0 22.5	Amos & Smith 74 NHP 10.5 knots	Victoria Steam Fishing Co Ltd Grimsby
1929 Sold to Lindsey Steam Fishing Co Ltd, Grimsby. 29.08.1939 Rqd by the Royal Navy as a minesweeper No. FY 1595. 09.11.1944 returned. 1961 Vessel sold for scrap to Vereenigde Utrechtie Ijzehandel, Holland. Sep 1961 Arrived Utrecht for breaking up.					
WINDWARD HO 144065 H243 Steam Trawler	435 20.05.1920 00.11.1920	263 105	125.0 23.0	Amos & Smith 78 NHP 10.5 knots	S T White & Co Ltd Hull
16.04.1926 Sold to Seaward Fishing Co Ltd, Hull. 1927 to Hudson Bros Ltd, Hull. 13.11.1929 to H Croft Baker Ltd, Grimsby (GY158). 1930 to Strand Steam Fishing Co Ltd, Grimsby. 29.08.1939 Rqd by the Royal Navy as a minesweeper No. FY 574. 28.06.1946 returned. 1951 to Diamonds Steam Fishing Co Ltd, Grimsby renamed OKINO. 1962 Sold to BISCO and allocated to Thos Young & Sons Ltd. 24.01.1962 Arrived Sunderland for breaking up.					
ROSA MARIS 144070 H248 Steam Trawler	436 24.05.1920 00.11.1920	246 92	117.4 22.0	C.D.Holmes 75 NHP 10 knots	Wilberforce Steam Fishing Co Ltd Hull.
1926 to Lancashire Steam Fishing Co Ltd, Fleetwood (FD43). 16.01.1929 Vessel wrecked on Red Rocks Eriskey. All crew rescued.					
NODZU 143528 CF1 Steam Trawler	437 30.09.1920 30.12.1920	281 110	128.5 23.5	C.D.Holmes 85 NHP 10.5 knots	Neale & West Ltd Cardiff
1928 Sold to Cam & Sons Pty Ltd Sydney Australia renamed OLIVE CAM. 06.10.1939 Rqd by the Royal Australian Navy as a minesweeper No. FY 76. 24.05.1946 returned. 02.11.1954 Vessel wrecked after striking a submerged rock on Mowworry Point near Eden New, South Wales. Whilst seeking shelter from a gale.					
HIROSE 143532 CF4 Steam Trawler	438 30.09.1920 24.02.1921	282 110	128.5 23.5	C.D.Holmes 85 NHP 10.5 knots	Neale & West Ltd Cardiff
1930 Sold to Pettit & Youds, Milford Haven (M47). 11.04.1934 Vessel foundered approx 50 miles off Valentia.					
FARFIELD 145696 Steam Coaster	439 25.01.1921 28.07.1921	468 192	152.0 25.2	C.D.Holmes 85 RHP 10 knots	T. Coppack & Co Ltd. Chester
13.07.1941 Vessel sunk by German aircraft 7 miles off the South Stack Light. Eight crew lost one naval rating rescued.					
MICKLETON 144084 Steam Coaster	440 14.03.1921 11.08.1921	777 364	180.4 30.1	C.D.Holmes 109 NHP 10.2 knots	W.C.Bradley & Sons Hull
08.03.1941 Vessel wrecked on rocks at Red Head near Montrose on passage Aberdeen towards Blyth in ballast.					
REDESMERE 145870 Steam Coaster	441 23.03.1921 15.09.1921	345 133	135.0 23.1	C.D.Holmes 73 RHP 9.8 knots	Northwich Carrying Co Ltd Liverpool
1926 Sold to Ald Shipping Co Ltd, Bristol renamed BROCKLEY COMBE. 1937 to G Cooper & Co Ltd, Bristol renamed LOTHDALE. 1953 to Bremner & Co Ltd, Kirkwall renamed ORKNEY DAWN. 27.12.1956 Vessel sold to for scrap to Haulbowline Industries Ltd., Passage West, Cork for breaking up.					
HATCHMERE 145880 Steam Coaster	442 23.03.1921 06.10.1921	345 133	135.0 23.1	C.D.Holmes 73 RHP 9.8 knots	Northwich Carrying Co Ltd Liverpool
1926 Sold to Cement Marketing Co Liverpool. 21.12.1927 Vessel wrecked after striking rocks off the Antrim Coast and sank north of Whitehead on passage from Ardrossan towards Maghermorve with a cargo of coal.					
GARTH SHIRE Steel Lighter	443 08.02.1921 09.02.1921	101 98	70.0 17.1	N/A	Hobson & Co Hull
For use in the transhipment of cargo at the Hull Docks.					
GARTH CITY Steel Lighter	444 24.02.1921 25.02.1921	101 98	70.0 17.1	N/A	Hobson & Co Hull
For use in the transhipment of cargo at the Hull Docks.					

NAME Official No. Port Letters Numbers	Yard No. Launched Registered	Registered G Ton N Ton	 L Ft B Ft	Engine Builder Horse Power Reg'd Speed	OWNER (Built for)
H.C.B. (HULL) R Gas Light Float	445 13.01.1922 14.01.1922	22	40.0 12.0	N/A	Humber Conservancy Board Hull
For use in marking part of the navigable deep water channel in the River Humber.					
W. J. COOK 146479 H548 Steam Trawler	446 28.02.1922 08.06.1922	94 34	82.2 20.1	Goldie & McCulloch 33 NHP 8 knots	Cook Welton & Gemmell Ltd Hull
27.10.1923 Sold to R. Hollingsworth Hull.1926 to J Gomes Villa Real De St Antonio Portugal renamed CABO SPARTEL. 1928 to Serafin Romeu Fages Cadiz Spain renamed GARIFA *(converted to a tug).* 1949 to Enrique Lorenzo Vigo renamed PONDAL *(converted back to a fishing vessel),* *(6 cyl La Maquinista Terrestre Y Maritima of Barcelona diesel engine fitted).* 1976 Vessel deleted from Lloyds Register of Shipping on advice vessel was broken up.					
WM. GEMMELL 146483 H582 Steam Trawler	447 28.02.1922 00.06.1922	94 34	82.2 20.1	Goldie & McCulloch 33 NHP 8 knots	Cook Welton & Gemmell Ltd Hull
27.10.1923 Sold to R. Hollingsworth, Hull. 1926 Sold to J. Gomes Villa De St. Antonio, Portugal renamed CABO ESPICHEL 1928 to Serafin Romeu Fages, Cadiz, Spain renamed CIUDAO REAL. *(converted to a tug).* 1949 to Jose Enrique Lorenzo, Vigo renamed MURGUIA *(converted back to a fishing vessel),* *(6 cyl La Maquinista Terrestre Y Maritima of Barcelona diesel engine fitted).* 1976 to Alberto Manchon Hurtado, Vigo . 24.04.1976 Vessel wrecked in heavy weather 20 miles north of Konitra.					
C K WELTON 146493 H600 Steam Trawler	448 28.02.1922 28.06.1922	94 34	82.2 20.1	Goldie & McCulloch 33 NHP 8 knots	Cook Welton & Gemmell Ltd Hull
27.10.1923 Sold to R. Hollingsworth Hull. 1926 Sold to Fredericksen, Esbjerg, Denmark renamed VINCIT QUI PATITUR. 1942 to C Sörensen, Esbjerg, renamed GRÖNLAND I. 1947 to Hans Jacobsen & Hans Hellemguard, Klaksvig, Færoe Islands renamed SVINOYARBJAANI. 1950 to P/F Hugo Gardor, Klaksvig. 1950 Vessel sold for scrap to shipbreakers and broken up.					
N.E.R. No. 5 (3) 139913 Twin Screw Steam Tug	449 06.08.1922 13.12.1922	161	75.0 26.1	Amos & Smith 173 NHP 12 knots	North Eastern Railway Co York
Ordered by the North Eastern Railway Co, York for use at the company's docks at South Shields. 30.12.1922 Under the Railway Act of 1921 the ownership passed to the London and North Eastern Railway Co. 1937 to Tyne Improvement Commissioners renamed T.I.C.No. 2. 1955 to Newport Screw Towing Co renamed MONNOW. 1960 Vessel sold for scrap to Haulbowline Industries Ltd. Aug 1960 Arrived Passage West, Cork for breaking up.					
N.E.R. No. 6 139226 Twin Screw Steam Tug	450 06.12.1922 13.01.1923	190	95.0 24.1	Amos & Smith 159 NHP 12 knots	North Eastern Railway Co York
Ordered by the North Eastern Railway Co York for use at the company's docks at Hartlepool. 30.12.1922 Under the Railway Act of 1921 the ownership passed to the London and North Eastern Railway Co. 01.01.1948 to The British Transport Commission. 1960 to Newport Screw Towing Co renamed DUNHERON. 1964 Vessel sold for scrap to J Cashmore Newport. 12.02.1963 Breaking up commenced.					
LETTEN Steam Coaling Lighter	451 23.01.1924 1924	121 58	78.0 19.0	Plenty & Son 14 RHP 7 knots	Great Grimsby Coal Salt & Tanning Co Ltd Grimsby
For use in bunkering duties at Grimsby Docks.					
MOODY Steam Coaling Lighter	452 29.01.1924 1924	121 58	78.0 19.0	Plenty & Son 14 RHP 7 knots	Great Grimsby Coal Salt & Tanning Co Ltd Grimsby
For use in bunkering duties at Grimsby Docks.					
JEFFS Steam Coaling Lighter	453 26.02.1924 1924	121 58	78.0 19.0	Plenty & Son 14 RHP 7 knots	Great Grimsby Coal Salt & Tanning Co Ltd Grimsby
For use in bunkering duties at Grimsby Docks.					
BASKCOMB 146886 Steam Coaling Lighter	454 26.02.1924 1924	121 58	78.0 19.0	Plenty & Son 14 RHP 7 knots	Great Grimsby Coal Salt & Tanning Co Ltd Grimsby
For use in bunkering duties at Grimsby Docks.					

Yard No.426
1920 KYOTO as WYRE CORSAIR
Photo by courtesy of Peter Horsley

Yard No.435
1920 WINDWARD HO
Photo by courtesy of George Scales

Yard No.459
1924 ST. MERRYN
Photo:- Author's Collection

NAME Official No. Port Letters Numbers	Yard No. Launched Registered	Registered G Ton N Ton	 L Ft B Ft	Engine Builder Horse Power Reg'd Speed	OWNER (Built for)
Un-named Gas Light Float	455 20.03.1924 23.03.1924	22	40.0 12.0	N/A	Humber Conservancy Board Hull
For use in marking part of the navigable deep water channel in the River Humber.					
BATAVIA 146887 Motor Coaling Lighter	456 08.03.1924 1924	132 81	83.0 19.0	Widdop 70 BHP 6 knots	Standard Coal Supply Grimsby
For use in bunkering duties at Grimsby Docks.					
IMPERIALIST 148418 H143 Steam Trawler	457 13.12.1924 00.02.1925	488 226	160.7 27.1	Amos & Smith 99 NHP 11 knots	Hellyer Bros Ltd Hull
1938 Sold to L'Armement St Perrais, St Perrais, France renamed ADMINISTRATEUR DE BOURNAT. 1940 Seized by the Royal Navy renamed ALASTOR anti-submarine FY 266. Bought by the Royal Navy and renamed BRETWALDA. 13.10.1944 In collision with Dutch Submarine No. 015 (b 1931) in the Clyde. 08.10.1946 to St Andrew's Steam Fishing Co Ltd, Hull renamed WHITE NILE (H39). 11.01.1947 to Polish Government Fleet managed by "Dalmor" Przedsiobiorstwo Polowow, Dalekomorskich, Gdynia renamed JUPITER. 1960 Vessel sold to shipbreakers and broken up.					
ST. DONATS 148381 H35 Steam Trawler	458 21.06.1924 03.09.1924	349 146	140.3 24.0	C.D.Holmes 96 NHP 10.8 knots	Thomas Hamling & Co Ltd Hull
30.08.1939 Rqd by the Royal Navy as a mine-sweeper . 01.03.1941 Vessel sank following a collision with HMS COTSWOLD (b 1940) in the River Humber. Whilst serving with mine-sweeper group 17 based at Grimsby.					
ST. MERRYN 148384 H40 Steam Trawler	459 17.07.1924 25.09.1924	352 148	140.3 24.0	C.D.Holmes 96 NHP 10.8 knots	Thomas Hamling & Co Ltd Hull
01.09.1939 Rqd by the Royal Navy as a boom defence vessel based at Lyness renamed SPINET. 06.06.1946 returned and reverted. 06.07.1946 Sold to Grimsby Merchants Amalgamated Trawlers Ltd, Grimsby. 1953 to G F Sleights & Sons Ltd, Grimsby renamed RUBATO (GY84). 1956 Vessel sold for scrap to Jacques Bakker & Zonen, Belgium. 19.07.1956 Arrived Bruges for breaking up.					
ST. BRELADE 148392 H64 Steam Trawler	460 16.08.1924 23.10.1924	352 144	140.9 24.2	C.D.Holmes 96 NHP 11 knots	Thomas Hamling & Co Ltd Hull
26.05.1936 Sold to Arberjdernes Trawlerdeipt Andelsselskab, Trangisvaag, Færoe Islands renamed LEIVUR OSSURSON. 1954 Vessel sold to shipbreakers and broken up.					
ANDALUSITE 148401 H90 Steam Trawler	461 16.09.1924 10.11.1924	352 144	140.3 24.0	C.D.Holmes 96 NHP 11 knots	Kingston Steam Trawling Co Ltd Hull
13.09.1933 Sold to J Marr & Son Ltd, Fleetwood renamed CORENA. 10.07.1934 to City Steam Fishing Co, Hull. 09.09.1937 Transferred to Fleetwood (FD195). Aug 1939 Rqd by the Royal Navy as a minesweeper No. FY 709. 1946 returned. 1946 to J Craig, Aberdeen (A198). 24.08.1948 Vessel wrecked 6 miles north of Frederikshaab, Greenland. All crew rescued by Eskimos from Frederikshaab.					
ALALITE 148408 H101 Steam Trawler	462 02.10.1924 10.12.1924	352 144	140.3 24.0	C.D.Holmes 96 NHP 11 knots	Kingston Steam Trawling Co Ltd Hull
07.06.1933 Sold to Cia Portuguesa De Pesca Lisbon Portugal renamed ALCACER. 1975 Vessel deleted from Lloyds Register of Shipping.					
ST. LOUIS 148429 H153 Steam Trawler	463 30.12.1924 12.03.1925	352 144	140.3 24.0	C.D.Holmes 96 NHP 11 knots	Thomas Hamling & Co Ltd Hull
12.01.1930 Vessel sank after running aground on rocks in West Fjord, Norway whilst on passage from Hull to the Norwegian fishing grounds. Wreckage from the trawler was found but the circumstances of the stranding are unknown. All sixteen crew lost.					

Yard No.462
1924 ALALITE
Photo:- Author's Collection

Yard No.468
1925 GOTH
Photo:- Harry Cartlidge Collection

Yard No.480
1926 HANNES RÁDHERRA
Photo by courtesy of The Icelandic Maritime Museum, Hafnarfjördur

<table>
<tr><th rowspan="2">NAME
Official No.
Port Letters Numbers</th><th rowspan="2">Yard No.
Launched
Registered</th><th colspan="2">Registered</th><th rowspan="2">Engine Builder
Horse Power
Reg'd Speed</th><th rowspan="2">OWNER
(Built for)</th></tr>
<tr><th>G Ton
N Ton</th><th>L Ft
B Ft</th></tr>
<tr><td>ANDRADITE
148431
H176 Steam Trawler</td><td>464
26.01.1925
30.03.1925</td><td>352
150</td><td>140.3
24.0</td><td>C.D.Holmes
96 NHP
10.8 knots</td><td>Kingston Steam
Trawling Co Ltd
Hull</td></tr>
<tr><td colspan="6">06.07.1933 Sold to J Marr & Son Ltd, Fleetwood renamed ORILLA (FD191).
23.11.1935 to City Steam Fishing Co Ltd, Hull.
08.03.1939 to A/S Vaga Trolarfelag, Sörvaag, Færoe Islands renamed VESTURVARDI (VA214).
1952 to Polish Government Fleet managed by "Dalmor" Przedsiobiorstwo Polowow Dalekomorskich, Gdynia renamed MALY WOZ. 1960 Vessel sold to shipbreakers and broken up.</td></tr>
<tr><td>AXINITE
148441
H183 Steam Trawler</td><td>465
14.02.1925
00.05.1925</td><td>352
150</td><td>140.3
24.0</td><td>C.D.Holmes
96 NHP
10.8 knots</td><td>Kingston Steam
Trawling Co Ltd
Hull</td></tr>
<tr><td colspan="6">01.12.1925 Vessel left Hull for the Icelandic fishing grounds. 07.12.1925 Last contact made with another vessel.
10.12.1925 Vessel posted missing:- Lost with all hands.</td></tr>
<tr><td>ST. GATIEN
148454
H189 Steam Trawler</td><td>466
23.03.1925
00.05.1925</td><td>352
149</td><td>140.3
24.0</td><td>C.D.Holmes
96 NHP
11 knots</td><td>Thomas Hamling & Co Ltd
Hull</td></tr>
<tr><td colspan="6">06.03.1939 Sold to the Royal Navy as a minesweeper No. T97 renamed TAMARISK.
12.08.1940 Vessel sunk by German aircraft in the Thames Estuary off the North-east Spit buoy.</td></tr>
<tr><td>ST. CELESTIN
148458
H192 Steam Trawler</td><td>467
09.04.1925
00.06.1925</td><td>352
149</td><td>140.3
24.0</td><td>C.D.Holmes
96 NHP
10.8 knots</td><td>Thomas Hamling & Co Ltd
Hull</td></tr>
<tr><td colspan="6">01.04.1937 Sold to H Franklin Hull.
03.09.1939 Rqd by the Royal Navy as a boom defence vessel No. Z 104. Nov 1945 returned.
1945 to Shire Trawlers Ltd, Hull. 27.11.1946 to Lord Line Ltd, Hull renamed (1948) LORD PORTAL.
1953 to Associated Fisheries Ltd, Hull.
1954 Vessel sold for scrap to Van Heyghen Freres, Belgium. 14.05.1954 Arrived at Ghent for breaking up.</td></tr>
<tr><td>GOTH
148478
H211 Steam Trawler</td><td>468
08.06.1925
20.08.1925</td><td>394
174</td><td>147.5
25.1</td><td>Amos & Smith
99 NHP
10.5 knots</td><td>Hellyer Bros Ltd
Hull</td></tr>
<tr><td colspan="6">29.08.1939 Rqd by the Royal Navy as a minesweeper No. FY 649. Nov 1945 returned.
01.08.1945 Sold to Ocean Steam Fishing Co Ltd, Hull. 13.12.1946 to Wyre Steam Trawling Co Ltd, Fleetwood (FD52).
16.12.1948 Vessel disappeared whilst making for shelter at Adalvik north west Iceland in severe weather with the loss of all twenty-one crew. A wireless message from the GOTH stating her intentions to seek shelter was picked up by the Grimsby trawler LINCOLN CITY. 15.11.1997 The Icelandic trawler HELGA RE49 trawled up a funnel whilst fishing north north-west of Halo. It was taken into Reykjavik and later identified as belonging to the GOTH. The Funnel has now been returned to Fleetwood where the relatives of the men lost intend to preserve it as a memorial.</td></tr>
<tr><td>ANGLE
149013
H212 Steam Trawler</td><td>469
25.06.1925
05.09.1925</td><td>397
150</td><td>147.3
25.1</td><td>Amos & Smith
104 NHP
10.5 knots</td><td>Hellyer Bros Ltd
Hull</td></tr>
<tr><td colspan="6">1938 Sold to Hull Northern Fishing Co Ltd, Hull. 1938 to A/S Astrop & Co, Kristiansund, Norway.
1958 to A/S Stavtrål, Stavanger, renamed STAVTRÅL. 1959 to Asbjørn Støm-Blabstad , Stavanger renamed ANGLE.
1964 Vessel sold for scrap to Norwegian shipbreakers. Nov 1964 Breaking up commenced.</td></tr>
<tr><td>NORSE
149017
H219 Steam Trawler</td><td>470
22.07.1925
21.09.1925</td><td>394
174</td><td>147.5
25.1</td><td>Amos & Smith
99 NHP
10.5 knots</td><td>Hellyer Bros Ltd
Hull</td></tr>
<tr><td colspan="6">05.03.1929 Homeward bound to Hull in thick fog vessel was wrecked on a reef near Hvalsnes, Faxa-Floi, Keflavik south-west Iceland. Having exhausted the supply of distress flares the crew burned mattresses to attract attention. At first light the following day an Icelandic motor boat came alongside and took all the crew safely aboard and landed them at Reykjavik.</td></tr>
<tr><td>KELT
149026
H236 Steam Trawler</td><td>471
20.08.1925
19.10.1925</td><td>376
162</td><td>147.2
25.2</td><td>Amos & Smith
99 NHP
10.5 knots</td><td>Hellyer Bros Ltd
Hull</td></tr>
<tr><td colspan="6">19.11.1935 Sold to A / S Bergens Fiskeriselskap, Bergen, Norway.
1940 Rqd by the Royal Norwegian Navy as a patrol vessel based at Ofotfjord.
09.04.1940 Seized by German destroyer DIETHER VON ROEDER Z17 (b 1937) renamed KREBS No. NN 01 later V6301.
1946 Vessel deleted from Lloyds Register of Shipping.</td></tr>
</table>

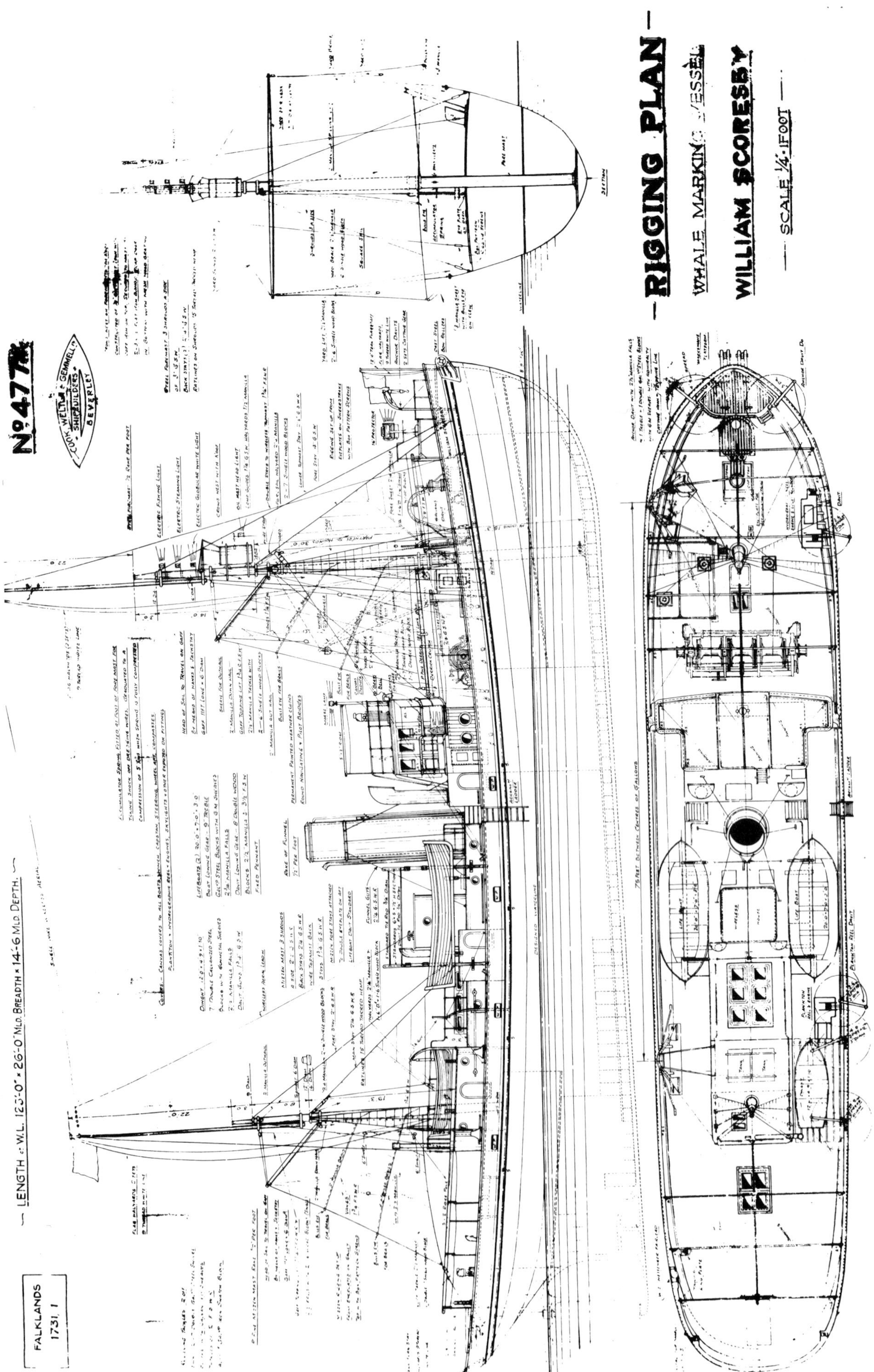

FALKLANDS
1731, 1
LENGTH at W.L. 125'-0" × 26'-0" MLD. BREADTH × 14'-6 MLD. DEPTH.
No 477
COOK, WELTON & GEMMELL LTD
SHIPBUILDERS
BEVERLEY
RIGGING PLAN
WILLIAM SCORESBY
SCALE 1/4"·1FOOT
75 FEET BETWEEN CENTRES OF GALLOWS
DESIGNED WATERLINE
SECTION

<table>
<tr><th>NAME
Official No.
Port Letters Numbers</th><th>Yard No.
Launched
Registered</th><th colspan="2">Registered</th><th>Engine Builder
Horse Power
Reg'd Speed</th><th>OWNER
(Built for)</th></tr>
<tr><th></th><th></th><th>G Ton
N Ton</th><th>L Ft
B Ft</th><th></th><th></th></tr>
<tr><td>PICT
149033
H250 Steam Trawler</td><td>472
04.09.1925
05.11.1925</td><td>394
174</td><td>147.5
25.1</td><td>Amos & Smith
116 NHP
11 knots</td><td>Hellyer Bros Ltd
Hull</td></tr>
<tr><td colspan="6">22.04.1935 Sold to Devon Fishing Co Ltd, Hull renamed ELBURY.
02.09.1939 Rqd by the Royal Navy as a minesweeper No. FY 656. 05.07.1945 returned.
23.11.943 to Pickering & Haldane's Steam Trawling Co Ltd, Hull. 1945 to Lord Line Ltd, Hull renamed LORD GORT.
14.11.1947 to Wyre Steam Trawling Co Ltd, Fleetwood renamed WYRE GENERAL (FD258).
1956 Vessel sold for scrap to B J Nijkerk S/A, Belgium. 19.03.1956 Sailed from Fleetwood to Boom for breaking up.</td></tr>
<tr><td>TERVANI
149041
H260 Steam Trawler</td><td>473
02.11.1925
17.12.1925</td><td>394
174</td><td>147.5
25.1</td><td>Amos & Smith
99 NHP
10.8 knots</td><td>Henriksen & Co Ltd
Hull</td></tr>
<tr><td colspan="6">27.01.1939 Sold to J F Kjolbro, Klaksvig Færoe Islands renamed NÆRÅBERG.
17.04.1941 Vessel sunk by German aircraft bombs. All crew rescued.</td></tr>
<tr><td>PELTON
149024
H228 Steam Trawler</td><td>474
04.09.1925
10.10.1925</td><td>358
141</td><td>140.4
24.0</td><td>C.D.Holmes
96 NHP
10.7 knots</td><td>F & T Ross Ltd
Hull</td></tr>
<tr><td colspan="6">31.08.1939 Rqd by the Royal Navy as a mine-sweeper .
24.12.1940 Vessel sunk by E-boat in the North Sea alongside No 5 buoy off Aldeburgh Suffolk.</td></tr>
<tr><td>BUNSEN
149045
H269 Steam Trawler</td><td>475
05.11.1925
06.01.1926</td><td>358
141</td><td>140.4
24.0</td><td>Amos & Smith
96 NHP
10.7 knots</td><td>F & T Ross Ltd
Hull</td></tr>
<tr><td colspan="6">26.04.1939 Sold to the Admiralty / Royal Navy as a boom defence vessel renamed JENNETT No. Z21.
1946 to J C Llewellyn Ltd, Hull renamed WESTHERON (H465). 22.09.1950 to Lord Line Hull renamed LORD BANN.
26.10.1951 Vessel sold as storage hulk to Stevedoring Co, Antwerp, Belgium. 21.12.1951 Resold for breaking up.</td></tr>
<tr><td>JUPITER

GK161 Steam Trawler</td><td>476
21.09.1925
26.11.1925</td><td>404
165</td><td>147.5
25.1</td><td>Amos & Smith
110 NHP
11 knots</td><td>Fiskiveidahlutafrlagid
Belgaum Hafnarfjord
Iceland</td></tr>
<tr><td colspan="6">09.04.1928 to H/F Jupiter, Reykjavik (RE61). 14.12.1929 to H/F Jupiter, Hafnarfjord.
21.08.1951 to Garautgerd Dyrfirdinga H/F, Thingeyri renamed GUDMUNDER JUNI (IS20).
21.06.1955 to Einari Sigurdssyni, Reykjavik.
29.07.1963 Vessel removed from fishing register after being scuttled for use as a breakwater for the slipway at Isafjord.</td></tr>
<tr><td>WILLIAM SCORESBY
148757
Research Ship</td><td>477
31.12.1925
14.06.1926</td><td>326
109</td><td>128.4
26.1</td><td>Amos & Smith
160 NHP
12 knots</td><td>Crown Agents for the Colonies
London</td></tr>
<tr><td colspan="6">1926 -1938 Vessel carried out seven separate commissions.
1927 Sold to Government of the Falkland Islands. 1929 Bestowed the title Royal Research Ship.
1930 - 1938 Employed in a series of cruises mainly concerned with whale marking activities.
1939 Rqd by the Royal Navy as a minesweeper No. J122. Jan 1947 returned.
1947 to the Admiralty. 1949 to National Institute of Oceanography, London.
Jan 1950 - Dec 1950 Last cruise mainly spent in the South Indian Ocean. Jan 1951 Laid up Portsmouth due to lack of funds.
20.05.1954 Vessel sold to BISCO (£1900) and allocated to Demellweek & Ridding Plymouth and broken up.</td></tr>
<tr><td>LADY BERYL
149058
H283 Steam Trawler</td><td>478
19.12.1925
04.02.1926</td><td>358
153</td><td>140.4
24.0</td><td>C.D.Holmes
96 NHP
11 knots</td><td>Jutland Amalgamated
Trawlers Ltd
Hull</td></tr>
<tr><td colspan="6">04.11.1935 Sold to Ocean Steam Fishing Co Ltd, Hull renamed OCEAN DUKE.
28.03.1938 to Charleson Smith Trawlers Ltd, Hull renamed STELLA RIGEL.
02.09.1939 Rqd by the Royal Navy as a minesweeper No. FY 657. 27.07.1945 returned.
08.06.1945 to Hull Merchants Amalgamated Trawlers Ltd, Hull renamed ALAMEIN.
16.02.1949 to Yolland Bros Ltd, Milford Haven.
04.08.1949 to St Andrew's Steam Fishing Co Ltd, Hull renamed LADY OLWEN.
1952 to G F Sleight, Grimsby renamed REMINDO (GY252). 28.04.1955 Whilst at anchor off Nypubakka Færoe Islands sheltering from a storm the anchor cable of the REMINDO parted and she was driven ashore on to rocks. Although the crew managed to fire off a distress flare they had no time to launch the lifeboat before the trawler slid off the rocks and sank. The North Shields trawler BEN MEIDIE SN340 (234 gt/ b 1917) which was anchored near by came to the rescue, launching her lifeboat she picked up three men from the sea, one man was swept away and lost. The BEN MEIDIE then recovered another eleven men who were clinging to a liferaft. Unfortunately three men died on the way to Thorshaven.</td></tr>
</table>

<table>
<tr><th rowspan="2">NAME
Official No.
Port Letters Numbers</th><th rowspan="2">Yard No.
Launched
Registered</th><th colspan="2">Registered</th><th rowspan="2">Engine Builder
Horse Power
Reg'd Speed</th><th rowspan="2">OWNER
(Built for)</th></tr>
<tr><th>G Ton
N Ton</th><th>L Ft
B Ft</th></tr>
<tr><td>LADY MADELEINE
149050
H278 Steam Trawler</td><td>479
21.11.1925
20.01.1926</td><td>358
153</td><td>140.4
24.0</td><td>C.D.Holmes
96 NHP
11 knots</td><td>Jutland Amalgamated
Trawlers Ltd
Hull</td></tr>
<tr><td colspan="6">15.06.1934 Sold to Clan Steam Fishing Co Ltd, Grimsby renamed CAMERON (GY65).
20.04.1939 to Loch Fishing Co Ltd, Hull renamed LOCH ALSH (H73).
22.04.1939 Rqd by the Royal Navy as a mine-sweeper.
30.01.1942 Disabled by German aircraft off the Norfolk coast taken in tow but sank approx 30 miles north-east of Skegness.</td></tr>
<tr><td>HANNES RÁDHERRA

RE268 Steam Trawler</td><td>480
16.01.1926
13.03.1926</td><td>451
183</td><td>151.0
25.6</td><td>Amos & Smith
118 NHP
11 knots</td><td>H / f Alliance
Reykjavik
Iceland</td></tr>
<tr><td colspan="6">14.02.1939 Vessel wrecked at Braufarholt near Kjalarnesi, Iceland.</td></tr>
<tr><td>SARDIUS
149069
H289 Steam Trawler</td><td>481
03.02.1926
27.03.1926</td><td>352
147</td><td>140.3
24.0</td><td>C.D.Holmes
96 NHP
11.3 knots</td><td>Kingston Steam
Trawling Co Ltd
Hull</td></tr>
<tr><td colspan="6">23.12.1935 Sold to Soc. Anon Armement Ostendais, Ostend, Belgium renamed CHRIST MAHLMAN.
1950 to Polish Government Fleet managed by "Dalmor" Przedsiobiorstwo Polowow Dalekomorskich, Gdynia renamed PLUTON. 1965 Vessel sold to shipbreakers and broken up.</td></tr>
<tr><td>TOURMALINE
149077
H290 Steam Trawler</td><td>482
04.03.1926
28.04.1926</td><td>352
147</td><td>140.3
24.0</td><td>C.D.Holmes
96 NHP
11 knots</td><td>Kingston Steam
Trawling Co Ltd
Hull</td></tr>
<tr><td colspan="6">16.03.1939 Sold to NV Motorvisscherij, Ostend, Belgium renamed VAN OOST (O296).
21.05.1940 Arrived at Milford Haven from Belgium.
07.07.1940 Rqd by the Royal Navy as an anti-submarine FY 330. 03.11.1945 returned.
16.01.1948 to Polish Government Fleet managed by "Dalmor" Przedsiobiorstwo Polowow Dalekomorskich, Gdynia renamed MERKURY (GDY120). 1961 Vessel sold to shipbreakers. 1962 Breaking up completed.</td></tr>
<tr><td>KINGSTON DIAMOND
149080
H294 Steam Trawler</td><td>483
31.03.1926
09.08.1926</td><td>352
147</td><td>140.3
24.0</td><td>C.D.Holmes
96 NHP
11 knots</td><td>Kingston Steam
Trawling Co Ltd
Hull</td></tr>
<tr><td colspan="6">First trawler of the company's fleet with the 'KINGSTON' prefix.
11.03.1939 Sold to NV Motorvisscherij, Ostend, Belgium renamed VAN DYCK (O298).
29.05.1940 Arrived at Fleetwood from Belgium.
12.02.1941 Rqd by the Royal Navy as an anti-submarine vessel No. FY 106. 11.11.1945 returned.
1948 to P/f Eidis Trolareefelag A/S, Ejde, Færoe Islands renamed EIDESKOLLUR (FD226).
1952 to P/f Nypan, Sandevaag, Færoe Islands renamed VENUS.
1960 Vessel sold for scrap to B J Nijkirk N V, Holland. 12.04.1960 Breaking up commenced at Boom.</td></tr>
<tr><td>KINGSTON PEARL
149083
H296 Steam Trawler</td><td>484
17.04.1926
12.08.1926</td><td>352
147</td><td>140.3
24.0</td><td>C.D.Holmes
96 NHP
11 knots</td><td>Kingston Steam
Trawling Co Ltd
Hull</td></tr>
<tr><td colspan="6">20.03.1939 Sold to Soc. Anon Armement Ostendais, Ostend, Belgium renamed NAUTILUS (O160).
18.05.1940 Arrived at Fleetwood from Belgium.
08.02.1941 Rqd by the Royal Navy for miscellaneous uses renamed JAY No. M.06 (1944) renamed SANDMARTIN.
12.02.1946 returned and reverted. 1950 to Central Morska Importowa, Eksportowa, Poland renamed PERSEUSZ.
03.06.1952 Vessel struck a submerged wreck and sank off Szezecin Poland.</td></tr>
<tr><td>KINGSTON GARNET
160047
H323 Steam Trawler</td><td>485
30.04.1927
22.06.1927</td><td>352
146</td><td>140.3
24.0</td><td>C.D.Holmes
96 NHP
10.9 knots</td><td>Kingston Steam
Trawling Co Ltd
Hull</td></tr>
<tr><td colspan="6">11.03.1939 Sold to NV Motorvisscherij, Ostend, Belgium renamed VAN ORLEY (O299).
18.05.1940 Arrived at Fleetwood from Belgium.
08.02.1941 Rqd by the Royal Navy as an anti-submarine vessel based at Liverpool .
04.05.1941 Vessel sunk by German aircraft bombs off the River Mersey. Wreck raised in Nov 1941 and broken up.</td></tr>
<tr><td>KINGSTON EMERALD
160048
H350 Steam Trawler</td><td>486
17.05.1927
30.06.1927</td><td>352
146</td><td>140.3
24.0</td><td>C.D.Holmes
96 NHP
10.9 knots</td><td>Kingston Steam
Trawling Co Ltd
Hull</td></tr>
<tr><td colspan="6">15.03.1938 Sold to Suomen Kalastus O/Y Finska Fiskeri A/B, Hangö, Finland renamed AUNUS.
1952 Vessel sold for scrap to Octaaf Van Der Bon, Belgium. Mar 1952 Arrived at Ostend for breaking up.</td></tr>
</table>

Yard No.488
1927 KINGSTON ONYX as WESTHOPE
Photo:- Author's Collection

Yard No.500
1928 ST. SEBASTIAN
Photo:- Author's Collection

Yard No.512
1928 FLEMING
Photo:- Harry Cartlidge Collection

<table>
<tr><th rowspan="2">NAME
Official No.
Port Letters Numbers</th><th rowspan="2">Yard No.
Launched
Registered</th><th colspan="2">Registered</th><th rowspan="2">Engine Builder
Horse Power
Reg'd Speed</th><th rowspan="2">OWNER
(Built for)</th></tr>
<tr><th>G Ton
N Ton</th><th>L Ft
B Ft</th></tr>
<tr><td>KINGSTON TOPAZ
160054
H352 Steam Trawler</td><td>487
01.06.1927
20.07.1927</td><td>352
145</td><td>140.3
24.0</td><td>C.D.Holmes
96 NHP
11 knots</td><td>Kingston Steam
Trawling Co Ltd
Hull</td></tr>
<tr><td colspan="6">(1937 Lengthened to 151.5 ft 357 Gross tons) Work carried out by Smiths Dock Co Ltd, Middlesbrough.
30.08.1939 Rqd by the Royal Navy as an armed boarding / anti-submarine vessel No. FY 4.31. 17.11.1945 returned.
03.08.1945 Sold to Grimsby Motor Trawlers Ltd, Grimsby renamed (1946) HAWKINS (GY93).
30.07.1949 to Trawlers Grimsby Ltd, Grimsby.10.04.1953 to Derwent Trawlers Ltd, Grimsby.
Nov 1953 to Yorkshire Trawlers Ltd, Grimsby.
1956 Vessel sold to BISCO and allocated to J J King & Co Ltd. 23.10.1956 Arrived Gateshead for breaking up.</td></tr>
<tr><td>KINGSTON ONYX
160057
H365 Steam Trawler</td><td>488
18.06.1927
11.08.1927</td><td>352
145</td><td>140.3
24.0</td><td>C.D.Holmes
96 NHP
10.8 knots</td><td>Kingston Steam
Trawling Co Ltd
Hull</td></tr>
<tr><td colspan="6">(1937 Lengthened to 151.5 ft 357 Gross tons) Work carried out by Smiths Dock Co Ltd, Middlesbrough.
31.08.1939 Rqd by the Royal Navy as an armed boarding / anti-submarine vessel No. FY 4.54. 02.09.1944 returned.
09.10.1945 Sold to Parkholme Trawlers Ltd, Grimsby renamed MOORSOM (GY119).
1947 to J C Llewellin, Milford Haven renamed WESTHOPE (H590). 03.01.1949 to St Andrew's Steam Fishing Co, Hull .
1956 Vessel sold to BISCO and allocated to Clayton & Davie Ltd. 24.04.1956 Arrived Dunston on Tyne for breaking up.</td></tr>
<tr><td>ST. MELANTE
160061
H367 Steam Trawler</td><td>489
15.08.1927
27.09.1927</td><td>358
155</td><td>140.4
24.0</td><td>C.D.Holmes
96 NHP
10.8 knots</td><td>Thomas Hamling & Co Ltd
Hull</td></tr>
<tr><td colspan="6">28.08.1939 Rqd by the Royal Navy as a minesweeper No. FY 753. 21.06.1946 returned.
06.07.1945 Sold to Grimsby Merchants Amalgamated Trawlers Ltd, Grimsby (GY80).
1950 to Grimsby Merchants Amalgamated Trawlers Ltd, Grimsby renamed WOMERSLEY.
1953 to G F Sleight, Grimsby renamed RAPALLO.
1956 Vessel sold for scrap to Jacques Bakker & Zonen, Belgium. 14.07.1956 Arrived Bruges for breaking up.</td></tr>
<tr><td>ST. ALEXANDRA
160093
H373 Steam Trawler</td><td>490
10.12.1927
12.01.1928</td><td>359
156</td><td>140.4
24.0</td><td>C.D.Holmes
96 NHP
10.8 knots</td><td>Thomas Hamling & Co Ltd
Hull</td></tr>
<tr><td colspan="6">11.03.1939 Sold to the Royal Navy as a minesweeper No. T96 renamed LARCH.
1946 to Westholme Fishing Co Ltd, Milford Haven (M138).
1947 to J C Llewellin, Milford Haven renamed WESTHILL (H470) managed by St Andrew's Steam Fishing Co, Hull.
15.09.1950 to J Marr & Son Ltd, Hull.
1952 Vessel sold to BISCO and allocated to Thos Young & Sons Ltd. 10.10.1952 Arrived Sunderland for breaking up.</td></tr>
<tr><td>ST. DELPHINE
160096
H380 Steam Trawler</td><td>491
31.12.1927
07.02.1928</td><td>359
156</td><td>140.4
24.0</td><td>C.D.Holmes
96 NHP
10.8 knots</td><td>Thomas Hamling & Co Ltd
Hull</td></tr>
<tr><td colspan="6">09.03.1939 Vessel sank following a collision in the River Humber with the trawler AQUAMARINE H388 (see Yard No. 492) near the entrance to St Andrew's Dock after returning from Admiralty trials off Flamborough Head. Thirteen of the crew were picked up by other shipping but the skipper and two crew were lost. Oct 1939 Wreck dispersed by explosives.</td></tr>
<tr><td>AQUAMARINE
160098
H388 Steam Trawler</td><td>492
28.01.1928
23.02.1928</td><td>352
145</td><td>140.3
24.0</td><td>C.D.Holmes
96 NHP
11 knots</td><td>Kingston Steam
Trawling Co Ltd
Hull</td></tr>
<tr><td colspan="6">(1937 Lengthened to 151.5 ft 357 Gross tons) Work carried out by Smiths Dock Co Ltd, Middlesbrough.
30.08.1939 Rqd by the Royal Navy as an armed boarding / anti-submarine vessel No. FY 4.00. 21.09.1944 returned.
24.08.1945 Sold to Grimsby Motor Trawlers Ltd, Grimsby renamed HARGOOD (GY97).
16.11.1948 to J C Llewellin, Milford Haven renamed WESTHAZE (H589)managed by St Andrew's Steam Fishing Co, Hull.
1955 Vessel sold to BISCO and allocated to J J King & Co Ltd. 19.07.1955 Arrived Gateshead for breaking up.</td></tr>
<tr><td>CHALCEDONY
160099
H392 Steam Trawler</td><td>493
11.02.1928
13.03.1928</td><td>352
145</td><td>140.3
24.0</td><td>C.D.Holmes
96 NHP
11.2 knots</td><td>Kingston Steam
Trawling Co Ltd
Hull</td></tr>
<tr><td colspan="6">(1937 Lengthened to 151.5 ft 357 Gross tons) Work carried out by Smiths Dock Co Ltd, Middlesbrough.
26.08.1939 Rqd by the Royal Navy as a mine-sweeper / auxiliary patrol vessel No. FY 4.124. 13.05.1946 returned.
09.10.1945 Sold to Parkholme Trawlers Ltd, Grimsby renamed LAFOREY (GY109).
1948 to Wyre Steam Trawling Co Ltd, Fleetwood renamed WYRE MARINER (FD34).
1954 Vessel sold for scrap to Haulbowline Industries. 16.11.1954 Arrived Passage West for breaking up.</td></tr>
<tr><td>ST. LEANDER
160103
H420 Steam Trawler</td><td>494
05.04.1928
07.05.1928</td><td>357
147</td><td>140.4
24.0</td><td>C.D.Holmes
96 NHP
10.9 knots</td><td>Thomas Hamling & Co Ltd
Hull</td></tr>
<tr><td colspan="6">24.02.1938 Vessel sank in 25 minutes following a collision with trawler LADY ROSEMARY H442 (see Yard No.496) off Andenaes Lighthouse, Norway. All fifteen crew took to the lifeboat and were taken aboard by the LADY ROSEMARY.</td></tr>
</table>

NAME Official No. Port Letters Numbers	Yard No. Launched Registered	Registered G Ton N Ton	 L Ft B Ft	Engine Builder Horse Power Reg'd Speed	OWNER (Built for)
ST. JOAN 160120 H456 Steam Trawler	495 08.05.1928 03.08.1928	359 147	140.4 24.0	C.D.Holmes 96 NHP 10.9 knots	St Andrew's Steam Fishing Co Ltd Hull
20.02.1939 Sold to Soc. Anon Armement Ostendais, Belgium renamed TRANSPORT. 23.10.1945 Vessel sank in heavy weather in approx position 51° 37'N 003° 18'E.					
LADY ROSEMARY 160113 H442 Steam Trawler	496 19.05.1928 07.07.1928	357 153	140.4 24.0	C.D.Holmes 96 NHP 11 knots	Jutland Amalgamated Trawlers Ltd Hull
04.03.1937 Sold to Great Grimsby & East Coast Steam Fishing Co Ltd, Grimsby renamed DALMATIA (GY374). Sep 1939 Rqd by the Royal Navy as a minesweeper No. FY 844. 1946 returned. 1946 to Manor Steamship Co Ltd, Milford Haven (M140). 24.04.1946 to J C Llewellin, Milford Haven renamed WESTHAWK (H474). managed by St Andrew's Steam Fishing Co, Hull. 22.09.1950 to J Marr & Son Ltd, Hull. 1952 Vessel sold to BISCO and allocated to J J King & Co Ltd. 25.11.1952 Arrived Gateshead for breaking up.					
VENDORA 146909 GY466 Steam Trawler	497 21.06.1928 05.08.1928	344 160	140.4 24.0	C.D.Holmes 96 NHP 11 knots	Atlas Steam Fishing Co Ltd Grimsby
1938 Sold to P/F Uvak A/S, Thorshaven, Færoe Islands renamed NORDBUGVIN. 1948 to P/F Hellufassur, Kvivik, Færoe Islands renamed EGIL. 24.10.1949 Vessel sank after stranding off Bear Island.					
EMBASSY 146910 GY469 Steam Trawler	498 05.07.1928 26.09.1928	345 159	140.4 24.0	C.D.Holmes 96 NHP 11 knots	Letten Bros Grimsby
1932 Sold to E C Grant, Grimsby. 1935 Clan Steam Fishing Co Ltd, Grimsby renamed WIGMORE. 18.11.1939 Vessel torpedoed and sunk by U-18 (Captain Mengerson) at 2330 hrs 25 miles north by west of Rattray Head. All sixteen crew lost. The WIGMORE was fishing out of Fleetwood at the time of her loss.					
ST. ROMANUS 160106 H426 Steam Trawler	499 24.04.1928 06.06.1928	357 154	140.4 24.0	C.D.Holmes 96 NHP 10.7 knots	Thomas Hamling & Co Ltd Hull
02.03.1939 Sold to the Royal Navy as a minesweeper No. T54. renamed OAK. 23.03.1946 to St Andrew's Steam Fishing Co Ltd, Hull renamed ST. STEPHEN (H299). 06.05.1949 to Cairo Fishing Co Ltd, Hull renamed LADY JUNE. 02.02.1950 to G F Sleight & Sons Ltd, Grimsby renamed (1952) RECEPTO (GY254). 1956 Vessel sold for scrap to Jacques Bakker & Zonen, Belgium. 22.08.1956 Arrived Bruges for breaking up.					
ST. SEBASTIAN 160805 H470 Steam Trawler	500 02.08.1928 04.10.1928	357 154	140.4 24.0	C.D.Holmes 96 NHP 10.7 knots	Thomas Hamling & Co Ltd Hull
29.09.1938 Vessel wrecked near Cape Duner on the north coast of Bear Island, as a result of her request for assistance the trawlers KINGSTON CAIRNGORM H175 (see Yard No.601), LOCH OSKAIG H431 (534 gt/ b1937), CAPE DUNER H174 (455 gt/ b1935), DAVY H332 (see Yard No.612), LE TIGER GY398 (516 gt/ b 1937), and MILDENHALL GY124 (466 gt/ b 1938) arrived at her position. Due to rough seas and gale force winds it was not possible to attempt a rescue by boat. So it was decided to land a rescue party with crew members from the CAPE DUNER and DAVY on the sheltered eastern side of the island. During the hours of darkness the ST. SEBASTIAN was swept by heavy seas and all eighteen crew were lost.					
AMETHYST 160117 H455 Steam Trawler	501 05.06.1928 21.07.1928	352 145	140.3 24.0	C.D.Holmes 96 NHP 11 knots	Kingston Steam Trawling Co Ltd Hull
(1937 Lengthened to 151.5 ft 357 Gross tons) Work carried out by Smiths Dock Co Ltd, Middlesbrough. 24.01.1937 Vessel sank off Kinnaird Head near Fraserburgh Scotland during a storm. All crew were lost.					
LADY RACHAEL 160798 H457 Steam Trawler	502 17.07.1928 20.08.1928	357 153	140.4 24.0	C.D.Holmes 96 NHP 10.6 knots	Jutland Amalgamated Trawlers Ltd Hull
04.03.1937 Sold to Standard Steam Fishing Co Ltd, Grimsby renamed SOLOMON (GY372). Aug 1939 Rqd by the Royal Navy as a mine-sweeper. 01.04.1942 Vessel sunk by mine north of Cromer 2.7 miles off the 57C buoy.					
ST. IRENE 160808 H472 Steam Trawler	503 18.08.1928 16.10.1928	357 154	140.4 24.0	C.D.Holmes 96 NHP 10.6 knots	Thomas Hamling & Co Ltd Hull
03.03.1939 Sold to the Royal Navy for use as a minesweeper No. T91 renamed MYRTLE. 14.06.1940 Vessel sunk by mine in the Thames estuary.					

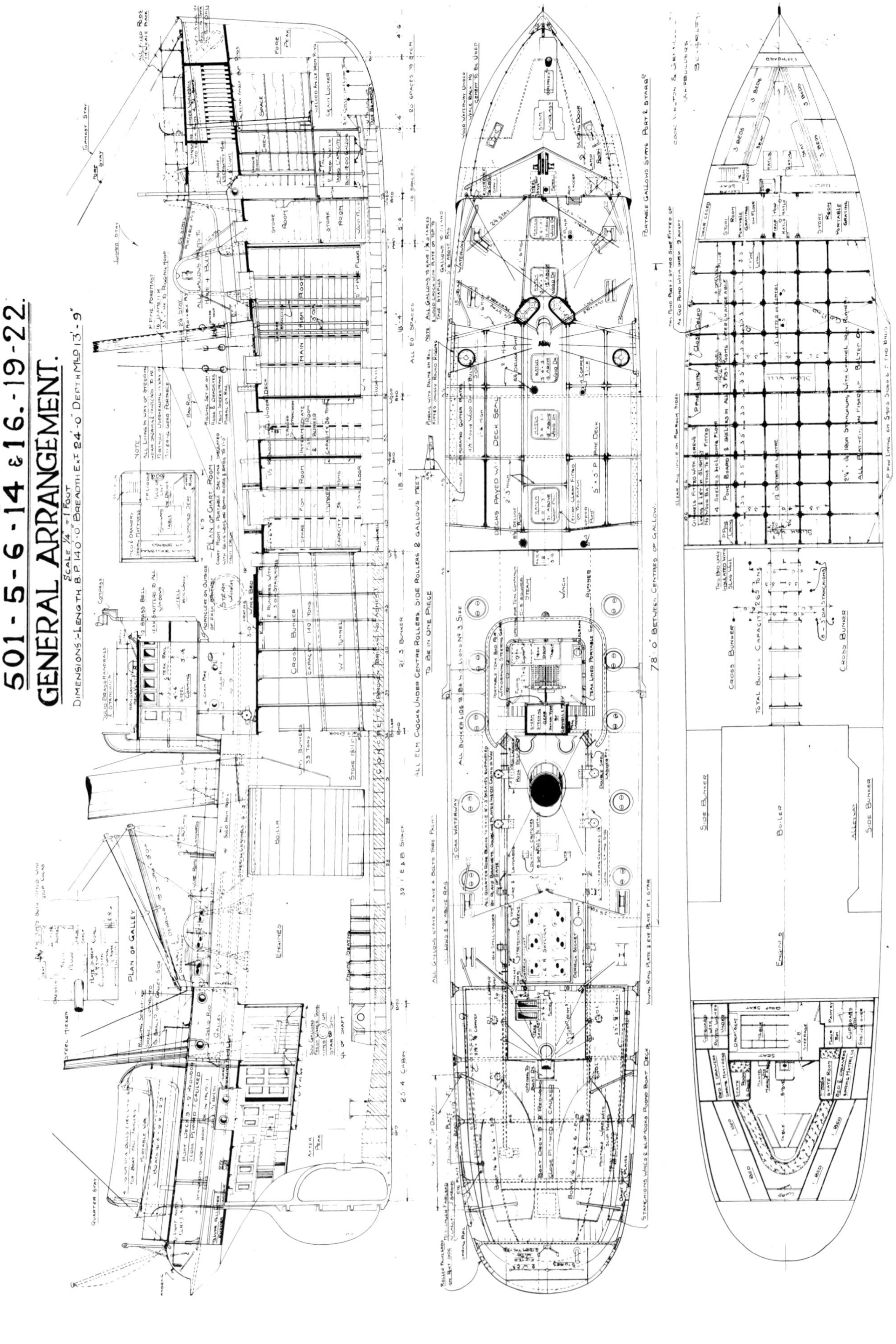
501-5-6-14 & 16.-19-22.
GENERAL ARRANGEMENT.
SCALE 1/4" = 1 FOOT
DIMENSIONS:-LENGTH B.P 140'-0" BREADTH ExT 24'-0" DEPTH MLD 13'-9"

NAME Official No. Port Letters Numbers	Yard No. Launched Registered	Registered G Ton N Ton	 L Ft B Ft	Engine Builder Horse Power Reg'd Speed	OWNER (Built for)
ST. ROSE 160811 H492 Steam Trawler	504 04.09.1928 30.10.1928	357 154	140.4 24.0	C.D.Holmes 96 NHP 10.6 knots	Thomas Hamling & Co Ltd Hull
1939 Sold to the Royal Navy for use as a minesweeper No. T86 renamed REDWOOD. 19.12.1945 to NV Visch Onderneming De Vam, Ijmuiden, Holland (1947) renamed MARY. 1956 Vessel sold to shipbreakers and broken up.					
KINGSTON JASPER 160813 H494 Steam Trawler	505 17.09.1928 07.11.1928	352 154	140.3 24.0	C.D.Holmes 96 NHP 11.4 knots	Kingston Steam Trawling Co Ltd Hull
13.02.1929 Left Hull for the Icelandic fishing grounds. 16.02.1929 Vessel wrecked at Medalland, south Iceland. during a blizzard. Local farmers saw the trawler's distress rockets and came to the assistance of the stranded vessel's crew. A breeches buoy was rigged and all twelve crew were brought ashore and taken on a four day journey on ponies to Reykjavik.					
KINGSTON BERYL 160814 H499 Steam Trawler	506 02.10.1928 19.11.1928	352 149	140.3 24.0	C.D.Holmes 96 NHP 11.4 knots	Kingston Steam Trawling Co Ltd Hull
(1939 Lengthened to 151.5 ft 357 Gross tons) Work carried out by Smiths Dock Co Ltd, Middlesbrough. 26.08.1939 Rqd by the Royal Navy as an armed boarding/anti-submarine vessel No. FY 4.03. 23rd anti-submarine group. 25.12.1943 Vessel sank after running onto two British floating mines whilst on convoy escort duties north of Ireland approx position 56° 12'N 007° 30'W. All twenty-eight crew lost.					
LOCH LEVEN 148957 A379 Steam Trawler	507 16.10.1928 04.12.1928	357 154	140.4 24.0	C.D.Holmes 96 NHP 10.6 knots	Loch Line Steam Trawling & Fishing Co Ltd Aberdeen
20.01.1930 Sold to Hellyer Bros Ltd, Hull (H186). 23.08.1939 to Caledonian Fishing Co Ltd, Hull. 31.08.1939 Rqd by the Royal Navy as a minesweeper No. FY 642. 06.02.1946 returned. 22.01.1946 to A & M Smith Ltd, Hull. 1948 to United Trawlers Ltd, Milford Haven renamed GEORGE HASTINGS. 1954 Vessel sold to BISCO, allocated to Rees Shipbreaking Co Ltd. Jun 1954 Left Fleetwood for Llanelli for breaking up.					
SISAPON 160962 GY493 Steam Trawler	508 30.10.1928 27.12.1928	326 133	137.2 23.6	Amos & Smith 92 NHP 10.5 knots	Standard Steam Fishing Co Ltd Grimsby
01.09.1939 Rqd by the Royal Navy as a mine-sweeper . 12.06.1940 Vessel sunk by mine off Harwich.					
LOYAL 160963 GY501 Steam Trawler	509 12.08.1928 23.01.1929	326 133	137.2 23.6	Amos & Smith 92 NHP 10.5 knots	Loyal Steam Fishing Co Ltd Grimsby
18.12.1939 The LOYAL rescued all thirteen crew of the Hull trawler LORD FISHER H264 *(see Yard No.301).* which was wrecked on the north coast Iceland. 19.02.1939 Vessel wrecked south of Hammerfest in the Norwegian Fjords. Eight of the LOYAL's crew were taken off by the trawler PICT H162 (462 gt/ b 1936). The skipper and three crew remained on board to supervise salvage attempts with the Norwegian salvage vessel JASON (295 gt/ b 1908). But due to severe weather the four crewmen were taken off and the salvage attempt had to be abandoned and the vessel foundered.					
NIGHT WATCH 160964 GY26 Steam Trawler	510 12.12.1928 14.02.1929	348 160	140.2 24.6	Amos & Smith 91 NHP 10.5 knots	Nocturne Steam Fishing Co Ltd Grimsby
02.10.1937 Stranded at Sem Island. 1938 Salvaged and returned to Grimsby. Feb 1939 Sold to Markham Cook, Grimsby renamed MURMANSK (GY45). Aug 1939 to Shire Trawlers Ltd, Grimsby. 01.06.1940 Rqd by the Royal Navy as a mine-sweeper . 17.06.1940 Grounded at Brest and abandoned. 1942 Salved by the German Navy and used as patrol boat PB06. 1944 Vessel reported missing :- War loss.					
LORINDA 148320 FD182 Steam Trawler	511 28.11.1928 22.12.1928	348 165	140.2 24.6	C.D.Holmes 96 NHP 10.8 knots	Fleetwood Steam Fishing Co Ltd Fleetwood
1939 Sold to Shire Trawlers Ltd, Grimsby (GY220). 04.09.1939 Rqd by the Royal Navy as a mine-sweeper . 20.08.1941 Vessel foundered after being damaged by a fire in the engine room off Freetown West Africa.					
FLEMING 160820 H3 Steam Trawler	512 29.12.1928 30.01.1929	356 145	140.2 24.6	C.D.Holmes 96 NHP 10.9 knots	F & T Ross Ltd Hull
30.08.1939 Rqd by the Royal Navy as a mine-sweeper . 24.07.1940 Vessel sunk by German Aircraft in the Thames estuary.					

<table>
<tr><th rowspan="2">NAME
Official No.
Port Letters Numbers</th><th rowspan="2">Yard No.
Launched
Registered</th><th colspan="2">Registered</th><th rowspan="2">Engine Builder
Horse Power
Reg'd Speed</th><th rowspan="2">OWNER
(Built for)</th></tr>
<tr><th>G Ton
N Ton</th><th>L Ft
B Ft</th></tr>
<tr><td>CAPEL
160822
H17 Steam Trawler</td><td>513
12.01.1929
14.02.1929</td><td>356
145</td><td>140.2
24.6</td><td>C.D.Holmes
96 NHP
10.9 knots</td><td>F & T Ross Ltd
Hull</td></tr>
<tr><td colspan="6">26.04.1939 Sold to Boyd Line Hull renamed ARCTIC HUNTER.
Aug 1939 Rqd by the Royal Navy as a minesweeper No. FY 1614. May 1945 returned.
05.09.1950 Lord Line Hull renamed LORD FOYLE.
1952 Vessel sold to BISCO and allocated to Thos Young & Sons Ltd. 06.10.1952 Arrived Sunderland for breaking up.</td></tr>
<tr><td>KINGSTON SAPPHIRE
160824
H39 Steam Trawler</td><td>514
28.01.1929
27.02.1929</td><td>352
149</td><td>140.3
24.0</td><td>C.D.Holmes
96 NHP
10.9 knots</td><td>Kingston Steam
Trawling Co Ltd
Hull</td></tr>
<tr><td colspan="6">(1939 Lengthened to 151.5 ft 357 Gross tons) Work carried out by Smiths Dock Co Ltd, Middlesbrough.
4.09.1939 Rqd by the Royal Navy as an armed boarding vessel No. FY 4.81. Based at Gibraltar.
05.10.1940 Vessel torpedoed and sunk by the Italian Submarine NANI (Captain Polizzi) (b 1938) West of Gibraltar in approx position 36° N 007° W. Twenty-eight crew were rescued by a Spanish tanker after spending fifteen days in the ship's lifeboat and landed at Huelua. Thirteen crew lost.</td></tr>
<tr><td>MONIMIA
160825
H43 Steam Trawler</td><td>515
12.02.1929
19.03.1929</td><td>374
156</td><td>140.3
24.6</td><td>C.D.Holmes
96 NHP
10.9 knots</td><td>Henriksen & Co Ltd
Hull</td></tr>
<tr><td colspan="6">Aug 1939 Rqd by the Royal Navy as a minesweeper No. FY 677. 30.05.1946 returned.
1947 Stranded at Norway. 14.02.1948 Sold to Scarisbrick Steam Trawling Co Ltd, Fleetwood (FD266).
1956 Vessel sold for scrap to B J Nijkerk S/A, Belgium. 24.05.1956 Left Fleetwood for Antwerp for breaking up.</td></tr>
<tr><td>KINGSTON JACINTH
160828
H44 Steam Trawler</td><td>516
28.02.1929
03.04.1929</td><td>352
149</td><td>140.3
24.0</td><td>C.D.Holmes
96 NHP
10.7 knots</td><td>Kingston Steam
Trawling Co Ltd
Hull</td></tr>
<tr><td colspan="6">(1939 Lengthened to 151.5 ft 357 Gross tons) Work carried out by Smiths Dock Co Ltd, Middlesbrough.
Aug 1939 Rqd by the Royal Navy as an armed boarding vessel No. FY 4.45.
12.01.1943 Vessel sunk by mine off Portsmouth 4 cables south of EA 5 buoy, 11 miles east south-east of Selsey Bill .</td></tr>
<tr><td>VARANGA
160968
GY61 Steam Trawler</td><td>517
14.03.1929
25.04.1929</td><td>361
171</td><td>140.3
24.6</td><td>C.D.Holmes
96 NHP
10.8 knots</td><td>Letten Bros Ltd
Grimsby</td></tr>
<tr><td colspan="6">1930 Sold to Atlas Steam Fishing Co Ltd, Grimsby.
29.08.1939 Rqd by the Royal Navy as a minesweeper No. FY 1625. 1945 returned.
16.09.1945 to Hudson Bros. Ltd, Hull. 1946 to Iago Steam Trawlers Ltd, London renamed RED CRUSADER (LO462).
1955 Vessel sold for scrap to Jacques Bakker & Zonen, Belgium. 16.04.1955 Arrived Bruges for breaking up.</td></tr>
<tr><td>HAMMOND
160970
GY80 Steam Trawler</td><td>518
28.03.1929
14.05.1929</td><td>351
148</td><td>140.0
24.1</td><td>Amos & Smith
91 NHP
10.7 knots</td><td>Perihelion Steam
Fishing Co Ltd
Grimsby</td></tr>
<tr><td colspan="6">1935 Sold To Cia. Portuguesa de Pessca, Lisbon, Portugal renamed ALCÔA.
1986 Vessel deleted from Lloyds Register of Shipping.</td></tr>
<tr><td>KINGSTON TURQUOISE
160834
H45 Steam Trawler</td><td>519
27.04.1929
23.05.1929</td><td>352
149</td><td>140.8
24.0</td><td>C.D.Holmes
96 NHP
10.9 knots</td><td>Kingston Steam
Trawling Co Ltd
Hull</td></tr>
<tr><td colspan="6">(1937 Lengthened to 151.5 ft 357 Gross tons) Work carried out by Smiths Dock Co Ltd, Middlesbrough.
26.08.1939 Rqd by the Royal Navy as an armed boarding vessel (1940) anti-submarine No. FY 4.91. 27.11.1945 returned.
09.08.1945 Sold to Trawlers Grimsby Ltd, Grimsby renamed (1946) CUNNINGHAM (GY86).
Jan 1953 to Ravendale Trawlers, Grimsby. Apr 1953 to Derwent Trawlers, Grimsby.
1957 Vessel sold for scrap to Van den Bossche & Co, Belgium. 30.11.1957 Arrived Boom for breaking up.</td></tr>
<tr><td>LADY ELEANOR
160836
H50 Steam Trawler</td><td>520
11.05.1929
08.06.1929</td><td>360
149</td><td>140.2
24.6</td><td>C.D.Holmes
96 NHP
10.8 knots</td><td>Jutland Amalgamated
Trawlers Ltd
Hull</td></tr>
<tr><td colspan="6">12.03.1937 Sold to Loyal Steam Fishing Co Ltd, Grimsby renamed EQUERRY (GY375).
(1939 Lengthened to 151.5 ft 357 Gross tons) Work carried out by Smiths Dock Co Ltd, Middlesbrough.
Aug 1939 Rqd by the Royal Navy as a minesweeper No. FY 668. 24.10.1945 returned.
1957 Vessel sold to BISCO and allocated to C W Dorkin & Co Ltd.
07.09.1957 Left Grimsby for the River Tyne for breaking up.</td></tr>
</table>

<table>
<tr><th rowspan="2">NAME
Official No.
Port Letters Numbers</th><th rowspan="2">Yard No.
Launched
Registered</th><th colspan="2">Registered</th><th rowspan="2">Engine Builder
Horse Power
Reg'd Speed</th><th rowspan="2">OWNER
(Built for)</th></tr>
<tr><th>G Ton
N Ton</th><th>L Ft
B Ft</th></tr>
<tr><td>GAMBRI
160972
GY99 Steam Trawler</td><td>521
25.05.1929
27.06.1929</td><td>349
152</td><td>140.2
24.6</td><td>C.D.Holmes
96 NHP
11.1 knots</td><td>Grant & Baker Steam
Fishing Co Ltd
Grimsby</td></tr>
<tr><td colspan="6">1932 Sold to Howe Steam Fishing Co Ltd, Grimsby.
28.05.1934 to Marine Steam Fishing Co Ltd, Hull renamed RUNSWICK BAY (H33).
25.08.1939 Rqd by the Royal Navy as a minesweeper No. FY 750 with South Atlantic Command.
15.11.1942 with West African Command. 18.07.1946 returned.
26.06.1944 to Perihelion Steam Fishing Co, Grimsby.
1947 to Crampin Steam Fishing Co Ltd, Grimsby renamed HASSETT (GY489).
18.09.1953 Vessel wrecked in heavy weather at Aukeingill , 10 miles north of Wick, The Wick lifeboat found the HASSETT but was unable to get alongside due to rough seas and shoal water. The destroyer HMS SCORPION (b 1942) arrived and floodlit the wreck to assist the Coastguard rescue team. who managed to get a line to the trawler and fifteen crew were rescued by breeches buoy. Five other crewmen were swept overboard and lost.</td></tr>
<tr><td>KINGSTON PERIDOT
160840
H55 Steam Trawler</td><td>522
08.06.1929
11.07.1929</td><td>352
137</td><td>140.5
24.0</td><td>C.D.Holmes
96 NHP
11.1 knots</td><td>Kingston Steam
Trawling Co Ltd
Hull</td></tr>
<tr><td colspan="6">(1937 Lengthened to 151.5 ft 356 Gross tons) Work carried out by Smiths Dock Co Ltd, Middlesbrough.
31.08.1939 Rqd by the Royal Navy armed boarding vessel(1941) anti-submarine trawler No. FY 4.69. 07.12.1945 returned.
22.06.1940 KINGSTON PERIDOT towed the disabled Swedish destroyer PUKE (x Italian BETTINO RICASOLI b 1926) from near the Færoe Islands to Scapa Flow. This caused a major diplomatic incident.
09.08.1945 Sold to Grimsby Industries Ltd, Grimsby (GY89).
Sep 1945 to Trawlers Grimsby Ltd, Grimsby renamed (1946) STOCKHAM.
1948 to Wyre Steam Trawlers Ltd, Fleetwood WYRE MONITOR (FD304).
1954 Vessel sold for scrap Haulbowline Industries. 16.11.1954 Arrived Passage West, Cork for breaking up.</td></tr>
<tr><td>ST. HONORIOUS
160846
H66 Steam Trawler</td><td>523
25.06.1929
25.07.1929</td><td>357
155</td><td>140.3
24.0</td><td>C.D.Holmes
96 NHP
10.9 knots</td><td>Thomas Hamling & Co Ltd
Hull</td></tr>
<tr><td colspan="6">19.01.1933 Vessel wrecked Asmundarstadhir, north-east coast of Iceland. All crew rescued.</td></tr>
<tr><td>ST. GERONTIUS
160848
H69 Steam Trawler</td><td>524
09.07.1929
14.08.1929</td><td>357
155</td><td>140.3
24.0</td><td>C.D.Holmes
96 NHP
10.9 knots</td><td>Thomas Hamling & Co Ltd
Hull</td></tr>
<tr><td colspan="6">25.02.1939 Sold to the Royal Navy converted to a Berberis Class mine-sweeper renamed MAPLE No. T38.
1946 to NV Vissch Omderneming "De Vem", Ijmuiden, Holland renamed SUMATRA (IJM62).
1956 Vessel sold for scrap to Frank Rijsdyck, Holland. Jun 1956 Arrived at Hendrick Ido Antracht for breaking up.</td></tr>
<tr><td>BEVERLAC
160849
H72 Steam Trawler</td><td>525
23.07.1929
22.08.1929</td><td>352
150</td><td>140.3
24.0</td><td>C.D.Holmes
96 NHP
11.1 knots</td><td>W A Massey & Sons Ltd
Hull</td></tr>
<tr><td colspan="6">22.12.1938 Sold to Loch Fishing Co. Ltd, Hull renamed (06.02.1939) LOCH ERIBOLL.
04.08.1939 Rqd by the Royal Navy as a minesweeper No. FY 704.
12.10.1945 Vessel sank following a collision with the American cargo vessel ss SIDNEY SHERMAN (7244 gt/ b 1943) off Start Point, Orkney Island. Vessel lost whilst serving with mine-sweeper group 13 based at Grimsby.</td></tr>
<tr><td>GALVANI
160855
H88 Steam Trawler</td><td>526
07.08.1929
26.09.1929</td><td>353
138</td><td>140.3
24.0</td><td>C.D.Holmes
96 NHP
11.6 knots</td><td>F & T Ross Ltd
Hull</td></tr>
<tr><td colspan="6">08.06.1940 Rqd by the Royal Navy - auxiliary patrol vessel (1941) minesweeper No. 4.71. 28.08.1945 returned.
01.04.1946 Sold to Iago Steam Trawlers Ltd, London renamed RED SWORD (LO459).
11.08.1955 to Thos Hamling & Co Ltd, Hull (H80).
1955 Vessel sold to BISCO and allocated to C W Dorkin & Co Ltd. 26.03.1956 Arrived Sunderland for breaking up.</td></tr>
<tr><td>MARZ
160983
GY182 Steam Trawler</td><td>527
13.02.1929
19.03.1929</td><td>380
174</td><td>141.9
24.7</td><td>C.D.Holmes
96 NHP
10.7 knots</td><td>Rinovia Steam Fishing Co Ltd
Grimsby</td></tr>
<tr><td colspan="6">17.06.1932 Vessel wrecked on rocks to the west of the lighthouse, on the north side of the Island of Stroma, Pentland Firth. In dense fog whilst homeward bound from Iceland to Grimsby. A boat launched from the trawler capsized and one man was lost. Considerable difficulty was experienced in locating the trawler but eventually the Thurso lifeboat found the MARZ and took off the remaining fifteen crewmen and landed them at Scrabster.</td></tr>
<tr><td>DROMIO
160859
H94 Steam Trawler</td><td>528
23.09.1929
02.11.1929</td><td>380
143</td><td>140.9
25.5</td><td>Amos & Smith
129 NHP
10.8 knots</td><td>Hull Northern Fishing Co Ltd
Hull</td></tr>
<tr><td colspan="6">27.08.1939 Rqd by the Royal Navy as a mine-sweeper based at Sheerness.
22.12.1939 Vessel sank following a collision north of Whitby.</td></tr>
</table>

Yard No.525
1929 BEVERLAC
Photo:- Harry Cartlidge Collection

Yard No.531
1929 WESTRAY FIRTH
Photo:- Harry Cartlidge Collection

Yard No.550
1930 WELSBACH
Photo:- Harry Cartlidge Collection

<table>
<tr><th>NAME
Official No.
Port Letters Numbers</th><th>Yard No.
Launched
Registered</th><th colspan="2">Registered</th><th>Engine Builder
Horse Power
Reg'd Speed</th><th>OWNER
(Built for)</th></tr>
<tr><th></th><th></th><th>G Ton
N Ton</th><th>L Ft
B Ft</th><th></th><th></th></tr>
<tr><td>ORSINO
160865
H115 Steam Trawler</td><td>529
05.10.1929
19.11.1929</td><td>380
143</td><td>140.9
25.5</td><td>Amos & Smith
129 NHP
10.8 knots</td><td>Hull Northern Fishing Co Ltd
Hull</td></tr>
<tr><td colspan="6">01.04.1938 Sold to N V Zeèvisscherij Maats "Walrus" , Ijmuiden, Holland renamed WALRUS (IJM24).
1940 Rqd by the German Navy No. M3410 - V6510.
14.09.1943 Vessel sank by Royal Navy motor torpedo boats west of Scheveningen in approx position 52° 13'N 004° 09'E .</td></tr>
<tr><td>CASSIO
160870
H138 Steam Trawler</td><td>530
21.10.1929
28.11.1929</td><td>380
143</td><td>140.9
25.5</td><td>Amos & Smith
99 NHP
1085 knots</td><td>Hull Northern Fishing Co Ltd
Hull</td></tr>
<tr><td colspan="6">01.04.1938 Sold to N V Zeèvisscherij Maats "Flamingo", Ijmuiden, Holland renamed FLAMINGO (IJM25).
1942 Rqd by the German Navy No. M3420. 1945 returned.
1956 Vessel sold for scrap to Hansa Rohstoff Verwertung, Dusseldorf. Dec 1956 Arrived Dordrecht for breaking up.</td></tr>
<tr><td>SOLWAY FIRTH
160860
H107 Steam Trawler</td><td>531
24.08.1929
30.10.1929</td><td>358
154</td><td>140.3
24.0</td><td>C.D.Holmes
96 NHP
10.8 knots</td><td>J Stewart (Hull)
Trawling Co Ltd
Hull</td></tr>
<tr><td colspan="6">08.01.1931 Sold to Firth Steam Trawling Co Ltd, Hull. 20.06.1931 to H W Hall (Thos Hamling & Co Ltd), Hull.
09.01.1939 to Premier Steam Fishing Co Ltd, Grimsby renamed EPINE (GY7).
03.09.1939 Rqd by the Royal Navy as a minesweeper No. FY 682. Jan 1946 returned.
13.03.1948 Vessel wrecked on rocks at Snæfellsnes, Faxafloi west coast of Iceland in a severe gale and blizzard.
An Icelandic rescue party managed to get a line to the trawler and four crew were rescued by breeches buoy, one other managed to swim ashore but fourteen crew were lost as the wreck was swept by heavy seas.</td></tr>
<tr><td>WESTRAY FIRTH
160867
H125 Steam Trawler</td><td>532
07.10.1929
15.11.1929</td><td>358
154</td><td>140.3
24.0</td><td>C.D.Holmes
96 NHP
10.8 knots</td><td>J Stewart (Hull)
Trawling Co Ltd
Hull</td></tr>
<tr><td colspan="6">19.01.1931 Sold to Firth Steam Trawling Co Ltd, Hull. 15.06.1931 to H W Hall (Thos Hamling & Co Ltd), Hull.
09.01.1939 to Premier Steam Fishing Co Ltd, Grimsby renamed VILDA (GY4).
08.01.1940 Rqd by the Royal Navy as a boom defence vessel No. Z 118. 27.09.1946 returned.
1955 Vessel sold to BISCO and allocated to C W Dorkin & Co Ltd. 09.07.1955 Arrived Gateshead for breaking up.</td></tr>
<tr><td>VENUS

GK519 Steam Trawler</td><td>533
16.11.1929
19.12.1929</td><td>432
183</td><td>142.8
25.1</td><td>Amos & Smith
108 NHP
10.7 knots</td><td>H / F Belgaum
Hafnarfjordur
Iceland</td></tr>
<tr><td colspan="6">27.02.1937 Sold to Hlutafelaginu Venusi Hafnarfjord.
01.03.1962 Vessel sold to foreign shipbreakers and broken up.</td></tr>
<tr><td>LADY ENID
160873
H172 Steam Trawler</td><td>534
20.11.1929
20.12.1929</td><td>354
149</td><td>140.2
24.6</td><td>C.D.Holmes
96 NHP
11 knots</td><td>Jutland Amalgamated
Trawlers Ltd
Hull</td></tr>
<tr><td colspan="6">04.03.1937 Sold to Standard Steam Fishing Co Ltd, Grimsby renamed CURTANA (GY369).
31.08.1939 Rqd by the Royal Navy as a minesweeper No. FY 674. 08.05.1946 returned.
21.08.1953 to J. Marr & Son Ltd, Hull. 31.08.1953 Laid up at Alexandra Dock, Grimsby.
01.04.1954 Vessel sold for scrap to J.W. Draper & Son Grimsby and broken up at the fish dock slips.</td></tr>
<tr><td>LADY MARGOT
160875
H188 Steam Trawler</td><td>535
02.12.1929
08.01.1930</td><td>354
149</td><td>140.2
24.6</td><td>C.D.Holmes
96 NHP
11 knots</td><td>Jutland Amalgamated
Trawlers Ltd
Hull</td></tr>
<tr><td colspan="6">23.03.1937 Sold to Standard Steam Fishing Co Ltd, Grimsby renamed SICYON (GY376).
Sep 1939 Rqd by the Royal Navy as a minesweeper No. FY 669. 13.07.1946 returned.
21.08.1953 to J. Marr & Son Hull. 31.08.1953 Laid up at Alexandra Dock, Grimsby.
01.04. 1954 Vessel sold for scrap to J.W. Draper & Son, Grimsby and broken up at the fish dock slips.</td></tr>
<tr><td>WILLIAM WESNEY
160981
GY168 Steam Trawler</td><td>536
23.12.1929
03.02.1930</td><td>364
171</td><td>145.9
24.2</td><td>Amos & Smith
91 NHP
10.5 knots</td><td>Crampin Steam
Fishing Co Ltd
Grimsby</td></tr>
<tr><td colspan="6">16.09.1939 Rqd by the Royal Navy as a mine-sweeper.
07.11.1940 Vessel sunk by mine off Orfordness approx position 51° 33.8' N 001°33.6' E. Five crew lost.
Lost whilst serving with mine-sweeper group 5 based at Harwich.</td></tr>
<tr><td>LOCH INVER
148972
A89 Steam Trawler</td><td>537
15.01.1930
13.02.1930</td><td>356
151</td><td>140.3
24.0</td><td>C.D.Holmes
96 NHP
10.8 knots</td><td>A & M Smith Ltd
Aberdeen</td></tr>
<tr><td colspan="6">20.02.1930 Sold to Hellyer Bros, Hull (H195). 26.08.1935 to Caledonian Fishing Co Ltd, Hull.
May1940 Rqd by the Royal Navy an anti-submarine/auxiliary patrol vessel based at Harwich.
24.09.1940 Vessel posted missing:- lost with all hands presumed mined off Harwich.</td></tr>
</table>

<table>
<tr><th rowspan="2">NAME
Official No.
Port Letters Numbers</th><th rowspan="2">Yard No.
Launched
Registered</th><th colspan="2">Registered</th><th rowspan="2">Engine Builder
Horse Power
Reg'd Speed</th><th rowspan="2">OWNER
(Built for)</th></tr>
<tr><th>G Ton
N Ton</th><th>L Ft
B Ft</th></tr>
<tr><td>HOWE
160982
GY177 Steam Trawler</td><td>538
30.01.1930
27.02.1930</td><td>349
152</td><td>140.2
24.6</td><td>C.D.Holmes
96 NHP
11.1 knots</td><td>Howe Steam Fishing Co Ltd /
W Grant
Grimsby</td></tr>
<tr><td colspan="6">19.11.1931 Vessel wrecked on Cape Ruche west coast of Bear Island. The Hull trawler IMPERIALIST H143 (see Yard No.457) attempted a rescue from seaward but this proved to dangerous, and so twenty-five trawlers from Hull and Grimsby landed over one hundred men on the opposite side of the island to form rescue parties. After 60 hours the rescuers succeeded in reaching the wreck and all fifteen crew were hauled up the three hundred foot cliff to safety.</td></tr>
<tr><td>KINGSTON OLIVINE
160890
H209 Steam Trawler</td><td>539
15.03.1930
10.04.1930</td><td>363
162</td><td>140.3
24.6</td><td>C.D.Holmes
96 NHP
11 knots</td><td>Kingston Steam
Trawling Co Ltd
Hull</td></tr>
<tr><td colspan="6">(1937 Lengthened to 151.5 ft 378 Gross tons) Work carried out by Smiths Dock Co Ltd, Middlesbrough.
08.08.1939 Rqd by the Royal Navy as an anti-submarine trawler (1942) minesweeper No. FY 193. 11.05.1942 returned.
1947 Sold to Swansea Trawlers Ltd Swansea renamed LANGLAND BAY (SA72).
18.09.1947 to Eton Fishing Co, Hull. 26.05.1950 to Hudson Bros, Hull.
01.01.1953 to, Milford Haven Steam Trawling Co Ltd, Milford Haven.
1954 to Mason Trawlers , Fleetwood renamed MASONA (FD16).
1956 Vessel sold to The West of Scotland Shipbreaking Co Ltd. 02.11.1956 Arrived Troon for breaking up.</td></tr>
<tr><td>KINGSTON CORAL
160895
H241 Steam Trawler</td><td>540
17.04.1930
17.05.1930</td><td>365
137</td><td>141.3
24.6</td><td>C.D.Holmes
96 NHP
11 knots</td><td>Kingston Steam
Trawling Co Ltd
Hull</td></tr>
<tr><td colspan="6">25.11.1935 Sold to the Royal Navy converted to a Berberis Class minesweeper No. T19 renamed HOLLY.
May 1946 to P/f J F Kjolbro, Klaksvig, Færoe Islands renamed DRAGABERG.
1961 to Lars Gunderson & Per Olsen, Norway. 28.07.1961 Vessel sank after striking rocks off Faeringehavn, Greenland.</td></tr>
<tr><td>KINGSTON CYANITE
162175
H237 Steam Trawler</td><td>541
15.05.1930
12.06.1930</td><td>365
137</td><td>141.3
24.6</td><td>C.D.Holmes
96 NHP
11 knots</td><td>Kingston Steam
Trawling Co
Hull</td></tr>
<tr><td colspan="6">25.11.1935 Sold to the Royal Navy converted to a Berberis Class minesweeper No. T29 renamed LAUREL.
1944 wreck dispersal vessel No. FY 4.417 based at Port Tallbot.
1948 to Granton Trawlers Co Ltd Granton renamed STRATHYRE (GN46).
1951 to Clifton Steam Trawling Co Ltd, Fleetwood renamed PATRICIA HAGUE (FD58).
1955 Vessel sold to The West of Scotland Shipbreaking Co Ltd . 23.05.1955 Arrived Troon for breaking up.</td></tr>
<tr><td>AVANTURINE
160887
H197 Steam Trawler</td><td>542
01.03.1930
24.03.1930</td><td>296
130</td><td>128.9
24.0</td><td>C.D.Holmes
89 NHP
11 knots</td><td>Kingston Steam
Trawling Co Ltd
Hull</td></tr>
<tr><td colspan="6">04.06.1940 Rqd by the Royal Navy as an auxiliary patrol vessel. 1941 minesweeper No. FY 1886.
01.12.1943 Vessel sunk by E-boat torpedo off Beachy Head whilst under tow. All crew lost.</td></tr>
<tr><td>MALMATA
160984
GY199 Steam Trawler</td><td>543
20.03.1930
24.04.1930</td><td>355
169</td><td>140.4
24.7</td><td>Amos & Smith
91 NHP
11.2 knots</td><td>Malmata Fishing Co Ltd
Grimsby</td></tr>
<tr><td colspan="6">1936 Sold to Dalmatia Fishing Co, Grimsby renamed GREGORY.
30.08.1939 Rqd by the Royal Navy as an auxiliary patrol FY 1875. 04.07.1945 returned.
21.10.1939 to Crampin Steam Fishing Co Ltd, Grimsby.
1956 Vessel sold for scrap to Van Heyghen Freres, Belgium. 30.06.1956 Arrived Ghent for breaking up.</td></tr>
<tr><td>JERIA
160985
GY224 Steam Trawler</td><td>544
03.04.1930
15.05.1930</td><td>349
144</td><td>140.3
24.6</td><td>Amos & Smith
98 NHP
10.5 knots</td><td>Great Grimsby and East Coast
Steam Fishing Co Ltd
Grimsby</td></tr>
<tr><td colspan="6">23.01.1935 Vessel sank after being overwhelmed in severe weather in Breithi Bay, Iceland. Lost with all thirteen crew. The trawler STOKE CITY GY114 (422 gt/ b 1935) which responded to the distress call of the JERIA was herself badly damaged in a courageous attempt to reach the stricken trawler.</td></tr>
<tr><td>REGAL
160988
GY245 Steam Trawler</td><td>545
03.05.1930
03.06.1930</td><td>348
144</td><td>140.3
24.6</td><td>Amos & Smith
98 NHP
10.5 knots</td><td>Loyal Steam Fishing Co Ltd
Grimsby</td></tr>
<tr><td colspan="6">25.12.1937 Vessel wrecked off Gerdaholni near Utskalor during severe weather in the early hours of Christmas day. Four crew were rescued by breeches buoy the other nine crew landed safely ashore in the ship's boat. The Icelandic gunboat THOR made all haste to the scene arriving at midday but all the crew were by then safely ashore.</td></tr>
</table>

Yard No.551
1930 LADY ELSA as ETRURIA
Photo by courtesy of The Grimsby Evening Telegraph

Yard No.557A
1930 MALAYAN
Photo:- Author's Collection

Yard No.563
1931 LACENNIA
Photo by courtesy of The Grimsby Evening Telegraph

<table>
<tr><td rowspan="2">NAME
Official No.
Port Letters Numbers</td><td rowspan="2">Yard No.
Launched
Registered</td><td colspan="2">Registered</td><td rowspan="2">Engine Builder
Horse Power
Reg'd Speed</td><td rowspan="2">OWNER
(Built for)</td></tr>
<tr><td>G Ton
N Ton</td><td>L Ft
B Ft</td></tr>
<tr><td>SILANION
160992
GY246 Steam Trawler</td><td>546
29.05.1930
01.07.1930</td><td>349
144</td><td>140.3
24.6</td><td>Amos & Smith
98 NHP
10.5 knots</td><td>Standard Steam
Fishing Co Ltd
Grimsby</td></tr>
<tr><td colspan="6">25.02.1933 Vessel wrecked at Torness Point, south coast of Hoy, Orkney Islands Pentland Firth whilst outward bound from Grimsby to Iceland. Distress rockets were fired, these were seen by lighthouse men at Dunnet Head and a short while later the Longhope lifeboat arrived alongside the stricken trawler and took off her thirteen crewmen.</td></tr>
<tr><td>VINUR
160993
GY249 Steam Trawler</td><td>547
12.06.1930
16.07.1930</td><td>406
161</td><td>142.7
25.1</td><td>Amos & Smith
99 NHP
10.9 knots</td><td>Vinur Steam Fishing Co Ltd
Grimsby</td></tr>
<tr><td colspan="6">Built for Little & Olgeirrsson but sold before completion. 1936 renamed BRITISH.
27.08.1939 Rqd by the Royal Navy as a minesweeper No. FY 506. 11.01.1946 returned.
1942 to Northern Trawlers Ltd, Grimsby.1954 to Wyre Steam Trawlers Ltd, Fleetwood renamed WYRE BRITISH (FD24).
1957 Vessel sold for scrap to Van Heyghen Freres, Belgium. 19.10.1957 Arrived Ghent for breaking up.</td></tr>
<tr><td>LEONIDAS
162186
H267 Steam Trawler</td><td>548
26.06.1930
31.07.1930</td><td>369
159</td><td>140.3
24.6</td><td>Amos & Smith
99 NHP
10.7 knots</td><td>Christensen & Co Ltd
Hull</td></tr>
<tr><td colspan="6">(1937 Lengthened to 151.5 ft 390 Gross tons) Work carried out by Smiths Dock Co Ltd, Middlesbrough.
17.05.1938 Sold to Hudson Steam Fishing Co Ltd, Hull renamed CAPE BARRACOUTA.
26.08.1939 Rqd by the Royal Navy as a mine-sweeper. 30.10.1939 returned.
03.06.1940 Rqd by the Royal Navy as an auxiliary patrol vessel (1941) minesweeper No. 4.122. 17.08.1946 returned.
24.01.1945 to Hudson Bros Trawlers Ltd, Hull. 28.04.1947 to Trawlers Grimsby Ltd, Grimsby (GY479).
1948 to Heward Trawlers Ltd, Fleetwood renamed NEW PRINCE (LO471).
1959 Vessel sold for scrap to Van Heyghen Freres, Belgium. 18.06.1959 Left Fleetwood for Ghent for breaking up.</td></tr>
<tr><td>ARKWRIGHT
162198
H314 Steam Trawler</td><td>549
30.07.1930
10.09.1930</td><td>369
149</td><td>143.5
24.5</td><td>C.D.Holmes
96 NHP
10.4 knots</td><td>F & T Ross Ltd
Hull</td></tr>
<tr><td colspan="6">31.08.1939 Rqd by the Royal Navy as a minesweeper No. FY 653. 1946 returned.
01.04.1946 Sold to Iago Steam Trawlers Ltd, London renamed RED CHARGER (LO460).
28.03.1955 to J Marr & Son Ltd, Hull. 1955 Vessel sold to BISCO allocated to The West of Scotland Shipbreaking Co Ltd.
03.06.1955 Arrived Troon for breaking up.</td></tr>
<tr><td>WELSBACH
162188
H277 Steam Trawler</td><td>550
10.07.1930
08.08.1930</td><td>369
149</td><td>143.6
24.5</td><td>C.D.Holmes
96 NHP
10.4 knots</td><td>F & T Ross Ltd
Hull</td></tr>
<tr><td colspan="6">Sep 1939 Rqd by the Royal Navy as a minesweeper No. FY 652 renamed WELLSBACH. 16.05.1946 returned.
1946 Sold to Wyre Trawlers, Fleetwood renamed WYRE WARRIOR (FD178).
1955 Vessel sold for scrap to Jacques Bakker & Zonen, Belgium.
20.03.1955 Left Fleetwood towards Bruges but towed into Milford Haven with engine trouble.
02.04.1955 Departed Milford Haven under tow by the trawler RED CRUSADER LO462 (see Yard No. 517) also bound for the breakers yard. 09.04.1955 Arrived Bruges for breaking up.</td></tr>
<tr><td>LADY ELSA
162195
H287 Steam Trawler</td><td>551
26.07.1930
24.08.1930</td><td>373
158</td><td>143.5
24.7</td><td>C.D.Holmes
96 NHP
11 knots</td><td>Jutland Amalgamated
Trawlers Ltd
Hull</td></tr>
<tr><td colspan="6">05.03.1937 Sold to Great Grimsby and East Coast Steam Fishing Co Ltd, Grimsby renamed ETRURIA (GY365).
(1939 Lengthened to 159.2 ft 373 Gross tons) Work carried out by Smiths Dock Co Ltd, Middlesbrough.
18.12.1939 Damaged by German aircraft bombs 20 miles south-east of Duncansby Head Scotland.
31.05.1940 Rqd by the Royal Navy as an auxiliary patrol vessel (1941) boom defence vessel No. Z 187. 1946 returned.
1953 Vessel sold for scrap (£2,425) to B J Nijkirk S/A, Belgium.07.05.1954 Departed Grimsby for Antwerp for breaking up.</td></tr>
<tr><td>ST. JUST
162200
H320 Steam Trawler</td><td>552
23.08.1930
23.09.1930</td><td>377
158</td><td>145.0
24.6</td><td>C.D.Holmes
96 NHP
11.2 knots</td><td>St Andrew's Steam
Fishing Co Ltd
Hull</td></tr>
<tr><td colspan="6">(1938 Lengthened to 158.2 ft 394 Gross tons) Work carried out by Smiths Dock Co Ltd, Middlesbrough.
Sep 1939 Rqd by the Royal Navy as a minesweeper No. FY 673 renamed FIREFLY.
29.10.1945 returned and reverted. 31.08.1943 Sold to Heward Trawlers Ltd, Fleetwood (LO434).
1961 Vessel sold for scrap to Haulbowline Industries Ltd.01.03.1961 Arrived Passage West Cork for breaking up.</td></tr>
<tr><td>GALLEON
160994
GY269 Steam Trawler</td><td>553
30.08.1930
30.09.1930</td><td>362
173</td><td>145.9
24.2</td><td>Amos & Smith
91 NHP
11 knots</td><td>Perihelion Steam
Fishing Co Ltd
Grimsby</td></tr>
<tr><td colspan="6">1938 Sold to Premier Steam Fishing Co Ltd, Grimsby renamed CALVI.
13.09.1939 Rqd by the Royal Navy as a mine-sweeper / 1940 based at Dover .
29.05.1940 Vessel sunk by German aircraft bombs whilst embarking Allied troops at Dunkirk during the evacuation.</td></tr>
</table>

<table>
<tr><th rowspan="2">NAME
Official No.
Port Letters Numbers</th><th rowspan="2">Yard No.
Launched
Registered</th><th colspan="2">Registered</th><th rowspan="2">Engine Builder
Horse Power
Reg'd Speed</th><th rowspan="2">OWNER
(Built for)</th></tr>
<tr><th>G Ton
N Ton</th><th>L Ft
B Ft</th></tr>
<tr><td>GEORGE AUNGER
160996
GY285 Steam Trawler</td><td>554
11.09.1930
14.10.1930</td><td>363
173</td><td>145.9
24.2</td><td>Amos & Smith
91 NHP
10.9 knots</td><td>Bunch Steam Fishing Co Ltd
Grimsby</td></tr>
<tr><td colspan="6">1935 renamed SANDHAM. Jun 1938 Sold to W. Butt, Grimsby.
Jul 1938 Sold to Premier Steam Fishing Co Ltd, Grimsby renamed BURKE.
13.09.1939 Rqd by the Royal Navy as a minesweeper No. FY 605 North Atlantic Command.
(1944) wreck dispersal vessel. 1946 returned.
16.07.1955 Vessel sold for scrap to B J Nijkirk S/A, Belgium and broken up at Antwerp.</td></tr>
<tr><td>KOPANES
162202
H502 Steam Trawler</td><td>555
24.09.1930
28.10.1930</td><td>397
151</td><td>142.7
25.1</td><td>Amos & Smith
99 NHP
10.7 knots</td><td>Oddsson & Co Ltd
Hull</td></tr>
<tr><td colspan="6">03.10.1933 Sold to W B Willey & Sons Ltd, Hull renamed GRAMPIAN. 18.01.1939 to East Riding Fishing Co Ltd, Hull.
(1939 Lengthened to 158.7 ft 409 Gross tons) Work carried out by Smiths Dock Co Ltd, Middlesbrough.
Sep 1939 Rqd by the Royal Navy as a minesweeper No. FY 546. 05.03.1946 returned.
01.01.1940 to Hudson Bros Ltd, Hull renamed (1946) CAPE PEMBROKE.
11.12.1946 to Ocean Steam Trawling Co Ltd, Hull renamed FROBISHER.
03.12.1948 to Short Blue Fishing Co Ltd, London (LO15).
1957 Vessel sold for scrap to Van Heyghen Freres, Belgium. 24.10.1957 Left Fleetwood for Ghent for breaking up.</td></tr>
<tr><td>RYLSTON
162204
H343 Steam Trawler</td><td>556
08.10.1930
10.11.1930</td><td>380
154</td><td>143.4
24.7</td><td>C.D.Holmes
104 NHP
10.9 knots</td><td>Henriksen & Co Ltd
Hull</td></tr>
<tr><td colspan="6">1939 renamed TERVANI.
(1939 Lengthened to 159.0 ft 409 Gross tons) Work carried out by Smiths Dock Co Ltd, Middlesbrough.
05.06.1940 Rqd by the Royal Navy as an auxiliary patrol vessel (1941) minesweeper No. FY 4.110.
07.02.1943 (at approx 2327 hrs) Vessel sunk by Italian submarine ACCIAIO (Commanded by Captain Beltrami) (b 1941) off Cape Bougaroni, Algeria in approx position 37° 02'N 006°15'E.</td></tr>
<tr><td>TUNISIAN
161001
GY319 Steam Trawler</td><td>557
11.10.1930
15.11.1930</td><td>238
93</td><td>122.6
22.1</td><td>C.D.Holmes
77 NHP
10.2 knots</td><td>Sir Thomas Robinson
& Sons Ltd
Grimsby</td></tr>
<tr><td colspan="6">20.10.1939 Rqd by the Royal Navy as a boom defence vessel No. Z 128.
09.07.1942 Vessel sunk by mine off Harwich 2.5 miles east of Languard Point.</td></tr>
<tr><td>MALAYAN
161002
GY322 Steam Trawler</td><td>557A
23.10.1930
25.11.1930</td><td>238
93</td><td>122.6
22.1</td><td>C.D.Holmes
77 NHP
10.2 knots</td><td>Sir Thomas Robinson
& Sons Ltd
Grimsby</td></tr>
<tr><td colspan="6">31.08.1939 Rqd by the Royal Navy as a minesweeper No. FY 596 renamed STONEFLY.
14.09.1945 returned and reverted.
23.01.1962 to Meletious N Sofras, Piræus, Greece renamed RITSA. 1965 renamed LINDOS.
1977 to Nicolaos Drouzas, Piræus. 1985 to General Maritime Enterprises Antwerp Ltd, Piræus.
1985 Vessel sold for scrap to shipbreakers in Greece and broken up.</td></tr>
<tr><td>ROSS
161005
GY329 Steam Trawler</td><td>558
24.11.1930
12.01.1931</td><td>348
153</td><td>140.2
24.6</td><td>C.D.Holmes
96 NHP
10.7 knots</td><td>Rugby Steam Fishing Co Ltd
Grimsby</td></tr>
<tr><td colspan="6">09.03.1934 Sold to Marine Steam Fishing Co Ltd, Hull renamed FILEY BAY (H27).
31.08.1939 Rqd by the Royal Navy as a minesweeper No. FY 679. 31.05.1945 returned.
18.10.1945 to Trawlers Grimsby Ltd, Grimsby (GY135).
1953 to Derwent Trawlers Ltd, Grimsby. 1955 to G F Sleight, Grimsby.
1956 Vessel sold for scrap to Van Heyghen Freres, Belgium. 26.07.1956 Arrived Ghent for breaking up.</td></tr>
<tr><td>Not Built</td><td>559</td><td></td><td></td><td></td><td></td></tr>
<tr><td>NORSE
162209
H348 Steam Trawler</td><td>560
06.11.1930
15.12.1930</td><td>351
138</td><td>140.3
24.6</td><td>C.D.Holmes
96 NHP
10.6 knots</td><td>Hellyer Bros Ltd
Hull</td></tr>
<tr><td colspan="6">1939 Sold to Shire Trawlers Ltd, Grimsby (GY197).
29.08.1939 Rqd by the Royal Navy as a minesweeper No. FY 1628. Mediterranean Command. 10.11.1944 returned.
01.04.1946 to p/f Jacob Haroldsen's Efterfölgere, Fuglefjord, Færoe Islands renamed KROSS-STEINUR.
Oct 1955 Vessel sold for scrap to H J Hansen, Odense, Denmark and broken up.</td></tr>
<tr><td>ANGUS
162211
H362 Steam Trawler</td><td>560A
20.11.1930
23.12.1930</td><td>351
138</td><td>140.3
24.6</td><td>C.D.Holmes
96 NHP
10.9 knots</td><td>Hull Northern Fishing Co Ltd
Hull</td></tr>
<tr><td colspan="6">07.04.1938 Stranded on Fitfail Head Foula Island Shetlands.
08.04.1938 Vessel foundered in deep water whilst an Aberdeen trawler was trying to tow her to port. All crew rescued.</td></tr>
</table>

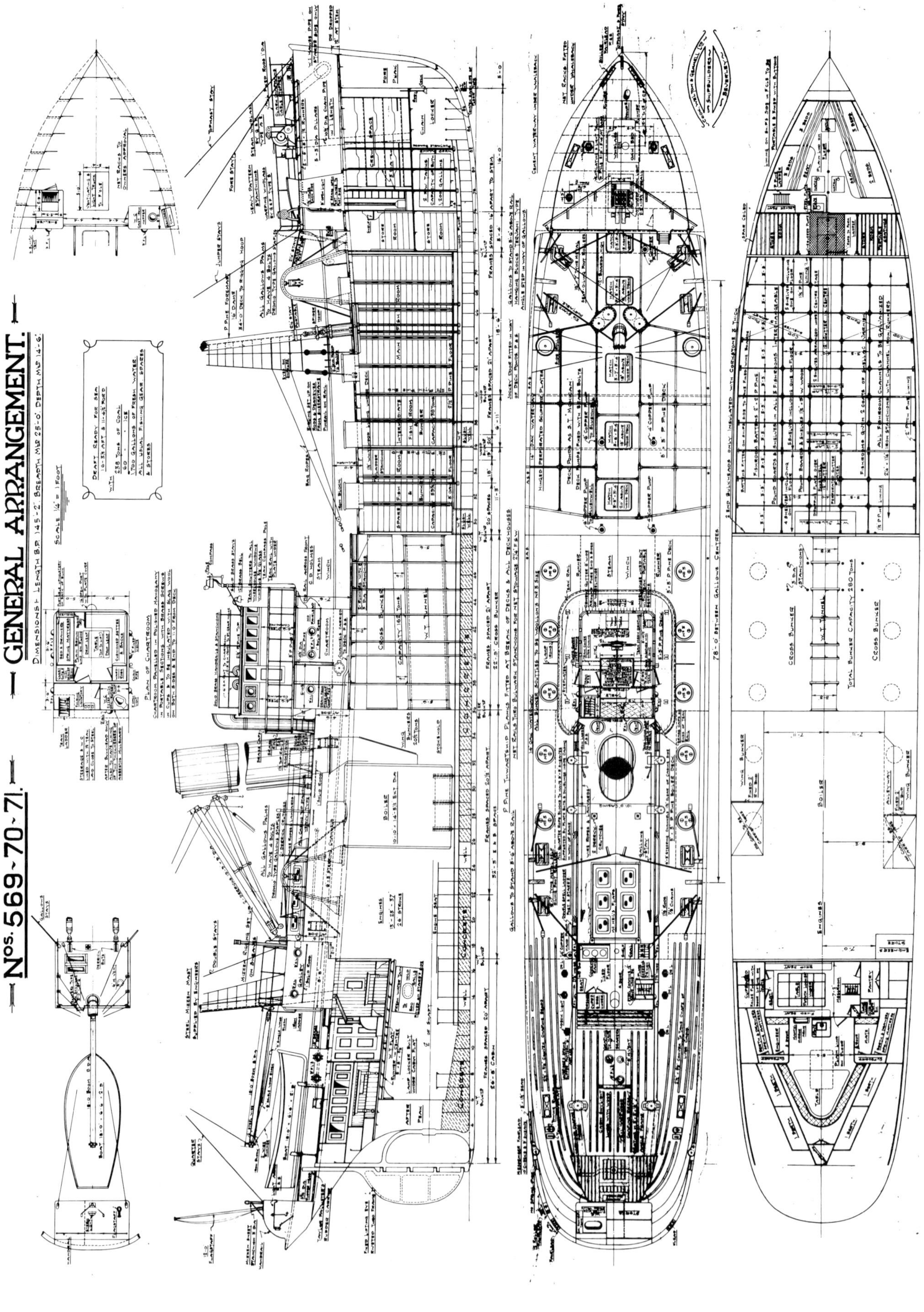
Nos. 569-70-71.
GENERAL ARRANGEMENT.
DIMENSIONS:- LENGTH B.P. 145'-2" BREADTH MLD 25'-0" DEPTH MLD 14'-6"
SCALE 1/4" = 1 FOOT

<table>
<tr><th rowspan="2">NAME
Official No.
Port Letters Numbers</th><th rowspan="2">Yard No.
Launched
Registered</th><th colspan="2">Registered</th><th rowspan="2">Engine Builder
Horse Power
Reg'd Speed</th><th rowspan="2">OWNER
(Built for)</th></tr>
<tr><th>G Ton
N Ton</th><th>L Ft
B Ft</th></tr>
<tr><td>EDWARDIAN
161004
GY328 Steam Trawler</td><td>561
06.12.1930
12.01.1931</td><td>348
148</td><td>140.3
24.6</td><td>Amos & Smith
96 NHP
10.5 knots</td><td>Loyal Steam Fishing Co Ltd
Grimsby</td></tr>
<tr><td colspan="6">Sep 1939 Rqd by the Royal Navy as a minesweeper No. FY 691. 08.01.1946 returned.
06.08.1948 Sold to Devon Fishing Co Ltd, Hull renamed OPHELIA (H576). 31.10.1952 to Hellyer Bros Ltd, Hull.
1954 Vessel sold to BISCO and allocated to J J King & Co Ltd. 08.01.1955 Arrived Gateshead for breaking up.</td></tr>
<tr><td>SOLON
161006
GY337 Steam Trawler</td><td>562
20.12.1930
28.01.1931</td><td>348
148</td><td>140.3
24.6</td><td>Amos & Smith
96 NHP
10.5 knots</td><td>Standard Steam
Fishing Co Ltd
Grimsby</td></tr>
<tr><td colspan="6">Sep 1939 Rqd by the Royal Navy as a minesweeper No. FY 601. 04.06.1946 returned.
06.08.1948 Sold to Devon Fishing Co Ltd, Hull renamed ORSINO (H579). 31.10.1952 to Hellyer Bros Ltd, Hull.
1954 Vessel sold to BISCO and allocated to J J King & Co Ltd. 08.01.1955 Arrived Gateshead for breaking up.</td></tr>
<tr><td>LACENNIA
161007
GY345 Steam Trawler</td><td>563
07.01.1931
09.02.1931</td><td>348
148</td><td>129.0
24.0</td><td>Amos & Smith
96 NHP
10.5 knots</td><td>Great Grimsby & East Coast
Steam Fishing Co Ltd
Grimsby</td></tr>
<tr><td colspan="6">Sep 1939 Rqd by the Royal Navy as a minesweeper No. FY 712. 16.04.1946 returned.
1954 Vessel sold for scrap (£2,225) to B J Nijkirk S/A, Belgium. 07.05.1954 Arrived Antwerp for breaking up.</td></tr>
<tr><td>SIBERITE
162242
H378 Steam Trawler</td><td>564
20.05.1931
02.07.1931</td><td>295
131</td><td>129.0
24.0</td><td>C.D.Holmes
89 NHP
11 knots</td><td>Kingston Steam
Trawling Co Ltd
Hull</td></tr>
<tr><td colspan="6">16.03.1936 Vessel wrecked under the high cliffs of Rora Head, Isle of Hoy, Orkney Islands during heavy rain
which obscured the shore, whilst homeward bound to Hull from the North Færoese fishing grounds.
All eleven crewmen were rescued by the Stromness lifeboat.</td></tr>
<tr><td>EUCLASE
162245
H384 Steam Trawler</td><td>565
30.05.1931
07.07.1931</td><td>295
131</td><td>129.0
24.0</td><td>C.D.Holmes
89 NHP
11.2 knots</td><td>Kingston Steam
Trawling Co Ltd
Hull</td></tr>
<tr><td colspan="6">12.02.1940 Rqd by the Royal Navy as a minesweeper No. FY 1636. 04.04.1946 returned.
20.02.1948 Sold to Lothian Trawlers Co Ltd, Granton (GN51).
22.09.1955 Vessel wrecked 2 miles south of Duncansby Head. 26.09.1955 Salvaging attempts abandoned.</td></tr>
<tr><td>BLAKKUR
162861
GY378 Steam Trawler</td><td>566
27.08.1931
06.10.1931</td><td>403
166</td><td>142.7
25.1</td><td>Amos & Smith
99 NHP
11 knots</td><td>Rinovia Steam Fishing Co Ltd
Grimsby</td></tr>
<tr><td colspan="6">1938 renamed RINOVIA no change of owner. 31.08.1939 Rqd by the Royal Navy as a mine-sweeper .
Sep 1940 Grounded at Dartmouth and re-floated.
02.11.1940 Vessel sunk by mine off Falmouth Bay 2.9 miles off St. Anthony Light.</td></tr>
<tr><td>WALPOLE
162862
GY385 Steam Trawler</td><td>567
14.09.1931
15.10.1931</td><td>387
185</td><td>142.2
24.9</td><td>C.D.Holmes
105 NHP
11 knots</td><td>E C Grant
Grimsby</td></tr>
<tr><td colspan="6">01.09.1939 Rqd by the Royal Navy as a minesweeper No. FY 681 renamed WATERFLY.
17.09.1942 Vessel sunk by German aircraft off Dungeness in approx position 50° 49.5'N 000° 54'E.
Vessel lost whilst serving with mine-sweeper group 46 based at Dover.</td></tr>
<tr><td>MOHICAN
162256
H391 Steam Trawler</td><td>568
12.10.1931
06.11.1931</td><td>374
152</td><td>145.8
24.6</td><td>C.D.Holmes
96 NHP
11.2 knots</td><td>Hellyer Bros Ltd
Hull</td></tr>
<tr><td colspan="6">19.04.1939 Vessel wrecked after stranding at Rangar Sands, Marker Fjord, south coast Iceland. All fourteen crew were
rescued by an Icelandic shore party using breeches buoy. Rough seas had prevented the crew reaching shore by ship's boat.
Attempts by the Icelandic gunboat AEGIR (162 gt/ b 1906) to tow the MOHICAN free were unsuccessful.</td></tr>
<tr><td>BASUTO
162260
H401 Steam Trawler</td><td>569
12.12.1931
09.01.1932</td><td>381
151</td><td>145.8
25.1</td><td>C.D.Holmes
102 NHP
11.2 knots</td><td>Hellyer Bros Ltd
Hull</td></tr>
<tr><td colspan="6">(1939 Lengthened to 161.0 ft 388 Gross tons) Work carried out by Smiths Dock Co Ltd, Middlesbrough.
Jan 1940 Rqd by the Royal Navy as a boom defence vessel No. Z. 106. Jan 1946 returned.
04.09.1945 Sold to Lord Line Ltd, Hull renamed (13.06.1947) LORD MONTGOMERY (Jun 1947 Fitted for fuel Oil).
1953 to Associated Fisheries Ltd, Hull. 13.09.1954 to Wyre Trawlers Ltd, Fleetwood (FD13).
1963 Vessel sold for scrap to The West of Scotland Shipbreaking Co Ltd. 01.09.1963 Arrived Troon for breaking up.</td></tr>
</table>

Yard No.566
1931 BLAKKUR
Photo by courtesy of George Scales

Yard No.572
1932 ALMANDINE
Photo:- Harry Cartlidge Collection

Yard No.577
1934 PENTLAND FIRTH
Photo:- Author's Collection

<table>
<tr><th rowspan="2">NAME
Official No.
Port Letters Numbers</th><th rowspan="2">Yard No.
Launched
Registered</th><th colspan="2">Registered</th><th rowspan="2">Engine Builder
Horse Power
Reg'd Speed</th><th rowspan="2">OWNER
(Built for)</th></tr>
<tr><th>G Ton
N Ton</th><th>L Ft
B Ft</th></tr>
<tr><td>BALTHASAR
162263
H405 Steam Trawler</td><td>570
29.12.1931
21.01.1932</td><td>381
151</td><td>145.8
25.1</td><td>C.D.Holmes
102 NHP
11.2 knots</td><td>Hull Northern Fishing Co Ltd
Hull</td></tr>
<tr><td colspan="6">01.11.1935 Sold to the Royal Navy converted to a Gem Class anti-submarine vessel No. T14 renamed JASPER.
01.12.1942 Vessel sunk by E-boat No.S81 in the English Channel in approx position 50° 10'N 003° 48'W).
Lost whilst serving with the 2nd anti-submarine group based at Plymouth.</td></tr>
<tr><td>NEGRO
162264
H406 Steam Trawler</td><td>571
11.01.1932
03.02.1932</td><td>381
151</td><td>145.8
25.1</td><td>C.D.Holmes
102 NHP
11.2 knots</td><td>Hellyer Bros Ltd
Hull</td></tr>
<tr><td colspan="6">(1939 Lengthened to 161.1 ft 402 Gross tons) Work carried out by Smiths Dock Co Ltd, Middlesbrough.
05.09.1939 Rqd by the Royal Navy as a minesweeper No. FY 717. 12.05.1945 returned.
04.09.1945 Sold to Lord Line Ltd, Hull renamed LORD PORTAL.
04.11.1947 to Ocean Steam Trawling Co Ltd, Hull renamed VIAN.
1957 Vessel sold for scrap to Van Heyghen Freres, Belgium . 28.11.1957 Arrived Ghent for breaking up.</td></tr>
<tr><td>ALMANDINE
163097
H415 Steam Trawler</td><td>572
05.04.1932
12.05.1932</td><td>294
135</td><td>129.0
24.0</td><td>C.D.Holmes
89 NHP
11 knots</td><td>Kingston Steam
Trawling Co Ltd
Hull</td></tr>
<tr><td colspan="6">30.08.1939 Rqd by the Royal Navy as a minesweeper No. FY 645. 22.05.1946 returned.
30.09.1948 Sold to Milford Fishing Ltd, Milford Haven.
1963 Vessel sold for scrap to The West of Scotland Shipbreaking Co Ltd. 01.10.1963 Arrived Troon for breaking up.</td></tr>
<tr><td>PYROPE
163100
H424 Steam Trawler</td><td>573
07.04.1932
19.05.1932</td><td>295
135</td><td>129.0
24.0</td><td>C.D.Holmes
89 NHP
11.3 knots</td><td>Kingston Steam
Trawling Co Ltd
Hull</td></tr>
<tr><td colspan="6">31.08.1939 Rqd by the Royal Navy as a mine-sweeper .
12.08.1940 Vessel sunk by German aircraft in the Thames estuary off North East Spit buoy.
Vessel lost whilst serving with mine-sweeper group No. 2 based at Sheerness.</td></tr>
<tr><td>RIFSNES
163118
H451 Steam Trawler</td><td>574
17.10.1932
21.11.1932</td><td>423
163</td><td>144.7
25.1</td><td>C.D.Holmes
99 NHP
11 knots</td><td>J Oddsson & Co Ltd
Hull</td></tr>
<tr><td colspan="6">26.08.1939 Rqd by the Royal Navy as a mine-sweeper based at Yarmouth .
20.05.1940 Vessel sunk by German aircraft off Ostend three crew lost.</td></tr>
<tr><td>LADY LILIAN
163132
H467 Steam Trawler</td><td>575
28.03.1933
27.04.1933</td><td>392
150</td><td>151.9
25.6</td><td>C.D.Holmes
102 NHP
11.5 knots</td><td>Jutland Amalgamated
Trawlers Ltd
Hull</td></tr>
<tr><td colspan="6">27.01.1939 Sold to the Royal Navy converted to a Gem Class anti-submarine vessel No. T56 renamed JADE.
10.04.1942 Vessel sunk by German aircraft bombs during an air raid on Grand Harbour, Malta.
Dec 1943 broken up en situ. Vessel lost whilst serving with 4th anti-submarine group based at Malta.</td></tr>
<tr><td>ST. ARCADIUS
163139
H482 Steam Trawler</td><td>576
11.05.1933
15.06.1933</td><td>403
156</td><td>151.5
25.6</td><td>C.D.Holmes
102 NHP
11.4 knots</td><td>Thomas Hamling & Co Ltd
Hull</td></tr>
<tr><td colspan="6">08.08.1939 Rqd by the Royal Navy as an anti-submarine vessel No. FY 135.
16.10.1939 Transferred to the French Navy as an auxiliary patrol vessel No. P 135 renamed LA NANTAISE.
03.07.1940 Seized by the Royal Navy whilst in a British port used as an anti-submarine vessel No. FY 360.
08.07.1945 Vessel sank following a collision with ss HELENCREST (5233 gt/ b 1941) in the Downs.</td></tr>
<tr><td>ST. AMANDUS
163154
H505 Steam Trawler</td><td>576A
10.08.1933
20.08.1933</td><td>400
152</td><td>151.5
25.6</td><td>C.D.Holmes
102 NHP
11.3 knots</td><td>Thomas Hamling & Co Ltd
Hull</td></tr>
<tr><td colspan="6">27.07.1939 Rqd by the Royal Navy as an anti-submarine vessel No. FY 176.
16.10.1939 Transferred to the French Navy as an auxiliary patrol vessel No. P 132 renamed LA CANCALAISE.
30.04.1940 Vessel sank after being mined off Dyke Light-vessel off Calais.</td></tr>
<tr><td>ST. ANDRONICUS
163171
H536 Steam Trawler</td><td>576B
04.11.1933
15.12.1933</td><td>398
151</td><td>151.5
25.6</td><td>C.D.Holmes
102 NHP
11.4 knots</td><td>Thomas Hamling & Co Ltd
Hull</td></tr>
<tr><td colspan="6">02.08.1939 Rqd by the Royal Navy as an anti-submarine vessel No. FY 111.
16.10.1939 Transferred to the French Navy as an auxiliary patrol vessel No. P 134 renamed LA ORIENTAISE.
21.05.1940 Scuttled at Boulogne (in port for repairs) raised and repaired for use by the German Navy No. PA2 - V1516 - M3853 14.06.1944 Damaged by RAF bombs at Nantes and scuttled / raised 1946.
1947 Sold to Pecheries Delpierre, Boulogne, France renamed COLBERT.
26.04.1955 Vessel sank following a collision with the French trawler FISHER BANK (268 gt/ b 1948) 7 miles north-west of Cape Gris Nez. Twelve crew were picked up by the FISHER BANK. Nine crew lost</td></tr>
</table>

NAME Official No. Port Letters Numbers	Yard No. Launched Registered	Registered G Ton N Ton	 L Ft B Ft	Engine Builder Horse Power Reg'd Speed	OWNER (Built for)
PENTLAND FIRTH 163955 H123 Steam Trawler	577 26.09.1934 22.11.1934	485 189	164.4 27.3	C.D.Holmes 154 NHP 12.3 knots	Firth Steam Trawling Co Ltd Hull
14.11.1939 Sold to the Royal Navy as an anti-submarine vessel No. FY 108. 25.02.1942 Loaned to the United States Navy *(Royal Navy crew)* for north Atlantic anti-submarine work. 19.09.1942 Vessel sank following a collision with the fleet mine-sweeper/ patrol vessel USS CHAFFINCH No. AM81 off New York 2.9 miles west north-west of Ambrose Light-vessel in approx position 40° 25.3'N 073° 55.1'W. The wreck was considered a danger to shipping and was dispersed by explosives.					
ARAB 163160 H516 Steam Trawler	578 06.09.1933 12.10.1933	422 162	154.6 25.6	C.D.Holmes 111 NHP 11.4 knots	Hellyer Bros Ltd Hull
19.11.1935 Sold to the Royal Navy for conversion to a Berberis Class minesweeper No. T01 renamed CEDAR. 1946 to Iago Steam Trawlers Ltd, London renamed RED GAUNTLET. 10.08.1947 Vessel wrecked on a reef at South Cape Spitzbergen. All twenty crew and two Norwegian gutters were safely taken aboard the Grimsby trawler NORTHERN SPRAY GY190 (655 gt/ b 1936).					
LORENZO 163162 H518 Steam Trawler	579 21.09.1933 28.10.1933	424 163	154.6 25.6	C.D.Holmes 111 NHP 11.4 knots	Hull Northern Fishing Co Ltd Hull
14.01.1939 Sold to Loyal Steam Fishing Co Ltd, Grimsby renamed REGAL (GY28). Aug 1939 Rqd by the Royal Navy as a mine-sweeper / anti-submarine trawler No. FY 180. 1945 returned. Mar 1946 to The Hull Ice Co Ltd, Hull. 1946 to Great Grimsby & East Coast Steam Fishing Co Ltd, Grimsby renamed NUBIA (GY208). 18.06.1948 to Henriksen & Co Ltd, Hull renamed TERVANI (H530). 17.12.1956 to Fern Leaf Co Ltd / Hewett, Fleetwood (FD61). 18.08.1959 to Sun Trawlers Ltd , Fleetwood. 1959 Vessel sold for scrap to Jacques Bakker & Zonen, Belgium. 13.10.1959 Arrived Bruges for breaking up.					
PICADOR 163165 H520 Steam Trawler	580 04.10.1933 09.11.1933	424 163	154.6 25.6	C.D.Holmes 111 NHP 11.5 knots	Hellyer Bros Ltd Hull
25.05.1936 Vessel sank following a collision in thick fog with the London registered Oil tanker SAN SALVADOR (3808 gt/ b 1924) off Aldbrough East Yorkshire whilst returning to Hull from Bear Island fishing grounds. Twelve crew were rescued by the SAN SALVADOR. Six crew lost.					
BASQUE 163166 H521 Steam Trawler	581 19.10.1933 21.11.1933	424 162	154.6 25.6	C.D.Holmes 111 NHP 11.6 knots	Hellyer Bros Ltd Hull
14.01.1939 Sold to Great Grimsby & East Coast Steam Fishing Co Ltd, Grimsby renamed ISTRIA (GY41). Aug 1939 Rqd by the Royal Navy as an anti-submarine trawler No. FY 150. Nov 1946 returned. Nov 1946 to Wendover Steam Fishing Co, Grimsby (GY129). 14.01.1947 to Thos. Hamling & Co Ltd, Hull renamed ST. ARCADIUS (H363). 24.11.1947 to Eton Fishing Co Ltd, Hull renamed REPTONIAN. 14.08.1951 to Dinas Steam Trawling Co Ltd , Fleetwood (FD171). 28.08.1950 to J Marr & Son Ltd, Fleetwood. 1959 Vessel sold to BISCO and allocated to Thos W Ward Ltd. 10.01.1959 Arrived Preston for breaking up.					
LOCH SEAFORTH 163167 H529 Steam Trawler	582 23.10.1933 29.11.1933	424 161	154.6 25.6	C.D.Holmes 111 NHP 12 knots	Loch Fishing Co of Hull Ltd Hull
16.03.1939 Sold to Fiskveiidafelagid Alliance, Reykyavik, Iceland renamed JON OLAFSSON (RE279). 1942 War loss posted missing. 21.10.1942 Vessel left Fleetwood for Reykjavik last sighted 22.10.1942. All thirteen crew lost.					
KINGSTON ALALITE 163172 H538 Steam Trawler	583 18.11.1933 19.12.1933	412 166	151.7 25.9	C.D.Holmes 111 NHP 11.8 knots	Kingston Steam Trawling Co Ltd Hull
11.08.1939 Rqd by the Royal Navy as an anti-submarine trawler No. FY 136. 10.11.1940 Vessel sunk by mine 5.7 cables from Plymouth Breakwater Light. Vessel lost whilst serving with the 9th anti-submarine group based at Plymouth.					
KINGSTON ANDALUSITE 163177 H15 Steam Trawler	584 17.01.1934 13.02.1934	416 168	151.7 25.9	C.D.Holmes 111 NHP 11.8 knots	Kingston Steam Trawling Co Ltd Hull
11.08.1939 Sold to the Royal Navy as an anti-submarine trawler No. FY 160. 1945 Sold back to Kingston Steam Trawling Co Ltd, Hull (H133). 12.02.1948 to Victoria Fishing Co Ltd, Hull renamed MILYNA. 10.11.1955 to Hudson Bros, Hull. 1956 Vessel sold for scrap to Jacques Bakker & Zonen, Belgium .05.04.1956 Arrived Bruges for breaking up.					

Yard No.586
1933 LADY ADELAIDE as RED KNIGHT
Photo by courtesy of Peter Horsley

Yard No.592
1934 LADY MADELEINE
Photo by courtesy of Peter Horsley

Yard No.602
1935 KINGSTON CHRYSOBERYL
Photo:- Author's Collection

<table>
<tr><th rowspan="2">NAME
Official No.
Port Letters Numbers</th><th rowspan="2">Yard No.
Launched
Registered</th><th colspan="2">Registered</th><th rowspan="2">Engine Builder
Horse Power
Reg'd Speed</th><th rowspan="2">OWNER
(Built for)</th></tr>
<tr><th>G Ton
N Ton</th><th>L Ft
B Ft</th></tr>
<tr><td>ALEXANDRITE
163175
H7 Steam Trawler</td><td>585
21.12.1933
23.01.1934</td><td>313
139</td><td>131.0
24.6</td><td>C.D.Holmes
89 NHP
11.3 knots</td><td>Kingston Steam
Trawling Co Ltd
Hull</td></tr>
<tr><td colspan="6">28.08.1939 Rqd by the Royal Navy as a minesweeper No. FY 560. 01.11.1945 returned.
23.09.1949 Sold to J Marr & Son Ltd, Fleetwood. 04.12.1951 to North Star Steam Fishing Co Ltd, Aberdeen.
1963 Vessel sold to Motherwell Machinery & Scrap Co Ltd. 02.11.1963 Arrived Grangemouth for breaking up.</td></tr>
<tr><td>LADY ADELAIDE
163173
H4 Steam Trawler</td><td>586
04.12.1933
10.01.1934</td><td>394
150</td><td>151.9
25.6</td><td>C.D.Holmes
102 NHP
11.5 knots</td><td>Jutland Amalgamated
Trawlers Ltd
Hull</td></tr>
<tr><td colspan="6">27.01.1939 Sold the Royal Navy as a minesweeper No. T34 renamed BERYL.
1946 to Iago Steam Trawlers Ltd, London renamed RED KNIGHT (LO445). (Feb 1947 Fitted for Fuel Oil).
1962 Vessel sold for scrap to Thos W Ward Ltd. 27.11.1962 Arrived Barrow for breaking up.</td></tr>
<tr><td>DERVISH
163176
H8 Steam Trawler</td><td>587
18.12.1933
29.01.1934</td><td>426
166</td><td>154.6
25.6</td><td>C.D.Holmes
111 NHP
11.5 knots</td><td>Hellyer Bros Ltd
Hull</td></tr>
<tr><td colspan="6">09.10.1935 Sold to the Royal Navy for conversion to a Gem Class anti-submarine vessel No. T22 renamed PEARL.
09.04.1946 to J Marr & Son Ltd, Hull renamed WESTELLA (H349).
25.06.1948 to Pegasus Fishing Co, Fleetwood (FD318). 15.08.1951 to Iago Steam Trawlers Ltd, London.
1952 to Dinas Steam Trawling Co Ltd, Fleetwood. 30.05.1959 to J Marr & Son Ltd, Fleetwood.
1959 Vessel sold for scrap to Van Heyghen Freres, Belgium. 18.08.1959 Arrived Ghent for breaking up.</td></tr>
<tr><td>ANDRADITE
163179
H26 Steam Trawler</td><td>588
01.02.1934
27.02.1934</td><td>313
139</td><td>131.0
24.6</td><td>C.D.Holmes
89 NHP
11.4 knots</td><td>Kingston Steam
Trawling Co Ltd
Hull</td></tr>
<tr><td colspan="6">28.08.1939 Rqd by the Royal Navy as a minesweeper No. FY 559. 18.01.1946 returned.
23.02.1949 Sold to J Marr & Son Ltd, Fleetwood.
07.03.1957 Vessel wrecked in Castlebay Barra Island Outer Hebrides. All crew rescued.</td></tr>
<tr><td>KINGSTON GALENA
163186
H31 Steam Trawler</td><td>589
15.02.1934
13.03.1934</td><td>415
168</td><td>151.7
25.9</td><td>C.D.Holmes
111 NHP
11.9 knots</td><td>Kingston Steam
Trawling Co Ltd
Hull</td></tr>
<tr><td colspan="6">12.08.1939 Sold to the Royal Navy as an anti-submarine vessel No. FY 145.
24.07.1940 Vessel sunk by German aircraft bombs off Dover.
Lost whilst serving with the 9th anti-submarine group based at Dover.</td></tr>
<tr><td>BRONTES
163191
H41 Steam Trawler</td><td>590
03.03.1934
31.03.1934</td><td>424
159</td><td>154.6
25.6</td><td>C.D.Holmes
111 NHP
11.7 knots</td><td>Henriksen & Co Ltd
Hull</td></tr>
<tr><td colspan="6">14.08.1939 Sold to the Royal Navy as a minesweeper No. FY 118.
1945 Sold back to Henriksen & Co Ltd, Hull (H236).
1959 Vessel sold for scrap to Van Heyghen Freres, Belgium. 20.06.1959 Arrived Ghent for breaking up.</td></tr>
<tr><td>ST. ATTALUS
163927
H48 Steam Trawler</td><td>591
03.04.1934
22.05.1934</td><td>399
154</td><td>151.6
25.6</td><td>C.D.Holmes
102 NHP
11.5 knots</td><td>Thomas Hamling & Co Ltd
Hull</td></tr>
<tr><td colspan="6">27.07.1939 Sold to the Royal Navy as an anti-submarine vessel No. FY 183.
16.10.1939 Transferred to the French Navy as an auxiliary patrol vessel No. P133 renamed LA HAVRAISE.
27.11.1942 Scuttled at Toulen. 1943 raised and repaired for use by the German Navy No. VJ6078.
09.06.1944 Vessel torpedoed and sunk by French submarine CASABIANCA (b 1935) off La Ciotat Pos'n 43°08'N 05°36'E.</td></tr>
<tr><td>LADY MADELEINE
163938
H85 Steam Trawler</td><td>592
31.07.1934
30.08.1934</td><td>390
145</td><td>151.9
25.6</td><td>C.D.Holmes
105 NHP
11.6 knots</td><td>Jutland Amalgamated
Trawlers Ltd
Hull</td></tr>
<tr><td colspan="6">27.01.1939 Sold to the Royal Navy as an anti-submarine vessel No. T90 renamed MOONSTONE.
19.06.1940 Whilst on patrol in the Red Sea the MOONSTONE captured the Italian submarine GALILEO GALILEI (b 1934) with depth charges and gunfire. Escorted to Aden repaired and renamed HMS EUROPA and served with Royal Navy.
Apr 1946 to Iago Steam Trawlers Ltd, London renamed RED LANCER (LO442). (Jan 1947 Fitted for Fuel Oil).
1964 Vessel sold for scrap to Lacmots Ltd Glasgow. 27.01.1964 Left Fleetwood for Glasson Docks for breaking up.</td></tr>
<tr><td>KINGSTON CORNELIAN
163932
H75 Steam Trawler</td><td>593
12.06.1934
23.07.1934</td><td>449
174</td><td>160.6
26.6</td><td>C.D.Holmes
117 NHP
11.6 knots</td><td>Kingston Steam
Trawling Co Ltd
Hull</td></tr>
<tr><td colspan="6">16.08.1939 Sold to the Royal Navy as an anti-submarine vessel No. FY 121.
05.01.1940 Vessel sank following a collision east of Gibraltar with the French liner CHEILA (8920 gt/ b 1934).
The KINGSTON CORNELIAN's depth charges exploded as she sank. All crew lost.
Lost whilst serving with the 7th Anti-submarine group based at Gibraltar.</td></tr>
</table>

<table>
<tr><th rowspan="2">NAME
Official No.
Port Letters Numbers</th><th rowspan="2">Yard No.
Launched
Registered</th><th colspan="2">Registered</th><th rowspan="2">Engine Builder
Horse Power
Reg'd Speed</th><th rowspan="2">OWNER
(Built for)</th></tr>
<tr><th>G Ton
N Ton</th><th>L Ft
B Ft</th></tr>
<tr><td>ARAGONITE
163934
H79 Steam Trawler</td><td>594
27.06.1934
26.07.1934</td><td>315
138</td><td>133.2
24.5</td><td>C.D.Holmes
89 NHP
11.3 knots</td><td>Kingston Steam
Trawling Co Ltd
Hull</td></tr>
<tr><td colspan="6">26.08.1939 Rqd by the Royal Navy as a minesweeper based at Dover. 22.11.1939 Vessel sunk by mine, beached but broke in two and sank 1 mile off Deal in approx position 51°14' 08" N 001°24'59" E.</td></tr>
<tr><td>ST. ACHILLEUS
163957
H127 Steam Trawler</td><td>595
11.10.1934
05.12.1934</td><td>484
189</td><td>164.4
27.3</td><td>C.D.Holmes
154 NHP
12.3 knots</td><td>Thomas Hamling & Co Ltd
Hull</td></tr>
<tr><td colspan="6">28.08.1939 Rqd by the Royal Navy as an anti-submarine vessel No. FY 152.
31.05.1940 Vessel sunk by mine off Dunkirk during allied forces withdrawal operations.
Vessel lost whilst serving with the 11th anti-submarine group based at Harwich.</td></tr>
<tr><td>ACHROITE
163935
H81 Steam Trawler</td><td>596
30.06.1934
09.08.1934</td><td>314
138</td><td>133.2
24.5</td><td>C.D.Holmes
89 NHP
11.4 knots</td><td>Kingston Steam
Trawling Co Ltd
Hull</td></tr>
<tr><td colspan="6">31.08.1939 Rqd by the Royal Navy as a minesweeper No. FY 914. 28.08.1945 returned .
11.08.1949 Sold to J Marr & Son Ltd, Hull. 29.01.1952 to J Marr & Son Ltd, Fleetwood.
14.05.1960 to Cevic Steam Fishing Co Ltd, Fleetwood.
1963 Vessel sold for scrap to Haulbowline Industries Ltd . 04.02.1963 on delivery to Passage West she developed engine trouble off the Coningbeg Light-vessel and was escorted into Rosslare. She broke adrift and ran ashore (06.02.1963) on Rosslare Strand approx 5 miles north-west of Rosslare Lighthouse. 11.02.1963 In a full storm she was driven further ashore. The wreck was sold to P Roche Killinich who broke her up "in situ".</td></tr>
<tr><td>LADY LAVINIA
163962
H160 Steam Trawler</td><td>597
07.01.1935
04.02.1935</td><td>417
157</td><td>155.7
26.1</td><td>C.D.Holmes
105 NHP
12.1 knots</td><td>Jutland Amalgamated
Trawlers Ltd
Hull</td></tr>
<tr><td colspan="6">05.03.1938 Vessel sank in a severe storm in the vicinity of Sula Lighthouse Norway whilst on passage to Hull from Bear Island. On the 5 March the last communication from the LADY LAVINIA was with the Hull trawler LORD AUSTIN H483 (473 gt/ b 1937) when she reported being hove to in a severe gale off west coast Norway approx position 65°N 007°W.
All sixteen crew lost.</td></tr>
<tr><td>VITALITY
163972
Water Boat</td><td>598
23.02.1935
14.03.1935</td><td>63
36</td><td>58.0
16.0</td><td>Plenty & Sons
27 BHP
6 knots</td><td>Hull Trawler Supply Co Ltd
Hull</td></tr>
<tr><td colspan="6">The VITALITY had a 113 tons fresh water capacity for bunkering trawlers in St Andrew's (Fish Dock) Dock Hull.</td></tr>
<tr><td>KINGSTON CHRYSOLITE
163967
H169 Steam Trawler</td><td>599
22.01.1935
28.02.1935</td><td>448
174</td><td>160.6
26.6</td><td>C.D.Holmes
117 NHP
12.3 knots</td><td>Kingston Steam
Trawling Co Ltd
Hull</td></tr>
<tr><td colspan="6">12.08.1939 Sold to the Royal Navy as an anti-submarine trawler No. FY 184.
1945 Sold back to Kingston Steam Trawling Co Ltd, Hull (H205).
1956 Vessel sold to BISCO and allocated to Clayton & Davie Ltd. 27.03.1956 Arrived Dunston for breaking up.</td></tr>
<tr><td>KINGSTON CEYLONITE
163971
H173 Steam Trawler</td><td>600
06.02.1935
13.03.1935</td><td>448
174</td><td>160.6
26.6</td><td>C.D.Holmes
117 NHP
12.3 knots</td><td>Kingston Steam
Trawling Co Ltd
Hull</td></tr>
<tr><td colspan="6">15.11.1939 Sold to the Royal Navy as an anti-submarine trawler No. FY 214.
25.02.1942 Loaned to the United States Navy (Royal Navy crew) for north Atlantic anti-submarine work.
15.06.1942 Vessel sunk by mine off Norfolk Virginia in Chesapeake Bay. Eighteen (all British) crew lost fourteen rescued. She was one of four ships to run into the same mine-field the others were USN destroyer BAINBRIDGE, US tankers ESSO AUGUSTA (11237 gt/ b 1940) and ROBERT C. TUTTLE (11615 gt/ b 1940) the latter vessel was salved.</td></tr>
<tr><td>KINGSTON CAIRNGORM
163976
H175 Steam Trawler</td><td>601
21.02.1935
01.04.1935</td><td>448
174</td><td>160.6
26.6</td><td>C.D.Holmes
117 NHP
12.2 knots</td><td>Kingston Steam
Trawling Co Ltd
Hull</td></tr>
<tr><td colspan="6">18.09.1939 Rqd by the Royal Navy as an anti-submarine vessel .
Jun 1940 Stranded but re-floated and repaired at Portsmouth. 17.10.1940 Vessel sunk by mine in the English Channel.
Lost whilst serving with the 27th anti-submarine group based at Portsmouth.</td></tr>
<tr><td>KINGSTON CHRYSOBERYL
163978
H177 Steam Trawler</td><td>602
09.03.1935
07.05.1935</td><td>448
174</td><td>160.6
26.6</td><td>C.D.Holmes
117 NHP
12.2 knots</td><td>Kingston Steam
Trawling Co Ltd
Hull</td></tr>
<tr><td colspan="6">18.09.1939 Rqd by the Royal Navy as an anti-submarine trawler No. FY 236. 31.03.1945 returned.
1955 Vessel sold for scrap to Jacques Bakker & Zonen, Belgium.. 18.03.1955 Arrived Bruges for breaking up.</td></tr>
</table>

<table>
<tr><th rowspan="2">NAME
Official No.
Port Letters Numbers</th><th rowspan="2">Yard No.
Launched
Registered</th><th colspan="2">Registered</th><th rowspan="2">Engine Builder
Horse Power
Reg'd Speed</th><th rowspan="2">OWNER
(Built for)</th></tr>
<tr><th>G Ton
N Ton</th><th>L Ft
B Ft</th></tr>
<tr><td>ROYAL JUBILEE
163995
Passenger Pleasure Ship</td><td>603
04.07.1935
18.07.1935</td><td>60
41</td><td>69.6
17.0</td><td>Bergius (Twin)
132 BHP
9 knots</td><td>Crawford & Pockley
Bridlington</td></tr>
<tr><td colspan="6">1938 Sold to St.Mawes Ferry Co Ltd Falmouth renamed NEW ROSELAND for use as the Falmouth to St.Mawes ferry.
1955 Withdrawn from service. Re-sold for private use.</td></tr>
<tr><td>THORNWICK BAY
164012
H226 Steam Trawler</td><td>604
28.08.1935
18.01.1936</td><td>437
171</td><td>155.7
26.1</td><td>Amos & Smith
112 NHP
11.5 knots</td><td>Marine Steam Fishing Co Ltd,
Hull</td></tr>
<tr><td colspan="6">10.08.1939 Sold to the Royal Navy as an anti-submarine trawler No. FY 179.
1946 Sold back to the Marine Steam Fishing Co Ltd, Hull (H241). 18.05.1951 to St Andrew's Steam Fishing Co Ltd, Hull.
07.03.1952 to Trawlers Grimsby Ltd, Grimsby (GY250). 1953 to Derwent Trawlers Ltd, Grimsby.
1955 to Dennis Roberts Fishing Co Ltd, Grimsby renamed AFRIDI.
1959 Vessel sold for scrap to Eisen Und Metall KG Lehr & Co, Germany. 01.03.1959 Arrived Bremerhaven for breaking up.</td></tr>
<tr><td>LADY BERYL
164006
H222 Steam Trawler</td><td>605
12.11.1935
12.12.1935</td><td>417
157</td><td>155.7
26.1</td><td>C D Holmes
117 NHP
12.4 knots</td><td>Jutland Amalgamated
Trawlers Ltd
Hull</td></tr>
<tr><td colspan="6">03.08.1939 Sold to the Royal Navy as an anti-submarine trawler No. FY 100.
1945 Sold back to Jutland Amalgamated Trawlers Ltd, Hull (H151).
14.02.1948 to Newington Trawlers Ltd, Hull renamed (30.11.1949) WARWICK DEEPING.
1959 Vessel sold for scrap to Van Heyghen Freres, Belgium. 23.10.1959 Arrived Ghent for breaking up.</td></tr>
<tr><td>LADY PHILOMENA
164018
H230 Steam Trawler</td><td>606
09.01.1936
06.02.1936</td><td>417
157</td><td>155.7
26.1</td><td>C D Holmes
117 NHP
12.4 knots</td><td>Jutland Amalgamated
Trawlers Ltd
Hull</td></tr>
<tr><td colspan="6">09.10.1939 Sold to the Royal Navy as an anti-submarine trawler No. FY 148.
1945 Sold back to Jutland Amalgamated Trawlers Ltd, Hull (H167).
18.01.1946 to Thomas Hamling & Co Ltd, Hull renamed (23.01.1947) ST. ATTALUS.
13.01.1948 to Ocean Steam Trawling Co Ltd, Hull renamed (02.02.1948) ONSLOW.
1954 to Hessle Fishing Co Ltd, Hull. 31.10.1956 to Mason Trawlers Ltd, Fleetwood (FD50).
1960 Vessel sold to Thos W Ward Ltd. 11.05.1960 Arrived Preston for breaking up.</td></tr>
<tr><td>KINGSTON CYANITE
164019
H254 Steam Trawler</td><td>607
25.01.1936
02.03.1936</td><td>433
166</td><td>162.2
26.6</td><td>C.D.Holmes
117 NHP
12.3 knots</td><td>Kingston Steam
Trawling Co Ltd
Hull</td></tr>
<tr><td colspan="6">27.09.1939 Rqd by the Royal Navy as an anti-submarine trawler No. FY 217.
1941 - 10.09.1945 Mediterranean command. 13.05.1946 returned (H237).
1957 Vessel sold for scrap to Jacques Bakker & Zonen, Belgium. 12.11.1957 Arrived Bruges for breaking up.</td></tr>
<tr><td>KINGSTON CORAL
164021
H241 Steam Trawler</td><td>608
08.02.1936
17.03.1936</td><td>433
166</td><td>162.2
26.6</td><td>C.D.Holmes
117 NHP
12.5 knots</td><td>Kingston Steam
Trawling Co Ltd
Hull</td></tr>
<tr><td colspan="6">28.09.1939 Rqd by the Royal Navy as an anti-submarine trawler No. FY 215.
1942 - 03.09.1945 Mediterranean command. 20.03.1946 returned (H242).
1956 Vessel sold to BISCO and allocated to Clayton & Davie Ltd. 27.03.1956 Arrived Dunston for breaking up.</td></tr>
<tr><td>KINGSTON CAMEO
164917
H272 Steam Trawler</td><td>609
27.02.1936
15.04.1936</td><td>433
166</td><td>162.2
26.6</td><td>C.D.Holmes
117 NHP
12.5 knots</td><td>Kingston Steam
Trawling Co Ltd
Hull</td></tr>
<tr><td colspan="6">14.04.1937 Vessel sank following a collision with the coaster Goole registered ss FAXFLEET (843 gt/ b 1916)
20 miles NE of the Spurn Light-vessel (River Humber). All crew rescued.</td></tr>
<tr><td>KINGSTON CRYSTAL
164921
H281 Steam Trawler</td><td>610
22.03.1936
06.05.1936</td><td>433
166</td><td>162.2
26.6</td><td>C.D.Holmes
117 NHP
12.5knots</td><td>Kingston Steam
Trawling Co Ltd
Hull</td></tr>
<tr><td colspan="6">19.09.1939 Rqd by the Royal Navy as an anti-submarine trawler No. FY 216.
1942 - 03.01.1946 Mediterranean command. 28.03.1946 returned.
1958 Vessel sold for scrap to Van Heyghen Freres, Belgium. 31.12.1958 Arrived Ghent for breaking up.</td></tr>
<tr><td>CAPE COMORIN
164924
H291 Steam Trawler</td><td>611
08.04.1936
15.05.1936</td><td>504
192</td><td>166.6
27.7</td><td>C.D.Holmes
132 NHP
12 knots</td><td>Hudson Bros Ltd
Hull</td></tr>
<tr><td colspan="6">14.08.1939 Sold to the Royal Navy as an anti-submarine trawler No. FY 143.
1945 Sold back to Hudson Bros Ltd, Hull (H139).
10.11.1955 to Victoria Fishing Co Ltd, Hull renamed (15.12.1955) OLVINA.
15.08.1960 to Irvin & Johnson, Cape Town, South Africa renamed LOBELIA.
1968 Vessel stripped for spare parts. 27.09.1968 Hulk scuttled off Cape Town to form an artificial reef.</td></tr>
</table>

Yard No.604
1935 THORNWICK BAY
Photo:- Harry Cartlidge Collection

Yard No.612
1936 DAVY as RED FALCON
Photo by courtesy of Peter Horsley

Yard No.624
1936 VICTRIX
Photo:- Author's Collection

NAME Official No. Port Letters Numbers	Yard No. Launched Registered	Registered		Engine Builder Horse Power Reg'd Speed	OWNER (Built for)
		G Ton N Ton	L Ft B Ft		
DAVY 164954 H322 Steam Trawler	612 08.07.1936 20.08.1936	449 171	161.3 27.2	C.D.Holmes 114 NHP 11.9 knots	F & T Ross Ltd Hull
12.08.1939 Sold to the Royal Navy as an anti-submarine trawler No. FY 147. 1945 Sold back to F & T Ross Ltd, Hull (H213). 17.11.1951 to Hudson Bros Ltd, Hull renamed (26.11.1951) CAPE BARFLEUR. 07.09.1954 to Iago Steam Trawlers Ltd, London renamed (13.09.1954) RED FALCON (LO4). 14/15.12.1959 Vessel lost off Skerryvore, Scotland on her way home from Iceland. All nineteen crew lost. Last heard from when she was abeam of Skerryvore Lighthouse.					
ST. CATHAN 164964 H353 Steam Trawler	613 19.08.1936 02.10.1936	564 210	172.2 29.1	C.D.Holmes 157 NHP 12.3 knots	Thomas Hamling & Co Ltd Hull
09.09.1939 Rqd by the Royal Navy as an anti-submarine trawler No. FY 234. 25.02.1942 Loaned to the United States Navy *(Royal Navy crew)* for north Atlantic anti-submarine work. Oct 1945 returned. 11.04.1942 Vessel sank following a collision with the Dutch cargo vessel ss HEBE (1140 gt/ b 1916) which also sank off Georgetown, South Carolina in approx position 33° 09.N 078° 16.4'W.					
ST. GORAN 164966 H356 Steam Trawler	614 05.09.1936 22.10.1936	564 210	172.2 29.1	C.D.Holmes 157 NHP 12.3 knots	Thomas Hamling & Co Ltd Hull
09.09.1939 Rqd by the Royal Navy as an anti-submarine trawler. 03.05.1940 Damaged by German aircraft bombs off Namsos during allied troop evacuations, scuttled by allied forces. Vessel lost whilst serving with the 15th anti-submarine group based at Aberdeen *(on loan to the home fleet)*.					
LADY SHIRLEY 165653 H464 Steam Trawler	615 25.02.1937 19.04.1937	472 177	163.5 27.2	C.D.Holmes 120 NHP 12 knots	Jutland Amalgamated Trawlers Ltd Hull
27..05.1940 Rqd by the Royal Navy as an anti-submarine trawler. Based at Gibraltar with the 31st Anti-submarine group. 04.10.1941 HMT LADY SHIRLEY commanded by Lt Commander Callaway DSO of the RANVR sank U-boat U111 using depth charges and gunfire. One crewman was lost in the action. The U-boat commander and seven submariners were lost, thirty-seven crew were rescued and picked up by trawler. The action took place west-southwest of Tenerife. 11.12.1941 Vessel sunk by torpedo from U374 (Commanded by Unno Von Fischel) in the Straits of Gibraltar. Lost with all thirty-three crew (four officers and twenty-nine ratings).					
LADY JEANETTE 165658 H466 Steam Trawler	616 20.03.1937 01.05.1937	472 177	163.5 27.2	C.D.Holmes 120 NHP 12 knots	Jutland Amalgamated Trawlers Ltd Hull
08.03.1939 Vessel ran aground on a sand-bank and capsized off Hessle Foreshore (River Humber) after the anchor cable parted in gale force winds and a strong tide. Nine crew were lost and nine rescued by local shipping. Attempts by a German salvage company to raise the trawler failed and in Oct 1939 the wreck was dispersed by explosives.					
ST. KENAN 164975 H360 Steam Trawler	617 01.10.1936 16.11.1936	564 210	172.2 29.1	C.D.Holmes 157 NHP 12.3 knots	Thomas Hamling & Co Ltd Hull
09.09.1939 Rqd by the Royal Navy as an anti-submarine trawler No. FY 264. 06.02.1946 returned. 28.11.1951 Sold to Boyd Line Ltd, Hull renamed ARCTIC INVADER. *(Oct 1955 Fitted for Fuel Oil)*. 1966 Vessel sold for scrap to Scrapping Co SA, Belgium. 23.08.1966 Arrived Antwerp for breaking up.					
ST. LOMAN 164991 H381 Steam Trawler	618 15.10.1936 07.12.1936	564 210	172.2 29.1	C.D.Holmes 157 NHP 12.3 knots	Thomas Hamling & Co Ltd Hull
09.09.1939 Rqd by the Royal Navy as an anti-submarine trawler No. FY 276. 02.07.1946 returned. 25.02.1942 Loaned to the United States Navy *(RN crew)* for North Atlantic anti-submarine work. Oct 1945 returned. 04.12.1951 Sold to Boyd Line Ltd, Hull renamed ARCTIC ADVENTURER. *(Jun 1953 Fitted for Fuel Oil)*. 08.12.1964 Vessel suffered a boiler explosion in which three engine room crew lost their lives whilst outward bound for the Norwegian fishing grounds in a position 90 miles east of Dunbar Scotland. The disabled vessel was towed back to Hull by the trawler ST. MATTHEW H201 *(see Yard No.918)*. Repairs were not economic so she was sold for scrap to Van Heyghen Freres, Belgium. 25.01.1965 Arrived Ghent for breaking up.					
ST. NECTAN 164996 H411 Steam Trawler	619 02.11.1936 11.01.1937	564 210	172.2 29.1	C.D.Holmes 157 NHP 12.3 knots	Thomas Hamling & Co Ltd Hull
29.05.1940 Rqd by the Royal Navy as an auxiliary patrol / anti-submarine trawler No. FY 4.139. 1946 returned. *(May 1953 Fitted for Fuel Oil)*. 1967 Vessel sold for scrap to Scrapping Co SA, Belgium. 09.04.1967 Left Hull in tow for breaking up at Antwerp.					

NAME Official No. Port Letters Numbers	Yard No. Launched Registered	Registered G Ton N Ton	 L Ft B Ft	Engine Builder Horse Power Reg'd Speed	OWNER (Built for)
ST. NIDAN 164999 H412 Steam Trawler	620 30.11.1936 20.01.1937	564 210	172.2 29.1	C.D.Holmes 157 NHP 12.3 knots	Thomas Hamling & Co Ltd Hull
28.10.1939 Vessel captured and sunk by gunfire by U59 (Commander Jürst). and explosive charge north of Cape Wrath in approx position 59° 50'N 004° 20'W. All crew rescued.					
Not Built	621				
LADY ROSEMARY 165678 H477 Steam Trawler	622 09.08.1937 22.09.1937	472 177	163.5 27.3	C.D.Holmes 120 NHP 12.3 knots	Jutland Amalgamated Trawlers Ltd Hull
28.05.1940 Rqd by the Royal Navy as an anti-submarine trawler No. FY 253 / auxiliary patrol vessel No. FY 4.150. Feb 1942 Loaned to the United States Navy *(Royal Navy crew)* for North Atlantic anti-submarine work. Oct 1942 returned to Royal Naval duties.18.05.1946 returned. 14.11.1942 Sold to Kingston Steam Trawling Co Ltd, Hull renamed (1946) KINGSTON RUBY. 1963 Vessel sold for scrap to Van Heyghen Freres, Belgium. 20.03.1963 Arrived Ghent for breaking up.					
LADY HOGARTH 165681 H479 Steam Trawler	623 07.09.1937 22.10.1937	472 177	163.5 27.3	C.D.Holmes 120 NHP 12.3 knots	Jutland Amalgamated Trawlers Ltd Hull
1939 Rqd by the Royal Navy as an anti-submarine trawler / auxiliary patrol vessel No. FY 4.89. 31.05.1940 Loaned to the United States Navy *(RN crew)* for North Atlantic anti-submarine work.12.05.1946 returned. 14.11.1942 Sold to Kingston Steam Trawling Co Ltd, Hull renamed (1946) KINGSTON EMERALD. 22.12.1951 to West Dock Steam Fishing Co Ltd, Hull renamed STAXTON WYKE. 23.08.1959 Vessel sank following a collision with bulk carrier ss DALHANNA (11452 gt/ b 1958) in thick fog 10 miles south of Flamborough Head whilst homeward bound from the Icelandic fishing grounds to Hull. Fifteen survivors were picked up by the DALHANNA and five were crew lost.					
VICTRIX 165004 H428 Steam Trawler	624 15.12.1936 11.02.1937	472 176	163.5 27.3	C.D.Holmes 120 NHP 12.4 knots	Henriksen & Co Ltd Hull
30.09.1939 Rqd by the Royal Navy as an anti-submarine trawler No. FY 244. 19.12.1945 returned. *(Jun 1955 Fitted for Fuel Oil).* 1966 Vessel sold for scrap to Scrapping Co SA, Belgium. 23.03.1966 Left Hull under tow for breaking up at Ghent.					
ITALIA CAESAR 164428 GY442 Steam Trawler	625 27.04.1937 14.07.1937	518 283	173.0 28.6	Amos & Smith 135 NHP 12.8 knots	Earl Steam Fishing Co Ltd Grimsby
1938 Sold to Jutland Amalgamated Trawlers Ltd, Hull renamed LADY ELSA. (H532). 03.08.1939 Sold to the Royal Navy as an anti-submarine trawler No. FY 124. 25.03.1941 In collision with Norwegian submarine B1 (b 1922) near Cambletown sustained bow damage. 10.02.1942 Loaned to the United States Navy *(RN crew)* for North Atlantic anti-submarine work. Oct 1942 returned. Jan 1946 Sold back to Jutland Amalgamated Trawlers Ltd, Hull (H286). 02.11.1950 to Associated Fishing Trawling Co Ltd, Hull renamed LORD TAY. 26.06.1953 to Lord Line Ltd, Hull. *(Jan 1954 Fitted for Fuel Oil).* 03.09.1964 Severely damage by fire which broke out in her engine room whilst alongside at Hull. 1964 Vessel sold for scrap (£6,992) to Thos W Ward. 20.11.1964 Arrived Grays, Essex for breaking up.					
EL CAPITAN 164429 GY450 Steam Trawler	626 15.05.1937 28.07.1937	514 280	173.0 28.6	Amos & Smith 135 NHP 12.8 knots	Earl Steam Fishing Co Ltd Grimsby
1938 Sold to Crampin Steam Fishing Co Ltd, Grimsby renamed WELLARD. Aug 1939 Sold to the Royal Navy as an anti-submarine trawler No. FY 137. 25.02.1942 Loaned to the United States Navy *(RN crew)* for North Atlantic anti-submarine work. Oct 1942 returned. Jul 1946 Sold back to Crampin Steam Fishing Co, Grimsby (GY300), and managed by Hull Ice Co Ltd, Hull. Nov 1946 transferred to her owners at Grimsby. 1961 Vessel sold for scrap to Van Heyghen Freres, Belgium. 31.08.1961 Arrived Ghent for breaking up.					
VISENDA 164421 GY377 Steam Trawler	627 30.01.1937 05.04.1937	455 185	161.6 27.2	C.D.Holmes 120 NHP 12 knots	Atlas Steam Fishing Co Ltd Grimsby.
28.08.1939 Rqd by the Royal Navy as an anti-submarine trawler No. FY 138. 08.02.1946 returned. 23.03.1941 HMT VISENDA sank U551 with depth-charges south of Iceland in approx position 63° 37'N 016° 47'W. All forty-five crew of the German submarine were lost. 1959 Vessel sold for scrap to Jacques Bakker & Zonen, Belgium. 27.02.1959 Arrived Bruges for breaking up.					
Not Built	628-629-630-631-632-633 Orders cancelled due to a slump in the fishing industry.				

Yard No.626
1937 EL CAPITAN as WELLARD
Photo by courtesy of The Grimsby Evening Telegraph

Yard No.634
1937 ST. ELSTAN
Photo:- Author's Collection

Yard No.649
1938 FORTO (towing SACRAMENTO)
Photo:- Author's Collection

NAME Official No. Port Letters Numbers	Yard No. Launched Registered	Registered G Ton N Ton	 L Ft B Ft	Engine Builder Horse Power Reg'd Speed	OWNER (Built for)
ST. ELSTAN 165685 H484 Steam Trawler	634 23.09.1937 16.11.1937	564 209	172.2 29.1	C.D.Holmes 157 NHP 12.4 knots	Thomas Hamling & Co Ltd Hull.
09.09.1939 Rqd by the Royal Navy as an anti-submarine trawler No. FY 240. 15.12.1945 returned. *(Jul 1949 Fitted for Fuel Oil).* 1966 Vessel sold for scrap to Scrapping Co S.R.L, Belgium. 06.01.1966 Left Hull for breaking up in Ghent.					
ST. WISTAN 165690 H486 Steam Trawler	635 21.10.1937 10.12.1937	564 209	172.2 29.1	C.D.Holmes 157 NHP 12.4 knots	Thomas Hamling & Co Ltd Hull.
31.05.1940 Rqd by the Royal Navy as an anti-submarine trawler / auxiliary patrol vessel No. FY 4.015. *(Sep 1953 Fitted for Fuel Oil).* 1941 Served with South Atlantic command. 1942 Served with West Atlantic command. 19.05.1946 returned. 1966 Vessel sold for scrap to Scrapping Co S.R.L, Belgium. 06.01.1966 Left Hull for breaking up in Ghent.					
Not Built	636-637-638 Orders cancelled due to a slump in the fishing industry.				
ADMIRAL HAWKE 165669 H476 Steam Trawler	639 24.06.1937 12.08.1937	507 195	166.2 28.1	C.D.Holmes 132 NHP 12.5 knots	C H Smith & Co Ltd Hull.
30.07.1938 Sold to Charleson & Smith Ltd, Hull renamed (07.11.1938) STELLA CAPELLA. 14.08.1939 Sold to the Royal Navy as an anti-submarine trawler No. FY 107. 11.03.1942 *(at approx 0211 hrs)* Vessel sunk by torpedo by U701 (Commander Degen) in Icelandic waters in approx position 64° 48'N 013° 20'W. The U-boat observed the trawler sinking 2 ½ minutes after being hit. Lost whilst serving with the 41st anti-submarine group based at Iceland.					
KINGSTON AGATE 165692 H489 Steam Trawler	640 18.11.1937 23.12.1937	464 168	164.0 27.2	C.D.Holmes 155 NHP 12.5 knots	Kingston Steam Trawling Co Ltd Hull.
18.09.1939 Rqd by the Royal Navy as an anti-submarine trawler / armed boarding FY 212. 03.01.1946 returned. *(Mar 1950 Fitted for Fuel Oil).* 1963 Vessel sold for scrap to Jos de Smedt, Belgium. 03.10.1963 Arrived Antwerp (Brucht) for breaking up.					
BARNETT 164432 GY454 Steam Trawler	641 26.07.1937 29.09.1937	483 202	166.2 28.1	C.D.Holmes 132 NHP 12.5 knots	Crampin Steam Fishing Co Ltd Grimsby.
Aug 1939 Sold to the Royal Navy as anti-submarine FY 117 renamed BLACKFLY. 15.05.1944 HMT BLACKFLY and HMS KILMARNOCK (Ex US Navy PCE 837 B1943) attacked and sank U731 off Tangiers. Jul 1946 Sold back to Crampin Steam Fishing Co, Grimsby (GY200) renamed BARNETT. 1960 Vessel sold for scrap (£6,581) to Van Heyghen Freres, Belgium. 30.09.1960 Arrived Ghent for breaking up.					
EQUALITY 165699 Water Boat	642 03.03.1938 1938	66 37	64.0 16.0	Plenty & Sons 27 BHP 6 knots	Hull Trawler Supply Co Ltd Hull.
135 tons Fresh Water capacity for use at St Andrew's Dock for bunkering trawlers.					
JAMES ROCK-BREAKER VII Rock-breaking Pontoon	643 03.02.1938 08.04.1938	251 169	105.0 33.0	N/A	James Dredging Towage & Transport Co Ltd London.
08.04.1938 Left Hull in tow for Southampton.					
BOYS OWN 165703 Passenger Pleasure Ship	644 17.03.1938 09.04.1938	52 27	69.0 17.0	Bergius (Twin) 176 BHP 9.5 knots	John, Jim and Walter Newby Bridlington
16.11.1939 Rqd by the Royal Navy for harbour patrol duties / boom defence vessel. 28.04.1942 Sold to the Royal Navy. Feb 1946 Sold back to Newby Bros, Bridlington. 07.03.1946 returned to Cook Welton & Gemmell for conversion back to a Passenger Pleasure Ship *(155 passengers).* 15.04.1946 Left Beverley for Bridlington for her first trip. 1960 to Trevor Silverwood, Flamborough renovated and renamed FLAMBORIAN. 1966 to Desmond Connelly, Bridlington. 1993 to Julian Connelly, Bridlington. 1995 to Andrea Connelly, Bridlington. Jun 1998 to Croson Ltd and the Bournemouth Poole & Swanage Steam Packet Co Ltd renamed SWANAGE QUEEN. 1999 Vessel still in service.					
YORKSHIRE BELLE 165707 Passenger Pleasure Ship	645 07.05.1938 19.05.1938	75 30	76.0 17.0	Bergius (Twin) 176 BHP 9.5 knots	Crawford & Pockley Bridlington
23.11.1939 Rqd by the Royal Navy patrol duties / boom defence vessel. 11.04.1941 Vessel sunk by mine 3.5 cables from Haile Sand Fort, River Humber. All crew lost.					

NAME Official No. Port Letters Numbers	Yard No. Launched Registered	Registered G Ton N Ton	 L Ft B Ft	Engine Builder Horse Power Reg'd Speed	OWNER (Built for)
FOREMOST 90	646	143	85.0	C.D.Holmes	James Dredging Towage &
166553	02.07.1938		24.0	NHP	Transport Co Ltd
Steam Tug	31.08.1938			11 knots	London.
1939 Sold to the Royal Navy No.C64 based at Devonport for fleet fuelling duties. 1959 renamed FOREMOST. 24.10.1967 Vessel sold for scrap to Jos de Smedt, Antwerp, Belgium and broken up.					
FOREMOST 91	647	143	85.0	C.D.Holmes	James Dredging Towage &
166571	16.07.1938		24.0	NHP	Transport Co Ltd
Steam Tug	13.09.1938			11 knots	London.
1939 Sold to the Royal Navy No.C11 based at Portsmouth for fleet fuelling duties. 1959 renamed REGARD. 25.05.1966 Vessel sold for scrap to Jos de Smedt, Antwerp, Belgium and broken up.					
FOREMOST 93	648	116	85.0	C.D.Holmes	James Dredging Towage &
166607	12.09.1938		24.0	NHP	Transport Co Ltd
Steam Tug	23.11.1938			11 knots	London.
1939 Vessel deleted from Lloyds Register of Shipping.					
FORTO	649	180	101.2	Amos & Smith	Ellerman's
167047	12.11.1938		25.8	106 NHP	Wilson Line
Steam Tug	12.01.1939			11.5 knots	Hull
13.03.1968 Sold to United Towing Co Ltd, Hull. 1968 Vessel sold for scrap to Hughes Bolckow Ltd. 15.06.1968 Arrived Blyth for breaking up.					
LADY LILIAN	650	581	178.1	C.D. Holmes	Jutland Amalgamated
167076	02.09.1939	214	30.0	165 NHP	Trawlers Ltd
H229 Steam Trawler	09.11.1939			12.8 knots	Hull
23.01.1940 Rqd by the Royal Navy as an anti-submarine trawler . 16.03.1941 Vessel sunk by German aircraft 150 miles west by south of Bloody Foreland West of Ireland in approx position 54°18'N 012°10'W. Bombs exploded under the trawler splitting the hull causing her to sink in ten minutes. Lost whilst serving with the anti-submarine trawler force based at Belfast.					
LADY MADELEINE	651	581	178.1	C.D.Holmes	Jutland Amalgamated
167077	14.09.1939	214	30.0	165 NHP	Trawlers Ltd
H243 Steam Trawler	30.11.1939			12.8 knots	Hull
24.01.1940 Rqd by the Royal Navy as an anti-submarine trawler No. FY 283. 13.02.1946 returned. 14.11.1942 Sold to Kingston Steam Trawling Co Ltd, Hull renamed (04.04.1946) KINGSTON DIAMOND. *(Dec 1949 Fitted for Fuel Oil).* 25.10.1963 to Wyre Trawlers, Fleetwood (FD84). 1965 Vessel sold for scrap to Smith & Houston Ltd, Port Glasgow. 08.04.1965 Left Fleetwood for Glasson Dock for breaking up.					

Yard No.651
1939 LADY MADELEINE as KINGSTON DIAMOND
Photo:- Author's Collection

Yard No.653
1940 H.M.T. BLACKTHORN
Photo:- Author's Collection

Yard No.655
1940 ST. ZENO
Photo:- Author's Collection

Yard No.663
1941 H.M.S. AZALEA
Photo by courtesy of The Imperial War Museum

Vessels built at Beverley 1939 to 1945.

<table>
<tr><th rowspan="2">NAME
Official No.
PLN Vessel Type</th><th rowspan="2">Yard No.
Ordered
Laid Down</th><th rowspan="2">
Launched
Completed</th><th colspan="2">Registered</th><th rowspan="2">Engine Builder
Horse Power
Reg'd Speed</th><th rowspan="2">OWNER</th></tr>
<tr><th>G Ton
N Ton</th><th>L Ft
B Ft</th></tr>
<tr><td>BIRCH
T 93
Tree Class</td><td>652
05.06.1939
21.08.1939</td><td>
11.11.1939
17.04.1940</td><td>452
144</td><td>150.0
27.6</td><td>C.D.Holmes
850 IHP
11.5 knots</td><td>The Admiralty
Whitehall
London</td></tr>
<tr><td colspan="7">09.05.1947 Sold to Vosper Ltd Portsmouth. 1955 renamed MAGNOLIA P14 Official No.186786.
(converted to a motor trawler) (Length 153.8 Ft 479 Gross tons).
12.01.1955 Vessel transferred to Hull and managed by St Andrew's Steam Fishing Co Ltd, Hull.
28.08.1962 to N V Vischhandel Reed Ijsf. & Hoelhuis V/H, Scheveningen, Holland renamed FRANK.
1964 Vessel sold for scrap to shipbreakers and broken up.</td></tr>
<tr><td>BLACKTHORN
T 100
Tree Class</td><td>653
05.06.1939
25.08.1939</td><td>
29.11.1939
31.05.1940</td><td>452
144</td><td>150.0
27.6</td><td>C.D.Holmes
850 IHP
11.5 knots</td><td>The Admiralty
Whitehall
London</td></tr>
<tr><td colspan="7">09.05.1947 Sold to Vosper Ltd Portsmouth renamed MAYTHORN P57 Official No.182741.
(converted to a motor trawler) (Length 153.8 Ft 479 Gross tons). Based at Milford Haven.
03.07.1954 Vessel transferred to Hull and managed by St Andrew's Steam Fishing Co Ltd, Hull.
31.03.1955 to A/S Bergens Fiskerisellska, Bergen, Norway renamed KLAN.
1963 to Olav Ostervold, Bergen renamed JAN OVE. 1971 Vessel sold for scrap to shipbreakers and broken up.</td></tr>
<tr><td>ST APOLLO
167088
H351 Steam Trawler</td><td>654
1939
1939</td><td>
14.12.1939
25.06.1940</td><td>608
207</td><td>178.1
30.0</td><td>C.D.Holmes
165 NHP
12 knots</td><td>Firth Steam
Trawling Co Ltd
Hull</td></tr>
<tr><td colspan="7">20.02.1940 Rqd by the Royal Navy as an anti-submarine trawler .
22.11.1941 Vessel sank following a collision with the 'S' Class Destroyer HMS SARDONYX (b 1919) off the Hebrides.
Vessel lost whilst serving with the Clyde escort group based at Greenock.</td></tr>
<tr><td>ST ZENO
167090
H255 Steam Trawler</td><td>655
1939
1939</td><td>
12.02.1940
18.07.1940</td><td>608
207</td><td>178.1
30.0</td><td>C.D.Holmes
165 NHP
12 knots</td><td>Thomas Hamling
& Co Ltd
Hull</td></tr>
<tr><td colspan="7">26.03.1940 Rqd by the Royal Navy as an anti-submarine trawler No.FY.280. 10.05.1946 returned.
25.02.1942 Loaned to the United States Navy (Royal Navy crew) for North Atlantic anti-submarine work. Oct 1942 returned.
1943 Sold to Firth Steam Trawling Co Ltd, Hull. (Dec 1949 Fitted for Fuel Oil).
17.01.1952 to Henriksen & Co Ltd, Hull renamed BANYERS.
1966 Vessel sold for scrap to Scrapping Company S.R.L, Belgium. 26.11.1966 Arrived Antwerp for breaking up.</td></tr>
<tr><td>VIZALMA
166636
GY101 Steam Trawler</td><td>656
1939
1939</td><td>
11.04.1940
12.08.1940</td><td>572
207</td><td>178.1
30.0</td><td>C.D.Holmes
165 NHP
12 knots</td><td>Atlas Steam
Fishing Co Ltd
Grimsby</td></tr>
<tr><td colspan="7">15.06.1940 Rqd by the Royal Navy as an anti-submarine trawler No.FY.286. 23.12.1945 returned.
(Sep 1949 Fitted for Fuel Oil).
1964 Vessel sold for scrap to Clayton and Davie Ltd. 04.11.1964 Arrived Dunston on Tyne for breaking up.</td></tr>
<tr><td>Not Built</td><td colspan="6">657-658-659-660-661-662 Orders cancelled due to War.</td></tr>
<tr><td>AZALEA
K 25
Flower Class Corvette</td><td>663
1939
15.11.1939</td><td>
08.07.1940
27.01.1941</td><td>721
261</td><td>192.9
33.0</td><td>C.D.Holmes
2800 IHP
16 knots</td><td>The Admiralty
Whitehall
London</td></tr>
<tr><td colspan="7">1946 Sold to Soc. Anon Maritime Et Commerciale, Switzerland renamed NORTE (converted to a cargo vessel).
registered in Panama (860 Gross tons 353 Net tons). 1953 to Navegacáo Riograndense, Porto Alegre, Brazil.
19.01.1955 Vessel sank following a collision with Brazilian registered ss TAMBAHU (1731 gt/ b 1905) off Cape Santa Marta south of Floriannopolis.</td></tr>
<tr><td>BEGONIA
K 66
Flower Class Corvette</td><td>664
1939
13.04.1940</td><td>
18.09.1940
03.03.1941</td><td>721
261</td><td>192.9
33.0</td><td>C.D.Holmes
2800 IHP
16 knots</td><td>The Admiralty
Whitehall
London</td></tr>
<tr><td colspan="7">16.03.1942 Commissioned into the US Navy renamed IMPULSE No.PG68. 22.08.1945 returned and reverted.
1946 Sold to Wheelcock Marden, Hong Kong renamed BEGONLOCK Official No.181545 (converted to a cargo vessel)
(Length 189.9 ft 721 Gross tons 262 Net tons).
1949 to Adrilleros Luzurinaga S.A, Pasajes renamed FUNICIONES MOLINAO.
1951 to Astrilleros Luzuriago S.A, Bilbao renamed ASTILUZU.
1955 to Naviera Compostela S.A, Corunna renamed RIO MERO.
07.02.1970 On a voyage from the Canary Islands to Valencia ran aground off Punta de Las Entinas in Position 36° 41'N 002° 46'W. 1970 Vessel sold for scrap to Spanish shipbreakers.</td></tr>
</table>

NAME	Yard No.		Registered		Engine Builder	OWNER
Official No.	Ordered	Launched	G Ton	L Ft	Horse Power	
PLN Vessel Type	Laid Down	Completed	N Ton	B Ft	Reg'd Speed	
GAVOTTE	665		452	150.0	C.D.Holmes	The Admiralty
T 115	09.09.1939	07.05.1940	142	27.6	850 IHP	Whitehall
Dance Class	08.12.1939	24.08.1940			11.5 knots	London
1946 Sold to the Italian Navy renamed RD312. Nov 1965 Vessel placed on disposal list:- used as target vessel.						
HORNPIPE	666		452	150.0	C.D.Holmes	The Admiralty
T 120	09.09.1939	21.05.1940	142	27.6	850 IHP	Whitehall
Dance Class	08.12.1939	14.09.1940			11.5 knots	London
16.03.1946 Sold to the Italian Navy renamed RD316. Nov 1965 Vessel placed on disposal list:- used as target vessel.						
HAMLET	667		452	150.0	C.D.Holmes	The Admiralty
T 167	12.12.1939	24.07.1940	142	27.6	950 IHP	Whitehall
Shakesperian Class	21.02.1940	23.12.1940			12 knots	London
30.01.1947 Sold to Partrederiet, Reidun, Norway renamed EIFONN. 1950 to Soc.Nav.Laennaise, Toulon, France renamed FORT LAMALGUE *(converted to a cargo vessel) (fitted for fuel oil) (Length 153.6 ft 491 Gross tons 172 Net tons).* 1954 to Paolo Caruso & Co, Trapani, Italy renamed UNION. 1956 renamed ITACA *(Ansaldo 7cyl 525 BHP diesel engine fitted).* 1974 to C Kavadas, Piræus, Greece renamed NICOLAS K. 1976 to G Carponis, Piræus. 23.06.1976 Vessel sank 90 miles west of Tel-Aviv after engine failure and developing leaks on passage from Limasol to Aqaba.						
HORATIO	668		452	150.0	C.D.Holmes	The Admiralty
T 153	12.12.1939	08.08.1940	142	27.6	950 IHP	Whitehall
Shakesperian Class	12.03.1940	27.01.1941			12 knots	London
07.01.1943 Vessel sunk in the Scarpanto Channel torpedoed by an Italian E Boat. MA/SB. Thirty-two crew lost, two taken prisoner. Lost whilst serving with the 8th Minesweeper / Anti-submarine group based at Oran Western Mediterranean.						
JULIET	669		452	150.0	C.D.Holmes	The Admiralty
T 136	12.12.1939	02.10.1940	142	27.6	950 IHP	Whitehall
Shakesperian Class	23.05.1940	20.03.1941			12 knots	London
1947 Sold to Regent Shippers London renamed PETERJON Official No.181762 *(converted to a cargo vessel) (Length 173.8 ft 585 Gross tons 259 Net tons) (Crossley Bros 8 cyl diesel engine fitted).* 1951 to Limerick Steam-ship Co Ltd London renamed PLASSY re-assessed *(563 Gross Tons 233 Net Tons).* 08.03.1960 Vessel ran aground on passage from Liverpool towards Galway on Finnis Rock in Galway Bay, Arran Isle.						
LAERTES	670		452	150.0	C.D.Holmes	The Admiralty
T 137	12.12.1939	16.10.1940	142	27.6	950 IHP	Whitehall
Shakesperian Class	23.05.1940	09.04.1941			12 knots	London
25.07.1942 Vessel sunk torpedoed by U201 (Captain Schnee) at 2305 hours in approx Position 06°00'N 014° 17'W. Lost whilst serving with the 1st Minesweeper / Anti-submarine group based at Freetown.						
ARRAN	671		452	150.0	C.D.Holmes	The Admiralty
T 06	06.04.1940	16.11.1940	142	27.6	850 IHP	Whitehall
Isles Class	25.07.1940	29.04.1941			12 knots	London
02.10.1946 Sold to NV Verre Visscheri Maats, Holland renamed ASSAN REIS *(458 Gross tons 168 Net tons).* 1952 to Schhliiienz Hagemann Hochsee und Garfrikrfisch GmBH, Kiel, Germany renamed PROFESSOR HENKING. 1956 to Reinhold Kienass, Büdelsdorf renamed BERTA KIENASS *(Motorenf 7 cyl diesel engine fitted).* 31.01.1962 Vessel sank on passage from Amsterdam to Copenhagen off Texel Island in approx position 51° 53'N 004° 41'E All passengers and crew lost.						
BALTA	672		452	150.0	C.D.Holmes	The Admiralty
T 50	06.04.1940	02.12.1940	142	27.6	850 IHP	Whitehall
Isles Class	10.08.1940	16.05.1941			12 knots	London
12.07.1946 Sold to Tai Chong Cheang Steam Ship Co, Shanghai, China renamed CHING HAI *(converted to a cargo vessel) (478 Gross ton 184 Net tons).* 1992 Vessel deleted from Lloyds Register of Shipping.						
BRORA	673		452	150.0	C.D.Holmes	The Admiralty
T 99	06.04.1940	18.12.1940	142	27.6	850 IHP	Whitehall
Isles Class	13.08.1940	04.06.1941			12 knots	London
06.09.1941 Vessel wrecked in the Hebrides.						
HOXA	674		452	150.0	C.D.Holmes	The Admiralty
T 16	27.05.1940	15.01.1941	142	27.6	850 IHP	Whitehall
Isles Class	20.09.1940	20.06.1941			12 knots	London
1946 Sold to Ming Sung Industrial Co Ltd, Shanghai, China renamed SUNG HWEI *(452 Gross tons 144 Net tons).* 1992 Vessel deleted from Lloyds Register of Shipping.						

<table>
<tr><th rowspan="2">NAME
Official No.
PLN Vessel Type</th><th rowspan="2">Yard No.
Ordered
Laid Down</th><th rowspan="2">
Launched
Completed</th><th colspan="2">Registered</th><th rowspan="2">Engine Builder
Horse Power
Reg'd Speed</th><th rowspan="2">OWNER</th></tr>
<tr><th>G Ton
N Ton</th><th>L Ft
B Ft</th></tr>
<tr><td>HOY
T 114
Isles Class</td><td>675
27.05.1940
20.10.1940</td><td>
01.02.1941
08.07.1941</td><td>452
142</td><td>150.0
27.6</td><td>C.D.Holmes
850 IHP
12 knots</td><td>The Admiralty
Whitehall
London</td></tr>
<tr><td colspan="7">Mar 1946 Sold to USSR Government Merchant Fleet, Vladivostok renamed DUNAY(converted to a cargo vessel)
(Length 153.6 ft 516 Gross tons 223 Net tons) (6cyl Russian diesel engine fitted).
1990 Vessel deleted from Lloyds Register of Shipping.</td></tr>
<tr><td>INCHCOLM
T 18
Isles Class</td><td>676
27.05.1940
20.10.1940</td><td>
03.03.1941
28.07.1941</td><td>452
142</td><td>150.0
27.6</td><td>C.D.Holmes
850 IHP
12 knots</td><td>The Admiralty
Whitehall
London</td></tr>
<tr><td colspan="7">Jun 1946 Sold to War Department (Royal Army Service Corps - Wreck dispersal).
1947 (converted to a cargo vessel) (Length 164.5 ft 453 Gross tons 183 Net tons).
1953 Sold to G A Ferguson, Lerwick (Apr 1953 fitted for fuel oil).
1953 to Giacomo Federici Di Giovanni, Rome, Italy renamed CELESTE AIDA.
(1958 Motorenwerk 6cyl 500 BHP diesel engine fitted).
1965 to Antonio Schiano Di Cola, Naples renamed ANNA GEMMA. 1976 to Zeus Shipping Co, Greece renamed ZEUS.
1976 to Constantinos Dagadakis, Piræus renamed AGIOS IOANNIS R. 1999 Vessel still in service.</td></tr>
<tr><td>MULL
T 110
Isles Class</td><td>677
22.07.1940
19.10.1940</td><td>
27.03.1941
19.08.1941</td><td>452
142</td><td>150.0
27.6</td><td>C.D.Holmes
850 IHP
12 knots</td><td>The Admiralty
Whitehall
London</td></tr>
<tr><td colspan="7">27.04.1946 Sold to the Ministry of Defence Army Dept - Wreck dispersal.
16.02.1962 Vessel ran aground in Loch Tarbert later salved. Jan 1974 Vessel placed on disposal list.</td></tr>
<tr><td>PLADDA
T 144
Isles Class</td><td>678
22.07.1940
29.12.1940</td><td>
16.04.1941
05.09.1941</td><td>452
142</td><td>150.0
27.6</td><td>C.D.Holmes
850 IHP
12 knots</td><td>The Admiralty
Whitehall
London</td></tr>
<tr><td colspan="7">May 1946 Loaned to Rangoon Harbour Authorities. Dec 1946 returned.
1947 Sold to Gythfeldt & Co Ltd, Singapore Official No. 173119. 1949 to Siamese owners.
1950 Vessel deleted from Lloyds Register of Shipping.</td></tr>
<tr><td>HILDASAY
T 173
Isles Class</td><td>679
13.09.1940
26.12.1940</td><td>
29.04.1941
30.09.1941</td><td>452
142</td><td>150.0
27.6</td><td>C.D.Holmes
850 IHP
12 knots</td><td>The Admiralty
Whitehall
London</td></tr>
<tr><td colspan="7">21.06.1945 Vessel wrecked on a reef near Kilindini Mombassa.
Lost whilst serving with the East African Patrol Flotilla based at Kilindini.</td></tr>
<tr><td>KILLEGRAY
T 174
Isles Class</td><td>680
13.09.1940
29.01.1941</td><td>
27.05.1941
07.11.1941</td><td>452
142</td><td>150.0
27.6</td><td>C.D.Holmes
850 IHP
12 knots</td><td>The Admiralty
Whitehall
London</td></tr>
<tr><td colspan="7">15.10.1941 Sold to the Royal New Zealand Navy. 30.01.1946 Paid Off to the Royal New Zealand Reserve at Auckland.
10.09.1958 Vessel sold for scrap to G A Sparrey and broken up at Auckland.</td></tr>
<tr><td>SCARBA
T 175
Isles Class</td><td>681
13.09.1940
06.03.1941</td><td>
25.06.1941
25.11.1941</td><td>452
142</td><td>150.0
27.6</td><td>C.D.Holmes
850 IHP
12 knots</td><td>The Admiralty
Whitehall
London</td></tr>
<tr><td colspan="7">Oct 1941 Sold to the Royal New Zealand Navy. 21.03.1946 Paid Off to the Royal New Zealand Reserve at Auckland.
10.09.1958 Vessel sold for scrap to G A Sparrey and broken up at Auckland.</td></tr>
<tr><td>BIRDLIP
T 218
Hills Class</td><td>682
20.11.1940
01.03.1941</td><td>
09.07.1941
23.12.1941</td><td>510
160</td><td>166.3
28.0</td><td>C.D.Holmes
970 IHP
11 knots</td><td>The Admiralty
Whitehall
London</td></tr>
<tr><td colspan="7">13.06.1944 Vessel sunk torpedoed by U547 (Captain Niemeyer) off the West African coast
in approx Position 05° 09'N 001° 36'W. Lost whilst serving with the 2nd Anti-submarine group based at Freetown.</td></tr>
<tr><td>BUTSER
T 219
Hills Class</td><td>683
20.11.1940
01.04.1941</td><td>
29.07.1941
16.01.1942</td><td>510
160</td><td>166.3
28.0</td><td>C.D.Holmes
970 IHP
11 knots</td><td>The Admiralty
Whitehall
London</td></tr>
<tr><td colspan="7">10.04.1946 Sold to Devon Fishing Co Ltd, Hull renamed BALTHAZAR H359 Official No.181282.
(538 Gross tons 210 Net tons) (Nov 1946 fitted for fuel oil).
11.01.1952 to Loyal Steam Fishing Co Ltd, Grimsby renamed ROYAL MARINE (GY213).
11.04.1960 to Wyre Trawlers Ltd Fleetwood (FD63).
25.07.1963 Vessel abandoned south of the Mull of Galloway after a fire in the stoke hold. On being towed back to Fleetwood the ROYAL MARINE was found to be damaged beyond repair and laid up.
1963 Vessel sold for scrap to West of Scotland Shipbreaking Co Ltd. 22.10.1963 Left Fleetwood for Troon for breaking up.</td></tr>
</table>

Yard No.686
1942 H.M.T. YES TOR as STELLA CARINA
Photo:- Harry Cartlidge Collection

Yard No.689
1942 H.M.T. INKPEN
Photo by courtesy of Hull Maritime Museum

Yard No.706
1943 H.M.T. COLDSTREAMER
Photo:- Author's Collection

NAME	Yard No.		Registered		Engine Builder	OWNER
Official No.	Ordered	Launched	G Ton	L Ft	Horse Power	
PLN Vessel Type	Laid Down	Completed	N Ton	B Ft	Reg'd Speed	
DUNCTON	684		510	166.3	C.D.Holmes	The Admiralty
T 220	18.01.1941	06.09.1941	160	28.0	970 IHP	Whitehall
Hills Class	02.05.1941	11.02.1942			11 knots	London
10.04.1946 Sold to Marine Steam Fishing Co Ltd renamed COLWYN BAY H387 Official No. 181294. *(517 Gross tons 190 Net tons). (Mar 1953 fitted for fuel oil).* 18.05.1951 to St Andrew's Steam Fishing Co Ltd, Hull. 15.04.1955 Transferred to Grimsby. 11.04.1956 Transferred to Hull. 1964 Vessel sold for scrap to Arie Rijsdijk Boss & Zonen, Holland. 29.02.1964 Arrived Hendrik Ido Ambacht for breaking up.						
PORTSDOWN	685		510	166.3	C.D.Holmes	The Admiralty
T 221	18.01.1941	24.09.1941	160	28.0	970 IHP	Whitehall
Hills Class	07.05.1941	06.03.1942			11 knots	London
10.04.1946 Sold to Hull Merchants Amalgamated Trawlers Ltd, Hull renamed SOLLUM H369 Official No. 181287. *(505 Gross tons 186 Net tons) (Dec 1949 fitted for fuel oil).* 21.01.1949 to Derwent Trawlers Ltd, Grimsby renamed HARGOOD (GY8). 24.06.1955 to Iago Steam Trawlers Ltd London renamed RED SABRE (LO71). 1964 Vessel sold for scrap to Haulbowline Industries Ltd Eire. 21.12.1964 Arrived Passage West Cork for breaking up.						
YES TOR	686		510	166.3	C.D.Holmes	The Admiralty
T 222	18.01.1941	21.10.1941	160	28.0	970 IHP	Whitehall
Hills Class	04.06.1941	10.04.1942			11 knots	London
10.04.1946 Sold to Hudson Bros Ltd, Hull renamed CAPE CLEVELAND H355. Official No. 181280 *(522 Gross tons 197 Net tons) (Nov 1947 fitted for fuel oil).* 12.11.1947 to Clyde Trawlers Ltd, Hull renamed STELLA CARINA. 05.09.1949 to Hudson Bros Ltd, Hull renamed CAPE FINISTERRE. 24.01.1952 to Great Grimsby & East Coast Steam Fishing Co Ltd, Grimsby DRAGOON (GY222). 23.06.1960 to Wyre Trawlers Ltd Fleetwood (FD60). 1966 Vessel sold for scrap to West of Scotland Shipbreaking Co Ltd. 18.12.1966 Arrived Troon for breaking up.						
BREDON	687		510	166.3	C.D.Holmes	The Admiralty
T 223	15.03.1941	20.11.1941	160	28.0	970 IHP	Whitehall
Hills Class	12.07.1941	29.04.1942			11 knots	London
08.02.1943 Vessel sunk torpedoed by U521 (Captain Bargsten) in the North Atlantic in approx Position 29° 49'N 014° 05'W. Lost whilst serving with the 2nd Anti-submarine group based at Freetown.						
DUNKERY	688		510	166.3	C.D.Holmes	The Admiralty
T 224	15.03.1941	04.12.1941	160	28.0	970 IHP	Whitehall
Hills Class	11.07.1941	29.05.1942			11 knots	London
10.04.1946 Sold to Hellyer Bros, Hull renamed SPANIARD H366 Official No. 181283. *(542 Gross tons 220 Net tons) (Jan 1947 fitted for fuel oil).* 01.03.1948 to Northern Fishing Co, Hull. 22.03.1949 Vessel wrecked off Sletnes Lighthouse near Gamvik, Finnmark, north Norway. All crew rescued.						
INKPEN	689		510	166.3	C.D.Holmes	The Admiralty
T 225	15.03.1941	22.12.1941	160	28.0	970 IHP	Whitehall
Hills Class	13.08.1941	19.06.1942			11 knots	London
22.10.1946 Sold to East Riding Trawlers Ltd, Hull renamed STELLA CAPELLA H358 Official No. 181281 *(504 Gross tons 191 Net tons) (Sep 1947 fitted for fuel oil).*01.09.1950 Transferred to Grimsby. 12.03.1951 Transferred to Hull managed by Charleson -Smith Trawlers Ltd, Hull. 1953 to Trawlers Grimsby Ltd, Grimsby. 1954 to Derwent Trawlers Ltd, Hull. 1960 to Ross Trawlers Ltd, Hull. 1963 to Hudson Bros, Hull. 1963 Vessel sold for scrap to Hughes Bolckow Ltd. 24.10.1963 Arrived Blyth for breaking up.						
BRESSAY	690		452	150.0	Amos & Smith	The Admiralty
T 214	17.05.1941	20.01.1942	142	27.6	850 IHP	Whitehall
Isles Class	27.09.1941	20.05.1942			12 knots	London
14.03.1946 Vessel sold to Belgium owners left Portland for Antwerp.						
EGILSAY	691		452	150.0	Amos & Smith	The Admiralty
T 215	17.05.1941	07.02.1942	142	27.6	850 IHP	Whitehall
Isles Class	01.10.1941	08.07.1942			12 knots	London
22.02.1946 Sold to Italian Navy No. DR 306. NATO fleet No. DR 5306 later M 5306. Nov 1965 Vessel placed on disposal list.						
ENSAY	692		452	150.0	Amos & Smith	The Admiralty
T 216	17.05.1941	05.03.1942	142	27.6	850 IHP	Whitehall
Isles Class	24.10.1941	01.08.1942			12 knots	London
16.02.1946 Sold to Italian Navy No. DR 314. NATO fleet No. DR 5314 later M 5314. Nov 1965 Vessel placed on disposal list. 29.09.1983 Vessel last seen at Cagliari as target ship.						

<table>
<tr><th rowspan="2">NAME
Official No.
PLN Vessel Type</th><th rowspan="2">Yard No.
Ordered
Laid Down</th><th rowspan="2">
Launched
Completed</th><th colspan="2">Registered</th><th rowspan="2">Engine Builder
Horse Power
Reg'd Speed</th><th rowspan="2">OWNER</th></tr>
<tr><th>G Ton
N Ton</th><th>L Ft
B Ft</th></tr>
<tr><td>RAASAY
T 292
Isles Class</td><td>693
16.06.1941
09.12.1941</td><td>
01.04.1942
16.09.1942</td><td>452
142</td><td>150.0
27.6</td><td>Amos & Smith
850 IHP
12 knots</td><td>The Admiralty
Whitehall
London</td></tr>
<tr><td colspan="7">1942 renamed SHEPPEY. 25.06.1946 Sold to Royal Army Service Corp. No. A35 - Wreck dispersal.
1959 Vessel sold for scrap to Demmelweek & Redding. 24.03.1959 Arrived Plymouth for breaking up.</td></tr>
<tr><td>WHALSAY
T 293
Isles Class</td><td>694
16.06.1941
09.12.1941</td><td>
04.04.1942
04.09.1942</td><td>452
142</td><td>150.0
27.6</td><td>Amos & Smith
850 IHP
12 knots</td><td>The Admiralty
Whitehall
London</td></tr>
<tr><td colspan="7">08.10.1943 Loaned to Portuguese Navy No.P4. 27.06.1945 returned.
11.06.1946 Sold to Portuguese Navy renamed SANTA MARIA . Apr 1971 Vessel placed on disposal list.</td></tr>
<tr><td>BERN
T 294
Isles Class</td><td>695
16.06.1941
24.12.1941</td><td>
02.05.1942
30.09.1942</td><td>452
142</td><td>150.0
27.6</td><td>Amos & Smith
850 IHP
12 knots</td><td>The Admiralty
Whitehall
London</td></tr>
<tr><td colspan="7">1946 Wreck dispersal vessel No. DV 4 (1956) Tank cleaning vessel No. P 410 - No. A 334.
30.08.1978 Vessel sold for scrap to Liguria Maritime. Nov 1978 Arrived Sittingbourne Kent for breaking up.</td></tr>
<tr><td>BRURAY
T 236
Isles Class</td><td>696
27.07.1941
17.02.1941</td><td>
16.05.1942
02.12.1942</td><td>452
142</td><td>150.0
27.6</td><td>Amos & Smith
850 IHP
12 knots</td><td>The Admiralty
Whitehall
London</td></tr>
<tr><td colspan="7">08.10.1943 Loaned to Portuguese Navy No. P1. 11.02.1946 Sold to Portuguese Navy renamed SAN MIGUEL.
1957 Vessel sold for scrap to shipbreakers in Lisbon and broken up.</td></tr>
<tr><td>SCALPAY
T 237
Isles Class</td><td>697
24.07.1941
14.02.1942</td><td>
02.06.1942
21.10.1942</td><td>452
142</td><td>150.0
27.6</td><td>C D Holmes
850 IHP
12 knots</td><td>The Admiralty
Whitehall
London</td></tr>
<tr><td colspan="7">1946 Wreck dispersal vessel No. DV 15.
1948 Sold to W Ripon Ltd London Official No.181928 (converted to a salvage vessel).
(Length 164.5 ft 475 Gross tons 155 Net tons) (M.W.M. Benz 6cyl diesel engine fitted).
1953 to 'Sorima' Soc Ricuperi Marittimi, Genoa, Italy. 1958 to Pasquale Di Donna, Torre Del Greco.
1964 to Ciro Garofano, Torre Del Greco.
Aug 1967 Vessel wrecked near Capo Mannu. 1968 Vessel sold for scrap to M A Esposito and broken up.</td></tr>
<tr><td>GWEAL
T 246
Isles Class</td><td>698
24.10.1941
12.03.1942</td><td>
17.06.1942
04.11.1942</td><td>452
142</td><td>150.0
27.6</td><td>Amos & Smith
850 IHP
12 knots</td><td>The Admiralty
Whitehall
London</td></tr>
<tr><td colspan="7">Launched as BRORERAY Sep 1942 renamed GWEAL.
1946 Sold to Johannes Ostensjo & Co A/S, Haugesund, Norwayrenamed VELOX (converted to a cargo vessel).
(Length 152.8 ft 508 Gross tons 250 Net tons) (Harland & Wolff 5cyl diesel engine fitted).
1965 to The Peoples Republic of China. 1991 Vessel deleted from Lloyds Register of Shipping.</td></tr>
<tr><td>NEAVE
T 247
Isles Class</td><td>699
24.10.1941
11.04.1942</td><td>
16.07.1942
18.11.1942</td><td>452
142</td><td>150.0
27.6</td><td>Amos & Smith
850 IHP
12 knots</td><td>The Admiralty
Whitehall
London</td></tr>
<tr><td colspan="7">1946 Wreck dispersal vessel No. DV 14. (1948) No. A 342.
01.07.1951 Sold to British Wheeler Process Ltd Liverpool renamed TULIPBANK (converted to a petroleum sludge carrier).
Official No.185455 (Length 153.8 ft 478 Gross tons 170 Net tons) (Jan 1953 fitted for fuel oil).
1964 to Barclay Curle & Co Ltd, Liverpool. 1965 to Elderslie Tank & Boiler Cleaning Co, Liverpool.
1975 to Beacon Cleaning Services (Scotland) Ltd, Liverpool. 1976 to Kelvin Beacon Ltd, Liverpool.
04.06.1979 to Northern Counties Shipping Co Ltd, Douglas, Isle of Man.
1979 Vessel sold for scrap to Rodridge Engineering Ltd, Hartlepool and broken up.</td></tr>
<tr><td>ULVA
T 248
Isles Class</td><td>700
24.10.1941
14.04.1942</td><td>
30.07.1942
16.12.1942</td><td>452
142</td><td>150.0
27.6</td><td>Amos & Smith
850 IHP
12 knots</td><td>The Admiralty
Whitehall
London</td></tr>
<tr><td colspan="7">1946 Sold for mercantile use renamed SALVO.
1948 Sold to A/S D/S Erling Lindo, Haugesund, Norway renamed PLICO (converted to a cargo vessel).
(Length 154.2 ft 516 Gross tons 264 Net tons) (Crossley Bros 8cyl diesel engine fitted).
1950 to R Boerma, Groningen, Holland renamed SURINAM. 1951 to A A Reid, Monrovia renamed ANNE T WILLIAM.
(1957 Ansaldo 5cyl diesel engine fitted). 1966 to W A Sanchez, Castries, St Lucia.
1977 Vessel deleted from Lloyds Register of Shipping.</td></tr>
</table>

MILITARY CLASS

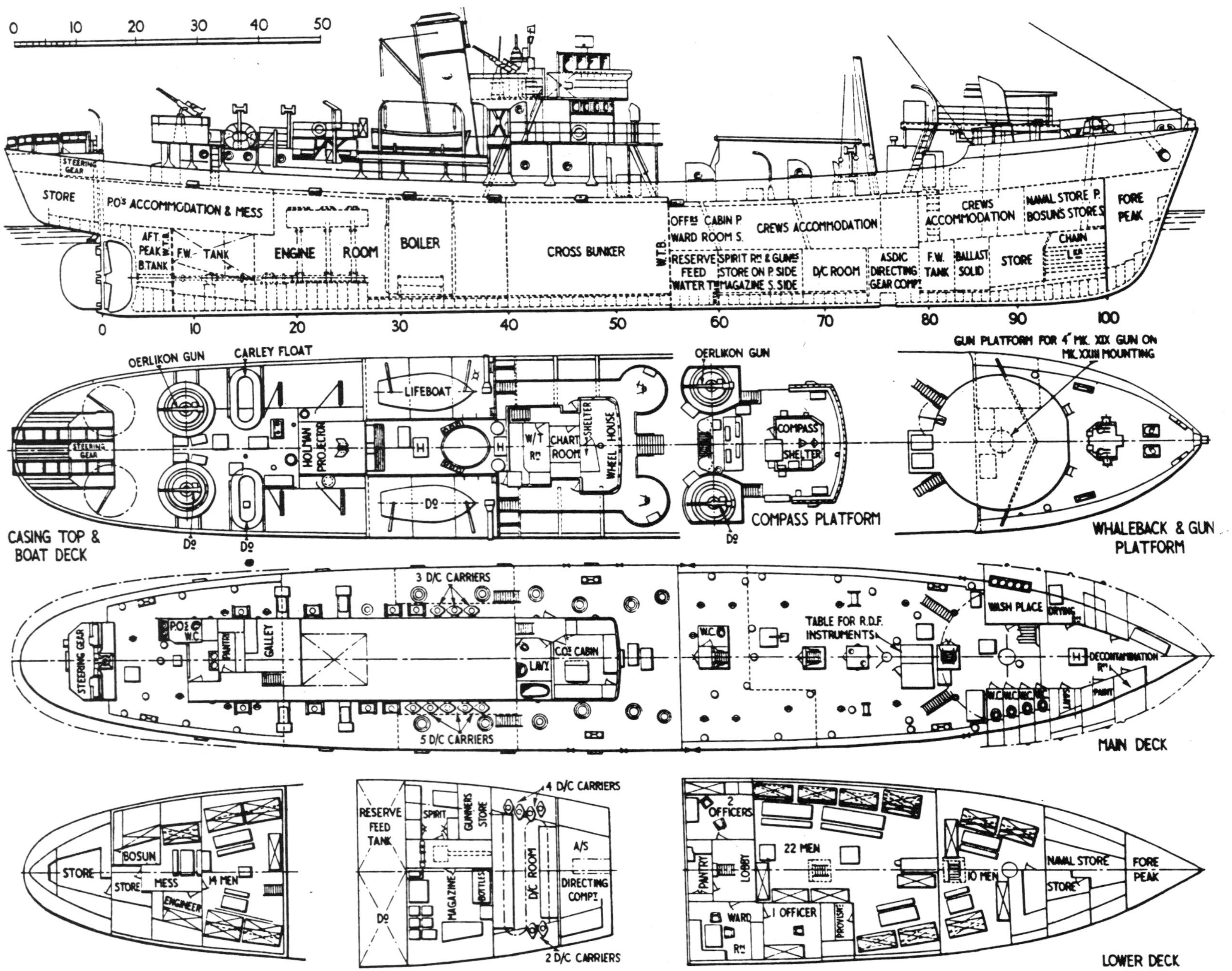

<table>
<tr><th>NAME
Official No.
PLN Vessel Type</th><th>Yard No.
Ordered
Laid Down</th><th>
Launched
Completed</th><th colspan="2">Registered</th><th>Engine Builder
Horse Power
Reg'd Speed</th><th>OWNER</th></tr>
<tr><th></th><th></th><th></th><th>G Ton
N Ton</th><th>L Ft
B Ft</th><th></th><th></th></tr>
<tr><td>HAYLING
T 271
Isles Class</td><td>701
01.01.1942
14.04.1942</td><td>
17.08.1942
31.12.1942</td><td>452
142</td><td>150.0
27.6</td><td>Amos & Smith
850 IHP
12 knots</td><td>The Admiralty
Whitehall
London</td></tr>
<tr><td colspan="7">08.10.1943 Loaned to Portuguese Navy No. P3. 02.07.1945 returned.
11.06.1946 Sold to Portuguese Navy renamed TERCEIRA. 1957 Vessel placed on disposal list.</td></tr>
<tr><td>LUNDY
T 272
Isles Class</td><td>702
01.01.1942
06.06.1942</td><td>
29.08.1942
15.01.1943</td><td>452
142</td><td>150.0
27.6</td><td>Amos & Smith
850 IHP
12 knots</td><td>The Admiralty
Whitehall
London</td></tr>
<tr><td colspan="7">1946 Wreck dispersal vessel No. DV 12. (1950) No. P 46. (1957) Tank cleaning vessel No. A 366.
1981 Vessel laid up for disposal at Portsmouth. 04.08.1982 Used and sunk as a target vessel.</td></tr>
<tr><td>GRENADIER
T 334
Military Class</td><td>703
07.02.1942
13.06.1942</td><td>
26.09.1942
10.02.1943</td><td>579
181</td><td>175.0
30.0</td><td>C.D.Holmes
1000 IHP
11 knots</td><td>The Admiralty
Whitehall
London</td></tr>
<tr><td colspan="7">20.04.1946 Sold to Great Grimsby & East Coast Steam Fishing Co Ltd, Grimsby renamed ISERNIA GY448
Official No. 166655. (580 Gross tons 207 Net tons) (Dec 1946 fitted for fuel oil).
16.11.1965 Damaged by fire in stoke hold. 19.11.1965 Grounded at the entrance of Peterhead harbour.
1966 Vessel sold for scrap to Arie Rijsdijk Boss & Zonen 22.01.1966 Arrived Hendrik Ido Ambacht for breaking up.</td></tr>
<tr><td>LANCER
T 335
Military Class</td><td>704
07.02.1942
03.07.1942</td><td>
26.10.1942
26.02.1943</td><td>579
181</td><td>175.0
30.0</td><td>C.D.Holmes
1000 IHP
11 knots</td><td>The Admiralty
Whitehall
London</td></tr>
<tr><td colspan="7">20.04.1946 Sold to East Riding Trawlers Ltd, Hull renamed STELLA ORION H379 Official No. 181293.
(575 Gross tons 228 Net tons) (Sep 1949 fitted for fuel oil).
02.01.1951 to Trawlers Grimsby Ltd, Grimsby managed by Charleson - Smith Trawlers Ltd, Hull.
07.11.1955 Vessel wrecked at Maalay, Vestfjorden, Norway outward bound for the Barents Sea. All twenty crew rescued by a Norwegian vessel. Attempts to re-float the trawler by the Norwegian salvage tug ULLER (319 gt/ b 1943) failed.</td></tr>
<tr><td>SAPPER
T 336
Military Class</td><td>705
07.02.1942
10.08.1942</td><td>
11.11.1942
19.03.1943</td><td>579
181</td><td>175.0
30.0</td><td>C.D.Holmes
1000 IHP
11 knots</td><td>The Admiralty
Whitehall
London</td></tr>
<tr><td colspan="7">20.04.1946 Sold to Hudson Bros Ltd, Hull renamed CAPE GLOUCESTER H395 Official No. 181295.
(624 Gross tons 279 Net tons) (Jun 1949 fitted for fuel oil).
28.12.1956 to Henriksen & Co Ltd, Hull renamed ADMETUS.
1966 Vessel sold for scrap to Scrapping Co, Belgium. 10.05.1966 Left Hull for Antwerp for breaking up.</td></tr>
<tr><td>COLDSTREAMER
T 337
Military Class</td><td>706
16.04.1942
12.08.1942</td><td>
10.12.1942
09.04.1943</td><td>579
181</td><td>175.0
30.0</td><td>C.D.Holmes
1000 IHP
11 knots</td><td>The Admiralty
Whitehall
London</td></tr>
<tr><td colspan="7">1946 Sold to Hellyer Bros Ltd, Hull renamed ESQUIMAUX H297 Official No. 181271.
(619 Gross tons 234 Net tons) (Apr 1947 fitted for fuel oil). 01.03.1948 to Devon Fishing Co Ltd, Hull.
05.05.1956 to West Dock Steam Fishing Co Ltd, Hull renamed DUNSLEY WYKE. 29.06.1966 to Hellyer Bros Ltd, Hull.
1967 Vessel sold for scrap to Scrapping Co, Belgium. 19.02.1967 Arrived Antwerp for breaking up.</td></tr>
<tr><td>FUSILIER
T 305
Military Class</td><td>707
16.04.1942
12.09.1942</td><td>
23.12.1942
30.04.1943</td><td>579
181</td><td>175.0
30.0</td><td>C.D.Holmes
1000 IHP
11 knots</td><td>The Admiralty
Whitehall
London</td></tr>
<tr><td colspan="7">1946 Sold to Standard Steam Fishing Co Ltd, Grimsby renamed SERRON GY309 Official No. 166647.
(578 Gross tons 212 Net tons) (Jul 1947 fitted for fuel oil).
1965 Vessel sold for scrap to Thos W Ward Ltd, Preston. 13.01.1965 Arrived Grays, River Thames for breaking up.</td></tr>
<tr><td>BOMBARDIER
T 304
Military Class</td><td>708
28.05.1942
16.10.1942</td><td>
23.01.1943
15.05.1943</td><td>579
181</td><td>175.0
30.0</td><td>C.D.Holmes
1000 IHP
11 knots</td><td>The Admiralty
Whitehall
London</td></tr>
<tr><td colspan="7">1946 Sold to Hellyer Bros Ltd, Hull. renamed NORMAN H289 Official No. 181272.
(629 Gross tons 244 Net tons). 01.03.1948 to Northern Fishing Co Ltd, Hull.
04.10.1952 Vessel wrecked in thick fog on Skerries east of Cape Farewell, South Greenland. Twenty crew lost one rescued.</td></tr>
<tr><td>BLACKBIRD
M 15
Controlled mine-layer</td><td>709
29.05.1942
03.11.1942</td><td>
20.02.1943
09.06.1943</td><td>442
149</td><td>150.0
27.6</td><td>C.D.Holmes
850 IHP
12 knots</td><td>The Admiralty
Whitehall
London</td></tr>
<tr><td colspan="7">Ordered as SHEPPEY Isles Class (Nov 1942) modified and renamed BLACKBIRD.
1949 Sold to Gwent Co Aberdeen renamed GOODMAR A639 Official No. 182024 (449 Gross tons 165 Net tons).
1951 to Mary A Johannesson & others Aberdeen. 1953 to G J Livanos, Piræus, Greece renamed IASON.
13.03.1953 Vessel sank after losing power in rough seas near Cape Spartivento on passage from Piræus towards Trapani.</td></tr>
</table>

NAME Official No. PLN Vessel Type	Yard No. Ordered Laid Down	 Launched Completed	Registered G Ton N Ton	 L Ft B Ft	Engine Builder Horse Power Reg'd Speed	OWNER
DABCHICK M 22 Controlled mine-layer	710 29.05.1942 20.11.1942	 09.03.1943 08.07.1943	442 149	150.0 27.6	C.D.Holmes 850 IHP 12 knots	The Admiralty Whitehall London
Ordered as THORNEY Isles Class (Nov 1942) modified and renamed DABCHICK. 1945 Royal Navy reserve. 1954 Sold to the Royal Malaysian Navy renamed PENYU No. N22 (1958) renamed SRI JOHOR. 1959 Vessel placed on disposal list.						
ANNET T 341 Isles Class	711 07.07.1942 21.12.1942	 25.03.1943 19.06.1943	456 144	150.0 27.6	C.D.Holmes 850 IHP 12 knots	The Admiralty Whitehall London
1946 Wreck dispersal vessel No. DV 2 then No. A 328. 28.05.1958 Sold to The Scottish Fisheries Inspectorate as a Patrol Vessel renamed ULVA Official No. 303455. Nov 1971 Withdrawn from service and laid up for disposal. Dec 1971 Vessel sold for scrap to W H Arnott Young Ltd. Jan 1972 Arrived Dalmuir for breaking up.						
BRYHER T 350 Isles Class	712 07.07.1942 28.12.1942	 08.04.1943 24.08.1943	456 144	150.0 27.6	C.D.Holmes 850 IHP 12 knots	The Admiralty Whitehall London
18.02.1947 Sold to Johannes Östensjö, Haugesund, Norway renamed ESKIMO (1950) renamed ZERO. 1953 *(Converted to a Refrigerated cargo vessel) (Length 181.4 ft 650 Gross tons 278 Net tons)* *(Mirrlees Bickerton & Day 6cyl diesel engine fitted).* 1960 to The Peoples Republic of China. 1981 Deleted from Lloyds Register of Shipping.						
FARNE T 353 Isles Class	713 30.07.1942 21.01.1943	 22.04.1943 07.09.1943	456 144	150.0 27.6	C.D.Holmes 850 IHP 12 knots	The Admiralty Whitehall London
Dec 1946 Sold to Rederi A/S Ranvik, Oslo, Norway *(converted to a cargo vessel)* *(Length 154 ft 497 Gross tons 180 Net tons).* 23.02.1949 Vessel departed Szczecin to Larvik with a cargo of coal. 24.02.1949 Wreckage washed ashore near Halmsted. Posted missing presumed sunk by mine in the Kattegat:- lost with all hands.						
FLATHOLM T 354 Isles Class	714 30.07.1942 23.02.1943	 08.05.1943 20.08.1943	456 144	150.0 27.6	C.D.Holmes 850 IHP 12 knots	The Admiralty Whitehall London
1946 Wreck dispersal vessel No. DV 9 (1951) No. A 337. 31.08.1960 Vessel sold for scrap to Scrapping Company S.R.L Belgium. 03.09.1960 Arrived Antwerp for breaking up.						
GANILLY T 376 Isles Class	715 30.07.1942 03.03.1943	 22.05.1943 03.09.1943	456 144	150.0 27.6	C.D.Holmes 850 IHP 12 knots	The Admiralty Whitehall London
05.07.1944 Vessel sunk by mine in the English Channel. Lost whilst serving with the 33rd Minesweeper / Anti-submarine group based at Plymouth.						
LINDISFARNE T 361 Isles Class	716 30.07.1942 12.03.1943	 17.06.1943 07.09.1943	456 144	150.0 27.6	C.D.Holmes 850 IHP 12 knots	The Admiralty Whitehall London
1946 Wreck dispersal vessel No. DV 11 (1950) No. P 44. 1958 Vessel sold for scrap to shipbreakers. 26.04.1958 Arrived Dover for breaking up.						
MINALTO T 362 Isles Class	717 29.08.1942 14.04.1943	 03.07.1943 05.10.1943	456 144	150.0 27.6	C.D.Holmes 850 IHP 12 knots	The Admiralty Whitehall London
1947 Sold to Sigurd Svorig, Bergen, Norway renamed LILLEN *(converted to a cargo vessel).* *(Length 154.3 ft 499 Gross Tons 216 Net Tons) (British Auxiliaries Ltd 7cyl diesel engine fitted).* 1956 to Partenreed M S Agricola Washbaylinie MmbH, Osten, Germany renamed AGRICOLA. 1958 to Otto Arens, Lubeck renamed HOLSTENTOR. 1961 Horst Melz, Esterbrugge renamed TRAVE. 1964 to Mediteranska Plovidba, Korcula, Yugoslavia renamed PERNA. 1971 to Obalna Plovidba 'Vela Luka', Dubrovnik. 1972 to Dalmatinska Plovidba, Dubrovnik. 28.08.1978 Vessel fell off slipway whilst under repair at Vranjic. Dec 1978 Sold for scrap to Brodaspas and broken up.						
ROSEVEAN T 363 Isles Class	718 29.08.1942 15.04.1943	 17.07.1943 16.10.1943	456 144	150.0 27.6	C.D.Holmes 850 IHP 12 knots	The Admiralty Whitehall London
Mar 1946 Sold to Cie Marocaine des Pécheries, Casablanca, Morocco renamed EL RESZK *(439 Gross tons 196 Net tons) (1948 British Polar 7 cyl diesel engine fitted).* 02.05.1957 Vessel wrecked on a reef near Punta Galha.						

NAME Official No. PLN Vessel Type	Yard No. Ordered Laid Down	Launched Completed	Registered G Ton N Ton	 L Ft B Ft	Engine Builder Horse Power Reg'd Speed	OWNER
GULLAND T 365 Isles Class	719 04.11.1942 30.04.1943	 05.08.1943 30.10.1943	456 144	150.0 27.6	C.D.Holmes 850 IHP 12 knots	The Admiralty Whitehall London
Mar 1946 Sold to F Daems, Antwerp, Belgium. *(Length 154 ft 497 Gross tons 180 Net tons) (diesel engine fitted).* 1947 to Anton Steen, Bergen, Norway renamed HENKEN. 1949 to Arab Navigation & Transport Co, Aden renamed ARAB TRADER. 13.04.1951 Vessel wrecked near Mombassa, Kenya, East Africa.						
KITTERN T 382 Isles Class	720 04.11.1942 27.05.1943	 21.08.1943 13.11.1943	456 144	150.0 27.6	C.D.Holmes 850 IHP 12 knots	The Admiralty Whitehall London
1946 Sold to Ahlgren & Coppelens Rederi K /S, Oslo, Norway renamed BONITA *(converted to a cargo vessel).* *(Length 154.8 ft 466 Gross tons 251 Net tons) (Sep 1947 fitted for fuel oil).* 1949 to Norsksibs Hypothekbank A / S, Oslo renamed STAT, (1950) renamed HELEN TOLA, (1951) renamed STAT. 1951 to Ezra Deep Sea Fishing Co Ltd , Tel Aviv, Israel renamed D'VORA. *(1953 Refrigeration machinery fitted).* 1954 to C H Products, Yarmouth Official No.186392. 1955 to Mercury Fisheries Ltd Yarmouth.*(1957 Crossley Bros 6cyl diesel engine fitted).* 1958 to Ministry of Trade & Industry for the Province of Nova Scotia. 1959 to R Duval, Halifax, Nova Scotia. 1962 to North Shipping & Transport Ltd Halifax, Nova Scotia. 1964 to Harvey Bros Co Ltd Halifax, Nova Scotia. 27.12.1968 Vessel wrecked at Fox River, Gaspe, Quebec after developing leaks in bad weather and abandoned by her crew.						
MEWSTONE T 374 Isles Class	721 04.11.1942 08.06.1943	 16.09.1943 26.11.1943	456 144	150.0 27.6	C.D.Holmes 850 IHP 12 knots	The Admiralty Whitehall London
10.04.1946 Sold to B Nesje, Bergen, Norway (1948) renamed VINGTOR *(converted to a cargo vessel).* *(Length 154 ft 499 Gross tons 180 Net tons) (diesel engine fitted).* Jan 1949 Vessel suffered an engine break-down in approx position 37° 10'N 009° E. The ms VERNON (4609 gt/ b 1947) attempted to tow the VINGTOR to safety but inflicted collision damage on her, resulting in the crew having to abandon ship. The stricken vessel later drifted ashore and was wrecked between Cap Serret and Cap Negro.						
SKOGHOLM T 376 Isles Class	722 04.11.1942 02.06.1943	 29.09.1943 10.12.1943	456 144	150.0 27.6	C.D.Holmes 850 IHP 12 knots	The Admiralty Whitehall London
1946 Sold to George Stellberg , Bergen, Norway renamed SKOKHOLM. *(1948 Converted to a cargo vessel).* *(Length 160.7 ft 586 Gross tons 244 Net tons).* 1950 to Franz Preukschat, Flensburg, Germany renamed HOCHMEISTER. 1951 *(Motorenfabrik 6cyl diesel engine fitted).* 1958 to George Latrou, Piræus, Greece renamed GRIGOROUSA. 1965 to N Diakos & Partners, Piræus renamed STELIOS. 1978 to Fenia Makris Shipping, Piræus renamed FENIA. 21.08.1985 Vessel reported to have been lost in the Red Sea.						
AILSA CRAIG T 377 Isles Class	723 13.12.1942 26.07.1943	 16.10.1943 24.12.1943	456 144	150.0 27.6	C.D.Holmes 850 IHP 12 knots	The Admiralty Whitehall London
1946 Sold to Skibs A/S Veas Rederi, Stavanger, Norway renamed VESLEMOY. *(1947 Converted to a tanker).* *(Length 179.6 ft 657 Gross Tons 246 Net Tons).* 1952 to A / S Chr Christensen, Oslo renamed TORAN. 19.02.1955 Vessel sank in ice between Sandefjord and Arendal Langesund Fjord.						
BENBECULA T 379 Isles Class	724 13.12.1942 21.07.1943	 28.10.1943 13.01.1944	456 144	150.0 27.6	C.D.Holmes 850 IHP 12 knots	The Admiralty Whitehall London
12.03.1946 HM Customs & Excise renamed VIGILANT. 1982 Vessel sold to Albert Yard & Motor Packet Services Southampton *(Converted to an accommodation ship).*						
CROWLIN T 380 Isles Class	725 13.12.1942 16.08.1943	 15.11.1943 28.01.1944	456 144	150.0 27.6	C.D.Holmes 850 IHP 12 knots	The Admiralty Whitehall London
1946 Sold to Express-Service A / S, Norway renamed HANS HUMMERSUND *(converted to a cargo vessel).* *(Length 153.2 ft 574 Gross tons 280 Net tons) (M.A.N. 6cyl diesel engine fitted).* 1948 to Crowlin Frozen Food Transport Co, Puerto Cortes, Honduras renamed CROWLIN. 31.03.1954 Vessel found floating, completely capsized, off Stavanger whilst on passage from Gydinia to Kopervik. 01.01.1954 The upside down hulk was towed into Stavanger but examination failed to reveal any trace of her sixteen crew. The CROWLIN is believed to have capsized during the night of 30-31.03.1954 in heavy seas. 10.04.1954 Vessel uprighted. 12.04.1954 Refloated . Apr 1955 to Govert Grindhaug, Kopervik, Norway refitted and renamed THERMO. 1961 to Navigation Maritime Bulgare Varna, Bulgaria renamed CHERNOMORETZ. 1964 to Red Sea Development Corp, Massawa, Ethiopia renamed AXUM. (1977) renamed DIRE DEWA. 04.03.1977 Vessel sank inside Massawa Port. 20.02.1979 Vessel re-floated, sold for scrap to shipbreakers and broken up.						

Yard No.715
1943 H.M.T. GANILLY
Photo:- Author's Collection

Yard No.726
1944 H.M.T. CALVAY as WM. FENTON
Photo by courtesy of Hull Maritime Museum

Yard No.733
1944 H.M.T. HOME GUARD
Photo by courtesy of Hull Maritime Museum

<table>
<tr><th rowspan="2">NAME
Official No.
PLN Vessel Type</th><th rowspan="2">Yard No.
Ordered
Laid Down</th><th rowspan="2">Launched
Completed</th><th colspan="2">Registered</th><th rowspan="2">Engine Builder
Horse Power
Reg'd Speed</th><th rowspan="2">OWNER</th></tr>
<tr><th>G Ton
N Ton</th><th>L Ft
B Ft</th></tr>
<tr><td>**CALVAY**
T 383
Isles Class</td><td>726
20.03.1943
20.09.1943</td><td>
29.11.1943
16.02.1944</td><td>456
144</td><td>150.0
27.6</td><td>C.D.Holmes
850 IHP
12 knots</td><td>The Admiralty
Whitehall
London</td></tr>
<tr><td colspan="7">Nov 1946 Sold to Humber Pilots Steam Cutter Co Ltd, Hull renamed WM. FENTON
Official No.181352 *(Length 153.8 ft 561 Gross tons 202 Net tons).* 1953 Registered for Pilot Service.
1975 Vessel sold for scrap to Hughes Bolckow Ltd. Oct 1975 Arrived Blyth for breaking up.</td></tr>
<tr><td>**COLSAY**
T 384
Isles Class</td><td>727
20.03.1943
21.09.1943</td><td>
14.12.1943
04.03.1944</td><td>456
144</td><td>150.0
27.6</td><td>C.D.Holmes
850 IHP
12 knots</td><td>The Admiralty
Whitehall
London</td></tr>
<tr><td colspan="7">02.11.1944 Vessel sunk by German human torpedo off Ostend.</td></tr>
<tr><td>**FUDAY**
T 385
Isles Class</td><td>728
20.03.1943
01.10.1943</td><td>
01.01.1944
24.03.1944</td><td>456
144</td><td>150.0
27.6</td><td>C.D.Holmes
850 IHP
12 knots</td><td>The Admiralty
Whitehall
London</td></tr>
<tr><td colspan="7">1946 Sold to N V Verre Visscherij Maats, Ijmuiden, Holland renamed SIMON DE DANSER (IJM43).
(Length 161.0 ft 462 Gross tons 168 Net tons).
1952 to Schlienz-Hagemann Hochhsee und Gerfrierfisch, Kiel, Germany renamed PROF HEINCKE (SO117).
1953 to Fritz Wilberg & LP Paesleme, Rio de Janeiro, Brazil renamed CAROLA.
1958 to Empressa De Nav E Pesca Vieira Ltda, Santos renamed ORION 1 *(A/S Volund 6cyl 660 BHP diesel engine fitted).*
1993 Vessel deleted from Lloyds Register of Shipping.</td></tr>
<tr><td>**GILSAY**
T 386
Isles Class</td><td>729
20.03.1943
01.11.1943</td><td>
29.01.1944
12.04.1944</td><td>456
144</td><td>150.0
27.6</td><td>C.D.Holmes
850 IHP
12 knots</td><td>The Admiralty
Whitehall
London</td></tr>
<tr><td colspan="7">1944 renamed HARRIS. 24.03.1947 Sold to Anders Lynga Sandal, Farsund, Norway renamed LYNGÅS
(converted to a cargo vessel) (Length 174.6 ft 682 Gross tons 278 Net tons).
1950 to Soc Nav Caennaise, Toulon, France renamed FORT MALBOUSQUET.
1952 to Gill Amin Steam Ship Co Private Ltd, Bombay, India renamed SHEILA MARGARET (1964) renamed ASHARE.
07.08.1964 Vessel driven ashore by a cyclone near Bombay.
16.04.1965 Re-floated and sold for scrap to Putco Private Ltd, Bombay and broken up at Darukhana (Bombay).</td></tr>
<tr><td>**HANNARAY**
T 389
Isles Class</td><td>730
20.03.1943
02.11.1943</td><td>
12.02.1944
03.05.1944</td><td>456
144</td><td>150.0
27.6</td><td>C.D.Holmes
850 IHP
12 knots</td><td>The Admiralty
Whitehall
London</td></tr>
<tr><td colspan="7">1947 Sold to Friedrich Beutelrock, Lubeck, Germany renamed WODAN
(Length 161.5 ft 493 Gross tons 221 Net tons) (1952 Masch. Kiel A.G. 6cyl 300 BHP diesel engine fitted).
1965 to Johannes Nagel, Lubeck. 1966 to Parten Reedere Wodan, Lubeck. 1968 to Reederei Woden, Lubeck.
1973 to Roger Carlsson, Panama. 1980 to Isa Ltd, Panama renamed ISA.
23.04.1980 Vessel wrecked on Ile Avache, near Aux Cayes, Haiti.</td></tr>
<tr><td>**HASCOSAY**
T 390
Isles Class</td><td>731
20.03.1943
19.11.1943</td><td>
28.03.1944
26.05.1944</td><td>456
144</td><td>150.0
27.6</td><td>C.D.Holmes
850 IHP
12 knots</td><td>The Admiralty
Whitehall
London</td></tr>
<tr><td colspan="7">1947 Sold to E Karavias & G Manolessos, Piræus, Greece renamed YPAPANDI *(converted to a cargo vessel).*
(Length 153.8 ft 497 Gross tons 190 Net tons). 13.01.1952 Vessel left Alexandropoulis on passage towards Piræus.
17.01.1952 Vessel reported missing (3 days overdue):- lost with all hands.</td></tr>
<tr><td>**GUARDSMAN**
T 393
Military Class</td><td>732
20.03.1943
28.01.1944</td><td>
07.06.1944
27.08.1944</td><td>579
181</td><td>175.0
30.0</td><td>C.D.Holmes
1000 IHP
11 knots</td><td>The Admiralty
Whitehall
London</td></tr>
<tr><td colspan="7">10.04.1946 Sold to Great Grimsby & East Coast Steam Fishing Co Ltd, Grimsby renamed THURINGIA GY321
Official No.166648. *(581 Gross tons 209 Net tons) (Aug 1947 fitted for fuel oil).* Mar 1966 to Northern Trawlers, Grimsby.
1966 Vessel sold for scrap to Clayton & Davie Ltd. 30.10.1966 Arrived Dunston on Tyne for breaking up.</td></tr>
<tr><td>**HOME GUARD**
T 394
Military Class</td><td>733
20.03.1943
17.02.1944</td><td>
08.07.1944
19.09.1944</td><td>579
181</td><td>175.0
30.0</td><td>C.D.Holmes
1000 IHP
11 knots</td><td>The Admiralty
Whitehall
London</td></tr>
<tr><td colspan="7">10.04.1946 Sold to Loyal Steam Fishing Co Ltd, Grimsby renamed LOYAL GY344
Official No. 166650 *(581 Gross tons 213 Net tons) (Nov 1947 fitted for fuel oil).* Jan 1966 to Northern Trawlers, Grimsby.
1966 Vessel sold for scrap to Scrapping Co, Willerbroek, Belgium. 02.07.1966 Arrived Antwerp for breaking up.</td></tr>
</table>

Yard No.734
1944 H.M.T. ROYAL MARINE as SISAPON
Photo by courtesy of The Grimsby Evening Telegraph

Yard No.736
1944 H.M.T. WHITETHROAT
Photo:- Author's Collection

Yard No.746
1945 H.M.T. WIAY
Photo:- Author's Collection

NAME Official No. PLN Vessel Type	Yard No. Ordered Laid Down	 Launched Completed	Registered G Ton N Ton	 L Ft B Ft	Engine Builder Horse Power Reg'd Speed	OWNER
ROYAL MARINE T 395 Military Class	734 20.03.1943 30.03.1944	 22.07.1944 30.10.1944	579 181	175.0 30.0	C.D.Holmes 1000 IHP 11 knots	The Admiralty Whitehall London
10.04.1946 Sold to Standard Steam Fishing Co Ltd, Grimsby renamed SISAPON GY381 Official No.166653. *(581 Gross tons 212 Net tons) (Oct 1947 fitted for fuel oil).* 26.03.1965 to Wyre Trawlers Ltd, Fleetwood (FD92). 12.05.1967 Vessel sold for scrap to Scrapping Co, Belgium. 15.06.1967 Breaking up commenced at Antwerp.						
STONECHAT M 25 Isles Class	735 16.04.1943 23.02.1944	 22.08.1944 12.11.1944	443 151	150.0 27.6	C.D.Holmes 850 IHP 12 knots	The Admiralty Whitehall London
Completed for the Royal Canadian Navy - controlled mine-layer. 1946 returned. 1963 Laid up for disposal. 26.09.1966 Sold for mercantile use but sale cancelled. 12.03.1967 Vessel sold for scrap to West of Scotland Shipbreaking Co Ltd and broken up at Troon.						
WHITETHROAT M 03 Isles Class	736 16.04.1943 15.05.1944	 06.09.1944 12.12.1944	443 151	150.0 27.6	C.D.Holmes 850 IHP 12 knots	The Admiralty Whitehall London
Completed for the Royal Canadian Navy - controlled mine layer. (1950) No.AGH113. 1967 Sold to Davis Trading Co, Vancouver *(converted to a survey vessel).* Oct 1967 Vessel sold for scrap to shipbreakers and broken up at Vancouver.						
SANDRAY J 424 Isles Class (Dan Layer)	737 16.04.1943 10.06.1944	 05.10.1944 27.12.1944	443 151	150.0 27.6	C.D.Holmes 850 IHP 12 knots	The Admiralty Whitehall London
1947 renumbered M 424. 15.12.1960 Sold to owners in Honduras but sale cancelled. 1962 Vessel sold for scrap to Van Heyghen Freres. 10.04.1962 Arrived Bruges for breaking up.						
SCARAVAY J 425 Isles Class (Dan Layer)	738 16.04.1943 17.06.1944	 22.10.1944 14.01.1945	443 151	150.0 27.6	C.D.Holmes 850 IHP 12 knots	The Admiralty Whitehall London
Nov 1946 Sold to N V Scheepv Maats, Holland renamed HOLLAND (1951) renamed HOLLAND II *(converted to a salvage tug) (Length 164.2 ft 460 Gross tons 128 Net tons) (1946 fitted for fuel oil).* 1954 to National Iranian Oil Co Mehdi Karoon , Iran renamed GIEV. 28.12.1974 Vessel sank following a fire which gutted the engine room in approx Position 28° 19'N 050° 15'E.						
SHILLAY J 426 Isles Class (Dan Layer)	739 16.04.1943 26.07.1944	 15.11.1944 30.01.1945	443 151	150.0 27.6	C.D.Holmes 850 IHP 12 knots	The Admiralty Whitehall London
1947 renumbered M 426. 1958 Vessel laid up at Malta and placed on disposal list. 1959 Sold to shipbreakers for breaking up in Italy but resold for mercantile use. 1961 Sold to Camillo Bartoli, Savona, Italy renamed FEDERICO BARTOLI *(converted to a cargo vessel).* *(Length 164.5 ft 483 Gross tons 237 Net tons). (Motorenwerk 6cyl 800 BHP diesel engine fitted).* 1966 to Giuseppe Messina, Genoa renamed MONT BLANC *(converted to a wine tanker).* 1987 Vessel sold for scrap to shipbreakers and broken up in Vado Ligure, Italy.						
SURSAY J 427 Isles Class (Dan Layer)	740 16.04.1943 25.08.1944	 16.12.1944 26.02.1945	443 151	150.0 27.6	C.D.Holmes 850 IHP 12 knots	The Admiralty Whitehall London
1947 renumbered M 427. 26.09.1966 Sold for mercantile use but sale cancelled. 02.03.1967 Vessel sold for scrap to West of Scotland Shipbreaking Co Ltd.15.04.1967 Arrived Troon for breaking up.						
TAHAY J 452 Isles Class (Dan Layer)	741 16.04.1943 26.08.1944	 31.12.1944 25.03.1945	443 151	150.0 27.6	C.D.Holmes 850 IHP 12 knots	The Admiralty Whitehall London
1947 renumbered M 452. 1963 Vessel sold for scrap to West of Scotland Shipbreaking Co Ltd. 31.07.1963 Arrived Troon for breaking up.						
TOCOGAY J 451 Isles Class (Dan Layer)	742 16.04.1943 13.09.1944	 07.02.1945 19.04.1945	443 151	150.0 27.6	C.D.Holmes 850 IHP 12 knots	The Admiralty Whitehall London
1947 renumbered M 81. 1958 Sold to Greek owners renamed ANNA *(converted to a cargo vessel).* *(Length 154.6 ft 475 Gross tons 241 Net tons) (fitted for fuel oil).*1961 to Stefanos M Baxevanis, Piræus renamed ELMA *(1961 Russki 6cyl diesel engine fitted).* 1968 to Dem G Kallimasias, Piræus renamed KYRIAKI. renamed (1974) RINO. 1980 Vessel sold for scrap to Mrs Ourania Papatriandafilloy, and broken up at Piræus.						

NAME Official No. PLN Vessel Type	Yard No. Ordered Laid Down	Launched Completed	Registered G Ton N Ton	 L Ft B Ft	Engine Builder Horse Power Reg'd Speed	OWNER
TRODDAY J 431 Isles Class (Dan Layer)	743 16.04.1943 26.10.1944	 03.03.1945 13.05.1945	443 151	150.0 27.6	C.D.Holmes 850 IHP 12 knots	The Admiralty Whitehall London
1947 renumbered M 431. Jul 1959 Vessel laid up at Malta and placed on disposal list. 25.07.1960 Sold to shipbreakers for breaking up in Italy but resold for mercantile use. 1961 to "S.A.T.I.M" S A Transporti Internazionali Maritimi, Savona, Italy renamed NICOLA JACOVITTI *(converted to a tanker) (Length191.8 ft 726 Gross tons 322 Net tons) (1961 Franco Tosi 5cyl 1300 BHP diesel engine fitted).* 1962 to Silvio Bonaso, Genoa renamed ANTONELLA. renamed (1971) NANDO. 1975 to Bulktransport SrL, Genoa renamed FRAI. 1977 to Agip Tanzania Ltd Dar-es-Salam. renamed HODARI. 1994 Vessel reported laid up at Dar-es-Salam.						
VACEASAY J 432 Isles Class (Dan Layer)	744 16.04.1943 27.10.1944	 17.03.1945 29.05.1945	443 151	150.0 27.6	C.D.Holmes 850 IHP 12 knots	The Admiralty Whitehall London
1947 renumbered M 432. 16.02.1967 Vessel sold for scrap to Pounds Shipowners & Shipbreakers. May 1968 Re-sold to Jacques Bakker & Zonen, Belgium. 10.05.1968 Arrived Bruges for breaking up.						
VALLAY J 434 Isles Class (Dan Layer)	745 16.04.1943 22.11.1944	 10.04.1945 13.06.1945	443 151	150.0 27.6	C.D.Holmes 850 IHP 12 knots	The Admiralty Whitehall London
1947 renumbered M 434. Jul 1959 Vessel laid up at Malta and placed on disposal list.						
WIAY J 441 Isles Class (Dan Layer)	746 16.04.1943 03.01.1945	 26.04.1945 17.07.1945	443 151	150.0 27.6	C.D.Holmes 850 IHP 12 knots	The Admiralty Whitehall London
15.12.1960 Sold to Honduran owners renamed ENRICO CARLO. Sale cancelled vessel sold for scrap.						
L.C.T (3) 7037 Tank Landing Craft	747	 25.04.1944 05.06.1944	303 247	175 31	2 Stirling Admiralty Petrol Engines	The Admiralty Whitehall London
L.C.T (3) 7038 Tank Landing Craft	748	 11.05.1944 08.07.1944	303 247	175 31	2 Stirling Admiralty Petrol Engines	The Admiralty Whitehall London
EMPIRE MAYPORT 180449 Type C Coaster	749 17.02.1945	 14.06.1945 25.09.1945	394 112	140.0 27.1	Amos & Smith 450 IHP 10.1 knots	Ministry of War Transport London
Vessel managed by Singapore Straits Steam Ship Co Ltd, London. 14.08.1946 Sold to Singapore Straits Steam Ship Co Ltd, London renamed MENTAKAB. 1953 to Shun Cheong Steam Navigation Co Ltd, Hong Kong renamed DEBORA. 1958 to Soc Franco - Chinoise de Transp Marit & Fluviaux SARL, Marseilles, France. 1962 to Mercantile Maritimes, Penang, Malaya. 1965 to Progress Shipping Co Ltd, Panama renamed BRIGHTSTAR. 21.01.1966 Vessel wrecked on a reef near Da Nang in approx position Lat 15° 32'N Long 009° 09'E.						
EMPIRE MAYBURY 1880458 Type C Coaster	750 22.03.1945	 10.07.1945 30.10.1945	394 112	140.0 27.1	Amos & Smith 450 IHP 10.1 knots	Ministry of War Transport London
Vessel managed by United Africa Co Ltd London.01.07.1947 Sold to Ho-Hong (Steam Ship) Co Ltd renamed HONG ANN. 1954 to Pacific Shipowners Ltd, Singapore renamed AI SOKULA. 1963 to Milne Bros, Majura, Marshall Islands (USA) renamed NEI RAETE II. 1995 Vessel deleted from Lloyds Register of Shipping continued existence in doubt.						
Not Built	751-752 Allocated to Ministry of War Transport but not taken up.					
EMPIRE PEGGY 180446 Warrior Class Steam Tug	753 06.01.1945	 14.05.1945 28.07.1945	259	105.9 30.0	C.D.Holmes 1000 IHP 12 knots	Ministry of War Transport London
Vessel managed by Townend Bros Ferries for Ministry of War Transport.30.08.1945 Sailed to Bombay thence to Singapore. 16.11.1945 Arrived Singapore allocated to B.R.N.O Saigon. 16.05.1946 to French Navy at Medan. 19.04.1948 returned. 1949 to Sold to William & Co Pty Ltd, Brisbane, Australia renamed CORINGA. 1961 Sold to Queensland Tug Co Pty Ltd, Brisbane. 1974 to Northern Salvage Pty Ltd renamed EMPIRE PEGGY. 1977 to VA & RVA Tonkin. 20.05.1977 Breaking up commenced at Cairns.						
EMPIRE PAM Warrior Class Steam Tug	754 24.03.1945	 29.08.1945 16.01.1945	259	105.1 30.1	C.D.Holmes 1000 IHP 12 knots	Ministry of War Transport London
1946 Sold to Société de Remmorquage et d'Assistance, Morocco renamed EL HANK. 1947 to Société Chérifienne de Remmorquage et d'Assistance renamed EL BARAKA. 1999 Vessel still in service.						

Vessels built at Beverley 1945 to 1963

<table>
<tr><th colspan="2">NAME
Official No.
Port Letters Numbers</th><th>Yard No.
Launched
Registered</th><th colspan="2">Registered</th><th>Engine Builder
Horse Power
Reg'd Speed</th><th>OWNER
(Built for)</th></tr>
<tr><th colspan="2"></th><th></th><th>G Ton
N Ton</th><th>L Ft
B Ft</th><th></th><th></th></tr>
<tr><td>ABY
180326
FD138</td><td>
Coal Fired
Steam Trawler</td><td>755
22.09.1945
27.11.1945</td><td>361
139</td><td>136.1
25.2</td><td>C.D.Holmes
600 IHP
11.7 knots</td><td>Seddon Fishing Co Ltd
Fleetwood</td></tr>
<tr><td colspan="7">1949 Sold to Neale & West Ltd, Cardiff renamed CHAFFCOMBE (CF18).
20.06.1956 to Don Fishing Co Ltd, Aberdeen renamed BOSTON GANNET (FD30) Nov 1956 (Fitted for fuel oil).
1963 Vessel sold for scrap to West of Scotland Shipbreaking Co Ltd.18.10.1963 Breaking up commenced at Troon.</td></tr>
<tr><td>BULBY
180327
FD147</td><td>
Coal Fired
Steam Trawler</td><td>756
08.10.1945
01.01.1946</td><td>361
139</td><td>136.1
25.2</td><td>C.D.Holmes
600 IHP
11.9 knots</td><td>Seddon Fishing Co Ltd
Fleetwood</td></tr>
<tr><td colspan="7">27.07.1949 Sold to J Marr & Son Ltd, Fleetwood.27.12.1953 to National Trawling & Fishing Co, Cape Town, South Africa.
20.04.1960 Sank the former Hull trawler CAPE MATAPAN H238 (321 gt/ b 1925) following a collision 2 miles off Cape Town. 1968 Vessel stripped of reusable parts.
Dec 1968 Hulk scuttled at 'Irvin Johnson Reef' in False Bay, Cape Town to form an artificial reef.</td></tr>
<tr><td>NAVENA
180328
FD149</td><td>
Coal Fired
Steam Trawler</td><td>757
25.10.1945
07.01.1946</td><td>361
139</td><td>136.1
25.2</td><td>C.D.Holmes
600 IHP
11.8 knots</td><td>J Marr & Son Ltd
Fleetwood</td></tr>
<tr><td colspan="7">30.12.1946 Sold to Kingston Steam Trawling Co Ltd, Hull renamed (24.02.1947) IOLITE (H372).
11.04.1949 to J Marr & Son Ltd, Hull. 09.02.1951 to National Trawling & Fishing Co, Cape Town, South Africa (CTA51).
1969 Vessel stripped of reusable parts. 21.03.1969 Hulk scuttled at 'Irvin Johnson Reef' in False Bay, Cape Town.</td></tr>
<tr><td>ST. BOTOLPH
180469
H188</td><td>
Coal Fired
Steam Trawler</td><td>758
21.11.1945
22.01.1946</td><td>361
139</td><td>136.1
25.2</td><td>C.D.Holmes
600 IHP
11.8 knots</td><td>St Andrew's Steam
Fishing Co Ltd
Hull</td></tr>
<tr><td colspan="7">1946 Sold to Neale & West Ltd, Cardiff (CF8). Nov 1956 (Fitted for fuel oil).
20.06.1956 to St Christopher Steam Fishing Co Ltd, Fleetwood (FD31).
Sep 1963 Vessel sold for scrap to Lacmots Ltd Glasgow. 11.11.1963 Breaking up commenced at Glasson Dock.</td></tr>
<tr><td>EMPIRE TEST</td><td>

Coastal Tanker</td><td>759</td><td></td><td>190.0
34.0</td><td>C.D.Holmes</td><td>Ministry of War Transport
London</td></tr>
<tr><td colspan="7">14.07.1945 Laid down but later removed order cancelled.</td></tr>
<tr><td>EMPIRE DOROTHY</td><td>

Warrior Class Steam Tug</td><td>760
27.07.1945
09.10.1945</td><td>260</td><td>105.9
30.1</td><td>C.D.Holmes
1000 IHP
10.9 knots</td><td>Ministry of War Transport
London</td></tr>
<tr><td colspan="7">14.10.1945 Sailed for the Far East via Bombay & Singapore. Dec 1945 Arrived Japan.
12.03.1946 At Port Swettenham in service of Harbour Board. 17.03.1947 to the Government of the Federation of Malaya.
1958 to the Malayan Railway Co, Penang renamed DOROTHY. 1964 returned to Port Swettenham Authority.
1970 to Straits Engineers (Singapore) Pte Ltd , Panama renamed STRAITS WINNER.
1975 to World Dredging Lt, Panama (Cummins 12cyl 12 knots diesel engine fitted).
1981 Vessel sold to shipbreakers and broken up.</td></tr>
<tr><td>JOSENA
180473
H207</td><td>
Coal Fired
Steam Trawler</td><td>761
21.12.1945
14.02.1946</td><td>361
139</td><td>136.1
25.2</td><td>C.D.Holmes
600 IHP
11.8 knots</td><td>Trident Steam Fishing Co Ltd
Hull</td></tr>
<tr><td colspan="7">24.03.1947 Sold to Polish Government Fleet managed by "Dalmor" Przedsiobiorstwo Polowow Dalekomorskich, Gdynia, Poland renamed SYRIUSZ. 1969 Vessel sold to shipbreakers and broken up.</td></tr>
<tr><td>BORELLA
180481
H240</td><td>
Coal Fired
Steam Trawler</td><td>762
19.01.1946
26.03.1946</td><td>524
186</td><td>165.3
27.7</td><td>Amos & Smith
800 IHP
12.2 knots</td><td>City Steam Fishing Co Ltd
Hull</td></tr>
<tr><td colspan="7">23.12.1948 Sold to Dinas Steam Trawling Co Ltd , Fleetwood.
02.07.1953 to National Trawling & Fishing Co, Cape Town, South Africa (CTA62).
20.07.1953 Left Hull. 20.08.1953 Arrived Cape Town (first South African trawler with radar).
1971 Vessel stripped of reusable parts. 01.03.1971 Hulk scuttled in Simonstown Bay by the South African Navy.</td></tr>
<tr><td>ST. JOHN
180483
H284</td><td>
Oil Fired
Steam Trawler</td><td>763
20.02.1946
16.04.1946</td><td>536
192</td><td>166.9
27.7</td><td>C.D.Holmes
1000 IHP
12.5 knots</td><td>St Andrew's Steam
Fishing Co Ltd
Hull</td></tr>
<tr><td colspan="7">The first fuel oil burning trawler built for the Hull fleet.
20.08.1948 Sold to Newington Steam Trawling Co Ltd, Hull renamed ANTHONY HOPE .
01.01.1957 to Consolidated Fisheries Ltd, Grimsby renamed ASTON VILLA (GY42).
1965 Vessel sold for scrap to Arie Rijsdijk, Holland. 03.06.1965 Arrived Dordrecht for breaking up.</td></tr>
</table>

<table>
<tr><th>NAME
Official No.
Port Letters Numbers</th><th>Yard No.
Launched
Registered</th><th colspan="2">Registered</th><th>Engine Builder
Horse Power
Reg'd Speed</th><th>OWNER
(Built for)</th></tr>
<tr><th></th><th></th><th>G Ton
N Ton</th><th>L Ft
B Ft</th><th></th><th></th></tr>
<tr><td>ST. MATTHEW
181267 Oil Fired
H284 Steam Trawler</td><td>764
16.05.1946
16.07.1946</td><td>536
192</td><td>166.9
27.7</td><td>C.D.Holmes
1000 IHP
12.6 knots</td><td>St Andrew's Steam Fishing Co Ltd
Hull</td></tr>
<tr><td colspan="6">04.10.1951 Sold to Zwicker & Co Ltd Lunenburg, Nova Scotia, Canada.
15.09.1955 to St Andrew's Steam Fishing Co Ltd, Hull (H70).
01.01.1957 to Consolidated Fisheries Ltd, Grimsby renamed (18.01.1957) WOLVERHAMPTON WANDERERS (GY31).
22.12.1957 The WOLVERHAMPTON WANDERERS assisted by FARADAY (Yard No.781) rescued the fourteen crew of the coaster mv BOSWORTH (865 gt/ b 1946) which was in distress 120 miles off Aberdeen.
1967 Vessel sold for scrap to Clayton & Davie Ltd. 22.06.1967 Arrived Dunston on Tyne for breaking up.</td></tr>
<tr><td>BREUGHEL
Oil Fired
O299 Steam Trawler</td><td>765
01.06.1946
31.07.1946</td><td>534
191</td><td>166.9
27.6</td><td>C.D.Holmes
1000 IHP
12.6 knots</td><td>NV Motorvisserij
Ostend
Belgium</td></tr>
<tr><td colspan="6">28.11.1955 Sold to St Andrew's Steam Fishing Co, Hull renamed ST. PETER (H102) Official No. 186693.
1965 Vessel sold for scrap to Clayton & Davie Ltd. 14.05.1965 Arrived Dunston on Tyne for breaking up.</td></tr>
<tr><td>THORINA
181277
H318 Motor Trawler</td><td>766
19.03.1946
04.10.1946</td><td>338
116</td><td>136.8
25.6</td><td>Ruston &
Hornsby
600 BHP
10.5 knots</td><td>J Marr & Son Ltd
Hull</td></tr>
<tr><td colspan="6">06.06.1947 Sold to NV Vissch Ijmuiden, Holland (IJM33).
1962 to Claridge Trawlers Ltd, Lowestoft renamed ST. GEORGES (LT402).
1981 Vessel sold for scrap after being scuttled during the making of the James Bond film "For Your Eyes Only".</td></tr>
<tr><td>RUBENS
Oil Fired
O297 Steam Trawler</td><td>767
17.04.1946
21.06.1946</td><td>536
201</td><td>166.9
27.7</td><td>C.D.Holmes
1000 IHP
12.8 knots</td><td>NV Motorvisserij
Ostend
Belgium</td></tr>
<tr><td colspan="6">14.10.1955 Sold to St Andrew's Steam Fishing Co Ltd, Hull renamed ST. CRISPIN (H86) Official No. 186688.
15.03.1956 Vessel driven ashore in heavy seas after propeller had been fouled by fishing gear on sands near Kudhafljot SE coast of Iceland. All twenty crew were rescued by Icelandic farmers using breeches-buoy.
14.04.1956 Vessel refloated and taken to Reykjavik for repairs. 18.05.1956 Returned to Hull.
1965 Vessel sold for scrap to Van Heyghen Freres, Belgium. 12.03.1965 Arrived Ghent for breaking up.</td></tr>
<tr><td>SOUTHELLA
181275 Oil Fired
H303 Steam Trawler</td><td>768
02.07.1946
02.09.1946</td><td>536
192</td><td>166.9
27.7</td><td>C.D.Holmes
1000 IHP
12.9 knots</td><td>J Marr & Son Ltd
Hull</td></tr>
<tr><td colspan="6">1965 Vessel sold for scrap to Van Heyghen Freres, Belgium. 25.01.1965 Arrived Ghent for breaking up.</td></tr>
<tr><td>MICHEL BERNARD
Coal Fired
B2360 Steam Trawler</td><td>769
18.07.1946
26.09.1946</td><td>299
116</td><td>130.0
24.8</td><td>C.D.Holmes
650 IHP
11.3 knots</td><td>Vve Léon Ferton
Boulogne
France</td></tr>
<tr><td colspan="6">1954 Sold to Association Rochelaise de Peche a Vapeur, La Rochelle, France renamed DADAS (LR4470).
1957 to Simon Gaury, La Rochelle (Masch. Kiel A.G. 8cyl 920 BHP 11.5 knots diesel engine fitted).
1974 Vessel sold for scrap to Steelnorte, Spain. 15.03.1974 Breaking up commenced at San Esteban de Prava.</td></tr>
<tr><td>JACQUES COLIN
Coal Fired
B2366 Steam Trawler</td><td>770
17.07.1946
14.10.1946</td><td>295
116</td><td>130.0
24.7</td><td>C.D.Holmes
650 IHP
10.9 knots</td><td>Colin & Rabé
Boulogne
France</td></tr>
<tr><td colspan="6">15.11.1954 Sold to Boston Deep Sea Fishing Co Ltd, Fleetwood renamed BOSTON AVENGER (FD3) Official No. 185295. 01.04.1955 to St Christopher Steam Fishing Co Ltd, Fleetwood.
1956 to Findus, Hammerfest, Norway renamed RAIRO (F32H). 21.04.1956 Left Fleetwood for Norway.
1968 to Rueggens Trålrederi A/S, Hammerfest, renamed NILS OLUF.
1971 Vessel sold for scrap to Hovding Shipsopurning. 19.10.1971 Breaking up commenced at Sandesjoen.</td></tr>
<tr><td>AUNIS
Coal Fired
LR4042 Steam Trawler</td><td>771
28.09.1946
14.12.1946</td><td>299
116</td><td>130.0
24.7</td><td>C.D.Holmes
650 IHP
10.9 knots</td><td>Association Rochelaise
de Peche a Vapeur
La Rochelle France</td></tr>
<tr><td colspan="6">1951 Sold to Boston Deep Sea Fishing Co Ltd, Fleetwood renamed NOBEL (FD69) Official No. 180343.
1957 to Milford Fisheries Ltd, Fleetwood. 1963 to Merchants (Milford Haven) Ltd, Milford Haven (M118).
1965 Vessel sold for scrap to Haulbowline, Cork, Ireland. 26.05.1965 Arrived Passage West for breaking up.</td></tr>
<tr><td>ARTOIS
Coal Fired
LR4049 Steam Trawler</td><td>772
06.12.1946
27.01.1947</td><td>295
116</td><td>130.0
24.7</td><td>C.D.Holmes
650 IHP
10.8 knots</td><td>Association Rochelaise
de Peche a Vapeur
La Rochelle France</td></tr>
<tr><td colspan="6">1951 Sold to Grange Fishing Co Ltd, Fleetwood renamed BRACONVALE (FD80) Official No. 180344.
19.12.1955 to Hammerfest Havfiske A/L, Hammerfest, Norway renamed MASI (F29H).
1970 Vessel sold for scrap to Anda Brodrene A/S, Stavanger. 31.03.1970 Breaking up commenced.</td></tr>
</table>

Yard No.757
1945 NAVENA
Photo:- Author's Collection

Yard No.764
1946 ST. MATTHEW
Photo:- Beverley Shipyard Collection

Yard No.773
1947 EDMOND - RENE
Photo by courtesy of Jack Daussy

<table>
<tr><th rowspan="2">NAME
Official No.
Port Letters Numbers</th><th rowspan="2">Yard No.
Launched
Registered</th><th colspan="2">Registered</th><th rowspan="2">Engine Builder
Horse Power
Reg'd Speed</th><th rowspan="2">OWNER
(Built for)</th></tr>
<tr><th>G Ton
N Ton</th><th>L Ft
B Ft</th></tr>
<tr><td>EDMOND-RENE
Oil Fired
F1053 Steam Trawler</td><td>773
20.05.1947
24.07.1947</td><td>336
139</td><td>130.0
25.0</td><td>C.D.Holmes
650 IHP
10.5 knots</td><td>Louis & Edmond Leporc
Fecamp
France</td></tr>
<tr><td colspan="6">14.03.1954 Sold to P& A Deconinck, Boulogne renamed SAINTE-IDE (B2669).
Apr 1958 to Levacher Lecanu, Fecamp renamed FRANC PICARD (F1157).
1959 to Craig Stores (AB) Ltd, Aberdeen (A396) Official No. 301582. 20.11.1959 left Fecamp for Aberdeen.
1966 Vessel sold for scrap to P & W Maclellan. 29.09.1966 Arrived Bo'ness for breaking up.</td></tr>
<tr><td>SOUVENIR
Oil Fired
F1038 Steam Trawler</td><td>774
23.05.1947
16.09.1947</td><td>295
139</td><td>130.0
25.0</td><td>C.D.Holmes
650 IHP
10.7 knots</td><td>Arm Vve J Bajard
Fecamp
France</td></tr>
<tr><td colspan="6">08.04.1954 Registration of vessel transferred to Boulogne (B2679).
1959 to Craig Stores (AB) Ltd, Aberdeen (A397) Official No. 301584. 20.11.1959 left Fecamp for Aberdeen.
1966 Vessel sold for scrap to P & W Maclellan. 21.11.1966 Arrived Bo'ness for breaking up.</td></tr>
<tr><td>VAN DER WEYDEN
Oil Fired
O293 Steam Trawler</td><td>775
01.08.1946
05.11.1946</td><td>323
118</td><td>129.0
25.7</td><td>C.D.Holmes
700 IHP
11.4 knots</td><td>NV Motorvisserij
Ostend
Belgium</td></tr>
<tr><td colspan="6">17.04.1951 Sold to Boston Deep-Sea Fishing Co Ltd, Fleetwood renamed BOSTON CANBERRA (FD68)
Official No. 180342. 16.10.1955 to Hammerfest Havfiske A/L, Hammerfest, Norway renamed GARGIA.
(Lengthened 158.6 ft 374 Gross tons 126 Net tons).
1970 Vessel sold for scrap to A/S H Berling Shipsopphugging, Sandnesjoen. 09.07.1970 Breaking up commenced.</td></tr>
<tr><td>VAN ORLEY
Oil Fired
O294 Steam Trawler</td><td>776
30.08.1946
03.12.1946</td><td>323
118</td><td>129.0
25.7</td><td>C.D. Holmes
700 IHP
11.3 knots</td><td>NV Motorvisserij
Ostend
Belgium</td></tr>
<tr><td colspan="6">17.04.1951 Sold to Boston Deep-Sea Fishing Co Ltd, Fleetwood renamed BOSTON ATTACKER (FD92)
Official No. 180345. 1952 to Canadian Government renamed MAPLE LEAF and given as a gift to Ceylon.
1971 Vessel deleted from Lloyds Register of Shipping.</td></tr>
<tr><td>ALLAN WATER
181298
H420 Motor Trawler</td><td>777
26.09.1946
31.03.1947</td><td>339
119</td><td>133.5
25.6</td><td>C.D. Holmes
750 BHP
11.3 knots</td><td>Great Western Fishing Co Ltd
Hull</td></tr>
<tr><td colspan="6">Original engine by Klöckner Humboldt Deutz under licence to C. D. Holmes.
04.03.1948 Vessel transferred to Fleetwood. 1953 Sold to Vissc Onderneming V/H, Ijmuiden, Holland (IJM34).
1964 to Claridge Trawlers Ltd, Lowestoft renamed ST. DAVIDS (LT494).
1966 (Ruston &Hornsby 6cyl 100 BHP 12.5 knots diesel engine fitted).
1980 Vessel sold for scrap to Medway Secondary Metals Ltd. 05.01.1981 Breaking up commenced at Rainham, Kent.</td></tr>
<tr><td>ST. CRISPIN
181296 Oil Fired
H399 Steam Trawler</td><td>778
13.11.1946
21.03.1947</td><td>559
202</td><td>170.8
29.2</td><td>C.D.Holmes
1000 IHP
12.2 knots</td><td>West Hartlepool Steam
Navigation Co Ltd
Hull</td></tr>
<tr><td colspan="6">Originally to have been named CORAL QUEEN (11.11.1946) but renamed before launch.
17.05.1951 Sold to J Marr & Son Ltd, Hull renamed JUNELLA (25.11.1962) renamed FARNELLA.
The name was changed to release her former name for use on the new freezer trawler JUNELLA H347.
1965 Vessel sold for scrap to P & W Maclellan. 09.12.1965 Arrived Bo'ness for breaking up.</td></tr>
<tr><td>AKUREY
Oil Fired
RE95 Steam Trawler</td><td>779
15.04.1947
21.07.1947</td><td>673
230</td><td>177.7
30.1</td><td>C.D.Holmes
1250 IHP
12.8 knots</td><td>The Government of
Iceland</td></tr>
<tr><td colspan="6">10.09.1947 Sold to Akurey H/F, Reykjavik, Iceland. 22.07.1952 to Fiskiveidahlutafelaginu Akurey, Akranes (AK77).
01.09.1966 to Bjarne Bendiksen. 1968 Erling Pettersen, Tromso, Norway renamed AKEROY (1968) renamed PETREL.
1970 (Klöckner - Humbolt - Deutz 8 cyl 1500 BHP diesel engine fitted). 1976 renamed PETREL V.
1978 to Techno Maritime Ltd, Ottawa, Canada. (converted to a research / survey vessel.)
1998 (Owners name change) Techno - Navigation, St John's, Newfoundland .</td></tr>
<tr><td>HVALFELL
Oil Fired
RE282 Steam Trawler</td><td>780
20.06.1947
23.09.1947</td><td>644
217</td><td>177.7
30.1</td><td>C.D.Holmes
1250 IHP
13.1 knots</td><td>Mjolnir H/F
Reykjavik
Iceland</td></tr>
<tr><td colspan="6">24.02.1961 Sold to Sildar Fiskimjolsverksmidjunn H/F, Reyjkavik. 02.07.1969 Removed from Icelandic Fishing Register.
1969 Vessel sold for scrap to Jos de Smedt, Antwerp, Belgium. 14.07.1969 Breaking up commenced.</td></tr>
</table>

Yard No.781
1947 NÓLSOYAR PÁLL
Photo:- Author's Collection

Yard No.787
1947 RÖDULL
Photo by courtesy of The Icelandic Maritime Museum, Hafnarfjördur

Yard No.793
1947 YORKSHIRE BELLE
Photo:- Author's Collection

<table>
<tr><th>NAME
Official No.
Port Letters Numbers</th><th>Yard No.
Launched
Registered</th><th colspan="2">Registered</th><th>Engine Builder
Horse Power
Reg'd Speed</th><th>OWNER
(Built for)</th></tr>
<tr><th></th><th></th><th>G Ton
N Ton</th><th>L Ft
B Ft</th><th></th><th></th></tr>
<tr><td>NOLSOYAR PALL
Oil Fired
TN10 Steam Trawler</td><td>781
08.01.1947
24.04.1947</td><td>538
183</td><td>169.1
29.2</td><td>C.D.Holmes
1000 IHP
13.0 knots</td><td>Chr. Holm Jacobsen
Thorshaven
Færoe Island</td></tr>
<tr><td colspan="6">03.11.1951 Sold to F & T Ross Ltd, Hull renamed FARADAY (H195) Official No. 185098.
22.12.1957 Went to the assistance of the coaster mv BOSWORTH which had developed a bad list in heavy seas.
Four of the crew boarded the stricken vessel and attached a tow rope, she was towed safely into Aberdeen (see Yard No.764).
06.07.1959 to Newington Steam Trawling Co Ltd, Hull renamed PETER CHEYNEY. 31.12.1966 Laid up at Hull.
1967 Vessel sold for scrap to P & W Maclellan. 23.02.1967 Left Hull for breaking up Bo'ness.</td></tr>
<tr><td>JÓANNES PATURSSON
Oil Fired
TN350 Steam Trawler</td><td>782
25.01.1947
20.05.1947</td><td>538
183</td><td>169.2
29.2</td><td>C.D.Holmes
1000 IHP
12.9 knots</td><td>Partafelagid Uvak
Thorshaven
Færoe Island</td></tr>
<tr><td colspan="6">1952 Sold to Partafelagid JF Kjolbro Klaksvig.
1965 Vessel sold for scrap to Clayton & Davie Ltd. 20.09.1965 Arrived Dunston on Tyne for breaking up.</td></tr>
<tr><td>GEIR
Oil Fired
RE241 Steam Trawler</td><td>783
21.07.1947
20.10.1947</td><td>644
217</td><td>177.7
30.1</td><td>C.D.Holmes
1250 IHP
13.3 knots</td><td>Hronn H/F
Reykjavik
Iceland</td></tr>
<tr><td colspan="6">24.02.1961 Sold to Sildar Fiskimjolsverksmidjunn H/F, Reyjkavik. 02.07.1969 Removed from Icelandic Fishing Register.
1969 Vessel sold for scrap to Jos de Smedt, Antwerp, Belgium. 14.07.1969 Breaking up commenced.</td></tr>
<tr><td>FYLKIR
Oil Fired
RE161 Steam Trawler</td><td>784
14.10.1947
13.02.1948</td><td>722
252</td><td>184.1
30.1</td><td>C.D.Holmes
1250 IHP
12.9 knots</td><td>Fylkir H/F
Reykjavik
Iceland</td></tr>
<tr><td colspan="6">14.11.1956 Whilst fishing approx 25 miles north of Straumnes, Iceland vessel trawled up a mine which exploded alongside causing her to sink. The crew of thirty-two men were rescued by the Icelandic trawler HAFLIDI SI 2 (see Yard No.780).</td></tr>
<tr><td>LORELLA
181320 Oil Fired
H455 Steam Trawler</td><td>785
20.08.1947
12.11.1947</td><td>559
202</td><td>170.8
29.2</td><td>C.D.Holmes
925 IHP
13.5 knots</td><td>City Steam Fishing Co Ltd
Hull</td></tr>
<tr><td colspan="6">26/27.01.1955 Vessel capsized due to a build up of ice in severe weather 90 miles north-east of the North Cape of Iceland along with the Hull trawler RODERIGO H135 (see Yard No.824). All twenty crew lost.</td></tr>
<tr><td>GODANES
Oil Fired
NK105 Steam Trawler</td><td>786
17.09.1947
18.12.1947</td><td>644
219</td><td>177.7
30.1</td><td>C.D.Holmes
1250 IHP
13.0 knots</td><td>Godanes H/F
Neskaupstador
Iceland</td></tr>
<tr><td colspan="6">03.01.1957 Vessel wrecked at Faereyjar, Færoe Islands.
The skipper was lost but twenty-three crew were rescued by a Færoese ship.</td></tr>
<tr><td>RÖDULL
Oil Fired
GK518 Steam Trawler</td><td>787
01.12.1947
16.03.1948</td><td>722
253</td><td>184.1
30.1</td><td>C.D.Holmes
1250 IHP
12.8 knots</td><td>Venus H/F
Hafnarfjordur
Iceland</td></tr>
<tr><td colspan="6">1974 Vessel sold for scrap to W H Arnott Young & Co Ltd, Dalmuir. 07.10.1974 Arrived Greenock for breaking up.</td></tr>
<tr><td>ISBORG
Oil Fired
IS250 Steam Trawler</td><td>788
31.12.1947
26.04.1948</td><td>644
217</td><td>177.7
30.1</td><td>C.D.Holmes
1250 IHP
12.9 knots</td><td>Isafjardarkaupst, Isafjordur
Iceland</td></tr>
<tr><td colspan="6">1963 Converted to cargo vessel. (Length 172.9 ft 615 gross tons) (Skandiaverken 8 cyl 750 BHP diesel engine fitted).
1971 Sold to Gudmunder A Gudmundsson H/F, Reykjavik.1974 to Naviera Simoun SA, Honduras renamed MARIA SISSY.
1976 S Ioannides & E Ferentinon, Piræus, Greece renamed CATERA.
1977 to Simoun Cia Nav SA, Panama. 1977 to Tamana Cia SA, Panama renamed NUEVA ISBORG.
1991 Vessel deleted from Lloyds Register of Shipping. - continued existence in doubt.</td></tr>
<tr><td>MARGARET WICKS
180333 Oil Fired
FD265 Steam Trawler</td><td>789
01.11.1947
26.01.1948</td><td>366
137</td><td>136.9
26.1</td><td>C.D.Holmes
600 IHP
10.9 knots</td><td>Clifton Steam Fishing Ltd
Fleetwood</td></tr>
<tr><td colspan="6">07.07.1956 Sold to Boston Deep-Sea Fishing Co Ltd, Fleetwood .1963 Sold to Aberdeen Near Water Trawlers, Aberdeen.
07.02.1963 Transferred to Aberdeen.13.05.1963 Returned to Fleetwood.
08.12.1963 Ran aground on rocks on Mull of Oa Isle of Islay. All fourteen crew were rescued by breeches-buoy.
15.12.1963 Re-floated by the Admiralty Tug DISPENSER (775 gt/ b 1943) and taken to Port Glasgow.
1964 Vessel sold for scrap to Shipbreaking Industries. 12.02.1964 Arrived Faslane for breaking up.</td></tr>
</table>

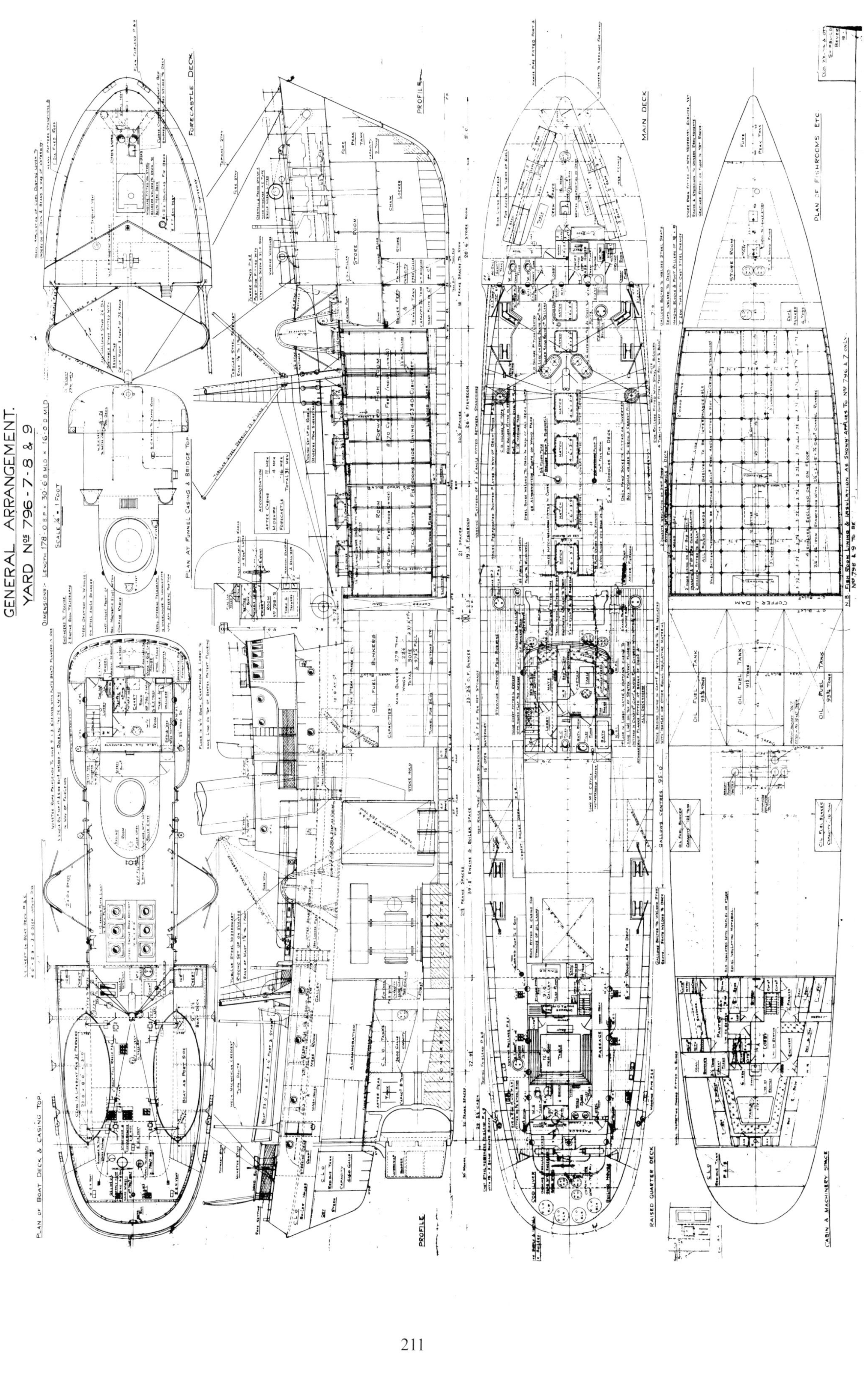
GENERAL ARRANGEMENT.
YARD Nos 796-7-8 & 9
DIMENSIONS:- LENGTH 178'-0 B.P. x 30'-6 B MLD x 16'-0 D MLD
SCALE 1/8" = 1 FOOT
FORECASTLE DECK
PLAN AT FUNNEL CASING & BRIDGE TOP
PLAN OF BOAT DECK & CASING TOP
PROFILE
MAIN DECK
RAISED QUARTER DECK
PLAN OF FISHROOMS ETC
CABIN & MACHINERY SPACE

<table>
<tr><th rowspan="2">NAME
Official No.
Port Letters Numbers</th><th rowspan="2">Yard No.
Launched
Registered</th><th colspan="2">Registered</th><th rowspan="2">Engine Builder
Horse Power
Reg'd Speed</th><th rowspan="2">OWNER
(Built for)</th></tr>
<tr><th>G Ton
N Ton</th><th>L Ft
B Ft</th></tr>
<tr><td>GARDAR ÞORSTEINSSON
(THORSTEINSSON)
GK3 Oil Fired Steam Trawler</td><td>790
28.01.1948
12.06.1948</td><td>722
252</td><td>184.1
30.1</td><td>C.D.Holmes
1250 IHP
13.1 knots</td><td>Utgerdarfelagid
Hrimlax H/F & Svidi H/F
Hafnarfjord Iceland</td></tr>
<tr><td colspan="6">24.07.1951 Sold to Baejarsjodi Siglufjardarkaupstadar, Siglufjord renamed HAFLIDI (SI 2).
02.05.1969 to Uterdarfelagi Siglufjardar H/F, Siglufjord.
08.12.1972 Vessel foundered whilst laid up at Siglufjord. 09.12.1972 refloated.
1973 Vessel sold for scrap to W H Arnott Young & Co Ltd, Dalmuir. 15.06.1973 Arrived Greenock for breaking up.</td></tr>
<tr><td>SKÚLI MAGNÚSSON
Oil Fired
RE202 Steam Trawler</td><td>791
28.02.1948
30.06.1948</td><td>722
252</td><td>184.1
30.1</td><td>C.D.Holmes
1000 IHP
13.1 knots</td><td>Baejarutgerd
Reykjavikur Reykjavik
Iceland</td></tr>
<tr><td colspan="6">01.08.1967 Vessel deleted from the Icelandic Fishing Register.
1967 Vessel sold for scrap to Van Heyghen Freres, Belgium . Feb1968 Breaking up commenced at Ghent.</td></tr>
<tr><td>JON FORSETI
Oil Fired
RE108 Steam Trawler</td><td>792
25.03.1948
23.07.1948</td><td>722
253</td><td>184.1
30.1</td><td>C.D.Holmes
1250 IHP
12.9 knots</td><td>Alliance H/F
Reykjavik
Iceland</td></tr>
<tr><td colspan="6">09.06.1966 Sold to Henriksen & Co Ltd, Hull renamed LARISSA (H266) Official No. 308549.
18.04.1968 Vessel sold for scrap to Thos W Ward Ltd. Jun 1968 Arrived Inverkeithing for breaking up.</td></tr>
<tr><td>YORKSHIRE BELLE
181302
Passenger Pleasure Vessel</td><td>793
22.05.1947
30.05.1947</td><td>70
32</td><td>80.2
19.4</td><td>Crosslley (twin)
120 BHP (each)
10.3 knots</td><td>Bride Hall Pockley
Bridlington</td></tr>
<tr><td colspan="6">12.03.1951 Vessel returned to Cook Welton & Gemmell, Beverley for modifications
(Two Gardiner 8 cyl 152 BHP diesel engines fitted). 27.04.1951 Returned to Bridlington.
22.09.1969 Ownership passed to John Cross Pockley & Thomas Marshall Neeham , Bridlington.
1973 to J T Bogg, Arthur Stirke Cook & J F Bogg, Bridlington.
11.02.1982 to Peter G Richardson & Roy Simpson, Bridlington. 1999 Vessel still in service.</td></tr>
<tr><td>ST. CHAD
181344 Oil Fired
H575 Steam Trawler</td><td>794
24.04.1948
23.08.1948</td><td>689
249</td><td>181.7
30.7</td><td>C.D.Holmes
1075 IHP
13.3 knots</td><td>St Andrew's Steam
Fishing Co Ltd
Hull</td></tr>
<tr><td colspan="6">26.04.1951 Sold to Charleson - Smith Ltd, Hull renamed STELLA POLARIS renamed (26.11.1965) ROSS POLARIS.
01.10.1967 to Hudson Bros (Trawlers), Hull. 13.12.1967 Laid up at Hull. 30.12.1967 Transferred to Grimsby.
04.04.1968 Vessel sold for scrap to Van Heyghen Freres, Belgium. Sep 1968 Breaking up commenced at Ghent .</td></tr>
<tr><td>BOSTON SEAFIRE
181351 Oil Fired
H584 Steam Trawler</td><td>795
24.05.1948
06.10.1948</td><td>689
249</td><td>181.7
30.7</td><td>C.D.Holmes
1075 IHP
13.4 knots</td><td>Boston Deep Sea Fisheries Ltd
Hull</td></tr>
<tr><td colspan="6">19.01.1952 Sold to Hudson Bros (Trawlers) Ltd, Hull renamed CAPE TARIFA.
05.02.1960 Company passed to Ross Group Ltd, Hull renamed (26.11.1965) ROSS TARIFA.
27.09.1967 Transferred to Grimsby. 1968 Vessel sold for scrap to Van Heyghen Freres Belgium.
07.03.1968 Vessel broke away from the tug MOORCOCK (272 gt/ b 1959) whilst on passage to the breakers yard at Bruges
Ran aground on the Goodwin Sands 1.25 miles east of the Goodwin Light-vessel. and subsequently sank into the sand.</td></tr>
<tr><td>KINGSTON SARDIUS
181354 Oil Fired
H588 Steam Trawler</td><td>796
10.06.1948
27.10.1948</td><td>686
245</td><td>181.7
30.8</td><td>C.D.Holmes
1000 IHP
13.2 knots</td><td>Kingston Steam Trawling
Co Ltd
Hull</td></tr>
<tr><td colspan="6">29.06.1966 Sold to Hellyer Bros Ltd, Hull.
1968 Vessel sold for scrap to Van Den Bossche, Belgium. 19.12.1968 Arrived Boom for breaking up.</td></tr>
<tr><td>KINGSTON PERIDOT
181356 Oil Fired
H591 Steam Trawler</td><td>797
10.07.1948
25.11.1948</td><td>658
232</td><td>181.7
30.8</td><td>C.D.Holmes
1000 IHP
12.9 knots</td><td>Kingston Steam Trawling
Co Ltd
Hull</td></tr>
<tr><td colspan="6">29.06.1966 Sold to Hellyer Bros Ltd, Hull.
26/27.01.1968 Vessel sank off Kopasker Iceland in gale force winds and freezing weather conditions.
30.01.1968 Icelandic search parties found wreckage but no survivors. All twenty crew lost.</td></tr>
<tr><td>ST. APOLLO
181359 Oil Fired
H592 Steam Trawler</td><td>798
06.09.1948
23.12.1948</td><td>658
232</td><td>181.7
30.8</td><td>C.D.Holmes
1000 IHP
13.3 knots</td><td>Thomas Hamling & Co Ltd
Hull</td></tr>
<tr><td colspan="6">09.11.1956 Sold to Firth Steam Trawling Co Ltd, Hull.
11.10.1960 Sank the Belgian trawler RUBENS (see Yard No.810) in collision 30 miles off the south east coast of Iceland.
All the RUBENS crew were taken aboard the ST. APOLLO and landed at Hull.
03.07.1973 Vessel sold for scrap to Albert Draper & Son Ltd, Hull.
25.06.1974 Breaking up commenced at the Victoria Dock slipway.</td></tr>
</table>

Yard No.799
1948 ST. LEANDER
Photo:- Beverley Shipyard Collection

Yard No.805
1949 BOMBARDIER
Photo:- Beverley Shipyard Collection

Yard No.807
1949 CAYTON BAY
Photo:- Beverley Shipyard Collection

<table>
<tr><th rowspan="2">NAME
Official No.
Port Letters Numbers</th><th rowspan="2">Yard No.
Launched
Registered</th><th colspan="2">Registered</th><th rowspan="2">Engine Builder
Horse Power
Reg'd Speed</th><th rowspan="2">OWNER
(Built for)</th></tr>
<tr><th>G Ton
N Ton</th><th>L Ft
B Ft</th></tr>
<tr><td>ST. LEANDER
183383 Oil Fired
H19 Steam Trawler</td><td>799
05.10.1948
08.02.1949</td><td>658
232</td><td>181.7
30.8</td><td>C.D.Holmes
1000 IHP
12.5 knots</td><td>Thomas Hamling & Co Ltd
Hull</td></tr>
<tr><td colspan="6">09.01.1951 Vessel sank following a collision with the trawler DAVY H213 (see Yard No.612) whilst manoeuvring off St Andrew's Dock, Hull. The ST. LEANDER drifted to Barton Ness and was taken in tow but capsized after grounding on the Hessle Flats. All crew were rescued by river craft. Apr-Aug 1951 Salvage attempts were carried out by three vessels of the Liverpool and Glasgow Salvage Association. These proved unsuccessful. 31.03.1952 The wreck was blown up.</td></tr>
<tr><td>PRINCESS ELIZABETH
182626 Oil Fired
GY590 Steam Trawler</td><td>800
07.08.1948
06.12.1948</td><td>568
206</td><td>170.2
29.2</td><td>C.D.Holmes
1000 IHP
13.2 knots</td><td>North Cape Fishing Co Ltd
Grimsby</td></tr>
<tr><td colspan="6">Originally ordered by NV Motorvisserij, Ostend, Belgium.
28.09.1949 Sold to Sold to Firth Steam Trawling Co Ltd, Hull renamed ST. RONAN (H86).
12.10.1952 Wrecked on the outermost rock of the Men of Mey, St Johns Point, Caithness, Scotland whilst outward bound for Greenland. All twenty crew were taken off by a boat from Stromness and landed at Mey harbour.</td></tr>
<tr><td>PRINCE PHILIP
183387 Oil Fired
H32 Steam Trawler</td><td>801
04.11.1948
18.02.1949</td><td>568
206</td><td>170.7
29.2</td><td>C.D.Holmes
1000 IHP
13.2 knots</td><td>North Cape Fishing Co Ltd
Hull</td></tr>
<tr><td colspan="6">Originally ordered by NV Motorvisserij, Ostend, Belgium.
08.07.1955 Sold to Derwent Trawlers, Grimsby renamed HARGOOD (GY7).
01.01.1958 to Charleson - Smith Trawlers Ltd, Hull renamed STELLA RIGEL (H170).
21.12.1962 Vessel wrecked at Vestor Falle 7 miles north west of Fugloy lighthouse off the north coast of Norway. The twenty crew took to life-rafts and were rescued by the Norwegian fishing vessel SIV.</td></tr>
<tr><td>FARNELLA
183389 Oil Fired
H41 Steam Trawler</td><td>802
20.11.1948
09.03.1949</td><td>684
246</td><td>181.7
30.8</td><td>C.D.Holmes
1075 IHP
13.4 knots</td><td>J Marr & Son Ltd
Hull</td></tr>
<tr><td colspan="6">12.01.1952 Sold to Kingston Steam Trawling Co Ltd, Hull renamed KINGSTON ANDALUSITE.
29.06.1966 to Hellyer Bros Ltd, Hull.
05.02.1968 Vessel stranded whilst entering Isafjördr, Iceland. 06.02.1968 Refloated but declared a Constructive Total Loss.
14.02.1969 Vessel sold for scrap to Van Den Bossche, Belgium. Apr 1969 Breaking up commenced at Boom.</td></tr>
<tr><td>SWANELLA
183391 Oil Fired
H42 Steam Trawler</td><td>803
18.12.1948
25.03.1949</td><td>684
246</td><td>181.7
30.8</td><td>C.D.Holmes
1075 IHP
13.4 knots</td><td>J Marr & Son Ltd
Hull</td></tr>
<tr><td colspan="6">04.03.1952 Sold to Firth Steam Trawling Co Ltd, Hull renamed ST. AMANT.
Jun 1973 Sold for scrap to Albert Draper & Son, Hull. 02.09.1973 Arrived Victoria Dock Slipway for breaking up.</td></tr>
<tr><td>PRINCE CHARLES
183412 Oil Fired
H85 Steam Trawler</td><td>804
14.05.1949
26.08.1949</td><td>712
262</td><td>181.7
30.7</td><td>C.D.Holmes
1075 IHP
13.4 knots</td><td>North Cape Fishing Co Ltd
Hull</td></tr>
<tr><td colspan="6">27.04.1951 Sold to Hudson Bros (Trawlers) Ltd, Hull renamed CAPE DUNER.
05.02.1960 Company passed to Ross Group Ltd, Grimsby renamed (26.11.1965) ROSS DUNER.
27.09.1967 Transferred to Grimsby. 1968 Vessel sold for scrap to Van Heyghen Freres, Belgium (see Yard No.795).
06.03.1968 Vessel broke away from the tug MOORCOCK off the South Falls Buoy whilst on passage to the breakers yard at Bruges Belgium. 07.03.1968 Ran aground near Dunkirk. 13.03.1968 Vessel refloated and towed to Bruges for breaking up.</td></tr>
<tr><td>BOMBARDIER
182633 Oil Fired
GY30 Steam Trawler</td><td>805
17.01.1949
13.05.1949</td><td>661
255</td><td>181.7
30.6</td><td>C.D.Holmes
1075 IHP
13.8 knots</td><td>Supreme Fish Curing Co Ltd
Grimsby</td></tr>
<tr><td colspan="6">24.01.1966 Sold to Northern Trawlers Ltd, Grimsby.
24.05.1968 Vessel sold for scrap to Jos de Smedt, Belgium. Jul 1968 Arrived Antwerp for breaking up.</td></tr>
<tr><td>VINDORA
182634 Oil Fired
GY40 Steam Trawler</td><td>806
16.02.1949
16.06.1949</td><td>640
240</td><td>181.7
30.6</td><td>C.D.Holmes
1075 IHP
13.6 knots</td><td>Atlas Steam Fishing Co Ltd
Grimsby</td></tr>
<tr><td colspan="6">24.01.1966 Sold to Northern Trawlers Ltd, Grimsby.
1968 Vessel sold for scrap to Jos de Smedt, Belgium. 30.04.1968 Breaking up commenced at Antwerp.</td></tr>
<tr><td>CAYTON BAY
183400 Coal Fired
H72 Steam Trawler</td><td>807
01.03.1949
27.05.1949</td><td>580
209</td><td>171.5
29.2</td><td>C.D.Holmes
1000 IHP
12.2 knots</td><td>Marine Steam Fishing Co Ltd
Hull</td></tr>
<tr><td colspan="6">Last coal burner built at Beverley for Hull owners.
07.02.1952 Sold to J Marr & Son Ltd, Hull renamed (11.02.1952) BAYELLA. Aug 1955 (Fitted for fuel oil).
Sep 1956 Towed the disabled Hull trawler STELLA ARCTURUS H216 (579 gt/ b 1946) to Hull from Spitsbergen.
20.10.1966 Vessel sold to for scrap(£6500) to Scrapping Co, Belgium. 26.11.1966 Arrived Antwerp for breaking up.</td></tr>
</table>

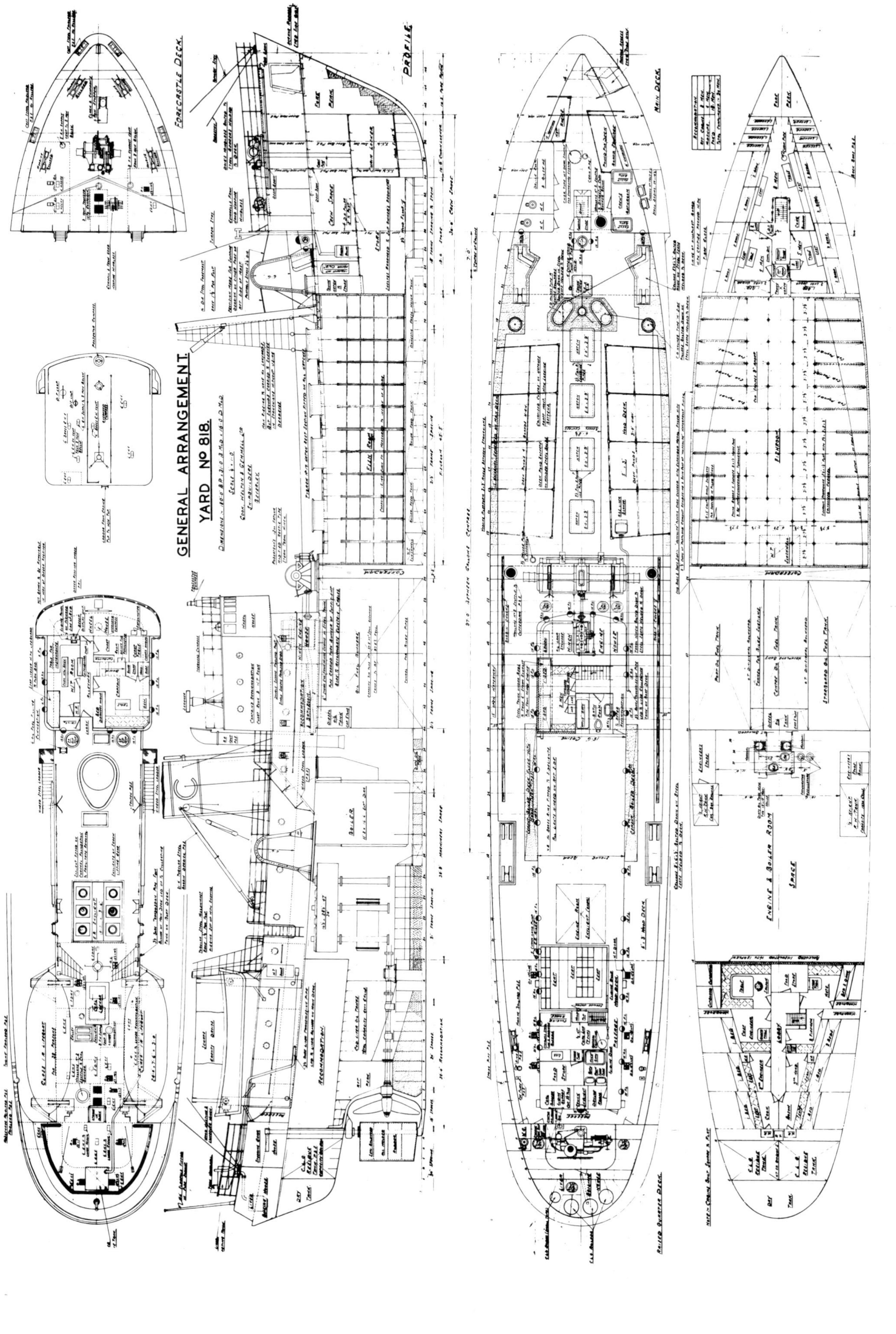
GENERAL ARRANGEMENT
YARD No 818.
PROFILE
FORECASTLE DECK
MAIN DECK
RAISED QUARTER DECK
ENGINE & BOILER ROOM SPACE

NAME Official No. Port Letters Numbers	Yard No. Launched Registered	Registered G Ton N Ton	 L Ft B Ft	Engine Builder Horse Power Reg'd Speed	OWNER (Built for)
STARELLA 183404 Oil Fired H75 Steam Trawler	808 31.03.1949 06.07.1949	684 242	181.7 30.7	C.D.Holmes 1075 IHP 13.5 knots	City Steam Fishing Co Ltd Hull
22.11.1958 Sold to Henriksen & Co Ltd, Hull renamed MILETUS. 16.10.1969 Vessel sold for scrap to Clayton & Davie Ltd for breaking up at Dunston on Tyne.					
LANCER 182635 Oil Fired GY65 Steam Trawler	809 14.04.1949 27.07.1949	668 243	183.4 30.7	C.D.Holmes 1100 IHP 13.6 knots	Loyal Steam Fishing Co Ltd Grimsby
1954 LANCER recorded the shortest trip to Iceland from the Humber. 22.07.1954 to 30.07.1954 (eight days seven hours), dock to dock. Fishing time at south-east Iceland, two days eighteen hours. Landed 1.100 kits. Grossed £4,238. 24.01.1966 Sold to Northern Trawlers Ltd, Grimsby. 1968 Vessel sold for scrap to Jos de Smedt, Belgium. 05.09.1968 Arrived at Antwerp for breaking up.					
RUDOLF Ice Breaker Harbour Tug	810 30.05.1949 17.09.1949	179 63	83.4 26.7	Amos & Smith 450 IHP 11 knots	Goteborgs Bogserings & Bårgnings A/B Gothenburg Sweden
1963 *(Ruston & Hornsby 8 cyl 1500 BHP diesel engine fitted).* 1972 Sold to A/S EM Z Svitzers Bjergnings Enterprise, Fredericia, Denmark renamed VOLUND. 1981 to Jannu-Hinaus O/Y Helsinki / Helsingfors, Finland renamed AMAZON 2000. 1989 to Rederi Alfons Hakans & Co, Helsinki renamed RUDOLF. 1995 to Parnu Port Authority, Lehtma, Estonia. 1999 Vessel still in Service.					
Not Built	811	Turn allocated to Iago Steam Fishing Co London but not taken up			
LIFEGUARD 182639 Oil Fired GY94 Steam Trawler	812 12.07.1949 05.10.1949	668 243	183.4 30.7	C.D.Holmes 1100 IHP 14 knots	Loyal Steam Fishing Co Ltd Grimsby
Apr 1954 Due to superstition a new PLN was acquired (GY395). Her former PLN GY94 added up to unlucky thirteen. The change followed the loss on the 08.02.1954 of the LAFOREY GY85 (609 gt/ b 1949) on the Norwegian coast with all her crew. 24.01.1966 Sold to Northern Trawlers Ltd, Grimsby. 1968 Vessel sold for scrap to Jos de Smedt, Belgium. 22.05.1968 Breaking up commenced at Antwerp.					
NORTHERN PRINCESS 182640 Oil Fired GY110 Steam Trawler	813 24.08.1949 09.11.1949	677 252	181.7 31.1	C.D.Holmes 1075 IHP 12.9 knots	Northern Trawlers Ltd Grimsby
29.10.1969 Vessel sold for scrap to Clayton & Davie Ltd. Jan 1970 Arrived at Dunston on Tyne for breaking.					
NORTHERN PRINCE 182641 Oil Fired GY121 Steam Trawler	814 26.09.1949 09.12.1949	677 251	181.7 31.7	C.D.Holmes 1075 IHP 13.0 knots	Northern Trawlers Ltd Grimsby
1975 Sold to British United Trawlers, Grimsby. 25.06.1975 Vessel sold for scrap to C F Booth Rotherham . Allocated to Blyth Shipbreakers & Repairers Ltd. 03.02.1976 Arrived Blyth for breaking up.					
NORTHERN QUEEN 182642 Oil Fired GY124 Steam Trawler	815 10.10.1949 09.01.1950	677 251	181.7 31.7	C.D.Holmes 1075 IHP 12.8 knots	Northern Trawlers Ltd Grimsby
1971 Refurbished by Humber Graving Dock at Immingham (£60,000). 1975 Sold to British United Trawlers, Grimsby. 21.04.1976 Vessel sold for scrap to Kibon Vickers Sheffield allocated to London Demolition Shipbreakers. 09.08.1976 Left Grimsby in tow for Dartford for breaking up.					
KINGSTON GARNET 183425 Oil Fired H106 Steam Trawler	816 03.11.1949 07.02.1950	717 243	183.4 30.7	C.D.Holmes 1000 IHP 12.9 knots	Kingston Steam Trawling Co Ltd Hull
29.06.1966 Sold to Hellyer Bros Ltd, Hull. 1968 Vessel sold for scrap to Hughes Bolckow Ltd . 14.12.1968 Arrived Blyth for breaking up.					
KINGSTON ZIRCON 183430 Oil Fired H108 Steam Trawler	817 07.12.1949 09.03.1950	717 243	183.4 30.7	C.D.Holmes 1000 IHP 12.9 knots	Kingston Steam Trawling Co Ltd Hull
29.06.1966 Sold to Hellyer Bros Ltd, Hull. 1968 Vessel sold for scrap to Hughes Bolckow Ltd . 14.12.1968 Arrived Blyth for breaking up.					
YARDLEY 182646 Oil Fired GY81 Steam Trawler	818 21.01.1950 14.04.1950	703 259	183.5 31.1	C.D.Holmes 1200 IHP 12.7 knots	Crampin Steam Fishing Co Ltd Grimsby
24.03.1965 Sold to Ross Group, Grimsby renamed (26.11.1965) ROSS HOWE. 25.06.1966 to Hudson Bros (Trawlers) Ltd, Hull (H422). 21.03.1967 Transferred to Grimsby. 1968 Vessel sold for scrap to Van Heyghen Freres, Belgium. May 1968 Breaking up commenced at Antwerp.					

Yard No.815
1949 NORTHERN QUEEN
Photo:- Beverley Shipyard Collection

Yard No.819
1950 THOMAS TOMPIAN
Photo:- Beverley Shipyard Collection

Yard No.829
1950 KINGSTON JADE
Photo:- Beverley Shipyard Collection

NAME Official No. Port Letters Numbers	Yard No. Launched Registered	Registered G Ton N Ton	 L Ft B Ft	Engine Builder Horse Power Reg'd Speed	OWNER (Built for)
THOMAS TOMPION 182649 Oil Fired GY126 Steam Trawler	819 06.02.1950 04.05.1950	590 211	174.4 29.5	C.D.Holmes 1000 IHP 12.5 knots	H Croft Baker Grimsby
Jul 1957 Sold to Derwent Trawlers Ltd, Grimsby. 01.01.1958 to Charleson - Smith Trawlers Ltd, Hull renamed STELLA PROCYON (H184) renamed (26.11.1965) ROSS PROCYON. 01.10.1967 to Hudson Bros (Trawlers) Ltd, Hull. 1968 Vessel sold for scrap to Jos De Smelt, Belgium. 25.10.1968 Arrived Antwerp for breaking up.					
ALAMEIN 183439 Oil Fired H123 Steam Trawler	820 08.03.1950 01.06.1950	661 239	181.7 30.7	C.D.Holmes 1000 IHP 12.5 knots	Hull Merchants Amalgamated Trawlers Ltd Hull
22.08.1955 Sold to Charleson - Smith Trawlers Ltd, Hull renamed STELLA ANTARES. 26.11.1965 renamed ROSS ANTARES. 01.10.1967 to Hudson Bros (Trawlers) Ltd, Hull. 1968 Vessel sold for scrap to P & W McLellan Ltd. 05.09.1968 Left Hull for the Tyne for breaking up.					
ST. BRITWIN 183443 Oil Fired H124 Steam Trawler	821 06.04.1950 18.05.1950	742 272	183.4 30.8	C.D.Holmes 1000 IHP 12.8 knots	Thomas Hamling & Co Ltd Hull
15.04.1975 Laid up at Hull. 1975 Vessel sold for scrap to C F Booth Rotherham . Allocated to Blyth Shipbreakers & Repairers Ltd. 22.10.1975 Arrived Blyth for breaking up.					
ST. ALCUIN 183446 Oil Fired H125 Steam Trawler	822 02.05.1950 25.07.1950	742 271	183.4 30.8	C.D.Holmes 1000 IHP 12.8 knots	Thomas Hamling & Co Ltd Hull
12.06.1974 Vessel sold for scrap to Albert Draper & Son Ltd, Hull. 24.06.1974 Arrived Victoria Dock for breaking up.					
Not Built	823	Turn allocated to Standard Steam Fishing Co, Grimsby but not taken up			
PRINCESS ELIZABETH 183449 Oil Fired H135 Steam Trawler	824 02.06.1950 15.09.1950	810 289	189.1 32.2	C.D.Holmes 1100 IHP 12.9 knots	St Andrew's Steam Fishing Co Ltd Hull
All crew accommodation arranged amidships and aft for a total of thirty-seven. First British trawler fitted with a Fishmeal processing plant situated in the forecastle. Ten tons of fish offal resulted in 2.5 tons of fishmeal per twenty-four hours. 06.04.1951 Sold to Devon Fishing Co Ltd, Hull. renamed (12.04.1951) RODERIGO. 31.01.1952 to Hellyer Bros Ltd, Hull. 27.01.1955 Vessel capsized due to a build up of ice in severe weather 90 miles north-east of the North Cape of Iceland along with the Hull trawler LORELLA H455 *(see Yard No.785).* All twenty crew lost.					
Not Built	825	Turn allocated to P/F Uvak Thorshaven but not taken up.			
KINGSTON ONYX 182453 Oil Fired H140 Steam Trawler	826 16.08.1950 30.10.1950	794 287	188.8 32.1	C.D.Holmes 1200 IHP 13.0 knots	Kingston Steam Trawling Co Ltd Hull
21.03.1963 Vessel stranded near Andenes. 07.04.1963 Refloated by the Norwegian salvage vessels PARAT (176 gt/ b 1963) and ULLER (319 gt/ b 1943) and towed to Harstad for repairs. 29.06.1966 Sold to Hellyer Bros Ltd, Hull. 28.04.1975 Vessel sold for scrap to Belcon Shipping & Trading Co Ltd. May1975 re-sold to Medway Secondary Metals Ltd. 10.05.1975 Left Hull for Gillingham Kent. 01.09.1975 breaking up commenced.					
KINGSTON TOPAZ 183459 Oil Fired H145 Steam Trawler	827 28.09.1950 11.12.1950	794 287	188.8 32.1	C.D.Holmes 1200 IHP 13.0 knots	Kingston Steam Trawling Co Ltd Hull
29.06.1966 Sold to Hellyer Bros Ltd, Hull. 28.04.1975 Vessel sold for scrap to Group Six Demolition. Jun 1975 Arrived Sittingbourne Kent for breaking up.					
VAN DYCK Oil Fired 0298 Steam Trawler	828 01.07.1950 00.09.1950	599 219	170.2 29.2	C.D.Holmes 925 IHP 12.9 knots	NV Motorvisserij Ostend Belgium
06.03.1964 Sold to Thomas Hamling & Co Ltd, Hull renamed ST. ROMANUS (H223) Official No. 305741. 11.01.1968 Vessel presumed to have sank in severe weather in the North Sea whilst outward bound towards the Norwegian fishing grounds in approx position 57° 57'N 001° 35'E . All twenty crew lost.					
KINGSTON JADE 183465 Oil Fired H149 Steam Trawler	829 28.10.1950 02.02.1951	794 287	188.8 32.1	C.D.Holmes 1200 IHP 13.2 knots	Kingston Steam Trawling Co Ltd Hull
29.06.1966 Sold to Hellyer Bros Ltd, Hull. 09.04.1975 Vessel sold for scrap to Albert Draper & Son Ltd, Hull. 26.04.1975 Arrived Victoria Dock Slipway for breaking up.					

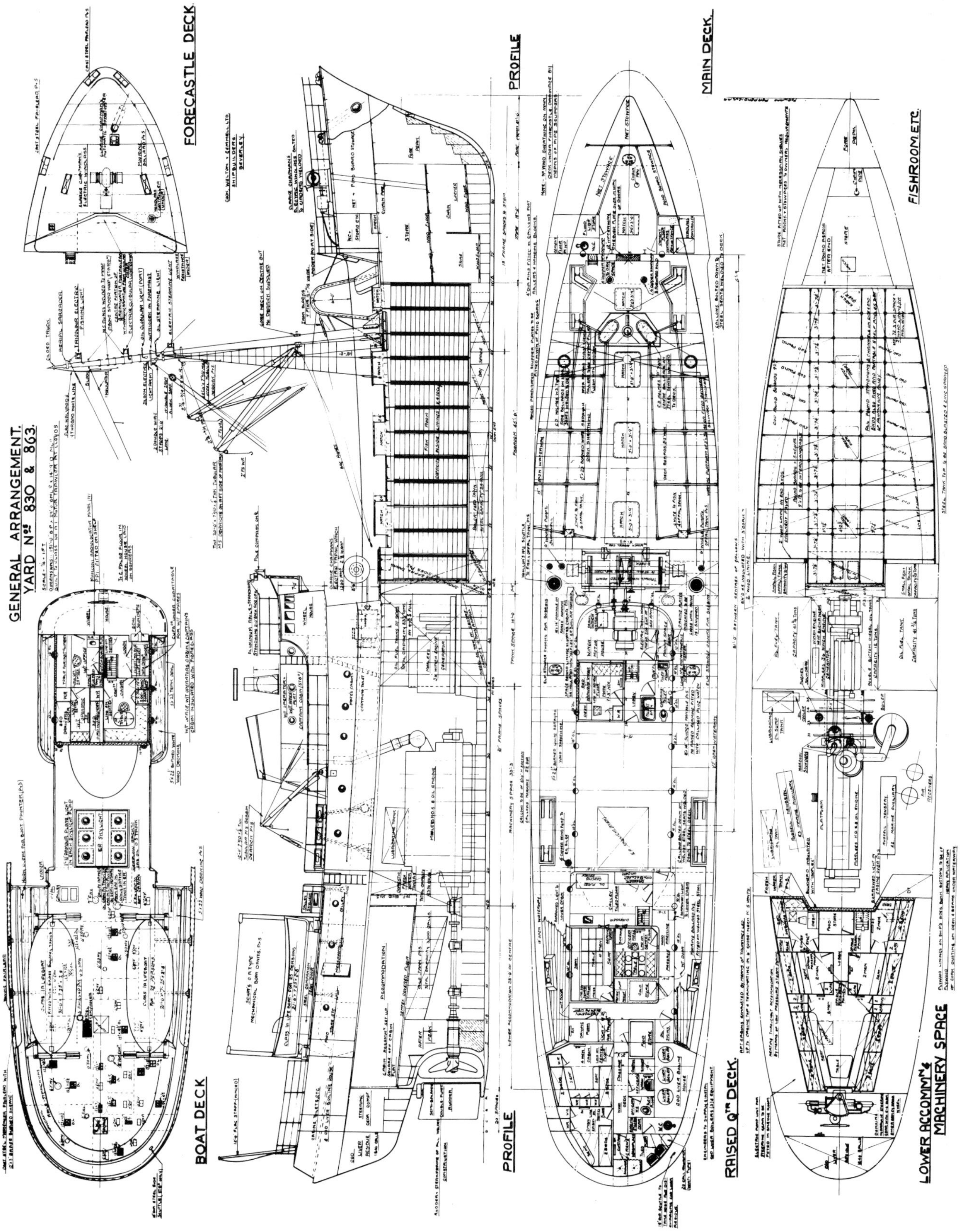
GENERAL ARRANGEMENT.
YARD No. 830 & 863.
FORECASTLE DECK
PROFILE
MAIN DECK
FISHROOM ETC.
BOAT DECK
PROFILE
RAISED Qr DECK.
LOWER ACCOMMn & MACHINERY SPACE

NAME Official No. Port Letters Numbers	Yard No. Launched Registered	Registered G Ton N Ton	 L Ft B Ft	Engine Builder Horse Power Reg'd Speed	OWNER (Built for)
PRINCESS ANNE 185150 H268 Motor Trawler	830 22.08.1952 05.06.1953	498 150	169.1 29.1	Mirrlees Bickerton Day 1050 BHP 12.1 knots	St Andrew's Steam Fishing Co Ltd Hull
08.05.1954 Sold to Pecheries de la Marine, Bolougne, France renamed SAINT JUST 11 (B2672). 17.03.1967 to Wyre Trawlers Ltd, Fleetwood renamed WYRE GLEANER. (FD269). 09.07.1971 to British United Trawlers(Finance) Ltd, Hull. 02.06.1976 Last landing. 1976 Vessel sold for scrap to Mayer Newman. 24.07.1976 Left Fleetwood for Hayle for breaking up.					
Not Built	831- 832-833 Turns allocated to Standard Steam Fishing Co, Grimsby but not taken up.				
ST. KEVERNE 183470 Oil Fired H158 Steam Trawler	834 12.12.1950 19.03.1951	794 286	188.8 32.2	C.D.Holmes 1150 IHP 13.4 knots	Thomas Hamling & Co Ltd Hull
Nov 1974 Vessel sold for scrap to Hughes Bolckow Ltd . 04.11.1974 Arrived Blyth for breaking up.					
ST. LEGER 185089 Oil Fired H178 Steam Trawler	835 09.04.1951 22.06.1951	794 286	188.8 32.2	C.D.Holmes 1150 IHP 13.4 knots	Thomas Hamling & Co Ltd Hull
1975 Vessel sold for scrap to F C Booth, Rotherham. Allocated to Doncaster Construction (Shipbreaking Co Ltd). 24.10.1975 Breaking up commenced at Grimsby.					
KINGSTON JACINTH 185106 Oil Fired H198 Steam Trawler	836 03.11.1951 28.01.1952	794 287	188.8 32.2	C.D.Holmes 1200 IHP 13.4 knots	Kingston Steam Trawling Co Ltd Hull
29.06.1966 Sold to Hellyer Bros Ltd, Hull. 11.08.1971 Vessel severely damaged by fire whilst at the port of Seydisfjördr Iceland for engine repairs. Damage to the bridge and accommodation was extensive and one crewman died in the fire which was finally extinguished by the local fire services. The KINGSTON JACINTH was towed back to Hull by the trawler LORD LOVAT H148 (713 gt/ b 1951). 1976 Vessel sold for scrap to Medway Secondary Metals Ltd . 31.03.1976 Left Hull for Gillingham, Kent for breaking up.					
Not Built	837 Turn allocated to Kingston Steam Trawling Co Ltd, Hull but not taken up.				
NORTHELLA 183471 Oil Fired H159 Steam Trawler	838 11.01.1951 14.04.1951	787 280	188.5 32.1	C.D.Holmes 1250 IHP 13.6 knots	J Marr & Son Ltd Hull
06.03.1956 Sold to P/f Sjørnan Westermanhavn Færoe Islands renamed GULLBERG. 1964 to P/f Saturn Thorshaven. 30.06.1965 to Henriksen & Co Ltd, Hull renamed (03.09.1965) CALYDON (H253). 15.02.1973 Company wound up. 04.05.1973 Vessel sold for scrap to Albert Draper & Son, Hull. May 1973 Arrived Victoria Dock Slipway and broken up.					
VELIA 185136 H239 Motor Trawler	839 04.06.1951 31.10.1952	296 117	128.2 26.6	Mirrlees Bickerton & Day 700 BHP 11.2 knots	J Marr & Son Ltd Hull
05.11.1952 Left Hull on her maiden voyage and landed her first catch at Fleetwood where she was to be based (FD116). 1959 *(lengthened 131 ft 317 Gross Tons by Humber St Andrew's Engineering Co Ltd, Hull).* 26.04.1960 re-registered. 1963 Sold to Ocean Pesca S.R.I, Mazara Del Vallo, Italy renamed SALVATORE GIACALONE. 17.07.1963 Left Fleetwood for Italy. 1999 Vessel still in service.					
Not Built	840 Turn allocated to Hull Merchants Amalg. Trawlers but not taken up. 841 Turn allocated to Boyd Line Ltd, Hull but not taken up. 842 Turn allocated to Basil Parkes, Hull but not taken up.				
VANESSA 184912 Oil Fired GY257 Steam Trawler	843 10.07.1952 02.10.1952	661 237	181.4 31.1	C.D.Holmes 1100 IHP 12.4 knots	Atlas Steam Fishing Co Ltd Grimsby
24.01.1966 Sold to Northern Trawlers Ltd, Grimsby. 30.12.1974 Vessel sold for scrap to Albert Draper & Son, Hull. 01.02.1975 Arrived at Victoria Dock slipway for breaking up.					
Not Built	844 Turn allocated to H Croft Baker, Grimsby but not taken up.				
VAN EYCK Oil Fired O293 Steam Trawler	845 07.05.1951 18.07.1951	576 207	170.1 29.2	C.D.Holmes 900 IHP 12.9 knots	NV Motorvisserij Ostend Belgium
11.09.1959 Sold to North Cape Fishing Co Ltd, Grimsby renamed NORTH HOLME (GY76) Official No. 168620. 24.03.1961 to NV Motorvisserij, Ostend, Belgium renamed VAN EYCK. 08.02.1964 to Thomas Hamling & Co Ltd, Hull renamed ST. ACHILLEUS (H215). 31.12.1968 Vessel sold for scrap to P & W McLellan Ltd . Feb 1969 Arrived Bo'ness for breaking up.					
Not Built	846 Order cancelled.				

Yard No.845
1951 VAN EYCK
Photo by courtesy of Ian Spashett, Skyfotos

Yard No.852
1951 HILDENA
Photo:- Beverley Shipyard Collection

Yard No.854
1953 H.M.S. BRONINGTON
Photo:- Author's Collection

<table>
<tr><th rowspan="2">NAME
Official No.
Port Letters Numbers</th><th rowspan="2">Yard No.
Launched
Registered</th><th colspan="2">Registered</th><th rowspan="2">Engine Builder
Horse Power
Reg'd Speed</th><th rowspan="2">OWNER
(Built for)</th></tr>
<tr><th>G Ton
N Ton</th><th>L Ft
B Ft</th></tr>
<tr><td>VAN ORLEY
Oil Fired
O294 Steam Trawler</td><td>847
24.05.1951
12.09.1951</td><td>576
207</td><td>170.2
29.2</td><td>C.D.Holmes
900 IHP
12.9 knots</td><td>NV Motorvisserij
Ostend
Belgium</td></tr>
<tr><td colspan="6">14.04.1964 to Thomas Hamling & Co Ltd, Hull renamed ST. ANDRONICAS (H241). Official No. 305744.
19.12.1968 Vessel sold for scrap to P & W McLellan Ltd . Feb1969 Arrived Bo'ness for breaking up.</td></tr>
<tr><td>VAN OOST
Oil Fired
O296 Steam Trawler</td><td>848
20.07.1951
00.11.1951</td><td>576
185.4</td><td>170.2
29.2</td><td>C.D.Holmes
900 IHP
13.0 knots</td><td>NV Motorvisserij
Ostend
Belgium</td></tr>
<tr><td colspan="6">17.09.1959 Sold to North Cape Fishing Co Ltd, Grimsby renamed NORTH CAPE (GY75) Official No. 168619.
24.03.1961 NV Motorvisserij, Ostend, Belgium renamed VAN OOST.
08.02.1964 Thomas Hamling & Co Ltd, Hull renamed ST. ARCADIUS (H207).
1968 Vessel sold for scrap to Jos de Smedt, Belgium. 22.07.1968 Arrived Antwerp under tow for breaking up.</td></tr>
<tr><td>Not Built</td><td>849</td><td colspan="4">Turn allocated to Marine Steam Fishing Co Ltd, Hull but not taken up.</td></tr>
<tr><td>NESS No. 27
Light Float</td><td>850
18.12.1950
12.01.1952</td><td>25</td><td>40.0
16.0</td><td>N/A</td><td>Humber Conservancy Board
Hull</td></tr>
<tr><td colspan="6">12.01.1952 Delivered to Princess Dock, Hull. For use in marking the Navigable deep water channel in the River Humber.</td></tr>
<tr><td>Un-named
Light Float</td><td>851
18.12.1950
12.01.1952</td><td>25</td><td>40.0
16.0</td><td>N/A</td><td>Humber Conservancy Board
Hull</td></tr>
<tr><td colspan="6">12.01.1952 Delivered to Princess Dock, Hull. For use in marking the Navigable deep water channel in the River Humber.</td></tr>
<tr><td>HILDINA
185119
H222 Motor Trawler</td><td>852
21.08.1951
29.04.1952</td><td>296
117</td><td>128.2
26.6</td><td>Mirrlees
Bickerton & Day
700 BHP 11 knots</td><td>City Steam Fishing Co Ltd
Hull</td></tr>
<tr><td colspan="6">26.11.1953 Transferred to Fleetwood. 01.12.1953 Vessel capsized in rough seas after trawl came fast on the sea bed whilst fishing approx 50 miles north by west from Sule Skerry, Scotland. Eight crewmen rescued by the Fleetwood trawler VELIA FD116 (see Yard No.839). Six crew lost.</td></tr>
<tr><td>HMS BRINTON
M 1114
Coniston (Ton) Class</td><td>853
08.08.1952
04.03.1954</td><td>425</td><td>140.0
28.9</td><td>Mirrlees
2500 BHP
15 knots</td><td>The Admiralty
Whitehall
London</td></tr>
<tr><td colspan="6">Wooden hulled coastal minesweeper built for the Royal Navy (Intended name BLUE BEETLE).
(This class was to be named after insects pre-fixed with different colours to denote specification levels).
01.10.1993 Vessel placed on disposal list. Aug 1995 Still listed and working in Portsmouth.</td></tr>
<tr><td>HMS BRONINGTON
M 1115
Coniston (Ton) Class</td><td>854
19.03.1953
04.06.1954</td><td>425</td><td>140.0
28.9</td><td>Mirrlees
2500 BHP
15 knots</td><td>The Admiralty
Whitehall
London</td></tr>
<tr><td colspan="6">Wooden hulled coastal minesweeper built for the Royal Navy. (Intended name GREEN BEETLE).
1954 Re-named HMS HUMBER depot ship of the Hull division of the Royal Navy Voluntary Reserve.
1958 Returned to the Royal Navy re-named HMS BRONINGTON.
09.02.1976 HRH Prince Charles took over HMS BRONINGTON at Rosyth Dockyard his first command.
24.01.1989 Vessel towed from Portsmouth by the tug ROBUST (b 1974) to Manchester to become a Museum Ship.</td></tr>
<tr><td>IRVANA
185291
FD152 Motor Trawler</td><td>855
19.09.1951
06.01.1953</td><td>296
117</td><td>123.6
26.6</td><td>Mirrlees
Bickerton & Day
700 BHP 11 knots</td><td>J. Marr & Son Ltd
Fleetwood</td></tr>
<tr><td colspan="6">1959 (Lengthened to 131 ft 317 Gross Tons by Humber St Andrew's Engineering Co Ltd, Hull). 14.01.1960 re-registered.
23.03.1964 Vessel ran aground after dragging her anchor at Red Bay near Cushendun Co Antrim Northern Ireland.
All crew abandoned the trawler in liferafts and safely landed ashore.
24.04.1964 Refloated and sold for scrap to Shipbreaking Industries. 10.06.1964 Arrived Faslane for breaking up.</td></tr>
<tr><td>IDENA
185288
FD136 Motor Trawler</td><td>856
28.02.1952
12.02.1953</td><td>296
117</td><td>123.6
26.6</td><td>Mirrlees
Bickerton & Day
772 BHP 11 knots</td><td>J. Marr & Son Ltd
Fleetwood</td></tr>
<tr><td colspan="6">1959 (Lengthened to 131 ft 317 Gross Tons by Humber St Andrew's Engineering Co Ltd, Hull).
1967 Sold to P & J Johnstone, Aberdeen (A793). 1969 to Ranger Fishing Co Ltd, Aberdeen.
1971 to Putford Enterprises Ltd , Aberdeen renamed (1974) FALKIRK. (Converted to Oil Rig Stand-by Safety Vessel).
1978 to Christian Salveson Ltd, Leith. Aug 1978 to George Craig & Sons, Aberdeen renamed GRAMPIAN FALCON.
29.05.1986 to Bon Voyage Enterprises(Inc), Nassau, Bahamas renamed MIAMI CLIPPER.
(Converted to an Auxiliary sailing vessel). 1999 Vessel still in service.</td></tr>
</table>

NAME Official No. Port Letters Numbers	Yard No. Launched Registered	Registered G Ton N Ton	 L Ft B Ft	Engine Builder Horse Power Reg'd Speed	OWNER (Built for)
BANNERDALE H 185107 Estuarial Spirit Lighter	857 31.12.1951 11.02.1952	173 109	138.0 17.6	Gardner 152 BHP 9 knots	John Harker Ltd Knottingley Yorkshire
For use on Humber, Trent, and Inland Waterway system. Also for ship bunkering services.					
BAYSDALE H 185109 Estuarial Spirit Lighter	858 16.02.1952 13.03.1952	173 109	138.0 17.6	Gardner 152 BHP 9 knots	John Harker Ltd Knottingley Yorkshire
For use on Humber, Trent, and Inland Waterway system. Also for ship bunkering services.					
EASEDALE H 185120 Estuarial Spirit Lighter	859 15.04.1952 19.05.1952	173 109	132.0 17.6	Gleniffer 120 BHP 9 knots	John Harker Ltd Knottingley Yorkshire
For use on Humber, Trent, and Inland Waterway system. Also for ship bunkering services.					
ENNERDALE H 185126 Estuarial Spirit Lighter	860 24.05.1952 30.06.1952	173 109	132.0 17.6	Gleniffer 120 BHP 9 knots	John Harker Ltd Knottingley Yorkshire
For use on Humber, Trent, and Inland Waterway system. Also for ship bunkering services.					
KIRKELLA 185114 Oil Fired H209 Steam Trawler	861 15.01.1952 27.03.1952	790 286	190.2 32.1	C.D.Holmes 1250 IHP 13.5 knots	J. Marr & Son Ltd Hull
1955 Winner of the Silver Cod Trophy (the largest total catch for the year) 46589x10 stone kits-339 days at sea- £123,525. 23.06.1959 Transferred to the Dinas Steam Trawling Co Ltd, Fleetwood. 01.04.1963 Sold to Boyd Line Ltd, Hull renamed ARCTIC GALLIARD renamed (27.06.1973) ARCTIC OUTLAW. Name changed to release her former name for use on the new freezer trawler ARCTIC GALLIARD H195 (1660 gt/ b 1973). 1974 Vessel sold for scrap to Albert Draper & Son, Hull. 09.03.1974 Arrived at the Victoria Dock slipway for breaking up.					
HMS DARLESTON M 1127 Coniston (Ton) Class	862 25.09.1953 15.09..1954	425	140.0 28.9	Mirrlees 2500 BHP 15 knots	The Admiralty Whitehall London
Wooden hulled coastal minesweeper built for the Royal Navy. (Intended name GREEN CICALA). 1960 Transferred to the Malaysian Navy renamed MAHAMIRU . May 1990 Took part in the Malaysian Fleet review.					
BOSTON JAVELIN 308719 B2655 Motor Trawler	863 26.08.1952 08.09.1953	498 177	151.0 29.1	Mirrlees Bickerton & Day 810 BHP 11.5 knots	Boston Deep Sea Fisheries Co Ltd Fleetwood
Sold before completion to Armement Pécheries de la Mosinie, Boulogne, France renamed SAINT CLAUDE II. May 1965 to Le Garroc & L Soublin, Fecamp (F1219). 19.12.1966 to Lagarde Lecanu & Leporc Lecanu, Fecamp renamed SAINT CLAUDE . 24.01.1968 to Wyre Trawlers Ltd, Fleetwood renamed WYRE CORSAIR (FD27). 09.07.1971 to British United Trawlers(Finance) Ltd, Hull. 1976 Vessel sold for scrap to Mayer Newman & Co Ltd . 21.11.1976 Arrived Hayle for breaking up.					
ST. CELESTIN 185129 Oil Fired H232 Steam Trawler	864 12.05.1952 19.08.1952	790 287	188.5 32.2	C.D.Holmes 1200 IHP knots	Thomas Hamling & Co Ltd Hull
27.05.1956 Vessel sank following a collision with Hull trawler ARCTIC VIKING H452 (533 gt/ b 1937) whilst fishing 45 miles WSW of Bear Island. Even though the sea was calm she sank within five minutes. The crew managed to launch one ten man liferaft onto which fifteen men climbed, four others clung on to the side of the raft and were picked up by the ARCTIC VIKING. The skipper swam to floating wreckage and was rescued by the Grimsby trawler THOMAS TOMPION *(see Yard No.819).* which later transferred him the ARCTIC VIKING. All the crew were saved.					
ST. BARTHOLOMEW 184913 Oil Fired GY178 Steam Trawler	865 20.11.1952 16.04.1953	635 234	175.6 29.7	C.D.Holmes 925 IHP knots	North Cape Fishing Co Ltd Grimsby
1954 Sold to NV Motorvisserij, Ostend, Belgium renamed VAN DER WEYDEN (O295). 30.03.1957 Ran aground in thick fog on the south-east coast of Iceland all crew rescued. 31.05.1957 Caught fire during salvage operations and was so badly damaged the salvage was abandoned.					
Not built	866				

Yard No.864
1952 ST. CELESTIN
Photo:- Beverley Shipyard Collection

Yard No.868
1952 ABEILLE No. 15
Photo:- Beverley Shipyard Collection

Yard No.874
1953 TERN
Photo:- Beverley Shipyard Collection

<table>
<tr><th rowspan="2">NAME
Official No.
Port Letters Numbers</th><th rowspan="2">Yard No.
Launched
Registered</th><th colspan="2">Registered</th><th rowspan="2">Engine Builder
Horse Power
Reg'd Speed</th><th rowspan="2">OWNER
(Built for)</th></tr>
<tr><th>G Ton
N Ton</th><th>L Ft
B Ft</th></tr>
<tr><td>BRUCELLA
185158
H291 Motor Trawler</td><td>867
30.05.1953
12.10.1953</td><td>678
248</td><td>175.1
31.7</td><td>British Polar
1220 BHP
13 knots</td><td>J Marr & Son Ltd
Hull</td></tr>
<tr><td colspan="6">08.09.1961 Sold to City Steam Fishing Co Ltd, Hull. 04.03.1965 J Marr & Son Ltd, Hull.
26.04.1975 Vessel sprang a leak 135 miles off the Icelandic coast. The skipper remained on board but ordered the nineteen crew to take to the liferafts and were picked up by the Icelandic vessel MANAFOSS (3004 gt/ b 1971)and later landed at Aberdeen. The Icelandic gunboat TYR (631 gt/ b 1952) came to the assistance of the BRUCELLA and divers were able to patch up the leak. The TYR then towed the BRUCELLA into Reykjavik for repairs and eventual return to Hull.
1977 Vessel sold for scrap to Albert Draper & Son, Hull. 21.02. 1977 Arrived at the Victoria Dock slipway for breaking up.</td></tr>
<tr><td>ABEILLE 15

Steam Tug</td><td>868
20.12.1952
29.06.1953</td><td>401
347</td><td>137.1
34.2</td><td>C.D.Holmes
1500 IHP
12 knots</td><td>Soc Cherbouurgeoise De
Remorquage et de Sauvatage
Le Havre France</td></tr>
<tr><td colspan="6">1958 Owners name change Soc Cherbouurgeoise De Remorquage et de Sauvatage 'Les Abeilles', Le Havre.
1964 Owners name change Les Abeilles Soc De Remorquage et de Sauvatage, Le Havere.
1966 (Nydqvist & Holm A/B 9 cyl 2100 BHP diesel engine fitted).
1970 Owners name change Progemar (Société Provencale de Gestion Maritime), Le Havere.
1980 Sold to Asturamerican Shipping Co Inc, Panama renamed SUZANNE M. 1987 Vessel sank in the Mississippi Delta.</td></tr>
<tr><td>HMS HAZLETON
M 1142
Coniston (Ton) Class</td><td>869
06.02.1954
03.02.1955</td><td>425</td><td>140.0
28.9</td><td>Mirrlees
2500 BHP
15 knots</td><td>The Admiralty
Whitehall
London</td></tr>
<tr><td colspan="6">Wooden hulled coastal minesweeper built for the Royal Navy (Intended name BLUE FIREFLY).
1955 Transferred to South African Navy renamed KAAPSTAD. 1987 Vessel placed on disposal list.</td></tr>
<tr><td>HMS HEXTON
M 1143
Coniston (Ton) Class</td><td>870
19.06.1954
26.09.1955</td><td>425</td><td>140.0
28.9</td><td>Mirrlees
2500 BHP
15 knots</td><td>The Admiralty
Whitehall
London</td></tr>
<tr><td colspan="6">Wooden hulled coastal minesweeper built for the Royal Navy (Intended name GREEN FIREFLY).
1963 Transferred to the Malaysian Navy renamed LEDANG. May 1990 Took part in the Malaysian Fleet review.</td></tr>
<tr><td>ELLA HEWETT
185862 Oil Fired
LO47 Steam Trawler</td><td>871
04.12.1952
19.03.1953</td><td>595
217</td><td>166.9
29.3</td><td>C.D.Holmes
925 IHP
13 knots</td><td>Heward Fishing Co Ltd
Fleetwood</td></tr>
<tr><td colspan="6">03.11.1962 Vessel sank after striking the wreck of the cruiser HMS DRAKE (b 1901) whilst landing an injured crewman in Church Bay, Rathlin, Northern Ireland. All nineteen crew were taken off the trawler by the Portrush lifeboat.
18 to 29.09.1978 Wreck blown up by the Royal Navy due to causing oil pollution.</td></tr>
<tr><td>BLAKEDALE H
185137
Estuarial Spirit Lighter</td><td>872
19.09.1952
05.11.1952</td><td>160
77</td><td>138.0
17.6</td><td>Gleniffer
120 BHP
9 knots</td><td>John Harker Ltd
Knottingley
Yorkshire</td></tr>
<tr><td colspan="6">For use on Humber, Trent, and Inland Waterway system. Also for ship bunkering services.</td></tr>
<tr><td>BRANSDALE H
185157
Estuarial Spirit Lighter</td><td>873
12.08.1953
09.10.1953</td><td>160
77</td><td>138.0
17.6</td><td>Gleniffer
120 BHP
9 knots</td><td>John Harker Ltd
Knottingley
Yorkshire</td></tr>
<tr><td colspan="6">For use on Humber, Trent, and Inland Waterway system. Also for ship bunkering services.</td></tr>
<tr><td>TERN
185979
Refrigerated Motor Cargo Vessel</td><td>874
30.06.1953
19.11.1953</td><td>1028
481</td><td>196.6
34.0</td><td>British Polar
BHP
11 knots</td><td>The General Steam
Navigation Co Ltd
London</td></tr>
<tr><td colspan="6">1964 Sold to Avra Nav Inc, Liberia renamed AVRA. 1965 to Mediterranean Fruit Carriers, Piræus, Greece.
1970 to Magnum Shipping Co Ltd, Panama renamed ARGYRO. 1970 to Zulemar SA, Panama renamed DEBORAH I.
1991 Vessel deleted from Lloyds Register of Shipping. - continued existence in doubt.</td></tr>
<tr><td>BURCOM SAND
186667
Twin Grab Hopper Dredger</td><td>875
20.04.1954
05.10.1954</td><td>678
249</td><td>156.0
34.1</td><td>Ruston & Hornsby
720 BHP
9.5 knots</td><td>British Transport
Commission
Hull</td></tr>
<tr><td colspan="6">1963 Owners name change British Transport Docks Board, Hull. 1975 Sold to D Cook Dredging Ltd, Hull.
1989 Vessel sold for scrap to New Holland Shipyard Co Ltd, Lincolnshire.03.01.1989 Arrived New Holland for breaking up.</td></tr>
<tr><td>Not Built</td><td colspan="5">876-877-878-879 Turns allocated to J Harker (for Oil Barges) but not taken up.</td></tr>
</table>

NAME Official No. Port Letters Numbers	Yard No. Launched Registered	Registered G Ton N Ton	 L Ft B Ft	Engine Builder Horse Power Reg'd Speed	OWNER (Built for)
LANCELLA 185151 Oil Fired H290 Steam Trawler	880 03.04.1953 18.07.1953	790 286	190.2 32.1	C.D.Holmes 1325 IHP 13.5 knots	J. Marr & Son Ltd Hull
Jan 1955 The skipper of the LANCELLA made an heroic bid to reach the Hull trawlers LORELLA H455 *(see Yard No.785)* and RODERIGO H135 *(see Yard No.824)*. He steamed from the shelter of the Icelandic coast until fifty miles north of the North Cape where visibility was down to zero. Severe icing put his own ship in jeopardy and so had to abandon the search. 1956 Winner of the Silver Cod Trophy (the largest total catch for the year) 45936 x10 stone kits-340 days at sea-£131,633. Vessel sold for scrap to Hughes Bolckow Ltd . 27.02.1974 Arrived Blyth for breaking up.					
GEORGE IRVIN 191928 Coal Fired CTA138 Steam Trawler	881 03.10.1953 06.01.1954	535 184	173.6 28.1	C.D.Holmes 850 IHP 9.5 knots	East Fishing Ltd Cape Town South Africa
09.01.1954 Left Hull on delivery voyage, 21/22.01.1954 Bunkered at Dakar. Distance steamed 6293 nautical miles 29 days on passage. 08.02.1954 Arrived Cape Town. 1970 Vessel sold for spare parts to South African Metals Ltd. 01.12.1970 Breaking up commenced. Hulk subsequently scuttled at Irvin Johnson Reef in False Bay, Cape Town.					
REDCLIFFE Light Float	882 11.08.1953 11.09.1953	25	40 10	N/A	Humber Conservancy Board Hull
Used in marking the Navigable deep water channel in the River Humber.12.09.1953 Delivered to King George Dock, Hull.					
BTC 32 Dumb Hopper Barge	883 24.11.1953 10.12.1953	430	140.0 30.0	N/A	British Transport Commission Hull
For use in dredging operations. 11.12.1953 Delivered to Alexandra Dock, Hull.					
BTC 33 Dumb Hopper Barge	884 23.12.1953 11.01.1954	430	140.0 30.0	N/A	British Transport Commission Hull
For use in dredging operations. 12.01.1954 Delivered to Alexandra Dock, Hull.					
BTC 34 Dumb Hopper Barge	885 22.01.1954 23.02.1954	329	140.0 30.0	N/A	British Transport Commission Hull
For use in dredging operations. 24.02.1954 Delivered to Alexandra Dock, Hull.					
BTC 35 Dumb Hopper Barge	886 08.03.1954 02.04.1954	329	140.0 30.0	N/A	British Transport Commission Hull
For use in dredging operations. 03.04.1954 Delivered to Victoria Dock, Hull.					
SHELL FARMER 186308 Motor Spirit Tanker	887 08.07.1955 08.10.1955	313 174	137.0 29.0	Blackstone 324 BHP 9 knots	Shell-Mex & BP Ltd London
Classed for use on the River Trent and Humber. 1975 Sold to A Cornish London renamed COAST FARMER. 1976 to A M R Twine London. 1976 to Northwood (Farnham) Ltd Surrey. 1978 Vessel deleted from Lloyds Register of shipping (re-classed).					
HMS DILSTON M 1168 Coniston (Ton) Class	888 15.11.1954 21.06.1955	425	140.0 28.9	Napier 2500 BHP 15 knots	The Admiralty Whitehall London
Wooden hulled coastal minesweeper built for the Royal Navy. 1964 Transferred to the Malaysian Navy renamed JERAI. May 1990 Took part in the Malaysian Fleet review.					
HMS PENSTON M 1169 Coniston (Ton) Class	889 09.05.1955 09.03.1956	425	140.0 28.9	Mirrlees 2500 BHP 15 knots	The Admiralty Whitehall London
Wooden hulled coastal minesweeper built for the Royal Navy . 1968 Placed on disposal list. 28.01.1970 Vessel sold for scrap to Metal Recovery Ltd and broken up at Newhaven.					
HMS PICTON M 1170 Coniston (Ton) Class	890 20.10.1955 19.07.1956	425	140.0 28.9	Mirrlees 2500 BHP 15 knots	The Admiralty Whitehall London
Wooden hulled coastal minesweeper built for the Royal Navy. 1968 Placed on disposal list. 28.07.1969 Vessel sold for scrap to shipbreakers and broken up at Queensborough.					

<table>
<tr><th rowspan="2">NAME
Official No.
Port Letters Numbers</th><th rowspan="2">Yard No.
Launched
Registered</th><th colspan="2">Registered</th><th rowspan="2">Engine Builder
Horse Power
Reg'd Speed</th><th rowspan="2">OWNER
(Built for)</th></tr>
<tr><th>G Ton
N Ton</th><th>L Ft
B Ft</th></tr>
<tr><td>HMS WILKIESTON
M 1192
Coniston (Ton) Class</td><td>891
26.06.1956
24.07.1957</td><td>425</td><td>140.0
28.9</td><td>Mirrlees
2500 BHP
15 knots</td><td>The Admiralty
Whitehall
London</td></tr>
<tr><td colspan="6">Wooden hulled coastal minesweeper built for the Royal Navy. 1972 Vessel placed on disposal (for sale) list.</td></tr>
<tr><td>PIET RETIEF
191932 Coal Fired
CTA140 Steam Trawler</td><td>892
20.05.1954
27.07.1954</td><td>452
151</td><td>141.0
27.1</td><td>C.D.Holmes
650 IHP
9.5 knots</td><td>Irvin & Johnson Ltd
Cape Town
South Africa</td></tr>
<tr><td colspan="6">28.07.1954 Left Hull on delivery voyage, 09.08.1954 Bunkered at Dakar.
Distance steamed 6412 nautical miles 33 days on passage. 30.08.1954 Arrived Cape Town.
1972 Vessel stripped of reusable parts. 10.01.1972 Hulk scuttled off Table Bay.</td></tr>
<tr><td>LOUIS TRICHARDT
191934 Coal Fired
CTA146 Steam Trawler</td><td>893
01.07.1954
29.08.1954</td><td>452
151</td><td>141.0
27.1</td><td>C.D.Holmes
650 IHP
9.5 knots</td><td>Irvin & Johnson Ltd
Cape Town
South Africa</td></tr>
<tr><td colspan="6">01.10.1954 Left Hull on delivery voyage. 14.10.1954 Bunkered at Dakar.
Distance steamed 6293 nautical miles 33 days on passage. 02.11.1954 Arrived Cape Town.
1972 Vessel stripped of reusable parts.10.02.1972 Hulk scuttled off Robben Island, Cape Town.</td></tr>
<tr><td>KINGSTON EMERALD
186671 Oil Fired
H49 Steam Trawler</td><td>894
31.08.1954
13.12.1954</td><td>811
288</td><td>189.4
32.1</td><td>C.D.Holmes
1300 IHP
13.5 knots</td><td>Kingston Steam
Trawling Co Ltd
Hull</td></tr>
<tr><td colspan="6">29.06.1966 Sold to Hellyer Bros Ltd, Hull. 1970 Winner of the Hull Distant Water Challenge Shield. (for the greatest value of catch for the year calculated on a points basis) 36526 x 10 stone kits-£232,682.
18.11.1973 The KINGSTON EMERALD rescued all eleven crew from the Swedish freighter GAPERN (2286 gt/ b 1972) which sank in a gale 50 miles east of the Tyne.
26.03.1976 Vessel sold for scrap to London Demolition (UK) Ltd . 19.09.1976 Arrived on the Medway for breaking up.</td></tr>
<tr><td>KINGSTON TURQUOISE
186674 Oil Fired
H50 Steam Trawler</td><td>895
15.10.1954
16.02.1955</td><td>811
288</td><td>189.4
32.1</td><td>C.D.Holmes
1300 IHP
13.5 knots</td><td>Kingston Steam
Trawling Co Ltd
Hull</td></tr>
<tr><td colspan="6">22.01.1965 Vessel sank after striking the North Shoal 14 miles north north-west of Hoy Head, Orkney Islands whilst homeward bound to Hull from Iceland. The trawler's engine room rapidly flooded and she sank in four minutes. Nineteen crew managed to climb into two liferafts but one man was swept away and lost. A Shacklelton aircraft responding to the 'MAYDAY' located the rafts and dropped flares to aid the Stromness lifeboat which came and picked up the survivors.</td></tr>
<tr><td>KINGSTON SAPPHIRE
186691 Oil Fired
H95 Steam Trawler</td><td>896
22.06.1955
16.11.1955</td><td>811
288</td><td>189.4
32.1</td><td>C.D.Holmes
1300 BHP
13.5 knots</td><td>Kingston Steam Trawling
Co Ltd
Hull</td></tr>
<tr><td colspan="6">29.06.1966 Sold to Hellyer Bros Ltd, Hull.
02.04.1976 Vessel sold for scrap to London Demolition (UK) Ltd . Oct 1976 Laid up in Hull.
16.05.1977 Arrived Shadwell Quay London for breaking up.</td></tr>
<tr><td>MADAIRA REEF
Boat Beacon</td><td>897
09.03.1954
10.04.1954</td><td>70</td><td>55.0
22.0</td><td>N/A</td><td>The Gas Accumulator Co Ltd
London</td></tr>
<tr><td colspan="6">For use in marking navigable deep water channels and reefs for The Persian Gulf Lighting Service Ltd.</td></tr>
<tr><td>CABLE BANK
Boat Beacon</td><td>898
09.03.1954
06.06.1954</td><td>70</td><td>55.0
22.0</td><td>N/A</td><td>The Gas Accumulator Co Ltd
London</td></tr>
<tr><td colspan="6">For use in marking navigable deep water channels and reefs for The Persian Gulf Lighting Service Ltd.</td></tr>
<tr><td>MARINIA
186179
Motor Tug</td><td>899
16.10.1954
29.01.1955</td><td>392
41</td><td>127.0
29.10</td><td>British Polar
960 BHP
12 knots</td><td>Overseas Towage &
Salvage Co Ltd
London</td></tr>
<tr><td colspan="6">1966 Sold to Salvage Engineers (HK) Ltd, Hong Kong renamed SALVANA.
1969 to Selco (Singapore) Ltd, Singapore. 1976 to Vistamarine Ltd, Singapore. 1978 to Orion Leasing, Singapore.
1982 to Transpac Marine SA (Panama), Manila, Philippines renamed MARANAW.
1986 Vessel sold for scrap to Boy Aquario, Manila. 20.11.1986 Commenced breaking up at Metro Manila.</td></tr>
<tr><td>STIFF BANK
Boat Beacon</td><td>900
22.04.1954
26.05.1954</td><td>70</td><td>55.0
22.0</td><td>N/A</td><td>The Gas Accumulator Co Ltd
London</td></tr>
<tr><td colspan="6">For use in marking navigable deep water channels and reefs for The Persian Gulf Lighting Service Ltd.
27.05.1954 Delivered to King George Dock, Hull. For transhipment to the Persian Gulf.</td></tr>
</table>

Yard No.881
1953 GEORGE IRVIN
Photo:- Beverley Shipyard Collection

Yard No.902
1955 MARBELLA
Photo by courtesy of J Marr & Son Ltd

Yard No.907
1956 STELLA AQUILA
Photo:- Beverley Shipyard Collection

NAME Official No. Port Letters Numbers	Yard No. Launched Registered	Registered G Ton N Ton	 L Ft B Ft	Engine Builder Horse Power Reg'd Speed	OWNER (Built for)
Un-named Boat Beacon	900A 17.07.1957 26.09.1957	70	55.0 22.0	N/A	The Gas Accumulator Co Ltd London
For use in marking navigable deep water channels and reefs for The Persian Gulf Lighting Service Ltd. 27.09.1954 Delivered to King George Dock, Hull. For transhipment to the Persian Gulf.					
Un-named Boat Beacon	900B 17.07.1957 26.10.1957	70	55.0 22.0	N/A	The Gas Accumulator Co Ltd London
For use in marking navigable deep water channels and reefs for The Persian Gulf Lighting Service Ltd. 27.09.1954 Delivered to King George Dock, Hull. For transhipment to the Persian Gulf.					
Un-named Boat Beacon	900C 08.09.1959 29.11.1959	70	55.0 22.0	N/A	The Gas Accumulator Co Ltd London
For use in marking navigable deep water channels and reefs for The Persian Gulf Lighting Service Ltd. 30.11.1959 Delivered to King George Dock, Hull. For transhipment to the Persian Gulf.					
PRINCESS ANNE 185299 FD15 Motor Trawler	901 11.12.1954 06.04.1955	421 144	137.6 28.4	British Polar 960 BHP 11.5 knots	St Andrew's Steam Fishing Co Ltd Fleetwood
08.10.1963 Vessel transferred to Hull. 10.03.1965 Transferred back to Fleetwood. 1971 Transferred to Lowestoft (LT740). 1973 renamed BOSTON WELLINGTON. 1974 Vessel sold for scrap to Scrap Metal By-Products. 1975 Re-sold to Skainberry Ltd Lowestoft renamed MELICIA. 1976 Vessel deleted from Lloyds Register of Shipping.					
MARBELLA 186678 Oil Fired H52 Steam Trawler	902 11.02.1955 16.06.1955	793 279	185.11 32.5	C.D.Holmes 1325 IHP 13.5 knots	J. Marr & Son Ltd Hull
01.02.1965 Sold to Boyd Line Ltd, Hull renamed (26.02.1965) ARCTIC BRIGAND. 1967 First trawler to be Awarded the Hull Distant Water Challenge Shield. (for the greatest value of catch for the year calculated on a points basis) 38,806 x 10 stone kits-£134,462. 1975 Vessel sold for scrap to Jacques Bakker & Zonen, Belgium. 05.07.1975 Arrived Bruges for breaking up.					
ST. BARTHOLOMEW 185300 FD27 Motor Trawler	903 12.03.1955 16.06.1955	421 144	137.6 28.4	British Polar 960 BHP 11.5 knots	St Andrew's Steam Fishing Co Ltd Fleetwood
01.01.1964 Sold to Iago Steam Trawling Co Ltd, Fleetwood. 1965 to Partrederiet Utheim, Kristiansund, Norway renamed BJOGNA. 05.05.1965 Left Fleetwood for Norway. 1972 Owners name changed to Sigmund Utheim Partrederie. 1977 to Per OG Reidar Smadal, Alesund. 1980 to Kare Misje & Co, Alesund renamed NAUTIK renamed (1983) NAUTIKA. 1985 to Tamis Ltd, Aberdeen Stand -by Safety Vessel.1990 to Cam Offshore Ltd Aberdeen renamed CAM VANGUARD. 1993 to John Crowson, Aberdeen renamed JON PAUL. (1998) renamed CAM VANGUARD. 1999 Vessel still in service.					
GROOTE SCHUUR 191938 Coal Fired CTA129 Steam Trawler	904 28.03.1955 12.07.1955	453 151	141.0 27.4	C.D.Holmes 750 IHP 10 knots	East Fishing Ltd Cape Town South Africa
Dec 1971 Vessel stripped of reusable parts. 03.02.1972 Hulk scuttled off Robben Island, Cape Town.					
GROOTE CONSTANTIA 191939 Coal Fired CTA139 Steam Trawler	905 18.10.1955 11.02.1956	453 151	141.0 27.4	C.D.Holmes 750 IHP 10 knots	National Trawling & Fishing Co Ltd Cape Town South Africa
Dec 1971 Vessel stripped of reusable parts. 10.02.1972 Hulk scuttled off Robben Island, Cape Town.					
THORNELLA 186686 Oil Fired H84 Steam Trawler	906 20.05.1955 22.09.1955	793 279	190.3 32.5	C.D.Holmes 1325 IHP 13.5 knots	J. Marr & Son Ltd Hull
1956 Top earning British trawler grossed £129,563. 03.04.1973 Vessel sold for scrap to Clayton & Davie Ltd. Apr 1973 Arrived at Dunston on Tyne for breaking up.					
STELLA AQUILA 186702 Oil Fired H114 Steam Trawler	907 16.11.1956 21.03.1956	780 286	185.0 32.5	Amos & Smith 1350 IHP 14 knots	Derwent Trawlers Ltd Hull
Managed by Charleson - Smith Trawlers Ltd, Hull. 16.08.1965 to Hudson Bros (Trawlers) Ltd, Hull renamed (26.11.1965) ROSS AQUILA. 16.03.1971 Whilst having new furnaces fitted at Hull a fire broke out in the engine room which took five fire-engines over an hour to bring under control. This caused considerable damage to the engine room and bridge. Twenty workmen who were aboard escaped uninjured. The trawler was eventually repaired and returned to service. 19.05.1975 Vessel sold for scrap to Desguaces Y Salvametos, Spain. 15.07.1975 Arrived Aviles for breaking up.					

Yard No.909
1956 BOSTON FURY
Photo:- Beverley Shipyard Collection

Yard No.912
1955 CHINA BAKER (being loaded on board the BRAUNFELS)
Photo:- Beverley Shipyard Collection

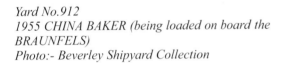

Yard No.913
1956 SAMUEL HEWETT
Photo:- Beverley Shipyard Collection

NAME Official No. Port Letters Numbers	Yard No. Launched Registered	Registered G Ton N Ton	 L Ft B Ft	Engine Builder Horse Power Reg'd Speed	OWNER (Built for)
ST. CHAD 186698 H20 Motor Trawler	908 22.06.1955 06.01.1956	575 210	160.5 30.5	Mirrlees Bickerton & Day 1050 BHP 13 knots	St Andrew's Steam Fishing Co Ltd Hull
24.10.1968 Sold to Boston Deep Sea Fisheries Ltd Hull. 30.03.1973 Vessel driven ashore and wrecked at Ritur Huk, Isafjordur, north-west Iceland whilst sheltering in a blizzard and severe gale. The eighteen crew took to liferafts and reached the shore in Isafjördur, they were taken aboard the support tug STATESMAN (1167 gt/ b 1966) and then transferred to the support / mother ship OTHELLO H389 (1113 gt/ b 1966).					
BOSTON FURY 184934 GY188 Motor Trawler	909 19.09.1956 23.02.1956	577 210	160.5 30.4	Mirrlees Bickerton & Day 1050 BHP 13 knots	Boston Deep Sea Fisheries Co Ltd Grimsby
14.08.1961 Sold to Abunda Steam Fishing Co Ltd, Grimsby renamed (25.08.1961) ABUNDA . 22.12.1966 to Newton Trawlers Ltd, Grimsby renamed VOLESUS. 01.01.1975 to North Cape Fishing Co Ltd, Hull. 19.05.1978 to C J Else (Gibraltar) Ltd, Gibraltar. for use as a Wreck recovery / salvage vessel. 1979 to H K Vickers & Sons Engineering Ltd. Sep 1979 to Maritime Sunshine SA, Panama. 1987 to Chepo Shipping Co SA, Panama. 1998 Deleted from Lloyds Register of Shipping - Vessel's continued existence in doubt.					
Not Built	910				
ST. CHRISTOPHER 300397 H88 Motor Trawler	910A 10.01.1958 18.04.1958	603 213	161.11 30.5	Mirrlees Bickerton & Day 1250 BHP 13 knots	St Andrew's Steam Fishing Co Ltd Hull
12.02.1960 to Eton Steam Fishing Co Ltd, Hull. 21.04.1961 to F & T Ross Ltd, Hull. 21.07.1961 Sold to Abunda Steam Fishing Co Ltd, Grimsby renamed (14.08.1961) ORATAVA (GY669). 12.09.1968 to Irvin & Johnson, Cape Town, South Africa (CTA304). 1983 Vessel stripped of reusable parts. 27.06.1983 Hulk scuttled off Robben Island, Cape Town.					
SHELL STEELMAKER 187363 Oil Barge	911 05.12.1956 01.03.1956	303 189	139.3 21.9	Lister Blackstone 324 BHP 9.5 knots	Shell - Mex & BP Ltd London
Classed for carrying Petroleum in bulk in the Bristol Channel the limiting port seawards was Swansea. 1970 Sold to J P Knight (London) Ltd London renamed KINGSCLERE. 1983 Vessel sold for scrap to Henderson - Morez Kent. May 1993 Commenced breaking up at Northfleet Gravesend.					
SHELL TRAVELLER 187716 Oil Barge	911A 31.10.1957 28.01.1958	303 189	139.3 21.9	Lister Blackstone 324 BHP 9.5 knots	Shell - Mex & BP Ltd London
Classed for carrying Petroleum in bulk in the Bristol Channel / River Severn the limiting port seawards was Swansea. 1970 Sold to Celtic Coasters Ltd, Cork renamed CELTIC 1 (for service in Cork harbour). 1972 Vessel sold for scrap to Haulbowline Industries Ltd. Mar1972 Commenced breaking up at Passage West Co, Cork.					
CHINA BAKAR Lightship	912 22.08.1955 30.01.1956	150	70.0 27.0	N/A	The Gas Accumulator Co Ltd (Rangoon) London
For use in marking navigable channel. at Rangoon. 16.02.1956 Loaded at Immingham aboard the German cargo vessel BRAUNFELS (6977 gt/ b 1951) for shipment to Rangoon.					
SPIT Boat Beacon	912A 27.11.1957 23.03.1958	130	70.0 27.0	N/A	The Gas Accumulator Co Ltd (Rangoon) London
For use in marking navigable channel at Rangoon. 24.03.1958 Delivered to Albert Dock, Hull.					
Un-named Light Float	P1 02.02.1956	25	33.0 14.0	N/A	The Gas Accumulator Co Ltd London
For use by the Pakistan Light service for marking the anchorage at Chalna East Pakistan. 12.04.1956 Delivered to Victoria Dock, Hull for transhipment to London. Apr 1956 Loaded on the ss MAIPURA (9748 gt/ b 1952).					
Un-named Light Float	P2 02.02.1956	25	33.0 14.0	N/A	The Gas Accumulator Co Ltd London
For use by the Pakistan Light service for marking the anchorage at Chalna East Pakistan. 12.04.1956 Delivered to Victoria Dock, Hull for transhipment to London. Apr 1956 Loaded on the ss MAIPURA.					
Un-named Light Float	P3 11.02.1956	25	33.0 14.0	N/A	The Gas Accumulator Co Ltd London
For use by the Pakistan Light service for marking the anchorage at Chalna East Pakistan. 12.04.1956 Delivered to Victoria Dock, Hull for transhipment to London. Apr 1956 Loaded on the ss MAIPURA.					

Yard No.915
1956 CAPE ADAIR
Photo:- Beverley Shipyard Collection

Yard No.916
1956 VELINDA
Photo:- Beverley Shipyard Collection

Yard No.920
1957 ARCTIC RANGER
Photo:- Beverley Shipyard Collection

NAME Official No. Port Letters Numbers	Yard No. Launched Registered	Registered G Ton N Ton	 L Ft B Ft	Engine Builder Horse Power Reg'd Speed	OWNER (Built for)
Un-named Light Float	P4 11.02.1956	25	33.0 14.0	N/A	The Gas Accumulator Co Ltd London
For use by the Pakistan Light service for marking the anchorage at Chalna East Pakistan. 12.04.1956 Delivered to Victoria Dock, Hull for transhipment to London. Apr 1956 Loaded on the ss MAIPURA.					
SAMUEL HEWETT 187405 Oil Fired LO117 Steam Trawler	913 16.03.1956 28.05.1956	589 219	166.7 29.3	C.D.Holmes 925 IHP 12.5 knots	Heward Trawlers Ltd Fleetwood
1968 Vessel sold for scrap to W H Arnott Young & Co Ltd, Dalmuir. 21.10.1968 Arrived Troon for breaking up.					
CAPE COLOMBIA 186713 Oil Fired H118 Steam Trawler	914 27.04.1956 31.07.1956	806 298	185.0 32.1	C.D.Holmes 1400 IHP 13.5 knots	Hudson Bros (Trawlers) Ltd Hull
First British distant water trawler built with a bulbous bow. 05.02.1960 Company sold to Ross Group Ltd, Grimsby renamed (22.11.1965) ROSS COLUMBIA. 14.03.1967 Sold to Boyd Line Ltd, Hull renamed (03.05.1967) ARCTIC AVENGER. 1976 Vessel sold for scrap to Mayer Newman Dismantling Ltd (Erith). 16.03.1976 Left Hull for Sheerness for breaking up.					
CAPE ADAIR 186716 Oil Fired H119 Steam Trawler	915 26.05.1956 19.09.1956	806 298	185.0 32.1	C.D.Holmes 1400 IHP 13.5 knots	Hudson Bros (Trawlers) Ltd Hull
05.02.1960 Sold to Ross Group Ltd, Grimsby renamed (26.11.1965) ROSS ADAIR. 29.08.1967 Transferred to Grimsby. 1968 Vessel sold for scrap to Clayton & Davie Ltd. 11.07.1968 Arrived Dunston on Tyne for breaking up.					
VELINDA 184948 Oil Fired GY29 Steam Trawler	916 12.07.1956 24.10.1956	778 296	185.0 32.5	C.D.Holmes 1350 IHP 13.5 knots	Atlas Steam Fishing Co Ltd Grimsby
First Beverley built trawler to have the deckhouse on the port side fully extended for crew accommodation. 24.01.1966 Sold to Northern Trawlers Ltd, Grimsby. 12.02.1975 Whilst homeward bound to Grimsby the VELINDA was in collision with the outward bound Hull trawler ROSS CANAVERAL H 267 (805 gt/ b 1963) at the mouth of the River Humber. Laid up, repairs found to be uneconomic. 05.08.1975 Vessel sold for scrap to Celviet Ltd (Lincoln). May 1976 Re-sold to Bruges Scheeppssloperij NV, Holland. 27.05.1976 Arrived Bruges for breaking up.					
RUBENS Oil Fired O297 Steam Trawler	917 22.09.1956 01.01.1957	810 298	185.0 32.5	C.D.Holmes 1350 IHP 13.5 knots	NV Motorvisserij Ostend Belgium
11.10.1960 Vessel sank following a collision with the Hull trawler ST. APOLLO H592 *(see Yard No.798)* whilst fishing 30 miles off the south east coast of Iceland. All the RUBENS crew were taken aboard the ST. APOLLO and landed at Hull.					
BREUGHEL Oil Fired O299 Steam Trawler	918 23.10.1956 30.01.1957	810 298	185.0 32.5	C.D.Holmes 1350 IHP 13.5 knots	NV Motorvisserij Ostend Belgium
25.04.1961 Sold to North Cape Fishing Co Ltd, Grimsby renamed ST. MATTHEW (H201) Official No. 301660. Jan 1965 to St Andrew's Steam Fishing Co Ltd, Hull. Oct 1968 to Boston Deep Sea Fisheries Co Ltd, Hull. 05.03.1969 to Helleyer Bros Ltd, Hull renamed MACBETH. 20.03.1976 Vessel sold for scrap to London Demolition (UK) Ltd . 01.09.1976 Arrived River Medway for breaking up.					
SWANELLA 186739 Oil Fired H141 Steam Trawler	919 21.11.1956 06.03.1957	823 297	185.2 32.5	C.D.Holmes 1350 IHP 13.5 knots	J Marr & Son Ltd Hull
23.07.1962 Sold to Henriksen & Co Ltd, Hull renamed (24.10.1962) TARCHON. 03.05.1973 to Newington Steam Trawling Co Ltd, Hull renamed RUDYARD KIPLING. 12.11.1974 Vessel sold for scrap to Joaquin Otero Gonzalez & Co, Spain. 22.11.1974 Arrived Vigo for breaking up.					
ARCTIC RANGER 300375 Oil Fired H155 Steam Trawler	920 14.05.1957 18.10.1957	867 316	192.4 32.6	C.D.Holmes 1400 IHP 13.5 knots	Boyd Line Ltd Hull
The ARCTIC RANGER was the first British trawler fitted with Auto Helmsman. The last Hull steam trawler in service. 1976 Featured in the Television series "Snacker" under the mock name DYNASTY NEPTUNE. 1976 Vessel sold for scrap to Albert Draper & Son, Hull. 25.10.1976 Arrived at Victoria Dock slipway for breaking up.					
ST. LOMAN 300383 Oil Fired H156 Steam Trawler	921 01.07.1957 27.11.1957	895 326	190.0 33.1	C.D.Holmes 1600 IHP 13.5 knots	Thomas Hamling & Co Ltd Hull
The ST. LOMAN had the biggest Gross Tonnage of any British built side fishing trawler. 01.01.1965 to Firth Steam Trawling Co Ltd, Hull. 1976 Vessel sold for scrap to Myer Newman Dismantling Ltd., (Erith). 25.03.1976 Arrived Milton Regis near Sittingbourne, Kent for breaking up.					

ST. DOMINIC YARD No. 925

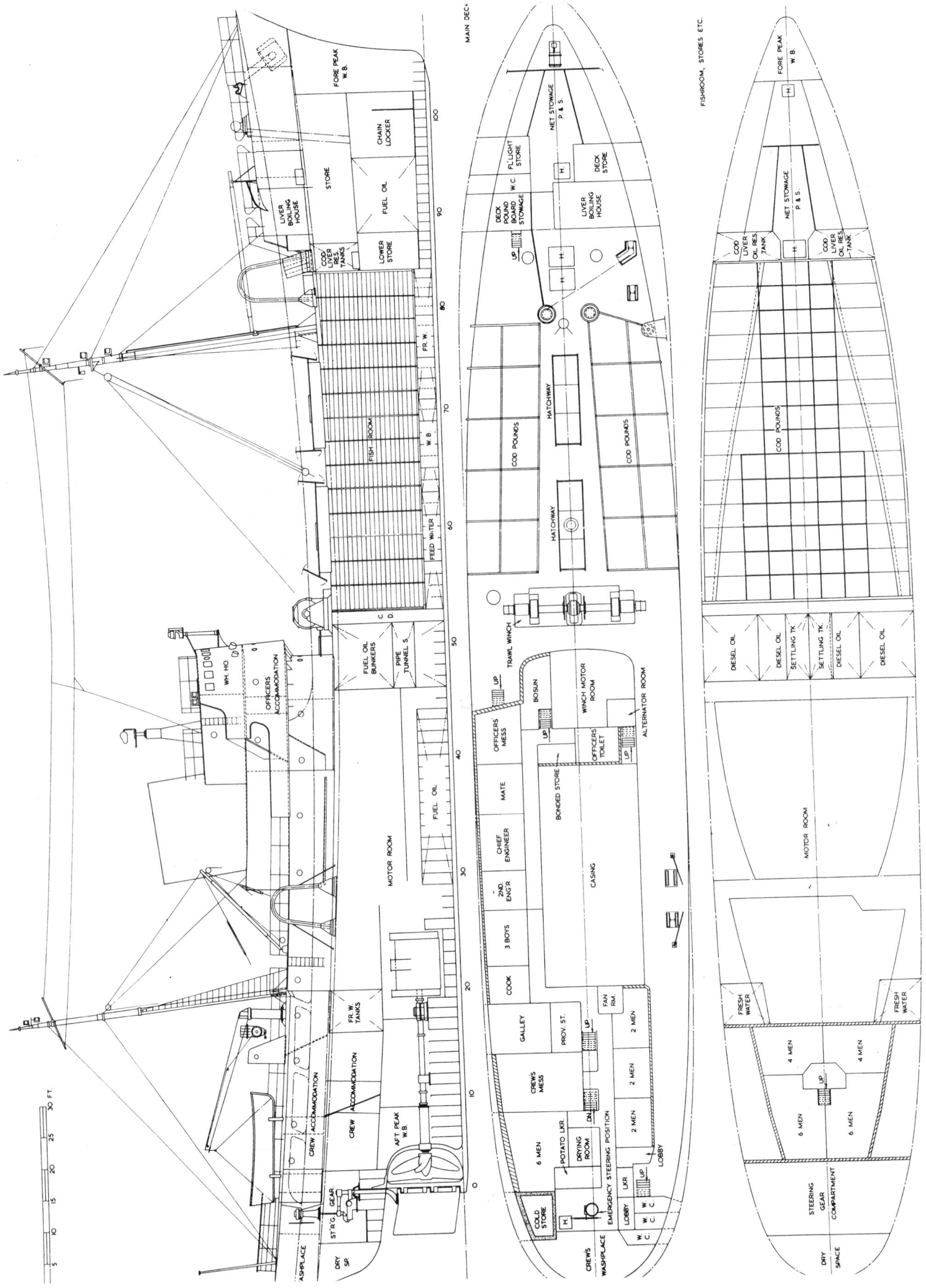

<table>
<tr><th rowspan="2">NAME
Official No.
Port Letters Numbers</th><th rowspan="2">Yard No.
Launched
Registered</th><th colspan="2">Registered</th><th rowspan="2">Engine Builder
Horse Power
Reg'd Speed</th><th rowspan="2">OWNER
(Built for)</th></tr>
<tr><th>G Ton
N Ton</th><th>L Ft
B Ft</th></tr>
<tr><td>CAPE TRAFALGAR
30037
H59 Diesel Electric Trawler</td><td>922
18.02.1957
03.09.1957</td><td>787
285</td><td>189.5
33.1</td><td>Mirrlees Bickerton
& Day
2400 BHP 14 knots</td><td>Hudson Bros (Trawlers) Ltd
Hull</td></tr>
<tr><td colspan="6">05.02.1960 Company sold to Ross Group Ltd, Grimsby renamed (26.11.1965) ROSS TRAFALGAR.
08.11.1967 Transferred to Grimsby. 09.09.1968 Returned to Hull.
1972 Winner of the Hull Distant Water Challenge Shield. (for the greatest value of catch for the year calculated on a points basis) 26813x 10stone kits-£269,529.
1978 Vessel sold for scrap to Albert Draper & Son, Hull. 04.09.1978 Arrived at the Victoria Dock slipway for breaking up.</td></tr>
<tr><td>LUCIDA
187859
FD437 Motor Trawler</td><td>923
05.12.1956
18.04.1957</td><td>392
141</td><td>134.0
27.6</td><td>Mirrlees Bickerton
& Day
932 BHP 12 knots</td><td>City Steam Fishing Co Ltd
Fleetwood</td></tr>
<tr><td colspan="6">05.01.1966 Transferred to Hull (H403) and lengthened (length 149.2 ft Gross tons 404). 21.01.1970 returned to Fleetwood.
27.04.1971 Sold to J Marr & Son Ltd, Fleetwood. 16.12.1974 Transferred to Oil Rig Stand-by Safety duties .
1980 Vessel sold for scrap to Albert Draper & Son, Hull. 18.03.1980 Arrived at the Victoria Dock slipway for breaking up.</td></tr>
<tr><td>JOSENA
187862
FD150 Motor Trawler</td><td>923A
13.07.1957
12.11.1957</td><td>392
141</td><td>134.0
27.6</td><td>Mirrlees Bickerton
& Day
932 BHP 12 knots</td><td>J Marr & Son Ltd
Fleetwood</td></tr>
<tr><td colspan="6">22.06.1973 Transferred to Oil Rig Stand-by Safety duties. 1975 Converted to an Oil Rig Stand-by Safety Vessel.
1983 Sold to Christ Compania Naviera S.A. Panama renamed CORMORAN. 1999 Vessel still in service.</td></tr>
<tr><td>JOSEPH CONRAD
300386 Oil Fired
H161 Steam Trawler</td><td>924
27.08.1957
07.01.1958</td><td>823
297</td><td>185.2
32.1</td><td>C.D.Holmes
1350 IHP
13.5 knots</td><td>Newington Steam
Trawling Co Ltd
Hull</td></tr>
<tr><td colspan="6">Last Steam Trawler built for a Hull Owner.
17.02.1972 (Stork Werkspoor 1500 BHP diesel engine fitted), by Zaanlandse SB Maats Holland. 10.05.1978 Laid up.
1980 Vessel sold for scrap to Albert Draper & Son, Hull. 15.08.1980 Arrived at the Victoria Dock slipway for breaking up.</td></tr>
<tr><td>ST. DOMINIC
300410
H116 Diesel Electric Trawler</td><td>925
20.05.1958
29.10.1958</td><td>829
302</td><td>185.0
34.5</td><td>Mirrlees Bickerton
& Day 3 x 760 BHP
13.5 knots</td><td>Thomas Hamling & Co Ltd
Hull</td></tr>
<tr><td colspan="6">Engine supplied by Metropolitan Vickers Ltd and installed by C D Holmes at Hull.
01.10.1979 Vessel sold for scrap to Henderson Morez Ltd London. Oct 1979 Arrived Dartford Kent for breaking up.</td></tr>
<tr><td>KIRSTENBOSCH
199251 Coal Fired
CTA124 Steam Trawler</td><td>926
26.12.1956
21.05.1957</td><td>453
151</td><td>141.0
27.4</td><td>C.D.Holmes
750 IHP
12 knots</td><td>National Trawling &
Fishing Co Ltd
Cape Town South Africa</td></tr>
<tr><td colspan="6">1972 Vessel stripped of reusable parts. 21.03.1972 Hulk scuttled in False Bay, South Africa to form an artificial reef.</td></tr>
<tr><td>PRINCE PHILIP
184939
GY218 Motor Trawler</td><td>927
16.01.1956
24.04.1956</td><td>577
210</td><td>160.9
30.3</td><td>Mirrlees Bickerton
& Day
1050 BHP 13 knots</td><td>F & T Ross Ltd
Grimsby</td></tr>
<tr><td colspan="6">12.08.1961 Sold to Abunda Fishing Co Ltd, Grimsby renamed BELGAUM.
01.01.1975 to The Iago Steam Fishing Co Ltd, Fleetwood. 1978 to Dominion Fishing Co Ltd, Fleetwood.
1979 Vessel sold for scrap to Medway Secondary Metals Ltd. 17.03.1979 Arrived Rainham Kent for breaking up.</td></tr>
<tr><td>ARSENAL
181394 Oil Fired
GY48 Steam Trawler</td><td>928
28.09.1957
10.02.1958</td><td>744
272</td><td>185.0
32.5</td><td>C.D.Holmes
1400 IHP
13.5 knots</td><td>Consolidated Fisheries Ltd
Grimsby</td></tr>
<tr><td colspan="6">1975 Vessel sold for scrap to Mayer Newman & Co Ltd . 12.03.1975 Arrived Fleetwood for breaking up.</td></tr>
<tr><td>PRINCE CHARLES
300404
H77 Motor Trawler</td><td>929
10.12.1957
14.03.1958</td><td>691
247</td><td>176.5
32.3</td><td>Holmes/Werkspoor
1350 BHP
14 knots</td><td>St Andrew's Steam
Fishing Co Ltd
Hull</td></tr>
<tr><td colspan="6">29.08.1960 Went to the assistance of the Hull trawler ST. HUBERT H142 (634 gt/ b 1950) 120 miles off Kirkenes, Norway. The ST. HUBERT had been severely damaged when a mine exploded on her fore-deck killing three of the crew. After six hours she began to sink and fifteen crewmen and two pleasure trippers took to the life-rafts and were picked up by the PRINCE CHARLES. The skipper later died of his injuries sustained by the mine blast.
1960 Winner of the Silver Cod Trophy (the largest total catch for the year) 39603x10 stone kits-346 days at sea-£152,139.
03.03.1960 to F & T Ross Ltd, Hull. 24.02.1961 to Premier Steam Fishing Co Ltd, Hull.
21.06.1965 to Robins Trawlers Ltd, Hull. 15.03.1974 to Boston Deep Sea Fisheries Ltd, Hull.
16.03.1976 Transferred to Grimsby.
1978 Vessel sold for scrap to Albert Draper & Son, Hull. 10.03.1978 Arrived at the Victoria Dock slipway for breaking up.</td></tr>
</table>

Yard No.929
1957 PRINCE CHARLES
Photo:- Beverley Shipyard Collection

Yard No.931
1958 NORTHELLA
Photo by courtesy of J Marr & Son Ltd

Yard No.935
1958 FOREMAN
Photo:- Beverley Shipyard Collection

<table>
<tr><th rowspan="2">NAME
Official No.
Port Letters Numbers</th><th rowspan="2">Yard No.
Launched
Registered</th><th colspan="2">Registered</th><th rowspan="2">Engine Builder
Horse Power
Reg'd Speed</th><th rowspan="2">OWNER
(Built for)</th></tr>
<tr><th>G Ton
N Ton</th><th>L Ft
B Ft</th></tr>
<tr><td>FYLKIR

RE171 Motor Trawler</td><td>930
08.02.1958
02.06.1958</td><td>598
204</td><td>176.6
32.7</td><td>Holmes/Werkspoor
1545 BHP
14 knots</td><td>Fylkir Ltd
Reykjavik
Iceland</td></tr>
<tr><td colspan="6">05.02.1966 Sold to Newington Steam Trawling Co Ltd, Hull renamed IAN FLEMING (H396) Official No. 308530.
25.12.1973 Vessel abandoned in a sinking condition after striking a rock off Havoey Sund, north Norway. Fifteen crew took to one life-raft and five crewmen including the skipper took to another, this capsized and three crewmen were lost.
A flotilla of small local boats responded to the distress call and picked up the seventeen survivors.</td></tr>
<tr><td>NORTHELLA
300404
H98 Motor Trawler</td><td>931
10.04.1958
17.07.1958</td><td>789
288</td><td>185.0
33.6</td><td>Holmes/Werkspoor
1700 BHP
15 knots</td><td>J Marr & Son Ltd
Hull</td></tr>
<tr><td colspan="6">1961 Winner of the Silver Cod Trophy (the largest total catch for the year) 41176 x10 stone kits-350 days at sea £162,062.
09.09.1963 Renamed PRIMELLA, name changed to release her former name for use on the new freezer trawler NORTHELLA H301 (1718 gt/ b 1964).
1968 Winner of the Silver Cod Trophy 40844 x 10 stone kits-348 days at sea £181,761.
17.03.1977 Landed last catch at Hull and laid up following an engine room fire.
1977 Vessel sold for scrap to Albert Draper & Son, Hull. 05.04.1977 Arrived at the Victoria Dock slipway for breaking up.</td></tr>
<tr><td>Not Built</td><td>932</td><td colspan="4">Turn allocated to Boston Deep Sea Fishing Co Ltd but not taken up.</td></tr>
<tr><td>KINGSTON PEARL
300413
H127 Motor Trawler</td><td>933
21.07.1958
27.11.1958</td><td>691
242</td><td>176.6
32.8</td><td>Holmes/Werkspoor
1450 BHP
13.5 knots</td><td>Kingston Steam
Trawling Co Ltd
Hull</td></tr>
<tr><td colspan="6">First Motor trawler built for this company. 29.06.1966 Sold to Hellyer Bros Ltd, Hull.
16.11.1973 Vessel beached following a collision with the bulk carrier KING ALFRED (29419 gt/ b 1968).
26.11.1973 Refloated and berthed at Grimsby for repairs. No casualties reported on either vessel .
20.11.1978 Vessel sold for scrap to Albert Draper & Son, Hull. 19.03.1980 Arrived at the Victoria Dock for breaking up.</td></tr>
<tr><td>KINGSTON BERYL
300419
H128 Motor Trawler</td><td>934
29.09.1958
16.01.1959</td><td>691
242</td><td>176.6
32.8</td><td>Holmes/Werkspoor
1450 BHP
13.5 knots</td><td>Kingston Steam
Trawling Co Ltd
Hull</td></tr>
<tr><td colspan="6">29.06.1966 Sold to Hellyer Bros Ltd, Hull.. The first British deep water trawler fitted with (Stone "Kamewa") controllable pitch propeller. 1971 Winner of the Hull Distant Water Challenge Shield (for the greatest value of catch for the year calculated on a points basis) 31108 x 10 stone kits £260,416.
1979 Vessel sold for scrap to Albert Draper & Son, Hull. 27.07.1979 Arrived at the Victoria Dock slipway for breaking up.</td></tr>
<tr><td>FOREMAN
301604
Motor Tug</td><td>935
30.12.1958
08.05.1959</td><td>227
19</td><td>100.2
25.6</td><td>Ruston Hornsby
1030 BHP
13 knots</td><td>United Towing Co Ltd
Hull</td></tr>
<tr><td colspan="6">First sea going motor tug owned by United Towing Co Ltd, Hull.
1972 Sold to C J King Bristol renamed SEA BRISTOLIAN.
1981 to Mustafaen Najabi & Co, Dubai renamed MANSCO TUG 4.
02.10.1981 Vessel driven ashore on to rocks in severe weather north of Pontevedra Bay whilst towing the AFRODITI P (3619 gt/ b 1967) from Vigo to Piræus, whilst on delivery voyage to Dubai, declared a constructive total loss.</td></tr>
<tr><td>BENELLA
300420
H132 Motor Trawler</td><td>936
16.10.1958
12.02.1959</td><td>789
288</td><td>185.0
33.6</td><td>C.D.Holmes
1700 BHP
15 knots</td><td>City Steam Fishing Co Ltd
Hull</td></tr>
<tr><td colspan="6">03.03.1965 Sold to J Marr & Son, Hull. 24.10.1977 Converted to an Oil Rig Stand-by Safety Vessel .
13.02.1978 Transferred to Fleetwood. 1991 to Cam Shipping Co Ltd, Aberdeen renamed CAM VICEROY.
01.11.1993 Vessel sold for scrap to Caravel Maritime Ltd. 15.11.1993 Left Grimsby for Rainham, Kent for breaking up.</td></tr>
<tr><td>SPURN No. 14

Light-vessel</td><td>937
29.01.1959
15.05.1959</td><td>300</td><td>107.0
26.0</td><td>N/A</td><td>Humber Conservancy Board
Hull</td></tr>
<tr><td colspan="6">For use in marking the start of the navigable deep water channel at the entrance to the River Humber.
11.12.1985 The SPURN Light-vessel was withdrawn from its station and replaced by a light float.
17.12.1986 Vessel towed to Portsmouth after being soled to Pounds Shipyard.
Aug 1988 to Mr & Mrs Roger Smith, Beaucette Marina, Guernsey for conversion to a yacht club.
12.09.1988 Moved to Conway for similar use, as the Lightships moorings restricted access for yachts at Beaucette Marina.
12.10.1990 to Milford Haven Port Authority as a tourist attraction. 14.03.1991 renamed HAVEN.
18.11.1998 to Irish Escapades for use as a floating activity centre in the Republic of Ireland.</td></tr>
<tr><td>PHYLLISIA
199269 Coal Fired
CTA126 Steam Trawler</td><td>938
09.04.1958
09.07.1958</td><td>453
151</td><td>141.0
27.4</td><td>C.D.Holmes
750 IHP
12 knots</td><td>B Gelcer (Pty) Ltd &
Irvin & Johnson
Cape Town South Africa</td></tr>
<tr><td colspan="6">03.05.1968 Vessel ran aground off Olifants Bosch, Cape Point, (nature reserve) South Africa.
17.05.1968 Salvage attempts were abandoned due to the trawler being badly holed in rough seas.</td></tr>
</table>

Yard No.941
1959 DISA
Photo:- Beverley Shipyard Collection

Yard No.944
1960 STELLA LEONIS
Photo:- Beverley Shipyard Collection

Yard No.946
1960 KINGSTON AMBER
Photo:- Beverley Shipyard Collection

NAME Official No. Port Letters Numbers	Yard No. Launched Registered	Registered G Ton N Ton	 L Ft B Ft	Engine Builder Horse Power Reg'd Speed	OWNER (Built for)
VIANOVA 168613 GY590 Motor Trawler	939 12.12.1958 14.04.1959	559 224	165.0 30.4	Mirrlees Bickerton & Day 1150 BHP 13.5 knots	Atlas Steam Fishing Co Ltd Grimsby
28.01.1966 to Northern Trawlers Ltd, Grimsby. 1971 to Ross Trawlers Ltd, Grimsby. 12.04.1980 Vessel sold for scrap to A & M Marine . May 1980 Arrived Hartlepool for breaking up.					
EDWINA 187865 FD162 Motor Trawler	940 05.06.1958 18.09.1958	392 141	134.0 27.6	Mirrlees Bickerton & Day 1012 BHP 12.5 knots	J Marr & Son Ltd Fleetwood
1973 Transferred to Oil Rig Stand-by Safety duties. 1983 Sold to G.L.A.D. Lines Panama as a Stand-by Safety Vessel. 1999 Vessel still in service.					
DISA 315322 Coal Fired CTA85 Steam Trawler	941 25.02.1959 22.05.1959	453 151	141.0 27.4	C.D.Holmes 750 IHP 10 knots	Irvin & Johnson Ltd Cape Town South Africa
Last steam trawler built at Beverley. 27.09.1967 Vessel sank following a collision in heavy weather with the Irvin & Johnson trawler LUPIN (340 gt/ b 1965) 4 miles off Green Point Lighthouse, Cape Town. Ten crew lost.					
ONWARD PROGRESS 187870 Coastal Bunkering Tanker	942 14.03.1959 10.06.1959	345 144	135.0 26.5	Crossley Bros 375 BHP 9 knots	Fleetwood Tankers Ltd B.A. Parkes Fleetwood
1974 Sold to C & R Shipping Ltd, Northfleet.1975 Converted to a Water Tanker for off-shore installations renamed NEW START. 1979 to I P Longford (Shipping) Ltd, London. 1992 Vessel deleted from Lloyds Register of Shipping - continued existence in doubt.					
BOSTON TYPHOON 301877 FD183 Motor Trawler	943 11.04.1959 09.07.1959	425 151	137.6 28.5	C.D.Holmes / Werkspoor 1065 BHP 12 knots	Boston Deep Sea Fishing Co Ltd Fleetwood
01.01.1964 Sold to Iago Steam Trawling Co Ltd, Fleetwood. 04.02.1968 Vessel stranded at the entrance to Isafjordur Iceland. 06.02.1968 Refloated. 28.08.1968 Sold to Irvin & Johnson Ltd, Cape Town, South Africa (CTA298). 25.04.1978 Vessel towed into Cape Town after being severely damaged by fire in the engine room on the 23.04.1978 56 miles north-west of Saldanha Bay approx position 32°43'S 016°50'E declared a Constructive total loss. 04.11.1978 Hulk scuttled off Robben Island to form an artificial reef.					
STELLA LEONIS 301641 H322 Motor Trawler	944 29.03.1960 26.07.1960	775 267	185.0 33.6	Mirrlees Bickerton & Day 1800 BHP 15 knots	Charleson-Smith Trawlers Ltd Hull
1963 Winner of the Silver Cod Trophy (the largest total catch for the year) 39556x10 stone kits-335 days at sea-£161,500. 1964 Winner of the Silver Cod Trophy 35505 x 10 stone kits-340 days at sea-£144,503. 26.11.1965 renamed ROSS LEONIS. 01.10.1967 Sold to Hudson Bros (Trawlers) Ltd Hull. 13.12.1976 Vessel on fire 50 miles off the Norwegian coast, escorted into Harstadt for repairs, suffered only minor damage and later returned to service. 1978 Vessel sold for scrap to Albert Draper & Son, Hull. 04.11.1978 Arrived at the Victoria Dock slipway for breaking up.					
ST. LOUIS B2803 Motor Trawler	945 15.11.1958 13.03.1959	690 285	176.6 32.8	Klöckner Humboldt Deutz 1600 BHP 13.75 knots	Pecheries de la Marine Boulogne France
1960 Winner of the French Fishing Industries, Ribbon Bleu (Presented to the top French trawler). 06.11.1968 Sold to Boston Deep Sea Fisheries Ltd, Grimsby renamed BOSTON COMANCHE (GY144) Official No.333954. 08.02.1979 Sold to Mayer Newman & Co Ltd for scrap. 17.03.1979 Arrived Medway Secondary Metals Ltd, Bloors Wharf, Rainham, Kent for breaking up.					
KINGSTON AMBER 301651 H326 Motor Trawler	946 28.07.1960 25.11.1960	785 270	190.0 33.11	C.D.Holmes / Werkspoor 2000 BHP 16 knots	Kingston Steam Trawling Co Ltd Hull
Reputed to be the fastest side fishing trawler in the British fleet. Reported to have achieved speeds of 18 knots. 29.06.1966 Sold to Hellyer Bros Ltd, Hull.. 20.11.1978 Laid up. 1980 Vessel sold for scrap to Henderson Morez. 10.03.1980 left Albert Dock, Hull under tow towards Gravesend. 14.08.1980 Severely damaged by fire at Gravesend during the removal of machinery.					
HMS CHILTON M 1215 Coniston (Ton) Class	947 15.05.1957 24.07.1958	425	140.0 28.9	Mirrlees 2500 BHP 15 knots	The Admiralty Whitehall London
Wooden hulled coastal minesweeper built for the Royal Navy. 1958 Sold on completion to South African Navy renamed EAST LONDON.					

Yard No.949
1959 BALNAGASK
Photo:- Beverley Shipyard Collection

Yard No.950
1959 WYRE CONQUEROR
Photo:- Beverley Shipyard Collection

Yard No.959
1960 ARCTIC CORSAIR
Photo:- Beverley Shipyard Collection

NAME Official No. Port Letters Numbers	Yard No. Launched Registered	Registered G Ton N Ton	 L Ft B Ft	Engine Builder Horse Power Reg'd Speed	OWNER (Built for)
WILLIAM WILBERFORCE 301616 H200 Motor Trawler	948 08.05.1959 11.09.1959	698 280	179.9 32.8	C.D.Holmes / Werkspoor 1550 BHP 14 knots	F & T Ross Ltd Hull.
05.04.1960 Sold to St Andrew's Steam Fishing Co Ltd, Hull. 14.04.1961 to Eton Fishing Co Ltd, Hull. 03.05.1965 to Parbel - Smith Ltd, Hull. 20.11.1968 Transferred to Grimsby (GY140). 01.01.1975 to Boston Deep Sea Fisheries Ltd, Grimsby. 1978 Vessel sold for scrap to Albert Draper & Son, Hull. 23.05.1978 Arrived at the Victoria Dock slipway for breaking up.					
BALNAGASK 301574 A294 Motor Trawler	949 27.05.1959 05.10.1959	211 73	99.7 23.4	National Gas & Oil Eng Co 500 BHP 11.5 knots	Aberdeen Near Water Trawlers Ltd Aberdeen
19.12.1961 Vessel ran aground in thick fog at Scotston Head 4 miles south of Rattray Head. Attempts to refloat the vessel failed due to being badly holed in rough seas. 03.03.1962 Declared a total loss.					
WYRE CONQUEROR 301879 FD187 Motor Trawler	950 25.07.1959 29.10.1959	398 135	136.0 27.7	Mirrlees Bickerton & Day 860 BHP 11.75 knots	Wyre Trawlers Ltd Fleetwood
07.04.1978 Transferred to Aberdeen (all Wyre fleet transferred by B.U.T.). 1979 Vessel sold for scrap to J Gibson Johnston Ltd, Hull.1979 re-sold to H Kitson Vickers & Sons Engineering Ltd, then re-sold to S Dalton Skip Hire Ltd. Dec 1979 Arrived Bo'ness for breaking up.					
WYRE VICTORY 301881 FD181 Motor Trawler	951 07.09.1959 09.01.1960	398 135	136.0 27.7	Mirrlees Bickerton & Day 860 BHP 11.75 knots	Wyre Trawlers Ltd Fleetwood
14.01.1976 Vessel sank four hours after stranding on an under-water reef near Oigh-Sgeir Lighthouse, Inner Hebrides whilst outward bound from Fleetwood to Iceland. Fifteen crewmen were picked up from a life-raft by her sister trawler WYRE CONQUEROR. Just before she sank the skipper, chief engineer and radio operator were also rescued.					
HIGHLAND LADY 301578 A387 Motor Trawler	952 23.07.1959 12.11.1959	211 74	100.2 23.4	National Gas & Oil Eng Co 500 BHP 11.5 knots	Don Fishing Co Aberdeen
1964 Sold to Boston Deep Sea Fisheries Ltd, Lowestoft renamed BOSTON JAVELIN (LT429). 1966 to Grimsby Near Water Trawlers Ltd, Grimsby. 1972 to Aristides Lambropoulos, Piræus Greece renamed DIONISSIOS SOLOMOS. 1973 to E Trikanzopoulos, Piræus. 1980 to G Georgiadis, Piræus renamed OCEANIS 1995 to Romay, Takaradi, Ghana 1999 still in service.					
HAZELHEAD 301579 A364 Motor Trawler	953 23.07.1959 18.11.1959	211 74	100.2 23.4	National Gas & Oil Eng Cc 500 BHP 11.5 knots	Aberdeen Near Water Trawlers Ltd Aberdeen
1963 Sold to Boston Deep Sea Fisheries Ltd, Lowestoft renamed BOSTON HUNTER (LT440). 1971 to Didrik G. Bentson, Norway renamed HUNTER. 1975 *(A/S Wichmann 900 BHP diesel engine fitted)..* 1985 renamed HATLOYTRAL. 1986 to Jan Dragnes Kopervik. 1990 Vessel sold for scrap to Anda Brodrene A/S, Norway. 21.11.1990 Breaking up commenced at Stavanger.					
ARUM 350000 CTA115 Motor Trawler	954 05.10.1959 28.01.1960	360 120	125.0 26.5	Burmeister & Wain 840 BHP 10 knots	Irvin & Johnson Ltd Cape Town South Africa
1979 Vessel stripped of reusable parts. 06.06.1979 Hulk scuttled in approx position Lat 33°52'S Long 018°17'E.					
LONDON TOWN 301043 LO70 Motor Trawler	955 22.09.1959 01.04.1960	228 79	105.0 23.1	Mirrlees Bickerton & Day 484 BHP 11.5 knots	Hewett Fishing Co Ltd Fleetwood
16.12.1980 Sold to Boston Deep Sea Fishing Co Ltd, Fleetwood for use as an Oil Rig Stand-by Safety Vessel. 1981 to Putford Enterprises, Milford Haven. 1982 to Antony James, Milford Haven. 1984 to Huxley Fishing Co Ltd, Lowestoft renamed GUANA. 1992 Vessel sold for scrap to Victor Montenegro Feijoo. 10.07.1992 Arrived Vigo for breaking up.					
WESTELLA 301629 H194 Motor Trawler	956 18.11.1959 18.03.1960	779 275	185.0 33.6	Mirrlees Bickerton & Day 1800 BHP 15 knots	J Marr & Son Ltd Hull
First trawler to be powered by Mirrlees 'Monarch' ALSDM *(6cyl turbo-charged direct reversing diesel engine).* 22.11.1978 Sold to the Paul Franklin Watson, Vancouver, Canada, (Sea Shepherd Group) renamed SEA SHEPHERD for use in the protection and study of marine creatures. 1979 The SEA SHEPHERD rammed the pirate whaler SIERRA (683 gt/ b 1960) off the Portuguese coast in a bid to put her out of action. (she allegedly had illegally killed an estimated 25,000 whales). Due to the damage inflicted the SIERRA put into port for repairs, were she was sunk by saboteurs using a limpet mine. 31.12.1979 The SEA SHEPHERD was scuttled by her skipper using explosives at No2 Dock Leixoes, Portugal to prevent her being seized by the authorities for compensation. Subsequently raised and sold for scrap.					

Yard No.961
1960 VIVARIA
Photo:- Beverley Shipyard Collection

Yard No.965
1960 SOMERSET MAUGHAM
Photo:- Beverley Shipyard Collection

Yard No.971
1961 PADGETT
Photo:- Beverley Shipyard Collection

NAME Official No. Port Letters Numbers	Yard No. Launched Registered	Registered G Ton N Ton	 L Ft B Ft	Engine Builder Horse Power Reg'd Speed	OWNER (Built for)
Not Built	957				
ARCTIC CAVALIER 301635 H204 Motor Trawler	958 18.01.1960 11.05.1960	764 256	187.1 33.6	Mirrlees Bickerton & Day 1800 BHP 15 knots	Boyd Line Hull
First Diesel engined trawler built for the Boyd Line.19.03.1981 Sold to James F Hodson, Grimsby. 1981 to Oasis Natigation S A Panama for fishing in the South Pacific. 1985 to Parque Acuatico y Club de Navegacion de Puntaranas, Costa Rica. 1999 Vessel still in service.					
ARCTIC CORSAIR 301638 H320 Motor Trawler	959 29.02.1960 15.06.1960	764 256	187.1 33.6	Mirrlees Bickerton & Day 1800 BHP 15 knots	Boyd Line Hull
14.09.1967 Vessel severely damaged in collision with the collier OLIVE in thick fog off Duncansby Head Scotland whilst homeward bound from Greenland. Both vessels attempted to reach Wick harbour but the ARCTIC CORSAIR had to be beached in Sinclair Bay to save her from sinking. She was refloated and after temporary repairs returned to Hull. Feb 1978 Converted to Pelagic fishing. 08.01.1981 Final trip before being laid up at Hull. 1985 Converted back to conventional fishing. 21.03.1985 Returned to fishing. 15.01.1988 Registration closed renamed ARCTIC CAVALIER name changed to release her former name for use on the freezer trawler ARCTIC CORSAIR H320 (ex HAVSTRAND 1266 gt/ b 1971). 18.06.1993 Vessel sold to Hull City Council and renamed ARCTIC CORSAIR moored in the river Hull for use as a museum ship. 09.05.1999 Officially opened to the public.					
ROYALIST 301171 LO50 Motor Trawler	960 16.03.1960 29.06.1960	228 79	105.0 23.1	Mirrlees Bickerton & Day 484 BHP 12 knots	Hewett Fishing Co Ltd Fleetwood
1981 Sold to Primrose Fishing Co Ltd , Fleetwood. 1981 to Putford Enterprises Ltd, Fleetwood. 1987 to Penfro Peche, Milford Haven (FD24). Rebuilt in Spain with port-side enclosed shelter deck and new bridge. 1999 Vessel still in service.					
VIVARIA 301840 GY648 Motor Trawler	961 12.05.1960 08.09.1960	744 272	185.0 33.6	Mirrlees Bickerton & Day 1800 BHP 15 knots	Atlas Steam Fishing Co Ltd Grimsby
Reputed to be the fastest side fishing trawler out of Grimsby. 28.01.1966 Sold to Northern Trawlers Ltd, Grimsby. Jun 1971 to Ross Trawlers Ltd, Grimsby 1979 Sold to Mr Valman machinery removed at West India Docks, London and hulk re-sold for breaking up .					
VIDAS Twin Screw Steel Yacht	962 31.03.1963 31.03.1963		49.0 14.1	Gardener	H G Briggs Scarborough
Built in the fitting shop. 31.03.1963 On completion she was lowered into the River Hull by crane.					
ROBERT HEWETT 302611 LO65 Motor Trawler	963 22.11.1960 14.03.1961	567 198	161.1 30.5	Mirrlees Bickerton & Day 1168 BHP 13.5 knots	Heward Trawlers Ltd Fleetwood
1979 Sold to Claridge Trawlers Ltd, Lowestoft renamed ST. LUKE *(converted to an Oil Rig Stand-by Safety Vessel).* 1989 to The Colne Shipping Co Ltd, Lowestoft. 1993 to Bristow Investments Ltd, Lowestoft. 1994 to Lowestoft Shipping III Ltd, Lowestoft. 1995 to Port Dickson Ltd, Lowestoft. 1996 to Charford Shipping IV Ltd, Lowestoft. 1997 to Bristow Investments Ltd, Lowestoft renamed (1999) VEESEA MERLIN. 1999 Vessel still in service.					
STARELLA 301645 H219 Motor Trawler	964 10.06.1960 06.10.1960	606 207	161.1 30.5	Mirrlees Bickerton & Day 1304 BHP 14 knots	J Marr & Son Ltd Hull
11.08.1969 Transferred to Fleetwood. 17.01.1973 Returned to Hull. 01.01.1975 Sold to Boyd Line Ltd, Hull renamed ARCTIC REBEL. 01.12.1976 Last British trawler to fish in Icelandic waters, she was ordered off the fishing grounds as the 200 mile exclusion limit came into force. 01.05.1979 to Huxley Fishing Co Ltd, Lowestoft renamed ST. MATTHEW*(converted to an Oil Rig Stand-by Safety Vessel).* 1986 Vessel sold for scrap to K & M Davies (Pembroke). 16.12.1986 Arrived Milford Haven for breaking up.					
SOMERSET MAUGHAM 301656 H329 Motor Trawler	965 22.09.1960 02.02.1961	789 275	189.7 33.6	C.D.Holmes / Werkspoor 2000 BHP 15 knots	Newington Steam Trawling Co Ltd Hull
First Diesel trawler built for Newington Steam Trawling Co Ltd, Hull. 1962 Winner of the Silver Cod Trophy (the largest total catch for the year) 46557x10 stone kits-351 days at sea-£146,183. 1965 Winner of the Silver Cod Trophy 37669 x 10 stone kits-326 days at sea-£157,942. 1966 Winner of the Silver Cod Trophy 39397 x 10 stone kits-343 days at sea-£165,655. 1967 Winner of the Silver Cod Trophy 39247 x 10 stone kits-339 days at sea-£139,924. 1978 Vessel sold for scrap to Albert Draper & Son, Hull. 19.09.1978 Arrived at the Victoria Dock slipway for breaking up.					

<table>
<tr><th rowspan="2">NAME
Official No.
Port Letters Numbers</th><th rowspan="2">Yard No.
Launched
Registered</th><th colspan="2">Registered</th><th rowspan="2">Engine Builder
Horse Power
Reg'd Speed</th><th rowspan="2">OWNER
(Built for)</th></tr>
<tr><th>G Ton
N Ton</th><th>L Ft
B Ft</th></tr>
<tr><td>ARLANDA
301890
FD206 Motor Trawler</td><td>966
02.05.1961
25.09.1961</td><td>431
153</td><td>137.2
26.10</td><td>Mirrlees Bickerton
& Day 1250 BHP
12 knots</td><td>City Steam Fishing Co Ltd
Fleetwood</td></tr>
<tr><td colspan="6">00.03.1962 Sold to Dinas Steam Trawling Co Ltd, Fleetwood. 04.01.1971 to Cevic Steam Fishing Co Ltd, Fleetwood.
04.06.1975 Vessel transferred to Oil Rig Stand-by Safety Vessel duties.
1977 to Kalleawo Ent Tema Ghana renamed TOHALE (converted to an Oil Rig Stand-by Safety Vessel).
24.01.1991 Vessel hulked at Takoradi.</td></tr>
<tr><td>LINARIA
350051
CTA.123 Motor Trawler</td><td>967
07.10.1960
17.01.1961</td><td>360
120</td><td>125.7
26.10</td><td>Alpha - Diesel
800 BHP
10 knots</td><td>National Trawling &
Fishing Co Ltd
Cape Town South Africa</td></tr>
<tr><td colspan="6">1982 Sold to H D Cottle & L Angelico, Cape Town, South Africa.
1983 to Atlantic Fishing Enterprises (Pty) Ltd, Cape Town renamed SOUTHERN HARRIER. 1999 Vessel still in service.</td></tr>
<tr><td>ARCTIC VANDAL
301677
H344 Motor Trawler</td><td>968
15.06.1961
14.11.1961</td><td>594
202</td><td>163.7
30.5</td><td>Mirrlees Bickerton
& Day 1400 BHP
14 knots</td><td>Boyd Line Ltd
Hull</td></tr>
<tr><td colspan="6">03.05.1979 Sold to Huxley Fishing Co Ltd, Lowestoft renamed ST. PAUL (converted to an Oil Rig Stand-by Safety Vessel).
1990 The Colne Shipping Co Ltd, Lowestoft. 1996 to Charford Shipping IV Ltd, Lowestoft. 1999 Vessel still in service.</td></tr>
<tr><td>TRUEMAN
301851
GY659 Motor Trawler</td><td>969
22.12.1960
20.04.1961</td><td>412
139</td><td>137.2
28.5</td><td>C.D.Holmes /
Werkspoor
1050 BHP 12 knots</td><td>Crampin Steam
Fishing Co Ltd
Grimsby</td></tr>
<tr><td colspan="6">29.09.1963 Whilst steaming through the Norwegian fjords the TRUEMAN suffered an accommodation fire in which two crewmen lost there lives.
23.03.1965 Sold to Ross Trawlers (Goweroak) Ltd, Grimsby renamed (24.11.1965) ROSS JUPITER .
12.09.1968 to Irvin & Johnson, Cape Town, South Africa (CTA293).
1994 to Viking Fishing Co (Pty) Ltd, Cape Town. 1999 Vessel still in service.</td></tr>
<tr><td>PRINCESS ELIZABETH
301887
FD213 Motor Trawler</td><td>970
19.01.1961
17.05.1961</td><td>419
143</td><td>137.2
28.4</td><td>C.D.Holmes /
Werkspoor
1055 BHP 12 knots</td><td>F & T Ross Ltd
Fleetwood</td></tr>
<tr><td colspan="6">19.05.1961 Sold to Boston Deep Sea Fisheries Ltd, Fleetwood. Mar 1962 to F & T Ross Ltd, Hull.
09.10.1962 Transferred to Grimsby. 03.05.1965 to Brixham Trawlers Ltd, Hull. 31.05.1966 to F & T Ross Ltd, Hull.
13.01.1967 to Brixham Trawlers Ltd, Hull. 21.11.1968 (GY143).
29.08.1969 to Irvin & Johnson Ltd, Cape Town, South Africa (CTA51).
1983 Vessel stripped of reusable parts. 27.06.1983 Hulk scuttled off Robben Island, Cape Town.</td></tr>
<tr><td>PADGETT
303276
GY660 Motor Trawler</td><td>971
20.02.1961
26.07.1961</td><td>413
138</td><td>137.2
28.5</td><td>C.D.Holmes /
Werkspoor
1050 BHP 12 knots</td><td>Bunch Steam
Fishing Co Ltd
Grimsby</td></tr>
<tr><td colspan="6">23.03.1965 Sold to Ross Trawlers (Goweroak) Ltd, Grimsby renamed (09.12.1965) ROSS JUNO.
10.12.1982 to Ulex Shipping Co S.A, Panama renamed NATALY.
1990 to Lesamar S.C.L. Vigo, Spain renamed LESAMAR UNO. 1995 to Montajes Cies S.L. Vigo.
1996 to Compania Pesquera de Cana S.A, Kingstown, St Vincent & The Grenadines renamed ALMIKE.
1999 Vessel still in service.</td></tr>
<tr><td>CAPE OTRANTO
301692
H227 Diesel Electric Trawler</td><td>972
28.07.1961
24.05.1962</td><td>823
237</td><td>198.1
34.5</td><td>Mirrlees Bickerton
& Day
2775 BHP 15 knots</td><td>Hudson Bros (Trawlers) Ltd
Hull</td></tr>
<tr><td colspan="6">Built for Hudson Bros (Trawlers) Ltd, Hull which was then a subsidiary of Ross Group Ltd, Grimsby
(Largest conventional trawler built at Beverley) renamed (26.11.1965) ROSS OTRANTO.
27.09.1979 Vessel sold for scrap to José Oliveira Gomez, Spain. 02.09.1980 Arrived Vigo for breaking up.</td></tr>
<tr><td>BOSTON WEELSBY
303278
GY671 Motor Trawler</td><td>973
20.03.1961
12.09.1961</td><td>412
140</td><td>137.2
28.4</td><td>C.D.Holmes /
Werkspoor
1050 BHP 12 knots</td><td>Boston Deep Sea
Fisheries Ltd
Grimsby</td></tr>
<tr><td colspan="6">20.09.1962 Sold to F & T Ross Ltd, Hull. 03.05.1965 to St Christopher's Steam Fishing Co Ltd, Grimsby.
04.02.1968 Whilst returning from the Icelandic fishing grounds she was seriously damaged by a heavy sea to the west of the Færoe Islands. The Aberdeen trawler BEN BHRACKIE A814 (443 gt/ b 1966) came to the aid of the BOSTON WEELSBY and towed her into Thorshavn for repairs. 19.09.1969 to Irvin Johnson Ltd, Cape Town, South Africa (CTA47).
1984 Vessel stripped of reusable parts. 26.07.1984 Hulk scuttled off Robben Island, Cape Town.</td></tr>
</table>

Yard No.972
1961 CAPE OTRANTO
Photo:- Beverley Shipyard Collection

Yard No.974
1961 BOSTON WELLVALE
Photo:- Beverley Shipyard Collection

Yard No.976
1961 ST. GERONTIUS
Photo:- Beverley Shipyard Collection

<table>
<tr><th rowspan="2">NAME
Official No.
Port Letters Numbers</th><th rowspan="2">Yard No.
Launched
Registered</th><th colspan="2">Registered</th><th rowspan="2">Engine Builder
Horse Power
Reg'd Speed</th><th rowspan="2">OWNER
(Built for)</th></tr>
<tr><th>G Ton
N Ton</th><th>L Ft
B Ft</th></tr>
<tr><td>BOSTON WELLVALE
301893
FD209 Motor Trawler</td><td>974
30.06.1961
14.12.1961</td><td>419
143</td><td>137.2
28.4</td><td>C.D.Holmes /
Werkspoor
1050 BHP 12 knots</td><td>Boston Deep Sea Fishing
Co Ltd
Fleetwood</td></tr>
<tr><td colspan="6">Jun 1962 Whilst fishing off St Kilda the vessel suffered an accommodation fire. No casualties.
25.11.1966 Sold to North Cape Fishing Co Ltd, Grimsby.
22.12.1966 Vessel ran ashore on Cape Arnanes in a gale and snow storm whilst proceeding to Isafjordhur to have her radar repaired. An Icelandic rescue party answered the distress call and took off all seventeen crew using breeches buoy.
08.08.1967 refloated and sold for breaking up. Vessel taken to Hafnarfjordur and refitted by an Icelandic company.
1971 returned to service, by Stalskip H/F Iceland renamed RAN (PLN GK42).
29.05.1980 to Issfodin H/F, Gardur renamed INGOLFUR.
16.03.1984 to Nidursuduverks Midjunni H/F, Isafirdi renamed ARNANES (IS42). 08.03.1985 to Torfnesi H/F, Isafirdi.
08.04.1988 to Saedori H/F, Siglufirdi (SI70). 1999 to Thormodur Rammi-Saeberg, Guaymas, Mexico. 1999 Still in service.</td></tr>
<tr><td>BERTIL

Ice Breaker Harbour Tug</td><td>975
21.05.1961
18.09.1962</td><td>42</td><td>54.7
16.1</td><td>Ruston & Hornsby
300 SHP
11 knots</td><td>Goteborg Bogserings &
Bårgungs A/B
Gothenburg Sweden</td></tr>
<tr><td colspan="6">1984 Sold to The Swedish Maritime Administration Gothenburg renamed VILHEIM HANSEN.
For use on the River Göta for maintenance and ice breaking duties. 1999 Vessel still in service.</td></tr>
<tr><td>ST. GERONTIUS
301682
H350 Motor Trawler</td><td>976
28.09.1961
07.03.1962</td><td>659
221</td><td>173.6
32.2</td><td>C.D.Holmes /
Werkspoor
1380 BHP 14 knots</td><td>Thomas Hamling & Co Ltd
Hull</td></tr>
<tr><td colspan="6">30.11.1979 Registration cancelled vessel laid up.
1980 Vessel sold for scrap to Albert Draper & Son, Hull. 11.10.1980 Arrived at the Victoria Dock slipway for breaking up.</td></tr>
<tr><td>NERINE
350291
CTA572 Motor Trawler</td><td>977
07.05.1962
26.11.1962</td><td>360
120</td><td>125.7
26.10</td><td>Alpha Diesel
840 BHP
10 knots</td><td>Irvin & Johnson Ltd
Cape Town
South Africa</td></tr>
<tr><td colspan="6">1982 Vessel stripped of reusable parts. 19.06.1982 Hulk scuttled about 40 miles south of Cape Point.</td></tr>
<tr><td>Un-named

Light Float</td><td>978
16.10.1962</td><td>25</td><td>40.0
16.0</td><td>N/A</td><td>Humber Conservancy Board
Hull</td></tr>
<tr><td colspan="6">16.10.1962 Delivered to Princes Dock, Hull. For use in marking the Navigable deep water channel in the River Humber.</td></tr>
<tr><td>Un-named

Light Float</td><td>978A
16.10.1962</td><td>25</td><td>40.0
16.0</td><td>N/A</td><td>Humber Conservancy Board
Hull</td></tr>
<tr><td colspan="6">16.10.1962 Delivered to Princes Dock, Hull. For use in marking the Navigable deep water channel in the River Humber.</td></tr>
<tr><td>LORD JELLICOE
301694
H228 Motor Trawler</td><td>979
24.11.1961
05.06.1962</td><td>594
224</td><td>163.7
30.5</td><td>Mirrlees Bickerton
& Day 1400 BHP
14 knots</td><td>Lord Line Ltd
Hull</td></tr>
<tr><td colspan="6">16.04.1963 Transferred to Grimsby managed by Northern Trawlers Ltd, Grimsby (GY709).
24.03.1966 Sold to Northern Trawlers Ltd, Grimsby. Jun 1971 to Ross Trawlers Ltd, Grimsby.
01.02.1981 to Colne Shipping Co Ltd, Lowestoft renamed ST. LOUIS, (converted to an Oil Rig Stand-by Safety Vessel).
1983 to Dagon Fishing Co Ltd, Lowestoft. 1989 to Colne Shipping Co Ltd, Lowestoft.
1995 to Atlantic Consolidated Ltd, Lowestoft. 1996 to Charford Shipping IV Ltd, Lowestoft. 1999 Vessel still in service.</td></tr>
<tr><td>NORTHERN REWARD
303299
GY694 Motor Trawler</td><td>980
09.01.1962
20.07.1962</td><td>576
194</td><td>163.7
30.5</td><td>Mirrlees Bickerton
& Day 1400 BHP
14 knots</td><td>Northern Trawlers Ltd
Grimsby</td></tr>
<tr><td colspan="6">Jun 1971 Sold to Ross Trawlers Ltd, Grimsby. 01.02.1981 to Colne Shipping Co Ltd, Lowestoft renamed ST. ELIZABETH.
(converted to an Oil Rig Stand-by Safety Vessel). 1995 to Bristow Investments Ltd, Lowestoft.
1996 to Charford Shipping IV Ltd, Lowestoft. 1999 to Bristow Investments Ltd, Lowestoft. 1999 Vessel still in service</td></tr>
<tr><td>LORD ST. VINCENT
303809
H261 Motor Trawler</td><td>981
09.03.1962
12.09.1962</td><td>594
224</td><td>163.7
30.5</td><td>Mirrlees Bickerton
& Day 1400 BHP
14 knots</td><td>Lord Line Ltd
Hull</td></tr>
<tr><td colspan="6">03.05.1963 Managed by Hellyer Bros Ltd, Hull. 29.06.1966 to Hellyer Bros Ltd, Hull.
26.10.1979 Registration cancelled vessel laid up. 13.03.1980 Sold to Drifter Trawlers Ltd, Lowestoft renamed ST. ANNE,
(converted to an Oil Rig Stand-by Safety Vessel). 1989 to Colne Shipping Co Ltd, Lowestoft.
1995 to Port Dickson Ltd, Lowestoft. 1996 to Charford Shipping IV Ltd, Lowestoft.
1999 to Port Dickson Ltd, Lowestoft renamed VEESEA HAWK 1999 Vessel still in service</td></tr>
</table>

NAME Official No. Port Letters Numbers	Yard No. Launched Registered	Registered G Ton N Ton	 L Ft B Ft	Engine Builder Horse Power Reg'd Speed	OWNER (Built for)
NORTHERN GIFT 304780 GY704 Motor Trawler	982 05.04.1962 29.10.1962	576 194	163.7 30.5	Mirrlees Bickerton & Day 1400 BHP 14 knots	Northern Trawlers Ltd Grimsby
15.05.1974 Whilst outward bound for Iceland in thick fog the NORTHERN GIFT was in collision with the German freighter BROOK (1517 gt/ b 1967) near the Bull Light-vessel. With the trawler badly holed and in danger of sinking the twenty one crew were taken aboard the pilot cutter CAPTAIN HOLMES. The ROSS KHARTOUM GY120 (507 gt/ b 1958) took the NORTHER GIFT in tow but it became clear she would not make it back to Grimsby so she was beached at Spurn Bight near the Humber lifeboat station . 20.05.1974 Refloated and returned to Grimsby for repairs. 18.12.1980 Sold to The Dagon Fishing Co Ltd, Lowestoft renamed ST. DAVIDS, Oil Rig Stand-by Safety Vessel. 1987 Vessel sold for scrap to Liguria Maritime Ltd. 29.07.1987 Arrived Milton Creek for breaking up.					
LADY ELSIE 304783 Motor Tug	983 31.10.1962 31.01.1963	159	85.0 24.0	Ruston & Hornsby 920 BHP 11 knots	J H Pigott & Son Ltd Grimsby
1969 to Union des Remorquers de`l Ocean, Bordeaux, France renamed TALMONT. 1984 to Apostolos Bros Shipping Agencies, Limassol, Cyprus. 1994 Vessel deleted from Lloyds Register of Shipping.					
LADY THERESA 307568 Motor Tug	984 13.12.1962 22.03.1963	159	85.0 24.0	Ruston & Hornsby 920 BHP 11 knots	J H Pigott & Son Ltd Grimsby
The last commercial vessel to be built at Beverley by Cook, Welton and Gemmell Ltd. 1974 to Weldwood Transportation Vancouver Canada renamed WELDWOOD SPIRIT renamed (1994) COMOX ARGUS. 1999 Vessel still in service.					
LADY CECILIA 304786 Motor Tug	985 25.07.1963 20.11.1963	159	85.0 24.0	Ruston & Hornsby 920 BHP 11 knots	J H Pigott & Son Ltd Grimsby
Order completed by Charles D Holmes & Co Ltd Beverley. 1964 to Port of Varna Authority, Bulgaria renamed SATURN. 1999 Vessel still in service.					

Yard No.982
1962 NORTHERN GIFT
Photo:- Beverley Shipyard Collection

GLOSSARY

Headings G Ton = Gross Tons. N Ton = Net Tons. L Ft = Length in Feet. B Ft = Breadth in Feet.
Horse Power :- NHP = Notional HP. IHP = Indicated HP. BHP = Brake HP.

Text Fishing vessel :- Pot Letters and Numbers in brackets indicate subsequent changes.
Fishing vessels often changed their base port but retained their oiginal PLN.

Not all vessels requisitioned by the Royal Navy were issued wiith Pennant numbers, these were vessels either sunk or returned in the early years of the 1939-1945 war.

Vessels deleted from Lloyds Register of Shipping:- Continued existence in doubt.

BISCO = British Iron & Steel Corporation

gt/ b = Gross tons / Year built

BIBLIOGRAPHY

Hull Shipping Registers, Grimsby Shipping Registers, Lloyds Register of Shipping, Lloyds Casualty and Loss Books, Lloyds War Loss Books, Hull News, Hull Times, Hull Daily Mail, Grimsby Evening Telegraph, Fishing News and Trawling Times.

INDEX

BULLDOG	82	03.03.1892	32
BUNSEN	*475*	*05.11.1925*	159
BURCOM SAND	*875*	*20.04.1954*	225
BUTSER	*683*	*29.07.1941*	192
BUTTERFLY	201	10.02.1898	49
BY GEORGE	*291*	*17.01.1914*	119
C K WELTON	*448*	*28.02.1922*	153
CABLE BANK	*898*	*09.03.1954*	227
CADET	*308*	*07.09.1914*	122
CAIRO	*6*	*10.05.1902*	69
CALIBAN	*218*	*15.07.1911*	104
CALPHURNIA	*187*	*16.09.1909*	100
CALVAY	*726*	*29.11.1943*	201
CAMBODIA	*207*	*04.01.1911*	103
CAMBRIA	71	27.06.1891	31
CANDACE	313	19.11.1902	64
CANTATRICE	*317*	*04.02.1915*	124
CAPE ADAIR	*915*	*26.05.1956*	233
CAPE COLOMBIA	*914*	*27.04.1956*	233
CAPE COMORIN	*611*	*08.04.1936*	182
CAPE OTRANTO	*972*	*28.07.1961*	244
CAPE TOWN	*169*	*15.08.1908*	97
CAPE TRAFALGAR	*922*	*18.02.1957*	235
CAPEL	*513*	*12.01.1929*	166
CARDINAL	*255*	*26.10.1912*	111
CARENCY	*340A*	*20.04.1916*	130
CARIAMA	*42*	*04.02.1904*	75
CARIEDA	*275*	*21.06.1913*	117
CARILON	*325*	*28.04.1915*	126
CASSANDRA	*92*	*16.10.1905*	83
CASSIO	*530*	*21.10.1929*	169
CAVALIER	314	13.02.1902	65
CAYTON BAY	*807*	*01.03.1949*	214
CECIL RHODES	318	04.02.1902	65
CEDAR	*182*	*19.06.1909*	98
CELESTIAL EMPIRE	192	05.09.1897	48
CEYLON	52	02.07.1890	28
CHALCEDONY	*493*	*11.02.1928*	162
CHAMONIX	*367*	*28.08.1919*	138
CHAMPION	108	11.01.1894	36
CHANTICLEER	122	05.06.1894	39
CHARLES BOYES	*388*	*14.02.1918*	142
CHARLES ANTRAM	*417*	*18.06.1919*	148
CHIEFTAIN	97	04.02.1893	35
CHIEFTAIN	*86*	*28.09.1905*	82
CHINA BAKAR	*912*	*22.08.1955*	231
CHINDWIN	21	03.12.1887	24
CHRISTOPHER	*208*	*17.01.1911*	103
CHRYSOLITE	259	20.03.1900	58
CICERO	*129*	*18.12.1906*	89
CITY OF BIRMINGHAM	78	00.07.1891	32
CITY OF EXETER	123	03.07.1894	39
CITY OF GLOUCESTER	147	18.09.1895	41
CITY OF HULL	204	26.02.1898	49
CITY OF LONDON	289	17.06.1901	62
CITY OF WAKEFIELD	64	14.02.1891	31
CLAIRE	*148*	*29.06.1907*	92
CLAUDIA	127	20.08.1894	39
CLEOPATRA	228	13.03.1899	54
CLYDE	130	00.00.1894	40
COLDSTREAMER	*706*	*10.12.1942*	197
COLLINGWOOD	*11*	*11.07.1902*	70
COLONIAL EMPIRE	209	07.04.1898	51
COLSAY	*727*	*14.12.1943*	201
COMMANDER BOYLE	*316 (1)*	*17.02.1915*	124
COMMANDER NASMITH	*316 (2)*	*17.02.1915*	124
COMRADE	173	10.10.1896	45
CONDOR	119	00.04.1894	39
CONDOR	*79*	*04.07.1905*	80
CONGO	181	16.02.1897	47
CONQUEROR	291	31.07.1901	62
CONSORT	*185*	*02.09.1909*	100
CORCYRA	*288A*	*12.02.1914*	118
CORIENTES	*201*	*09.06.1910*	101

CORNELIA	124	21.07.1894	39
CORNELIAN	261	15.04.1900	58
CORTINA	*270*	*24.04.1913*	115
CORYTHAIX	*202*	*24.08.1910*	101
COUNCILLOR	169	26.08.1896	45
COURSER	*43*	*08.02.1904*	75
COURSER	*78*	*18.05.1905*	80
COURTIER	*203*	*25.06.1910*	101
COURTLAND	*61*	*13.10.1904*	78
CROWLIN	*725*	*15.11.1943*	199
CROXBY	*214*	*01.05.1911*	104
CRUSADER	358	22.12.1903	68
CRYSTAL	151	20.11.1895	43
CUCKOO	154	30.01.1896	43
CURLEW	139	16.03.1895	41
CYPRUS	88	00.05.1892	33
CYRANO	274	27.08.1900	59
DABCHICK	*710*	*09.03.1943*	198
DALE CASTLE	93	14.04.1892	35
DANE	193	00.07.1897	48
DANE	*22*	*03.03.1903*	72
DANE	*211*	*02.02.1911*	103
DAUNTLESS	286	03.04.1901	62
DAVY	*612*	*08.07.1936*	184
DE LA POLE	*228*	*11.10.1911*	106
DEER HOUND	40	01.11.1889	27
DEFENDER	354	10.10.1903	68
DELHI	*27*	*14.04.1903*	72
DERVISH	*587*	*18.12.1933*	180
DESDEMONA	296	03.10.1901	64
DESIDERATUM	73	08.07.1891	32
DESIREE	*257*	*29.10.1912*	111
DESTINN	*302*	*27.06.1914*	122
DIRECTOR GERLING	86	02.02.1892	33
DISA	*941*	*25.02.1959*	239
DOGBERRY	*179*	*22.05.1909*	98
DOGGER BANK	26	00.06.1888	25
DOMINICK ADDISON	*412*	*02.04.1919*	147
DONALDA	*301*	*28.03.1914*	121
DORCAS	*127*	*17.11.1906*	89
DOUGLAS	196	15.09.1897	48
DOURO	180	08.03.1897	47
DOVEY	194	00.08.1897	48
DROMIO	*195*	*09.06.1910*	101
DROMIO	*528*	*23.09.1929*	167
DUCHESS OF YORK	106	00.10.1893	36
DUKE OF WELLINGTON	197	00.02.1898	48
DUKE OF YORK	105	25.08.1893	36
DUNCTON	*684*	*06.09.1941*	194
DUNKERY	*688*	*04.12.1941*	194
DURBAN	195	09.09.1897	48
DYNAMO	*82*	*20.06.1905*	82
EARL ESSEX	*290*	*07.01.1914*	119
EARL HEREFORD	*110*	*10.04.1906*	86
EARL HOWARD	*305*	*27.07.1914*	122
EARL KITCHENER	*315*	*02.02.1915*	124
EARL LENNOX	*306*	*25.08.1914*	122
EARL OF SHAFTESBURY	*75*	*11.03.1905*	80
EARL WARWICK	*74*	*18.05.1905*	80
EASEDALE H	*859*	*15.04.1952*	223
EASTWARD HO	210	10.05.1898	51
EDITH	102	00.07.1893	36
EDMOND-RENE	*773*	*20.05.1947*	208
EDWARD B. CARGILL	206	00.07.1898	49
EDWARD ROBSON	35	29.06.1889	27
EDWARDIAN	*241*	*23.03.1912*	109
EDWARDIAN	*561*	*06.12.1930*	175
EDWINA	*940*	*05.06.1958*	239
EGILIAS AKERMAN	*410*	*18.03.1919*	147
EGILSAY	*691*	*07.02.1942*	194
EGYPT	60	29.12.1890	29
EL CAPITAN	*626*	*15.05.1937*	185
ELEANOR MARIA M	7	00.06.1885	23
ELECTRA	14	00.05.1886	24

ELECTRA	58	14.09.1904	78
ELK	13	21.08.1902	70
ELLA HEWETT	871	04.12.1952	225
EMBASSY	498	05.07.1928	163
EMPEROR	30	14.05.1903	73
EMPIRE PAM	754	29.08.1945	204
EMPIRE TEST	759	14.07.1945	205
EMPIRE DOROTHY	760	27.07.1945	205
EMPIRE MAYBURY	750	10.07.1945	204
EMPIRE MAYPORT	749	14.06.1945	204
EMPIRE PEGGY	753	14.05.1945	204
EMU	280	08.10.1900	61
ENCORE	282	03.12.1900	61
ENDYMION	281	10.11.1900	61
ENGLISHMAN	44	00.10.1889	28
ENNERDALE H	860	24.05.1952	223
ENSAY	692	05.03.1942	194
EQUALITY	642	03.03.1938	187
ERIN	33	11.07.1903	73
ERMINE	32	11.07.1903	73
EROICAN	288	15.01.1914	118
EROS	34	28.07.1903	73
EROS	139	15.04.1907	91
ESCALLONIA	209	16.03.1911	103
ESMERALDA	31	13.06.1903	73
ETRUSCAN	283	18.10.1913	118
EUCLASE	565	30.05.1931	175
EUDOCIA	61	10.02.1891	29
EXCELSIOR	34	01.06.1889	27
EXYAHNE	293	12.03.1914	119
FALCON	158	16.04.1896	44
FALSTAFF	125	04.10.1906	88
FARADAY	190	19.06.1897	48
FARFIELD	439	25.01.1921	152
FARNE	713	22.04.1943	198
FARNELLA	802	20.11.1948	214
FAWN	219	26.11.1898	52
FEDERAL	136	14.02.1907	91
FEZENTA	292	12.03.1914	119
FIDELIA	79	06.10.1891	32
FILEY	284	29.11.1913	118
FLANDRE	323	30.04.1915	126
FLATHOLM	714	08.05.1943	198
FLEMING	512	29.12.1928	165
FLORENCE	128	04.09.1894	39
FLYING WING	324	30.04.1915	126
FOREMAN	935	30.12.1958	237
FOREMOST 90	646	02.07.1938	188
FOREMOST 91	647	16.07.1938	188
FOREMOST 93	648	12.09.1938	188
FORTO	649	12.11.1938	188
FORTUNA	108	14.03.1906	86
FORWARD	205	06.06.1898	49
FORWARD HO	313	19.11.1914	123
FOXHOUND	39	26.08.1889	27
FRANCES	20	00.04.1888	24
FRANCONIA	126	01.08.1894	39
FRANKLIN	85	05.08.1905	82
FRASER	135	18.03.1907	91
FREDRICK BUSH	389	14.03.1918	142
FREESIA	210	03.04.1911	103
FUDAY	728	01.01.1944	201
FULMAR	223	23.02.1899	52
FUSILIER	707	23.12.1942	197
FYLKIR	784	14.10.1947	210
FYLKIR	930	08.02.1958	237
GABIR	186	02.09.1909	100
GADRA	183	05.08.1909	98
GALLEON	553	30.08.1930	172
GALVANI	526	07.08.1929	167
GAMBRI	343	16.09.1916	134
GAMBRI	521	25.05.1929	167
GAME COCK	94	22.09.1892	35
GANILLY	715	22.05.1943	198

GARDAR _ORSTEINSSON	790	28.01.1948	212
GARTH CITY	444	24.02.1921	152
GARTH SHIRE	443	08.02.1921	152
GARU	215	01.05.1911	104
GAUL	64	24.11.1905	78
GAVOTTE	665	07.05.1940	191
GAZE HOUND	72	00.07.1891	31
GEIR	783	21.07.1947	210
GELSINA	327	12.10.1915	127
GENERAL GORDON	221	17.01.1899	52
GENERAL GORDON	266	31.07.1900	59
GENERAL ROBERTS	23	01.03.1888	25
GEORGE	103	12.06.1893	36
GEORGE ADGELL	418	18.06.1919	148
GEORGE AIKEN	407	19.12.1918	145
GEORGE AUNGER	376	20.09.1917	139
GEORGE AUNGER	554	11.09.1930	173
GEORGE COCHRAN	397	28.06.1918	143
GEORGE IRVIN	881	03.10.1953	226
GIBRALTAR	58	15.11.1890	29
GIBRALTAR	170	15.08.1908	97
GILSAY	729	29.01.1944	201
GODANES	786	17.09.1947	210
GOLDEN ERA	37	08.10.1903	73
GONZALO	107	09.06.1906	85
GOOD & BLANCHARD	8	00.09.1885	23
GOOD HOPE	346	17.01.1903	66
GOOD LUCK	249	18.07.1912	110
GOTH	468	08.06.1925	157
GOZO	3	27.02.1902	69
GRAPHIC	42	14.09.1889	27
GREAT ADMIRAL	160	07.12.1907	93
GREBE	121	02.10.1906	88
GRECIAN	153	18.01.1896	43
GRECIAN EMPIRE	244	09.10.1899	55
GRENADA	151	29.06.1907	92
GRENADIER	703	26.09.1942	197
GREYHOUND	43	27.11.1889	28
GRIFFITH GRIFFITH	401	27.08.1918	144
GRIMSBY	288	06.05.1901	62
GROOTE CONSTANTIA	905	18.10.1955	229
GROOTE SCHUUR	904	28.03.1955	229
GUARDSMAN	732	07.06.1944	201
GUERNSEY	133	12.02.1895	40
GULLAND	719	05.08.1943	199
GWEAL	698	17.06.1942	195
H.C.B. (HULL) R	445	13.01.1922	153
HAMLET	667	24.07.1940	191
HAMMOND	518	28.03.1929	166
HANDYMAN	175	22.02.1909	97
HANNARAY	730	12.02.1944	201
HANNES RÁDHERRA	480	16.01.1926	160
HARRIER	176	21.12.1896	45
HASCOSAY	731	28.03.1944	201
HATCHMERE	442	23.03.1921	152
HATFIELD	157	10.10.1907	93
HATSUSE	369	13.09.1919	138
HAWK	200	27.01.1898	49
HAWTHORN	8	07.07.1902	69
HAYLING	701	17.08.1942	197
HAZELHEAD	953	23.07.1959	241
HELIOS	338	03.12.1902	66
HELVETIA	203	09.05.1898	49
HELVETIA	353	30.09.1916	135
HENE CASTLE	210A	08.08.1898	51
HERCULES	99	06.04.1893	35
HERCULES	35	26.08.1903	73
HEREWOOD	24	23.04.1888	25
HERO	105	10.05.1906	85
HERON	11	22.03.1886	23
HERON	77	14.03.1891	32
HIGHLAND LADY	952	23.07.1959	241
HILDASAY	679	29.04.1941	192
HILDINA	852	21.08.1951	222

HIROSE	*438*	*30.09.1920*	152
HMS BRINTON	*853*	*08.08.1952*	222
HMS BRONINGTON	*854*	*19.03.1953*	222
HMS CHILTON	*947*	*15.07.1957*	239
HMS DARLESTON	*862*	*25.09.1953*	223
HMS DILSTON	*888*	*15.11.1954*	226
HMS HAZLETON	*869*	*06.02.1954*	225
HMS HEXTON	*870*	*19.06.1954*	225
HMS PENSTON	*889*	*09.05.1955*	226
HMS PICTON	*890*	*20.10.1955*	226
HMS WILKIESTON	*891*	*26.06.1956*	227
HOBART	*7*	*24.05.1902*	69
HOME GUARD	*733*	*08.07.1944*	201
HONORIA	160	11.05.1896	44
HOPE	10	00.00.1886	23
HORATIO	*668*	*08.08.1940*	191
HORNPIPE	*666*	*21.05.1940*	191
HORNSEA	245	08.11.1899	56
HORUS	237	08.08.1899	55
HOUBARA	*221*	*29.07.1911*	104
HOWE	*538*	*30.01.1930*	170
HOXA	*674*	*15.01.1941*	191
HOY	*675*	*01.02.1941*	192
HUGH BLACK	*340J*	*09.05.1917*	131
HUMBER	109	00.00.1893	37
HUNTSMAN	*1*	*13.02.1902*	69
HVALFELL	*780*	*20.06.1947*	208
IAGO	*153*	*25.07.1907*	93
IDENA	*856*	*28.02.1952*	222
IJIUN	*427*	*23.03.1920*	150
ILUSTRA	*295*	*14.03.1914*	119
IMPERIA	*254*	*14.09.1912*	111
IMPERIAL QUEEN	186	19.05.1897	47
IMPERIALIST	*39*	*07.11.1903*	75
IMPERIALIST	*213*	*04.03.1911*	104
IMPERIALIST	*457*	*13.12.1924*	155
INCHCOLM	*676*	*03.03.1941*	192
INDIAN EMPIRE	191	00.06.1897	48
INDUSTRIA	18	00.02.1887	24
INKPEN	*689*	*22.12.1941*	194
INVICTA	*109*	*10.04.1906*	86
IOLANTHE	161	30.05.1896	44
IONA	*60*	*24.09.1904*	78
IRANIAN	*224*	*13.11.1911*	106
IRELAND	183	15.04.1897	47
IRISHMAN	159	20.02.1896	44
IRRAWADDY	9	00.12.1885	23
IRVANA	*855*	*19.09.1951*	222
ISAAC ARTHAN	*413*	*01.05.1919*	147
ISBORG	*788*	*31.12.1947*	210
ISERNIA	234	10.05.1899	54
ISIS	232	29.04.1899	54
ITALIA CAESAR	*625*	*27.04.1937*	185
JÓANNES PATURSSON	*782*	*25.01.1947*	210
JACAMAR	*220*	*15.07.1911*	104
JACINTH	171	24.08.1896	45
JACKDAW	148	16.10.1895	41
JACQUES COLIN	*770*	*17.07.1946*	206
JAMAICA	163	26.03.1896	44
JAMES BERRY	*340K*	*09.05.1917*	132
JAMES CARRUTHERS	*256*	*09.09.1912*	111
JAMES ROCK-BREAKER VII	*643*	*03.02.1938*	187
JAPAN	*57*	*14.08.1904*	76
JEFFS	*453*	*26.02.1924*	153
JELLICOE	*319*	*19.12.1914*	124
JERIA	238	26.07.1899	55
JERIA	*348*	*17.07.1916*	135
JERIA	*544*	*03.04.1930*	170
JESSICA	*97*	*17.01.1906*	83
JOHANNESBURG	*17*	*19.11.1902*	70
JOHN AIKENHEAD	*408*	*19.12.1918*	145
JOHN ANDERSON	*375*	*20.09.1917*	139
JOHN APPELBY	*357*	*30.01.1917*	136
JOHN ARTHUR	*358*	*10.02.1917*	136
JOHN ASHLEY	*409*	*18.03.1919*	147
JOHN BAPTISH	*391*	*29.04.1918*	143
JOHN BATEMAN	*394*	*29.04.1918*	143
JOHN BOMKWORTH	*392*	*29.04.1918*	143
JOHN BRENNAN	*374*	*04.09.1917*	139
JOHN BRICE	*373*	*22.08.1917*	139
JOHN BROOKER	*340M*	*09.06.1917*	132
JOHN BURLINGHAM	*363*	*21.04.1917*	138
JOHN GAUNTLET	*400*	*12.08.1918*	144
JOHN GRAHAM	*399*	*27.07.1918*	144
JOHN GULIPSTER	*403*	*24.09.1918*	144
JOHN SHERBURN	317	21.07.1902	65
JON FORSETI	*792*	*25.03.1948*	205
JOSENA	*761*	*21.12.1945*	212
JOSENA	*923A*	*13.07.1957*	235
JOSEPH BARRATT	*381*	*02.11.1917*	140
JOSEPH BUTTON	*379*	*17.12.1917*	140
JOSEPH CONRAD	*924*	*27.08.1957*	235
JOSHUA ARABIN	*415*	*01.05.1919*	148
JULIET	*103*	*27.02.1906*	103
JULIET	*669*	*02.10.1940*	191
JUPITER	*476*	*21.09.1925*	159
KARI SOLMUNDARSON	*425*	*05.03.1920*	150
KASTORIA	257	06.03.1900	58
KASTORIA	*349*	*28.10.1916*	135
KELT	*471*	*20.08.1925*	157
KENNYMORE	*261B*	*14.01.1914*	113
KESTREL	157	02.04.1896	43
KHARTOUM	241	11.07.1899	55
KILCHATTAN	*405*	*13.04.1918*	145
KILCHVAN	*406*	*13.07.1918*	145
KILCLIEF	*407A*	*08.09.1918*	145
KILCLOGHER	*408A*	*24.11.1918*	145
KILLEGRAY	*680*	*27.05.1941*	192
KIMBERLEY	*15*	*04.10.1902*	70
KING EDWARD	*2*	*15.03.1902*	69
KING EDWARD VII	293	15.08.1901	62
KINGFISHER	*84*	*03.08.1905*	82
KINGS GREY	*318*	*19.12.1914*	124
KINGSTON AGATE	*640*	*18.11.1937*	187
KINGSTON ALALITE	*583*	*18.11.1933*	178
KINGSTON AMBER	*946*	*28.07.1960*	239
KINGSTON ANDALUSITE	*584*	*17.01.1934*	178
KINGSTON BERYL	*506*	*02.10.1928*	165
KINGSTON BERYL	*934*	*29.09.1958*	237
KINGSTON CAIRNGORM	*601*	*21.02.1935*	181
KINGSTON CAMEO	*609*	*27.02.1936*	182
KINGSTON CEYLONITE	*600*	*06.02.1935*	181
KINGSTON CHRYSOBERYL	*602*	*09.03.1935*	181
KINGSTON CHRYSOLITE	*599*	*22.01.1935*	181
KINGSTON CORAL	*540*	*17.04.1930*	170
KINGSTON CORAL	*608*	*08.02.1936*	182
KINGSTON CORNELIAN	*593*	*12.06.1934*	180
KINGSTON CRYSTAL	*610*	*22.03.1936*	182
KINGSTON CYANITE	*541*	*15.05.1930*	170
KINGSTON CYANITE	*607*	*25.01.1936*	182
KINGSTON DIAMOND	*483*	*31.03.1926*	160
KINGSTON EMERALD	*486*	*17.05.1927*	160
KINGSTON EMERALD	*894*	*31.08.1954*	227
KINGSTON GALENA	*589*	*15.02.1934*	180
KINGSTON GARNET	*485*	*30.04.1927*	160
KINGSTON GARNET	*816*	*03.11.1949*	216
KINGSTON JACINTH	*516*	*28.02.1929*	166
KINGSTON JACINTH	*836*	*03.11.1951*	220
KINGSTON JADE	*829*	*28.10.1950*	218
KINGSTON JASPER	*505*	*17.09.1928*	165
KINGSTON OLIVINE	*539*	*15.03.1930*	170
KINGSTON ONYX	*488*	*18.06.1927*	162
KINGSTON ONYX	*826*	*16.08.1950*	218
KINGSTON PEARL	*484*	*17.04.1926*	160
KINGSTON PEARL	*933*	*21.07.1958*	237
KINGSTON PERIDOT	*522*	*08.06.1929*	167
KINGSTON PERIDOT	*797*	*10.07.1948*	212
KINGSTON SAPPHIRE	*514*	*28.01.1929*	166

KINGSTON SAPPHIRE	896	22.06.1955	227
KINGSTON SARDIUS	796	10.06.1948	212
KINGSTON TOPAZ	487	01.06.1927	162
KINGSTON TOPAZ	827	28.09.1950	218
KINGSTON TURQUOISE	519	27.04.1929	166
KINGSTON TURQUOISE	895	15.10.1954	227
KINGSTON ZIRCON	817	07.12.1949	216
KINGSWAY	62	09.11.1904	78
KINSMAN	161	22.02.1908	95
KIRKELLA	861	15.01.1952	223
KIRSTENBOSCH	926	20.12.1956	235
KITTERN	720	21.08.1943	199
KLONDYKE	216	20.08.1898	52
KONG FREDERIK III	181	07.06.1909	98
KOPANES	555	24.09.1930	173
KYOTO	426	23.03.1920	150
L.C.T (3)	748	11.05.1944	204
L.C.T (3)	747	25.04.1944	204
LA CHAMPAGNE	302	16.12.1901	64
LA FLANDRE	315	09.04.1902	65
LABORE ET HONORE	104	03.07.1893	36
LABRADOR	118	05.04.1894	37
LACENNIA	563	07.01.1931	175
LACONIA	258	30.04.1900	58
LADY ADELAIDE	586	04.12.1933	180
LADY BERYL	478	19.12.1925	159
LADY BERYL	605	12.11.1935	182
LADY CECILIA	985	25.07.1963	247
LADY ELEANOR	520	11.05.1929	166
LADY ELSA	551	26.07.1930	172
LADY ELSIE	983	31.10.1962	247
LADY ENID	534	20.11.1929	169
LADY HOGARTH	623	07.09.1937	185
LADY JEANETTE	616	20.03.1937	184
LADY LAVINIA	597	07.01.1935	181
LADY LILIAN	575	28.03.1933	177
LADY LILIAN	650	02.09.1939	188
LADY MADELEINE	479	21.11.1925	160
LADY MADELEINE	592	31.07.1934	180
LADY MADELEINE	651	14.09.1939	188
LADY MARGOT	535	02.12.1929	169
LADY PHILOMENA	606	09.01.1936	182
LADY RACHAEL	502	17.07.1928	163
LADY ROSEMARY	496	19.05.1928	162
LADY ROSEMARY	622	09.08.1937	185
LADY SHIRLEY	615	25.02.1937	184
LADY THERESA	984	13.12.1962	247
LADYBIRD	277	27.11.1900	61
LADYSMITH	19	02.02.1903	72
LAERTES	670	16.10.1940	191
LANCELLA	880	03.04.1953	226
LANCER	704	26.10.1942	197
LANCER	809	14.04.1949	216
LANSDOWNE	178	00.00.1897	47
LAPAGERIA	341	08.02.1916	134
LARK	12	00.05.1886	24
LARK	188	31.05.1897	48
LEONATO	178	08.05.1909	98
LEONIDAS	548	26.06.1930	172
LETTEN	451	23.01.1924	153
LIBYAN	282	18.10.1913	117
LIFEGUARD	812	12.07.1949	216
LINARIA	967	07.10.1960	244
LINDISFARNE	716	17.06.1943	198
LINNET	13	04.06.1886	24
LINNET	189	03.06.1897	48
LIVINGSTONE	253	19.01.1900	56
LOCH INVER	537	15.01.1930	169
LOCH LEVEN	507	16.10.1928	165
LOCH SEAFORTH	582	23.10.1933	178
LONDON TOWN	955	22.09.1959	241
LORD SALISBURY	336	15.10.1902	66
LORD ALVERSTONE	340G	27.04.1917	131
LORD C. BERESFORD	174	23.11.1896	45

LORD CHANCELLOR	28	00.09.1888	25
LORD FISHER	311	06.10.1914	123
LORD HENEAGE	176	10.03.1909	97
LORD JELLICOE	979	24.11.1961	246
LORD NELSON	179	21.01.1897	47
LORD ROSEBERY	301	22.11.1901	64
LORD SELBOURNE	340F	27.04.1917	131
LORD ST. VINCENT	981	09.03.1962	246
LORD WOLSELEY	56	27.08.1904	76
LORELLA	785	20.08.1947	210
LORENZO	579	21.09.1933	178
LORINDA	511	28.11.1928	165
LOROONE	266	11.01.1913	114
LOUIS BOTHA	338	05.02.1916	129
LOUIS TRICHARDT	893	01.07.1954	227
LOUISE	46	19.05.1904	75
LOYAL	509	12.08.1928	165
LUCIDA	923	05.12.1956	235
LUCKNOW	26	14.04.1903	72
LUNDY	168	16.06.1908	95
LUNDY	702	29.08.1942	197
LYCURGUS	49	17.04.1890	28
LYSANDER	38	10.10.1903	75
MACFARLANE	171	29.08.1908	97
MACKENZIE	325	16.09.1902	65
MACKENZIE	226	12.09.1911	106
MADAIRA REEF	897	09.03.1954	227
MAFEKING	18	19.11.1902	70
MAGNETA	3	00.05.1885	23
MAGPIE	155	04.02.1896	43
MAI	423	20.02.1920	150
MALABAR	28	27.01.1903	72
MALAYAN	557A	23.10.1930	173
MALMATA	543	20.03.1930	170
MANDALAY	53	14.07.1890	28
MANILA	150	02.10.1895	43
MARBELLA	902	11.02.1955	229
MARCONI	36	02.10.1903	73
MARGARET WICKS	789	01.11.1947	210
MARGUERITE	146	24.06.1895	41
MARIE	306	11.02.1902	64
MARINIA	899	16.10.1954	227
MARTABAN	57	02.10.1890	29
MARTHE	268	10.02.1913	114
MARTINETA	190	16.10.1909	100
MARZ	527	13.02.1929	167
MASTIFF	75	05.09.1891	32
MAURITIUS	5	10.04.1902	69
MAYFLY	246	07.10.1899	56
MEDIAN	165	30.04.1908	95
MEDIAN	365A	17.05.1919	138
MELBOURNE	90	00.05.1892	33
MERCIA	283	24.12.1900	61
MERCURY	278	13.09.1900	61
MERRIE ISLINGTON	81	19.11.1891	32
MEWSTONE	721	16.09.1943	199
MICHAEL GRIFFITH	402	05.09.1918	144
MICHEL BERNARD	769	18.07.1946	206
MICKLETON	440	14.03.1921	152
MIKADO	81	05.06.1905	80
MINALTO	717	03.07.1943	198
MINERVA	279	27.09.1900	61
MINORU	184	05.08.1909	98
MIRANDA	98	13.02.1906	83
MITRES	356	24.07.1917	136
MIZPAH	30	00.11.1888	25
MOHICAN	568	12.10.1931	175
MONARCH	167	05.07.1896	44
MONIMIA	248	15.06.1912	110
MONIMIA	515	12.02.1929	166
MONTREAL	98	30.03.1893	35
MOODY	452	29.01.1924	153
MOONSTONE	45	19.05.1904	75
MOORE	69	24.12.1904	79

MOPSA	156	13.08.1907	93
MORAVIA	263	24.05.1900	58
MORAVIA	350	28.10.1916	135
MORVINA	303	27.06.1914	122
MULL	677	27.03.1941	192
MYNA	229	24.10.1911	107
N.E.R. No. 5 (3)	449	06.08.1922	153
N.E.R. No. 6	450	06.12.1922	153
NARBERTH CASTLE	212	06.10.1898	51
NARVAL	205	23.07.1910	103
NAVENA	757	25.10.1945	205
NEAVE	699	16.07.1942	195
NEGRO	571	11.01.1932	177
NEMROD	191	29.11.1909	100
NEPTUNE	290	06.07.1901	62
NERINE	977	07.05.1962	246
NERISSA	102	27.02.1906	85
NESS No.27	850	18.12.1950	222
NEW ZEALAND	213	09.06.1898	51
NEWINGTON	225	02.03.1899	54
NIGHT WATCH	510	12.12.1928	165
NIGHT-HAWK	216	29.04.1911	104
NIL DESPERANDUM	33	16.03.1889	27
NINUS	240	06.03.1912	109
NJORDUR	424	20.02.1920	150
NODZU	437	30.09.1920	152
NOLSOYAR PALL	781	08.01.1947	210
NORMAN	115	08.02.1894	37
NORMAN	16	15.11.1902	70
NORMAN	212	15.02.1911	104
NORSE	470	22.07.1925	157
NORSE	560	06.11.1930	173
NORTH SEA	70	22.05.1891	31
NORTHELLA	838	11.01.1951	220
NORTHELLA	931	10.04.1958	237
NORTHERN GIFT	982	05.04.1962	247
NORTHERN PRINCE	814	26.09.1949	216
NORTHERN PRINCESS	813	24.08.1949	216
NORTHERN QUEEN	815	10.10.1949	216
NORTHERN REWARD	980	09.01.1962	246
NORTHUMBRIA	116	23.06.1906	86
NORTHWARD HO	231	08.04.1899	54
NOVELLI	336	09.12.1915	129
NUBIA	353	27.08.1903	68
OBERON	93	31.10.1905	83
OCTAVIA	99	13.02.1906	85
OLIVER CROMWELL	250	20.11.1899	56
OLYMPIA	71	23.01.1905	79
OLYMPIA	354	22.05.1917	135
ONWARD PROGRESS	942	14.03.1959	239
OPHIR	341	14.02.1902	66
ORIZABA	162	21.01.1908	95
ORSINO	529	05.10.1929	169
ORVICTO	339	05.02.1916	130
OSIRIS	220	16.11.1898	52
OSPREY	112	14.09.1893	37
OSPREY	137	00.00.1895	40
OSTRICH	41	16.07.1889	27
OSTRICH	347	12.03.1903	66
OSWALDIAN	355	24.07.1917	136
OTHELLO	294	29.10.1901	62
OTHELLO	152	13.07.1907	92
OTTER HOUND	48	22.03.1890	28
OTTILIE	294	12.03.1914	119
PADGETT	971	20.02.1961	244
PAMELA	219	30.05.1911	104
PARTHIAN	223	15.08.1911	106
PASSING	261	05.06.1913	113
PATRICK BOWE	386	17.01.1918	142
PAVLOVA	244	20.04.1912	109
PELICAN	145	05.05.1895	41
PELTON	474	04.09.1925	159
PENELOPE	142	07.09.1895	41
PENGUIN	136	11.05.1895	40

PENTLAND FIRTH	577	26.09.1934	178
PERICLES	23	13.03.1903	72
PERICLES	196	25.06.1910	101
PERSIAN	319	24.06.1902	65
PERSIAN EMPIRE	243	21.08.1899	55
PERTH	226	21.09.1898	54
PETER BLUMBERRY	378	18.10.1917	140
PETREL	111	10.08.1893	37
PHAROS	275	10.12.1900	61
PHILIP GODBY	404	24.09.1918	145
PHILIP MAXTED	38	13.05.1889	27
PHINEAS BEARD	383	24.11.1917	142
PHOEBE	104	12.04.1906	85
PHYLLISIA	938	09.04.1958	237
PICADOR	580	04.10.1933	178
PICT	472	04.09.1925	159
PICTON CASTLE	92	00.03.1892	33
PIET RETIEF	892	20.05.1954	227
PLADDA	678	16.04.1941	192
PLATO	297	24.10.1901	64
PLOVER	4	00.09.1885	23
PLUTARCH	21	15.01.1903	72
POINTER	273	02.07.1900	59
POINTZ CASTLE	208	26.08.1898	51
POONAH	25	31.03.1903	72
PORTIA	138	30.03.1895	40
PORTSDOWN	685	24.09.1941	194
PRECURSOR	1	21.01.1885	23
PREMIER	168	28.07.1896	45
PRESIDENT LUDWIG	85	03.03.1892	33
PRETORIA	14	22.09.1902	70
PRETORIA	114	23.06.1906	86
PRIDE OF THE HUMBER	107	11.12.1893	36
PRIME MINISTER	27	28.07.1888	25
PRINCE CHARLES	47	17.02.1904	75
PRINCE CHARLES	804	14.05.1949	214
PRINCE CHARLES	929	10.12.1957	235
PRINCE CONSORT	54	06.08.1890	29
PRINCE OF WALES	62	28.02.1891	29
PRINCE PHILIP	801	04.11.1948	214
PRINCE PHILIP	927	16.01.1956	235
PRINCESS MARIE JOSÉ	314	17.12.1914	123
PRINCESS ANNE	830	22.08.1952	220
PRINCESS ANNE	901	11.12.1954	229
PRINCESS ELIZABETH	800	07.08.1948	214
PRINCESS ELIZABETH	824	02.06.1950	218
PRINCESS ELIZABETH	970	19.01.1961	244
PRINCESS LOUISE	83	31.08.1905	82
PRINCESS VICTORIA	350	27.08.1903	68
PRINCESSE MARIE-JOSE	138	15.04.1907	91
PURITAN	254	03.02.1900	56
PYROPE	573	07.04.1932	177
QUAIL	120	02.10.1906	88
QUEBEC	89	00.05.1892	33
QUEEN	272	01.08.1900	59
QUEEN ALEXANDRA	292	20.07.1901	62
QUEENSLAND	100	01.05.1893	36
QUERCIA	238	07.02.1912	109
RAASAY	693	01.04.1942	195
RADO	352	29.06.1903	68
RAETIA	242	23.03.1912	109
RALCO	230	09.11.1911	107
RAMBLER	202	12.03.1898	49
RAMESES	129	16.10.1894	40
RANGOON	25	00.05.1888	25
RAPIO	174	24.02.1909	97
RAYMONT	372	05.03.1916	139
RAYON D'OR	245	15.06.1912	110
REBONO	247	18.07.1912	110
REBOUNDO	429	20.04.1920	150
RECEPTO	299	06.06.1914	121
RECOLO	234	23.12.1911	107
RECONO	331	14.08.1915	127
RECORDIA	187	00.04.1897	48

RECORDO	193	14.02.1910	100
RECTO	51	18.05.1904	76
REDCLIFFE	882	11.08.1953	226
REDESMERE	441	23.03.1921	152
REFINO	351	08.06.1903	68
REFUNDO	360	27.11.1916	136
REGAL	112	10.05.1906	86
REGAL	545	03.05.1930	170
REGARDO	330	01.07.1915	127
REINDEER	12	18.09.1902	70
RELEVO	235	23.01.1912	107
RELONZO	298	11.05.1914	121
REMAGIO	269	08.03.1913	114
REMARKO	297	27.04.1914	121
REMEXO	246	18.06.1912	110
REMINDO	361	26.02.1917	136
RENARRO	272	08.05.1913	115
RENCO	200	09.06.1910	101
RENOVO	54	16.07.1904	76
RENOWN	137	14.02.1907	91
RENZO	263	11.01.1913	113
REPERIO	147	14.05.1907	92
REPORTO	164	16.04.1908	95
REPRO	197	13.04.1910	101
RESERCHO	362	26.02.1917	138
RESMILO	359	27.11.1916	136
RESOLUTE	29	00.10.1888	25
RESOLVO	278	20.08.1913	117
RESONO	194	12.03.1910	100
RESPARKO	333	06.12.1915	127
RESPONSO	231	09.11.1911	107
RESTRIVO	300B	10.06.1914	121
RETAKO	300	06.06.1914	121
RETRIEVER	80	21.10.1891	32
RETRUDO	280	02.09.1913	117
RETURNO	300A	10.06.1914	121
REVELLO	163	02.04.1908	95
REVERTO	50	18.05.1904	76
REVIGO	145	15.04.1907	92
RHODESIA	229	31.12.1898	54
RIANO	117	25.06.1906	88
RIBY	206	06.09.1910	103
RICHARD BACON	382	02.11.1917	140
RICHARD BAGLEY	340L	09.06.1917	132
RICHARD CROFTS	396	13.06.1918	143
RICHARD SIMPSON	47	22.02.1890	28
RIDEO	149	25.06.1907	92
RIFSNES	574	17.10.1932	177
RIGHTO	428	09.02.1920	150
RIGOLETTO	118	25.07.1906	88
RIPARVO	273	07.06.1913	115
RISKATO	332	09.11.1915	127
RISTANGO	279	02.09.1913	117
RIVIERE	335	09.11.1915	129
ROBERT BETSON	364	21.04.1917	138
ROBERT BOWEN	390	14.03.1918	142
ROBERT HEWETT	963	22.11.1960	243
ROCHE CASTLE	211	05.09.1898	51
RODINO	264	25.01.1913	113
RODNEY	124	22.08.1906	88
RODOSTO	267	11.02.1913	114
RÖDULL	787	01.12.1947	210
ROLULO	173	06.02.1909	97
ROMAN	141	16.03.1907	91
ROMAN EMPIRE	217	26.10.1898	52
ROMANOFF	276	10.09.1900	61
ROMEO	20	17.12.1902	72
RONONIA	271	24.04.1913	115
RONSO	329	01.07.1915	127
ROSA MARIS	436	24.05.1920	152
ROSALIND	251	08.12.1899	56
ROSALIND	89	02.09.1905	82
ROSARENO	10	24.07.1902	70
ROSCO	9	24.07.1902	69

ROSE	17	00.01.1887	24
ROSEVEAN	718	17.07.1943	198
ROSS	558	24.11.1930	173
ROTO	53	29.06.1904	76
ROWSAY	237	23.12.1911	107
ROWSLEY	251	17.08.1912	110
ROYAL JUBILEE	603	04.07.1935	182
ROYAL MARINE	734	22.07.1944	203
ROYALIST	207A	01.09.1898	51
ROYALIST	960	16.03.1960	243
ROYALLIEU	269	11.07.1900	59
ROYALLIEU	143	14.05.1907	91
ROYALO	334	06.12.1915	129
RUBENS	767	17.04.1946	206
RUBENS	917	22.09.1956	233
RUDOLF	810	30.05.1949	216
RUGBY	267	14.06.1900	59
RUGBY	342	20.07.1916	134
RUSSELL	123	25.07.1906	88
RYLSTON	556	08.10.1930	173
SABREUR	340C	22.05.1916	130
SABRINA	175	04.01.1897	45
SAINT MALO	227	08.09.1911	106
SALACON	68	10.01.1905	79
SALVINI	337	09.12.1915	129
SAMUEL HEWETT	913	16.03.1956	233
SAN PEDRO	56	14.09.1890	29
SANDRAY	737	05.10.1944	203
SANDRINGHAM	77	23.03.1905	80
SANSON	140	25.06.1907	91
SAPPER	705	11.11.1942	197
SARDIUS	481	03.02.1926	160
SARGON	184	02.03.1897	47
SARGON	146	08.04.1913	92
SARPEDON	199	07.03.1898	49
SARPEDON	347	18.04.1916	134
SATELLITE	116	00.00.1894	37
SATYRION	235	24.05.1899	54
SAXON	131	20.10.1894	40
SAXON	300	14.01.1902	64
SAXON	154	11.09.1907	93
SCALPAY	697	02.06.1942	195
SCARAVAY	738	22.10.1944	203
SCARBA	681	25.06.1941	192
SCARRON	271A	19.07.1913	115
SCHIPPERKE	225	12.06.1911	106
SCOTLAND	182	17.03.1897	47
SCOTSMAN	285	09.03.1901	62
SCOTSMAN	327	13.11.1902	65
SEA HORSE	299	17.09.1901	64
SEA KING	303	23.12.1901	64
SEA LION	305	10.02.1902	64
SEA MONARCH	322	31.05.1915	126
SEA SWEEPER	321	31.05.1915	126
SEAGULL	252	14.12.1899	56
SEAWARD HO	312	19.11.1914	123
SEDDON	346	20.05.1916	134
SEMIRAMIS	155	26.08.1907	93
SENATOR	73	08.03.1905	79
SERAPION	256	20.02.1900	58
SERIEMA	189	02.10.1909	100
SESOSTRIS	320	14.09.1915	126
SETHON	260	29.03.1900	58
SETHON	345	22.04.1916	134
SETI	166	15.06.1896	44
SETTER	74	22.08.1891	32
SHAKESPEARE	207	00.05.1898	49
SHAMROCK	249	23.10.1899	56
SHELDON	239	23.02.1912	109
SHELL FARMER	887	08.07.1955	226
SHELL STEELMAKER	911	05.12.1956	231
SHELL TRAVELLER	911A	21.10.1957	231
SHERATON	115	19.11.1906	86
SHIELDS	287	06.05.1901	62

SHILLAY	739	15.11.1944	203
SIALKOT	253	28.09.1912	111
SIBERITE	564	20.05.1931	175
SICYON	113	24.05.1906	86
SIHON	198	24.02.1898	49
SILANION	262	16.05.1900	58
SILANION	356	24.10.1903	68
SILANION	546	29.05.1930	172
SILICIA	258	27.11.1912	111
SIMERSON	274A	30.09.1913	115
SIMPSON	352	02.09.1916	135
SINGAPORE	248	03.05.1900	56
SIR ALBERT ROLLIT	32	30.11.1888	25
SIR FRANCIS DRAKE	345	20.12.1902	66
SIR JAMES RECKITT	177	22.04.1909	97
SIR JOHN FRENCH	310	06.10.1914	123
SIR JOHN JELLICOE	309	22.09.1914	123
SIR REDVERS BULLER	144	00.00.1895	41
SISAPON	67	26.11.1904	79
SISAPON	508	30.10.1928	165
SKOGHOLM	722	29.09.1943	199
SKÚLI MAGNÚSSON	791	28.02.1948	210
SKÚLI FÓGETI	368	25.10.1919	138
SLEDMERE	87	28.03.1892	33
SLEUTH HOUND	65	25.10.1890	31
SOLON	185	23.03.1897	47
SOLON	243	20.04.1912	109
SOLON	562	20.12.1930	175
SOLWAY FIRTH	531	24.08.1929	169
SOMERSET MAUGHAN	965	22.09.1960	243
SOPHRON	233	26.04.1899	54
SOPHRON	348	25.05.1903	66
SOUTH COATES	295	20.10.1901	62
SOUTHELLA	768	02.07.1946	206
SOUVENIR	774	23.05.1947	208
SPARTA	63	07.04.1891	31
SPARTAN	110	12.07.1893	37
SPIT	912A	26.11.1957	231
SPRINGFIELD	114	11.10.1893	37
SPURN No.14	937	29.01.1959	237
ST. ACHILLEUS	595	11.10.1934	181
ST. ALCUIN	822	02.05.1950	218
ST. ALEXANDRA	490	10.12.1927	162
ST. AMANDUS	576A	10.08.1933	177
ST. ANDRONICUS	576B	04.11.1933	177
ST. APOLLO	654	14.12.1939	190
ST. APOLLO	798	06.09.1948	212
ST. ARCADIUS	576	11.05.1933	177
ST. ATTALUS	591	03.04.1934	180
ST. BARTHOLOMEW	865	20.11.1952	223
ST. BARTHOLOMEW	903	12.03.1955	229
ST. BERNARD	264	19.04.1900	59
ST. BOTOLPH	758	21.11.1945	205
ST. BRELADE	460	16.08.1924	155
ST. BRITWIN	821	06.04.1950	218
ST. CATHAN	613	19.08.1936	184
ST. CELESTIN	467	09.04.1925	157
ST. CELESTIN	864	12.05.1952	223
ST. CHAD	794	24.04.1948	212
ST. CHAD	908	22.06.1955	231
ST. CHRISTOPHER	910A	10.01.1958	231
ST. CLAIR	357	23.11.1903	68
ST. CRISPIN	778	13.11.1946	208
ST. DELPHINE	491	31.12.1927	162
ST. DOMINIC	925	20.05.1958	235
ST. DONATS	458	21.06.1924	155
ST. ELMO	286	15.11.1913	118
ST. ELSTAN	634	23.09.1937	187
ST. GATIEN	466	23.03.1925	157
ST. GERONTIUS	524	09.07.1929	167
ST. GERONTIUS	976	28.09.1961	246
ST. GORAN	614	05.09.1936	184
ST. HONORIOUS	523	25.06.1929	167
ST. HUBERT	344	19.06.1916	134

ST. IRENE	503	18.08.1928	163
ST. IVES	172	10.12.1908	97
ST. JOAN	495	08.05.1928	163
ST. JOHN	763	20.02.1946	205
ST. JOHNS	198	12.05.1910	101
ST. JUST	552	23.08.1930	172
ST. KENAN	617	01.10.1936	184
ST. KEVERNE	834	12.12.1950	220
ST. KILDA	59	30.08.1904	78
ST. LEANDER	494	05.04.1928	162
ST. LEANDER	799	05.10.1948	214
ST. LEGER	835	09.04.1951	220
ST. LOMAN	618	15.10.1936	184
ST. LOMAN	921	01.07.1957	233
ST. LOUIS	463	30.12.1924	155
ST. LOUIS	945	15.11.1958	239
ST. LUCIA	134	03.01.1907	91
ST. MATTHEW	764	16.05.1946	206
ST. MELANTE	489	15.08.1927	162
ST. MERRYN	459	17.07.1924	155
ST. NECTAN	619	02.11.1936	184
ST. NIDAN	620	30.11.1936	185
ST. ROMANUS	499	24.04.1928	163
ST. ROSE	504	04.09.1928	165
ST. SEBASTIAN	500	02.08.1928	163
ST. VINCENT	133	03.01.1907	89
ST. WISTAN	635	21.10.1937	187
ST. ZENO	655	12.02.1940	190
STAG HOUND	45	27.12.1889	28
STALWART	307	24.08.1914	122
STARELLA	808	31.03.1949	216
STARELLA	964	11.06.1960	243
STAUNTON	142	21.10.1907	91
STELLA AQUILA	907	16.11.1956	229
STELLA LEONIS	944	29.03.1960	239
STIFF BANK	900	22.04.1954	227
STONECHAT	735	22.08.1944	203
STORK	101	17.05.1893	36
STORK	255	17.02.1900	58
STORM COCK	95	22.10.1892	35
STORNOWAY	199	25.05.1910	101
STRATON	236	12.06.1899	55
STREPHON	218	24.08.1898	52
STREPHON	259	27.11.1912	111
STRONSAY	232	21.11.1911	107
STRYMON	240	09.09.1899	55
STURTON	434	20.04.1920	152
SUNCLOUD	252	31.08.1912	110
SURSAY	740	16.12.1944	203
SUSARION	351	30.08.1916	135
SWAN	335	20.09.1902	65
SWANELLA	803	18.12.1948	214
SWANELLA	919	21.11.1956	233
SWEEPER	262	24.02.1914	113
SWIFT	84	02.01.1892	33
SYDNEY	91	00.06.1892	33
SYRIAN	52	29.06.1904	76
TAHAY	741	31.12.1944	203
TANJORE	29	27.01.1903	73
TARTAN	250	12.08.1912	110
TASMANIA	59	15.12.1890	29
TERN	874	30.06.1953	225
TERRIER	76	17.09.1891	32
TERVANI	287	18.10.1913	118
TERVANI	473	02.11.1925	159
TETNEY	188	16.08.1909	100
TEUTON	214	01.07.1898	51
THANET	4	10.05.1902	69
THE BANYERS	296	09.04.1914	119
THE PRINCE	48	20.04.1904	76
THE PRINCESS	49	20.04.1904	76
THE TETRARCH	277	22.07.1913	117
THEBAN	281	30.09.1913	117
THOMAS ADNEY	411	02.04.1919	147

THOMAS ALEXANDER	420	18.07.1919	149
THOMAS ALLEN	419	18.07.1919	148
THOMAS ALTOFT	416	02.06.1919	148
THOMAS BARTLETT	393	29.05.1918	143
THOMAS BLACKHORN	340N	07.07.1917	132
THOMAS BOOTH	387	14.02.1918	142
THOMAS BOUDIGE	422	15.08.1919	149
THOMAS BUCKLEY	340P	07.07.1917	132
THOMAS CONNOLLY	384	29.11.1917	142
THOMAS HAMLING	359	02.01.1904	68
THOMAS TOMPION	819	06.02.1950	218
THORINA	766	19.03.1946	206
THORNELLA	906	23.05.1955	229
THORNWICK BAY	604	28.08.1935	182
THUNDERSTONE	276	21.06.1913	117
THURINGIA	144	08.04.1913	92
TITAN	24	31.01.1903	72
TOBAGO	247	15.11.1899	56
TOCOGAY	742	07.02.1945	203
TOPAZ	152	18.12.1895	43
TOR BAY	268	18.06.1900	59
TORFRIDA	36	00.02.1889	27
TORONTO	162	04.03.1896	44
TOUCHSTONE	130	18.01.1907	89
TOURACO	158	07.11.1907	93
TOURMALINE	482	04.03.1926	160
TRIER	204	08.08.1910	103
TRINIDAD	164	12.09.1896	84
TRODDAY	743	03.03.1945	204
TROJAN	215	06.08.1898	52
TRUEMAN	969	22.12.1960	244
TRYGON	167	30.06.1908	95
TUGELA	270	05.11.1900	59
TUNISIAN	122	06.09.1906	88
TUNISIAN	557	11.10.1930	173
TURQUOISE	170	12.08.1896	45
TUSCAN	87	06.07.1905	82
TYNDRUM	337	21.10.1902	66
UGANDA	120	04.05.1894	39
ULUNDI	121	04.05.1894	39
ULVA	700	30.07.1942	195
Un-named Boat Beacon	900A	17.07.1957	229
Un-named Boat Beacon	900B	17.07.1957	229
Un-named Boat Beacon	900C	08.09.1959	229
Un-named Gas Float	978	29.10.1962	246
Un-named Gas Float	978A	29.10.1962	246
Un-named Light Float	455	20.03.1924	155
Un-named Light Float	851	18.12.1950	222
Un-named Light Float	P1	02.02.1956	231
Un-named Light Float	P2	11.02.1956	231
Un-named Light Float	P3	11.02.1956	231
Un-named Light Float	P4	11.02.1956	233
Un-named Lightship	132	00.00.1894	40
UNDINE	37	15.04.1889	27
UNITIA	269A	19.07.1913	114
UNITY	5	00.06.1885	23
VACEASAY	744	17.03.1945	204
VALERIA	140	10.07.1895	41
VALESCA	340B	02.05.1916	130
VALKYRIE	113	07.10.1893	37
VALKYRIE	41	23.12.1903	75
VALLAY	745	10.04.1945	204
VALMONT	340	08.01.1916	130
VAN DER WEYDEN	775	01.08.1946	208
VAN DYCK	828	01.07.1950	218
VAN EYCK	845	07.05.1951	220
VAN OOST	848	20.07.1951	222
VAN ORLEY	776	30.08.1946	208
VAN ORLEY	847	24.05.1951	222
VANESSA	843	10.07.1952	220
VANGUARD	22	01.03.1888	24
VARANGA	517	14.03.1929	166
VELIA	839	04.06.1951	220
VELINDA	916	12.07.1956	233

VENDORA	497	21.06.1928	163
VENUS	533	16.11.1929	169
VERA	150	27.07.1907	92
VIANOVA	939	12.12.1958	239
VICTORIA	50	08.05.1890	28
VICTORIAN	265	25.06.1900	59
VICTRIX	624	15.12.1936	185
VIDAS	962	31.03.1963	243
VIKING	230	29.03.1899	54
VINDELECIA	274	17.09.1913	115
VINDORA	806	16.02.1949	214
VINUR	547	12.06.1930	172
VIOLA	96	17.01.1906	83
VIRGINIAN	131	22.10.1906	89
VISENDA	627	30.01.1937	185
VITALITY	598	23.02.1935	181
VIVANTI	328	12.10.1915	127
VIVARIA	961	12.05.1960	243
VIZALMA	656	11.04.1940	190
VULTURE	239	28.06.1899	55
W J COOK	446	28.02.1922	153
WALLENA	261A	17.12.1913	113
WALPOLE	567	14.09.1931	175
WALTER S BAILEY	316	12.04.1902	65
WALWYNS CASTLE	209A	23.06.1898	51
WAR LORD	304	27.07.1914	122
WAR DUKE	340E	11.01.1917	131
WAR GREY	340D	28.12.1916	131
WAR WING	326	29.04.1915	127
WARLAND	265	11.12.1912	114
WARSTAR	289	12.02.1914	119
WATCHFUL	40	02.12.1903	75
WELSBACH	550	10.07.1930	172
WELSHMAN	125	00.06.1894	39
WESSEX	320	23.07.1902	65
WESTELLA	956	18.11.1959	241
WESTRAY	233	07.12.1911	107
WESTRAY FIRTH	532	07.10.1929	169
WHALSAY	694	04.04.1942	195
WHITETHROAT	736	06.09.1944	203
WIAY	746	26.04.1945	204
WILBERFORCE	177	24.12.1896	45
WILLIAM BELL	385	17.01.1918	142
WILLIAM BRADY	380	17.12.1917	140
WILLIAM BROWIS	377	18.10.1917	140
WILLIAM CALDWELL	395	12.06.1918	143
WILLIAM DARNOLD	398	11.07.1918	144
WILLIAM SCORESBY	477	31.12.1925	159
WILLIAM WESNEY	536	23.12.1929	169
WILLIAM WILBERFORCE	948	08.05.1959	241
WINDWARD HO	326	18.08.1902	65
WINDWARD HO	435	20.05.1920	152
WM. GEMMELL	447	28.02.1922	153
WOLF HOUND	67	25.04.1891	31
WORSLEY	260	09.12.1912	111
WYRE CONQUEROR	950	25.07.1959	241
WYRE VICTORY	951	07.09.1959	241
YARDLEY	818	21.01.1950	216
YES TOR	686	21.10.1941	194
YORICK	180	05.06.1909	98
YORKSHIRE BELLE	645	07.05.1938	187
YORKSHIRE BELLE	793	22.05.1947	212
ZEBEDEE	31	00.12.1888	25
ZENOBIA	55	14.09.1890	29